Northwestern University
STUDIES IN *Phenomenology &*
Existential Philosophy

Freedom and Nature:
The Voluntary and the Involuntary

Paul Ricoeur

Translated, with an Introduction by

Freedom and Nature: The Voluntary and the Involuntary

Erazim V. Kohák

NORTHWESTERN UNIVERSITY PRESS

1966

À MONSIEUR GABRIEL MARCEL

Hommage Respectueux

See the sky. Is there no constellation
called "Rider"? For this is strangely impressed
on us: this earthy pride. And a second,
who drives and holds it and whom it bears.

Is not the sinewy nature of our being
just like this, spurred on and then reined in?
Track and turning. Yet at a touch, understanding.
New open spaces. And the two are one.

But *are* they? Or do both not mean
the way they take together? Already
table and pasture utterly divide them.

Even the starry union is deceptive
But let us now be glad a while
to believe the figure. That's enough.
—Rainer Maria Rilke *

* From *Sonnets to Orpheus,* trans. M. D. Herter Norton (New York, W. W. Norton, 1942), p. 37. Reprinted with permission of the publisher.

TRANSLATOR'S INTRODUCTION:

The Philosophy of Paul Ricoeur

[1] THE PHILOSOPHY OF THE WILL

1. Bibliographical Data

Le Volontaire et l'involontaire, presented below as
Freedom and Nature: The Voluntary and the Involuntary, first
appeared in Paris in 1950 as the first volume of Paul Ricoeur's
La Philosophie de la volonté. As Ricoeur outlined the task in a
paper concerning the application of phenomenology to the will,
read before the International Colloquium on Phenomenology in
Brussels the following year,[1] the entire work was to consist of
three volumes, the first devoted to the eidetics of the will, the
second and third volumes dealing with empirics and poetics.

The second volume was published in 1960 under the title
Finitude et culpabilité. It undertakes the projected task of empirics of the will in two parts. The first part, published separately
as L'Homme faillible (and, in English translation, as Fallible
Man),[2] still falls broadly within the limits of descriptive phenomenology. In contrast with the first volume, however, it is concerned
with the existential possibilities of man's being: specifically, the
possibility of evil. The second part, published the same year under
the title La Symbolique du mal, continues the task of empirics of
the will, but its focus is no longer possibility, but rather the experienced fact of evil as it is expressed in symbol and myth.

This transition requires a basic change of methodology. While
both earlier volumes employed a descriptive phenomenology to

1. "Les Méthodes et tâches de la phénoménologie de la volonté," in Les
Problèmes actuels de la phénoménologie, ed. van Breda (Paris, 1952).
2. Trans. Charles Kelbley (Chicago, 1965).

[xi]

describe overt meanings, *La Symbolique du mal*, like the projected third volume, *Poetics of the Will*, must resort to a hermeneutic phenomenology of latent meanings. Ricoeur recognizes this problem in the *Symbolique*, and deals with it in detail in his most recent publication, *De l'interpretation*. This volume applies the basic insight of phenomenology of will to the question of meaning and its expression, thus resolving the methodological problems of the second volume of *Philosophy of the Will* and laying the groundwork for a future *Poetics of the Will*.

2. Methodological and Terminological Data

RICOEUR'S WRITINGS have received an enthusiastic reception among his students in France and America as well as among the few philosophers familiar with the terminology and concerns of contemporary existential phenomenology. However, Ricoeur's phenomenological methodology and the terminology derived from it tend to lend to his work a rather esoteric ring among audiences accustomed either to recent British philosophy or to Sartrean existentialism. Yet the difficulty here is far less significant than the very real parallels between the French and the American philosophical scenes. Just as American philosophy has tended towards a polarization between linguistic analysis and the more extreme representatives of existentialism, so recent French philosophical debate has tended to become a dialogue between materialism and idealism in an existentialist garb.

The brilliant success of Sartre's novels and plays and the increasing influence of Marxism in the postwar years sharpened the dichotomy of subject and object which has plagued French philosophy since Descartes and obscured the very existence of the *tiers monde* of French philosophy represented by men like Gabriel Marcel, to whom Ricoeur dedicated the first volume of his *Philosophy of the Will*. To English-speaking audiences, Marcel is familiar only as a minor existentialist thinker. Yet if existentialism is identified with Sartre's radical opposition of the subject as being-for-itself to an alien, meaningless object, being-in-itself, this is grossly inaccurate. For Marcel's central intuition, expressed in the concept of incarnation, is precisely one of an ultimate ontological unity of man's being-in-the-world and so stands in clear contrast to the dichotomy of subject and object which materialism and idealism—even in existentialist garb—take as their datum. The problem for Marcel and for the philosophical *tiers monde* he represents is not one of relating the subject and the object, or of reducing one of them to the other, but rather one of describing the polar structure of their ultimate unity.

The philosophy of Paul Ricoeur brings this philosophical third force into the forefront of contemporary thought. Ricoeur accepts Marcel's basic insight, the ultimate unity of subject and object in incarnation, but unlike Marcel, Mounier, and other *tiers monde* thinkers, Ricoeur finds in phenomenology a methodological tool adequate to the task of elaborating it into a systematic philosophy of man's being in the world.

Central to Ricoeur's methodological apparatus is the concept of intentionality, brought to the fore by Brentano and elaborated by Edmund Husserl. Intentionality here provides a disciplined expression for the vague recognition of unity of experience by recognizing that consciousness is always a consciousness *of*. . . . This does not mean simply that a discreet, given subject is conscious of an equally discreet object, but rather that the basic datum of experience at its most immediate level is the intentional unity of subject and object from which both the concept of a pure subject and of a pure object are subsequently derived by reflexive consciousness. As recent experiments on sensory deprivation have confirmed, there is no consciousness unless it is a consciousness *of* an object—and, conversely, an object presents itself as an object only *for* a consciousness.

Yet the intentional unity of experience is immediately polarized in thought—or, to use Husserl's more precise term, in *thematic* awareness. In reflection the intentional correlate of consciousness is inevitably objectified and opposed to the reflecting subject. How, then, can we reach the level of intentional unity of experience in understanding?

This precisely is the function of the much misinterpreted technique of *bracketing*. Husserl himself referred to it increasingly in his middle and later works, yet never gave it a strict definition. Bracketing is the deliberate suspension—not denial —of the objectifying standpoint and of the causal explanation derived from it. In imposing the phenomenological brackets, we deliberately choose not to consider our experience in terms of causal relations of objects conceived as discreet entities existing somehow "out there." Following Husserl, we can say that what is suspended is the question of existence or non-existence as an empirical fact, as a set of causal relations among "objective" objects observed by a disinterested observer. Instead, we choose to see experience (including "existence" in the existentialist sense of man's mode of being-in-the-world) as it in fact immediately presents itself, that is, as a structure of *meanings*, of intentional relations of subject engaged in a "world." Thus, by imposing the phenomenological brackets we transform the contents of experience from a physical world of objects into a world of *phenomena*, that is, objects as meanings presenting themselves to a consciousness. It is this radically human world which then becomes the proper subject for philosophy as a phenomeno-logy.

Two points need to be noted with respect to the technique of bracketing. The first point is that bracketing might, as in the later Husserl, lead to a triumph of subjectivity, but cannot of itself be considered a triumph of subjecti*vism*. The meanings with which it deals are not arbitrary products of consciousness, but intentional relations which unite the subject and the object in experience. Thus a river is an obstacle because I wish to cross it —but also because it is too deep for wading. While Husserlian bracketing corrects the objectivistic prejudice by recognizing that the object is object *for* consciousness, a phenomenon, it can reject the subjectivistic prejudice equally in its recognition that the phenomenon is the *presence* of an object to consciousness.

The second point we need to make is that a philosophy within brackets—a phenomeno*logy*—is possible because experience as immediately experienced is not James's buzzing, booming confusion, but presents a structure of its own. Again, the recognition is not new—John Duns Scotus spoke of common natures, and the early phenomenologists formulated the concept of *Wesenschau*, idea-perception, which is often misleadingly translated as intuition. Husserl, wary of becoming entangled in the debate about the ontological status of essences, used the Greek term *eidos* to refer to the immediately given structures of experience. Following this usage, the imposition of a second set of brackets, suspending the effects and vicissitudes of particular actual existence within the phenomenological brackets, has come to be called "eidetic bracketing."

Paul Ricoeur, in approaching the problems of incarnation, of being-in-the-world, relies heavily on Husserlian techniques. Thus the entire project of the *Philosophy of the Will* is carried out within phenomenological brackets, as an intentional analysis. In addition, in the first volume, eidetic bracketing enables Ricoeur to separate the essential structure of man's being-in-the-world from its special existential characteristics. Yet in spite of the extensive use he makes of Husserl, Ricoeur is scrupulously careful to avoid any reduction of the world to the subject. While the dichotomy of the subject and the object is not, Ricoeur believes, metaphysically ultimate, it is nonetheless real, and both of its poles must receive full recognition.

Ricoeur presents his basic methodological principle, through which he seeks to avoid either reduction or polarization of subject and object, in the somewhat cryptic formula that "the voluntary is *by reason of* the involuntary while the involuntary is *for* the voluntary." We could paraphrase this assertion in less precise but more familiar terminology by saying that while nature makes freedom actual, freedom makes nature meaningful, and neither can ultimately be separated from the other. The reasons which motivate my decision, the body which I am, even the personal and historical conditions of my being are not simply external limitations imposed upon me, but rather the organ in and through which I am actual. I am not identical with them, yet I am at all only through them and in them. While my freedom is actual only in and through my nature, the voluntary only by reason of the involuntary, that very "nature," that involuntary, becomes meaningful only in relation to the Cogito incarnate in and through it. Whatever may or may not be the case means nothing unless an "I" appropriates it as the motive of decision, as the organ of action, and as the condition of its being. Husserl's use of the Greek term *hyle* describes it quite appropriately: it is my freedom which transforms it into a meaningful "nature" while it itself becomes actual through it.

This basic principle of reciprocity of the voluntary and the involuntary serves also as Ricoeur's guide in bridging the gap between phenomenology and the empirical sciences. Unlike the existentialists, Ricoeur rejects neither traditional philosophy nor empirical science, but rather makes extensive use of both. Since freedom is incarnate in nature, empirical description of nature is prima facie relevant evidence for philosophy. But since philosophy, as Ricoeur understands it, is intentional analysis of the *subject's* being-in-the-world, it has to approach empirical science "diagnostically," as a description of "symptoms," that is, description of the ways in which the Cogito becomes actual in the world, and apply to it its own question, the question of the underlying intentional structure manifest through the objective form. The term *diagnostics* refers to this process of uncovering intentional structures embodied in empirical descriptions.

Similarly the "hermeneutics" to which Ricoeur turns at length in *De l'interpretation* is a complement to diagnostics on the other end of the spectrum. While the term diagnostics refers to uncovering intentional structures or meanings latent in objective, empirical description, so hermeneutics refers to the uncovering of latent meanings of symbolic and mystical expressions of experience.

3. The Project of the *Philosophy of the Will*

IN LIGHT OF THE methodological data which we have examined above we can begin to understand the project of the *Philosophy of the Will*. Ricoeur speaks of the first volume as an *eidetics* of the will because its task is a phenomenological description of the essential—eidetic—structures of man's being-in-the-world. The task is carried out within double brackets: phenomenological brackets excluding the concerns of objectifying consciousness, and eidetic brackets which exclude the special characteristics of actual existence as such. It is, as Ricoeur states in his Introduction,[3] a study of man's fundamental possibilities.

The term *empirics*, which Ricoeur used to describe the task of the second volume, reflects the removal of the eidetic brackets. No longer are the special characteristics of actual existence excluded: actual existence, its possibilities and actualities, are now the subject matter. Yet the task is still not an empirical explanation in the usual sense. The phenomenological brackets remain —the approach is still one of intentional analysis rather than causal explanation and the question of ontological status remains in suspension.

Finally, the term *poetics*, which Ricoeur uses in projecting the third volume of the *Philosophy of the Will*, distinguishes intentional analysis of the vision of a reconciled humanity from poetry as the term empirics distinguished intentional analysis of actual existence from its empirical explanation. The tasks, as the terms, are parallel: the vision of Transcendence and reconciliation is as much a part of man's being as the experience of the fault, and poetry in the broadest sense is the evocation of that vision. Thus a phenomenology of man's being-in-the-world remains incomplete as long as it does not include an intentional analysis of this vision. But again the poetics of the will continues to operate within phenomenological brackets. The question of the ontological status of Transcendence and reconciliation remains in suspension.

3. See p. 3.

[2] EIDETICS OF THE WILL: FREEDOM AND NATURE

THE FIRST VOLUME of Ricoeur's *Philosophy of the Will* is an intentional analysis of man's fundamental possibilities, carried out within double brackets. This methodological decision has a far-reaching significance. It excludes from consideration two dimensions of experience which, while they cannot be derived from the eidetic structure of man's being as incarnate Cogito, are nonetheless crucial aspects of his actual existence: the dimensions of Transcendence and of the fault.

Ricoeur's concept of the fault [*la faute*] is broad, and neither French nor English provides a term which would do it full justice. It expresses the basic awareness that all is not right with the world, that existence as I live it is always a flawed existence. This is the awareness expressed in symbols of evil and myths of the fall, in the Platonic myth of the world running backwards, as well as in the philosophical concepts of the fall or of the bondage of passions. Using the term in its broadest sense (rather than in Ricoeur's own more restricted, clinical sense), we can say that the concept of the fault points to the *pathological* distortion of existence.

Linked closely with the pathological distortion of existence are the encounter with Transcendence and the eschatological vision of innocence which confront existence with the hope of restoration and healing. As the fault represents existential distortion of man's being, so the vision of Transcendence points to the hope of reconciliation represented in existence by those rare glimpses which reveal the fault as a distortion rather than as an essential feature of man's being. A comprehensive understanding of man has to take both these dimensions of man's being into account. The problem, however, is precisely that the dimensions of fault and of Transcendence introduce an opacity into existence. Existence, as we approach it in experience, is always existence distorted by the fault. Yet the fault—as all the pathological—is not intelligible in itself, but only in terms of the essential structure which it distorts. The bondage of passions, when it is not conceived as a bondage of freedom but as the essential human condition, inevitably leads to a view of man which either loses sight of freedom altogether, reducing man to an essentially passive victim of a radically alien nature, or asserts freedom in a spasm of Promethean defiance which rejects nature altogether—and with it freedom which is actual only as incarnate in nature. Thus an eidetic analysis of the essential structures of man's being, apart from their existential distortions, is a prerequisite for an understanding of existence.

A parallel consideration applies to the second, eschatological dimension of man's existence. The confrontation with Transcendence and the vision of innocence may in fact be what reveals the fault as a fault. But as the fault masks the essential unity of man's being, so the vision of innocence masks its real polarity. A premature consideration of Transcendence reduces it to a *deus ex machina*, barring a genuine recognition of the problem with a facile, verbal solution. We can return to the poetics of Transcendence only after we have carried out an eidetic analysis of man's being-in-the-world within the rigorous brackets which exclude both the fact of existential distortion and the hope of reconciliation.

Motives and Decision. One incidental effect of this double bracketing is that Ricoeur's first volume operates in an area familiar to traditional philosophy under the topics of free will and determinism, mind and body, and freedom and fate. Yet there is a basic difference in approach. While traditional philosophy tended to assume a dualism of the voluntary and the involuntary, Ricoeur's guiding principle is their reciprocity, the "primacy of conciliation over paradox." [4]

Ricoeur opens his analysis by applying this principle to the moment of decision in which the involuntary is most clearly linked with the voluntary. Following the program outlined in his paper, "The Methods and Tasks of Phenomenology of the Will," [5] Ricoeur now argues that a decision, like an act of intellection, has an intentional correlate. Unlike a wish, a decision intends its object as something *to be done by me,* and unlike a command, as something which depends on me, *is within my power.* At the same time decision has a reflexive dimension: I define myself in its object, commit myself, bind myself. Thus the act of deciding is the central and constitutive act of my mode of being.

Yet even in this central voluntary act the involuntary dimension is never far removed. For there are no decisions without motives. I decide not only to . . . , but also because. . . . Apart from motives there are no decisions, only happenings. To be sure, a motive is not a cause: it is not effective and cannot be understood apart from the decision *of which* it is the motive. Still, the centrality of motives in a decision gives that decision a continuity with the involuntary. Material value ethics and the philosophical

4. See below, p. 341.
5. van Breda, *op. cit.*

naturalism akin to it seek these motives in my body and the world, in terms of needs and desires. Yet Ricoeur's detailed analysis shows that need is not self-explanatory but is a lack and a desire which acquire definitive direction only as appropriated by a will. Similarly, desires, as pleasure, pain, ease, or challenge, constitute only the raw material of motivation, confused and contradictory, which assumes the form of definite motives only as it is received by the voluntary. It is this aspect of motives which lends a certain persuasiveness to formalism in ethics which sees reason as dominant and equates freedom with its sovereignty over desire. But as Ricoeur's analysis of formalism clearly shows, the Kantian rational law is only a minimal ethical rule which remains purely formal apart from a recognition of the material value of the other. Thus the polarity of the voluntary and the involuntary persists in motivation: motives are motives for a will—while a will is a definite will only by reasons of motives. In terms of our earlier translation, motives make a will actual, will makes motives meaningful.

This polarity stands out clearly in the *process* of choosing. As against Sartre, Ricoeur sees the hesitating consciousness not as nothing, but as a unity of search, trying out projects in a conditional mode. Yet as against cosmological interpretations, Ricoeur sees the hesitating consciousness as genuinely conditional, as not yet definite, not yet an object. Because of its intimate connection with motives, the will is not a nothing, a spontaneity rejecting all reasons, but because of its power of shifting attention, of considering or not considering motives, neither is it simply a process of necessary deductive reasoning from premises (motives) to conclusion (decision).

Thus Ricoeur points out that two readings of the process of deciding are possible: in terms of the continuity of motives and choice, and in terms of the freedom creating novelty in the act of choosing. Both are necessary, yet neither is adequate: the first fails to do justice to the freedom of attention which injects a genuine element of novelty into choice, the second to the role of motive in choice which it paradoxically acknowledges when it constitutes the choosing will as the ultimate *reason* for choice. In this paradoxical reaffirmation lies the key to the dialectic unity of the voluntary and the involuntary in deciding: the choosing will does not create novelty *ex nihilo,* but appropriates the involuntary into the process as the willed motive of. . . .

Movement and Action. The intimate dialectic of the voluntary and the involuntary becomes more visibly polarized in the second moment of the eidetic structure of the will, in action and movement. Decision and action, as Ricoeur sees them, are continuous: genuine decision entails the possibility of action and is fulfilled by it. Yet they are as distinct as idea and reality. This is what makes action—as distinct from a project of action—difficult to reach phenomenologically. It is nevertheless possible because action is an extension or an incarnation of a will. Thus it shares the will's intentionality: its intentional object is the change it effects in the world.

Movement here emerges as the organ of Cogito's practical incarnation. Normally it remains in the margins of the consciousness which passes through it, takes it for granted in its preoccupation with its intention. However, it is brought to thematic awareness in effort, that is, in will's need to overcome bodily inertia in acting and, more intimately still, in the Cogito's need to subdue the body sufficiently to make thought possible. Thus in a way the core of the study of man as the unity of the voluntary and the involuntary, as incarnate Cogito, lies in the ways the will uses the involuntary as an organ and the ways the involuntary lends itself to such use. The danger of misinterpretation is also greatest here, in the temptation, to which behaviorism and Gestalt psychology are equally prone, to attribute independent intelligibility to the involuntary by confounding the observing Cogito with the observed body. The task of clarification of the mystery of incarnation here depends precisely on recognizing the primordial unity of man in act, the genuine duality of actor and observer viewpoints, and the second-level unity of the incarnate Cogito which uses an original, underived involuntary as its organ, thereby inscribing itself into the texture of the world. The primary tool of Ricoeur's clarification here is a careful analysis of the spontaneity and availability of the involuntary in action as presented in preformed skills and in the spontaneity of emotion and of habit.

Two points stand out clearly in Ricoeur's analysis of preformed ("instinctive") skills (as, for example, the basic and unlearned coordination of sight and touch). One is an affirmation of the continuity of the perceiving and the acting Cogito. While in man's case such preformed skills are no more than a minimum on which learning and habituation must build, learning is possible at all only because of my given initial hold on the world which they represent. The second point is negative: while my preformed skills represent an involuntary form or organ, it is not possible to reduce voluntary action to them as its alleged involuntary essence. Unlike the truly involuntary reflexes of defense or assimilation, Ricoeur shows that the preformed skills are not rigid and incoercible, but rather eminently educable and subject to voluntary control. The alleged ideo-motor reflex, which attempts to reduce voluntary action to involuntary imitation, is in this sense not a reflex at all—it, too, might serve to regulate the form which voluntary action can assume, but only a pathological fading of the will can give it a capacity for involuntary action. Seeing a laborer use a hammer might suggest to me a way of fastening one piece of wood to another, but it is not of itself enough to make me start hammering. Thus the involuntary of preformed or instinctive skills is involuntary only with respect to the form which my action might follow, but not with respect to the *whether* of a voluntary act. Neither reflexes nor "instinct," but emotion or habit might be the area in which the will is ultimately secondary to the involuntary.

Yet Ricoeur finds good and sufficient reason for considering emotion, too, an organ rather than a motive of willing, offering means rather than ends—the means of effective action. This is not difficult to establish with respect to the emotions whose basic mode is *wonder*. These emotions lend an affective coloring and vibration to my encounter with the world, helping to bridge the distance between perception and action. But even the emotions whose mode is *shock* ultimately support Ricoeur's contention. Even they, as he shows, include an element of valuation and judgment: only a world about which I care, in which I intend, can shock me. Though the will is overwhelmed and broken, it is not enslaved. Only in passion is the will an enslaved will rather than either sovereign or defeated will. But while emotion provides the corporeal point of entry and an alibi for passion, it is not passion. Passion is a mental rather than a corporeal phenomenon —it is the vertigo to which the will chooses to yield, a bondage which the will imposes on itself. The true corporeal involuntary, emotion, remains in principle an organ rather than a master of the voluntary.

Similarly, in his treatment of habit Ricoeur remains faithful to his basic methodological rule that the reciprocity of the voluntary and the involuntary is intelligible in light of the voluntary which appropriates it in receiving and transforming it into an organ of its act. But here, as in the earlier chapters, the receptivity of the voluntary is as real as its primacy, and it is precisely the real spontaneity of the involuntary which makes possible the naturalistic reduction of the voluntary—as well as the defective forms of conduct reflected in this misinterpretation. Thus it is the givenness of our preformed skills which makes it possible to confuse them with reflexes, just as it is the spontaneity of emotion which makes it available as an alibi. Similarly, it is the real spontaneity of habitual conduct which makes possible both its misinterpretation as involuntary automatism and its degeneration into involuntary automatism. In principle, habit is the organ which most increases the efficacy of willing and frees the will from preoccupation with means, enabling it to focus on ends. In providing willing with easy, familiar patterns of action, habit reinforces willing. But it is a double-edged tool which also presents a temptation and an opportunity for a degradation of active willing. Its spontaneity is also an inertia: the weak or tired will sees in its easy, readily available pattern not just a tool for effective action but also a relief from responsibility, a substitute for such action. Thus the ultimate significance of habit—as well as of preformed skills and of emotion—depends on the effort which determines whether the will uses them or yields to them.

Effort represents the culmination of the dialectic of the voluntary and the involuntary on the level of action. The ideal limit of voluntary movement is effortless movement, the gracious ease of freedom in full harmony with its organs. In this sense the need for effort is itself a sign of disharmony, of the resistance of the involuntary—whether as inertia of mind or body which I must overcome in act, or as the impulse outburst which I must control. But the resistance is not an absolute one: already the fact that I experience resistance shows that my willing is partly successful. The involuntary here is still relative to a will and lends itself to use by the voluntary. Thus building up docile habits of action aids the will in overcoming both inertia and impulse—as Ricoeur beautifully points out, gymnastics is relevant to ethics. On the other hand, it is the relative involuntary of emotion which aids the will in mobilizing its resources and breaking through the inertia of habit and the customary. The dialectic is never one of sheer effort—"will power"—conquering sheer involuntary emotion or habit, but rather of voluntary effort using docile aspects of the involuntary to overcome those aspects which oppose it in a given situation. Thus effort is the epitome of incarnate freedom: freedom appropriating a body and a world. As in the case of decision, so in the case of action the involuntary is an involuntary *for* a will, yet willing is possible only by reason of the involuntary organ it appropriates.

And yet in spite of the privileged position of voluntary movement as the quintessence of incarnate will, a philosophy of effort is not the whole of a philosophy of man. The idealism of *praxis* encounters its limit in *theoria,* in knowledge which is not simply experience of resistance but a presence of a genuinely *other.*

Condition and Consent. Analysis of man in terms of the will and the involuntary relative to it must confront one other difficult problem: the problem of the absolutely involuntary. The will not only brings out a relative involuntary with its purposes, but it also confronts the absolute involuntary of accidents of character type, of an unconscious, and ultimately of sheer biological life, birth, and death. I am not only incarnate in the sense of being myself *through* limited mental and physical organs, but also in the sense of what Heidegger called *Geworfenheit,* in the sense of being stuck with the particularity of my situation. Have we here reached the ultimate involuntary, or can this still be understood in terms of the will?

The latter is precisely what *consent* makes possible. This ultimate act of the will is not simply a passive acknowledgment of necessity but its active adoption in the decision to accept it as mine and in the strange effort of patience which realizes this decision. Thus, as Ricoeur observes, what is at stake in consent is "the ultimate reconciliation of freedom and nature." [6] On this level the two forms of the dialectic of the voluntary and the involuntary which Ricoeur examines in the first two parts of the book reach an ultimate stage: the involuntary of the organ in movement as the absolutely involuntary character (what common usage calls "temperament"), the involuntary of motive in decision as the absolutely involuntary unconscious. In addition, a third problem arises: the ultimate problem of the relation of the will to the world as encountered in the whole complex of nature— life in all its significance—and history. The first two problems can be considered primarily psychological problems of applicability of subjective reflexion to objective reasoning; the third is a philosophical problem of ultimate compatibility of freedom and nature. To the extent to which these two are essentially incompatible, the only possibilities for the will are defiance or surrender. Consent would then become either impossible—or a masked surrender.

Character. The guiding insight of Ricoeur's analysis of the absolute involuntary of character is that it is precisely as necessity is experienced internally at the limits of objective knowledge that it can be matched by voluntary consent. Only as I recognize my

6. See below, p. 346.

temperament as an incoercible datum can I begin to use it in my service.

The empirical ethology with which Ricoeur deals has not figured prominently in Anglo-Saxon philosophical discussion and much of its terminology—especially that of the Dutch ethologists to whom he refers—tends to acquire a rather quaint and dated flavor in translation. In American practice, descriptive transcription of statistical material is rare. Yet the full relevance of Ricoeur's analysis stands out clearly when we recognize that the various IQ, scholastic, or vocational aptitude test scores with which we label our students and ourselves function no less as character portraits than the various combinations of emotivity, activity, or primarity which the Dutch and French researchers label as nervous, phlegmatic, or other character types. With the inevitable increase in administrative reliance on objective indices of temperament—however described—a philosophical analysis of the problem of character becomes crucially important.

When such analysis is absent, interpretation of statistical profiles falls back on a common-sense view of character. Yet common sense is quite ambiguous at this point, regarding character on the one hand as a set of external traits which identify and typify my behavior and on the other hand as my innermost unique way of being. Empirical ethology, which Ricoeur examines at length, resolves the ambiguity by rejecting the second alternative. Rather, it describes and hypostatizes character types which it construes as causal factors—possibly further reducible to unconscious and even genetic factors—determining my behavior. So conceived, character becomes objective necessity not assimilable to freedom. In order to rediscover character as my freedom's way of being, philosophy has to approach it from the viewpoint of the freedom whose vehicle is character. This freedom remains present—albeit in a concealed way—even in empirical ethology: it is an I, a subjectivity, who constructs the ideal type and reduces myself to them. But empirical ethology can do more than indicate symptomatically the presence of freedom: it can also serve as a means of articulating the fleeting experience of my character as my freedom's unique way of being in the world. For this, finally, is the truth of the involuntary of character: my freedom is not an abstract freedom but a concrete, incarnate freedom which is real in a particular, determinate way. Yet it remains a freedom: while the character, or temperament, through which I am free determines the style of my acts, it does not determine their intention. Only if we can keep this clearly in mind can we, both as administrators and administered, use and profit from empirical indicators without becoming victimized and spellbound by them.

The Unconscious. The ambiguous availability and danger of the concept of character also marks the other objective index of subjectivity, whose popular and administrative use again far exceeds its strictly clinical application—the concept of the unconscious. Ricoeur's treatment of the unconscious in this volume raises one technical question: it was written before his exhaustive research in Freud and was strongly affected by Karl Jaspers' and Roland Dalbiez' interpretation of Freud and Freudianism. Eighteen years later, in *De l'interpretation,* Ricoeur's interpretation of Freud is much more profound and much more systematic. To what extent are Ricoeur's comments in *The Voluntary and the Involuntary* still valid?

I believe that the discontinuity in Ricoeur's thought is much more apparent than real, and that while Ricoeur's work on Freud adds much and changes the perspective from which we need to view his earlier comments, it detracts nothing from their validity. The different perspectives are implicit in Ricoeur's later work on Freud which recognizes Freud's methodological ambiguity and vacillation between a naturalistic mental physics and a profound intentional analysis. For our purposes we can project this difference in terms of a difference between Freudianism which succumbed by and large to the fascination of Freudian energetics of the unconscious and Freud's own mature philosophical insight which Ricoeur's later work uncovers. In light of this work, the section in the present volume dealing with the unconscious appears valid in its positive assertions, and, negatively, as a critique of Freudianism rather than of Freud at his best. Thus it remains both acute and accurate, for whatever deeper meaning may lie concealed in Freud's work, Freud as he is still understood in the vast body of popular Freudian literature and common psychological and philosophical debate is still the Freud of the Freudians.

Ricoeur approaches the problem in the context of the broader, more basic problem of the *hidden* which not only resists my effort but also *deceives* me. An analysis of the unconscious as a hidden nature is possible only if we bracket the bondage of passion, the self-deception which a fascinated consciousness works on itself and which constitutes a major part of the hidden. Such deception is possible because consciousness can lie to itself—and lose awareness of its deception. Thus it is not involuntary, but a self-deceived voluntary, a bondage which freedom imposes on itself.

Only when we resolutely bracket the hidden as self-deception does the truly involuntary pole of the hidden emerge: the hidden as an aspect rather than as a defect of consciousness. But any attempt at an intentional analysis of my unconscious encounters the difficulty that I have no experience of it: it is really unconscious. I can approach it only through objective description which I reappropriate subjective as the *condition* of a freedom in the world.

Before such an approach becomes possible, Ricoeur points out, we need to overcome a double obstacle, the dogmatism of consciousness which insists that consciousness is fully transparent to itself, and the realism of the unconscious which would attribute to the unconscious a will and thought of its own, construing it as a second, involuntary myself. The evidence offered by Ricoeur's analysis, the facts presented by psychoanalysis, as well as the untenable polarization of experience between a sovereign, unsituated consciousness and a meaningless world which absorbs even my body, a polarization entailed by such dogmatism, are sufficient grounds for rejecting the dogmatism of transparent consciousness. But in turn the Freudian realism of the unconscious requires criticism. The root of this illusion is the assumption that consciousness, when dealing with the other, is unconscious. Yet while such consciousness does not include an explicit judgment about the self, it is still present to itself in a way which an explicit judgment formulates and expresses overtly. Ricoeur extends this relation step by step to all aspects of the Freudian unconscious, showing that the unconscious is not yet thought but rather impersonal matter which thought uses. Thus the "memory" of a dream, in its overt form, is always a retrospective interpretation of the unarticulated affective matter which lends itself to it but which is not yet identical with it. Like the ethological concept of character, psychoanalytic conception of the unconscious mediates the affective matter of the unconscious which receives explicit form from the intention of a subject.

This basic relation of the unconscious as *hyle*, truly involuntary but real only as it is given form by consciousness and will, guides Ricoeur's critique of Freudian geneticism, the tendency to reduce all higher manifestations to "lower" drives. The truth of the position lies in its recognition of undifferentiated affective matter in terms of which freedom becomes real freedom; its danger lies in its availability as an alibi. Thus, while formulating such affective matter in terms of the lowest forms can serve a valid clinical function, it is ultimately dangerous and degrading for consciousness. Though the matter of my acts may be given, the intention and so the significance they have are mine. Thus, while Ricoeur recognizes and stresses the full value of psychoanalysis and of its objectification of consciousness and the unconscious, he also recognizes the ultimate primacy of phenomenology of intentionality to it. While the voluntary, in this area again, is by reason of the involuntary, the involuntary becomes meaningful and actual only *for* the voluntary.

Life. The pattern which emerges from Ricoeur's analysis of character and the unconscious as forms of absolute involuntary applies, *mutatis mutandis,* to its third and most radical form, the brute fact of organic life, not in its dimension of a docile tool for willing but as sheer datum with which I am confronted and on which I depend. Here again there is no distinct subjective experience to guide us and objective description must serve not only a diagnostic but also a mediating function. Ricoeur examines it from three viewpoints. The first of these is life as structure, with its own teleology independent of willing in which both naturalism and supernaturalism see ultimate explanation of the teleology of willing. Secondly, life is a process, a growth on which eidetic analysis casts light through an examination of the patterns which make it a meaningful process rather than random change. Finally, Ricoeur turns to life as the brute datum of my birth, underscoring —like the death which I also encounter first of all objectively as an empirical law—the experience of my radical contingence. Each of these viewpoints presents the Cogito with a temptation to lose itself in a total explanation. Only in the difficult act of consent does the will transform this absolute involuntary from a restriction of its freedom into its unique individuality. My freedom is real *because* it is incarnate in the structure which is my life; it is *realized*—"historialized"—in the process of growth to which it gives unity and meaning; it is, finally, real because it is located by birth in an actual historical context.

However, consent is won from a refusal and this poses the basic, philosophical problem of eidetics of the will which Ricoeur faces in his magnificent final chapter. Only the *refusal* of my submergence in a nature continuum, the refusal which *rejects* my condition and wrenches me out of nature as freedom, makes *freedom's consent* possible. Without a refusal, there is only the fact of the nature continuum, not yet consent.

Here we leave psychological considerations behind and enter upon truly philosophical ground. For beneath the dualism of reflexion resolved in earlier chapters, Ricoeur recognizes a rupture in being. Though we might say that this rupture becomes actual only in the act of thought, this act is the fundamental human act, and on its ultimately ontological level the negative moment is an essential moment of freedom's affirmation. Because necessity is also a negation of freedom, rejection is essential to consent. The will which can consent is born of refusal. The creative act of rejection destroys the nature continuum more basically than reflexion. Freedom can consent to the necessity of character, the unconscious, and life as its act only because it rejects them as a necessity inflicted upon it.

Here we are operating at the very limit of eidetics. In the last instance consent implies a value judgment: freedom can consent to necessity because the universe is a possible home of freedom. And, in a universe in which the experience of evil is real and persistent, it is also an act of *hope*—the hope that in spite of its persistence evil is not an original aspect of the universe, and that the hope of ultimate reconciliation is not an impossible hope. Two basic philosophical models help us trace this difficult dialectic. First is the Stoic model of ultimately imperfect consent, consent made possible by a radical expulsion of evil and affectivity from the Cogito which wins itself in the acceptance of the rational Whole. The second is the hyperbolic consent of Orphism which submerges the Cogito in a frenzied plunge into the whirlpool of process—die and become! Yet ultimate consent must retain both the Cogito and the world. The guiding thread for such consent is the element common to both Stoicism and Orphism, the element of adoration in which Ricoeur sees a second Copernican revolution in philosophy. While the first Copernican revolution won the Cogito by placing man at the center of the universe, the note of adoration makes consent possible by replacing man with Transcendence as the center of reality. Only because the first revolution won the Cogito can the second revolution be a consent rather than surrender. Here the Cogito appropriates both Stoic and Orphic consent, gaining from the one the assurance of itself as sovereign and from the other involuntary emotive impetus which serves as a vehicle enabling it to recognize the limits of its sovereignty and its ultimate consent.

Thus it is appropriate that Ricoeur concludes his eidetics of the will by speaking of "une liberté seulement humaine"—a freedom which is only and uniquely a human freedom. What this means emerges clearly when we contrast it with the ideal limits which freedom projects. Human freedom is like the ideal limit, the divine freedom, in the sovereignty of its fiat, but radically unlike such hypothetical freedom since it is and remains a motivated freedom. Yet it falls short of the ideal of an omniscient, fully rational freedom because it acts in time and space, on the basis of a knowledge which is always incomplete, and its acts always involve an element of risk. Similarly, it falls short of the ideal of an effortless, graceful freedom in full harmony with its organs, and finally of the ideal of a fully human freedom, unlimited by particularity.

Human freedom is a willing, not a creative freedom. It is a freedom which in decision, effort, and consent unites the poles separated by understanding, a freedom which becomes actual in embracing its particularity. Human freedom is finally an incarnate freedom. This is its limitation—and its grandeur.

[3] EMPIRICS AND POETICS OF THE WILL

1. The Fallible Man

WITH THE RECOGNITION that human freedom is incarnate freedom we reach the limit of eidetics of the will. But while eidetics of the will provides us with an indispensable tool for understanding the vicissitudes of existence, it is not yet a full understanding of man. Man is not only *essentially* an incarnate freedom, but also actual freedom under the actual, disruptive conditions of existence. Thus a full understanding of man must include also *empirics* of the will which would elucidate the actual conditions of existence as reflected in consciousness and as presented in unreflecting expressions as symbol and myth.

This is the task which Ricoeur undertakes in the second volume of the *Philosophy of the Will: Finitude et culpabilité*. The first part of this volume, *The Fallible Man,* is still a descriptive phenomenology, though now a descriptive phenomenology of existence as it is reflected in consciousness. Thus it deals still with possibility, albeit existential rather than essential possibility —the possibility of evil. Here consciousness reveals the essential *ambiguity* of man's existence as the root of man's "fallibility"— his capacity for evil. In a triple movement of transcendental, practical, and affective dialectic and synthesis, Ricoeur here seeks to show that the Cogito in cognition, connation, and sensation is essentially a precarious, unstable synthesis of a finite and an infinite pole. This ambiguity and instability of existence is the opening through which evil can enter.

Can—but need not. Even after we have analyzed man's fallibility, we have not yet reached the level of the experienced *fact* of evil. Ricoeur's second movement in the second volume is an attempt to reach the very experience of evil—not its reflexive formulation in consciousness which removes it to the level of possibility, but the prereflexive experience of the fact of evil. This movement, presented in the second part of the second volume, *La Symbolique du mal*, requires a change in subject matter and a change in methodology. The subject matter so far was presented in the form of contents of consciousness, and so reflexive. However, in seeking experience itself, we have to turn to those areas in which the Cogito *acts itself out* rather than reflects on itself. In principle this could take the form of analysis of cultural forms, society, economic structures, dreams, or other forms of relatively unreflecting self-expression. Ricoeur chooses the most radical form of self-expression, at the same time more primordial and less affected by reflection and momentary influences than the forms we have suggested. In the symbolic expressions of evil and their systematization in myths, concrete experience presents itself for philosophical analysis.

However, this shift in subject matter demands a corresponding shift in methodology. Experience expressed in myths is always ciphered experience: its latent meaning is expressed through a level of overt meaning which simultaneously reveals and distorts it. In dealing with myth, we can no longer simply describe the overt, but must uncover the latent layer of meaning. Phenomenology here becomes a hermeneutic rather than a descriptive phenomenology.

2. Symbol and Hermeneutic Phenomenology

RICOEUR OUTLINES A FULL THEORY of symbolic expression and hermeneutic interpretation in the first part of his most recent publication, *De l'interpretation*. Here he details the two-layer structure of meaning characteristic of symbol which is neither a simple substitution of one set of signs for another nor any reference beyond the sign to an idea or an object, but rather a peculiar relationship of sharing in or representing, *pars pro toto*, a second layer of meaning. The relationship can be seen more clearly in the case of symbolic acts: the act of a white and a Negro student eating lunch together at a previously segregated lunch counter at the same time *is* integration and is ultimately significant as a symbol, representing social change *pars pro toto* as well as participating in it. (The example is mine rather than Ricoeur's.) In the same way, a specific evil act has its overt meaning—that is, it itself is evil—yet receives an ultimate significance as a symbolic expression of a flawed existence. On the other hand, instances of healing, for instance, in the New Testament, are both the presence and the symbol of the Kingdom of God.

The task of hermeneutic phenomenology is precisely to recognize the universal latent significance made manifest through the overt meaning of myth and symbol. Thus a hermeneutics must combine the attitude of trust with an attitude of suspicion, a willingness to listen to what is revealed through the symbol and a suspicion which would protect it from being misled by its overt meaning.

Ricoeur's previously published *La Symbolique du mal* is such a hermeneutic phenomenology of symbolic and mythical expression of prereflexive experience of actual evil, both as act and as fact. It is in the analysis of a series of symbols of evil as stain, sin, and guilt that Ricoeur succeeds in showing the unity of the paradoxical relation of man as agent and patient, as act and fact, or, in the terminology of the first volume, as freedom and nature, the voluntary and the involuntary, in existence. Here evil as fact infecting me from the outside (stain) appears as involving me in a broken relationship (sin) to which I consent (guilt): as the myth of Adam shows, I am seduced, and let myself be seduced. The various types of myth in which the symbols of evil are systematized can be subsumed within the basic myth of Adam which expresses the unity of the voluntary and the involuntary in existing man as *bound freedom,* and this freedom-in-bondage as the central motif of human existence.

3. Transcendence and the Vision of Innocence

THE VISION OF INCARNATION as essentially neutral and of evil as a fault leads to the third part of a comprehensive view of man, the hope of healing. The eidetic analysis of the first volume described the neutral structure of incarnation in terms of the polarity of the voluntary and the involuntary, whose existential condition the second volume describes as the distortion which Ricoeur characterizes as bound freedom. The distortion is revealed as such rather than as an essential condition of incarnate freedom in light of a vision of innocence, a vision of healing which would bind the polarities of the voluntary and the involuntary in the unity of reconciliation.

The evocation of this vision escapes the competence of eidetics and empirics alike. Rather, it would be a phenomenology of the vision of reconciliation which poetry, in its widest sense, evokes, and so a task of the *Poetics of the Will*, the yet unwritten third volume of the *Philosophy of the Will*. Ricoeur's published writings suggest two dimensions to which such poetics would have to turn: the dimension of promise and the dimension of hope. The dimension of the promise is present, as a token of reconciliation, in those rare experiences which offer us glimpses of reconciliation: the graceful, effortless movements of a dancer, the unity of understanding and will surpassed in moments of love. In such instances the voluntary and the involuntary meet fleetingly in a unity beyond conflict, a unity of reconciliation. But there is a second dimension. The significance of these moments of experience lies not only in their reality as a token of reconciliation, but also in the latent vision of ultimate restoration to which they point. This is the dimension of hope, and a comprehensive vision of man has to include a phenomenology of this dimension of experience as well.

Yet even when that task has been completed, a crucial final question still remains. Can we ever remove the phenomenological brackets and say not only that the description of man's being in the world we have presented is an accurate account of the way he experiences his being, but also it is—true? That is a question which can be postponed but never eliminated by phenomenological bracketing. Because it involves transcendental position, it lies beyond the competence of phenomenology. Conversely, because it inevitably includes the subject, it lies beyond the competence of "objective" explanation. The question remains, but the answer it receives may ultimately be an act of faith.

*   *   *

The philosophy of Paul Ricoeur, as we have tried to outline it above, brings to fruition the possibility of a comprehensive view of man's being in the world contained in Brentano's intentional psychology and Husserl's phenomenology. In elaborating the conception of incarnate Cogito as a philosophical guideline rather than as a mystery, Ricoeur resolves precisely the dichotomy of being-for-itself and being-in-itself which had driven earlier existentialist thinkers to mysticism or materialism. At the same time his insistence that the Cogito is actual in and through the world makes a diagnostic use of empirical investigation possible, opening a line of communication between philosophy and the human and social sciences.

But while this can be suggested in an outline, Ricoeur's *Philosophy of the Will,* like Hegel's *Phenomenology of the Mind,* defies summary, and for a similar reason. Ricoeur takes seriously the fact that freedom is actual only in a world. He is not content with a theoretical structure which could be summarized in an outline, but elaborates his insight concretely in a series of detailed analyses of specific topics. The monographs which become sections of the book, as the consideration of instinct, emotion, habit, character, the unconscious, life, etc., each worthy of separate attention, become in his hands steps in a comprehensive understanding of man. It is this wealth of detail, inevitably lost in summary, which makes Ricoeur's work more than just another speculative construction but rather a genuine philosophical synthesis. Joseph Moreau has written that ". . . the originality and depth of a philosophy is not measured by the astonishment it causes or the acclaim it draws, but by the perspectives it opens up on the great doctrines of the past and the insight it receives from them." [7] The philosophy of Paul Ricoeur meets this challenge.

[4] MECHANICS OF TRANSLATION

THE NEED TO COMMENT on the mechanics of translation testifies to the accuracy of Ricoeur's observations. In a world of pure consciousness, a translation could be a perfectly transparent glass, affording the reader a direct, undistorted view of the original work. But ideas, like men, are actual only as they become incarnate in a language which has an inertia of its own. Even languages as closely related as French and English are not perfectly isomorphic, and philosophical audiences as different as the continental and the Anglo-Saxon in our time are even less so. In preparing the present translation, I have attempted to intrude as little as possible on the flow of the argument. Yet a few comments, as a sample of my approach, might be helpful.

1. Le caractère

SOME OF RICOEUR'S TERMS are problematic because of their specialized application. Thus for instance the term *caractère.* In Ricoeur's usage, it refers to the unique "style" in which I do whatever I do. The content is ultimately immaterial: my basic

7. *La Conscience et l'être* (Paris, 1958), p. 156.

caractère does not determine whether I shall choose this or that possibility, good or evil. It does, however, mark my choice with the peculiar style of a nervous, placid, or other *caractère*.

In colloquial English, this style would be described as my "temperament," the unchanging style which, for instance, a militant, extroverted alcoholic will carry over into his new life as a militant, extroverted teetotaler. The German cognate of the term appears in Ach's work, *Ueber den Willensakt und das Temperament*. Unfortunately, the term "temperament" has not received wide currency in English scholarly writings. English-speaking ethologists, as for instance W. H. Sheldon, have been concerned with the much broader concept of personality which includes not only my constant style but also a range of acquired contents and preferences as well. Thus while the term has many advantages (especially in the plural: "personality types" would be an acceptable equivalent of *caractères*), it is not suitable for Ricoeur's much narrower use.

Nor is the cognate, "character," any more acceptable. Character in English has definite moral overtones: it is the specifically moral aspect of personality, subject, as personality, to training and voluntary change. Thus, colloquially, "temperament" remains by far the best equivalent of Ricoeur's particular use of *caractère*. However, in great part because of the fatal lure of a cognate for translators, "character" has been the term most frequently used in translations from French and German. Thus Klages' *Vorschule der Charakterkunde* appeared in English as *The Science of Character* and, more recently, the term has been used in translating Mounier's remarkable volume, *Traité du caractère*. The usage, unfortunate and misleading in many respects, received formal sanction in the third edition of *The Concise Oxford Dictionary* which defines ethology as "science of character formation."

Thus, while I believe a better case could be made for rendering the term as "temperament," the force of precedent and the attraction of a cognate together constitute too strong an objection. Accordingly, after much hesitation and experimentation, I have decided to translate Ricoeur's *caractère* as "character," with the hope that the reader will bear in mind that the colloquial connotations of "temperament" rather than of "character" are intended.

2. La faute

SOME OF RICOEUR'S TERMS pose special difficulty because of the original use which Ricoeur makes of them. Foremost among these is *la faute*. As we noted earlier, this term reflects Ricoeur's basic intuition of a world out of kilter, of basic disruption marking all existence. In conversation Ricoeur has stated that he had sought the most neutral term which would express this sense of radical disruption.

In the process of translation, I have experimented with several terms: fall, disruption, corruption, flaw, and others. The theological connotations of "fall" proved unsupportable. "Flaw" has the advantage of neutrality, but is hopelessly awkward in most English constructions, especially in adjectival use. "Corruption" has the great advantage of suggesting the central intuition that *la faute* is not metaphysically original. Perhaps the most faithful—and stylistically impossible—rendering would have been simply "the trouble," in the sense of that fine colloquialism, "the trouble with the world is . . ." Any of these terms might have been used. After much hesitation, I have finally settled on the cognate, "the fault," in part because of its obvious availability, and even more because it is the term used by Kelbley in the previously published English version of the first part of the second volume of the *Philosophy of the Will: Fallible Man*.

3. Comprendre

A SIMILAR PROBLEM is connected with Ricoeur's term *comprendre*, which I have rendered as "understand." In light of the eidetic task which he has set for himself in the first volume, Ricoeur distinguishes sharply between understanding and explanation. He uses "explanation" in the sense of explaining away, that is, reducing a phenomenon to the causal factors to which it can be attributed. By contrast, "to understand" has a specifically nonreductive meaning: to understand means to appropriate, to grasp a phenomenon in its full significance for the Cogito.

4. L'émotion, la durée

RICOEUR HIMSELF provides the guidelines for the rendering of these two terms. The first of them, *l'émotion* (esp. in Part II, Chap. 2, 2) seems at first sight to be an equivalent of English "feeling." However, Ricoeur's analysis (page 252 below), clearly indicates that "emotion" is the more accurate rendering, even though it produces some awkward phrases.

Similarly, *la durée*, rendered "duration" in translations of Bergson's work (as well as below, in the cases where a static emphasis prevails), has more frequently the dynamic value of English "process." Ricoeur's usage confirms this reading: in translating from German, Ricoeur uses *la durée* to translate the German *Prozess*.

5. Designer à vide

COMPARISON WITH THE GERMAN is less useful in the case of another problematic expression, *designer à vide*, which corresponds to Husserl's *leere Meinung*. In substantive form, this can be rendered very satisfactorily as "empty intention," and I have so rendered it when possible. Unfortunately, Ricoeur usually uses the verbal construction rather than the noun, and the accurate translation "to intend emptily" is so incredibly awkward that it badly disrupts the flow of the argument. I have therefore put the nontechnical expression "in general" to a specific technical use, translating *designer à vide* as "intending in general," contrasting this with the expression "intending specifically." Here common usage ("Did you have anything specific in mind?"—"No, I was thinking of it in general") provides adequate warrant for such use.

6. La conscience

ANOTHER CLASS OF TERMS poses a special difficulty because it covers the intention of more than one English term. Foremost, in this class is the recurring term, *la conscience*, equivalent variously to English "consciousness," "conscience," and "awareness." In translating it, I have on occasion done violence to English usage for the sake of philosophical consistency and rendered it "consciousness" even in expressions where "awareness" would have been more usual, reserving the term "conscience" for the few passages where this specific meaning is indicated by context.

7. Le pouvoir

THE TERM *pouvoir* belongs to the same class of problems. While "power" is its most obvious equivalent, Ricoeur's use of it is analogous to a use of "power" now obsolete in English, covering the related meanings of "potency," "ability," "capacity," and on occasions "possibility." After extensive experimentation, I have, with some misgivings, used both "power" and its related terms, depending on context, in an attempt to retain all the shades of meaning, and I have used juxtaposition to indicate their basic equivalence.

8. Le corps propre

ONE FINAL EXAMPLE must suffice to indicate the approach used. The term *le corps propre* indicates the body which I am and as I am it, in contrast with the body as observed. I have heard it translated "proper body," testifying to the fascination for the translator of cognates between French and English. Yet *le corps propre* obviously does not have the significance of a "proper body" —the hopelessly clumsy translation, "an own body," is more faithful to its meaning. So is yet a third translation, "a person's body." With some misgivings, I have settled on the term "personal body." While some of the intimate flavor of *le corps propre*, body-as-myself, is lost, the unobtrusiveness of the term provides considerable compensation.

There have, of course, been many more terminological decisions which had to be made, and often equally good case could be made for several quite different terms. I am far from certain that my choice was always the best possible. As the examples above show, I have tried to produce English text which could stand on its own philosophical feet as a work of philosophy. Thus my basic guide was fidelity to the meaning of the text rather than substitution of cognates. However, wherever more than one interpretation of the text is possible, I have tried to arrive at a neutral translation even at the cost of violence to good English usage.

For reasons of terminological consistency, I have in most cases prepared my own translation of quotations in languages other than English, identifying passages in Ricoeur's fashion by chapter and paragraph which are uniform in various editions. Whenever the work referred to is available in English, I have identified the English edition in the bibliography. In all cases where I have used an existing translation—principally in the case of the lengthy quotations from Rilke in Part III, Chap. 3—I have identified the translator and the page of the quote in translation in a footnote.

* * *

At the end of this undertaking, which has been both strenuous and rewarding, I should like to express my appreciation to Professor Ricoeur for his advice on several points of the text, to Professor John H. Lavely, Chairman of the Department of Philosophy of Boston University, to my colleagues in the department for their help and encouragement, and to the Graduate School of

Boston University for a research grant which saved me much tedious secretarial work. I am indebted to Derek Kelly for compiling the index.

A special appreciation is also due to Mrs. Frances Macpherson Kohák, who did not type, proofread, or in any other way collaborate in the preparation of the manuscript, but who throughout the sometimes nightmarish year of long weekends, longer evenings, and sleepless nights assumed cheerfully and competently all the many chores which normally make demands on my time, unfailingly providing me with a cheerful and calm home at a time when I contributed little to it besides the rattling of a worn temper and worn typewriter. More than anyone else, she has made this translation possible. If translations carried dedications, I know of no one to whom this translation would be more fittingly dedicated.

ERAZIM V. KOHÁK

Boston University
Thanksgiving, 1965

Contents

GENERAL INTRODUCTION: 3
QUESTION OF METHOD

1 *Descriptive Method and Its Limits*   4
2 *Abstraction of the Fault*   20
3 *Abstraction of Transcendence*   29

PART I   DECISION: CHOICE AND ITS MOTIVES   35

CHAPTER 1: PURE DESCRIPTION OF "DECIDING"   37

1 *Intentionality of Decision: The Project*   41
2 *Imputation of Myself: "Se Decider"—*   55
  Making up My Mind
3 *Motivation of Willing*   66

CHAPTER 2: MOTIVATION AND THE CORPOREAL   85
            INVOLUNTARY

1 *Need and Pleasure*   88
2 *Motives and Values on the Organic Level*   104
3 *Body and the Total Field of Motivation*   122

CHAPTER 3: HISTORY OF DECISION: FROM   135
            HESITATION TO CHOICE

1 *Hesitation*   137
2 *The Process of Attention*   149
3 *Choice*   163
4 *Determination and Indetermination*   181

xl / CONTENTS

PART II   VOLUNTARY MOTION AND HUMAN   199
CAPABILITIES

CHAPTER 1: PURE DESCRIPTION OF ACTING   201
AND MOVING

1   Intentionality of Acting and Moving   205
2   Moving and Dualism   216

CHAPTER 2: BODILY SPONTANEITY   231

1   Preformed Skills   231
2   Emotion   250
3   Habit   280

CHAPTER 3: MOVING AND EFFORT   308

1   Effort, Emotion, and Habit   312
2   Effort and "Motor Intention"   318
3   Being Able and Willing   327
4   Limits of a Philosophy of Effort: Effort and Knowledge   331

PART III   CONSENTING: CONSENT AND   339
NECESSITY

CHAPTER 1: THE PROBLEMS OF CONSENT   341

1   The Third Cycle of the Involuntary   341
2   Consent: Pure Description   343

CHAPTER 2: EXPERIENCED NECESSITY   355

1   Character   355
2   The Unconscious   373
3   Life: Structure   409
4   Life: Growth and Genesis   425
5   Life: Birth   433

CHAPTER 3: THE WAY OF CONSENT   444

1   Necessity as Non-Being and the Refusal   444
2   From Refusal to Consent   466

CONCLUSION: AN ONLY HUMAN FREEDOM   482

BIBLIOGRAPHY   487

Index   495

Freedom and Nature:
The Voluntary and the Involuntary

GENERAL INTRODUCTION:
QUESTION OF METHOD

THE STUDY OF relations between the Voluntary and the Involuntary forms the first part of a more extensive whole bearing the general title *Philosophy of the Will*. Thus the problems included in this volume and the method used in it are delimited by an act of abstraction which must be justified in this introduction since the fundamental structures of the voluntary and the involuntary which we shall seek to *describe* and *understand* acquire their full significance only when the abstraction which enables us to elaborate them is removed.

In effect, pure description and pure understanding of the Voluntary and the Involuntary are constituted by bracketing the fault which profoundly alters man's intelligibility and by bracketing the Transcendence which hides within it the ultimate origin of subjectivity.

It might seem strange to call a study descriptive when it is conducted within the limits of an abstraction which suspends such important aspects of man. We must therefore point out at the start that a description is not necessarily an empirical description, that is, a picture of the forms of man's actual voluntary activities. Daily forms of human willing present themselves as ramifications and, more exactly, as a distortion of certain fundamental structures which alone can furnish a guiding thread to the human maze. Such ramifications and distortions—which we shall investigate in the principle of passions and which we might call the fault or moral evil—indispensably require this particular abstraction capable of revealing man's structures or *fundamental possibilities*.

This abstraction is in some respects akin to what Husserl calls eidetic reduction, that is, bracketing of the fact and elaborating the idea or meaning. Husserl, however, was not concerned with focusing man's empirical reality around one fundamental fact, such as the already given degradation of the will and its disguise in the shades of passion. In contrast we shall see that all our considerations drive us away from the famous and obscure transcendental reduction which, we believe, is an obstacle to genuine understanding of personal body.

Thus this study is in some ways an eidetic of the voluntary and the involuntary, providing we remain constantly on guard against any Platonizing interpretation of essences and consider them simply as meanings or principles of intelligibility of the broad voluntary and involuntary functions. The essences of willing are what I understand in terms of a single model, specifically an imaginary model, when I say "project," "motive," "need," "effort," "character," and so on. A schematic understanding of these key functions precedes any empirical, inductive study undertaken according to experimental methods borrowed from natural sciences. Such an immediate understanding of the voluntary and the involuntary is what we have sought to elaborate first of all.

[1] DESCRIPTIVE METHOD AND ITS LIMITS

1. Fundamental Structures of the Voluntary and the Involuntary

THE FIRST PRINCIPLE which guided our description is the methodological contrast between description and explanation. To explain always means to move from the complex to the simple. As applied to psychology, this rule, which gives the natural sciences their force, led to building up man like a house, first laying down a foundation of a psychology of the involuntary, then topping these initial functional levels with a supplementary level called "will." The assumption is that in psychology need, habit, etc., have a meaning *of their own* to which the meaning of the will can be added if, that is, it is not derived from them. It does not consider the possibility that will might be already entailed in a full understanding of the involuntary.

In contrast, the initial situation revealed by description is *the reciprocity of the involuntary and the voluntary*. Need, emotion, habit, etc., acquire a complete significance only in relation to a will which they solicit, dispose, and generally affect, and which in turn determines their significance, that is, determines them by its choice, moves them by its effort, and adopts them by its consent. The involuntary has no meaning of its own. Only the relation of the voluntary and the involuntary is intelligible. Description is understanding in terms of this relation.

This reciprocity of the voluntary and the involuntary leaves no doubt even about the direction in which we must read their relations. Not only does the involuntary have no meaning of its own, but understanding proceeds from the top down, and not from the bottom up. Far from the voluntary being derivable from the involuntary, it is, on the contrary, the understanding of the voluntary which comes first in man. I understand myself in the first place as he who says "I will." The involuntary refers to the will as that which gives it its motives and capacities, its foundations, and even its limits. This reversal of perspective is only one aspect of the Copernican revolution which in its many forms is philosophy's first achievement. All of man's partial functions focus around his central function which the Stoics called the directing principle. This means that while for explanation the simple is the reason for the complex, for description and understanding the one is the reason for the many. The will is the one which brings order to the many of the involuntary.

This is why the various parts of this descriptive study will always begin with a description of the voluntary aspect, after which we shall consider what involuntary structures are needed to make that act or that aspect of the will intelligible. We shall then describe such involuntary functions in their partial intelligibility and finally show their integration in the voluntary synthesis which makes them fully understandable.[1]

We shall have an opportunity to emphasize at length some methodological corollaries of this principle of reciprocity between the voluntary and the involuntary. Thus it is enough to note two principles in passing. If the so-called elements of mental life are not intelligible in themselves, we can find no meaning in a purported primitive automatic behavior from which voluntary spon-

---

1. While its intention is very different, our enterprise of description and understanding touches at this point on the genetic explanation which M. Pradines attempts in his *Traité de psychologie générale* (Paris, 1943). The author shows that the appearance of a superior function in the course of phylogenesis brings with it a transformation which is "in a way retrospective" (vol. I, p. viii). Functions which appear simple to analytic psychology are often derived from subsequent evolution; thus it is the complex which precedes the simple and "thus fixes, in ontogenesis, an erroneous appearance of succession and derivation" (p. ix). Our intention is to understand the functional reciprocity which Pradines explains by his "law of reciprocal genesis" in terms of a phenomenology of the subject.

taneity could be derived by secondary complication, flexibility, or correction. Similarly, we are led to reject any inherent intelligibility of the pathological: in relation to the human synthesis of the voluntary and the involuntary, products of disintegration are new and aberrant. All attempts to understand the normal in terms of the products of pathological dissociation rest on the illusion that the simplification which sickness often produces uncovers simple elements already present in the normal, which had been merely elaborated and disguised by the phenomena of a higher level and deprived of their original form. This illusion is not an error of abnormal psychology but of normal psychology. The possibility of understanding the normal directly, without recourse to the pathological, will justify this corollary of our fundamental principle.[2]

The first task posed by the reciprocal understanding of the voluntary and the involuntary is to distinguish the most natural *articulations* of willing. The practice of the descriptive method itself effectively teaches us that the description of the practical function of the Cogito and its opposition to the theoretical functions of perception and judgment (existential judgments, judgments of relation, of quality, etc.) cannot be pushed very far without introducing important distinctions within the realm of functions itself, between imperative functions and the indicative functions which are wholly opposed to them.

The first attempts at description imposed on us a triadic interpretation of the act of the will. To say "I will" means first "I decide," secondly "I move my body," thirdly "I consent." Full justification of this principle of analysis lies in the execution of this plan itself. Nonetheless we might suggest, at least schematically, how these three moments are determined.

Here we need to appeal to a principle which extends beyond the limits of psychology of the will and which unites psychology as a whole. Any function is constituted by its type of object, or, as Husserl says, by its intentionality. We express it differently by saying that consciousness constitutes itself by the type of object to which it projects itself. All consciousness is a consciousness of. . . . This golden rule of Husserlian phenomenology is too well known today to require further comment. On the other hand, its application to the problems of the voluntary and the involuntary

<hr>

2. Morbid ontogenesis, writes Pradines, *op. cit.,* p. xii, "is, rather, necrogenesis. . . . The illness *creates* disorder and is not content with freeing a suppressed order. It creates madness in which the point at issue is never considered." Similarly, cf. Kurt Goldstein, *Der Aufbau des Organismus* (The Hague, 1934), pp. 2–3 and especially pp. 266–82.

is singularly delicate. The sample descriptions given in *Ideas I* and *II* are devoted primarily to perception and to the constitution of objects of knowledge.[3] The difficulty is to identify the status an object might have as the correlate of consciousness in the context of practical functions. The articulations of "the willed" as correlate of willing is precisely what directs our description.

1. The willed is first of all that on which I decide, the *project* I form: it contains the direction of action to be done by me in accord with my abilities.

2. Now a project is unreal, or rather a type of the unreal. Its inscription into the real by action constitutes the second structure of the will: the voluntary movement. Here the great difficulty is to identify the intentional structure of consciousness insofar as it is an effective action, an action carried out. The relation between acting and action will be the guiding theme of the second part of this description.

3. But there remains a residuum. The will does not resolve into an empty project and its practical execution in action. It consists also of acquiescence to the necessity which it can neither propose nor change. This third trait of willing is, admittedly, not immediately evident: it is brought to our attention by a detour into the involuntary to which it is a response, and of which we have not yet spoken.

Thus by virtue of the principle of reciprocity between the voluntary and the involuntary, the articulations of willing which we have sketched here guide us in turn into the realm of the involuntary. We can even say that one valuable consequence of the reversal of perspective posited in principle above is that it provides us with an order for dealing with the "elementary" functions which by themselves present no clear sequence. Involuntary functions thus can be differentiated and ordered according to their reference to this or that aspect of willing.

1. The decision stands in an original relation not only to the project which is its specific object, but also to the motives which justify it. To understand a project means to understand it in terms of *reasons* for it—whether reasonable or not. I decide this because . . . ; the "because" of *motivation*, which is itself an original "because," is the first structural element joining the involuntary and the voluntary. It makes it possible to relate a number of functions such as need, pleasure and pain, etc., to the center of perspective, the "I" of the Cogito.

3. A phenomenology of sensing and action is, however, adumbrated in *Ideas*, trans. W. R. B. Gibson (New York, 1931, 1962), §§ 95, 115, 123.

2. Voluntary motion, in addition to its typical intentional structure, implies a special reference to the more or less submissive abilities which are its *organs,* as previously the motives were the reasons for the decision. Thus it is possible to compare different psychological functions as potential organs of willing: habit is the most familiar and least disputable example of this.

3. Not all the involuntary is motive or organ of the will. There is also the inevitable, the absolutely involuntary with respect to decision and effort. This type of the involuntary, whether in the form of character, of the unconscious, of biological life, etc., is the terminus of that original act of willing which at first is even more hidden than its terminus: to this I consent.

2. Description of the Cogito and Scientific Objectivity

MAN'S BODY and the host of problems connected with it enters on the scene together with the involuntary. The task of describing the voluntary and the involuntary is in effect one of becoming receptive to Cogito's *complete* experience, including even its most diffuse affective margins. Need has to be treated as an "I have need of . . . ," habit as "I have the habit of . . . ," character as my character. Intentionality on the one hand and reference to a self on the other, which are the marks of a subject, are not easy to understand, especially since any consideration of the subject is more at home on the level of theoretical representation. Even the psychological indications (that is, the intending of a specific object and through that intention a subject-region) seem unknowable: what, for instance, would *my* unconscious mean?

The body is better known as an empirical object elaborated by experimental sciences. We have a biology, endowed with an objectivity which appears to be the only conceivable objectivity, for knowing the objectivity of facts within a nature encompassed by *laws* of an inductive kind. Conceiving of the body as an object thus tends to divorce knowledge of the involuntary from the Cogito and bit by bit makes all psychology fall on the side of natural sciences. In this way psychology develops as an empirical science of mental facts, conceived as one class within the greater class of facts in general. In becoming a fact, the experience of consciousness becomes degraded and loses its two distinctive characteristics: its intentionality and its reference to an "I" which lives in its experience. To be sure, the concept of a mental fact is a monstrosity: if it pretends to be a fact, it does so only by contamination from the object-body which alone has the privilege of being exposed among objects. But if it wants to be mental, it can do so only by virtue of recollection of conscious experiencing and of the fringes of subjectivity illegitimately dragged to the level of empirical fact to which psychology claims to have transplanted it.

Now as the involuntary becomes degraded into an empirical fact, the voluntary for its part is purely and simply dissipated: the "I will" as free initiative is annulled because it has no empirical meaning unless as a certain style of behavior which is no more than an elaboration of simple conduct following from the empirical objectification of the involuntary. Thus to understand the relations between the involuntary and the voluntary we must constantly reconquer the Cogito grasped in the first person from the natural standpoint.

This reconquest can make use of the Cartesian Cogito. Descartes, however, compounded the difficulty by relating the soul and the body to two heterogeneous lines of intelligibility, assigning the soul to reflexion and the body to geometry. Thus he instituted an epistemological dualism doomed to conceive of man as divided. He warns us, however, that "whatever pertains to the union of the soul and the body . . . is most clearly known by the senses." [4] And he adds, "It is by emphasizing solely ordinary life and discourse, and refraining from meditation and study of all that makes use of the imagination that we learn to conceive of the union of the soul and the body." [5] "For this," he states more strongly, "we must conceive of them as one, and together conceive of them as two, which is contradictory." [6]

The reconquest of the Cogito must be complete: we can only discover the body and the involuntary which it sustains in the context of the Cogito itself. The Cogito's experience, taken as a whole, includes "I desire," "I can," "I intend," and, in a general way, my existence as a body. A common subjectivity is the basis for the homogeneity of voluntary and involuntary structures. Our description, yielding to what appears to the consideration of the self, thus moves into a unique universe of discourse concerning the subjectivity of the integral Cogito. The nexus of the voluntary and the involuntary does not lie at the boundary of two universes of discourse, one of which would be reflection concerning thought and the other concerning the physical aspects of the

4. Descartes, *Letter to Princess Elizabeth*, June 28, 1643.
5. *Ibid.*
6. *Ibid.* This entire letter specifically clarifies the *Treatise on Passions*.

body: Cogito's intuition is the intuition of a body conjoined to a willing which submits to it and governs it. It is the meaning of the body as a source of motives, as a cluster of capacities, and even as necessary nature. Our task will in effect be one of discovering even necessity in the first person, as the nature which I am. Motivation, motion, and necessity are intrasubjective relations. There is a phenomenological eidetics of the body as the body belonging to a self, and of its relations to the willing "I."

Here some explanation is needed to specify what should be understood by subject body and generally by the Cogito in the first person. The opposition of subject body and object body does not in any way coincide with the opposition of the two points of view, towards myself, as such, unique, and towards other bodies, outside of myself. The question is a more complex one of the opposition of two attitudes, both of which can have recourse to introspection or extrospection, but within two different frames of mind.

What in effect characterizes empirical psychology is not in the first instance its preference for external knowledge, but its reduction of *acts* (with their intentionality and their reference to an Ego) to *facts*. Could we say that *acts* are better known from the "inside" and *facts* from the "outside"? That is only partly true. For introspection itself can be degraded to a knowledge of *facts* if it omits the mental as intentional act and as someone's act. That is what happened to empirical interpretation of introspection in Hume and Condillac. Introspection can be interpreted in a naturalistic sense if it translates acts into the language of anonymous facts, homogeneous with other natural facts, that "there are" sensations as "there are" atoms. Empiricism is a discourse in the mode of "there is." Inversely, knowledge of subjectivity cannot be reduced to introspection just as empirical psychology cannot be reduced to a psychology of behavior. Its essence is to respect the originality of the Cogito as a cluster of the subject's intentional acts. But the subject is myself *and* yourself.

These remarks are decisive for understanding the concept of a personal body. A personal body is someone's body, a subject's body, *my* body, and *your* body. For while introspection can be naturalized, external knowledge can in turn be personalized. Empathy (*Einfuehlung*) is precisely the reading of the body of another as indicating acts which have a subjective aim and origin. Thus subjectivity is both "internal" and "external." It is the subject function of someone's acts. By communicating with another, I have a different relation to a body which is neither included in my perception of my own body, nor inserted in an empirical acquaintance with the world. I discover body in the second person, body as motive, organ, and nature of another person. I read decision, effort, and consent in it. It is then not an empirical object, a thing. The concepts of subjectivity (of the voluntary and the involuntary) are formed by gathering experience derived from multiple subjects. On the one hand, my consciousness is profoundly transformed by the reoccurrence of the other's consciousness in it. I treat myself as a you which in its external appearance is a presentation to the other. From this viewpoint, to know myself is to anticipate my presentation to a you. On the other hand, knowledge of myself is always to some extent the guide for deciphering the other, even if the other is in the first place and principally an original revelation of empathy. The you is an other myself. Thus the concepts of subjectivity, valid directly for *my fellow man* and going beyond the sphere of *my* subjectivity, are formed in mutual contact of reflection and introspection. We can see from this that the transition from the phenomenological to the naturalistic viewpoint does not take place by inversion of the internal and the external, but by a *degradation* of both. My body is displaced from my subjective realm, but likewise your body is displaced from its subjective *expression*. The inert and inexpressive body has become an object of science. The object body is the body of the other as well as my body severed from the subject which each affects and expresses. Thus we can go from an object body to a subject body only by a leap which goes beyond the order of things, just as we move from the latter to the former by diminution and suppression, such diminution and such suppression being made legitimate by the type of interest represented by the constitution of empirical science as a science of facts.

If the subjectivity of the Cogito is the intersubjectivity of the "I" function extended to the body itself as a personal body, can we say that objective-empirical knowledge of physical "facts" in biology and of involuntary and voluntary "facts" in naturalistic psychology is purely and simply bracketed? By no means. That might seem possible as long as we deal with generalities about the body as a personal body. But to the extent to which we wish to carry out pure description of the involuntary, articulated in terms of precise functions, we cannot pretend that we are unaware of the fact that the involuntary is often better known *empirically,* in its form, albeit degraded, of a natural event. Thus we need to enter into a close dialectic between the body as a personal body and the object body, and to establish specific relations between the description of the Cogito and classical empirical psychology.

These relations pose the second specific methodological problem at which we must glance in this introduction and whose solution can, admittedly, be elaborated only by actual use of the method, in the context of particular problems.

It is too easy to say that the body appears twice, once as a subject, then as an object, or more exactly the first time as the body of a subject, the second time as an anonymous empirical object. It would be vain to suppose that we can elegantly resolve the problem of dualism by substituting a dualism of viewpoints for a dualism of substances. The body of a subject and the body as anonymous empirical object do not coincide. We can superimpose two objects, but not a dimension of the Cogito and an object. The experienced body corresponds to a "behavior" of the will. It is thus an abstracted part, set apart from the subject as a whole. The object body, however, is not a part but itself a whole, a whole among other wholes in the uniform system of objects. It includes only *lateral* relations to other objects, not a subordination to a subjective realm. Hence the immanent relation of "I will" to the involuntary really has no counterpart in an objective *"hierarchy."* The dependence of my body on my self which wills in it and through it has nothing corresponding to it in the universe of discourse of empirical science except a body explained in terms of other bodies. This is why, as we shall see in detail, the experience of effort is always a stumbling block to empirical knowledge and is always *reduced* by it. We shall see in particular the obstacles to conveying effort as a *fact* in objective empirical language, for instance as a "hyperorganic" force, or as a *lacuna* amid facts, as in indeterminism. It is natural and necessary that the laws of empirical objectivity regularly triumph over all attempts to express the subjective experience of freedom on their level. But in turn this triumph of empirical science over indeterminism or over the hyperorganic force in the end represents a breakdown of uniform objectivity. This triumph itself, conceived as an obstacle to grasping freedom of the subject, leads us to change viewpoints. Freedom has no place among empirical objects; it requires a reversal of viewpoint and a discovery of the Cogito.

Does that mean that there is no relation between the body as mine or yours and the body as an object among the objects of science? There ought to be one, because it is the same body. But this correlation is not one of coincidence but of a *diagnostic*. That is, any moment of the Cogito can serve as an indication of a moment of the object body—movement, secretion, etc.—and each moment of the object body is an indication of a moment of the body belonging to a subject, whether of its overall affectivity or of some particular function. This relation is not at all *a priori*, but is gradually formed in a sign-learning process. Such analysis of symptoms, which we are here using with respect to the Cogito, is used by a doctor in service of empirical knowledge, an experience indicating a functioning or a functional disorder of the object body. But the two points of view are not cumulative; they are not even parallel. The use of the descriptive method shows that the lessons of biology or of empirical psychology are a *normal* path for discovering the subjective equivalent which is often quite ambiguous. In some cases it will appear almost impossible to discover the subjective indication, in the language of the Cogito, of a function or an occurrence which is well known in biology or in empirical psychology (for example, personality type or the unconscious; birth, on which we shall dwell at length, is perhaps the most remarkable instance).

This is why our method will be most receptive with respect to scientific psychology, even though it will make only diagnostic use of it. Description of the Cogito will frequently recover from empirical psychology the vestiges of a phenomenology which it discovers there in an objectified and in some way alienated form. But with equal frequency a phenomenological concept will be no more than a subjectivization of a concept far better known along an empirical path.

3. Pure (or Phenomenological) Description and Mystery

AT THIS STAGE of our reflection it might seem that a description of voluntary and involuntary structures could be developed in the atmosphere of an intelligibility devoid of mystery which is the usual atmosphere of Husserlian studies.

In reality, as we examine actual practice, the understanding of articulations between the voluntary and the involuntary which we call motivation, motion, conditioning, etc., becomes stymied in an invincible confusion. Far from being overcome by the discovery of a common subjective standard between willing and the body, the epistemic dualism seems in a way to be raised by the descriptive method to the essence of the Cogito itself. The triumph of description is distinction rather than a reuniting leap. Even in the first person, desire is something other than decision, movement is other than an idea, necessity is other than the will which consents to it. The Cogito is broken up within itself.

Reasons for this intimate internal rupture become apparent when we consider the natural inclination of reflection dealing with the Cogito. The Cogito tends to posit itself. Descartes' genius lies in having carried to the limit this intuition of a thought which returns to itself in positing itself and which takes into itself only an image of its body and an image of the other. The self becomes detached and exiles itself into what the Stoics have already called the circularity of the soul, free to posit all objects by a second movement within the circle which I form with myself. Self-consciousness tends to precede receiving of the other. That is the deepest reason for the expulsion of the body into the realm of objects.

Now this tendency on my part to return to myself cannot be overcome simply by willing to deal with the body as a personal body.

Extension of the Cogito to include personal body in reality requires more than a change of method: the Ego must more radically renounce the covert claim of all consciousness, must abandon its wish to posit itself, so that it can receive the nourishing and inspiring spontaneity which breaks the sterile circle of the self's constant return to itself.

But such rediscovery of roots is no longer mere understanding of structure. Description still retains something of the attitude of the onlooker: concepts of the voluntary and the involuntary, conceived as structures to be understood, still constitute a higher objectivity. To be sure, it is no longer an objectivity of things, an objectivity of an empirical nature, but an objectivity of concepts seen and mastered. The bond which in fact joins willing to its body requires a type of attention other than an intellectual attention to structures. It requires that I participate actively in *my incarnation as a mystery*. I need to pass from objectivity to existence.

This is why within each of the three broad sections the descriptive method will follow a transcending movement which appears ultimately alien to the native genius of Husserlian psychology. Initial elucidation of forms of willing by the way of simple description requires in each case a deepening in the direction of more fragile but more essential connections.

Descartes himself, more than he had suspected, leads us to change the order of thought. How can I regain the sense of being alternately given over to my body and also its master from the distinctions of understanding if not by a conversion of thought which, turning its back on holding clear and distinct ideas *at a distance from itself*, attempts to *identify* with the definite experience of existence which is myself in a corporal situation?

Here we can recognize Gabriel Marcel's approach which ties the rediscovery of incarnation to a bursting of thought by object, to a conversion from "objectivity" to "existence" or, as he says later, a reorientation from "problem" to "mystery." Meditation on Gabriel Marcel's work lies at the basis of the analyses in this book. However, we wanted to put that thought to the test in terms of specific problems posed by classical psychology (problem of need, habit, etc.). In addition we wanted to place ourselves at the meeting point of two demands: those of thought nourished by the mystery of *my* body, and those of thought concerned with the distinctions inherited from Husserlian descriptive method. Only carrying out this project will permit us to judge whether this intention is legitimate and viable.

The third methodological problem entailed by a theory of the voluntary and the involuntary is one of understanding how a *distinctive understanding* of subjective structures of the voluntary and an *encompassing sense* of the mystery of incarnation mutually complete and limit each other. In this respect this entire work is an exercise in method in which two requirements of philosophical thought—clarity and depth, a sense for distinctions and a sense for covert bonds—must constantly confront each other. On the one hand the meaning of "existence" excludes the meaning of "objectivity" only when the latter is already degraded —objectivity is not naturalism. To be sure, a psychology which pretends to treat the Cogito as a class of empirical facts which it calls mental facts or facts of consciousness and which it proclaims to be verifiable by methods of observation and induction used in natural sciences, a psychology which degrades the central experiences of subjectivity, such as intentionality, attention, motivation, etc., to the level of a physics of the mind, is in effect incapable of shedding light on my bodily existence in any profound sense. It has only a diagnostic value. There is, however, one clear analysis of the Cogito which we might well call objective in the sense that it poses various essences before thought as its objects, such as perceiving, imagining, or willing. Now among these essences there are also relational essences, that is, meanings which are relevant to the very connections of functions —as motivation, displacing of a general intention by a specific one, realization, or foundation of a complex act on a first-level act. These relations are understood as descriptive relations. Thus we are justified in assuming that a nonreductive yet descriptive thought, a thought which is not naturalistic but rather respects what presents itself as Cogito, in brief, the type of thought which Husserl calls phenomenology, might shed light on the evasive intuitions of the mystery of the bodily. In particular, it articulates the massive experience of being my body according to the different significations of my body as a source of motives, as a focus of abilities, or as a background of necessity.

Yet on the other hand, even though a particular objectivity— that of concepts of the Cogito—always provides a more subtle problematic for the sense of mystery than a naturalistic objectivity, it seems to us hopeless to believe that we might "save the phenomena" without the constant conversion which leads from the thought which posits concepts before itself to a thought which participates in existence. Even though conceptual thought is not necessarily a naturalistic reduction, it always starts with a definite loss of being. I appropriate what I understand, I lay a claim to it, I encompass it by a definite power of thought which sooner or later comes to regard itself as positing, forming, and constitutive with respect to objectivity. This loss of being which, with respect to the object, is a loss of presence, is with respect to the subject who articulates the knowledge of conceptual deincarnation: I exile myself into the void as the nondimensional subject. Thus on the one hand I appropriate reality, and on the other I cut myself off from its presence. Not even Husserlian phenomenology escapes this hidden danger. That is why it never takes my *existence* as a body really seriously, not even in the fifth *Cartesian Meditation*. My body is neither constituted in an objective sense, nor constitutive as a transcendental subject—it eludes this pair of opposites. It is the existing I.

This intuition could not have been reached in any of the "attitudes" proposed by Husserl. The transcendental "attitude" instituted by the transcendental reduction and the natural attitude alike avoid the presence of my corporal existence which is in a sense self-affirming. If I pay closer attention to this first underivable and uncharacterizable presence of my body, I also can no longer suspend the existence of a world extending that of my body as its horizon without seriously disrupting the very

Cogito which in losing the existence of the world also loses the existence of its body and finally its marks as a first person.

For this double set of reasons, philosophy of man appears to us as a living tension between an objectivity elaborated by a phenomenology to do justice to the Cogito (itself recovered from naturalism) and the sense of my incarnate existence. The latter constantly overflows the objectivity which in appearance respects it most but which by its very nature tends to eschew it. That is why the concepts we use, such as motivation, completion of a project, situation, etc., are *indications* of a living experience in which we are submerged more than signs of mastery which our intelligence exercises over our human condition. But in turn it is the task of philosophy to clarify existence itself by use of concepts. And this is the function of a descriptive phenomenology: it is the watershed separating romantic effusion and shallow intellectualism. This region of rational symptoms of existence may be reason itself to the extent to which it is distinguished from analytic understanding.[7]

4. The Stake, the Paradox, and Reconciliation

THESE SUCCESSIVE DEEPENINGS of the descriptive method call for one last consideration which should reveal some of the more remote intentions of this study. To participate in the mystery of incarnate existence means to adopt the internal rhythm of a *drama*.

In effect, if we wish to surpass epistemic dualism deriving solely from the demands of clarity and conceptual distinctness of thought, and if we wish to discover the actual bond of the body as mine to the self which sees it, yields to it, and governs it, we shall discover that this bond is itself a *polemic*.

A new dualism, a dualism of existence within the experienced unity, replaces epistemic dualism and suddenly endows it with a radical and, we might say, existential significance which goes singularly beyond the demands of method. Existence tends to break itself up. In effect the advent of consciousness is always to some degree the disruption of an intimate harmony.

7. In the language of Gabriel Marcel, we have attempted a *problematization* which would not degrade but would clarify by reference to the lived experience of incarnate freedom. We have found such problematization in a phenomenological eidetics, thus giving a partial response to the questions posed in Ricoeur, *G. Marcel et K. Jaspers* (Paris, 1948), pp. 369–70. In this we also follow some suggestions which Karl Jaspers makes in *Reason and Existenz*, trans. William Earle (New York, 1955), where reason is called *Das Verbindende* (that which binds, joins).

"Harmonious self . . ." said the youngest of the three Fates. Yet consciousness, as a capacity for judgment and refusal, recoils from the reality of her body and of objects. Will is the ability to deny.

By contrast, such recovery of the self from a spontaneous existence makes all spontaneity appear as a more or less injurious force. A dream of purity and integrity takes hold of consciousness which then conceives of itself as ideally complete, transparent, and capable of positing itself absolutely. The expulsion of the personal body beyond the circle of subjectivity, its ejection into the realm of objects considered at a distance, can from this viewpoint be interpreted as a revenge of a subjectivity which feels exposed, abandoned, thrown into the world, and has lost the naïveté of the original compact.

This drama reveals all its virulence in the third part, devoted to necessity. The involuntary appears to me as a hostile force, primarily as an invincible nature, a finite personality, an indefinite unconscious, and a contingent organic life.

But the drama is already present in the study of voluntary movement: effort is not only stimulation of docile capacities, but also a struggle against a resistance. Finally, the very ability to decide which is the theme of the first part is always to some extent a refusal, a discarding of rejected motives. In some way, the will always says "no." Thus bit by bit the relations of the involuntary to the voluntary reveal themselves in a perspective of *conflict*. The conviction which runs covertly through the most technical analyses is that the recapturing of consciousness is a loss of being since consciousness is opposed to its body and to all things, and seeks to close a circle with itself. The act of Cogito is not a pure act of self-positing: it lives on what it receives and in a dialogue with the conditions in which it is itself rooted. The act of myself is at the same time participation.

Thus the intention of this book is to understand the mystery as reconciliation, that is, as restoration, even on the clearest level of consciousness, of the original concord of vague consciousness with its body and its world. In this sense the theory of the voluntary and involuntary not only describes and understands, but also restores.

From the point of view of method, this final deepening of our quest opens the way for a consideration of the paradox. Consciousness is always in some degree both a disruption and a bond. This is why the structures which connect the voluntary and the involuntary are structures of rupture as well as of union. Behind these structures lies the paradox which culminates in the paradox of freedom and nature. Even on the level of existence, the paradox is a measure of the dualism of the objective level. There is no logical procedure by which nature could be derived from freedom (the involuntary from the voluntary), or freedom from nature. There is no *system* of nature and freedom.

But then what prevents the paradox from being destructive? How can freedom help being annulled by its very excess if it does not succeed in recovering its connection with a situation which would in some sense sustain it? A paradoxical ontology is possible only if it is covertly reconciled. The juncture of being appears in a blind intuition reflected in paradoxes; it is never what I observe, but rather what serves as occasion for the articulation of the great contrasts of freedom and nature. Perhaps, moreover, as Kant understood it in the exposition of postulates of practical reason, the conflicts of the voluntary and the involuntary, and especially the conflict of freedom and inexorable necessity, can be reconciled only in hope and in another age.

Thus this study of the voluntary and the involuntary is a limited contribution to a far broader schema which would be the reconciliation of a paradoxical and a reconciled ontology.[8]

Let us sum up in a few words the problems of method entailed by a reflection on the voluntary and the involuntary. The axis of the method is a *description* of the intentional, practical and affective structures of the Cogito in a Husserlian manner. But on the one hand understanding of the structures of the subject constantly refers to empirical and scientific knowledge which serves as a symptom of such intentional structures, while on the other hand fundamental articulations of these structures reveal the unity of man only by reference to a central mystery of incarnate existence. To be understood and rediscovered, this mystery which I am demands that I become one with it, that I participate in it so that I do not observe it as confronting me at a distance as an object. Such participation is at odds with the higher objectivity of phenomenology. Finally, because the mystery itself is under constant threat of disruption, the living bond which reunites the voluntary and involuntary aspects of man must be constantly actively reconquered. In particular, the mystery of that living bond needs to be rediscovered beyond the *paradoxes* in which the

8. Mikel Dufrenne and Paul Ricoeur, *K. Jaspers et la philosophie de l'existence* (Paris, 1947), pp. 379–93.

descriptive structures seem to end and which remain the broken language of subjectivity.

[2] ABSTRACTION OF THE FAULT

THE DIFFICULTIES of reconciling freedom and nature, especially the tendency of the "I" to close a circle with itself, implicitly raise the question of the fault which a description of the voluntary and the involuntary must abstract from consideration. In this introduction, we must justify this abstraction at least in principle.

1. Passions and the Law

IN THE FIRST PLACE we must specify the region of reality which is thus placed in brackets. In a word, it is *the universe of passions and of the law,* in the sense in which St. Paul contrasts the law which kills with the grace which gives life.

This work will not include a study of ambition, of hate, etc. Now we believe precisely that the passions are not entities alien to the will itself. Ambition and hate are the will itself, the will in its everyday aspect, concrete, real. This is why the exclusion of passions must be justified.

We shall endeavor later to show in detail that the passions are a distortion both of the involuntary and the voluntary. It is customary to include them with emotions of which they are said to be a more complex, more enduring, and more systematic form. In Descartes, the assimilation of passions to emotion is so complete that the treatise, *Concerning the Passions of the Soul,* is in fact a treatise of basic emotions and of their complications in the form of passions.[9] It is certainly true that our emotions are the seed of passions and that in a general way all the involuntary is a point of entry, an occasion for passions, and, as Gabriel Marcel says, an invitation to betrayal. This we shall show concretely with reference to need, pleasure, and habit as well as emotion.

But passion is not a degree of emotion: emotion belongs to

9. According to Descartes, passion is simply opposed to action (*Treatise on Passions*, arts. 1, 17, 27, etc.); we shall show later that the soul has two forms of passivity: the spontaneity of its body, according to which it receives its motives, its powers, and its necessary conditions in diverse ways, and its own passivity in its corrupt state, according to which it submits to the bondage it imposes on itself.

a fundamental nature which is the common keyboard serving both innocence and fault. Passions show the ravages wrought at the core of this essential nature by a principle which is at the same time active and belonging to nothingness. To hold the passions in suspension is to attempt to separate man's fundamental possibilities from this aberrant principle.

Such separation is not merely an abstraction of a pure involuntary, but also of a pure willing. For passions are just as much ramifications of willing as of the involuntary (for example, emotion)—ambition is a passionate form of the energy deployed in choice and in effort. Stendhalian "virtu," Nietzsche's "will to power," and passions depicted by dramatists and novelists generally are passionate forms of willing. Passions in effect proceed from the region of the will itself and not from the body. Passion finds its temptation and its means in the involuntary, but the spell comes from the soul. In this specific sense, the passions are the will itself. They seize the human totality by the head and make it an alienated totality. This is why no passion can be placed *among* even the synthetic functions of the voluntary or the involuntary. Each passion is a form of the human totality.

The abstraction of passions is also an abstraction of the law, the law in the actual concrete form which values assume in an order of passions. In this work we shall never speak of the law, but of *values* which motivate it. We consider the relation of the will to motives originative, and the relation to the values which justify choice fundamental. The will is fundamentally the ability to receive and approve values. But the willing-value nexus remains an abstraction and does not introduce us to concrete moral reality. Such a willing-value nexus is a fundamental possibility which is used differently by innocence and by the fault. It provides only a basis for the possibility of a principle of a morality in general. Real, concrete understanding of morality begins with the passions. Thus the words duty, law, remorse, etc., take on a different meaning. Values become obligatory after the manner of a hard law in reference to passions. In perverting the involuntary and the voluntary, the fault changes our fundamental relation to values and opens the true drama of morality which is the drama of a divided man. An ethical dualism rends man before any dualism of understanding or of existence. "The good that I would I do not, and the evil I would not I do." This mutual dependence of passions and the law is central: in the context of the fault, passions and the law form the vicious circle of actual existence. Passions eject values from man, alienate them in a hostile yet melancholy transcendence which is, strictly speaking, the law in St. Paul's sense of the word, the law without grace. In turn the law condemns without helping: it entices the fault by prohibition and precipitates the very internal decadence which it seems to be designed to hinder.

Thus it would seem imprudent to draw premature ethical conclusions from this essay. Moral significance of the quest for fundamental reconciliation between the soul and the body should remain suspended; its meaning remains hidden and requires a long detour in order to be perceived. At first it seems that the Greek ideal of measure and harmony is within our grasp. But such harmony is possible only at a point beyond our reach. In setting aside the fault we have set aside actual ethics, even though our analysis lacks nothing as a theory of values and of their relation of the will to them. Furthermore, far from being able to find repose in the wisdom of balance and self-possession, we shall call upon a consideration of the fault to destroy this myth of harmony which is a lie and an illusion of the ethical stage par excellence. The fault is an event with immense possibilities. At its outer limits it is a discovery of the infinite, an experience of the holy in reverse, of the holy in the demonic; it is sin in the strongest sense of the word. In this respect, the fault which alone could *pose* an ethical problem in its genuine context is also alone capable of *deposing* ethics considered as a closed order of law. It is related to God, it is before God, going beyond subjectivity by its very excess. Only later, among the fruits of the Spirit, can harmony be presented as a new ethic.

The greatest error we could make with respect to a fundamental ontology of willing and nature is to interpret it as an actual, immediate ethic. In celebrating the mastery of willing over nature, it would lead us falsely to eulogize the "Pharisee" and the "just": in promising self-possession prematurely, it would be a promise which cannot be kept.

2. The Fault

WE CANNOT HELP being impressed by the vastness of the domain placed in suspension by setting aside the fault. Have we bracketed what is most important? This first impression is reinforced if we consider the core from which moral evil proceeds, understanding this term in the widest sense of the pair, passions and the law. Without in any way attempting to elaborate here a complete theory of the fault we shall recapitulate some traits to which we shall constantly allude.

1) The principle of passions lies in a certain *bondage* which the soul imposes on itself: the soul binds itself. This bondage has nothing to do with determinism which is only a necessary rule binding *objects* together for a *theoretical* consciousness; the bondage of passions is something which happens to a subject, that is, to a freedom. Nor is the bondage a necessity revealing the absolutely involuntary, necessity in the first person, to which I am subject as long as I live, born of a woman. It is actually necessary to set aside the bondage of passions to understand the burden of that necessity, for the necessity to which I am subjected can still have a counterpart in a freedom which patience sustains by its consent. Bondage of passions introduces a new turn of events, so that we run the risk of missing the possible connection between experienced necessity and freedom. Starting with corruption, freedom, fascinated by a dream of self-positing, exiles itself. It curses necessity even while using it as an alibi for passions. Thus I appeal to my character to contest my responsibility, I speak of its tyranny and at the same time I sanctify my bondage in the name of a necessity which might have become fraternal. If it is the double effect of the fault to petrify necessity and dry up freedom, we must attempt a heroic penetration to the most elementary bonds which join even necessity to freedom.

2) The bondage of passions is a bondage to *Nothing*. All passion is *vanity*. Reproach, suspicion, concupiscence, envy, hurt, and grief are various names for chasing after the wind. This fiction, this lie, reveals the decisive role of imagination in the genesis of passion. Here again we shall not forget to note the points of least resistance where imagination might insinuate its myths and make the soul succumb to the charm of Nothing.

The last remark presents a new reason for holding the fault in suspension. The idea of Nothing is an inexhaustible source of error. As it is, negation already has an important place in fundamental ontology: the lack of need, the gaping hole of possibility opened by a project, the refusal inaugurating all voluntary affirmation, the negativity of finitude, the impotence indicated by death and even birth itself. But this negation must be set apart from the nothing of vanity which complicates and perverts it. Compared to suspicion in jealousy, feeding on its own fiction, the lack of hunger is still a type of fullness, a fullness of true anguish, and a truth of the body in contrast to the emptiness which is vanity and a lie of the soul.

Thus we must suspend this frightening power which constrains freedom to make itself unavailable by projecting the bondage it inflicts onto itself into an intentional *Nothing*.

3) Passion introduces an infinite, an excess, which is at the same time a painful infinite, perhaps even an obscure religion of suffering. All passion is unhappy. This trait is connected with the preceding: the projected nothing draws the soul into an endless pursuit and inaugurates the "bad infinite" of passion.

This false infinite needs to be placed in brackets to bring to light the authentic infinite of freedom, the infinite of which Descartes says that it makes us like God. In particular, only an authentic infinite, an infinite without disorder, can embrace its own finitude without feeling that it is denying itself. The possibility of consent cannot be understood unless we abstract that deification of willing which is in fact its demonization.

4) The fault is not an element of fundamental ontology homogeneous with other factors discovered by pure description, like motives, powers, conditions, and limits. It can be conceived only as an accident, an interruption, a fall. It does not constitute a part of a system together with the fundamental possibilities contained in willing and the involuntary. There can be no genesis of the fault starting with the voluntary or the involuntary, even though each aspect of that circular system (pleasure, power, custom, command, refusal, self-positing) constitutes an invitation to the fault. Rather, the fault remains an alien body in the essential structure of man. There is no principle of intelligibility of such disruption, analogous to the *mutual intelligibility* of involuntary and voluntary functions, in the sense that their essences complete each other within the human unity. The *fault is absurd*.[10]

Here we touch upon the methodological reason which demands most imperatively that we set the fault aside: the consideration of the fault and its ramifications in passions leads to a total recasting of method. There can be no eidetic description starting with an accident—only an empirical one. Deciphering the passions demands that we study man through the usages of life and ordinary discourse. This is why the study which will ultimately be devoted to the fault, to passions, and the law, will proceed by an entirely different method of convergence of concrete symptoms. That is the only method suited to a topography of the absurd.

It might seem humiliating to the philosopher to admit the presence of an absolute irrational in the heart of man, not merely

10. In this sense Lachelier vehemently holds that evil is incomprehensible.

as a *mystery* quickening the intelligence, but as a central and in a sense elementary opacity which obstructs the very access to intelligibility as much as to mystery. Might not the philosopher take exception to introducing the absurd on the pretext that it is dictated by a Christian theology of original sin? Yet if theology opens our eyes to an obscure segment of human reality, no methodological *a priori* should prevent the philosopher from having his eyes opened and henceforth reading man, his history and civilization, under the sign of the fall.

But though the fault has "entered the world," perhaps a method of abstraction will permit a description of the primordial possibilities which are not absurd.[11]

3. The Possibility of Abstracting the Fault

Is THE ABSTRACTION, which so many reasons demand, possible?

We could object that a description which abstracts such important characteristics of human reality is impossible. But we must not forget that an eidetic description can take as its springboard even an imperfect, truncated, distorted experience, or *even a purely imaginary one.* This last remark, which agrees with the Husserlian conception of eidetics,[12] is of capital importance for our proposal: we shall soon see what sustains the vision of a primordial connection between freedom and its body. Furthermore, the fault does not destroy the fundamental structures; it would be better to say that the voluntary and the involuntary, *as they are in themselves,* fall into the power of Nothing, like an occupied country surrendered intact to the enemy. This is why anthropology is possible.

We could then object that the eidetic pretends to describe an innocent existence which is not accessible to us. But it is not accurate to say that we are proposing a description of innocence, of, so to speak, innocent structures. Innocence does not reside in the structures, concepts, but in the actual, total man, just like the fault. Furthermore, innocence is not accessible to any description,

11. These remarks distinguish out treatment from the use which many present-day thinkers make of the idea of the fault. On the one hand they secularize it and incorporate it among other elements of human existence. On the other hand, to the extent to which it loses its primordial character, it contaminates fundamental ontology with a sort of diffuse absurdity. That is why we shall not place the fault among limit situations as did K. Jaspers, or in the structure of "care" as did Martin Heidegger in *Being and Time,* trans. Macquarrie and Robinson (New York, 1962), pp. H.175–H.180.

12. *Ideas,* §§ 4, 70.

even an empirical one, but rather to a concrete mythical approach whose nature we shall attempt to sketch later.[13] It is the myth of innocence which serves as the setting of all empirical description of the passions and of the fault. The fault is seen as a lost innocence, as a lost paradise. Thus the objection is right in refusing us a direct description of innocence. However, it is not the lost paradise of innocence which we propose to describe, but the structures which are the fundamental possibilities offered equally to innocence and to the fault as a common keyboard of human nature on which mythical innocence and empirical guilt play in different ways.

But, one might say, if corruption seizes the *whole* man, voluntary and involuntary, how can we describe possibilities apart from innocence or the fault. If such possibilities are not intact possibilities, aren't they neutral? At the same time, are we not separating the *depth* of human nature from a *superficial* fault or a *superficial* innocence? The objection leads us to the core of a problem which we shall have to resolve later: we need to understand that a fundamental nature subsists even within the most complete fault. The fault happens to freedom; the guilty will is a freedom in bondage and not a return to an animal or mineral nature from which freedom is absent. This is the price of the fault being a fault, that is to say, the fruit of freedom, object of remorse. *It is I who* makes myself a slave: I *impose* on myself the fault which *deprives* me of control over myself. Thus, difficult though it is, we must in some sense think of the fundamental nature of freedom and its bondage as superimposed. Man is not part free and part guilty; he is totally guilty, in the very heart of a total freedom as complete as the power to decide, to move, and to consent. If the fault were not complete, it would not be serious. If man ceased being this power to decide, to act, and to consent, he would cease to be a man, he would be an animal or a stone— the fault would no longer be a fault. The question is not one of proportion of freedom and fault. *This is why it is possible to abstract away the fault;* the empirical truth of man as bound is connected with the essential truth of man as free. It does not suppress it: I *am* free *and* this freedom *is* unavailable. To be sure, we must admit that this paradoxical coexistence of freedom and

13. Such a concrete mythical approach already belongs to a *Poetics of the Will.* The innocence of "before" cannot be reached except as tied to another myth of freedom "after" history; the hope of freedom revealed in the reminiscence of innocence. Thus the *Poetics* and the *Empirics of the Will* constantly interact. Finally, the fault itself, in penetrating the region of the holy, already participates in the *Poetics:* the sinner is closer to the saint than is the just man.

the fault poses most difficult problems; they are the subject of a later work within the *Philosophy of the Will.*

One last objection deserves to be taken into consideration: we can ask whether, since the fault seized man as a whole, we do not run the risk of introducing into our fundamental description traits which already belong to the guilty form of freedom. Isn't what we call freedom in good part aroused by the fault, or perhaps even initiated by it? Could it not be that man as we conceive of him and understand him begins with the fault?

This argument appears opposed to preceding arguments which considered freedom too lost to be reached. It seems to insinuate on the contrary, that freedom is an invention of the fault. But if we do not believe in the possibility of attaining freedom, at least ideally and as a horizon or limit of the fault, as a definite fundamental nature of the voluntary and the involuntary which would be the being into which the fault irrupted, all happens as if man began with the fault. The fault no longer presents itself as a lost innocence, but becomes constitutive. Freedom in bondage becomes the sole thinkable freedom; the absurd becomes fundamental. This movement from a theory of the fault as a fall to a theory of the fault as birth and unveiling of freedom seems to be outlined by Kierkegaard, who conjoins the two ideas most equivocally: that corruption is born of the intoxication of freedom and that consciousness is born of the fault.[14]

Without pretending that we have always practiced the abstraction of the fault correctly, we think that only a pure description of the voluntary and the involuntary apart from the fault can reveal the fault as a fall, as loss, as absurdity—in brief, set up the contrast which would bring out its full negative force. Pure description provides a setting, a *limit,* for a fundamental ontology. Even if this limit is partially inaccessible, it prohibits us from making the knowledge of the fault, of passions, and of the law into an ontology. It denounces what we could call in a special sense the phenomenality of guilty conscience in relation to the being of incarnate freedom.[15] But the phenomenon here is what hides more than it reveals; the phenomenon of the fault hides the being of human condition. It makes it unavailable. But, as we shall see, the being of freedom is limiting only as it is constitutive.

This precedence in principle of pure description of freedom

14. Dufrenne and Ricoeur, *op. cit.,* pp. 189–93, 391–93; Ricoeur, *op. cit.,* pp. 141–44.

15. In this sense, in the phrase presented above, "I *am* free *and* this freedom *is* unavailable," the word to be is not on the same level: freedom is more fundamental than the fault.

over empirical description of the fault does not exclude the possibility that there are some characteristics of such empirical descriptions which have given rise to an elaboration of freedom. As M. Nabert has recently shown, the fault is a privileged occasion for consideration of the self's initiative.[16] Man who is going to act or who is acting does not normally reflect on his fundamental self; only in memory and particularly in the retrospection of remorse does there appear to him suddenly, at the same time, at the center and outside of his act, a self which could and should be other. It is the fault which carries the self beyond the limits of its acts. Thus in passing through the fault consciousness reaches its fundamental freedom, experiencing it as in a way transparent.

Since there will perhaps never be an empirical approach to the fault without a mythical approach to innocence, we must also add that inspection of the fundamental possibilities of man in fact depends on the concrete myth of innocence. This is what gives us the desire to know man apart from his fault and puts a stop to an obsessive and exclusive representation of the world of passions and of the law. Subjectively, the myth of innocence reveals a fundamental nature which, however, is constituted solely by the force of the concepts introduced. It is the *courage* of the possible. At the same time it provides that *imaginary* experience of which we have spoken above in Husserlian terms and which serves as the springboard for the knowledge of human structures. Imagination, particularly, by recounting stories of primitive innocence, enchants and conjures up that diffuse sense of bodily mystery conjoined with our very essence as being free, without which pure description would be swallowed up in paradox. The myth of innocence is the desire, the courage, and the imaginary experience which sustains eidetic description of the voluntary and the involuntary.

These remarks only show that the psychological genesis of an over-all work shares something of its total scope, and that the methodological order according to which it will be presented does not coincide with the psychological succession of ideas. Though man moves beyond the fault through a myth of innocence, though man receives himself through remorse at the center of his freedom, we shall nonetheless attempt to *understand* the articulation of the voluntary and the involuntary by bracketing at the same time both the mythical consideration of innocence and the empirical consideration of the fault.

16. Jean Nabert, *Éléments pour une éthique* (Paris, 1943), pp. 3–19.

[3] ABSTRACTION OF TRANSCENDENCE

THE ABSTRACTION of Transcendence gives rise to difficulties no smaller than the abstraction of the fault. These two abstractions are in effect inseparable. The integral experience of the fault and its mythical counterpart, the vision of innocence, are closely linked with an affirmation of Transcendence—in one aspect, the integral experience of the fault is the fault experienced as before God, that is, as sin. This is why we cannot dissociate the fault and Transcendence. But above all Transcendence is what liberates freedom from the fault. Thus men live Transcendence, as purification and deliverance of their freedom, as salvation. Transcendence bursts forth on us in relation to a spiritual world in which there are real breaks. All other modes of access, which might appear as short cuts, are in fact alien to that concrete experience of Transcendence which is a sign of our rediscovered integrity. Captivity and deliverance of freedom are one and the same drama.

We can express it otherwise: as we have already suggested, the affirmation of Transcendence and the vision of innocence are linked by a subterranean affinity. The myths of innocence which reminiscence recounts as before history are paradoxically connected with the eschatological myth which experience recounts as at the end of time. Freedom remembers its integrity to the extent to which its expects a complete deliverance. The redemption of freedom by Transcendence is thus the secret soul of the vision of innocence. There is a Genesis only in the light of an Apocalypse.

That is enough to understand that we cannot suspend the fault without suspending Transcendence.

We shall not say, however, how difficult this abstraction is to sustain and how much equivocation it leaves in the doctrine of subjectivity. We should form an absolutely false idea of the Cogito if we conceived of it as a positing of the self by itself: the self as radical autonomy, not only moral but ontological, is precisely the fault. The Self—written with a capital S—is a product of separation. The ruse of the fault is to insinuate the belief that participation of the will in more fundamental being would be an alienation, the submission of a slave into the hands of Another. Thus the Self, taken in this special sense, is the I estranged from being; the Self is an alienated I.

Yet do we have a right to carry out such a dangerous abstraction of ontological roots of willing which resembles a methodological confirmation of the guilty disarrangement of the self? It is inevitable and even necessary. In effect, for us who exist always after the fault, the discovery of ontological roots of subjectivity is inseparable from the purification of myself, from a resistance to resistance, as Bergson said. This is why the doctrine of subjectivity cannot be completed in the thrust, so to speak, of fundamental description which does not include the most important vicissitude of actual will, namely its bondage. The completion of ontology can only be a liberation.

In addition, the completion of the ontology of the subject demands a new change of method, *moving on to a kind of "Poetics"* of the will, suitable to the new realities that need to be discovered. In a basic sense of the word, poetry is the art of conjuring up the world as created. It is in effect the order of creation which description holds in suspension.

This order of creation can appear to us concretely only as a death and a resurrection. It means for us *the death of Self*, as the illusion of positing of the self by the self, and the *gift of being* which heals the rents of freedom. We shall later attempt to suggest these radical experiences which would grasp willing at its source.

Thus phenomenology and all psychology constitute an abstraction from Poetics. We have just presented this abstraction as inevitable because of the close relation between the fault and Transcendence and because of the change of method demanded by the concrete approach of the inspiration of being in the heart of my self. But such abstraction is also necessary from a systematic point of view. Just as the bondage of the fault is constantly in danger of being understood—through a degradation to object—as a determinism destroying freedom rather than something which happens to freedom, so the death of the Self and the gift of being are in danger of being *objectivized* and thought of as a sort of violation of subjectivity, that is, as a constraint exercised on an object. The death of the Self touched by Transcendence and the grace which is the life-giving substance of this mortification happen to a freedom. In order to prepare an understanding of this highest mystery we need first of all to strive at length to understand freedom as a *rule* over motives, powers, and even over the necessity built into its very heart.

An understanding of freedom as responsibility for decision, action, and consent is a necessary stage on the way to surpassing objectivity which cannot be abandoned even though it involves the risk that the dialectic of Transcendence will be swallowed up in this dangerous stage. This entire work is no more than an aspect of this first Copernican revolution which restores to subjectivity its due. I need first of all to learn to think of my body as myself, that is to say, as reciprocal with the willing which I am. This surpassing of the object is not called in question again either by the doctrine of bondage or by that of Transcendence.

This concern lest we stop at the stage of myself undoubtedly explains why we have made no use of the concept of *Action* such as Maurice Blondel has used since 1893. We thought it necessary to take the time to explore the foundations of subjectivity at length before attempting to surpass it from within and, in a sense, by an excess of immanence. This method led us to stress the bond of freedom to Transcendence and the hiatus between the method of description of consciousness and the method of a *Poetics* of freedom. The concept of action, so broad and so precise, seems to us to acquire its full significance on the level of a Poetics or, better yet, of a spiritual analysis of the will, such as we find in Pascal, Dostoevski, Bergson, or Marcel. On this level there prevail essentially *unifying* concepts, beyond the diversity of acts and in particular beyond the duality of knowledge and of acting whose divergence in aim and object we have had to respect. Action is one such unitive concept. But it may be that Maurice Blondel underestimates the difficulties of the method of immanence, in particular those which proceed from the accident of the fault. Guilty freedom, broken between a powerless ethical inspiration and the strange effectiveness of the nothing at the heart of all its works, blocks the access to its own surpassing. Furthermore, the use of the method of immanence is inseparable from a deliverance of freedom by a Transcendence which becomes immanent to the extent to which the will purifies itself in becoming actively associated with its own liberation. Perhaps after all the work of Maurice Blondel is not only a method of immanence, but also a method of innocence. I often have the impression that through all the detours of Eidetics, Empirics, and Poetics of the will there runs the search for an onerous assurance which, to Blondel, is already given. . . .

A second consequence of the limitation of our method is that the notion of *love* plays no part in our analysis of willing. Love of beings among themselves appears to us too much a part of the love of beings towards Being to play a role outside the bounds of the poetic. The relation of a will to a will, when it is not one of imitation, commandment, solidarity, affective fusion, or social cohesion, but a friendly creation from within, belongs to that spiritual analysis which appeared to us to exceed the possibilities of a description of consciousness. That is why *"the other"* only appears in our analysis in a secondary and nonessential role, as affecting my decision, one motive among the motives from my body, from society, or from a universe of abstractions. We admit readily that the problem of the other is not really raised here, since the other becomes truly "thou" when he is no longer a motive or an obstacle for my decision but when he begets me in my very decision, inspires me in the heart of my freedom, and exercises on me an effect which is in some way seminal, akin to creative action. A study of encounters—which are not always misunderstandings—will serve us still later to initiate the poetics of freedom. But that is no longer the province of analysis of motives, capacities, and limits of the will such as we have been suggesting. This distinction between eidetics and poetics brings us in an unexpected fashion to dissociate intersubjectivity from love. The individual considered in the web of mutual inspirations —let us now call him a person—the individual surpassed by the "we" belongs already to an ecstasy, to a generosity which is a kind of mutual creation.

It is very much the case that to transcend my self is always to retain it at the same time as I suspend it as the supreme instance.

In relation to this first Copernican revolution, the poetics of the will ought to appear as a second Copernican revolution which displaces being from the center, without however returning to the rule of the object.

It is clear that this revolution at the very center of my self will be quite distinct from the general mentality of *transcendentalism.* The ideal genesis of nature and of temporality starting with a *transcendental ego* which would be the *a priori* condition of its possibility and perhaps even of its reality is in any case suspended by our method of description. We are considering my self as it presents itself, that is, as meeting and submitting to a necessity which it does not produce (cf. in particular our remarks on temporality in Parts I and III). In effect, it is urgent that the method of abstraction should reach at the same time transcendental problems posed in the spirit of critical idealism and the problems of Transcendence posed by a religious philosophy. In effect, the awareness of my concrete self risks being sacrificed to ambitious construction to which we lack the key in our incarnate condition. Perhaps even a faithful description of incarnate freedom does more than it would seem to dissolve the phantom of the transcendental Ego. Transcendence will appear to us later as an absolute positing of a presence which constantly precedes my own power of self-affirmation, even when the latter always seems to be on the verge of engulfing it. This is why the connection of Transcendence and freedom inevitably appears paradoxical. It will be the task of the third volume of this *Philosophy of the Will* to bring the difficulties of that paradox into full light. There is no thinkable system of freedom and Transcendence, any more than of freedom and nature. We shall be led to criticize systems which seek a conceptual harmonization of freedom and of Transcendence, whether by sacrificing one to the other, or by conjoining, without paradox, a half-freedom and a half-Transcendence. We hope to show the fruitfulness of an "a-logic of paradox" for recasting the old debates about freedom and grace (or predestination). I receive all, and this gift consists in this: that I am complete freedom in the very receiving of that gift. But the paradox of freedom and Transcendence can be sustained only as a mystery which it is the task of poetics to discern.

We can say no more about it in this introduction. As we shall see, the real difficulties arise in the conjunctions: how can freedom be itself and in bondage? How can it be set free as freedom and responsible in its very deliverance? We have seen that the method of abstraction, in spite of the danger of premature conclusions, is the sole means of posing the problem correctly and of showing that servitude and deliverance are things which happen to freedom.

Nor is this all. The virtue of the method of abstraction lies not only in relation to the future empirics and poetics of the will. Within the enterprise of pure description itself, the method of abstraction is the occasion for surpassing and deepening that "I" which is always on the point of closing in upon itself. The abstraction would actually be in vain if it were no more than a reduction of vision and an amputation of being. In suspending the fault and Transcendence, that is, bondage and inspiration, I can give full due to the experience of responsibility. This experience will not be annulled but rather ramified by bondage and by transcendent inspiration. Now this pure experience already represents a break in the circle which I form with my self; freedom transcends itself already in its body. Thanks to the abstraction of the fault and of Transcendence it is possible to restore the meaning of freedom understood as a dialogue with nature. Such abstraction is necessary in order to understand as much as possible the paradox and the mystery of incarnate freedom.

In turn the comprehension of incarnate freedom, protected by such abstraction, prepares the reintegration of aspects placed within brackets. In effect, in breaking up the narrow circle which the self tends to close with itself and in revealing an ability not only to posit, but also to receive at the heart of freedom, our meditation on incarnation prepares the conception of a far more intimate reception which freedom achieves in its very power of positing acts. Perhaps the body is an insecure form of Transcendence, and the patience which leans on the insurmountable bodily condition is a veiled form of yielding to Transcendence.

Need we say that once again the priority in principle of pure description over the poetics of the will does not exclude the possibility that the totality of themes might be elaborated simultaneously? Empirics and poetics gave rise to that description as their own prolegomenon. The myth of innocence and the assurance of unique creation beyond the rent of freedom and nature accompany, as hope, our search for a conciliation between the voluntary and the involuntary.

PART I

Decision: Choice and Its Motives

1 / Pure Description of "Deciding"

PURE DESCRIPTION, understood as an elucidation of meanings, has its limitations. The gushing reality of life can become shrouded in essences. But while it may finally be necessary to transcend the eidetic approach, we must first draw from it all that it can give us, especially delimiting of our principal concepts. The words decision, project, value, motive, and so on, have a meaning which we need to determine. Hence we shall first proceed to such analysis of meanings.

Here we shall move, as we said in the Introduction, from the higher to the lower, tying the meanings of the involuntary many to those of the voluntary one. We shall thus start with a direct description of the voluntary act in order to relate it subsequently to the involuntary.

Our point of departure will be equally circumscribed by the narrowest circle of abstraction. Eidetics is like an abstraction within the broad abstraction of the fault and Transcendence which will not be removed in this work. By contrast, eidetic abstraction can be removed at the end of the first chapter, which is devoted to pure description. Thus we shall regain:

a) the presence of the *body* which lends the concept of motive, brought up by pure description, its quality of existence;

b) the lived *duration* within which the abstract relations between decision and motive, project and self-determination, etc., achieve full realization. The eidetic approach forces us to describe these relations without reference to time or, if you wish, in instantaneous segments cut out of the flux of consciousness;

c) the *event* of the *fiat* which lends to the act of choice itself its quality of sovereign existence.

Thus there is something lost in description. But only a method of abstraction enables us to *understand* the fundamental meanings entailed by life, and when the brackets can be removed, the meanings won through arid abstraction will serve to clarify as much as possible the obscure gushing of freedom.[1]

The first distinction to justify is that between *decision* and voluntary *motion*. This distinction does not mean that a temporal interval need necessarily separate decision from execution. It was a defect of eclectic psychology that it presented an artificial image of reality by distinguishing different *phases* within the voluntary process: deliberation, decision, and execution. When we reintroduce duration into voluntary life, we shall criticize at length the temporal distinction between deliberation and decision. In contrast, a distinction between decision and action can be established here because the interval which separates them is not necessarily temporal but rather one of meaning. It is one thing to indicate an action in a *project*, another thing to act bodily *in conformity with the project*. The relation of decision to execution is one of a special type of idea (whose structure remains to be determined) to an action which fulfills it, somewhat as a perception filling an empty theoretical representation.[2]

This relation can be instantaneous, that is, the project and its execution can be simultaneous, the project remaining implicit as the ongoing meaning which I impose on my action. In that case we shall say that the action is projected to the extent to which the action itself is traced in the world by the body. This type of action which everyone calls voluntary corresponds to the

1. The reader will find vestiges of a purely descriptive phenomenology of the will in Hildebrand, "Die Idee der sittlichen Handlung," *Jahrbuch für Philosophie und phenomenologische Forschung*, vol. III; Pfänder, "Zur Psychologie der Gesinnungen," *ibid.*; Pfänder, *Motive und Motivation* (Leipzig, 1911[1], 1930); Hans Reiner, *Freiheit, Wollen, und Aktivität* (Halle, 1927). We can likewise extract it from the works of Kurt Lewin and his school (see below, Part II, chap. I, p. 201. Valuable analyses can be found in Stout, "Voluntary Action," *Mind* (1896); Shand, "Analysis of Attention," *Mind* (1894); "Attention and Will, A Study in Involuntary Action," *Mind* (1895); "Types of Will," *Mind* (1897); and especially Bradley, "The Definition of Will," Part I, *Mind* (1902), pp. 437 ff.; Part II, *ibid.* (1903), pp. 145 ff.; Part III, *ibid.* (1905), pp. 1 ff.; "On Active Attention," *Mind* (1902), pp. 1 ff.; "On Mental Conflict and Imputation," *Mind* (1902) pp. 289 ff.

2. Cf. Part II, chap. 1, p. 201 below. In defining the project as empty intention (one which designates *en vide, in general*) we may seem to depart from Bradley's definition which sees in volition the "self-realization of an idea with which the self is identified" ("The Definition of Will," Part I, *Mind* [1902], p. 437). But Bradley's definition embraces the totality of the three moments which we have here distinguished. Bradley did not account for the actual nature of the phenomenological and not necessarily temporal interval which separates the "resolution" as a voluntary act from "realization." It is true that we ourselves make this separation tenuous when we show that the project already lays hold on reality through the feeling of power or potency.

pattern of simply *controlled* actions. The project may even be so implicit that it is in a way lost in the action itself, as when I roll a cigarette while speaking. Yet I never doubt that my action is voluntary—in what sense is it so? It is voluntary in the sense that I could have projected it clearly in a given situation to which it is suited or at least one with which it is not incompatible. To the extent to which an automatic action is even minimally observed—in a sense out of the corner of my eye—and an explicit will could recognize it after the fact and go back over it, it begins to correspond to the pattern which we are trying to disentangle.[3]

The lower limit of voluntary action—which it is possible to posit at least theoretically even though most of the time it is difficult to recognize in fact—is the truly involuntary action, an explosive, impulsive action in which the subject cannot recognize himself and of which he says that it escaped him. Pathology and even a certain "psychopathology of everyday life" are familiar with such actions in the very margins of control, far removed from the will. Thus the distinction which we are examining and which is a distinction of meanings embraces an immense area of actual cases—from immediate realizations which have become automatic and in which the project is concealed within the action itself to postponed realizations. Such postponed realizations can in turn take an extended form in which the relation of the project to its execution is distended in the extreme, as previously it was extremely concentrated. A normal type of postponed action is one in which the decision is taken but its execution is subordinated to a signal which does not depend on me (material circumstances, bodily conditions, social events, etc.). What is remarkable is that the decision, cut off from its execution by a delay, by a blank, is nonetheless not indifferent to its execution. When I have decided to carry out a delicate proceeding I feel in a sense charged with it, in the way a battery is charged—the act is within my power, I am capable of it. Such power, such capability, already belongs to the order of action: it potentially fulfills the project on whose contemplated execution it is intent. We shall study this power at length in Part II. Of course this impression of power, of capability, can be contradicted in the course of events. The action might have been dreamed of and not willed. Only execution puts our intentions to the test. There are even cases in which I remain uncertain of my own decisions until I have seen the action in practice, as the combat soldier who does not know of what he is capable and what his determination to be

3. Cf. Part II, chap. 2, p. 231 below.

brave is worth until he has received a baptism of fire. But this very unease on the part of the agent concerning his own decisions confirms our analysis: the criterion, the proof of the subject, is the execution alone. A project, even when it is separated from its realization by an indefinite delay, still awaits its consecration from it. Yet we shall say this much: a decision can be separated in time from any corporal execution, yet it is the *power or capability for action* (or movement) which makes it an authentic decision. And since in fact we know this power only as we use it, execution is the sole criterion of the strength of the power itself. Eidetic analysis, however, does not need such verification, because it does not judge the value of actual acts, but rather defines only abstract possibilities. Thus it can lay down this theoretical rule: a decision implies that the project of an action is accompanied by a power or capability of movement which could realize the project. This theoretical rule permits us to distinguish, at least in principle, that is, in terms of structure, voluntary intentions from those which are not voluntary.

Two examples will help us understand this distinction. There is a difference in principle (even though it cannot be recognized in all cases) between a decision and a simple wish or command.[4] In both cases I can have a precise and even eager idea of what needs to be done, but the execution is not in my power,[5] either because it depends strictly on events, as when I wish for the end of the war, or because it depends strictly on the will of someone else, as when I give instructions to subordinates or agents empowered to execute my orders. As we shall see, the theoretical distinction can be masked by a tangle of attitudes. Thus the transition from a wish to conditional action is continuous, as when I project an excursion in case the weather is good. The condition is the object of a wish, but the action itself, to the extent to which it depends on me, is an authentic project. Similarly, an order is accompanied by the personal action of the man whom I command, for the order is an extension of the immediate action of direction or control.

Here we see the extreme flexibility in the analysis of detail allowed by pure description. However, we shall conclude that only a rigorous analysis of meanings can provide a guiding thread in

4. Concerning volition, wish, commandment, cf. Shand, "Types of Will," *Mind* (1897), pp. 289–325, and Bradley, "The Definition of Will," Part III, *Mind* (1904), pp. 1 ff. (re types of volition).

5. Cf. the concept of sphere of power in Pfänder, *Phänomenologie des Wollens* (Leipzig, 1899[1], 1930), pp. 82 ff., and the notion of *Machtbereich* in Hans Reiner, *Freiheit, Wollen, und Aktivität* (Halle, 1927), pp. 31 ff.

this maze of cases. This is why the eclectics, who have not gone on to such eidetic analysis, prudently stick to average experiences of explicit project and postponed action which present the fundamental relations of meaning most clearly, and inevitably consider these experiences as typical and normative. However, it is the relation of meanings still present even in the most unusual cases which is normative.

It is precisely such unusual cases which, by leading us to consider the extreme instance, permit us to pose the relation of the project to its execution clearly:

a) As shown in the extreme instance of automatic behavior exemplified in a purely impulsive and explosive action, an action is voluntary when consciousness can recognize even an extremely implicit intention in it, which could be affirmed after the fact as a potential project of a postponed action. Expressed negatively, this theoretical criterion allows us to say that a delay in execution of the project is not necessary for the existence of a *decision*.

b) Inversely, as it becomes apparent in the extreme instance of an action postponed indefinitely, to the point of becoming a simple wish or command, an intention is an authentic decision when the action it projects appears to be within the *power* of its author. This means that it could be executed without *delay*, if the conditions on which it depends were realized. Negatively: effective execution is not necessary for the existence of a decision.

These two corollaries which we have just added to the two criteria of voluntary decision in relation to action allow us to reject those definitions of volition which restrict the field of analysis illegitimately, for instance by demanding that the subject must be explicitly aware of a definite decision at the time of execution, or that the decision must be followed by the start of its execution.

[1] INTENTIONALITY OF DECISION: THE PROJECT

1. To Will Is to Think

RESOLUTELY TURNING OUR BACK on naturalism and all mental physics, we must provisionally renounce the search for some force under the name of "will" which would serve to focus more elementary impulses. The so-called "dynamic" psychology is often just as unaware of what consciousness is as old

empiricism. To be sure, we shall yet have to say why the naturalistic prejudice is easier to adopt in psychology of action than
in that of knowledge: the mode of thought which is the will certainly seems to be *also* a type of force in the hold which such
will exercises over the body, either as power under tension or as
effective motion. All this is true, and psychology of effort must
resolve this difficulty. A description of decision is interested in it
insofar as the ability to do adheres to the project of doing. Nonetheless we must at first neglect the will as force, promising to
come back to understand this force later as that which fulfills the
intention of the project.

The intention of the project is a thought. This means that
it belongs among acts in a broad sense. Descartes invites us to
take the word "thought" in a broad sense in the enumeration he
gives of various modes of thought in the *Meditations* or in the
Principles.[6] But Descartes puts us on the wrong track at the very
start when he defines thought in terms of self-consciousness. He
is looking for something other than we are, for the proof which
thought gives to itself of being an indubitable existence when
even things are subjected to doubt. By contrast, our entire analysis will strive to show the bonds between consciousness and the
world and not the isolation of a consciousness which retires into
itself. To be sure, all acts of thought are apt to be reflexive and
lend themselves to self-consciousness to some degree. The reflexive character of decision is stressed particularly by the French
expression "je *me* decide," literally, "I decide myself," or by the
English expression, "I make up *my mind*." Nonetheless, this self-
relatedness poses problems too difficult to be resolved first.
Thought can at first be understood better in terms of its least reflexive aspect, its intentional relation towards the other. Thus
we shall start by following another suggestion of language, that
various modes of thought are expressed by a transitive verb which
calls for an object to complement it. I perceive something, I desire, wish, for something. It is the basic nature of thought to
relate itself to an object. This extrasystematic relation prohibits
us from transplanting categories which govern the relation of
object to object from physics to psychology. It is a linguistic snare
(language is sometimes revealing in its sensitivity, though often
perturbing in its practical origins) to offer to the psychologist
acts of thought in the form of nouns. We speak of "a perception,"
"a volition," seemingly equating acts with things. With Husserl,
we shall call the centrifugal movement of thought turned towards

6. Descartes, *Meditations*, II; *Principles*, I:9, I:65.

an object intentionality: I am in that which I see, imagine, desire, or will. The first intention of thought is not to prove my existence to me, but to relate me to the perceived, imagined, or willed object. If we call "project" in the strict sense the object of a decision—the willed, that which I decide—we can say that to decide is to turn myself towards the project, to forget myself in the project, to be outside myself in the project, without taking time to observe myself willing.

Specifying the type of intention which aims at a project, we shall define it thus: *a decision signifies, that is, designates in general, a future action which depends on me and which is within my power.*

2. Decision and Judgment

DECISION IS A TYPE of "judging," that is, of acts which signify, which designate in general. Let us consider four types of judgment: the train will leave tomorrow at 5 o'clock; perhaps the weather will be good; I shall take the express at 5 o'clock; get me a ticket. These statements of an event, a wish, a project, and an order are types of judgment. What do they have in common?

Consider the Latin infinitive proposition which could be translated "I am to go on a trip." It expresses a level of meaning which might be common to very different acts all intending it in ways which again are quite different. "I am to go on a trip" is itself not a condition of things stated, or the content of a wish, or a project, or the structure of an order. It is a neutral signification which could be incorporated in acts of different quality. It will occur some day that "I shall go on a trip": here a positing of existence takes over the meaning and makes a statement of it. Oh, if it were true that "I shall go on a trip": here the meaning is at the same time called and held in suspension by its hypothetical modifier. In a decision the meaning is inserted into a positing of existence which is not stated but is affirmed as depending on me, as "to be done by me and susceptible to being done by me."

What then is the common meaning? Should we say that it is what understanding provides? Such formulation would again involve us dangerously in the circle of old discussions about the relation of faculties. Actually this meaning is distinguished only by abstraction from the concrete act of stating, wishing, ordering, or deciding. It is not at all an act of understanding which could have an autonomous existence and on which, secondarily, a state-

ment or a decision would be built. Still less is it a primitive judgment of existence modified afterwards as a wish or as a decision.
The infinitive absolute, "I am to go on a trip," is not a thought
or an act at all, but rather a level of meaning obtained by abstraction from acts of different "quality." A decision as practical judgment is not constructed upon a theoretical judgment of existence
conceived as the primitive form of judgment. We shall thus say
that the statement, the wish, the command, the decision, are
judgments because they are susceptible to an identical secondary
modification which abstracts an identical level of meaning from
them, expressed by the infinitive absolute or by a subordinate
clause beginning with "that": "that I shall go on a trip." This
proposition is not a judgment about that which I state, hope,
command, or will, but a convergent product of abstraction, formed
in the context of a reflexion on acts and their objects.

3. Designating in General (À Vide)

IN WHAT SENSE does the infinitive absolute common
to all classes of judgments signify? It signifies by *designating in
general* or "emptily" the structure of the event or the action
(whether stated, wished for, commanded, or willed).

Here we touch upon the difference which might exist generally between two ways of knowing an object: in general and
specifically (or "emptily" and "concretely"—*en vide et en plein*).[7]
For example, in the order of judgments of existence, I may designate an object having definite characteristics without in any way
seeing or imagining its characteristics. I understand it, even
though my intention is not specified by the stuff or flesh of a
presence or quasi-presence. This is the famous thought without
images, which is highly controversial even though it is illustrated
by the most ordinary comprehension which runs on and understands words without having the time to fill the meaning of such
words with as much as a promise of or attempts at images. When
an object is before me, I no longer designate it; I perceive it: I
eat it with my eyes. It fills my view and saturates the gaping void
of abstract signification. Even when I imagine the object, my
thought is filled with warm, colorful representations which, even
though tinged with non-existence or absence, are no less full.
Such imagination is even more deceptive because its absence
and its fullness mutually sharpen and irritate each other.

Such is the judgment of existence, and such is decision also:

7. Husserl, *Logische Untersuchungen* (Halle, 1922), studies I, V.

a designation in general, not of what is, but of what is to be done by me, what I am to do. Far from decision being an image —for example, as had been said, a motive image held in check by the mental constellation as a whole—an image is not even essential to decision. I do not have to imagine a train and treat myself to visions of myself at the ticket office. The image is more often an elaboration which translates itself in terms of highly varied effect; in a general sense imagination functions as the trigger in the tension of willing, mimicking the presence of the unreal. In an extreme case satisfaction with the image can charm me to such an extent that the imaginary becomes an alibi for the project and absolves me from the charge of carrying it out. It is true that the imaginary can also facilitate action: by painting the action for me in vivid colors, imagination carries me as on wings up to the pledge I make to myself. This double function of the imagination will be studied in more detail when we consider the concrete birth of a decision.

If an image is not essential to a decision, if it might even interfere with it, it is because the specific content of a judgment here is not a presence or a quasi-presence, but an action of my body, an action of which I am capable and which I do. The relation between the execution and the project in the practical order is the equivalent of the relation of perception or image to signification in theoretical order. Both a command and a wish each have a unique way of being fulfilled or carried out: by a happy event or by another's obedience.

Thus all judgments have in common the fact that they designate in general while the distinct quality of judgments represents a distinct way of being actualized. At the same time we recognize at least an eidetic standard common to decision and motion, to idea and movement—it is the agreement in meaning between idea and movement, the "covering" of a project by an action which has the same meaning. The latter actualizes the intention of the former within the same practical signification. This is why we said at the beginning that a movement is voluntary if its implicit meaning could be recognized after the fact as a project, that is, as a practical object designated potentially by an intention distinct from its execution. This is also why imagination can interfere with a project, for it also actualizes the project, albeit fictitiously. In fulfilling it with a quasi-presence in place of real movement, it frustrates its proper accomplishment in effective action. But it is also possible that this frustration is itself a movement which will stimulate it on the road to its accomplishment.

4. Categorical Affirmation of a Personal Action

THE DIFFERENCES in actualization of different modes of judging draw our attention to the structural difference of these modes. Project, wish, and command designate *practically*. These are basic modes of thought which language expresses by equally basic verbal modes, such as the subjunctive (would they would bring me something to eat!), conditional, imperative (let's go!), gerundive, passive, and so on (the indicative being generally the mode of theoretical judgment). These modes, moreover, mutually support each other and can be replaced by non-verbal forms, such as adverbs (out! forward!), adjectives (quiet!), nouns with or without prepositions (on your way! silence!), interjections in a strict sense (oh well!), conjunctions (thus), conventional signs, intonations, silences, gestures (banging a fist, pointing a finger, etc.).[8] One unique function connects these expressions and makes such substitutions possible: all practical judgments state that something is "to be done" and not "the case."

Further distinctions offer themselves within this broad dichotomy of practical and theoretical statements. Among all the acts which designate practically "that which is to be done," decision is distinguished by two traits: (1) It designates categorically (2) a personal action. In a decision I take a position (Fiat! so be it!); its categorical character distinguishes the decision from a whim which envisages a personal action but in an evasive way, just as a vague wish and a hesitant command. But further I take a position in relation to my own action; the project is to be done by me; it is I whom I commit and bind, I as the author of gestures and transformations in the world. I figure in the project—and so in the object willed—as the subject of the projected action. Even if I do not think of myself as *the one* who makes up *his* mind at that moment, though I do not stress the "It is I who . . ." of the verb of decision, I involve myself in the project, I impute to myself the action which is to be done. This is what distinguishes decision from a wish or a command in which the thing to be done is not my personal action but the course of things or the action of another, more often expressed by the conditional or the imperative.

To what extent might a decision nonetheless appear as a wish addressed to myself or a command which I give to myself? That is possible only by a change in the very meaning of the project. I can consider my action as something to wish for only by virtue

8. Ferdinand Brunot, *La Pensée et la langue* (Paris, 1926), pp. 557–73.

of a certain alienation which reabsorbs my personal conduct into the anonymous course of events and thus removes it from my control. This occurs in certain exceptional situations in which I do not know what I can expect of myself. For example, an emotion can deprive me of self-control to such an extent that, in relation to myself, I become like a falling stone, an explosion, or a tempest. Then my decision to confront it expresses itself as a wish: "Oh, if only I could master the event! If only I could hold out!" The alienation of my own body has broken down the boundaries which separated decision from a wish. The possibility of such confusion is inscribed in my bodily condition itself: my body has always a way of surprising me, escaping me, and deceiving me. It is the boundary of things which do not depend on me, as health, fortune, or good weather, and of things which do depend on me, as pure judgment.

For similar reasons, a command and a decision can be confused. Both are categorical affirmations. Furthermore, decision can be considered as a command which I give to myself to the extent to which my body appears to me not even as an anonymous mask of an alien force but as the autonomy of a person with its own intentions and its own initiative. Thus I converse with it, and it becomes a second person: "You shake, you old carcass, but if you knew. . . ." Though we may discount the rhetorical aspect which slips into such expressions, we must also admit that self-consciousness carries with it permanently the possibility of such redoubling, of such a dialogue with itself. My relation to myself is like that of a younger and an older brother: I respond for my part like an other who listens, imitates, obeys. In presence of value I sense myself more the younger; in face of an action in which my body is refractory, I feel more like the elder. This situation is far more basic and permanent than the alienation to which we referred above with respect to a wish. To think is to speak to myself, to will is to command myself. In this sense we speak of self-control and use the imperative in second person singular or even plural to express a decision: "Let's go, old man, we've got to get on!" This is the reason why medieval and even classical philosophy described decision as an *imperium*.

But in the end decision is not a true command, only a command by analogy. Pure description must start from the differences in principle among acts of thought and then, secondarily, show the situations which favor the analogy or even the confusion. My body is not another person. The duality arising in consciousness is a duality within the very heart of the first person: this is why the subject of the action intended in the project is the same subject who is implicit or explicit in the very act of deciding and intending the project: I who decide am the I who will do.

Here we need to reintroduce the sense of power which accompanies the intention of consciousness. It is this sense which binds the I projected as subject of an action to be done and the I glimpsed covertly as he who projects. It is myself who wills, it is I who is able to. It is myself who decides to be, who can do; and this capacity is what I project into the subject of action. It is of the essence of the power which is being tested to be objectified in an original way as the subject of action, but it is objectified in general just as the project itself. Here we can only note the role of the sense of power which will be analyzed in the context of description of action itself.[9]

This relation of the project to a personal action gives to decision an exceptional position among all practical judgments: decision posits me as the agent in my very intention of the action to be done. Hence its existential import is considerable: it is I who projects and does in projecting or doing something.

5. The Future Temporality of a Project

THE MOST IMPORTANT TRAIT of a project is undoubtedly its reference to the future. This temporal structure raises difficulties at least as complex as its intellectual structure. The two problems, as we shall see, are closely connected. The difficulty is this: does the future opened up by the decision presuppose a previous relation of consciousness to the future revealed, for instance, by theoretical consciousness? Or does willed future serve as a basis for future as known? Or does consciousness relate to its future and that of its world in a way which is more fundamental than any anticipation by will or knowledge? Thus these problems lead us again to the roots of consciousness and perhaps to the very limits of pure description.

Let us first attempt to describe the futurality of a project directly.

The project is pro-jected, that is, I decide for a time to come, no matter how near and imminent it may be. To decide is to anticipate. This is why the most remarkable type of decision is that in which a delay separates the project from its execution,

9. Pfänder, *op. cit.*, p. 91. The representation of doing, essential to willing, is the "representation of a future as introduced and accompanied by this *sense of doing.*"

though the possibility of having been anticipated accompanies even automatic forms of action sharing this structure. The project is thus the practical determination of what is to be. But this future is only intended; what I do depends on present action. This is why such intended future is not restricted to the continuous and irreversible [10] order of lived time. I leap from project to project across dead time, return to earlier moments, sketch the most interesting lines of future action, compress empty spaces, posit ends prior to the means which precede them, insert secondary projects into primary projects by gradual emendation or interpolation, and so on.[11] This is the pattern of human purposiveness which organizes time ahead of the present. Discontinuity and reversibility are the rule of time designated in general, in which only practical relations of the most outstanding accomplishments of action are indicated (in addition, actual carrying out of a projected action can itself be indicated, for instance to another, as information, model to imitate, or order to execute). In contrast, the action itself has no gaps. It contributes to building up the fullness of present time, fulfilling the promise of existence. A proposed order is not the experienced order, or, so to speak, the acted-out order.

But the future is also intended by a great number of acts which do not reach out to it as something within my power. Thus a command, a wish, a desire, or a fear represents a minimal instance whose lower limit is expectation of a future. Already, in the case of desire and fear, I weigh the future as a threat or a blessing which will injure or comfort me: I can only meet it and submit to it.

Yet are these two extreme ways of conceiving the future irreducible?

There are good reasons for suggesting alternately a reduction of one or the other to its alternative. Precisely this ambiguity indicates another problem.

At first it seems that I cannot form a project unless I first have an outline of dates, accomplishments, and future situations which can only be anticipated because they are essentially events beyond my control. I lodge my projects in the interstices of a world which is determined in its broad outlines by the course of planets, by the order of the whole. Furthermore, even my projects anticipate an action which sets various means in motion.

10. Reading "irreversible" for the "reversible" of the French text which appears to be a misprint.—Trans.
11. Gaston Bachelard, *Dialectique de la durée* (Paris, 1936).

Now the subordination of means to each other and to their ends presupposes a knowledge of succession and of causality—an end is never more than an effect conceived as the rule for constructing its cause. This is what all the old sayings about forewarning and forearming teach us. Thus we must say that I do not will the future, but *in* the future understood as an expected future. Roughly this is how an intellectually inclined mind reasons, paying little attention to structures more elementary than knowledge itself.

Yet a close examination suggests that we ought to reverse the functional relation. I do not foresee the future but *in* the future. Often, to foresee is simply to extrapolate a relation established in the past and to wait until a causal series or a set of causal series brings forth in the future an effect known in the past. But what permits us to say that there will be a future? Relations known in the past do not justify it, for the future of an older past is only a more recent past, and though it had been anticipated in the past, this was only possible by starting from a known past.

Let us generalize this remark. As stated, it does not apply to all cases: expectation can refer to a new phenomenon. But in that case the relation is known in the first place as necessary, that is, as non-temporal, and the question of how consciousness proceeds from non-temporal necessity to temporal expectation remains untouched. Expectation—fore-seeing—presupposes a future of the world which will make it possible, or, which amounts to the same thing, it presupposes that the consciousness bears itself ahead of itself, that it is outside itself in an original way which consists of being for a future, in having a future.

Thus we might be tempted to seek this thrust towards the future presupposed by foreseeing in desire, in fear, in the will, in brief, in practical consciousness. Going further, in order to stress the activity of consciousness and, perhaps, its ability to constitute and support being, we are tempted to say that the future is the *project* of consciousness itself, that it is but one of its references ahead of itself into the future, opening up a future by its project. The project would then be the very thrust of consciousness towards the future. We shall even note that consciousness does not constitute itself as past because it constitutes itself first of all as future, that is, as project, in testing the limits of its power of projecting. I leave the past behind only because I can no longer project it, whether in order to retain it or to efface it. Regret and remorse are like a will which flows back after breaking itself on an obstacle, while reconciled contemplation of the past in a peaceful memory is a consent to powerlessness. To remember is to fail to thrust forward.

Thus while expectation appeared to be an extrapolation from memory, to an analysis which gives the project primacy in the consciousness of future and gives to consciousness of future precedence over all other consciousness memory appears to be the limit of a project.

In effect our second analysis does not support the earlier one. I do not project a future, but *in* the future. I reduce the future to a project by force. Even in the practical order, desire and fear are not disguised forms of project. Besides, no device can remove the subordination of the project to expectation, to fore-seeing.

We might suppose that consciousness is oriented towards the future in a more basic sense than according to the partial structures of expectation and project. Already the role of anticipation in all modes of consciousness warns us that none of these modes can constitute or exhaust the ability of consciousness to designate the future, and we shall discover anticipation again in perception, in synesthetic consciousness, and even in reflexes. An incomplete temporal totality gives rise to a sense of incompleteness and imminence—a "protension," as Husserl puts it—which discord or delay in the resolution of a dissonance can carry to the level of anxiety. Could we say, for instance, that a melody develops such expectation only because of desire? But the case of temporal totalities is not an exception: all perception takes place in time, by tentative attempts, glimpses, and perspectives. To perceive a color as the color of a tree is to anticipate future glances as much as to retain past ones. I perceive this world as opening into a future. I foresee the future even in anguish and its imminence, in pleasure and its promise of satisfaction, just as in the reflex whose release precedes it itself (we shall verify this in the sneeze which Pascal does not deem in the least unworthy of consideration).

It would thus seem that the future temporality of each mode of consciousness is made possible by other aspects of the future which this mode does not constitute. This explains the vicious circle of project and expectation. It is also why each type of anticipation appears to be *in* the future, even though the future is not a body, a box, or a content. The preposition "in" indicates that if consciousness is future ("to be") for itself and the world is future for it, this future reference is not an act in the sense in which perceiving, imagining, doubting, or willing are acts turned towards a determined object, but rather is a *fundamental situa-*

tion which makes possible the future dimension of the project of expectation and of other acts. By expressing it this way we stress that the future direction is less a thrust than the condition of a thrust, as it also is the condition of fear, and that all fear in principle opens out towards my death. We cannot stress too much the extent to which consciousness is disarmed and powerless before its own drift into the future. It would be a great mistake to assume that only the past lies outside my control. The future is what I can neither hurry nor retard; it conditions the impatience of desire, the anxiety of fear, the wait of expectation, and finally subordinates the accomplishment of the project to the mercy of events. The past seems more basically beyond my control because it excludes the possibility that I might change it—it makes possible retrospection, but not action. But that there is a future which makes expectation and action possible is no less beyond my control. The future is the condition of an action, but it is not an action.

At this point one might say that phenomenological description should rise to the level of a *transcendental* phenomenology where what appears least willed is constituted by pure transcendental Ego, obtained by a reduction of the empirical Ego. We are not yet in a position to appreciate such transcendental philosophy. Rather, we are trying to pry loose pure description, which proceeds from the commitment to take things as they present themselves, from a theory of the transcendental constitution of the given. Pure description of the future dimension of consciousness does not include its conceptual genesis—for pure description, the project in the strict sense of the correlate of decision, is not constitutive of the future. Future temporality of consciousness is not reducible to its aptitude for making projects. It is important to resolve this ambiguity maintained by a semi-descriptive and semi-transcendental usage of expressions such as "consciousness 'as' a project," "consciousness 'as' a thrust," etc. Together with temporality in general, it belongs more to the order of the absolute involuntary, to the order of the inevitable, since it shifts that which I can will in the form of projects and whose execution to come depends on me to *consent,* as if it were a condition which I cannot will at all. The same consciousness which projects into the future consents to the "tempo" of duration and to the fullness of time for completion. In the eyes of wisdom which holds to the level of consciousness such as it presents itself it is essentially vain to suppose that a conceptual genesis of future temporality by transcendental consciousness would ever be more than a pure mental game. Such wisdom is one of a consciousness which acts within the context of a future dimension which it does not create. We can even recognize that a premature recourse to the idea of transcendental constitution interferes with our understanding of consciousness and of the absolutely unsurmountable necessities which it encounters in the privacy of its very core.[12]

6. The Project, the Possible, and Capability

WE STILL HAVE to reintroduce into our analysis an important element which we have held in suspension: the sense of power, or capability. We shall not approach it directly, since we can only suggest an analysis which already encroaches on the description of moving. We shall introduce it in terms of the idea of the *possible* which has the advantage of presenting itself first of all as an application of preceding discussion of the future. Similarly, classical authors link the study of possibility with that of "future contingents."

In what sense can we say that the will opens up possibilities in the very network of the actual?

The meaning of possibility involves the same ambiguity as that of the future: there is the possibility opened up by practical consciousness and the possibility which offers itself to theoretical consciousness. The latter is easier to understand—a possibility is what the order of things *permits*. It is possible that I shall take a train tomorrow because there is a train on that day. The possibility of my action is determined by the *entire* actual order of events which presents my action with a point of application, that is, by a collection of prohibitions and opportunities, obstacles, and feasible routes. That is the world of the voluntary agent— a complex collection of resistances and opportunities, of walls and of ways. Expressions such as "seizing an opportunity" or "missing a chance" are really quite revealing. These permissions which the actual offers are themselves marked with a variable index of certitude. Thus they are certain, probable, or merely possible, in the sense that the permission is, as to its modality, simply rather hypothetically calculated in light of conditions which are required in order for a given event to result. The possibility as permission to . . . can thus be in a possible mode, that is, subordinated to conditions which are more or less unknown or probable. This meaning of the possible, already complex since it consists of a permission and a mode of expectation, is the only

12. Cf. Part III, chap. 3, p. 444.

meaning which the possible has for theoretical consciousness. In this sense the possible is not prior, but logically posterior to the actual. It always has to be conceived by starting out from the actual or from retrospection on the actual. This is the valid part of the Bergsonian critique of the primacy of the possible over the actual. An event becomes possible—a specific possibility—because I project it. The presence of man in the world means that the possible precedes the actual and clears the way for it; a part of the actual is a voluntary realization of possibilities anticipated by a project. For a completely creative consciousness, the possible would be prior to the actual which would proceed from it by actualization, even though elimination of delay, ordinarily attributed to an inopportune or unfavorable actuality, would make the actualization indiscernible from the intention. But because the will is victim of necessities due to the irreducible fact of its bodily condition, it is constantly forced to harmonize the possibles it projects with the possibilities it expects, and can reconcile the latter with its freedom only by consent rather than by project.

Here a new fact is added to this double determination of the possible: what I project is possible only when there is a sense of capability or power which imparts its thrust and its force to the purely potential designation of the action which I am to do. The complete possibility which the will opens up is the project plus the power.

Thus we cannot rest content with transposing the analysis of the future to possibility. The harmony of my own possibilities with the possibilities which the world presents would be incomprehensible if the works of man and of the order of the world could not be fused into the same stuff of existence by the catalyst of voluntary motion. The possibility I project and the possibility I discover are knitted together by action. The man who boards a train joins possibility opened up by his project with the possibility offered by the railway company. An action, as a potency of my body, is outlined at the core of the project itself. The possible then is no longer absolutely blank; it is, so to speak, an "effective" possibility and no longer "up in the air." Here the verbal kinship of the words "potency" and "possibility" is revealing enough—the possible is what I can and not merely wish to do. Possibility thus acquires a consistency and almost physical density: it is on the way to actualization. It is the capacity of actualization of the project by the body. We shall study this sense of power or ability later, in the context of voluntary motion.

Let us just add that my body's capability is placed in a context of powerlessness. Each permission is a passage between the walls of prohibitions. These prohibitions are within myself, in modes which we shall study in Part III—character, the unconscious, organic structure, and birth. Thus the project, the capability in an indeterminate world, and impotence in a world which has an inflexible order, are closely linked to each other and the three moments of the possible are contemporaneous. It is the potency with which the body is charged which mediates between the possibility opened up by the project and the possibility permitted by the world as a way amid impossibilities. The connection of the three forms of the possible already suggests that of decision, motion, and consent.

And yet the notion of the possible is not exhausted by this triple determination of which the last two terms have barely been sketched. In each case the possibility to which we refer remains in the context of doing: the project is *to-do*, the capacity is *capacity for doing* (as movement is doing itself), consent refers to *impotence for doing*. But, in addition to this, possibility concerns also the being of the subject who projects the doing, the subject and not only the action. For in doing something, I *make* myself *be*. I am my own *capacity for being*. This unexpected theme proposes a reversal in the course of our analysis: leaving the intentional direction—according to which, to decide is to decide something—we must describe the reflexive direction of decision: *"je* me *decide"*: I make up *my* mind. When we have completed that analysis we shall be able to elucidate this last sense of possibility: the potential for being of willing itself.

[2] THE IMPUTATION OF MYSELF: *"se* DECIDER"— MAKING UP *my* MIND

1. *"Je* me *decide"*: I make up *my* mind

THIS REFERENCE of the decision to myself poses difficult problems. In what sense do I designate myself in designating a project, and say "It is *I who will do*, am doing, have done"?[13]

1) We must readily admit that we are not always aware of this reference: most of the time I am so involved in what I will

13. The method of experimental introspection used by Michotte and Prüm ("Le Choix volontaire et ses antécédents immédiats," *Arch. de Psych.*, vol. X [December, 1910], well highlights this consciousness of "it is myself who...," connected with the consciousness of "designating," of "turning oneself towards"; cf. pp. 132–34 and 187–298 of extracts from transcript.

that I do not notice myself willing; I have neither the need nor the occasion for laying a claim to my act and claiming authorship in one sense or another. Then isn't this self-reference always superadded to the voluntary act, and doesn't it even alter it profoundly, by inverting the centrifugal direction of consciousness turned toward the project and substituting for it an altogether different act, reflexive in character, which deflects the thrust of consciousness?

2) This uncertainty makes it necessary to relate the self-referential judgment, "it is I who ...," to a self-reference which is more basic than all judgment: relating looking *at* oneself to a determination *of* oneself. How is reflection already implied in the action of the self on itself which is contemporaneous with the decision?

3) These difficult analyses must lead us to the most obscure regions of metaphysical questions concerning the *power-of-being* which the *power-of-doing* inevitably leads us to raise.

2. The Reflexive Judgment: It Is I Who ...

DESCARTES had not the least doubt that self-consciousness was an inherent characteristic of thought: "It is so self-evident that it is I who doubts, who understands and who desires that nothing need be added to explain it" (*Second Meditation*). In the last analysis, Descartes surely is not wrong: a certain presence to myself must covertly accompany all intentional consciousness. We should form an oversimplified idea of this objective intention of consciousness if we considered reflection a secondary, alien act.[14] But on the other hand, the explicit judgment "it is I who ..." is not such an immediate self-presence clinging to the very thrust of consciousness. What then is the character of the project which makes it *available for* the distended apperception in which I impute the act to myself?

Let us start with situations in which self-affirmation is explicit and attempt to work our way back to the conditions which make it possible, as they are contained in any decision.

I form the consciousness of being the author of my acts in the world and, more generally, the author of my acts of thought, principally on the occasion of my contacts with an other, in a social context. Someone asks, who did that? I rise and reply, I did. Response—responsibility. To be responsible means to be

14. Cf. discussion below, Part III, chap. 2, p. 355, "The Unconscious."

ready to respond to such a question. But I can anticipate the question and lay a claim to responsibility which the other could neither note nor contest. Self-affirmation can then have the vainglorious overtone of self-satisfaction which calls on the other to attest and applaud; it is the other who certifies me as myself. Or again, rivalry, jealousy, harsh comparison, etc., present my consciousness of myself with a passionate orchestration whose difficult exegesis we shall have to undertake later.

And yet we sense that the other introduces nothing external but only evokes, by special revelatory power, that aptitude for imputing my acts to myself which is embedded even in my least reflexive acts. Life with the other might as well be our common dream, our analogous self-loss in the anonymous "they." Thus self-affirmation is a gesture of going out, of showing oneself, of bringing oneself to the fore and confronting oneself. "They" do not respond to the question, "who thinks so, who is making this noise?" because "they" is no-one. Some one must stand out of the mass in which each—or all—hide. In contrast with the "one," "I" take my act on myself, I assume it.[15]

All these expressions—to wake up, to take hold of oneself, to go forth, to show oneself, to confront—make self-consciousness appear as a breaking away: but I break away from others, since they are no-one, only as I break away from myself, inasmuch as I am alienated from myself, that is, surrendered to the others who are no-one. We need to seek the sources of self-consciousness in consciousness itself, with regard to which the others are no more than an occasion, an opportunity, but also a danger and a trap.

Now in waking up from anonymity I discover that I have no means of self-affirmation other than my acts themselves. "I" am only an aspect of my acts, the subject pole of my acts.[16] I have no means of affirming myself on the fringes of my acts. This is what the feeling of responsibility reveals to me.

Besides, it is after the fact, and in a situation of guilt, that reflection appears to itself as an articulation of a connection between the agent and the act which is more fundamental than all

15. G. Marcel, "The Ego and Its Relation to Others," in *Homo Viator*, trans. Crauford (Chicago, 1951), pp. 13 f.; *Creative Fidelity*, trans. Rostal (New York, 1964), re the act and the person, cf. pp. 104–20.

16. In this sense Husserl says that apart from its implication in its acts the self is not "a proper object of research": "if we abstract away its ways of relating itself [Beziehungsweisen] and behaving [Verhaltungsweisen], it is absolutely destitute of eidetic components and has not even any content which we could make explicit; it is in itself and for itself indescribable, pure Ego and nothing else," *Ideas*, § 80.

reflection. It is I who have done this. I accuse myself, and in accusing myself retrace the vestiges of my signature on the act. *Accusare:* to designate as the cause. At this stage we shall neglect the minor undertones of this consciousness wounded by itself; we shall forget the sting, the consciousness of fall and of indebtedness. An assurance irrupts in the heart of my affliction: the self is in its acts. As Nabert masterfully analyzed it, awareness of the fault opens the limits of my act and shows me an evil self at the roots of an evil act.[17]

But perhaps we can also capture this very feeling of responsibility which after the fact is reflected in a guilty conscience, and capture it directly in its thrust towards the act. Sometimes, in serious circumstances, when everyone shrinks back, I step forward and say, I take charge of these men, of this job. Here the feeling of responsibility, in the moment of commitment, crowns the highest self-affirmation and most decided exercise of control over a zone of reality for which I make myself responsible. It carries the double emphasis of myself and of the project. He who is responsible is prepared to respond for his acts, because he posits an equation of the will: this action is myself.

Now we are about to perceive a basic self-relation which is neither a reflected judgment nor a retrospective observation, but is implied in intentionality, in the projecting of the project.

Let us try to take up the analysis of the project once more and to discover there what sets off a possible reflection.

3. Prereflexive Imputation of Myself

THE TASK OF OUR ANALYSIS is to elaborate an aspect of the project which we might call the prereflexive imputation of myself. This implies a self-reference which is not yet self-observation, but rather a certain way of relating oneself or of behaving with respect to oneself, a non-speculative or, better, non-observant, way. It is an implication of the self rigorously contemporaneous with the very act of decision which in some sense is an act with reference to the self. This implication of the self must contain the germ of the possibility of reflection, contain the willing available to the *judgment* of responsibility, "it is I who. . . ."

French expresses this double and indivisible relation to the self and to the object of an intention by transitive verbs of pronominal form: "je *me* decide à . . ." (I decide to or I make up *my* mind), "je *me* souviens à . . ." (I remember . . .), "je *me*

17. Jean Nabert, *Éléments pour une éthique* (Paris, 1943), p. 6.

represent" (I imagine), "je *me* rejouis de . . ." (I rejoice at).[18] For the moment let us neglect the diversity of self-relation implied in these expressions, themselves diverse—this must be linked to the diversity of intentional relation. It is already apparent that this self-reference, whatever it may be, is not isolable from reference to the project, to whatever is represented, remembered, or rejoiced over. The self is not complete in itself. In particular it does not will itself in a void, but in its projects. I affirm myself in my acts. This is precisely what the feeling of responsibility teaches us: this action is myself.

But how is this possible?

As our point of departure we need to take an aspect of the project which we have stressed above—to decide is to designate a personal action. The "myself" figures in the project as that which will do and that which can do. I project my own self into the action to be done. Prior to all reflection about the self which I project, the myself summons itself, it inserts itself into the plan of action to be done; in a real sense it becomes *committed*. And, in becoming committed, it binds itself: it constrains its future appearance. It throws itself ahead of itself in posing itself as the object, as a direct complement of the project. In projecting myself thus, I objectify myself in a way, as I objectify myself in a signature which I will be able to recognize, identify as mine, as my sign.

Thus it is clear that the entire initial implication of myself is not a conscious relation or an observation. I behave actively in relation to myself, I determine *myself*. Once again French usage throws light on the situation: to determine my conduct is to determine myself—se *determiner*. Prereflexive self-imputation is active not observational.

But in this aspect decision is not, strictly speaking, available to explicit reflection. In effect there is always a subject "I," projecting and not projected. We could say that the more I determine myself as the grammatical object, as he who does, the more I forget myself as he from whom, here and now, as from grammatical subject, issues the determination of the self-projected as the agent who will realize the project.

18. Concerning the notion of assuming a position, cf. Hildebrand, *op. cit.*; Husserl, *op cit.*, § 113. (Similar construction occurs in other languages, as in German [*sich* entscheiden, *sich* erinnern, *sich* freuen] or in Czech [rozhodnouti *se*, těšiti *se*, pamatovati *se*], and is by no means peculiar to French or other romance languages. Unfortunately, except in circumlocutions [I make up *my* mind] or for emphasis [I made myself do it] it is not made explicit in English construction.—Trans.)

This initial analysis of the prereflexive self has to be completed by an inseparable second analysis: all acts carry with them a vague awareness of their subject-pole, their place of emission. This awareness does not suspend the direction of perceiving, imagining, or willing towards the object. Specifically in the acts which French expresses with reflexive constructions there is a juncture of the vague consciousness of being subject and of the subject as object, involved in the project, which takes place prior to all reflexive dissociation. A primordial identification resists the temptation to exile my self into the margins of its acts: an identification of the projecting and the projected myself. I am the myself which now wills (and projects) just as I am he who will do (and is projected). "This action is myself" means that there are no two selves, one projecting and one in the project; I affirm myself as the subject precisely in the object of my willing.

This difficult dialectic can also be clarified otherwise: the presence of the subject in his acts is likewise not a content of reflection in that it remains a presence of a subject. Distended reflection tends to make it an object of judgment: the feeling of responsibility orients this in some respects inevitable objectification in the direction of the specific objectification of the project. I meet myself in my project, I am involved in my project, the project of myself by myself. Self-consciousness is thus at the basis of the identity which is prior to judgment and conditions it, a presence of *projecting* subject and *projected* myself. We can understand reflexive judgment precisely by starting out with this prereflexive imputation of myself in my projects.[19]

We frequently imagine reflection as a turning about of consciousness which is at first outside of itself, then returns into itself and suspends its outward orientation. This forces us to regard consciousness turned towards the other as unconscious of itself and self-consciousness as corroding the consciousness which

19. Bradley, "The Definition of Will," Part II, *Mind* (1903), pp. 145 ff., tends to avoid this idea of imputation in which he sees a snare of substantialism and voluntarism; he makes the identification of myself with the idea the sole criterion of volition. The idea which my self *produces, changes*—briefly, the idea of an *agency*—appears to him to employ a suspect causality. (Bradley agrees, to be sure, that once execution has begun, the idea of change, in actualizing itself, in turn changes by its impact my perception of myself—my self which is one with the idea which transforms the actual; I modify reality equally.) If we remember to distinguish causality and imputation of my self in its acts, there is no reason to oppose this *identification* of the self with the project with the *action of the self on itself*, on the condition that we note that in its prereflexive form this determination of the self is effected "in" the project of the action itself.—Completed by his "On Mental Conflict and Imputation," *Mind* (1902), p. 289.

is directed towards something other than itself. Re-flection becomes retro-spection, disastrous for the pro-ject.

This scheme misses what is essential, the awareness of that practical reference to myself which is the very root of reflection. Explicit reflection, in the distended form of the judgment "it is I who . . . ," only raises a more primitive affirmation of myself to the dignity of discourse, a judgment which projects itself in the plan of an action. It makes the practical prereflexive affirmation thematic.

At the same time, reflection derives all its meaning as a moment of an interior dialectic by which I alternately accentuate myself and the project, exalting the one by the other. Nor is the consideration of responsibility anything else. But it is false to assume that self-consciousness is inherently disruptive. Auguste Comte in particular is mistaken about the meaning of introspection. In a great number of acts, awareness of myself is involved as an active ferment of the very thrust of consciousness towards its object. All the acts in which I "take a stand" (in relation to a reality, a fiction, a memory, or a project) are susceptible of being confirmed rather than changed by a more explicit self-consciousness. These are the acts which French expresses by reflexive constructions, se *souvenir* (to remember), se *representer* (to imagine), se *decider* (to decide). In all these acts an action on oneself is already involved in the movement which carries consciousness towards the past, the unreal, or the project; it is only stressed in the explicit judgment of which the judgment of responsibility is typical. It is a mistake to consider only the acts in which consciousness is dissipated and alienated, as anger and the passions in general; as soon as the passions inject themselves into emotion, I am beside myself, not in the sense that I turn towards another thing, but rather in the sense that I am deprived of myself, a victim of. . . . Self-consciousness is the decisive moment of taking hold of myself which opens up a high vision of freedom: in a flash of light, the alienation is suspended. Besides, emotion and passion are not the only examples of possessed or fascinated consciousness of which self-consciousness would become aware if it could enter the light of freedom: inauthentic consciousness, lost in the impersonal "they," provides another example. Thus when self-consciousness is relatively alienated, as in passion or in the "they," it constitutes a dialectic of rejection. On the other hand, it constitutes a dialectic of confirmation when consciousness is relatively its own mistress, as in the act of "taking a stand."

Still it remains true that, separated from this internal dialectic, reflexive judgment uproots itself from living, practical affirmation and becomes pure observation and self-satisfaction. It is the fate of self-consciousness to corrupt itself in all the cases in which it becomes pure observer. As it does so, it in fact suspends consciousness directed towards an action and towards the other in general. It is in contrast with this uprooted consciousness that consciousness, considered in its thrust towards the other, can be said to be forgotten by the self. Descartes calls this forward leap "generosity."

Later we shall consider the drift by which self-affirmation becomes complaisant observation. Faithful to our methodological rule, we shall here suspend the wanderings of consciousness fascinated by the Self and by Nothing, and we shall conceive of a self-affirmation, available for reflection, which is the common keyboard of innocent love of myself and of that fascinated self-consciousness. In this pure description follows the discourse of the Serpent: "Am I not who you are/this complaisance which rises/in your soul as it loves itself?/Finally, I am thanks to it/to that inimitable tang/which you find only in yourself!" [20]

4. Consciousness and Its Power of Being

SELF-DETERMINATION involved in the determination of a project leads us to the meaning of the word "possible" which we have reserved for the conclusion of our analysis of the possibility envisioned in the project. Am I who introduces possibilities into the world not ultimately myself possible? [21]

We shall approach this problem of the capacity for being inherent in the being which wills obliquely, starting with the foregoing analyses. Furthermore this can best be examined in a context far removed from the context of pure description and will have to be taken up anew when all the other elements of the doctrine of choice shall have been put in their place.

20. Valéry, "Ébauche du serpent," *Poésies* (Paris, 1936), p. 165. (Trans. Kohák.)

21. Cf. Karl Jaspers' analyses of possible existence which is "that which comports itself actively in relation to the self," *Philosophie* (Berlin, 1932), II, 35. But it is Heidegger who has gone furthest in this direction. "That entity which in its Being has this very Being as an issue, comports itself towards its Being as its most authentic possibility. In each case Dasein *is* its possibility and it 'has' this possibility, but not just as a property" (*op. cit.*, p. H.42). Commenting on Being "as an issue" [*es geht um*] in this passage, Heidegger here shows "self-projective Being towards its ownmost potentiality-for-being" (*ibid.*, p. H.191; trans. Macquarrie). Cf. primarily J.–P. Sartre, *Being and Nothingness*, trans. Barnes (New York, 1950), Part II, chap. 1, and Part IV, chap. 1.

We shall be guided by two methodological rules. First of all we shall have to begin with our prereflexive and active self-imputation rather than with explicit reflection: in particular, an unpremeditated consideration which would start with the spell or anxiety of power of being seems more likely to mislead the analysis than to aid it. The second rule: it is necessary to uncover the most primitive possibility of myself, which I launch within myself in making up *my* mind. This is the easiest analysis because it still refers to our analysis of the project. In effect, for a responsible being, that is, a being who *commits himself* in the project of an action which he at the same time recognizes as his, determining *oneself* is still one with determining his gesture *in the world*. We can thus search out what possibility of *myself* is simultaneous with the possibility of *action* opened up by the project. By this second means we shall avoid bringing prematurely into consideration the anxiety which is present not only on the level of rejection, but also on the level of engagement, at the dizzying edges of determination of the self and of the project. Thus we shall place ourselves on the prereflexive level of a will which makes the leap, which pro-jects the project.

Yet we could ask whether possibility still applies to my own self when I resolve *on something*? Does not the pro-jecting of the project separate me from potency by raising me to the level of act? Does not the reflexive form of the French expression, "*me* determiner," "to resolve myself," throw any light on this? In binding *myself*, as by an oath or a promise, is not all indetermination extinguished and all possibility with it?

And yet, as the analysis of anxiety will presently show, the possibility of indecision can be clarified only by a more basic possibility which I bring about by my very decision. We have started our description of decision by describing the project, that is, the object of decision, rather than by reflecting on the self who decides, in order to restrain the awareness that the will is first of all a thrust, a pro-ject, a leap—that is, an act, a "generosity." Now we have seen that the project *opens up* possibilities in the world by the very commitment which binds it. As long as I do not project anything, I do not chart possibilities within the actual. Our description of the project thus leads us to seek first of all those of my possibilities which I *open up* by deciding rather than those which I *lose* by it.

In deciding, I not only put an end to an antecedent confusion, but I also initiate a way for being what I am. This way is my "to be"—*a-venir*, future—and my possibility entailed by the project of my self. In what respect am I thus possible by starting with my own decision? First with respect to bodily gestures which would fulfill this possibility. To decide is to project a potential *myself* as the theme of proposed conduct for the body to follow. The possible which I am, in projecting a possible action, consists of a claim I make on my body. This possibility of myself is thus related to the capacity which the project both evokes and encounters in the body. It is the capacity for acting, insofar as my body's future is first possible before being actual (while in another respect the actual always precedes the possible, as awareness of the involuntary recognizes).

But I am also possible in another sense: in relation not only to my body's future reality, but also to the reality of my life-span and of decisions which I shall make in due time. Each decision I make uncovers a possible future, opens up some ways, closes others, and determines the outlines of new areas of indetermination offered as a possible course for subsequent decision. The possibility constituted within me by the project is thus always prior to myself as physical ability for realizing it and the subsequent capacity for deciding.

Such is my own covertly reflexive possibility which I initiate each time I form a project. It means that what I shall be is not *already* given but depends on what I shall do. My possible being depends on my possible doing.

Thus it should be apparent that the capacity of which we speak is not the bare potency of the metaphysicians—the undetermined "hyle"—which, at least logically, precedes the act. The first capacity we encounter is the capacity which an act opens up before itself. With respect to this capacity, indetermination understood as indecision is impotence.

Then reflection enters in, and with it mounting anxiety.

We have said that reflection can be in the first place a moment in the dialectic of the intercourse between the project and myself. What becomes of my capacity for being when I reflect on my responsibility along these lines? Its meaning still does not change: it is only stressed, together with the possibility of the project. As I am able to do I am also able to be. The moment of recoil leads me back to a stronger consciousness *of* the projected action. The more I commit myself and the more I am able to do, the more I am possible. I cannot affirm my potency for being unless I confirm it with acts. My possibility is in the first place my exercised ability.

It seems to me completely mistaken to tie the experience of

freedom to madness and dread. The experience of *exercised* freedom is free from anxiety and acquires the dramatic character which contemporary literature often attributes to it only under the condition of a profound alteration (which we shall examine later). The "generosity" which Descartes teaches is free of anxiety. The opposition of my being to the being of things, powerfully reinforced by my awareness of my own capacity for being, can very well move in the joyous mood which Descartes evokes in the *Treatise on Passions* and in his *Letters*. A thing is here, located, and determined by what is not itself, while freedom is not located, does not become aware of itself, does not discover itself as being already here until I observe it. It creates itself in doing and affirms itself to the extent to which it does—it is being which determines itself. Its potential being is not at all a gaping abyss, it is the actual task which freedom is for itself in the moment *in which it constitutes itself* by the decision it makes. Briefly, insofar as reflection on the capacity for being remains measured by actual exercise of the decision, it remains non-anguished. This is why it seems to me that the opposition of the being of consciousness as capacity for being and the being of things as determined being does not operate on the same level of analysis as the theme of anguish of freedom. This opposition can be made entirely within the context of a reflection on committed freedom, on the capacity for being exercised in self-determination. This is why we shall postpone the study of anguished hyper-reflection which would involve a study of the temporality of choice and of the properly existential dimension of freedom.[22]

But the analysis of imputation of myself, such as we are attempting in the context of pure description, offers but a hint of difficult problems which we can approach only at the cost of recasting our method. Pure description is not aware of the *history* of the project, of the conflicts, sustained by the body, from which hesitation proceeds, of the maturation of all discussions in duration, and of the growth of choice itself as an event. This is why words like thrust, leap, pro-ject, or act remain incomprehensible apart from an effort to correlate them with experienced history. This is also why we have been careful not to pass definitive judgments on *freedom* with respect to the capacity of willing and the capacity of being able. To understand freedom is to understand precisely the *history* which we have held in suspension. But history of consciousness introduces hesitation and choice. A new type of indetermination, a living possibility *tied to attention*, ap-

22. Cf. below, chap. 3, pp. 171–197.

pears to us here at the limit of understanding of essential structures—and at this point we cannot yet say to what extent these new analyses will make the initial conclusions of pure description once more questionable.

[3] MOTIVATION OF WILLING

THERE ARE NO DECISIONS without motives. This basic relation leads us to the boundaries of the central problem of the voluntary and the involuntary. In effect, in this initial relation the body enters into the voluntary synthesis even as it presents itself as an organ to moving and as invincible necessity to consent. Anticipating a general interpretation of the physical roots of motivation, we can say that it is at least in part because of the body that there is no freedom of indifference.

Description of a project as an opening of possibilities in the world and especially the possibilities of imputation of myself as self-determination can in effect create the impression that the will is an arbitrary decree. Relating the act of deciding to motives, which is the third aspect of pure description, checks such rash reasoning. The highest form of will is the will which has *its reasons*, that is, one which bears at the same time the mark of my initiative and the mark of its ancestry.

Thus our task will be first of all to distinguish the relation of motivation from all other relations, especially from the naturalistic conceptions. Secondly, we need to decide about a moral aspect of our investigation—if a motive is a value, should description of willing grow into a philosophy of value and entail an ethic? Finally, we need to correlate this new trait of decision with its relation to myself and to its object. In what sense can we say that I resolve on something and that I decide on it *because* it seems the best alternative?

1. The Essence of Motivation

THE RELATION OF DECISION to motives contains a snare and even an invitation to betray freedom. In this aspect willing lays itself open to a reductive naturalistic interpretation. Don't we say that "I want to do this *because* . . ."? The word "motive" itself suggests a motion, a movement which ought to be observable in the world of objects as a natural phenomenon. Language conspires to confuse a reason for acting with a *cause* and effort with effect. Action seems to be a set of effects whose causes motives are.

Thus we have to recognize the basic relationship of motives to decision at the very heart of Cogito and distinguish it from the relationship instituted on the level of objects between cause and effect.[23]

Without going back to the general reasons for contrasting the order of consciousness and the order of objects which we have presented in the introduction, we can contrast motive and cause directly.

It is the nature of a cause to be knowable and understood prior to its effects. A set of phenomena can be intelligible without reference to another set of phenomena which result from it. The cause confers its meaning on the effect: understanding proceeds irreversibly from cause to effect. On the other hand, it is the essence of a motive not to have a complete meaning apart from the decision which refers to it. I am not able to understand the motives first and in themselves, deriving an understanding of the decision secondarily from them. Their final meaning is tied in a basic way to that action of the self on the self which is decision. The will, in a single movement, determines both itself and the definitive form of its affective as well as its rational arguments. It imposes its decree on future existence and invokes its reasons: the self resolves in light of. . . . On the other hand, we must not say that decision causes its own motives: we shall presently distinguish a motive from a pretext, that is, from a pseudo-reason which the self offers to another—or to itself, considered as an other susceptible to deception. We can understand a pretext only in contrast with a genuine motive, and as a symptom of a covert real motive lying at the basis of decision. Thus the relation is reciprocal: the motive cannot serve as the basis for a decision unless a will bases itself on it. It determines the will only as the will determines itself.

Consider the nascent imagery in an expression like "basing my decision on . . ." etc. ("On what do you base your decision? It is without foundation.") That is the central metaphor. It is remarkable that in order to struggle against the abstract conceptualizations of naturalism, as Bergson realizes, the only help language offers us is the image. The image preserves the glow of mean-

23. Concerning contrast of motive and cause, see Pfänder, *op. cit.*, pp. 98–105, and especially *Motive und Motivation*, pp. 150–57. Along the same line, Michotte and Prüm, *op. cit.*, pp. 209–10: "reason, justification of choice," "reason for acting."

ing which enables language to designate the order of the Cogito.

Now the metaphor of "basing oneself" fits in with the metaphor of thrust. I base myself in order to be able to thrust forward. Every motive is a motive of . . . , a motive of a decision.[24]

This relation which—as all relations of voluntary and involuntary, of motion to its organs, of consent to necessity—is strictly circular, assures us that in the case of a motive, to determine is not to cause but to provide a basis for, to make legitimate, to justify.

From this it appears that it would be useless to try to bring together the language of psychology and the language of physics in order to integrate them into a general causal cosmology. In effect, on the level of empirically considered objects, causal explanation knows no limit. There are no gaps in determinism—it is total or not at all, its supremacy is in principle coextensive with empirical objectivity. To think of anything as an empirical object is to think of it in terms of law. Thus we must renounce the attempt to lodge fundamental structures of willing (project, self-determination, motivation, motion, consent, etc.) in the interstices of determinism, that is, in a general cosmology which would take phenomenal order of physical causality as its initial datum. This is why we need not seek to discover whether motivation is an aspect, a ramification, or on the contrary a limitation or a rupture of empirical causality: the problem itself is meaningless because it assumes a prior objectification and naturalization of the Cogito. Here there arises a kind of physics of the mind and the false dilemma which it implies: either we imagine a hierarchy of superimposed causalities, in which the higher completes the lower without being able to show how it would in fact fit in with biology and physics, or else we sacrifice consciousness to a monistic naturalism. Pure description starts by restoring the primordial status of consciousness in relation to objective structures which, besides, refer to the Cogito in turn, as a pure description of perception and of structures based on perception can show.[25]

24. Pfänder, *Motive und Motivation*: "This act of basing oneself on something in the operation of a voluntary act is a basic mental action. Only the mental act of basing oneself establishes the bond between the foundation and the voluntary act, and a possible motive becomes a genuine foundation of willing" (p. 152). Pfänder proposes to "take the word 'motive' solely in the sense of *foundation of willing which makes a demand*, and, correlatively, to understand by 'motivation' only the basic relation of foundation of willing which demands a *voluntary act based on it*" (p. 153).

25. Cf. below, chap. 3, p. 135. This is why we cannot call freedom "causality seen in retrospect": Schopenhauer, *On the Fourfold Root of the Principle of Sufficient Reason*, trans. Hildebrand (London, 1891), VIII, 43.

This distinction in principle between motive and cause can give us a guiding thread among recent psychologies of the will.

1) First of all it justifies us in having some reservations about the so-called "synthetic" or "Gestalt" psychologies which oppose psychological atomism but share its naturalistic prejudice. Opposing a mental whole to a composition of atoms or simple elements does not suffice to save the primordial status of the will: such a whole remains within the context of mental physics. It is an ambiguous notion which transports a glow of meaning borrowed from apperception of the self to the level of nature. Description then becomes involved in false problems such as that concerning the relation of the whole to a part. A motive is not a part; decision is not a whole—how could it be opposed to a part of myself and yet engender my self? [26] What is needed is to preserve the primordial status of the relation between motives and decision which a Gestalt psychology risks changing for the sake of a process of composition or totalization of psychic forces which remains enslaved by naturalistic modes of thought.

2) Bergsonian psychology, at least as presented in *Time and Free Will*, shares many prejudices of atomism. It is an illusion to interpret psychological determinism as an error concerning the succession of states of consciousness, as if identity of motives through time were a fundamental postulate of determinism. Bergson thinks he has transcended it in diluting states of consciousness and making them more flexible in process, but he never reaches the root of naturalization of consciousness. He cannot reach it because his stream-of-consciousness view of mental life does not break with the prejudice according to which a state of consciousness is a reality in that consciousness. A radical critique of psychological determinism consists entirely of the rediscovery of intentionality of conscious acts. Consciousness is not a natural phenomenon. Besides, a certain multiplicity, not of states but of acts of consciousness in time, is perfectly compatible with the relation of motive to decision. The meaning of such motive can be distinguished from others and preserved through duration. Besides, multiple, identifiable motives are not an attribute of determinism because they are not in nature. Rather, they enter into the act of decision according to absolutely irreducible, orig-

26. Concerning self-love, William James asks, "Who is the self who is loved in self-love?" *The Principles of Psychology* (New York, 1890), I, 139; P. Janet, who quotes him, asks, "Which is the self which wills?" *De l'angoisse à l'extasse* (Paris, 1926), I, 313. All these questions (together with Claparède's, "Does the will express the entire personality?") remain on the level of the inadequate relations of the whole to the part.

inal considerations. Nor does this originality demand, in order to be understood, that we should restructure our understanding of process.

An instantaneous segment permits us to demonstrate the alternately emerging, crossing, and recrossing relation of motive to decision at a given moment. The outline of a decision is relative to an outline of motives. Hesitation, which divides willing and holds it in suspension, is also a divided, evasive motivation. At every moment in our inquiry into choice we encounter the internal gesture of basing oneself on reasons. This is the same thing as saying that choice is not constrained and that motives do not determine it. The history of a decision is also a history of a motivation running through sketches, temptations, rejections, leaps, crises, and the decree. The same gesture determines and justifies me. The "because" of motivation seeks itself together with the possibility of the project. This is why we cannot completely correct psychological atomism by a *process psychology* if we have not recognized the basic essence of motivation.

But though Bergson's *Time and Free Will* is of little help for correcting the prejudices of classical psychology concerning the essence of motivation itself, it is this essay which in turn gives us the means for breaking out of the limits of a pure description tied to an instantaneous segment of duration. The conflict, the maturation, the choice are inseparable from time: Bergson teaches us that duration is the very life of our freedom. We shall keep it in mind when we attempt to give a breath of life to the skeleton of concepts which our first chapter attempted to establish.

3) One last comparison will permit us to specify the meaning of the relation between motive and decision. One intellectualistic tradition believes that it can save the primitive nature of the will by opposing motives to incentives. Incentives would then be affective and passionate, motives rational and moderate. Voluntary motivation would be a kind of practical reasoning in which decision would play the role of conclusion and motives the role of premises. The feeling of obligation which frequently accompanies such reasoning would be nothing else than the intellectual necessity which accompanies scientific reasoning.[27] We shall not encounter this type of opposition again; it presupposes that apart from rational judgment mental life is only a tributary of a naturalistic, causal explanation. This intellectualism shares with empiricism the prejudice that an incentive is a cause, and

27. Cf. the more complete discussion of intellectualism, below, chap. 3, p. 135.

that we do not get away from the rule of things except by clarity of reasoning. Thus we have to assure ourselves that a majority of our motives are made of no other stuff than our affective life. Our entire conception of the body, of the physical involuntary offered to the arbiter of "I will," rests on this conviction that it is the very thrust of the physical involuntary which *moves* our will, but by a *sui generis* motion which our free will appropriates in deciding. The relation of motives to decision is broader than the relation of premises to consequences in practical reasoning. Practical reasoning is only a pattern, devoid of all exemplary character. As we shall see later, examples of it are rare in real life. The prototype of rational decision is a sort of limit-instance in which even some basic traits of decision are reduced. Descartes was surely nearer to the truth when he linked practical decision to the impossibility of carrying out a rational analysis of a situation whose urgency in any case does not permit pursuing the clarification very far.

If intellectualism arbitrarily restricts motivation to the narrow body of practical reasoning, it does so because it considers the essence of motivation at the same time from the viewpoint of its exclusive causal rigor and from the viewpoint of its breadth which is receptive to the infinite diversity of experience.

In order for a tendency to function as a motive it is necessary and sufficient for it to make itself available to the reciprocal relation of affective or rational tendencies which incline willing and to a determination of the self by itself which is founded on them. The circular relation of motives and decision is the eidetic norm of all empirical observation. In this sense we could repeat the classical formula: motive inclines without compelling. But the term "compelling" has many meanings which we must distinguish. First of all, if necessity is synonymous with natural determinism, the formula should be interpreted as "a motive is not a cause." The second possibility is that necessity indicates the invincible depth of character, of the unconscious, and of life from which determinate motives arise and all that Jaspers calls the limit situations of human existence. Then the formula acquires a different meaning: it stresses the difference between an involuntary which is susceptible to being surrounded, faced, and changed, and which precisely is a motive, and the diffuse, enveloping, and incoercible involuntary which can no longer be a "motive of. . . ." This is the necessity in the first person which gives rise to still another dimension of free will—consent. Finally, the term "compel" could improperly indicate the bondage of passions, the captivity by Nothing. This is the bondage which we have bracketed in this analysis. The formula would then acquire a third meaning: motivation of a free will is more basic than the alienation of a fascinated consciousness.

2. Motive and Value: The Line Between Pure Description and Ethics

WE HAVE DELIMITED DESCRIPTION of motivation with respect to physics, and we need now to delimit it with respect to ethics. Now while it is easy to show the birth of a moral problem in the course of considering the motives of willing, it is rather difficult to trace the demarcation line between the two disciplines.

A motive represents and, so to speak, "historializes" values and their relations.[28] To give a reason is not to explain, but to justify, to legitimize, that is, to appeal to a right. But the values entailed by the thrust of the project do not necessarily take the form of value judgments, just as my self-imputation in a decision is only available to a reflection which would then make it explicit as a judgment of responsibility. Such reflection, while raising a motive to the level of a judged value, also makes it an occasion of contact between myself and the other. Thus I justify myself before . . . , in the eyes of, seek approval, contest or prevent disapproval, and in turn I learn to evaluate my acts in evaluating those of others. In brief, I reflect on value in the social context of praise and blame.[29] But reflection on the "they" and its inauthentic valuations, similar to those which elicited our considerations with regard to imputative judgment, leads to analogous

28. This abbreviated formula is freely inspired by Max Scheler, Der Formalismus in der Ethik und die materiale Wertethik (Halle, 1927), from which we have retained two ideas: (1) there is a way between formalism of duty and hedonism of the good (that is, utilitarianism and affectively oriented theories in general); (2) the material (non-formal) a prioris can reveal themselves only in terms of psychological feelings and the unfolding of history. We shall have occasion to show the connection of the a priori with individual affectivity, particularly in our study of organic motives in chap. 2. The relation of the a priori to history transcends the narrowly psychological framework of this work. Yet it is the most important problem of ethics. For what would have to be shown systematically in order to justify our expression, "historialization" of values, is that there are no moral constants, alongside of or above various judgments, feelings, and mores, but that, rather, varying history is a mode of appearance of a moral a priori. More than Scheler, we shall stress the necessary mediation through action and through history which prevents us from treating values as contemplative essences. That is why we refuse to harden our opposition to J.–P. Sartre's conception of value. It is no exaggeration to say that we decipher the good by our own devotion: an a prioristic interpretation of values will stretch that far.

29. Concerning approbation, see Le Senne, Traité de morale (Paris, 1942), pp. 325–29.

considerations here. Social valuation is only the occasion, sometimes an opportunity and often a degradation, of a more elementary power of valuation which constitutes the individual will. It
is the nature of the will to seek reasons; in terms of them it moves
beyond social valuation and finds roots and context in them.

Thus the reflexive character of valuation gives to the value
judgment a significance comparable to judgments of responsibility. Implicit evaluation, which movement brings out before
consciousness, remains a feeling contained *in* the project itself:
it is the project which has a value. When I reflect on the value
of the project, I partially set aside its thrust. Thus valuation is a
drawing back to question the legitimacy of my project and my
own value because the project is myself. Such recoil, such turning back towards value, can remain a moment of broader dialectic of thrust and reflection. But if the return to value is lasting,
if the project is suspended for a longer time or even abandoned
entirely, valuation becomes isolated from the thrust of consciousness toward action. This is why value judgments do not share
the future orientation of a project but rather express present
value, as "this is good." As they more generally lose any reference
to an imminent or postponed insertion of the project into the
world, their grammatical mode is no longer the imperative or
the gerundative, but the indicative of value.[30]

Under these conditions, where is the line between pure description of willing and ethics?

First of all it seems clear that ethics begins by abstracting
away the thrust of the project in which prereflexive valuation is
embedded. Consciousness constitutes itself as moral consciousness as it makes itself entirely a valuation, a reflection concerning
values. Such explicit valuation is undoubtedly a judgment, or,
more precisely, a comparison: this is better than that, right now
this is the best. This judgment, at the lowest rung of a situation,
has as a horizon or backdrop landmarks or value references which
are not evaluated actively each time, but rather form, for a given
consciousness at a given time of its development, a concrete, more
or less ordained table, or better, a configuration or a constellation
of fixed stars. These non-revaluated values form, so to speak, its
ethical firmament, its moral "habitus." The term "horizon of
value" well suggests what an ethical consciousness is: it is a

30. In this sense the scholastics distinguished speculative-practical judgments
(lying is wrong) and practical-practical judgments (I shall tell him all) tied to
the *imperium* of decision: between abstract injunction of the rule and the effective suggestion of concrete action there is the same distance as between the
infima species and the individual apprehended *hic et nunc*.

consciousness which, unlike a willing consciousness, moves from the reasons for its project to the reasons for its reasons, reopening the question of its value references and unceasingly questioning its proximate, remote, penultimate, and ultimate values and reevaluating its ethical firmament. To the extent to which it thus removes itself from its present project it places all its problems in a radical light and evaluates its life and its action as a whole. Ethics is such a radicalization. Now such questioning does not take place without another type of anxiety, which is no longer the anxiety of potential willing or potential doing but an anxiety of ultimate goals. In effect every project activates only a sector of values with respect to which the whole field of value serves as reference. In a given situation, I seek a point on which to base myself. I ordinarily find it in the totality of values not reevaluated at that moment, which in the course of the debate with myself reveal their motivating power in *that* situation. All my other values function as variables in a partial evaluation. This is what Bergson described in *Two Sources of Morality and Religion* under the name of the whole of obligation. But in great crises, on the occasion of a trial which radicalizes my very self, in face of a commotion which attacks me in my ultimate reasons, I turn to my fixed stars. Everything is changed. I can no longer ask for the horizon of value of *this* valuation. Suddenly, my ultimate values are no longer something which refers to. . . . But are my fixed stars fixed? How can we trace the ultimate tangents of reference, and what does "ultimate" mean? Anxiety about the ground of value seizes me; for the question "what does ultimate mean?" inevitably leads to another—"is there an ultimate in value?" The "ἀνάγκη στῆναι" becomes suspect. The *Grund* becomes *Abgrund*.

This anxiety, also, is an anxiety within reflection, and it is not certain that it could be unraveled within reflection. It could, if there existed something like a Platonic intuition of values and if the receptive aspect of reflection represented a closed field of an absolutely pure apperception in which absolute values would become manifest. Such intuition would in a sense mask the abyss which widens and becomes more radical as the question of my aims itself swells and grows to the proportions of an ultimate question.

For my part, I believe that there exists a certain emotional revelation of values in a given situation and that Max Scheler gave ethics a satisfactory orientation by his conception of the emotional *a priori*. But I also believe that he deceived himself when he conceived of that emotional intuition as independent of the thrust of my dedication, that is, of a project in act, and so could entertain illusions concerning the possibility of a pure ethics. This emotional intuition to which we shall return in time appears to be subjected to a peculiar condition which makes it unusual. Values only appear to me in proportion to my loyalty, that is, my active dedication. In our language of pure description we can say that value is valuable in relation to an eventual project, which means that values only appear to me in a historical, qualified situation within which I orient myself and seek to motivate my action. Motivation of a specific project is the basic context where moral judgments enter in. This is why we have said above that a motive "presents" or, so to speak, "historializes" a value or a value-context: following Josiah Royce and Gabriel Marcel, I should say that values are not timeless ideas but suprapersonal existences, thereby stressing that their appearance is tied to a definite *history* on which I collaborate actively with all the power of my dedication, briefly, a history which I invent. Yes, that is the paradox of value: it is not completely a product of history, it is not invented, it is recognized, respected, and discovered—but only to the extent of my capacity for making history, for inventing history. Royce especially insisted that only a loyalty of a collective (or rather community) character to what he calls a cause can bring forth the values which legitimize that cause; and the closer that cause comes to being a universally human cause, the closer we come to universal values. It is not certain that such loyalty is the only way along which values are historialized, or rather the way along which we *make* them historically present in our *making* of history. But it is enough for us to say, at the level of abstraction which we have adopted, that I encounter values in motivating a project (this project being itself a moment of a militant consciousness). If there is such a thing as a contemplation of the good, it is sustained only by the thrust of consciousness which incorporates its values in a project. Detached from this living dialectic of contemplation and decision, of legitimization and invention, a value judgment loses not only its function, but even its possibility. It is of the essence of value not to appear except as a possible motive of decision. I testify to a value only as its champion. This is the source of a certain deception which seems to accompany all theory of values. I do not see values as I see things. I see only those values which I am willing to serve. The very nature of value and of the seeing appropriate to it seems to enclose all theory of value in a circle.

On the one hand, will seeks its justification in values and turns to them to receive a blessing of the good; on the other hand valuation is only a moment in the initiative of the will which enlists in its service. I do not will unless I see, but I cease to see if I absolutely cease to will. That is the difference in principle which separates the truth of the good from the truth of an object. The attention which the latter requires activates only a pure understanding shorn of passions, while the attention demanded by the former mobilizes my whole being. Values are never given to an observer-consciousness impartiality and objectivity have no longer the same meaning in relation to value as in relation to empirical objects. This explains the gaps and the more or less lasting blindness which afflict our perception of the good.

Perhaps we shall now understand why pure reflection dealing with values, in the margins of any commitment, should be an undiminishing anxiety. For the second time, reflection appears as the subversion of a certain living relation which I must constantly rediscover as reflection annuls it. Just as self-imputation in a project cannot exile itself from that project without losing itself in the bad infinite of reflection, so evaluation, separated from loyalty, can only disappear in an endless question. We must constantly return to a second naïveté, suspend the reflection which itself suspends the living relation between valuation and project.

Only on this condition can we agree with Scheler's interpretation of the *emotive a priori*. Such *a priori* is defenseless against a critique which first expels it from history and action and then submits it to the dissolving action of a reflection which inevitably founders in a deadening doubt. But, replaced in its context of dedication, rediscovered as a new immediacy, prereflexive valuation is in effect really a kind of discovery of an *a priori* which transcends willing and which, in addition, is only perceived in unity of its aspects: truthfulness tied to love, love to justice, justice to equality, etc., without any one value ever having an isolated meaning. Nor can such an *a priori* be detached from the history or the civilization which presided at its birth: honor preserves its feudal aura, tolerance its eighteenth-century overtones, hospitality its Homeric resonance, etc. And yet it is the inexhaustible *a prioris*, illustrated very partially by an age or a social class, which give a nobility and a style to their age or social class. The task of ethics thus is to show explicitly those basic emotive acts which make consciousness sensitive to values. Kant himself inaugurated such description with his study of respect and of the sublime. But this sensitivity, at once humble and exalted, is only one possible mode of valuation, and valuation can be modulated in an infinity of other affective tones to conform with the noble, the heroic, the just, etc. Each emotive mode represents a different overstatement by a valuating consciousness which turns towards a sector of values of indeterminate extent. These values at the core of motivation in turn make the legitimization of a sector of projects possible.

Where then lies the line between pure description of willing and ethics? It is easier to show the passage from the one to the other than to point to the moment at which the line is crossed. Pure description of willing *calls* for a specifically moral consideration of valuation. What is the relation between valuation and the *a priori* on the one hand and history on the other? How can it be linked with the affective revelation of material *a priori* on the one hand, and on the other with formal criteria of universalization which Kant so successfully brought to light and which retain a subordinate but basic role in valuation? How can we retain the bond between valuation and closed problems, historically determined situations and persons whose destiny, vocation, and experience are limited, without destroying its other reference to an infinite mystery of sanctity which breaks down the limits of all value and which shines in the transparence of its appeal and its demands?

This consideration of valuation—which is ethics—is thus *called forth* by our pure description, though the latter at the same time betrays its fragile position on the margin of life. If ethics and practice cease to form a circle, both the one and the other become corrupted. Thus ethics is possible only as a reflection on the valuation entailed by the thrust of the project, and yet this reflection becomes impossible and founders in bottomless anxiety if it cuts the umbilical cord which ties it to the thrust, to the very generosity of freedom. This is the "exposed situation of ethical values" which always makes ethical considerations precarious. Reflection on valuation must alternately be outlined on the fringe of action and annulled by the movement of separation from action.

3. Motivation, Self-Determination, Project

THE CIRCLE of ethics and practice repeats the more basic circle of motive and decision. Every motive which "historializes" a value is a motive of . . . , and every decision which links willing to a value is a decision because. . . . The circle, in turn, is rooted in the even more elementary reciprocity of the involuntary and the voluntary, physical involuntary being the existential source of the first stratum of values and the affective sounding board of all values, even the most refined values. This circle thus figures in the central difficulty of pure description. How are determination by motive and self-determination linked together in decision?

To understand this nexus we must again start from the project. These two determinations, neither of which is causal determination of the empirical or naturalistic type, are two compatible and coherent dimensions of the project. The one points to the initiative of the thrust, the other to its basis.

More precisely, self-imputation and motivation indicate the liaison of a specific activity and receptivity at the heart of deciding. It would be a total misconception of man—and we shall progressively discover that man's condition has the being of Transcendence as its limiting index—if we considered willing a pure act. Activity has not only a contrary, but also a complement: a contrary in the passivity whose prototype is the bondage of passions, a complement in the passivity of which motives are a prime example and which is illustrated in still another way by the organs of voluntary motion and the necessity of a given condition. I do my acts to the extent to which I *accept* reasons for them. I provide the basis for the physical being of my actions even while I base myself on their value, that is, their moral being.

We can clarify this basic connection only by an exegesis of some revealing metaphors. We have already stressed the suggestive power of metaphors as they mutually annul each other as images and mutually convey their indirect meaning.

It is not an accident that the receptivity of willing expresses itself in metaphors taken from the senses. Perception is the prime model of receptivity and initial availability of consciousness. These are metaphors like "to listen," "listening," "voice," "word," "logos," "lending an ear to temptation," or "turning a deaf ear to all but one's duty." [31] The image of the trial develops this metaphor along other, rigid lines: the will is an arbiter (free or

31. Pfänder, *Motive und Motivation*, distinguishes the motive from a simple impulsive tendency by this correlative attitude of willing which hears a claim. Pfänder calls this *geistiges Gehör* (mental hearing), the focus of this receptivity the *Seelengeist* (mind of the soul), and opposes it to *Seelenleib* (body of the soul) (the peripheral self, says Hans Reiner for his part), which any tendency can unsettle and even force and violate (p. 155).

bound) who hears and advises. The eclectics have taken this metaphor at face value and canonized deliberation in the form of a
trial, with its pomp, its procedure, and, so to speak, its liturgy.
As we shall see, the complex argumentation of a trial is an
elaboration arising out of obstacles and checks of a more primitive, hidden attitude: namely, the brief drawing back, an un-
shaped question, a consultation without discourse.

Seeing: intuition—respect—light: *video meliora, deteriora
sequor* (I see the better, follow the worse).

Taste: bitter duty.

Through all the senses, consciousness receives what it does
not produce, at least does not produce from the perspective of a
description which remains true to the given, and excepts the
transcendental deduction of objects and values which we shall
not, in any case, consider as pure given of description.

The essential act of the senses consists of opening or closing,
of turning towards and turning away. This directing of the sense
which offers itself to its object is also the pattern of valuation.
As the intersubjective relation of receiving suggests in its elaborate form as hospitality, there can be no receiving without the
maturity of an I which receives in its area, in its environment,
in a word, in a zone which it actively qualifies and which is its
"home." [32] Reception is always the other side of the generosity
which irradiates and embraces the received being. This suggests
another cycle of metaphors of a more dynamic kind: I yield to
reasons, I support a party, I share in an opinion (in the eight-
eenth century, the expression was "to support with a will"), I
adopt a position, as a strange child received by his adoptive
father. These metaphors of adhesion, or better, of adherence,
insist on the movement which overcomes a distance, the humble
distance of respect and the sovereign distance of the judge. Thus
the improper intention of sensory metaphors is corrected. Seeing
remains observation: what I observe remains outside of myself,
but what I adopt penetrates within me, the willing and the value
are fused and united. This is the union which makes a value
into a motive . . . : I receive the value into the interior of my
consciousness. It is at home within me, and I see myself in light
of what it offers.

These initial reflections enable us to interpret the perilous
metaphor of commandment and obedience. This metaphor is borrowed from communication among consciousnesses, but it is

32. See Marcel, *Creative Fidelity*, pp. 82–103, concerning "being at home" and
"receiving."

analogous to the more intimate relation between value and project. Value is not necessarily an order received from an other, nor is the respect for a value necessarily the result of obedience to social authority outside of myself, but obedience is the occasion, the opportunity—and, again, sometimes the snare—which allows me to confront the problem of legitimacy. Another's command poses for me the question of legitimacy of his order, as well as the question of the legitimacy of my submission. Authentic obedience is one which consents, that is, which engenders in me reasons for obeying. Now a reason for obeying is a personal motive of decision. Thus we say that the essence of the voluntary act of the capacity for being involves at the same time something like a commandment—to the possible, the body, the world—and something like obedience—of known, respected, and accepted values.

We must, however, use this metaphor with caution—not only because of the equivocation which it creates between a social relation and a fundamental relation at the heart of consciousness, but also because of its moral and even Kantian overtones. Obedience to the imperative of obligation is not the whole of voluntary motivation. Affective variables cannot be excluded from voluntary motivation for descriptive reasons. Such an argument, which led Kant to constitute the relation of freedom to law in its somewhat chemical purity, is foreign to pure description. It seeks whatever relations could be necessary and *a priori* between the maxim of an action and a free will. But such methodological demand is foreign to us here—in contrast, we are attempting to uncover the relation between motive and project in all its amplitude, prior to any restriction imposed by the demands of an ethical *a priori*. In this respect Rauh's remarkable analyses, too often forgotten in our time, can help us restore the full scope of voluntary motivation. There is no *a priori* reason why we should not consider a desire as a motive or even as a value, provided that in receiving the desire the will bases itself on it in determining itself. In principle, all spontaneity, whether physical or not, can "incline without compelling" and serve as a basis for a sovereign decision. Thus, if we wish to restore to motivation all the breadth compatible with the concept in a strict sense, we cannot understand obedience as an indication of the receptivity to values considered as the essence of motivation, with all our other metaphors of hearing, seeing, adhesion, and receiving clustered around it. It is the convergence of all these metaphors which orients the mind towards the meaning of motivation, and the analysis of motivation must respect its full scope.

We could introduce one last metaphor, most important because it is the etymological source of the word motive, and most dangerous because it invites a naturalistic interpretation of willing. The motive is like a motion, an impulse. The will moves only when it is moved. This Aristotelian-sounding metaphor presented far fewer ambiguities in an age when the concept of motion had not been pushed by empirical experimentation with movement into space, into "locomotion," but rather embraced all change from one state to another. Under the influence of exact sciences, this margin of meaning has narrowed down and the excess meaning took refuge in metaphors like "what motive moved him to it?" or "I am inclined to think that. . . ." The motive is the *clinamen*, the inclination, of willing. To be sure, as we have often said, motion by value differs from physical motion as reason differs from cause and remains the obverse of self-determination by the self. But from the viewpoint of distinction of meanings, the analogy lies in the fact that a voluntary decision and a physical effect are both receptive, one with respect to its motives and the other with respect to its cause.

We have arrived at a point at which pure description already allows us to take sides against the famous freedom of indifference which repudiates the very essence of motivation. But at the same time pure description authorizes us to refuse the dilemma, either indeterminism or determinism. The latter confuses motive and cause and, in a general way, consciousness and nature, while the former omits the basic relation of project to motive.

Can we at least uncover this relation through the metaphors, at the juncture of activity and receptivity, of initiated possibility and received justification? There are privileged experiences which lead reflection close to this relation. First among these is the feeling of responsibility which we had begun to analyze above. Here the feeling of potency and the feeling of valuing become conjoined. If, in effect, I assume charge of things and beings for which I respond, it is to the extent to which I feel charged with them, that is, to which I receive responsibility for them. There is no authentic responsibility without the awareness of a mission confided in me by a legitimate power through a delegation which can even remain virtual (on part of my country, of a community, of all mankind). The responsible act is distinguished from the arbitrary act and even more from a stupid gamble—which is for

nothing, for laughs, for no one—by this consecration, this unc-
tion which value confers on action and by the hold it exercises
over me and to which I respond. In terms of this orientation by
a legitimizing value I can be not only responsible for . . . , but
also responsible to . . . ; for value, in the dangerous historical situation in which I become aware of it, is the suprapersonal bond
of a group of men to which I dedicate myself. I am responsible
to those who in some sense send me on a mission—particularly
to those whom some social differentiation raised up as specially
vigilant guardians of those threatened yet militant values. The
possibility of a principle of judgment passed on my action, of
blame and approbation, in a word, of sanction, is imbedded in
this legitimatization of my responsibility. It is enough that my
judge in some way bears the authority of those values for which
I battle. If I can thus be responsible to . . . , it is in this the first
place because my sovereignty is measured by an order of values
which have motivated it or which ought to motivate it.

In this mutual implication of value and ability the initiative
proceeds alternately from one and the other. One moment my
ability appears to me as an exalting availability in quest of a
cause worthy of its devotion, as the leisure of a freed slave who
does not yet know what use he'll make of his unearthed talent.[33]
A gap appears in history, a space opens up, for the possible, for
the unresolved, on which some value can be imposed. The next
moment, in contrast, the sense of a mission seizes a flickering life
and perhaps a sickly body and unveils powers within me which
I had not suspected. Wars, revolutions, domestic misfortunes,
philanthropic or religious vocations reveal these extraordinary
situations in which value clears the way to possibility. You ought
to, therefore you can, says a vocation. Then it seems necessary
to cut drastically into a world which does not seem capable of
having anticipated the role of that great design. Perhaps even
because of its intransigence—the intransigence of an Electra in
Giradoux—the value must appear destructive of an obstinately
non-porous historical reality. Thus in turn possibility seeks a
justification and a justification stimulates an initiative for its
devotion.

If now the primitive pact of the project, the determination of
the self by the self and of the motivating value breaks up, the
act of willing itself, which held them together, explodes: the un-

33. Cf. the freed slave in Saint-Exupéry, *Terre des hommes*, (Paris, 1939[1],
1948).

recognizable fragments are what we call arbitrary act, anxiety, scruple.

We are already familiar with *anxiety* of the potential ability without a project which would anchor it and engage it, but ability without a project is also potency without value. The same hyper-reflection which tires out the capacity for self-determination at the same time uproots it from the ground of values and leaves it suspended, with a gesture of sketching a determinate future, one of basing oneself on. . . . At the bottom of this impasse a half-turn is enough to rally the realm of projects and assemble the realm of values. If life begins beyond anxiety, there is a way back from there to here, to a naïveté, albeit a naïveté which has matured in the experience of anxiety.

In this way an *arbitrary act* can appear as a healthy reaction at the end of such hypercritical reflection about my capacity for being. I do something, something useless, perhaps vain, which, though it lacks the intensity of responsible acts, at least helps to crystallize a definite intention out of the chaos of unformed possibility. But if the arbitrary act in its turn reaches the level of deadening reflection, it will appear as despair, the despair of a vile freedom, that is, freedom without values. Reflection must force itself into this tunnel; for, by a wondrous movement, comparable to the discovery of the Cogito in the depth of doubt, the arbitrary act illuminates the relation of deciding with the light of rediscovered motive. Freedom passionately affirms itself because of itself, through respect for itself, respecting itself as its ultimate motive.

Hesitation or *scruple* is a corruption of the symmetrical willing of arbitrary act. It, too, is a kind of anxiety, arising from an endless reflection about value in the inability to decide. It, too, has lost the naïveté of a thrust and a basis. The gnawing worm of reflection uses it to corrupt the experience of value which is no longer an impetus but a stagnation. Reasons are endlessly questioned, held at a distance and criticized in a ratiocination which lives on the problematic mode. Now this anxiety of value proceeds from another shrinking of original generosity, as the will reduces its power by delay. It creates an inner void, a listening distance, a silence for value. But this suspension of potency is a disastrous loss of thrust: willing which does not commit itself or devote itself is also a willing which adheres to no value, because a value does not truly reveal itself until I adopt it, base myself on it, call on it as a motive of. . . . Thus potency and motive are corrupted simultaneously, testifying again by their solidarity in degeneration to their basic mutuality. Absence of act, negation of potency, shadow of value. . . .

All our analyses—whether they proceed from direct elucidation of concepts, from exegesis of revealing metaphors, or from the effort to clarify certain basic experiences—focus on the same definition of the essence of deciding. To decide means first of all to project a practical possibility of an action which depends on me, secondly to impute myself as the author responsible for the project, and finally to motivate my project by reasons and variables which "historialize" values capable of justifying them. In particular the bond of activity and receptivity indicates the fundamental limit of a freedom which is that of a man's will rather than the will of a Creator.

Next, introduction of the body and the corporal involuntary into our consideration—at the cost of explosion in method—will lead us to elucidate, within the limits of objectivity of essences, the actual existence of this human will, inclined by an existing body and sustaining the concrete event of choice in process.

2 / Motivation and the Corporeal Involuntary

INTRODUCTION: CORPOREAL EXISTENCE WITHIN LIMITS OF EIDETICS

MY BODY IS ONLY ONE SOURCE of motives among others, and I can evaluate and measure my life in terms of other goods. However, my body is the most basic source of motives, revealing a primordial stratum of values: the organic values. When I give preference to other values over these—when, as Plato puts it, I "exchange" my life for justice, for instance—I am no longer carrying on any purely academic debate. I really *stake my existence*, sacrifice myself. Thus all other values assume a serious, dramatic significance through a comparison with the values which enter history through my body.

It is my body which introduces this existential note; it is the initial existent, underivable, *involuntary*. Suddenly the entire abstract relation of willing to its motives comes to life; the brackets which shielded pure description are removed; the "I am" or "I exist" infinitely overwhelms the "I think."

But though pure description—which still remains on the level of an objectification of the structures of the Cogito—must, as we have shown in the introduction, be transcended, it may not be violated. It remains the task of understanding to comprehend as much as possible. This is why the relation of the corporeal involuntary to the will has to be *clarified* in light of previously *understood* relations between motive and project. My hunger, my thirst, my fear of pain, my desire for music, or my sympathy all refer to my willing in the form of motives. The circular relation of motive to project demands that I recognize my body as body-for-my-willing, and my willing as project-based-(in part)-on my

[85]

body. The involuntary is *for* the will and the will is *by reason* of the involuntary. Pure description thus fortifies us against the prejudices of naturalism and against its irreversible explanation of the higher by the lower.

But to clarify is not yet to understand, to lay hold of a structure. The corporeal involuntary is more than a mere illustration of pure relations described by eidetic analysis—it transcends all discourse. Our needs, in all senses of the word, are the material of which our motives are made. Now our needs are opaque not only to reasoning which would deduce them from the ability to think, but even to the light of reflection. To experience is always more than to understand. Not that hunger or thirst would not lend itself to any light of representation—quite the contrary, it is in them that need becomes real and significant, and through them enters the cycle of the will—but beyond all representation affectivity remains unreachable and really incomprehensible. In a general way, affectivity is the non-transparent aspect of the Cogito. We are right in saying, "of the Cogito." Affectivity is still a mode of thought in its widest sense. To feel is still to think, though feeling no longer represents objectivity, but rather reveals existence. Affectivity uncovers my bodily existence as the other pole of all the dense and heavy existence of the world. We can express it otherwise by saying that through feeling a personal body belongs to the subjectivity of the Cogito. But how can we reach feeling in its purity? All attempts to extend self-consciousness into the murky regions of need are to some extent deceptive. An introspection into the body is always a wager. We should have to be able to go beyond judgment in any form, indicative, imperative, conditional, etc., that is, beyond the self which orients itself in existence and assumes a position, and even beyond the representation which cloaks need with its objective intent. Admittedly, such regression could be only a feint—suggested by a kind of contortion —at regression or even self-denial of a clear consciousness which tries to penetrate to the very limits of its own extent.[1]

This opaqueness of affectivity leads us to seek the light which the Cogito refuses to itself in the objectification of need and of bodily existence. Everything invites us to treat involuntary organic life as an object, in the same way as stones, plants, and animals. The very fact that the will feels besieged by need and at

1. Concerning this "analytic regression to the immediate," cf. Pradines, *Philosophie de la sensation* (Paris, 1928–34), vol. II, *La Sensibilité élémentaire, Les Sens du besoin*, p. 9. Jean Nogue strongly emphasizes the difficulty of such "pure experience of life" by "reduction of the sensible," cf. *Le Signification du sensible* (Paris, 1936), p. 57.

times opposes it violently as if to eject it from consciousness places need midway between consciousness and foreign objects. Stoicism follows out this reasoning to the end and treats the body as a stranger. The bond which need establishes between my body and objects reinforces this temptation. To feed myself is to place myself on the level of reality of the objects on which I depend. While I transform them into myself, they drag me to the level of objects and make me a part of the great natural cycles—the cycles of water, carbon, nitrogen, etc. This view of things imposes itself not only on the observer, but also on the subject experiencing the need: the techniques by which I care for my body equate it with a machine to be repaired. Thus need stresses the essential ambiguity of the body: feeling integrates it with subjectivity, but it is our intimacy presented for observation, offered, exposed among things, and exposed to things. Here lies the temptation of naturalism, the invitation to deprive experience of the body of its personal traits and to treat it as any other object. And if all consciousness is gradually threatened by objective treatment, it is in the last analysis because the body is better known this way than in the privacy of self-consciousness. Thus the inevitable objectification of the body infects all experience of the self. The central, primitive fact of incarnation is simultaneously the first hallmark of all existence and the first invitation to treason.

But, in turn, while the opaqueness of affectivity invites us to treat the corporeal involuntary as an object, it is the breakdown of this objectification which leads us back to the interior of consciousness in order to take a gamble on introspection into personal body insofar as it is intelligible. We cannot stress too strongly how the reality of need is misrepresented by psycho-physiology. Description of need will be an excellent opportunity to test the usual schemas and to substitute for them the diagnostic relation between objective knowledge of the body and the living experience of incarnate Cogito to which we have referred in the introduction. I do not know need from the outside, as a natural event, but from within, as a lived need and, when needed, through empathy as yours; but I have an objective symptom of it in the deterioration of blood and tissue, and in the nervous or glandular reaction to such deterioration. On the one hand, this parallel tends irresistibly to explain consciousness by the body: the customs of life also suggest it—most of the time I need to act and it is enough to act on the body as a thing in order to change the way I experience it. On the other hand, the diagnostic relation which conjoins objective knowledge with Cogito's apperception brings about a truly

Copernican revolution. No longer is consciousness a symptom of the object-body, but rather the object-body is an indication of a personal body in which the Cogito shares as its very existence.

We can understand this language if we notice that the problem is never one of relating consciousness (a subject) to the body (an object). The link between consciousness and the body is already functioning and is experienced at the core of my subjectivity and your subjectivity. It is the adherence of affectivity to thought itself. As we shall gradually discover, all the relations of the involuntary to the "will," in the form of motives, organs of action, or experienced necessity, are aspects of this link, of this inherence of a personal body in the Cogito. The union of soul and body must be sought in the unique universe of discourse of the subjectivity of "I think" and of "you think." From this aspect the problem presents itself not in terms of the relation of two realities, consciousness and the body, but of the relation of two universes of discourse, two points of view of the same body, considered alternately as a personal body inherent in its Cogito and as object-body, presented among other objects. The diagnostic relation expresses this encounter of two universes of discourse.

This, then, is our task: to attempt to *clarify* the experience of the corporeal involuntary within the *limits* of eidetic analysis of motivation and in *tension* with objective, empirical treatment of the body.

[1] NEED AND PLEASURE

THE CORPOREAL INVOLUNTARY is but one source of motives among others; need in strict sense is in turn only a part of the corporeal involuntary. Thus our inquiry will consist of three cycles: (1) need in a strict sense, (2) the realm of the corporeal involuntary, and (3) the place of the values illustrated by the body among other motivating values. In contrast with their material diversity, this progressively broadening analysis should confirm the formal or eidetic unity of tendencies as motives.

1. The Nature of Need

WE SHALL ADMIT, with Pradines, that in a strict sense the term need pertains to alimentary or sexual assimilation, that is, to appetite. Thus we shall adopt Pradines' distinction between two major forms of our relational life. The first is the form of the living being tending to appropriate and assimilate things and beings which *complete* its existence and as such are linked with it (food, beverage, other sex). The other is the form of defensive functions which tend to repel that which *threatens* its existence and which is thus alien to it. We shall show subsequently why common language speaks of need in a broader sense, as need of light, music, friendship, etc. Initially there seem to be two reasons for this extension of meaning: needs in the broader sense bear a material resemblance to appetites in terms of the characteristic of *lack* which they entail and of the generalized affective revelation of a lacuna at the heart of existence. Secondly, the word "need" tends to cover the same area as motivation and to designate a form common to all motives, that is, inclining without compelling.

Let us therefore push on into pure affectivity in order to throw some light on those obscure traits in terms of which need (in the strict sense of the word) *lends itself* to motivation.

Appetite presents itself as an indigence and an exigence, an experienced lack of . . . and an impulse directed towards. . . .

Lack and impetus are experienced in the indivisible unity of an "affect." (We would say "affection" if the word did not also belong to the language of intersubjective feelings; we do not say "affective state" because the word "state" implies a rest, a cessation; only satiety would be a "state" in this sense.) More precisely, lack and impetus are experienced in the unity of an active affect, as opposed to pleasure and pain which are sense affects. Need is an affect since it is entirely an indigence whose urge drives towards that which would satisfy it.

But *what* does it lack, and *towards what* does it drive? Here reflection must turn towards the most abstruse and identify with pure experience of lack and urge, apart from any standpoint assumed by the will and even apart from any representation of the absent object.

In this retrogression towards purely organic functioning we can sense a lack and an urge which are not yet a perceived, imagined, or conceptualized intention. Yet it is not an indefinite lack, an indefinite urge, but a specific lack, a directed urge; I turn towards an other, a *specific* other, even though this direction is not given in a representation or even is not given at all. The lack from which I suffer, the lack I suffer, has a form. It is rather like a word which I have on the tip of my tongue and which I recognize when, having eliminated all words that do not fit the lack in question, I come across the word which fills the gap my demand represents. Its object is not here in flesh, because it must be sought, nor in representation because it is not in any way given—not even "given as absent," as J.–P. Sartre says of the imaginary. To imagine means to present the absent to myself, not to lack. A given (whether present or absent) is always relative to a giving, a gift, that is to say, to an encounter rather like grace. We can see what care we must use if we say that need affectively anticipates food, water, etc. . . . and has an "organic preconception" [2] of it: these words already belong to the scale of representation. There is no water or bread yet. But apart from representation it is not at all possible to speak of this selective unease. This specific absence, considered below the level of any representation of its object, is not distinct from the impetus, and the impetus, considered apart from the movement undertaken by willing, is no other than an uneasy, alert absence, an active, directed lack.

Thus we shall say negatively that need is not an *inner sensation*. First of all, the expression "inner" does not account for the other-directedness which is an essential aspect of need and which testifies that, as all acts of the Cogito, it is a consciousness of. . . . When I am hungry, I am an absence of . . . and an impetus towards. . . . Even without an image of bread, my hunger would still carry me beyond myself. Secondly, the expression "sensation" sacrifices the tense character of need which constitutes the underivable, basic nature of an active affect. It would be easy to explain the tendency of most psychologists to consider need as an internal sensation; for one thing, analyzing need into two elements, a sensation and a movement, permits the application of the convenient "stimulus-response" schematism to need. We could then speak of an internal stimulation as we speak of external stimulation, attributing the function of a stimulus to the alleged sensation. The parallelistic hypothesis especially suggests this erroneous language: it imagines that sensation *duplicates* certain physiological processes which are the true stimulus of motor reaction. Its defenders like to say that hunger "translates" into consciousness the organic defect which provokes nascent movements or tendencies.[3] But it is not true that need is the sensation of an organic defect satisfied by the sensation of a nascent movement. Such an assertion derives from a purely methodological prejudice according to which the affective is an awareness of

2. Pradines, *op. cit.*, pp. 13–15.

3. This is the language of Georges Dumas in *Nouveau traité de psychologie* (Paris, 1930–46), vol. II: "The need, that is, general or local internal sensations which translate the malfunctioning or gradual cessation of corresponding organic functions" (p. 487); also *ibid.*, pp. 475, 449–50.

the physiological, conceived after the manner of a translation into another language. The authors of this terminology admit, in any case, that such translation is perfectly unintelligible, in a sense different from the unintelligibility connected with affectivity as such. It is an unintelligibility which does not ground thought within the limits of any lived experience: in effect, such a "translation" has no meaning in objective terms, but neither is it lived by the subject. The absurdity of parallelism lies in seeking a passage of some sort between empirical knowledge of object-body and consciousness, and in positing that such passage is of an objective, albeit unknown, nature. This prejudice has to be broken, not only in general, but in each particular case. Need is not a sensation translating an organic defect and followed by a motor reaction. It is neither a sensation nor a reaction; it is a lack of . . . which is an action towards. . . . Thus the task of description is to recover the intentionality of need stressed by the expression "lack of . . ." from this aberrant objectification. Such intentionality excludes any possibility that need would translate an organic defect into consciousness. A need of . . . does not reveal my body to me but through my body reveals that which is not here and which I lack. I do not sense contractions and secretions—I am aware of the I-body as a whole lacking. . . . Neither organic difficulties nor movement are *that of which* I am aware; they are objective, empirical symptoms of an affective experience which belongs to thought, that is, to Cogito itself. This affective experience, as all *cogitatio,* has an intentional object. The I-body is implicated in it only as the subject-pole of the affect.

The second task of description is to shed light on the unity of the lack and of the impetus. In any case, the "stimulus-response" schema will not do, whether the stimulus is external or "internal." If need is an action, it is not a re-action but a pre-action, in principle prior to the sensation and the pleasure which would indicate that the need was being satisfied. But we also need to be able to uncover need as an active affect apart from the nascent distinction between lack and impetus. This is an intimacy which is most difficult to preserve intact. There are reasons for this nascent disjunction: it is emphasized by the higher level dissociation between the representation which clarifies the lack in terms of its own object and the voluntary movement which appropriates the impetus. In taking its stand, the will completes the separation of experience and need: while the impetus can be mastered by the will, the lack always remains uncoercible—I can refrain from eating, but I cannot help being hungry. And below the cleavage instituted by representation and by the will we can trace a rent in the experience of need. In effect, local painful or proto-painful sensations mingle with need and charge it with internal sensations with respect to which the impetus of need appears to be a secondary reaction. Now it is rather difficult to place these relations correctly with respect to the indivisible lack and impetus which affect the individual in his unity. I in my entirety am appetite; but at the same time a discomfort is localized in those regions which would be affected either by an ultimate satisfaction or by an encounter in which sensuous pleasure serves as a prelude to a profound joy. This localization of discomfort and pain which complicates the call of need should not disguise its illocalizable nature.[4] Here we find superimposed two aspects which are paradoxically joined in bodily existence, indivisible in appetite, divisible in pain and in inner sensations generally. Inner sensations relate need to a body other than my personal body. They are only sense-affects illustrating organic variety, as distinct from the active affect which is my life, non-localized and undivided, my life gaping as appetition for the other.

Thus we are able to press closer to the nature of need by distinguishing it from the pain which sometimes complicates it. In addition, the active affect is also duplicated by sense affects which range over the entire keyboard of the agreeable and disagreeable, from a certain cheerfulness of appetite up to the extremes of anxiety and frenzy (as, for example, in dipsomania). But even then this anxiety is not a pain. Pradines insists forcefully on this distinction which he very confidently interprets biologically and functionally: pain is tied to an external aggression, that is, to the intersection of the existent and the forces of nature. This is why it stimulates a re-action which avoids or repels the hostile agent. By contrast, a painful lack is inherent in need, prior to the encounter with the other. It moves towards this encounter; it is a lack which is active prior to it, and that is why it cannot in any sense be assimilated into a reflex to pain, to a concealed aversion.[5]

Thus need is at the same time distinct from a sensation of aggression and from a reflex to aggression. This distinction is crucial for our interpretation of the involuntary. We cannot repeat too often that a reflex is not assimilable to the will and must remain an alien body in the responsible conduct of the individual. On the other hand, it is the very nature of the impetus which is

4. Pradines, *op. cit.*, pp. 81–92.
5. Cf., on the other hand, Cellerier, "Les Éléments de la vie affective," *Revue philosophique* (1926).

indiscernible from the lack not to be a reflex, not to burst forth in an irrepressible fashion, but to be capable of "suspension" (following P. Janet's usage). It is because the impetus of need is not an automatic reflex that it can become a motive which inclines without compelling and that there are men who prefer to die of hunger rather than betray their friends.

2. Needs as Motives

GIVEN OVER TO MY BODY, subjected to the rhythm of my needs, I nonetheless do not cease to be a self which takes a stand, evaluates its life, exercises its control—or else charms itself and binds itself in a servitude whose entire fascination it draws from itself.

In view of my needs, how can I be a will?

In some way, need must lend itself to a relative integration into the unity of consciousness. Pure description leads us to pose the question thus: in terms of which trait can need be a motive on which willing can base itself in determining itself? Thus we must focus our inquiry at the intersection of the double analysis of the *form* of the motive and of the affective *matter* of the need as we have just seen it.

Our everyday experience assures us that we are not posing a false problem—our wisdom lies in good part at the *intersection* of our will and our needs. Man is man because of his ability to confront his needs and sometimes to sacrifice them. Now this must be structurally possible, that is, imbedded in the very nature of need. Though I am not the master of need in the sense of lack, I can reject it as reason for action. In this extreme experience man shows his humanity. Even the most banal life includes the pattern of such sacrifice: what we call "socialization of needs" presupposes that need lends itself to corrective action exercised on it by the needs of a properly human life (customs, rules of courtesy, the plan of one's life, etc.). But it is the experience of sacrifice which is most revealing. Accounts of expeditions to lands where water is scarce or to lands of extreme cold, or the testimony of combat soldiers are one long epic of victory over need. Man is capable of choosing between his hunger *and* something else. Non-satisfaction of needs can be not only accepted, but can even be systematically chosen, as the man who, constantly confronted with the choice between denunciation and a bit of bread, prefers honor to life, or as Gandhi chose not to eat in order to affect his adversary. A hunger strike is undoubtedly the rare experience which reveals the truly human nature of our needs just as, in a way, chastity (monastic or otherwise) makes sexuality into a human sexuality. These extreme situations are fundamental for a psychology of the involuntary. Needs can thus be one motive *among* others.

But the adherence of need to the most underivable bodily existence cannot make it into a motive *like* the others. Need is the primordial spontaneity of the body; as such, it originally and initially reveals values which set it apart from all other sources of motives. Through need, values *emerge* without my having posited them in my act-generating role: bread is good, wine is good. Before I will it, a value already appeals to me solely because I exist in flesh; it is already a reality in the world, a reality which reveals itself to me through the lack. This appeal, arising from my indigence, indicates a first rank of values which I have not engendered. Here the receptivity of willing with regard to values finds its first expression: need shows that a system of values cannot be deduced by starting from a purely formal need of coherence with itself, or by starting from a pure self-positing power of consciousness. The first non-deducible is the body as existing, life as value. The mark of all existents, it is what first reveals values. The passage from analytic logic to synthetic dialectic cannot account for the deviation which separates pure self-affirmation from that existing unease in terms of which bread and wine are first good. The mystery of incarnate Cogito ties willing to this first stratum of values with which motivation begins.

Under what conditions can need be a motive, if not *like* the others, at least among others?

We shall first point out a *negative* condition (which cannot be developed here because it lies at the intersection of the problem of motivation and the problem of motor execution). A need can become a motive only if the *conduct* which assures the satisfaction of that need is not an irresistible reflex.

Such precisely is the conduct activated by need—it is not a reflex. This is already true of animals, but in man's case the suspendable nature of the action accentuates it further. We shall learn in Part II that conduct connected with need is subject to double direction, by perceived signals and by tensions issuing from need itself, and that it is not an action following a rigid pattern. We shall see how these fundamental characteristics place "knowing-how" at the disposal of willing. Let us also add right away that suspension of action is aided by a certain diminution of "knowing-how" from animal to man. In the case of the animal it is a considerably complex spontaneous adaptation, if not infallible then at least adequate in the normal milieu characteristic of a given species. This relatively complete and unlearned "knowing-how" is what we call instinct. It leaves no organic problems unresolved and renders invention unnecessary, making the animal a constantly resolved problem. (We can affirm this without attributing to instinct the immutability and infallibility which classical authors attributed to it, a reality quite different from that attributed to it by empirical descriptions.) It is the instinctive conduct which decreases in the case of man. Man has quantitatively more instincts, if we include the new anxieties and new incentives which he invents, but he is less instinctive if we stress his loss of unlearned forms of conduct, spontaneously adapted to his milieu. It is characteristic that man must *learn* almost all basic forms of conduct, starting with the skills which are undoubtedly preformed but which would remain latent if they were not perfected by an acquired technique. This poverty of inherent movement opens an unlimited field to all invention and primarily to knowledge, language, and signs which direct our acts in conformity with the style of a civilization.

This plasticity of skills from the simple motive point of view at the same time reveals to us the positive condition of our control over need: it is the *representation,* the learned *knowledge* which regulates properly human conduct issuing from need. It is this in the first place which awakens need itself to consciousness of its object and raises it to the dignity of a motive for possible willing.

Thus we are led to seek the crossroads of need and willing in imagination—imagination of the missing thing and of action aimed towards the thing.

But in order really to understand how an image can perfect the blind experience of need, we must first of all understand the role of the perception whose role imagination assumes in absence of the thing. In effect, while the lack is in principle prior to perception, imagination is in principle posterior to it. Imagination cannot charge need's intentionality unless perception appraises it of its object and of the way to attain it. It is actually perception which *shows* food, liquids, etc. To be sure, as we have said, need, reduced to itself, is still not devoid of intentionality— the lack and the urge are specific (the organic defect, which is its objective symptom, is a selective emptiness). But, especially in the case of man, if knowledge of the object and of the means is not available to clarify the lack, the need remains a vaguely oriented distress. Such knowledge is the experience of satisfaction of the need experienced at least once. Its place is not only at the end of the need-cycle, when the object possessed and consumed is lost in the body, but also before the end, in the moment of sense-encounter, while the object is a presence still distinct from the body. This is the precious moment evoked by the imagination; but the moment of possession and of enjoyment, satisfying the need, suppresses the representation, for representation is always representation at a distance (this is true even of touch, which holds a peripheral position, advanced with respect to the viscera). "Even as a fruit's absorbed in the enjoying,/Even as within the mouth its body dying/changes into delight through dissolution. . . ." [6]

When the object of need is present to our senses, especially at a distance, as in sight or hearing, it is a stimulus, that is, it promises an enjoyment and, in proclaiming the future fullness of being, brings need to action pitch. Presence reinforces need because it shows the terminus of need without giving it, since enjoyment would no longer be either lack or absence, or even presence, but union. Now at the same time as presence awakens need, it gives it a form, *the form of the object.*

This is the decisive fact: a need which has recognized its object and whose program will no longer be only a lack and an impetus arising from the body, but will be a call coming from the outside, from a known object. I am no longer only pushed outward from within, but am also attracted outward by something within the world. Henceforth need truly has a known object which belongs to the perceptible constellation of the world. The world is full of affective signs which become attached to real sensible qualities and become indiscernible from them. These alluring qualities dress up things, perceived presences, as demands of need. Presence becomes the light of the lack; henceforth it is impossible to distinguish within total perception what is affective and what is actually observed. In this way need finds a language: the adjectives supplied by attributive propositions (great, light, delicious, etc.) are inseparably expressions of perception and of affectivity. Need has gradually entered the sphere of judgment: we can *say* something about it from the side of the object while

6. English version quoted from Paul Valéry, "Graveyard by the Sea," trans. C. D. Lewis, in *Selected Writings* (New York, New Directions, 1950[1], 1964), pp. 42–43. Copyright 1950 by New Directions. Reprinted with permission of the publisher.

at the same time experiencing it from the opposite pole of the subject, as the dense, opaque existence of body in distress.

We can come to understand the central role of imagination in this juncture of need and willing by starting from the intermingling of perception and need. The fundamental affective motive presented by the body to willing is need, extended by the imagination of its object, its program, its pleasure, and its satisfaction: what we commonly call the *desire* for, the wish for. . . . If imagination can play such a role, it is because contrary to common psychological opinion it itself is an intentional design projected into *absence*, a product of consciousness within actual nothing and not a mental *presence*.[7] Intentional as perception, it can, like perception, play such a role as it completes the virtual intentionality of need: absence gives a vivid, non-actual form to lack.

At this point the imaginary is the heir of the perceived. As Husserl puts it, it "presents" its properties. The alluring qualities of need appear through the imaginary. Thus the imaginary clarifies need as to its signification, shows it its object as other than itself, the itself depicted by a kind of quasi-observation, as J.–P. Sartre puts it. Even though it differs from the inexhaustible observation of a present thing, and though it is limited by prior knowledge, the quasi-observation of the absent object is the light of need just as the actual presence of the object would be.

Now what is remarkable is that the imaginary should be such a light in the absence of the object, thus *prior* to a new encounter and possession. Hunger becomes need *of bread* in the absence of bread, in the unity of experienced *lack* and quasi-observed *absence*. To be sure, at this point the objection arises that the imaginary is nothing, pure absence, negated existence, and that it should not play an exploratory role in the perfectly innerworldly concern of need. But imagination is undoubtedly not completely exhausted by a function of evasion and denial within the world. Imagination is also, and perhaps primarily, a militant power in the service of a diffuse sense of the future by which we anticipate the actual-to-be, as an absent actual at the basis of the world. As such it can mediate need and willing, each in its way directed towards the future of the world: the latter in order to open up new possibilities within it, the former in order to await there the fruit of achievement and encounter. Both carry us ahead of ourselves into a world which is at the same time indeterminate and

7. J.–P. Sartre, *Psychology of Imagination* (New York, 1948), pp. 4–21.

full of promises and threats. Imagination focuses this double anticipation of project and concern. Imagination which completely "negates" and carries us "elsewhere"—into an "elsewhere" which love of the exotic searches beyond distant seas and which is most frequently presented on a theatrical stage and evoked by characters in novels—this imagination is a luxury won from an imagination beset by concerns which does not depict a pure negation of the present, but rather an anticipated and still absent presence of things from whose lack we suffer. It is a lamp we point ahead to light up lack in terms of an entirely worldly absence, while need in turn tinges the imaginary with corporeal, concerned hue, quite different from aesthetic creations which sever its contact with its actual context.

We could still object that this synthesis of need and imagination in desire profoundly alters need: imagination in effect does not limit itself to *showing* to need its absent object as perception does, but rather charms and seduces. Since Montaigne and Pascal, moralists have stressed this deceptive power of the imaginary which mimics both presence and satisfaction and so fascinates consciousness. We are not yet in a position to understand this power of fascination proceeding from imagination: in the first place because we have not yet taken into account pleasure and the particular character which imagination assumes when it anticipates not only an objective presence, but also a pleasure or a pain; and moreover because according to our account imagination is *in addition* a privileged point of entry of what in subsequent works we shall call the fault. This corruption is in part binding oneself by nothing; the vanity "spreading to all things" is this captivity of which we are at the same time jailers and prisoners. But it is projected outside of us, as the nothing which lures, seduces, and captivates, as a magic potion which we drink in together with the world. The charm of imagination, the magic power of absence, thus seems to us to go back to a guilty consciousness, a consciousness which has already given in to temptation. There is no power within man capable of enslaving him; all the involuntary is for freedom, and consciousness can only be its own slave. Thus we shall attempt to bracket this fascination with the image, not without showing in passing how need, swollen by the imaginary, lends itself to this vertigo: this is what we shall do by introducing shortly the decisive trait of the analysis of desire— the anticipation of pleasure.

Thus if we return to the root of the imaginary, apart from its magic, up to its power of showing the object whose appeal is nothing but the echo of our needs echoed by the world, we shall reach the pure *representation* of absence.

Now absence can only be represented on the basis of a knowledge which provides the imaginary with an intellectual framework: I imagine what I know by having learned or invented it. To be sure, in contrast with abstract thought which designates in general and which can be without images, imaginative representation is a thought which designates an object as the senses do, cloaking knowledge with nascent movements, with affective sketches (of which we shall speak presently) which present the object, though absent, in effigy.[8] We must not lose sight of this sense quality of imagination. But the level of meaning of imagination remains knowledge; in terms of it the desire for bread or water is brought into the sphere of virtual judgments, into the region of discourse concerning the end and the means, and thus into the closed field of motivation. It is as knowledge that imagination which swells our desires is susceptible to coming under the control of the will and that our life itself can be *evaluated*. All of our power over our desires is relevant to this representative moment.

3. Value and the Imagination of Pleasure

OUR ENTIRE ANALYSIS so far has not touched on the most important aspect of desire, the anticipation of pleasure which gives the image of the object its full affective nuance and enriches the pure distress of need in a novel way.

As the imagination of an object and of the means for attaining it earlier, so also the imagination of pleasure must be understood by starting with the experience of pleasure itself. The parallel between the two analyses is that much closer because pleasure is contemporaneous with perception.

As perception, pleasure is in principle *posterior* to the tension of need: action precedes feeling. Pleasure is in no way autonomous, it indicates a need in process of being satisfied. This is well known—it has already been forcefully expressed by Aristotle and should be restated to bring out several related shades of meaning of that assertion. If, then, man is capable of pursuing pleasure for its own sake, making it an autonomous motive, pleasure is no longer the flower of youth, but rather a cut and already faded flower. Thus here again we need to discover the point of least resistance through which the fault can enter. One of the marks

8. *Ibid.*, pp. 81–136.

of man is indeed his ability to separate the sense affect from the active affect whose symptom it is by its sought-for goal. This separation takes place precisely in the imagination. But prior to being an invitation to the fault, imagination of pleasure is an attribute of actual pleasure which is secondary with respect to need.

Again, like perception, pleasure is an encounter—so, to be sure, is pain, but pain is an accident, while pleasure is an achievement.[9] More exactly, pleasure is an encounter *in* a perception. We should notice that pleasure actually points out and greets the moment when the object has entered within our borders but is not yet lost in our substance. Pleasure is only the penultimate phase of the cycle of need, whose last stage is possession and enjoyment in which the object is absorbed within us. Apart from the pleasure which is still diversified pleasure of the senses, such enjoyment is disconcertingly banal, but it is nonetheless satisfaction. Pleasure has no meaning apart from this satisfaction at which need aims through it. It is ambiguous in that it already presents the object for experience through the senses in anticipation of satisfied repose, and yet brings the tension of need to its highest pitch by emphasizing the fading duality of the body and its good. The object still pleases us, in a kind of pre-possession on the level of the senses, but as distinct from our deeper organic life, short of the intimacy of our viscera. It is likewise difficult to determine the status of pleasure in the fluid transition between the tendency and the condition, between lack and the satisfaction in which intentionality dies out. Only enjoyment is unambiguous, non-militant, and, moreover, unlocalizable: in it the consciousness of our profound divisibility, promising us to the dust, and the consciousness of our exposed, threatened periphery are completely absorbed in the paradoxical consciousness of an unformed, diffuse, and self-forgetful intimacy—as if my self experienced itself only on contact with an obstacle or at least when touched by an encounter which arouses its defenses and points out the diversity of its affected parts.

Specific, localized, and infinitely diversified pleasure, the pleasure of a thousand nuances, actually maintains complex relations with the senses: it is a pleasure of the senses, engendered in a sensation, gratuitous as all that is encountered and received. In this respect we are no more authors of our pleasure than of our pains. It depends on fortune just as much as on our own body which can engender only its own privations. It is the pleasure

9. Concerning this, cf. Pradines, *op. cit.*

of the senses and not ultimate satisfaction—the enjoyment or *fruitio*—which, by means of the imagination, is the object of human striving. We cannot refine satiety in any way, but we can refine the pleasures of touch, smell, taste, sight, and hearing. This is why we call them "sensible," in the same sense as sense-qualities—sensuousness and agreeable hedonic affectivity are, moreover, almost indiscernible (unlike pain which is itself a species of sensation involving touch). Similarly, it would require a long, slow corrective action on the part of our reflection to dissociate, in an impression, the meanings which pertain to our body (to which the impression offers satisfaction) from meanings pertaining to an object whose presence and structure the impression reveals. This story of the movement of our senses towards objectivity does not concern our subject. On the contrary, by dissociating itself from it, pure sensuousness brings out, by contrast and as residue, the pure function of pleasure which is to present an entity as *good* as well as *real*. This is the moment which imagination accentuates. Pleasure in fact enters motivation through the imagination: thus it is a moment in desire. *Desire is the present experience of need as lack and as urge, extended by the representation of the absent object and by anticipation of pleasure.* But what is this anticipation of pleasure? People often believe that pleasure itself cannot be imagined, only its measurable décor, its objective circumstances. There is the famous debate about affective memory: it has been said, and not without some semblance of truth, that we cannot imagine a pleasure as absent and not as given without having a foretaste of it in the form of motive emotional sketches, of an affective reliving which is some sense makes it present and given. That much is true, but it misinterprets the role of such present feeling. It is not this present feeling which I experience. Rather, I anticipate future pleasure in terms of this slender sense-affect through which I see ahead, as through an unreal, absent pleasure. The present feeling is the "affective image," the representative, the *analogon* (or whatever you wish to call it) of future pleasure.

It is possible to consider this affective image of future pleasure the most important part of desire, profoundly transforming the pure experience of *lack* and even the representation of the *absent* object. It gives flesh and even a kind of fullness to desire. The image of the absent is sustained by this strange presence which passes for its absence but which is rather like its advance emissary. This affective image has the force of a sense-affect—itself paradoxical, fluctuating between tension and possession, wanting and abundance, embattled and triumphant, it "presents" the enigmatic ambiguity of the sense-affect.

But this present image of absent pleasure is only the affective *matter* passing across the intentional horizon of imagination. Anticipation of pleasure also involves a formal aspect which belongs to the same order as *knowing*. We have already referred to these bits of knowledge stirred up by the imagination. But now, as imagination of a thing as existing, as having such and such properties and physico-chemical structure, implies a knowledge of reality, so imagination of pleasure implies a knowledge of value. To anticipate a pleasure means to be ready to say "this is good."

This is why a theory of affective imagination which would identify imagination with present feelings representing pleasure in its absence is at once irrecusable and insufficient. Such present feelings are products of abstraction, of that special abstraction which dissociates matter from form. Such an affective image lacks the intentional content of a concrete act, it lacks the "apprehension" which would bring it to life. Should we therefore say that this affective intention of pleasure-to-be is already an explicit value judgment? Not at all. A value judgment is itself a product of abstraction, born of reflection concerning the form of the intentional content. Besides, this reflection is quite common: whenever we *appreciate* the objects of our need we are making the affective apprehension involved in the imagination of pleasure explicit. We judge the goodness of bread and wine in terms of the affective image of anticipated pleasure, but imagination lends itself to the abstraction which raises it to the level of a value judgment.

The power of imagination to fascinate, to dupe, and to deceive, to which we have already alluded, has to be understood by starting from this function of affective anticipation and of latent valuation. The very imagination which seals the compact of our freedom and our body is also the instrument of our bondage and the occasion for corruption. To the guilty consciousness imagination does not simply show thing and value, but fascinates it by their very absence or rather by the image of absence which thereafter functions as the snare of a false presence. There must be a lie already ingrained at the heart of consciousness. Here we stand at the source of a psychology of temptation: imagination tempts and seduces by the absence it represents and depicts. Through it need in turn not only demands, but also tempts and seduces. Starting with this seduction, imaginary pleasure can be uprooted from need and pursued for itself, endlessly refined in quantity, duration, intensity, etc. Fascination henceforth stimulates itself; but it always functions through imagination because the course of pleasure separated from need as its standard proceeds through invention which would deserve the name of creation if it did not function completely uselessly. The traits of human conduct which are most remarkable with respect to man's needs proceed from this fascinated imagination. By themselves, needs have a settled level of meaning whose model is the closed cycle. This is the standard of sobriety taught by the wisdom of the most diverse creeds—Epicurean, Stoic, Christian. But human desire is without measure, infinite. Even in the alimentary order, and more obviously in the sexual order, there is something about human desire which sets it radically apart from a simple biological rhythm. Its actual point of satisfaction is masked by the fictitious demands which make even physical happiness itself a retreating horizon. Need is bewildered, misled about its own real demands. All human civilization, from its economy to its sciences and its arts, is marked by this trait of discontent and frenzy. The "bad infinity" of desire is the mover of history and, beyond that, of the technical determinisms which never give it its ends but only its means. Perhaps the meaning of pleasure can be rediscovered only at the end of wisdom, beyond the dilemma of hedonism and of puritanism which is the solution of fear and flight before pleasure and the body.

Our task here is to rediscover the essential function of pleasure and of the body in general with respect to willing. This is why we must again return from the seductive and seduced imagination to the temptation which is not yet fault, though it is an invitation to fault. The temptation is only the point of least resistance presented by human affectivity to the invasion of the vertigo. Imagination is not structurally the seat of calamities; by its nature, the will is stronger than the need brought to light by imagining a pleasure.

But let us close once more the parentheses which for a moment we half opened: we shall henceforth abstract this misstep of consciousness, of the fascinated imagination, of pleasure erected into a supreme, autonomous end. Indeed it is more important to understand how imagination *mediates* between need and willing before breaking the pact by false fascination. This is why we have considered imagination solely as the power of affective presentation and implicit evaluation of pleasure-to-be.

We already possess the principal elements of this analysis:

*Desire is the specific, directional experience of an active lack—
that is, need or active affect—clarified by the representation of
an absent object and of the means for attaining it, sustained by
basic affective feelings: by their matter, which is the affective
image of pleasure, these sense-affects represent pleasure to come;
by their form, which is imaginary apprehension of pleasure, they
make the need available to a judgment which designates the object of need as good, that is, available to a value judgment.*

Thus it is the anticipation of pleasure which adds overtones
of value to pure representation of absence. It introduces need
into the sphere of valuation; but just as the lack in need is an
involuntary which we cannot deduce from pure power of thought,
so anticipated pleasure reveals a spontaneous value which cannot be deduced from any formal principle of obligation. The anticipation which makes valuable or valuates is rooted in the
prior experience of pleasure, in an actual experience of satisfaction of need. Imagination can exercise its mediating function
only by starting with this living experience of pleasure: in anticipating a pleasure like one it has already experienced, imagination
plays the role of virtual knowledge of value. But in turn imagination of pleasure gives need the form of value; this form is inseparable—except in thought—from its matter, in the sense that it
is in the image of bodily pleasure that imagined pleasure shows
to consciousness the object of need as good and prepares the
most elementary value judgment. Thus in its matter affective
imagination clings to the living reality of the pleasure whose
image it is and to the living reality of bodily existence; in its form
it conceals a latent valuation, at the fringe of judgment, at the
point at which prereflexive feeling is a spontaneous belief concerning the good of the body. It is this form which confers on it,
as on other forms of motivation, the status of motive and makes
it comparable with other motives.

[2] MOTIVES AND VALUES ON THE ORGANIC LEVEL

THE RIGOROUS LIMITATIONS which we have imposed
on our analysis of need might give rise to the facile notion that
life can be reduced to a simple system of motives developed from
a handful of assimilative needs, and that the sole revelation of
positive value is pleasure: "good is what produces pleasure." Frequently it is held that it is enough to add "evil is what causes pain"

to present an over-all picture of motives and values on the organic level.

1) However, a more careful analysis of pain already shows that pain is not an opposite of pleasure within the same genus, but is *heterogeneous* with it.

2) Nor is the pair, pleasure-pain, itself the last word of organic concern: other tendencies, often discordant among themselves, come to complicate the clear schema of pleasure and pain.

3) But, curiously enough, another series of observations will lead us to attribute a positive value to the *difficult:* here the sensationalist psychology is blocked by certain intuitions of medieval, classical, and Nietzschean psychology which we find hard to reject.

4) All this leads us to think that there is no central will-to-live, with the different tendencies as its subordinate species: on the human level, organic life is undoubtedly a cluster of *heterogeneous* demands, revealing *discordant* values.

This ambiguity of organic life is what is really at stake in this analysis which would otherwise often appear as a rather uncertain unraveling. As a counterpart to this, we shall show that it is always *anticipating imagination* which transmutes the multiple sources of motives issuing from the body and which bestows a common form, a form lending itself to conventional value judgments: "this is good, that is bad." The word need in its broad sense as a synonym for desire (for instance, need of exercise, of music, needs arising from habit, need to struggle) expresses this latent valuation of expenditure of energy, of music, of habitual conduct, of struggle, etc., as good and desirable.

1. Pain as Evil

EVIL IS THE *opposite* of good. That much is clear: each positive value has an opposite with which it constitutes a genus. Under the cover of this obvious fact there arises the hasty judgment that pain is the opposite of pleasure. Isn't pleasure in fact what reveals the good, and pain what reveals evil?

If, however, we delve below the level of imagined pain, and of the fear which surrounds it, to the level of actual experience of pain, all symmetry suddenly disappears. Here again the objective, functional point of view serves as symptomatic of this obscure experience of affective life. Pradines, assuming this point of view, vehemently stresses the "functional heterogeneity of pleasure and pain." [10] First of all, pleasure is subordinated to an assimilatory activity directed towards a congeneric reality; pleasure emphasizes the fortunate *encounter* and signals the fusion of the thing and the living being in the intimacy of enjoyment. Secondly, in the cycle of needs pleasure follows a lack arising from a deep-seated indigence of the living being. This lack is the true opposite of pleasure. This lack affects the living being in its indivisible unity, and is only secondarily localizable. Thirdly, the assimilative activity which precedes pleasure is structured by an impetus rather than by a reflex and can be suspended, controlled, and appropriated by the will.

Pain is not comparable with pleasure, and in none of the three respects above does it appear as its opposite. In the first place, pain precedes a defensive activity whose function it is to repel whatever is strange and hostile to life. There is nothing prior to it which could be compared to the need preceding pleasure. In the case of pain, affectivity precedes activity. Secondly, pain is in no way comparable to a lack or an emptiness: it expresses a very positive aggression, a threat to the organism. Also, it is by its very nature localized, differentiated as the sense of touch to which it is narrowly bound, even though it is distinct from it from both anatomical and physiological points of view. Thus it belongs to a different dimension of experience than pleasure. It has its own opposite, the cessation of pain, which is a pleasure only by contrast, a pleasure of respite which is gradually absorbed in affective neutrality. Thirdly, action which follows pain is not comparable to the action which precedes pleasure. It is a reflex reaction rather than a pre-action guided by an impetus. The action which succeeds pain fully satisfies the requirements of the stimulus-response pattern which is frequently mistaken for the pattern of all action. This is why mastery over the body in pain no longer has the same meaning as the mastery over the body in need: the same man who can go on a hunger strike cannot keep from screaming with pain under torture. In the case of need it depends on his will whether he will suspend or complete the nascent movement towards nourishment, and when the will, fascinated by the imagination, resigns its function, we are faced with a true defeat of the will (though it is not a question of passing moral judgment on it). By contrast, under blows, stabs, burns, wounds, electric shocks, etc., the task of the will is not to suspend or complete an impetus but rather to superimpose itself as best

10. Pradines, "L'Hétérogeneité fonctionelle du plasir et de la douleur," *Rev. Phil.* (1927); *Les Sens du besoin*, pp. 12 ff., 27 ff., 81–92.

it can on a reflex alien to the realm under its control. Sometimes it may be able to restrain it and contain it, if it finds itself on the normal course of a voluntary action. Thus some repression of a cry, or a gesture, or of a grimace is possible to the extent to which the neuro-muscular mechanism still allows the organ to respond. But if the reflex escapes and explodes, we are not confronting a seduced will but a frustrated one. In this case man is broken rather than conquered. The man under torture is no longer really responsible for his cries.

In this sense we have to say that the pain we *undergo* is not a motive or a counter-motive of willing. On the other hand need is virtually a motive, because it stimulates an action of the "suspendable" kind, and permits a delay in order to build up an original action issuing from a representation.

But imagination profoundly transforms this situation, instituting a close similarity between anticipated pain and anticipated pleasure. Imagined pleasure is called desire—imagined pain is called fear. But while desire extends need which itself anticipates pleasure, fear reverses the order of precedence between action and the painful encounter. Fear can precede and ward off the threat just as need and desire preceded and sought pleasure. In this way imagination likens fear to a negative desire and fear reveals pain as evil, that is, as the opposite of the good.

Let us examine the different elements introduced by the imagination of pain:

1) To be afraid of suffering is in the first place to imagine objectively the things and beings which will be the agents, instruments, or intermediaries of suffering. But it is also to imagine affectively the pain itself. This affective imagining of pain, as that of pleasure, has a matter, a living substance which is a present feeling in face of the image of pain. In imagining vividly a stab, a burn, a bite, etc., I affectively see the pain *through* a present feeling which can subsequently spread out and swell into an impelling visceral emotion, giving it a limitless organic reverberation. In this way pain rules my flesh *before* being experienced. The imagination which anticipates it tends to imitate the affective fullness of desire. Even though fear is not sustained by the dull discomfort of a need, it develops an anxiety which can reach the level of terror preceding the great bodily experiences of suffering and torture. The objects represented as bearers of pain are then marked with negative indices, once more imitating the appeal radiating from objects of need. An instrument of torture repels as the object of need attracts. Henceforth the power of fascina-

tion and of vertigo, which can become attached to the imagination of suffering, is the same as that which attaches to the imagination of pleasure.

2) Starting from fear and bodily anticipation of pain there develop repelling movements which, unlike the reflex response of pain, precede the painful encounter. In this respect such defensive and offensive forms of conduct resemble alimentary and sexual forms. They are the supple, varied movements which are subject to suspension and appropriated by the will, as for instance flight, attack and, in an ulterior way, avoidance, watchfulness, ruse, and so on. These forms of conduct repel pursuit, chase, killing of the victim, sexual conquest, etc. They are not reflexes but forms of conduct governed by perceptions at a distance and eminently disciplinable: even though I can hardly keep from crying out under blows, I can keep from running away from the threat of blows. Here we have the real task for the will faced with pain. It is the fear of suffering rather than suffering undergone which is the motive I have to integrate, reject, or accept. Suffering which becomes accepted and sometimes willed adds its testimony to that which sacrificed need renders to the glory of human willing. A flight can be a fault, but the cry in suffering is not, because the will does not yield to the one and the other in the same way. Though it can be frustrated by a reflex, the will can only be conquered by itself, that is, by its own fascination, whether in the case of desire or in the case of fear. We could even say that if there is a problem for the will in suffering as undergone it is less one of holding onto its body, restraining the involuntary movement or the cry, than the problem of confronting the approaching suffering, that is, suffering represented before it is undergone. Endurance means continuing to suffer if an idea demands it. In this way desire and fear are united on the same side of the actions they respectively exhibit. In this way courage is also united: the struggle against cold, heat, hunger, thirst, fatigue, sleep, in spite of the basic difference of physical experience, is one and the same battle in which the struggle against reflexes has a minor part and in which acceptance of counter-motives issuing from the imagination holds the principal place. The martyrs of duty, science, faith, the pioneers of the polar regions, of deserts, glaciers, of space, or the fighters and heroes of liberty confront at the same time a body which is not a bundle of reflexes but of impeti and an imagination made to the measure of willing and of the body. To endure means to focus on the idea, the mission, the common cause, without considering the fascinating

image of possible pleasure and of approaching suffering. Thus the repelling movements which constitute defensive conduct are subject to a double command, just as the impulsive movements related to a lack: they are governed externally by signals received and internally by the affect which represents pain.[11]

3) *Through* this image which represents pain, I apprehend an eventual or imminent pain as *evil*. This apprehension, which imposes the form of thought on affective matter, is properly the moment of latent evaluation of pain. It is on this level that represented pain becomes truly a motive susceptible to being appreciated and eventually accepted as the hard road to the good. It is also on this level that a real symmetry of pleasure and pain is instituted, the symmetry of value and not of lived experience. "The functional heterogeneity of pleasure and pain" is thus surmounted in two opposite evaluations within the common genus of value on the organic level. To be sure, opposition of organic good and evil is only conceived as an opposition on the level of advanced reflection; it is apprehended in a prereflexive way in the opposition of the two affective imaginations, imagined pleasure and imagined pain. But in terms of their form, which is one of apprehension, these two imaginations lend themselves to an explicit knowledge relevant to the contradictory values of pleasure and of pain.

But there remains the deep-seated heterogeneity of pleasure and pain subsisting at the root of these two contradictory motives. Finally, a pleasure and a pain remain incomparable in their affective density. A desire is undergirded by a lived need which arises from the body and which cannot be likened to a pain; it is a privation which calls for a fullness and for positive pleasure. Should the need be assuaged, desire is deprived of its substance and evaporates; a desire nourished solely by imagination is artificial, adulterated, and hypersophisticated, a vain desire of the unhappy consciousness. Fear on the other hand is not supported

11. We might ask whether some preformed affective impressions pertaining to fear do not precede all experience, all the "apprenticeship" of pain, such as the ancestral fear awakened in certain animals by perception at a distance of the enemy of the species. Does this mean at least that these affective impressions would be comparable to the "organic preconception" of the object of need which precedes pleasure? No, for the supposed "organic preconception" of pain does not have the power of arousing defensive conduct when the noxious object is *absent*: though defensive conduct precedes the painful contact, it remains subordinated to the perception at a distance of danger. The preformed motor sets adapted to dangerous situations thus have an inner governor subordinated to the actual presence of perceived signs. The parallel with need thus is never complete. In addition, in the case of man such preformed defensive conducts have receded completely; the affective image which nourishes our fears is always learned.

by the body in the same way as desire: there are no negative needs which would give repulsion the organic density of appetition. It is imagination—imagination, it is true, which in terms of its matter is itself carnal—which supports the full weight of fear. This purely imaginative character is the natural condition of fear, even though it represents a transformation of desire by separation from actual need.

This deep-seated heterogeneity of pleasure and pain is essential to a psychology of the will because these two motives remain incomparable even as to their opposites. Pleasure has its own opposite, which is privation; pain has its own opposite, which is the absence of pain. This is why I can experience pleasure and pain simultaneously—who has not enjoyed a good meal or a pleasant show while suffering from a boil, a toothache, or a bunion? Pleasure and pain are not contraries within a homogeneous affective pair. Similarly, no affective calculus can tell me whether the pleasure which will put an end to a given privation is worth the pain which it would cost to obtain it. Is the negative pleasure of ceasing to suffer from a tooth irritated by cold worth the pain of giving up the positive pleasure of an iced drink on a hot summer afternoon? Pleasure and pain are not parts of the same series which would permit homogeneous classification—they are qualitatively different. Relative quantification on a scale of intensity whose poles they would be is equally excluded.

Thus the opposition of positive and negative value remains purely formal: it means only that pleasure and pain can participate in the same valuation, lend themselves to the same operation of affective motivation with opposite signs. But the heterogeneity of pleasure and pain as to their affective matter already makes it plain that life entails a plurality of value dimensions and introduces, at the root of choice, an essential ambiguity which is the principle of hesitation.

2. Complexity of Values on the Organic Level

THIS COMPLEXITY of organic tendencies—and the heterogeneity of goods and evils which it brings out—should be emphasized with added vigor: it even seems that bodily existence reveals other values than those of pleasure and of pain. These values are often hidden under the equivocal names of pleasure and pain which thereby lose their precise sense of organic satisfaction (related to an organic privation) and of physical pain (related to an aggression against the body). Pleasure and especially the act of pleasing oneself become coextensive with value on the organic level and designate the entire field of affective valuation on this level. Further, emotion gives to all valuation pertaining to other levels of value an organic echo, so that all sensibility can gradually adopt, by analogy or by resonance, the language of pleasure and pain. There is a pleasure and even an enjoyment of the beautiful, of numbers, even of divine presence. . . .

The agreeable and the disagreeable similarly cover an extremely ill-defined area of meaning: what suits me is, in a broad sense, that which awakens and touches positive affectivity. Thus to suit and to please become indiscernible, and pleasure in an organic sense is the lower stratum of the agreeable. It also happens that we give to the agreeable a more restricted meaning and oppose it to pleasure in order to designate affectivity which is not related to need but to happy exercise of the senses, of activity, and of intellect. But even in this sense the agreeable does not designate a special value but a confused mass of values of different levels.

We shall attempt to distinguish some special values on the organic level which, however, cannot be reduced to pleasure or to pain in the precise sense we have given to these sense affects nor to affective imagination which grafts itself on to them.

We shall not take the time for an examination of the useful and the non-useful (the useless and the indifferent). These values are for the most part subordinate rather than coordinate in a heterogeneous way with pleasure and pain. The useful is a positive value of the utensil (a tool, the good of use and consummation, a work of art) considered as a means of pleasure and absence of pain. The non-useful is a negative value of the utensil considered as a means of pain and privation. Thus "useful" and "non-useful" are values attached to means qua means. The useful can be related to other ends than those of the organic level. The useful can even enter into conflict with pleasure and pain, on the same level of life, without referring to ends other than the satisfaction of need or cessation of pain. It is enough that a good of the body should be evaluated not subjectively in terms of pleasure and absence of pain, but objectively from the functional point of view of biology. This is the attitude of the hygienist and the physician who, for instance, would consider food rations from the point of view of scientifically determined organic needs. The conflict of the useful and the agreeable reflects, for instance in the context of culinary art and of mores in general, the duality of points of view of the body and of life. But in fact this biological utility ultimately refers back to a utility which is properly instrumental with respect to an ultimate pleasure or a cessation of pain. The useful is a value-symptom of pleasure, as the body-object is the theoretical symptom of a personal body.

On the other hand we shall take time to examine the values "easy" and "difficult" which are remarkable because they are distinctly not derivable from pleasure and pain, and because they are in addition heterogeneous with each other. The easy is desirable in some respects, but so is the difficult. In other respects, these values are incommensurable with the earlier ones. The easy and the difficult neither resemble the sequence of pleasure and pain nor are themselves opposites within the same affective genus.

3. The Easy as Good

THE EASY IS RELATED to the absence or, better, the cessation of an obstacle or an impediment. Now an obstacle or an impediment represents a very general situation which cannot be reduced either to privation or to the kind of aggression which generates pain. But for reasons which we shall state later, an impeded function is expressed in the language of need: need to urinate, to breathe, need of movement and, in general, of activity and freedom.[12] Let us start with a simple case: the evacuatory reflex (urinary or excretory) inhibited by myself. Voluntary effort functions as a brake (an operative ligature or a functional difficulty can also play the same role): even though the mechanism of expulsion is absolutely undeducible from the impetus which proceeds from a lack or from responses to pain, the restrained movement imitates the impetus of need and the subjective tension of the lack. Imagination in effect extends the specific sensation of repletion by representative affective anticipation of the action which would free the function from restraint, of propitious places and of specific pleasure attached to such satisfaction. The common form of desire—understanding by this the positive valuation ("all the same, it would be good if I could . . .")—is imposed on the specific impetus which thereafter assumes the name of need of elimination. The easy is thus the value of release granted to a restrained function.

This pattern can be confirmed in terms of a number of reflex

12. Concerning impeded functions, cf. Pradines, *Les Sens du besoin.*

functions of very different physiological significance. The case of respiration is the most remarkable. Air is obviously an object of an assimilatory need. Since there is air all around us, this pseudo-need is continually being satisfied without a previous lack; furthermore this assimilation is governed by a reflex which in the last instance is not coercible (man can go on a hunger strike, but not on a breathing strike). It is not a conduct governed at the same time by perceived signs and by an organic lack. Yet inhibited respiration presents itself as a need, whether because the will inhibits it (passing through an evil-smelling place, diving, etc.) or because air becomes rarefied or contaminated. Here imagination seizes the discomfort and the impetus to seek air, picturing places where breathing is good, suggesting the pleasant quality of air in the fields or mountains, and impresses on the mind a belief in the value of a stay in the land of pure air. Here is a case where the agreeable borders on the easy: the easy is in the first place that which is unhindered.

These examples of hindered reflexes permit us to interpret the most important group of quasi-needs, those issuing from relational functions: use of the senses, expenditure of movement, or mental activity activating the innumerable aptitudes and talents created by civilization and culture. Inactivity functions as a hindrance: there is the lassitude of polar night or of silence, of sedentary work or of confinement. The impeded function extends itself in a happy imagination which permits us to speak of the need for exercise or expenditure of energy. To the sick man immobilized in an uncomfortable position, to turn over in his bed might at a given moment seem like the supreme good; to the prisoner confined to a cell, opening a door, crossing a street, turning the electric light off and on at any time, affirming himself by the most arbitrary and absurd activity is something which his imagination depicts as pleasures without equal, which, however, become dissipated in eventual exercise as a negative pleasure corresponding to the cessation of pain.

Excess of activity can also be experienced as a constraint. The forced labor of a convict, a slave, or an exploited laborer, or overwork forced on me by social or moral necessity make rest appear as a supremely desirable good. The struggle for liberation from work is sustained by an experience comparable to the struggle for bread.

In this way a moderate exercise of all functions, alternating with a similarly moderate rest, appears as a basic aspect of happiness in living, between the two excesses of forced inactivity and overwork. This moderate exercise is the second form which the easy assumes.

From this an easy transition leads us to the class of quasi-needs issuing from habit. Let us state in the first place that it is false that habit universally creates needs, that is, a desire to indulge in it.[13] Not infrequently habit creates not a need but revulsion. In addition, many technical and professional habits are affectively neutral. The need of a habitual action is actually secondary to the habit; it is an aspect which is sometimes present, at other times absent. These contradictory effects cannot be explained by habit but by its ingression into the deeper organic life of needs and sources of interest. I do not feel deprived of typing, of doing acrobatics, or of solving equations for the sole reason that I have mastered these activities and that I don't have an occasion to exercise them. They are inert tools which have no source of interest within themselves, though the need of earning a livelihood, a wish to surprise my acquaintances, etc., can suddenly animate these habits and attribute to them a demand of which they are devoid in themselves. If at times habit seems to create a need, it is by providing an *easy* outlet for preexistent needs which had previously been dormant. In effect habit, by providing a form for capacities, also gives form to the tension of need. The process of acting is what reveals need to itself; its vague intentionality acquires precision solely by establishing customary paths. It becomes fixed in its periodicity and its level of demand, settles on a precise category of objects, in brief, takes on a customary form and so comes to recognize itself in its end. A highly complex dialectic of ends and means is established: the need seeks an outlet and the knowledge of a practicable way heightens the tension of need. What we often call force of habit is no more than the tendency of a preexisting need to adopt a customary form which is easiest to satisfy. In extending need by an easy conduct, in showing to it *that* it can and *how* it can satisfy itself, the schema of available action in some way infects the need itself. This way the objects around us become suggestions for action: they show at the same time the coveted object and the form of action by which we shall reach it. They include at the same time a disinterested physiognomy, an appealing character, and a schema of action, all this narrowly conjoined in the expression, the allure, the air they offer to our vision. Thus an easy-chair reminds us that we are tired, it shows us a receptive

13. P. Guillaume, "Les Aspects affectifs de l'habitude," *J. de Ps.* (1935), Nos. 3, 4.

form which would give us rest, and outlines in our eye the gesture of sitting down. The attraction and the schema of an easy action are so well grounded in the object that our universe of perception is swollen with affective values and furrowed with possible lines of action. Usage unceasingly remodels the very face of our needs by this bias. It is the same thing to say "I am hungry" and "I'd love to cut myself a slice of that bread on the sideboard." Desire embraces the object of need as well as the customary motor schema.

If, then, habit affects need to the point of seeming to invent it, it does so in turn by the encounter of the acquired customary form and latent needs. The latter are always the true sources of need which overflow into quasi-needs. It is never true that habit creates a need—even the most artificial needs, such as needs of tranquilizers and stimulants, always refer to the genuine tissue of need in which exercise had worked a kind of derivative blood-letting. Usage never does more than reveal the primitive sources of motivation which then function along lines of least resistance. When a need dies out and there is no other need apt to take charge of the habit, the latter seems to us to create no longer a need but a disgust, as for example some obligation—professional or other —constraining us to carry out an action which we regard as beyond the point of saturation of genuine needs sustaining it.

But in and through these secondary, variable effects there remain the prerogatives of habit: its availability and its ease. The use of a familiar gesture may be accompanied by pleasure or disgust, but as to form it remains a disposition of the will to act according to a privileged pattern, to think and to feel along some comfortable customary models. Even though I find the action repugnant, if I am forced to act—to proofread an article without curiosity, apart from any pleasure of reading, understanding, communicating with another, working, or keeping busy—it is still the customary gesture, the easiest gesture, which offers itself spontaneously. It resists if I want to deflect it, even though I find it affectively repugnant.

Thus the case of neutral habits brings out the motif of *ease* which ordinarily coincides with that of *pleasure*. Imagination grasps the representation of the easy means, anticipates in it facilitation of its execution by means of a basic affective image and sees in it the value of ease. On a higher level of reflection, ease as such is explicitly regarded as desirable; it becomes constituted as an autonomous motive when it comes into conflict with pleasure, itself clearly valuated. Thus a new principle of hesitation appears at the root of choice. Which is better, the agreeable at the end of a painful road, or the easy road in the direction of a trivial pleasure?

When this motive of ease tends to become the center of valuation of my life, it assumes the more systematic form of the principle of economy whose many ramifications Jankélévich shows us. Perhaps it will establish a new point of least resistance in man's affective structure through which the vertigo of passion can insinuate itself. Paradoxical though it appears, there may exist passions of inertia and laziness along the line of the motive of ease, as there exist passions of pleasure along the line of motives proceeding from desire and fear, and passions of power along the line of motives of difficulty and struggle which we shall clarify presently.

4. The Difficult as Good

As WE MOVE beyond the well-delineated compass of need and pleasure and attempt to recognize other, broader reaches of the will to live, difficulties and uncertainties accumulate. It becomes apparent, however, that our analysis must break out decisively from the confines of organic concerns. Pleasure, pain, the useful, the agreeable, and the easy, in spite of their heterogeneity, still have the feel of a family bound together by the term *well-being*. Well-being is the composite end of *homo œconomicus*. It is for him that we produce, transform, exchange, and make plans. Yet can we be certain that positive pleasure, in relation to needs, cessation of pain in all its forms, and making easy all functions, whether primitive, acquired, or artificial, would advance the sway of the desirable? Nietzsche's criticism of such sensualistic, empiricistic interpretation of life is quite familiar: life, he tells us, aims not only at conservation, but also at expansion and domination. It seeks power, desires obstacles, and positively drives towards the *difficult*.[14] This interpretation of life finds an echo in psychology, particularly in some non-Freudian forms of psychoanalysis. While Freud tends to systematize all vital energies under the sole concept of libido which, while it centers on sexual drive, tends to cover the entire field of hedonic activity, Adler, for example, distinguishes an irreducible group of instincts which he calls the *Ichtriebe*.[15]

14. This is the penetrating insight of scholastic psychology, that the irascible is not reducible to the concupiscible, but aims at the arduous as the concupiscible aims at pleasure. Cf. below, Part II, chap. 2, p. 231.

15. Alfred Adler, *The Neurotic Constitution*, trans. Glueck and Lind (New York, 1917).

This is a rather troublesome question: psychology inspired by Nietzsche embraces under the name of will to power very different aspects of the life of consciousness which are difficult to distinguish. Within it we can recognize, for one, a power of practical affirmation and self-determination which in the present work we shall develop as will strictly speaking (deciding, moving, consenting), and also a complication of the will in passion and of vitality in the sense of passions of power illustrated by the Renaissance man so dear to Nietzsche. This makes it rather difficult to recognize the affective and active residues which belong clearly to the organic level. The truth is that the Nietzschean analysis cannot be superimposed on our pattern of the voluntary and the involuntary. It excludes the distinction between the will and organic life which is the cornerstone of our study of motivation, and it ignores the problem of the fault which is basic to our theory of passions. In our language the will to power is at the same time will, organic life, and passion. If, however, we distinguish the will, as the power of valuating, organic life, and the "bad infinite" of passions of violence and war, do there remain tendencies on the organic level which cannot be reduced to the quest for pleasure and avoidance of suffering? Does there remain an "irascible," a basic appetite for the *difficult?*

An affirmative answer to this question does not preclude the possibility that the "irascible" reveals itself empirically only through the passions of ambition, domination, or violence, just as the "concupiscible" reveals itself empirically through passions of pleasure and ease. Precisely in the irascible these passions find a point of least resistance, a temptation which the fascinated consciousness realizes in the fault.

Does biology offer us any objective indications, some symptoms of this tendency towards the difficult? This is precisely what is unclear; the testimony of biology on this point is doubtful. The chief reason for this is that biology never confronts us with a central will to live but rather with a cluster of functions tending towards a balance of internal context with respect to external context. The notions of balance and adaptation, which for the biologist always have a precise meaning, are worthless in a Nietzschean interpretation of life. To be sure, we can assume that biology only rarely shows us the living being in his unity and profusion within a diversity of functional equilibria. Only an examination of behavior could furnish us with a decisive diagnosis. Darwin already showed that strife is essential to life, that life includes an aggressive component, but the functional significance of this strife does not seem to favor the conception of a will to power: it is a struggle *for* life, that is, *for* eating, *for* reproduction, *for* avoiding being devoured, perishing from cold, etc. This struggle seems to be related strictly to need, as a means to an end, a struggle of organic forces united against death in order to establish an equilibrium which is constantly being disrupted: it is a struggle for equilibrium and not, so it seems, for excess or surplus.

And yet there are different aspects of behavior which seem to suggest a tendency towards the difficult not subordinated to need and in this respect relatively disinterested.

Already the example of play is bothersome enough: play seems to reveal a surplus of activity in life, a gratuitous expenditure, an activity for no reason. In watching young animals or young children at play we begin to think that life begins beyond actual danger and beyond equilibrium: life is generous. Perhaps for the living being this is a manner of being which surpasses deathlessness. Perhaps life is just this realm of leisure opening up for the living being when he is no longer hungry or thirsty, when he is out of danger and without hindrances. This tentative observation leads us to reconsider some aspects of pleasure itself which had been overshadowed before. It seems that pleasure conceals within itself elements of leisure and play which transcend simple indications of need, or, better, a nuance of the struggle not simply to live but to conquer. Pleasure, we shall say with Pradines, is a duality overcome, but it relishes the obstacle even while it anticipates the enjoyment: "difficulty," said Montaigne, "makes things worth while" (*Essays*, II.15).

The psychology of combat and of combative instincts contributes what might be the decisive testimony in this discussion. Such instincts apparently represent the peak of life's aggressiveness, its wish for power beyond its wish to survive. Play calls attention to the generosity which a living being attains when he reaches the fields of organic leisure beyond lack and pain. Struggle expresses the destructive, imperialistic side of this expansion. It testifies that war is an extension of a disturbing organic tendency with which passionate self-affirmation, a frenzy of auto-affirmation, becomes naturally allied. Peace is always an ethical conquest of the violent will to live; it proceeds from the affirmation of the supra-organic values of justice and brotherhood—life itself strives for effusion and destruction with an astonishing lack of discrimination.

But the most decisive testimony supporting the notion of an aggressive tendency of organic life is presented by the course of history. If the search for pleasure and ease and the fear of pain were the sole organic concerns animating activity, history would not be the *terrible* process it is, constantly sustained by the tragedy of ambition, power, catastrophe, and destruction. History would be economic history, history made by the *homo œconomicus*—and not political history, history made by the man of prey. History would be the history of well-being and of ill-being and not the history of power and resistance. The deviation between the actual course of history and theoretical schemata of sensualistic psychology must be bridged, from the level of psychology on, by taking an aggressive root of life into consideration. The taste for the terrible, with its latent scorn of pleasure and ease, its disturbing welcoming of suffering, definitely seems to be one of the primary components of the will to live.

Thus it appears that the taste for overcoming obstacles is *heterogeneous* with the search for pleasure of assimilation, the fear of suffering and the quest for ease. Sustained by the imagination, this tendency will appear as a need, but it is a need which is not initiated by any privation, aggression, or hindrance. Not having suffering in any form as its opposite pole, the pleasure in an obstacle never reaches the form of plenitude, of elimination of pain, of liberation from hindrances, in a word, of repose. It is the genuine pleasure of movement which alone reveals the authentic tensions of life beyond the twin avarice of desire and fear. It alone testifies to the heroic dimension, the Don Quixotic dimension of life contrasted to a Sancho Panza who is guided solely by the pleasures of possession, freedom from suffering, and ease.

If we trace out the suggestion of this analysis we shall be led to correct our earlier interpretations of the needs of expenditure of energy and of exercise. These needs—or quasi-needs—are essentially ambiguous, attracted by the two poles, the easy and the difficult. It would seem that life includes an attraction for obstacles which seems to be the primitive root of the will to power. But before deviating towards the Nietzschean myths of imperialism and war, imagination plays a mediating role between vital tendency and willing: it presents the obstacle and its physical make-up, it envisions in an original feeling the equally underivable pleasure of struggle, and thus suggests the *value* of energy.

Here is a new source of uncertainty concealed at the root of freedom: in effect the taste for obstacles is a tendency towards choosing suffering itself and sacrificing the pleasure of possession to the pure pleasure of conquest. This pleasure then adds to the more elementary complementary values of sustenance and sex which are still organic and spontaneous values, but which are in some ways disinterested and Utopian, the values of struggle.

5. Affective Confusion and the Heterogeneity of Organic Values

WE HAVE SAID at the start of the chapter that it is as affectivity that bodily existence transcends the intelligibility claimed by the essences of the Cogito. The study of pleasure, of pain, of the attraction of ease, and of the taste for the difficult gives a precise meaning to the topic of affective confusion.

The experience of different basic situations in which a living being is engaged—privation, aggression, hindrances, and obstacles—permits a composite, heterogeneous revelation of values even on the elementary organic level. The position of the body not only cannot be deduced from a possible self-positing act of the Cogito, but is not even a simple position. Affectivity forms no system; it illustrates disparate values in disparate pleasures and sufferings. Instead of the sole pair of pleasure and pain we have enumerated multiple affective series without even pretending to have completed the circle of value on the organic level. Each affective series represents a degree of intensity of value which permits in each case a homogeneous serialization between a negative and a positive pole, for example between privation and enjoyment, between external pain and the almost positive pleasure of security, etc.

Thus it becomes apparent that the conception of a will to live cannot be a simple one. It defines only a *level* of value, not a value or a pair of values. On this level, the "historialization" of values represents a kind of ἄπειρον, indefinite chaos at the root of the Cogito. There is no central tendency which we could call the will to live and of which the tendencies we have enumerated above would be derivative forms. There are, in fact, no sense affects which the various affective images of pleasure referring to assimilation, of absence of pain, and of ease and difficulty could be said to exemplify. This is also why there are no vital values which affective imagination could perceive *in* simple affective matter. Life, at least on the human level, is a complex, unresolved situation, an unresolved problem whose terms are neither clear nor consistent. Thus it is an open question posed to willing and this is finally why there is a problem of choice and a moral problem.

In the unity of the Cogito, experience on the organic level does not form a state within a state, with its own order. There is no organic order—it is rather a multiplicity which must be clarified and unified by the stroke of a de-cision.[16]

This conclusion might appear strange. Is life a pseudo-concept? Don't I have to choose, in extreme situations, between my life on the one hand and my friends, truth, my faith on the other? To be exact, if there are moments when my life appears to me united into one all-embracing value, it is not from the interior of indefinite, chequered, affective experience, but from the exterior, from the viewpoint of death. It is death which gives life its unity, in the sense that only a *catastrophic situation*, forcing me to choose between my life and those of my friends, has the power of posing the question of my existence. The possibility of this *simple* event, my death, my dying, suddenly unites all that I am as body in one equally simple embrace. From dying, life receives all the simplicity of which it is capable; in face of "deadly danger," [17] "being alive" thus appears as a total situation which has its simplicity, if not as an act I posit, then at least as a state of bodily existence itself.

This revelation of unity of living by sacrifice—whose richness of philosophical implications cannot be stressed enough—would itself be misinterpreted if we did not discern, behind the dying which unifies living, the affirmation of the values which imply my possible death and for which I risk my life.

In contrast with suicide, which is pure negation and destruction, sacrifice is entirely affirmative, affirming value and being, albeit without reference to my life. Thus we can say that my life only appears to me as a value when it is at the same time threatened and transcended, threatened by death and transcended by other values. Sacrifice unites the threat and the transcendence in a unique situation. This is why we could say that life itself is united by death *and* by other values. In the light of sacrifice we can say that "life" defines not a simple value but rather a simple *level* of values. Hence it is important to understand the values of

16. Along the same line, see the ambivalence at the root of freedom, J. Boutonier, *L'Angoisse* (Paris, 1955), pp. 269 ff. In Roland Dalbiez, *La Méthode psychanalytique et la doctrine freudienne* (Paris, 1936), II, 481–83, the author quotes Malinowski, *Sex and Repression in Savage Societies* (New York, 1927): plasticity of instincts in man calls for a properly human, ethical, and cultural regulation.

17. In German, deadly danger is expressed as *Lebensgefahr* (danger to life). Concerning the meaning of dying as revealing contingence, cf. below, Part III, chap. 3, p. 444, "Experience of Contingence and the Idea of Death."

the organic level by contrast with other values of different levels in order to see the full extent of the affective confusion and the heterogeneity of motives which sustain an act of willing.

[3] BODY AND THE TOTAL FIELD OF MOTIVATION

1. Level of History and Level of the Body

THE LIMIT EXPERIENCE of sacrifice stresses sufficiently that there are other sources of voluntary motivation beside organic concerns. But it is more difficult to try to enumerate even approximately these primary sources of motives. Such enumeration interests us only indirectly since our intention is to understand the relationship of the body to willing. Yet we cannot do without a consideration, brief though it may be, of other motives, since this consideration might throw light on willing itself. If, in effect, willing is the valuation of life, I broaden out the spread of my motivation by contrasting other values with my own life. But knowledge of these other motives is essential even for an understanding of the corporeal involuntary: the fact is that the body is not only a value among others, but also that it is in some way involved in the apprehension of all motives and through them of all values. It is the affective medium of all values: a value can reach me only as dignifying a motive, and no motive can incline me if it does not impress my sensibility. I reach values through the vibration of an affect. To broaden out the spread of values means at the same time to deploy affectivity to its broadest span.

The French sociological school accustomed us to seeking the difference between willing and desire in the role of collective representations. Similarly, Bergson's view in *Two Sources of Morality and Religion,* whose inadequacy he himself subsequently demonstrated, had a wide impact.

The reflections of the sociologists carry an indisputable power against all the theories which attempt to derive the will from variously refined, systematized, or sublimated organic concerns. Using the term "collective representations," they have made us aware, as against old empiricism, that it is the needs foreign to the organic level which give man his very quality of humanity. The organic level is not a human level, and it is quite natural to seek in "social context" what is not sufficiently explained by the "biological context" in the hope of rediscovering the ethical dualism of great philosophic tradition beyond the religious and philosophical agnosticism inherited from Comte and Spencer.[18]

Today we no longer need to repeat the excellent analyses of the influence of collective representations on abstract thought, memory, and even on organic needs carried out by the sociologists. What we do need to emphasize here is the contribution of these analyses to the psychology of the involuntary. Their chief interest is that they attract our attention to the basic sphere of feelings through which an individual consciousness finds itself *affected* by collective representations. The sociologists, to be sure, have a tendency to reduce the psychological level to a simple *fusion* of the social and the organic, to a passageway for collective representations. In this way they miss the essential moment of willing. We shall say more about this presently, but at least the sociologists have rightly noted that it is specific feelings which inject collective representations and tendencies into the cycle of representations and tendencies of the individual. Society, that is, must finally act out its role in the individual consciousness. Social imperatives are impressed in the individual consciousness and primarily in an original affectivity.[19] A specific fear or respect inclines our sensibility in the direction of commandments, and emotion, in conformity with its usual function, associates all the vibration of the body with the affective influence of our imperatives. Society penetrates into the individual through affects, and so is able to enter into competition with vital need within the psycho-organic walls themselves.

But while the sociological school has the merit of stressing the great extent to which collective representations are a source of motives distinct from organic needs it completely misses the relation between feelings attached to such representations and the will. Without previous analysis of the concepts of willing and of motives, and consequently without an eidetics of motivation, the will is in danger of appearing as an epiphenomenon of its own collective representations. In this respect the sociologically inspired language of the psychologists is particularly equivocal.

18. Ch. Blondel, "Les Volitions," in *Nouveau traité de psychologie,* ed. G. Dumas, vol. VI: "The Pauline conception of grace, the Kantian imperative, the collective representations of the sociologists are nothing other ... than a triple divergent interpretation of one properly human reality, as far as we can know; ... psycho-organic activity becomes voluntary activity only on condition of becoming sublimated, so to speak, in the action of collective representations" (pp. 321–24).

19. *Ibid.,* p. 233.

The will "translates" an "influence" exercised by representations which "penetrate" into consciousness. The imperatives "impose themselves"; the *fiat* is identified now with the imperative itself inasmuch as it dominates organic tendency, now with obedience to conscience, "a consenting obedience, if you will, but nonetheless obedience, because consciousness receives its law from without." The autonomy of consciousness becomes "a heteronomy which is not aware of itself," "group consciousness instilled in us." [20]

In reality, because of its phenomenological weakness, social psychology simply inserted its notion of group representations into a naturalistic psychology: collective representations became forces, tendencies which mechanically compete with organic tendencies.

Thus when we oppose the elite to the masses we are left without resources for understanding how an individual *rises* above his own collective representations. In the end we are forced to seek a deeper reason than such collective representations in the organic permeability of the individual to the apparently self-creating pressure of collective representations. [21] This is how we come to say that "the presence of collective representations alone is sufficient to make our activity a voluntary activity." [22]

Given such a "situated," "reflexive" consciousness, we are never forced to bother retracing the path of Cartesian doubt to the Cogito. "I think" means in the first place that I confront myself in order to evaluate. I am he who evaluates social imperatives.

This constant rediscovery of the Cogito does not in the least place me in a surly solitude; rather it teaches me to consider as a *motive* what I receive as *suggestion*. To evaluate means no more than this. The error of social psychology lies in having frequently chosen as its standard an inauthentic consciousness "which wills with a will which is already complete" and of having attempted to understand authentic willing as a refinement of such alienated consciousness, as an especially brilliant alienation.

On this voyage of rediscovery and in view of this elevation of willing, an eidetic analysis is an indispensable tool. While it tells me that to will is not to submit, it also reiterates that a motive is not a cause. Whether it is mechanistic or dynamistic, the implicit psychology of Durkheimian sociologists is always conceived in terms of mental physics.

An eidetic teaches me that though affectivity related to col-

20. *Ibid.*, pp. 355–66.
21. *Ibid.*, p. 360.
22. *Ibid.*, p. 363.

lective representation differs "materially" from affectivity on the organic level, it resembles it "formally" as motive of. . . .

This formal resemblance is valuable: it permits me to understand the relations between myself and my *body* and myself and my *history* in terms of a *mutual analogy*. History and my body are two levels of motivation, two roots of the involuntary. Just as I have not chosen my body, I have not chosen my historical situation, but both the one and the other are the locus of my responsibility. Between my body and myself and likewise between my history and myself there arises a circular relation one of whose forms is precisely the relation of motivation. History "historializes" values at a given moment and claims my adherence in a way *analogous* to that of my hunger, my thirst, or my sexuality. History inclines me just as my body does. This is why history is not already an object; [23] it becomes one only if I remove myself from it, in the same way as a personal body becomes an object-body for a pure, disembodied spectator, that is, for an unsituated spectator. As the affectivity of the organic level, fear and respect, it reveals to me values which illustrate my age. But in turn, though the unfolding of history has its own spontaneity and gives rise to values in its progress as my hunger gives rise to the value of bread, it is I who evaluate it, compare it, and decide. The receptivity of willing for social values, *like* the receptivity to organic values, stands in a reciprocal relation with my sovereign decision which appeals to received values. This receptivity only becomes passivity and bondage in surrender and alienation.

These apparently abstract considerations have an immediate political application: the objection of conscience to a tyrant— whether a man, a party, or a mob—is imbedded in the very structure of individual willing. Social motivation like bodily motivation can be judged and criticized. I confront the state as I confront my body. There are not two freedoms, a "civil" freedom and an "inner" freedom. There is only one free decision.

2. Obligation and Attraction

WHAT, THEN, IS THE AFFECTIVITY in terms of which consciousness becomes sensitive to social imperatives? The great affective transformation is the encounter with something superior, with a transcendence, not only in the improper, horizontal sense of an alternative alongside me, but also in the proper, vertical

23. R. Aron, *Introduction to the Philosophy of History*, trans. Irwin (Boston, 1961).

sense of an authority above me. There is a specific appeal which presents the good of the community in which I participate to my sensibility.

It is apparent that this appeal includes two contrary aspects: an attraction and an obligation which undoubtedly figure already on the level of the equivocal relation of myself to any transcendence which at the same time enhances and dominates it, satisfies it, and scars it. Consider a value like justice, whose historical forms vary, in part as a function of the inventive capacity and generosity of conscience which constantly prolongs its demands into ever new segments of common life. The demand of justice, historically embodied in essentially variable forms, has its root in the radical affirmation that the other *counts* as against me, that his needs count like mine, that his opinions proceed from a center of perspective and valuation which has the same dignity as I have. The other is a thou: this is the affirmation which covertly animates the maxim of justice, whether in its classical form of *"neminem lædere, suum cuique tribuere,"* or in its Kantian form, to treat each person as an end and never as a means. The demand of justice thus consists in principle of a decentering of perspective by which the perspective of the other—the need, the claim, of the other—balances my perspective.

This decentering is what my sensibility experiences variously as obligation and as attraction.

In one aspect this decentering is inevitably an obligation: in practice my own life is *humbled* by the values put into action by institutions and structures jointly constituted by the diverse demands of individual men. In the last instance it is the value of the other which humbles my own life. The feeling of being obligated to . . . expresses affectively the asymmetry of value between the value of my life and the value of the communities which make the life of the other in all its forms possible. Obligation shows that the decentering of perspective which the other inaugurates is an asymmetry of value.

But this feeling tends to become degraded under constraint— the facile identification of obligation and constraint is erroneous. Obligation has to do with freedom. Constraint is an aspect of bondage. Obligation motivates while constraint binds, concerns an inauthentic willing, an alienated freedom. Perhaps it represents the most formidable of all passions, the passion of inertia whose other outcropping we have encountered on the organic level in the taste for the easy. But this opposite of obligation attracts our attention to a fundamental aspect of obligation: social pressure tends toward its lower limit to the extent to which it remains diffuse, anonymous, and identified with a faceless "one" of lifeless prejudices: "one" thinks this or that, "one" does this and "one" does not do that. Obligation ceases to be a constraint when the values illustrated by mores assume someone's face, are borne by the thrust of a living decision, in short, when they are embodied by genuine persons. Bergson made a decisive contribution to this point in his *Two Sources* when he depicted the serious doubts which we shall stress later. It certainly seems that the constraint of social imperatives is connected with their anonymity.

Now this remark permits us to pass on to the other limit. The more a value like justice is embodied in a militant consciousness which imparts to it the thrust of its indignation and its generosity, the more that constraint becomes converted into an appeal. Constraint is a sign of a dehumanization of values which weigh like dead weight on consciousness; appeal is a sign of a creation, of a living "historialization" of values by men who are themselves alive. Constraint and appeal are the lower and upper limits of "collective representations."

But it would be a great mistake to think that the aspect of obligation can be eliminated together with constraint: this is one of the perils of Bergsonian analysis, as of the sociologically inspired psychology which takes inauthentic forms of the relations between willing and values as its standard. We shall presently return to this when we attempt to do justice to the Kantian analysis of obligation: "the call of heroes" does not supplant obligation. The feeling of obligation is not restricted to the anonymity of "one" but precedes the transcendence of community values with respect to organic values.

Rather, while constraint is the lower limit of obligation, the call or appeal is the upper limit of attraction which the good of communities seeking justice exercises on willing: "Happy are they who thirst and hunger after righteousness . . . ," for the demand for justice is like hunger and like thirst. This means that the faculty of desiring is broader than organic concern. I am a lacuna and a lack of something other than bread and water. Of what? Of entities? Of ideal forms which would bear the names justice, equality, solidarity? Shall we speak of "ideal dispositions" which would oppose us to organic dispositions? Here we are in danger of falling into the snare of dead abstractions. Justice, equality are never more than living rules of the integration of persons into a "we." In the last analysis, it is the other who counts. We must always return to this. It is thus the good of the other which I lack. The myself is empty with respect to the other myself. He completes me, just as food does. The being of the subject is not solipsistic; it is being-in-common. In this way the sphere of intersubjective relations can be the *analog* of the organic sphere and the world of needs can provide the fundamental *metaphor* of appetite: the alter-ego, like the non-ego—as for example nourishment—comes to fill up my lack.

If we start with this fundamental structure of intersubjectivity, values which render it possible can be attractive and not simply obligatory. The community is my good because it leads towards making me whole within a "we" where the lacuna of my being would be filled. In some moments of precious communion I sense tentatively that the isolated self is perhaps only a segment torn from such others who could have become a "thou" for me.

But in turn the community which completes me imposes obligations upon me because it leads towards making me whole only by transcending me as a will to live. Attraction is undoubtedly more basic than obligation, because obligation is only an idea of an attraction greater than the will to live connected with the idea of an obstacle to such will. The decentering of perspective from myself to yourself and to us is at the same time what I desire and what I fear, what makes me whole and what imposes obligations upon me. This is why the affectivity of the social level remains perforce equivocal.

But in that case in what sense can we say that the upper limit of attraction is vocation? In the sense that a call perhaps no longer belongs to the order of motivation, but exceeds it just as constraint falls short of it. There are some encounters which do not simply present me with reasons for living which I can evaluate and approve but which truly function as a conversion of the heart of willing and have the force of a genuine spiritual rebirth. Such encounters create freedom. They set me free. Friendship or love between two people can be like that. Thereafter, the very nature of the bond between myself and yourself is profoundly changed: it is no longer a social, public relation, but an essentially private relation which exceeds the rule of justice. At the same time the other is no longer the analog of my body: his willing no longer confronts me as a source of opinions which could *motivate* my willing. The relation of motivation is transcended and approaches a relation of creation. The effect of a friend on the very heart of willing, which is in a sense a "seminal" action, belongs

already to the order of the "poetics" which we are at present holding in suspension.

Thus the obligation and the attraction which we are here describing are restricted to that middle zone of public or civic relations with the other: that is, of the zone of the *"social,"* having as
its lower limit constraint or slavery in which there is no longer
society or right and in which willing is estranged, and for its upper
limit friendship in which there is no longer society or right but a
liberating vocation, and in which the will is no longer motivated
or counseled but created.[24] Undoubtedly it is the essence of intersubjectivity to be an unstable tension between the relation of
master and slave and the relation of communion. Political responsibility, however, is the zone in which freedom can never
have an alibi, either in the tyranny of the prince or in the dictator-
ship of the They, and in which the transformation of all civic
bonds into friendship is a Utopia.

In this middle zone, where the other is not yet the "thou" of
friendship but a "socius," a citizen—or, better, a fellow citizen—
a subject of right, there is no reason to believe that the other
represents a simple value in face of my life. It became apparent
above that similarly my life itself is not a simple value, but rather
a level of values which is in no way unified. There is a place for
choice inscribed already in the discord of affective motives which
gravitate around my life. The conflict of organic values taken in
a broad sense with the equally broad order of social values further
testifies to the necessity of choice. This is the conflict illustrated
by sacrifice; but the choice is still provoked by the internal conflict
of social values. We can, to be sure, state it radically, that the
other is what counts, but this value of the other is always seen
indirectly, through a labyrinth of social situations in which it becomes fragmented into incommensurable values: equality and
hierarchy, justice and order, etc. . . . It is not our task even to
sketch simply the conflicts which we should have to read "in"
history and never treat in an abstract, ideological manner. Let it
suffice to indicate that the historical situation of free choice is
even less simple than its bodily situation. We have by no means
exhausted the field of motivation of human willing. In the last
instance the incommensurability of values reveals itself essentially
in the *affective indistinctness of motives,* and in terms of this all
history is present in miniature in the involuntary life of each subject, affecting a personal will.

24. Bergsonianism might well involve the risk of missing the essence of the
social by its method of following the lower and upper limit.

3. "Material" and "Formal" Values

WE COULD HARDLY conclude our examination of involuntary motivation without bringing up the difficulty which arises even for psychology of the will from the Kantian interpretation of moral obligation. We can bring up this difficulty here only from the strictly limited viewpoint of a phenomenology of the voluntary and the involuntary. And as we have said above, our explicit phenomenology of motivation in turn involves a theory of values.

The implicit phenomenology of Kantianism is that the will is worthy of the name only when it is obeying an *a priori* principle distinct from the faculty of desiring, reason as a practical power. It would seem that there is no will here apart from the bond with reason, and that this bond ought to exclude all relations with sensibility. Kantianism is dominated by the problem of a *"pure"* will, independent of all empirical conditions, that is, of affective motivation.[25] The pure will is determined solely by reason as the practical power which commands it. Let us, for the moment, set aside the Kantian thesis according to which the only purely rational commandment which could determine a pure will is "formal" and not in any way "material."

However, the exclusion of the "faculty of desire" from the field of "pure" will presupposes a broad conception of human will which would bring us back precisely to a general theory of motivation. In effect the penchants of sensibility can enter into competition with the *"a priori* principle of willing" only within one and the same psychological framework, within one and the same field of motivation. The Kantian ethic itself presupposes a common standard among the inclinations summed up in the idea of happiness and the "principle of willing, according to which the action is produced without regard for any of the objects of the faculty of desire." [26] Conflict of duty and happiness presupposes a common standard of motivation. This shows two things. In the first place, affective inclinations cannot entail willing necessarily, or willing could never substitute rational motives for them; in other words, psychological determinism must be broken already on the level of the faculty of desire. Practical reason can determine willing only if sensibility does not entail rigid determination. "*A posteriori* inclinations" and "*a priori* principles" must thus share a common appearance as *motives*. The Kantian opposition of duty

25. Kant, *Fundamental Principles of Metaphysics of Morals*, sect. I.
26. *Ibid.*

and sensibility on an ethical level presupposes a broader phenomenology of motivation and decision which embraces even the
terms of the opposition.

But, secondly, we must go even further: not only must sensibility be capable of being related to willing as a motive which
inclines without compelling, but in turn a rational principle,
whatever it may be, must be capable of "touching" me in a manner analogous to that of sensible goods. Kant finally agrees with
this explicitly: *respect* is a *sui generis* feeling "which expresses
simply the consciousness I have of the *subordination* of my will
to a law without any other intermediary influences on my sensibility." [27] To be sure, Kant contrasts this feeling to all the others
as much as possible: it is said not to have been "received through
an influence as the feelings of desire and fear, but *spontaneously
produced* by a concept of reason." "Properly speaking," he tells us,
"respect is the representation of a value which interferes with my
self-love." [28] But this opposition cannot annul the deep-seated analogy which exists between respect and the affective pair, inclina-
tion-fear. Inasmuch as the law is the work of reason, and thus
my work, briefly, inasmuch as I am autonomous, I am spontaneously in accord with it as my desire is with pleasure; inasmuch
as it is opposed to my self-love, it is analogous with fear.

Thus in order to make Kantianism intelligible we must on the
one hand say that all human feeling, including the feelings of
desire and fear, are proportioned to willing, and on the other
hand that the most rational law "affects me" through a feeling
analogous to organic feelings. Kantianism as an ethic thus necessarily ingrains itself within a phenomenology which goes beyond
the *opposition* of reason and sensibility.

But even though Kantianism does not force us to reverse the
principles of our description of the voluntary and the involuntary,
does it not introduce an entirely new dimension of motivation
which in some sense brings about an internal revolution in the
very context within which, for a moment, it seemed we could include it? Respect, it has said, is a feeling which is not received
but spontaneous, because the law is the legislation of reason itself. This legislation of reason would be so homogeneous with
willing itself that the principle of obligation would no longer be
the *involuntary* which disposes but rather the self-determination

27. *Ibid.* and *Critique of Practical Reason*, I:iii; cf. also the reconciliation
between respect, the sublime, and admiration, *Critique and Judgment*, §§ 23,
27, 29.
28. *Foundations of Metaphysics of Morals*, Sect. I.

of a rational being. Duty would be myself as reason commanding myself as will. Beyond the motivation which disposes would lie not *appeal* but *autonomy*.[29]

It seems reasonable to approach this difficulty by attempting to place such rational legislation with respect to the *value of the other*. We have said above that it is the other and his rights which humble me and fulfill me. In addition, we have spoken of the respect for the other in the same terms as those which Kant uses to describe respect for the law. Kant precisely points out to us that "all respect for a person is properly nothing other than respect for the law (law of honesty, etc.) of which that person presents an instance." Here we are at the heart of the problem. Has not Kant stressed unduly the completely "formal" value of the universalization of our maxims? In particular, is not the prestige of the famous "formal" principle of universalization borrowed, purloined from the "material" value of the other? We could even ask whether, once we have restituted to the other his own value, underived from the law, this entirely formal principle retains any other function than to submit the authenticity of our feelings to a *critical* test. A project cannot be noxious to another if it is universalizable. But without the "material" value of the other and apart from this critical function, the "formal" value of non-contradiction loses all meaning. Such a formal criterion is a criterion of *control*. It is subordinate to the eruption of the concern for the other as other into my life; it presupposes a surge of *Mitsein* into *Selbstsein*, a surge revealed by a specific feeling of self-effacement and outward reach. Beside this controlling function the formal rule of universalization seems to have one other function, the function of a *substitute*, a *temporary expedient*. As Rauh masterfully pointed out,[30] I take refuge in a completely formal will of non-contradiction when I cease to live spontaneously, "passionately," the "material" values of social life. In a gap in feeling I rely on the law. Lacking fidelity to another, I content myself with remaining constant, with living in harmony with myself.[31]

It remains true that, brought back to this subordinate function, the formal rule of universalization of our maxims is irreducible. We have to give up trying to reduce it to the pressure of collective imperatives or even to the value of the other as other.

29. *Fundamental Principles of Metaphysics of Morals,* sect. I.
30. Kant, *Critique of Practical Reason,* I:i.
31. Marcel, *Creative Fidelity,* pp. 147 f.

It is a rule of good thought applied to action. It is the critical weapon of the individual. As such, the "formal" rule is not reducible to "material" values. Thus it poses a problem which at first is insoluble. In effect it does not motivate my action in the same way as "material" values: such a rule of good thought is in some sense consubstantial with the deliberating will, coinciding with the spontaneity of willing. In this sense Kant is surely right in saying that it expresses the autonomy of rational legislation. But this autonomy is nothing other than the *critical* autonomy of willing which tests its projects rationally and which, by this rational test, rises from an inherent to a built-up motivation. Strictly speaking, the formal autonomy is only the spontaneity of willing bound by its own rationality. Formal autonomy is only the rational obligation of remaining in agreement with itself in its deliberation. In this sense it does not express a contribution of a value, a good concerning which I deliberate, but the value of the operation of deliberation itself. In a narrow sense, in which motivation is reduced to the play of "material" values through the feelings which illustrate them, we could say the Kantian rule of universalization is not a motive but the duty of rational deliberation itself. But in a broad sense of the word motive, we could say that the concern to examine the situation rationally together with the values functioning in that situation can itself be a motive, a reason to which we appeal: "Let's see, let's reflect carefully!" Respect for the form of rational deliberation itself refers, as Kant well said, not to a thing or a person, but to a law.

To be sure, it is also true that in respecting its own rationality the will *receives* nothing, but spontaneously *produces* the feeling of respect in itself. It is also the only case where it produces a feeling in itself. But in so doing, the will does not produce a reason for doing this or that. Here it is not inclined either by its body or by another, either by its life or by history. It only produces a reason for reasoning and this reason again appears to it in a specific feeling, the respect for its own rationality. And, finally, what is it to respect its own rationality, if not concretely to create a zone of silence so that the respect for the other can speak as strongly as the devotion to my life? It is when I permit justice and not only my interest to speak, in brief, when I reach the "material" value of the other, that I most respect the "formal" value of my own rationality. I frequently say, to use a language less abstract than Kant's, that the only "formal" duty which enters the field of motivation is one of not consenting to limiting of the scope of motivation to "material" values depicted by desire and fear, and of holding it open to its broadest extent. "When you deliberate in your mind, accept the highest values, those whose seat is the other."

3 / History of Decision: From Hesitation to Choice

INTRODUCTION: TEMPORAL EXISTENCE WITHIN THE LIMITS OF EIDETICS

PURE DESCRIPTION, which opens the study of decision, offers only an intellectual regimen. Existence surges against eidetic limitations: existence of the body is the decisive fact which forced us to go beyond the eidetic point of view and to elucidate concrete life at the limits of intelligibility. In this way the completely pure idea of motive found its matter in need and pleasure, in pain, briefly, in affectivity. This initial surpassing of the eidetic calls forth a second one: existence is not only body, but also choice. The eidetic of decision held the actual birth of choice in suspension: the triple relation to the project ("I want *this*"), to itself ("I make up *my mind* to do this"), and to motive ("I decide *because* . . .") includes no reference to the *history* from which choice arises. Choice is the advance, the maturing, the growth which brings about the relation to project, to itself, and to the motive. The fact is that pure description could suppress existing history only by concentrating on an instantaneous segment and fixating an already performed choice in a non-temporal state. Within such a moment a simplified consciousness is guided by one single project, while at the same time it becomes determined as one and invokes, in an eternally petrified gesture, an invariable constellation of motives. This triple relation definitely has to do also with the hesitant consciousness: throughout that laborious history I am a deciding consciousness. But pure description always omits the history whose resolution choice is, the history in the course of which a choice is sought, lost, and found in attempted conflicts, moments of inertia, sudden, striking changes, or slow digestion.

Such consideration of the process of choice is intimately connected with the consideration of the bodily involuntary. On the one hand, the union of the voluntary and the involuntary by integration of bodily motives within the network of a concrete decision can only arise in a history in which we seek and invent a common standard of body and willing. The medium of human unity is duration, living motivation, the history of the union of soul and body. This union is a drama, that is, an internal action which takes time. Thus it is important to uncover this process in which basic relations are sketched and revealed. And in turn process can only be understood as a drama. Existence moves forward only by the double movement of corporeal spontaneity and voluntary control. Process has two aspects: it is undergone and carried out, it is an organic time which thrusts me into incarnate being and the art of guiding changes of mind. For an incarnate being, freedom is temporal: incarnation and temporality are one and the same human condition.

But while the history of choice is an extension of the discovery of the body, this new line of investigation, like the preceding one, takes place under the sign of eidetics. Process can only be elucidated in light of a non-temporal structure established by pure description. To be sure, in its existence the surging process remains absolutely underivable by ideas: but a minimal intelligibility of temporal condition of freedom comes from non-temporal essences at the vanishing point of pure description. Thus the process I am transcends the pure relations of decision to project, to myself, and to motives without transgressing upon them. It is a formed *decision* which makes the *formless* from which choice proceeds and even the progress of its *formation* intelligible. In light of these relations which we already understand history itself appears as the awakening, birth, and maturing of a meaning (essence or meaning do not in any way imply a Platonizing hypostatization). Specifically, pure description alone can protect a consideration of process from regressing towards a mental physics in which succession of moments would be conceived in terms of the idea of causality. This danger, of course, can never be completely avoided, because we have only inadequate concepts for the task of tracing this genesis, concepts which barely rise above the level of metaphors: awakening, growth, ripening, movement, journey, leap, development, unfolding, etc. . . . These metaphors are not dangerous if we protect them against themselves by pure relations such as project, self-determination, or motivation; they appear, then, between the limits of the intelligible and of actual experienced existence, as transparent indications of an inner experience which is at the same time an action.

[1] HESITATION

THE HISTORY of choice confirms one of the first requirements of pure description: the deciding will cannot be reduced to a terminal act, to a final *fiat* bursting suddenly into the warp and woof of an internal situation which makes no allowances for it. No matter how chaotic the indecision and how abrupt the choice may be, choice does not bring about a new type of consciousness. Even if it erupts as a sudden change in indecision, its leap takes place within a willing consciousness and its surge does not mean that prior to it the will was absent or null. I do not cease to exist as a body and as willing: hesitant willing, conquered willing, unavailable willing, or willing which decrees. The *fiat*, though it represents a discontinuity, springs from within a certain continuity of voluntary existence.

This is why it will be our first task to recognize in hesitation a certain mode of being of the capacity for choice.

Our second task will be to understand how decision advances and lives in the process from hesitation to choice.

Our third task will be to elucidate the event of choice itself as a resolution of a history, at the same time breaking and fulfilling it.

Finally there will remain the task of considering the philosophical difficulties brought about by a doctrine of freedom arising from the study of choice within the limits of and guided by elementary description.

1. Willing and Its Mode of Being in Hesitation

HESITATION IS A CHOICE being sought. This relation of hesitation to an eventual choice manifests itself in two ways. Hesitation presents itself at the same time as falling short of a choice and as an attempt at choosing, but the choice to which it refers is always conceived as absent, impossible, desired, delayed, or feared.

On the one hand, we speak of hesitation as an in-decision. This imperfection of willing is often experienced as painful: I sense a self-loss in it. It is an anxiety of not being at all, since I fail to be one. In hesitation I am many, and so am not. It would be a great mistake to identify the discovery of possibility, which is my very being, with that of indecision. The root possibility is not an indecision which destroys choice, but the power which initiates choice itself (cf. chap. 1, p. 37). Genuine possibility is one which I open in myself as I decide, that is, in opening possibilities in the world by an actual project. The mark of such possibility projected ahead of myself is the feeling of capacity or power which includes alerting the body, with all its abilities poised on the verge of actual action, awakened or encountered by the project in the reality of the body. Hesitation illustrates these truths in principle by a *reductio ad absurdum:* in the chaos of my intentions lurks the conviction of my powerlessness. I experience not my possibility, but my im-possibility: "I am not up to it," "I am not of my depth," "I am lost, swamped"—I feel powerless.

To be sure, this deficiency which characterizes hesitation also makes possible an exquisite feeling of abundance of power and enjoyment born precisely of the indecisive fecundity which always remains this side of choice, but this experience follows from a rather different situation than the somewhat naïve hesitation of a choice being sought. The refusal to choose or at least the postponement of choice, elevated into a way of life, presupposes a deflection of consciousness which contents itself with endless reflection. It is not at all turned towards an eventual project but towards a possibility in second degree: the possibility of winning possibility in choice. This experience of potential ability grows from an overriding clarity and is wrested from the naïve will which wills without being aware of itself as willing and which hesitates before a choice without being aware of itself as hesitating. Its basis is the hesitation-in-order-to-choose. We shall also attempt to recover the principle of this second degree possibility in which we sense a corruption of reflection and, so to speak, a reflexive concupiscence expressed, *inter alia,* by the myth of Narcissus.

On the other hand, hesitation has the positive significance of a willing, a perplexed willing seeking to orient itself. Three basic traits of the formed decision are outlined in it, and it is these outlines which show the defects of in-decision.

1) While unable to form a definite project I do not cease to be a consciousness absorbed in a diversity of practical aims representing actions which depend on me. I examine motives by referring to such tentative projects. In this respect, the intentional structure of a hesitating consciousness differs from that of a

deciding consciousness only in the *modality* of the projects among which consciousness is divided. To hesitate is to doubt—"I wonder whether . . . ," "What should I do? . . ." Here the imperative of decision is tried out in a conditional mode, but this modality does not destroy the basic type of project structure or annul the general volitional character of hesitation. The conditional note which marks nascent projects infects all the elements of the project. The indicator, "to do," which marks this or that suggested action with a practical mark, is itself conditional. If the future and the possibility which bring about decision were absent instead of being present in a conditional mode I should not feel myself in a world into which I have embarked in order to choose, in a world in which something needs to be done between involvement and resolution, something undetermined to determine. If the will emerged only at the end of deliberation, like the sword of the Gallic chieftain falling on the scale at the climax to outweigh the wealth of Rome, the future presented to the hesitating consciousness would be only the future of anticipation, obstructed by necessity, closed to action, briefly, a future which would make hesitation as such superfluous. I hesitate precisely because the world is an ironic question: and you, what will you do? Each tentative project is like a stammering response whose progress is delineated by an outline of closed and open roads, of obstacles and implements, of openings and blank walls. But this response is immediately overshadowed by another one. The unease of indecision contrasts a definite anticipation and an uncertain decision. The world moves on while I mark time. This gives rise to the impression of being submerged, borne by the tide: the rigor of anticipation overwhelms the vagueness of projected future. Thus we can see in what sense this or that course which I have not yet adopted is possible: as a held-up project, it is also possible in the sense of a foreseen possibility reflecting the consent of things as such. Moreover, this "theoretical" possibility allies itself with the "practical" possibility of the project itself. The latter is, however, in its turn cast in a conditional mode. Possibility, as the mode of all theoretical or practical judgment, as modification of the categorical mode (so as a formal concept) thus comes to complicate the real possibility opened up, so to speak, by any project. When I say, "It is possible, all things considered, that I shan't leave Paris," I indicate specifically the problematic character of my tentative project, while at the same time corporeal possibility, the partly aroused physical power itself, appears as undecided and unformed, and my vague project floats removed from the actual, without biting into reality. There is no definite power evoked in my body which would join projected possibilities to possibilities presented by the course of the world. My intentions remain, so to speak, disembodied, cerebral, and constantly in danger of turning towards the unreal, the imaginary, which annuls reality instead of representing its transformation.

2) But my unformed intentions float removed not only from things, but in a way also from myself, so that I cannot assert, this action is me. The imputation of the project is itself conditional. An irresponsible observer-consciousness which toys with the future is always ready to degrade and abolish the working will. This modification of the relation of the project to myself is part and parcel of the modification of the project: in effect I implicate myself in the project, the anticipated action is "to be done by me." I project myself as he who will do, I impute a future action to myself in identifying the projected "I" with the "I" which projects. Now in hesitation the uncertainty of the projected direction affects the I which will do. I do not know which I I shall be. Each possible project proposes an indefinite I. Thus the young man who has not yet chosen a vocation vaguely sees himself behind a desk or in a doctor's coat without yet affirming, this man is myself. I try myself out in various roles in the mode of "maybe." The conditional project appears alien to me because the I which it implicates is not categorically myself, I have not yet attached myself to one of the "myselves" floating before me. To hesitate means to try out different "selves," to attempt an imputation. There are not two "I"s, the I that will do and the I which is presently willing. Just as the affirmation of a project entails, in a type of recurrence, the affirmation of the I who will do, so also doubt with respect to a project is also doubt with respect to myself. I am not open to any accusation or conflict with another. Yet I am not nothing—I am a self in a conditional mode. I am ready to take upon myself an act which would engender me as a declared self. To hesitate is already to confront the "they," to tear away from the crowd. The perplexed isolation into which hesitation draws me is already a sign of my voluntary vocation: as a king without a kingdom, I am an inchoate consciousness which has not yet adopted its sphere of responsibility.

This indecisive status of my self calls forth some critical observations: this inchoate, problematic mode of myself must be grasped as it presents itself. We have no right to substitute for it the image of the triumphant self which is invariably one and which I build up beyond its own hesitations. This is a cosmological prejudice: the self is objectivized, posited in abstraction as an invariable entity, ornamented with sovereign attributes: non-spatiality, unity, identity, etc. Such an abstract representation is only a hypostatized image, like the immobile banks of a river or an immutable core from which multiple, intermittent rays emerge: an "I" subsisting in a non-temporal, intact identity beyond the time in which I hesitate, seek, and choose. We must take the radical significance of hesitation seriously. I form my self by starting with the unformed existence of subjectivity itself. In hesitation I am neither an absence of consciousness—as if I could leave myself and leave the scene vacant for a mode of existence other than existence as will—nor a triumphant consciousness —as if time were mere appearance, not to be taken seriously. I am a militant consciousness, that is, capable of modulation in the diverse modes of the categorical and the conditional. I must hold on to both these aspects of the situation equally firmly. On the one hand, in hesitation I already exist as will in terms of this very call to unity, to categorical affirmation which preserves me as subject of affirmation even in the midst of perplexity and makes me an unhappy consciousness. On the other hand, in hesitation I have no way of existing other than doubt and inconsistence it-self. Thus I am my own indecision; I have neither the right nor the means of "substantivizing" existence, consciousness, or will apart from their own deficiency, nor for "hypostatizing," even marginally, this call to choice, to unity, apart from the internal multiplicity which it never manages to escape. The hesitating consciousness expresses its call to unity only by surpassing itself in a painful self-consciousness, in an anguished, solitary self-presence; returning to myself, I am dread-fully conscious of ex-isting as a living wound. But this wounded consciousness of myself in which I am reunited is no other than the intentional conscious-ness divided among its attempted projects. Unity of apperception of my intimate division cannot replace the act of choice which alone would unify me in act. Rather, it serves to call attention to my own diffusion.

3) Finally, my self's indecision is an indetermination of mo-tives, which must also be uncovered between the two distinct limits of absence and of full determination.

On the one hand it is tempting to say that I am undetermined because there is as yet no relation to motives and such relation will appear only in light of a choice. Only choice would give me reasons, and to the extent to which I have not yet chosen, I have no reasons at all. But to this it would be necessary to reply that in hesitation I am actually a tentative project related to tentative motives. The pure relation of project to motive here sheds light on the unformed relation. The elaboration of a choice elaborates motives themselves. Motivation calls attention to a difference between sides or aspects of a situation, of proposed values, of the relation of values among themselves and with the situation. To restrict the meaning of these values and to restrict choice means the same thing. Choice never constitutes value, it always invokes it; a conditional project is one "based on" unstable motives. I literally cannot count on anything, support myself on anything firm. Hesitation is the experience of the support which fades away. In this experience, relation to motives is not absent but rather nascent.

But it is also possible to make the opposite assumption, that indecision comes from conflict of motives which are already constituted and as invariable as things themselves, so that each of them, were it the only motive present, would bring about a decision. Indecision then would be a decision inhibited by another, equally inhibited decision. This error, directly opposed to the preceding, also leads us to miss the significance of the problematic consciousness of decision. The first error was due to an inadequate acquaintance with the elementary relation of decision to motives, while the second construes motives as causes. But a cause is complete prior to the effect, while a motive exists only in its relation to a choice. While choice is a choice "because of" a motive, a motive is the motive of a choice. This eidetic rule elucidates the meaning of hesitation: where choice is in no way terminated, instinct, desire, or fear have not yet acquired their definitive meaning but rather present various "aspects": motivation is itself still in suspension. In indecision I am lost among confused motives.

Thus hesitation poses for understanding the impossible task of conceiving of a will which is and yet is not yet. The arithmetic of it is particularly misleading—the multiplicity of project and of my own self is not an "exact" multiplicity, since it assumes the unity of a call to choice and transcends itself in the unity of my presence to myself; and the unity in terms of which I conceive of this call, this receptivity, this solitude is not an "exact" unity since it is the revelation of a specific multiplicity which wounds my existence. In general, nascent, unformed existence resists clarity. To be sure, it is pure description which permits us to recognize the form in the unformed and to say that the unformed is the awakening form; it warns us that consciousness can arise only as formed consciousness, though in its own infancy it is not yet itself. But in turn eidetics presupposes its own surpassing in a certain tact, in a certain spirit of delicacy which uncovers the birth, awakening, and growth within the limits of mature forms. Thus it demands existence as history.

2. Body as Source of Indetermination

WHY SHOULD the will always have to start with indetermination? Why is man a history which builds up all meaning from a primordial disorder, all form from the unformed? We have to approach this from the side of motivation, or, more exactly, from the side of the body which supplies the formal concept of motive with its matter. It is because corporeal existence is a principle of disorder and of indetermination that I cannot, at the start, be a *determined* project, *self-determination,* apperception of *determinate* reasons. The project is confused and the self unformed *because* I am encumbered by the obscurity of my reasons, submerged in the essential passivity of existence which proceeds from the body. The body comes first as a "passion of the soul," —taking that word in its basic philosophical sense of passivity of received existence.

Thus it is incarnation which governs consideration of temporality. Because of the disorder of motives, motivation takes time, and choice has to be won from a hesitating consciousness. If we depicted freedom as integral, as completely existence-creating, we should not only miss the relation to motives in general and to corporeal motives in particular, but furthermore we could not justify time as freedom's *endeavor* because we should fail to perceive the bond of temporality and incarnation. This would destroy even the fundamental meaning of human freedom, knowing that choice is not a creation.

Let us elucidate this indetermination which the body imposes on the birth of choice in light of our preceding observations concerning organic values. Life, the corporeal involuntary, and the field of motivation in general do not constitute a system. We can also express the same thing differently: in a given moment there is no *present totality* of inclinations which would authorize us to draw up a balance sheet of needs, desires, and ideas brought about by a given situation. No more is there, among apprehended values, an *evident hierarchy* which would exhaustively resolve the inquiry concerning the good. Let us inquire successively into these two ideas of present totality and evident hierarchy.

Whether we take an isolated desire or the mental constellation at a given moment, I am always confronted with an incomplete harmony. This conception is a necessary consequence of our considerations of affectivity. Affectivity is essentially disordered. Confronted with an affective impression, I can endlessly ask, what is it? All meaning, summed up in these words, must be determined, defined, that is, understood by starting with a false infinite, with an indefinite, the affect.

> Who, if not the single wind, is sighing
> Alone here with distant diamonds dying?
> Whose sob so near myself is taking place?
>
> This hand whose touch is dreaming of my face,
> Absently answering some deep call,
> Awaits the tear my frailty will let fall
> When the clearest of my destinies, apart
> In silence brings to light a broken heart.[1]

Here lies the truth of the Stoic principle according to which bodily good and evil are opinions. Each need, each desire, is problematic as long as the self does not take an attitude towards it. To be sure, it confronts me with a definite immediacy, but this immediate presence is unformed and lends itself to endless inquiry. This is why time is important in self-knowledge. Under questioning, my desires take on endlessly new aspects which lend themselves to elucidation and confrontation which are always in a flux. Only time clarifies them. We must ascribe the incompleteness of the *totality* particularly to this imprecision of each desire: the reciprocal position of two or more desires is disordered and requires time to be determined. As we shall put it later, following classical formulation, it is indeed true that the last practical judgment of preference permits a choice, but in principle the field of motivation is limitless and always leaves room for a new indeterminate horizon whose progressive determination ceaselessly gives rise to new indeterminate horizons. There is no sum of existence.

Now this idea of myself as an open totality, as a field of inquiry enclosed by a horizon, is constantly reduced by the prejudices of mental physics. We formulate an image of a total field susceptible to quasi-geometrical representation. The Gestalt the-

1. Paul Valéry, "The Youngest of the Fates," trans. J. Mathews, from *Selected Writings of Paul Valéry* (New York, New Directions, 1950[1], 1964), pp. 14–15. Copyright 1950 by New Directions. Reprinted with permission of the publisher.

ory, we know, uses this type of metaphor without discretion.[2] Alleging that the body perceived in objective space is a spatial totality, the psychologist takes it upon himself to use the isomorphic prescription for constructing a dynamics of tensions oriented towards the interior of this closed, finite totality. Such closed, finite totality has no meaning for pure description of subjectivity.

It presupposes in the first place that each system of tensions is already objectively determined, that the time required for the resolution of these tensions and for the production of a dynamic resolution is only the physical time of a cosmic process, that is, a time which introduces no novelty. It supposes that resolution is already contained in the tensions, and that the indeterminateness of the resolution is dominated from the beginning by the determinateness of the tensions themselves. In brief, the basic type of affective indetermination is completely misconceived.

Secondly, such closed, finite totality presupposes a finite sum of these systems of unresolved tensions or tensions on the way to resolution. The total field is such a finite sum. Thus it misses the original type of indefinite consciousness, that "sea of reflection," the experience of which has left its marks on Kierkegaard and Nietzsche and from which Maine de Biran suffered cruelly. We cannot be too wary of this kind of topography and dynamics even though, of all the objective models, it describes consciousness in some respects most accurately. It destroys the basic character of consciousness: it reduces to the form of oriented tension the intentionality by which consciousness surpasses even the limits of the field laid down by the body and annuls the specific relation to myself which lies at the very heart of this intentionality, by reducing it to a special system of tensions within the interior of the total field. We shall see that it misses the original indetermination which our corporeal condition imposes on willing. There is no objective equivalent of the original disorder with which I start in choosing myself. The totality is never given, it is only a regulative rather than a constitutive idea in terms of which I conceive the possibility of seeking myself ceaselessly from horizon to horizon.

But if physics can make me miss the original condition of willing, ethics can lead to a similar mistake. In effect, we could object to the critique of the idea of totality that it is not necessary,

2. Concerning the Gestalt theory, cf. Part II, chap. I, pp. 201, below for a more thorough discussion of methodological principles. In the course of this work we shall see what descriptive richness we can find behind the systematizations of Gestalt theory.

in order to decide, to have drawn up a balance sheet, a sum of needs and desires involved in the situation. It is enough that "in" affectivity I read values whose *hierarchy* stands out clearly. But a theory of *a priori* values—whose truth or falsity is not the question here—can lead us to misunderstand the disorder from which choice emerges. Even if we suppose in effect that there is some such absolute hierarchy, the quest for choice is always something other than such possible intuition of moral essences and their order. The moralists proceed to a systematic evaluation of goods without reference to actual choice. The problem of choice remains one of an *evident* good, that is, of a good such as it appears here and now to a myself as such, in a given problematic situation.

Now the problem of the evident good repeats all the preceding difficulties and adds new ones. What would an evident good mean? It is a good which appears in an affective corporeal matrix which is not perceived in itself, unconnected to all reference to myself, but which is read precisely "in" a desire, a drive, or a tendency. The value has to be "tried out" as the actual meaning of the affect: to freeze the meaning of a desire is to fix its value emphasis. The application of an *a priori* value to affectivity is not instantaneous, but rather slowly tried out. Value as such and the value of *this* desire, *this* specific value, are something quite different. The test of *this* specific value is motivation itself.

If we now observe that all value is relative, that every "good" is a "better," we can sense that the difficulties concerning the idea of a totality arise once more in the notion of a hierarchy: the comparison of two or more values is always moving and incomplete, new points of view can always be considered, the evident hierarchy depends in part on knowing what "horizons" will be determined, that is, what values left in the shadows will be carried to the center of consciousness. The incompleteness of the totality makes the hierarchy precarious. The search for a hierarchy always remains an indefinite process.

But in addition to these difficulties, which are an extension of our preceding considerations of the indefinite consciousness there arise new ones which block the uncovering of an evident hierarchy more directly. Some of these relate to the demands of action, that is, conditions which the insertion of project into the world imposes on the development of the project itself. An action is concrete, urgent, excluding its opposites. This means in the first place that between the rule we accept and the concrete decision there always remains a distance comparable to that which theoretical thought discovers between the *infima species* which specifies the abstraction and the actual presence of an existing individual. We must constantly invent some original progression in order to embody a principle in an action which is in some respects without precedent, and this invention retains an irreducible character of inexactness. In the second place it means that the situation which serves as the context of our choice itself very frequently determines the outcome of our decisions. Thus every occasion has a terminus while reflection is in principle endless. Thirdly, it means that urgency imposes improvisation. The material realization of a project demands that we sacrifice points of view which can be compounded in thought and which we are doomed to separate in act. While observer-thought says, "both/and," the law of action in the world says "either/or." The options are cruel, and even compromises have a partiality which cuts a poor figure alongside the beautiful syntheses in which all values involved are safeguarded. But such beautiful syntheses, possible according to the laws of thought, are not jointly possible according to the law of action. Inexactitude, improvisation, and partiality are conditions which action imposes on the genesis of the project, and these conditions bring us back again to the corporeal condition of willing.

Finally, the evidence of the hierarchy of values is blocked by a final circumstance inherent in the corporeal condition: organic values found in affectivity are *not comparable* with each other and with other values. Insofar as I abstractly compare pleasure and duty, life of the body and the welfare of the community, hunger and honor, an obvious subordination might appear, but when I confront a given situation, doubt obscures everything. Isn't my life an extra-systematic value, since for me all the highest values would retreat into the shadows if I were to lose my life for them? These values would continue to exist only for others, they would be lost for me; to subordinate my life to other values is to risk losing myself and thus in a way losing everything. This shadow of death gives the theoretical hierarchy a dramatic significance and transforms what for the moralists was only a serene ordering of an idea with respect to another idea into a sacrifice. The primordial attachment to life constantly interferes with this dispassionate hierarchy and tends to make values incommensurable with each other. And in effect the commensurability of values can only appear under the conditions of abstraction, of forgetting the concrete choice which, as we know, is the very principle of moral reflection. When I am searching for an evident good, relative values which I compare are, so to speak, masked under the incognito of incommensurable affective signs: the point of hunger is incomparable with the refined sensation in which I sense the powerful concept of honor; and anxiety of death is absolutely heterogeneous with the appeal of the community in danger. Thus I have to read off a sovereign hierarchy of values under the incommensurable affective signs, under pleasure, the agreeable, the sublime, etc.

All these sources of disorder at the origin of choice fit together. Social history of each individual consciousness is already a part of this affective disorder; values tried out by others, illustrated by different historical periods, are inscribed within us and make even our ideals a chaos of values, even on the most abstract level of our moral consciousness. Values accumulate within us in sedimentary layers; there is within us a feudal conscience, gravitating around honor and knightly heroism, a Christian conscience centered on love and forgiveness, a bourgeois conscience whose tone is set by ideas of liberty and toleration, a modern conscience enamored of justice and equality: all the ages of mankind are thus represented within our consciousness.

Individual consciousness further reflects in its way the contemporary social topography as it concerns human history. Now society is not a homogeneous milieu, but is disjointed and divided against itself; from the outside it seems to present a series of concentric circles—humanity, nation, profession, family—at the center of which the individual would be lodged as a benchmark. As lived by a consciousness, these multiple circles represent the claims, obligations, pressures, and appeals which infringe upon each other and demand from us incompatible actions: social topography projects itself in contradictory affective signs and painful alternatives. Family groupings, professional groupings, cultural groupings, sports groupings, artistic groupings, religious groupings, and so on, tear us apart so that a person has to create his own unity, his independence, his originality, and to dare his own style of life. The person arises from his distortion among the conflicts of duties.

Other conflicts proceed from the purity of consciousness itself. These are primarily conflicts of ends and means. How often can legitimate aims be realized only by means which conscience rejects! Can I steal a document in order to establish the innocence of the accused? Can I permit restriction of freedom of thought and action in order to augment social justice—or use violence to assure order? But the most intimate conflicts arise in that region of the soul where intransigence of our principles encounters tact, the consideration we owe those we love. Anyone who wields authority encounters this cruel conflict of the person and the rule, of love and justice. This is no longer a clearly drawn conflict brought about by social diversity but a subtle twinge, a delicate distinction on which the certainty of a friendship or the harmony of a home depend.

All these conflicts, even the most spiritual and refined ones, are finally depicted in the confused sense of the whole. The hierarchy of goods always appears under the obscure coating of desire and under a type of problematic affectivity of endless horizons. The principle of hesitation lies in the bodily confusion to which human existence is subject. All history of choice proceeds from this hesitation.

[2] The Process of Attention

Decision advances and lives as process from hesitation to choice.

Our preceding analysis gave us a glimpse of the fundamental connection between temporality and incarnation; there remains the connection between decision itself and temporality, that is, to discover what power I have over the growth of a project in time. This quest which seems constantly to postpone the study of choice is actually the only possible introduction to the understanding of that terminal act: a choice completes something, it resolves a history. Furthermore, we are convinced that we shall implicitly resolve the problem of choice if we come to understand how we conduct the internal debate in that process. The working hypothesis which we shall put to the test is that the *power of stopping the debate* is no other than *the power of conducting it* and that this *control over the succession is attention.* Or to put it otherwise: *the control over process is attention in motion; choice in a sense is a fixing of attention.*[3] What follows will show at least that this assimilation of choice to the fixing of attention constitutes only one aspect of what we shall call the paradox of choice.

The appearance of attention on the scene seems to us decisive. This theme contains a whole tangle of concepts which we shall

3. Here Husserl's analysis in *Ideas*, §§ 35–37, 80–83, 114–15, and 122, joins that of St. Thomas, Descartes, and Malebranche. (J. Laporte, "Le Libre arbitre et l'attention chez St. Thomas," *Rev. de met, et morale* [1931, 1932, 1934]; "La Liberté selon Descartes," *ibid.* [1937]; "La Liberté selon Malebranche," *ibid.* [1938].)

ultimately have to disengage and which we shall first test together.

1) We cannot push a consideration of process very far without clarifying it in terms of attention. The idea of process as order of succession only brings out the *a priori* condition of personal development. This *a priori* condition constitutes a universal structure in which the personal marks of a venture do not appear. Now process, understood as a venture, as a personal development, is alternately undergone and carried out. The mark of the activity of process is attention; attention is succession carried out. In turn, attention can be understood only as a kind of change of object, as a shifting of view, briefly, as a function of process. Process and attention thus mutually imply each other.

2) The theory of attention, though it is easy to outline as far as it pertains to perception, must be capable of extension to the entire Cogito. In attention resides my whole power when I debate within myself. If all my power is in succession and if this power is attention, we can rise above the classical debate concerning deliberation and reject the dilemma of rationalism and irrationalism. Freedom does not belong exclusively to rational motives sweeping away affective motives (or inclinations). On the other hand, it does not belong exclusively to the surge from the deep which breaks through anonymous, dead, intellectual reasons. It occurs whenever I am in command of the succession, when the shifting of focus is in my power.

3) Attention and process, understood in terms of each other, should give us a more complete understanding of the fundamental role of imagination in the creation of decision. This in effect is the fundamental idea of analysis of motives, that all the forms of the involuntary are reflected in the imagination. This testing of values in imagination is here understood in terms of the universally imaginative character of attention. To pay attention is to see in a very broad, non-intellectualistic sense, that is, in a way to develop intuitively all the relations and all the values. Attention functions in the intuitive surroundings in which we try out most abstract values. In this way the three ideas of process, attention, and imagination become intertwined. But attention is what makes the others comprehensible.

1. Succession Undergone and Succession Carried Out: Attention

THE PROGRESS of decision through detours, stagnations, leaps, and returns is a succession. The voluntary quality of choice reflects the voluntary quality of the debate from which it in one way or another proceeds. How can the form of succession be said to be *voluntary*?

All previous analyses on the level of pure description held the role of succession in suspension: up to now we have considered time only as a future dimension of the project. But this temporal dimension of anticipation is not in the least time itself. Each instantaneous act has some future horizon. Even in hesitation the project, be it ever so nascent, ever so conditional, is also an uncertain view of a vague future, a vision which turns its back on the present moment. We are constantly turned towards tomorrow. It is always now. Time is the form according to which the present changes constantly as to its content, that is, it is the order of succession of moments which are always present, and which we express in a metaphor: time is the *flux* of the present. Now each present has by its very nature a horizon of anticipation (or, as Husserl has it, of protention) and a horizon of memory or, better, in the broadest sense of the word, of retention.[4] "The present is unceasingly *becoming* an other present," that means, "each anticipated future *becomes* present" and "the present *becomes* retained past." These three formulae contain the entire meaning of the words "to become." In effect they are not disparate but all of a piece; memory grows because there is always a present becoming past and there is always a present because there is always a future which points to the horizon.

But this triple formulation of becoming only expresses a form. The words, each future moment, each present moment, each past moment, do not in the least express the fact that this form is a subjectivity, that it is myself. On what condition would the form of becoming be the growth of a person, the development of a subject?

Posed in these terms, the problem has something unique about it: it is startling not to find the marks of subjectivity in time which yet is the typical mode of relation of subjectivity, as Kant and Bergson have shown in different ways. Should we say that the marks of subjectivity attach only to acts bound by the succession? That time is the form of subjectivity because it is the order of succession of perceptions, of imaginations, of memories, etc., in a word, of operations susceptible to being reached immediately by reflection? The marks of subjectivity must be sought in certain aspects of change itself, in the aspects which

4. Husserl, *Phenomenology of Internal Time Consciousness*, trans. Churchill (Bloomington, Ind., 1964), §§ 10 ff.; *Ideas*, § 81.

no mental physics can take into account, in the very form of succession: in the realization that succession can be experienced in an active or a passive mode. Succession represents the fundamental bipolarity of human existence with which this work is concerned: it is undergone *and* carried on. If process is a personal venture, it is because the preservation or the change of a perception, of a memory, of a desire, of a project, etc., in part depend on me, and in part do not depend on me. What radically does not depend on me is that time moves on: we have already alluded to this radically involuntary aspect of drifting from before to behind in relation to prevision and project. We shall return to it systematically when we consider necessity in the first person. But in turn the spontaneity of the Cogito and, more precisely, of the voluntary mode of internal debate consists in this, that we orient ourselves within the process, that we conduct the debate by calling forward witnesses. We are thus led to seek the voluntary marks of process as such and to confine the role of our *freedom* to a certain kind of maintaining or changing our motives and thus of maintaining or changing our projects.

We have just used the word freedom: in effect the introduction of process also introduces the problem of freedom. Up to now we have recognized only the instantaneous act of *willing* (whether inchoate or determinate), characterized by project, self-determination, and appeal to motives. The concept *free* refers to temporal activity in which are engendered the act, the emission, and the advance of process which constitute the very *existence* of the act. It is an adjective which best expresses this temporal birth which is not an act but the character of an act—of a power, of a desire, of a willing. This is why there is no redundancy in speaking of free willing. The noun *willing* designates the structure of the instantaneous act which we have analyzed eidetically at the start of this chapter. The adjective *free* indicates the mode of its birth in time; the word freedom is itself only a substantivized adjective. We can also make use of the adjective *voluntary* to characterize the temporal birth of *willing*. It is thus a synonym of *free*.

Wherein consists the free, the voluntary, in the growth of our motives and in the growth of our choice? Attention is this kind of mastering of the process whose flux itself is radically involuntary. In it arises the free or the voluntary; it is itself *attentive*, that is, not a distinct operation but the free mode of all *cogitationes*.

Attention does not at first present itself as the key to the problem of deliberation (to take up a classical expression which, as we shall point out later, seems to us a bit intellectualistic). Attention presents itself first as a mode of perception. By generalization we shall be able to extract from perceptive attention (or better, from attention as a mode of perceiving) the universal characteristics which make it a kind of production of permanence or change of thought in general, in the broad sense which Descartes gives to this word. A little later we shall understand why attention in its affective or intellectual forms retains certain characteristics of perception and always remains a perceiving in a very broad sense yet to be determined; the necessity of speaking of perceptive attention, which for a moment appears to be a detour, shall thus be justified.

Attention in perception is understood as free displacement of vision. Hence the analysis of attention suppresses its own object if it omits its fundamental temporal character. Static characteristics of attention, such as they appear in an instantaneous segment of consciousness, can only be understood with reference to a certain shift of vision. Language notes the place of attention by distinguishing seeing and looking at, hearing and listening, etc., not as two different acts but as two aspects of the same perception: to see is to *receive* the qualities of the object, to look at is to extract them *actively* from the background. Attention is thus in the first instance inseparable from the receptivity of the senses, or, to put it otherwise, from general intentionality which is the structure of all *cogitatio*. Attention is attention to . . .—not attention to the representation, as if it passed over perception once more in order to reflect on it. The intentionality of attention is initial, direct intentionality which goes beyond perceiving, and by which I become in some sense all things: I pay attention to the perceived thing itself.[5] Attention is secondly the active character of perception itself. In effect the same receptivity of senses can be experienced in a passive mode of fascination, obsession, etc., or in the active mode of attention.

What then are the marks of this active mode of attention? In the first place, a very special manner of appearance of the object: it becomes detached from the background with which I am not concerned but which is involved as the context of the object noted, "co-perceived." Husserl expresses this selection thus: "Das

5. Shand, "Analysis of Attention," *Mind* (1894). We can see the mistake of all psychological descriptions which, having confused the object of perception and representations "in" consciousness, interpret attention as a duplication of representation, as if I paid attention to my representations (as Wundt, *Principles of Physiological Psychology*, trans. Titchener [London, 1904], II, sect. IV).

Erfassen ist ein Herausfassen, jedes Wahrgenommene hat einen Erfahrungshintergrund": [6] the object stands out and acquires a special clarity, not in the sense of an outline in space or a clarity as to luminosity: those two words are metaphors for attention; [7] the plain and the obscure are not qualities of an object but rather characteristics of its appearance. Herein lies the secret of attention: when an object becomes detached from the background of which it is a part, it remains the same as to its meaning. I do not know another object, but rather the same one more clearly. It is really a strange action, an action which accentuates, yet brings out something already given. In paying attention to a part of the counterpoint, I do not change the meaning of the symphony, either the meaning which it might have in itself (whatever this might mean) or for the author, or for the performer, or for another listener, but the meaning which it has for me: I now hear better what I had heard less well earlier. We can sense that this remarkable meaning of attention dominates all subsequent reflection on the meaning of attention within the broad problems of truth and freedom. [8]

We cannot then understand this strange action without taking time into consideration. This distinction of the background and the object noted implies in principle that I can let the object slide into the background and bring out another object—or another aspect of the same object—from the background. Background means that it can become the foreground, that it lends itself to attention. Attention is this very movement of observation which, in displacing itself, *changes* the mode of appearance of objects and their aspects. In effect neither the world, nor even the least object, can be given all at once. Each object edges on actual perception, it is irrepressible. But the multiple attempts, the different faces or profiles which I must go through and name in order to posit the object in its unity, do not constitute an incoherent succession. Each attempt, each perspective noted, implies some other aspect in a mode of inattention; and thus each attentive observation includes in its context new aspects ready to be noted with attention. Thus the *object* itself guides me by the

6. "The apprehension is a singling out, every object having a background in experience," *Ideas*, trans. Gibson, § 35, p. 105.

7. Dallenbach makes the fortunate distinction between attributive and perceptive clarity.

8. Bradley gives a remarkable definition of attention: "To develop the object ideally for myself such as it is in itself and so to know it"; "the object itself, however developed by the process, cannot be considered changed." "On Active Attention," *Mind* (1901).

solicitations of its context; however, *I* orient myself among the appearances, *I* displace the main accent, *I* turn the object or perhaps *I* develop the same side in order to exhibit its multiple details, or *I* grasp it as part of a broader whole.

We note from this that attention is purest as observation is more interrogatory and docile. The lowest degree of attention is constituted by those anticipatory schemata with which we approach an object in order to recognize in it an expected presentation with which we agree in advance, as when a child looks for the head of a wolf in the clouds and branches on a hidden-picture puzzle. I am likewise more attentive when I am least attempting to "fill out" an empty perception intuitively and when I most diligently explore the field of perception. Thus it is neither preperception nor desire which makes for attention, but the naïveté of observation, the innocence of observation, the reception of the other as the other. Through this active availability I inscribe myself into the account of the object. The true name of attention is not anticipation but wonder; it is the opposite of precipitation and prevention. Error, Descartes reminds us, is in the first place memory, the memory of an intuition and not intuition, and Malebranche adds that preconceived notions obscure the truth in proportion to our inattention. Perhaps there is no act of attention in the sense in which Kant said that there can never be an act of good will; it is a limit, but one whose meaning we understand, and this meaning elucidates the degraded form of fascinated observation, which is then conceived as lack of attention, as an alienated freedom. This understanding suffices for a fundamental ontology of willing: it points out that the highest activity brings about greatest receptivity. The error of empirical psychology lies in having explained free attention by a bound attention. Association of ideas, principles of interest, laws or organization of the field of consciousness, etc., are expressions which annul the very essence of attention. When an idea is conceived as forcing another according to the necessity of contiguity or resemblance, when the object of my desire not only attracts my observation, but also draws it, occupies it, captures it, absorbs it, when the form and the content become distributed and reorganized according to laws of stress imposed by the distribution and reorganization of tensions issuing from the very forms of needs and quasi-needs constituting the total field, it is no longer I who orient myself. The "observing" has vanished, merged into its contrary: I have become a victim of the object.

Thus the essence of attention is that temporal shift of vision which turns towards or turns away from and thus makes an object appear such as it is in itself, that is, such as it already covertly was in the background.

Likewise the full distinction of the voluntary and the involuntary does not stand out apart from the temporal character of attention. In effect pure attention and fascination are equally characterized by the division of the field at a given moment between the illuminated foreground and the obscure background. An instantaneous segment of my mental life does not permit me to distinguish the voluntary or passive character of observation. What either is or isn't voluntary is the *becoming* of its division. In fascination, I have lost my power of changing the object: the flux of consciousness is, as it were, coagulated, congealed. Perhaps all fascinated consciousness retains a nostalgia for that free movement, as the "Swan" in Mallarmé. Attention is thus a mastery over the process, or more exactly the power of making appear, in accord with the rule of succession, objects or aspects of objects, by drawing them from the background or by letting them become effaced in the ground which constitutes the backdrop of inattention for any observation.

2. Attention and Deliberation: The False Dilemma of Intellectualism and Irrationalism

ATTENTION AS IT FUNCTIONS in perception is only the most striking example of attention in general which consists of turning towards or away from. . . . The act of looking must be generalized, following the double demand of a philosophy of the subject and of reflection concerning the form of succession. On the one hand attention is in effect possible wherever the Cogito in the broadest sense holds sway; as Descartes enumerated it, "not only hearing, willing, imagining, but also feeling here is the same as thinking." It is the active mode followed by all intentional acts of the Cogito so that even feeling can in some sense be an action. Attention is what relates all these intentional acts to me, as luminous rays to the core from which they emanate. Attention is what reveals the "I" in its acts and justifies me in adding to the definition of the Cogito, "for it is so self-evident that it is I who doubts, who listens, and who desires that there is no need to add anything to explain it." Even in sensation, the "I" is *my* vision.[9]

9. Cf. Malebranche, *De la recherche de la vérité*, Book VII, sect. i, § 4: "Attention of the mind is to the objects of mind what the fixed look of our eyes is to the objects of our eyes." Concerning the generalization of the "look," see Husserl, *Ideas*, § 35–37.

In addition, attention is possible wherever time is the form of subjectivity. It is the active mode of the temporal form; it is time in first person, active time. The "I" is the *mobility* of my vision even in sensation.

Let us apply this conception to our problem. How, let us ask, does a decision subsist in the process between hesitation and choice, and how can this process depend on us? The study of attention in perception contains the germ of an answer. Attention is something which unfolds in time, accentuating and bringing to light various alternative "aspects" of a disordered situation, the diverse "value aspects" of a practical puzzle.

Our study of hesitation has shown us that indefiniteness of the project was linked with indefiniteness of motives in general and with indefiniteness of affective motives in particular. Hesitation is thus linked with a certain passivity, the essential passivity of my corporeal existence. Now we can say that the clarification of our motives thanks to time depends on a certain activity, the essential activity of the free vision of attention. Time, which is the price of this clarity, is thus both the consequence and the counterpart of incarnation. Hence the problematic character of affectivity is on the one hand rooted in the corporeal indefiniteness and on the other hand is open to attentive inquiry. Starting with this, clarification consists on the one hand of disentangling values tangled in affectivity, and on the other hand of bringing together the successive tentative values within a progressively self-affirming idea. In this respect, attention to values resembles attention to things: it separates individual aspects of the same value from the context of that value, in order to confirm it by successive tests and by summing them up. When a value first begins to emerge, we leave it, consider something else, then return to the original profile of the value which stands out more clearly by contrast; another aspect of the situation arises which reveals a confusion within the idea, etc. No motive and no value is given all at once; an idea of value unifies under a simple rule of meaning a multiple succession of attempts. In this way, attention proceeds towards a separation of confounded aspects which it relates to different values and to a unification of scattered aspects which it relates to simple values. Motivation is clarified in time by this double operation of attention. In nascent and maturing motivation, attention shows definitely the difference between motive and cause. When we said that desire inclines without compelling, we stated negatively what we shall now formulate in positive terms: the definitive form of my desire depends on my attention. Bad faith consists in hiding behind a determinism. Only the omission of attention makes passion fateful. Apart from a theory of the fault, I affirm myself as a free vision in hunger, thirst, sexual desire, the will to power, and the wish of inertia, the impulse to imitate and obey, and the obligation and appeal issuing from the values of truth, justice, and love. This assurance that I am such free vision in time is one which I must constantly rediscover just as I must constantly rediscover the Cogito from which it is not distinct. No one can give it to me, or deprive me of it. It has no objective guarantee.

The recourse to attention, by posing the problem of freedom in a radical form, enables us to rise above the classical debate between intellectualism and anti-intellectualism and to refuse the false dilemma it poses.

On the one hand, it is false that determination by reasons rather than by impulses or desires is enough to make us free.[10] A rational development of ideas, a consideration linked by necessity akin to that of mathematical reasoning, is not in principle a free activity. In effect it is not enough to oppose an act of judgment to the tyranny of desire, to make much of this creation of truth in which ultimate consequences are discerned, moral implications exposed, and the parts in question related to the whole edifice of our happiness and our honor. We still have to say what it is that would make a judgment an action and not a determinism of ideas. This approach attempts to say that the highest decision, most worthy of the name freedom, is one which corresponds to the clearest and most comprehensive collation of our determining reasons. But it has not yet provided a conception of freedom insofar as it has only considered the mutual implication of objects of thought. This implication, though it is akin to geometric necessity and strongly contrasted with the fortuitous and mechanical connection of our image-association, does not by itself characterize thought as ours. What makes thought our act is the attention by which we receive and appropriate it. To adopt the level of clarity, to accept meditation rather than to take an unreflecting leap into action, is freedom not only in its terminus but also at the root of reason in virtue of an initial act of attention which from the beginning of the debate makes the problem to be resolved worth while. Attention lies at the source of the idea as an initial questioning aimed in the highest direction. Thus it is the default of freedom in attention which in some moments makes

10. Jean Nabert, *L'Expérience intérieure de la liberté* (Paris, 1924); re limits of determinism, see pp. 108–23.

all dialectic of ideas ineffective, boring, even inaccessible, and removes us from reason. Purity of the word, as Malebranche said, is always a response to the entreaty of attention.

But attention is not only the receptivity which sustains an idea in a given moment, it is also the mobility of vision which conducts the debate from moment to moment. The inherent force of ideas ceases to carry us along only if we continue to shift our attention along the multiple inflections suggested by the field of inattention attached to each distinct idea. Intellectualism pretends to believe that only one series of thoughts unfolds its implications in a section of the process under consideration: the truth is that we must constantly orient ourselves in a maze of intersections and badly marked roads. Practical problems are only rarely amenable to obvious interpretation. The order of action is the order of the probable. The heterogeneity of the values involved and the confusion of aspects of a situation make the problems of shifting more important than the problems of continuity, discontinuous passages more numerous than logical connections.

Hence rationality of a consideration not only fails to suffice to characterize my freedom, but it is not even necessary. It is always true that to deliberate is to raise our motives to the level of clarity and distinction, but it is not always true that these conform to what is commonly called rationality. An idea is clear when it stands at the center of our vision, when it is present to mind. Attention brings about its presence. And if distinction is the peak of clarity, the dissociations which it brings about apply to the realm of feelings as much as to that of ideas. A distinction is not always or even principally a rational operation in the sense of a train of thought conforming to deductive or dialectical logic. There can be only a calculus of personal interests, of means, of consequences, and of efficaciousness according to the rule of economy (maximum effect with minimum means) which assumes the appearance of a rational argument. Once the ends themselves are questioned, we run into incomparable qualities of existence each of which gives rise to a context and engenders attitudes by affinity and assonance, guided by a feel for the situation which is not susceptible to rigorous measurement.

Consequently the determination by even the most logically linked reasons and the determination by feelings less susceptible to being reduced to intellectual maxims equally depend on the freedom of the look which considers now this, now that, which reunites different aspects in one unique value and which dissociates confused elements into distinct values. Apart from this, it is the community of one and the same operation, of attention, which confers a common freedom on the two highly disparate forms of motivation, motivation by feeling and motivation by reason.

The same conviction permits us in turn to dismiss the pretensions of the Bergsonian type of irrationalism, as for example Bergson formulates it in the period of *Time and Free Will*. We owe too much to Bergson not to acknowledge our debt of gratitude to him. Many critical elements of Bergsonianism remain admirable, such as the critique of determinism as spatialization (and that of the anticipation resulting from it) which is so closely akin to the critique of communal objectification in our work and in other contemporary thought. Most of all he has taught us to conceive of freedom and process in terms of each other. By contrast, anti-intellectualism and pragmatism seem to us the most outdated aspects of the Bergsonian corpus. Reason appears to Bergson only as a train of thoughts which are dead and alien to life; in his eyes, our reasons are most of the time posthumous justifications of our choice. Adopting for a moment the language of determinism in order to destroy its foundation, he appeals to that "more attentive psychology" which "often shows us effects which precede their causes." [11] Thus rational motivation, rapidly discredited, returns to that deeper self from which all authentic decisions proceed. But we can ask whether Bergson has not omitted the essential function of attention and has not thus become caught in an opposition which can only take on a new meaning in the perspective of a consideration of attention: the opposition of alive and dead, of the superficial and the profound. In effect, by a curious reversal, the tyranny of dead reasons seems actually to give place to a vital, passionate necessity. "It is the profound myself which reemerges on the surface. The external crust breaks up, yielding to an irresistible thrust. . . ." [12] But what have we gained in thus returning to indistinct motives and vital coloration? We have to admit at once that such "irresistible thrusts" do not make us free. It is no help if enthusiasm is imbued with our entire mentality, it is no help that the somewhat spatial juxtaposition of ideas stamped by language and by society is replaced by a living interpenetration of continuous flux, it is no help even that

11. Bergson, *Time and Free Will*, trans. Pogson (New York, 1910). Translation in text mine from French original, *Essai sur les données immédiates de la conscience* (Paris, 1889), pp. 118–19.—Trans.
12. *Ibid.*, pp. 126–217.

I am present as a whole in an act—what is essential is that I should be the master of that flux rather than being subjected to it, in a word, that I should sustain it by attention, appropriate the very level on which I find myself. For my fault is precisely to remain on the level of the superficial myself; if not, how could we say with Bergson himself that "we often *abdicate* our freedom in most serious circumstances, and that by inertia or flabbiness, we *let* this same local process run its course when our entire personality *ought*, so to speak, vibrate. . . ."? [13] How should we speak of this "inexplicable distaste for willing" by which we "push back into the obscure depths of our being" [14] those deep feelings which erupt to the surface of our life in the moment of freedom? We would say that the surface self is the self from which attention has been omitted. Our deepest self consists of our power of turning our attention to the most earnest and precious values. This power of attention is what engenders our revolt against the values which seem to us as canceled as old stamps.

If we seek to understand the strictly methodological reasons which deflected Bergson's profound thought in the direction of a suspect irrationalism, we encounter a certain number of prejudices which he shares with his associationist opponents and which are due to the lack of a prefatory eidetic analysis. We can say that for him, as for them, a motive is not distinguished from a cause, and that it is necessary for him to immerse the clearest and most distinct outlines of motives in a changing fluidity in order to save the originality of the self. If we keep the distinction between motive and cause clearly in mind and if we rediscover the freedom of attention at the root of most distinct motives we are no longer compelled to link freedom with a process psychology which in the end simply and purely eliminates the very idea of motive together with the idea of distinction among motives. Bergson affirms that the plurality of motives comes from the reconstruction of mental reality in a sort of interior space where alternatives and their motives are juxtaposed, as two ways on an ideal map, as "inert, indifferent things awaiting our choice"; these "inert, so to speak solidified, alternatives" are not, he says, merely symbolic representations: "time is not a line along which we pass"; there are not two alternatives but "a multitude of successive and different states within whose web I disentangle, by an effort of imagination, two opposite directions . . . and a self which

13. *Ibid.*, p. 127. Ricoeur's italics.—Trans.
14. *Ibid.*

lives and develops due to the effect of these very hesitations until the free action detaches itself from it like overripe fruit." [15]

This analysis is not convincing because Bergson never distinguished acts and the correlates which they intend; he confuses them constantly under the name of states of consciousness. Likewise, the experienced succession of acts of hesitation, which he analyzed masterfully, does not permit him to understand that, through successive attempts, these multiple intentions could come to constitute a small number of points to consider and of motives whose meanings become progressively distinct and unified. A critique as profound as Bergson's critique of spatialization of experience does not itself in any way preclude the possibility of a real plurality of intentional motives arising within the infinity of continuous acts. Yet this plurality is not mental, it is not a plurality within consciousness as the focus of acts: it is an intentional plurality. This serious confusion taints all Bergsonian psychology which always seeks to elude the problem of clear conflicts and rationally enumerated alternatives, taking refuge in the clear-obscure realm of organic metaphors. We do not believe that there is any need to criticize the multiplicity of distinct reasons in order to save freedom. For this distinction among reasons, sentiments, and motives may itself be the work of freedom through the attention which guides it.

Yet more fundamentally, Bergson's thought instinctively refuses to name that power of attention because it would be an indeterminate power, a power of paying attention to this or that, of placing oneself on this or that level. Bergson, who at this point still remains too faithful to empiricism, would like freedom to be a fact and not a power, a capacity. This is undoubtedly the key to his tenacious criticism of the idea of possibility which runs all through his works. For him a power which is not actually determinate is always a retrospective illusion. *Time and Free Will* is an attempt to eliminate this idea of "equal possibility of two actions or two contrary wills." [16] The power of opting for the opposite alternative is only a retrospective impression of having had the power of choosing something else. This is precisely where the criticism of alternative as a posthumous spatialization comes in. We do not believe that we can eliminate from freedom this *potestas ad opposita* which is attention itself. We have just seen that the criticism of the spatialization of consciousness leaves the intentional plurality of grasped motives intact. On the other hand,

15. *Ibid.*, p. 137.
16. *Ibid.*, pp. 130–37.

it in fact appears that the impression of having been able to choose another alternative is not of a piece with the spatializing illusion—it is itself an immediate datum of consciousness. To be sure, we often do not formulate it until after the fact: the experience of the fault, as Nabert has shown,[17] does not belong to explanation but to the most primitive revelation of ourselves to which Bergson, incidentally, appeals. Retrospection does not invent a power which did not exist at the time of the act; it discovers it because after the fact it is no longer possible to hide it and to lie to oneself. The wasted or lost possibility arises before me as a living reproach: attention, *no longer preoccupied,* accuses me.

A doctrine of attention thus appears to us to be most perceptive and most respectful of the infinite richness of my motivation. The breadth of motivation which we have often defended finds its most basic subjective source here. On the one hand, rationality of motives is only a privileged form which the course of motivation adopts in certain favorable cases; on the other hand, the affective heat, the indivisible mass of our personality brings an enthusiasm and weight which no calculus and no dialectic can equal.

But freedom always remains that vision, that silence in which all voices echo. It is always attention which creates time, wins time, so that all these voices speak distinctly, that is to say, in a succession.

[3] CHOICE

1. The Event of Choice: Termination of Attention and Irruption of Project

IN THE PURE DESCRIPTION of the project, as we attempted it in the first chapter, the true character of decision remained hidden. As we had defined it, in an instantaneous segment, as the act of designating in general a future action which depends on me and which is in my power, we missed the fundamental characteristic of the act itself as a forward movement of my existence. Pure description remains the statics of acts. The projecting of the project, the active determination of the action and of myself, taken as a *passage* towards determination, briefly, the dynamics of the act, can only be clarified in a temporal perspective. Even if the act represents an eruption in the process

17. Nabert, *Éléments pour une éthique,* pp. 3–19.

as a momentary outburst—which, we shall see, is never more than part of the truth—that instant still is a modification of a process. The passage to the act from a myself which has the courage to face the act and which imputes it to itself in a prereflexive, disturbing way, the generous thrust of consciousness which makes the leap represented by a project, genuinely concern the birth of choice as an event. This is why we could say above that, apart from an attempt to correlate them with a lived history, words like thrust, leap, project, or act remain incomprehensible.[18] Put back in its place at the conclusion of a growth from which it proceeds, the project appears as a choice. In effect the description of the project within an instantaneous segment suspends the previous history of the project and the indetermination which it brings to an end. Choice is the event which resolves into a univocal project the antecedent indetermination which, in most favorable instances, is raised to the dignity of an alternative in the process of clarification of motives.

Now the event of choice stands in a peculiar relation to the process which precedes it: it *completes* it and at the same time *breaks it off*. A living dialectic constantly brings us back from one aspect of choice to the other: choice as the *peak* of previous growth and as the *surge* of novelty.

This paradoxical temporality of the act of choosing should permit us to throw new light on the fundamental paradox around which this entire first part revolves, the paradox of initiative and obedience, of activity and receptivity, of launched possibility and received justification. In effect this very paradox duplicates the paradox of existence chosen and existence undergone, reflected in the temporal paradox of an act which completes a process and breaks it off. This in fact is where this temporal paradox, which we shall examine at length, joins the paradox of activity and receptivity. The event of choice always permits two readings: on the one hand it is tied to the preceding examination whose end, or, more exactly, *resolution* it is; on the other hand it genuinely *inaugurates* the project as a simple intention of future action. Now it is easy to recognize in this resolution of examination the resolution of that very attention which we have considered in motion in the interior debate which it carried out. Thus it is this aspect of choice which all our previous analysis permits us to elucidate. Attention which becomes fixed on a certain constellation of motives is the receptive aspect of freedom; it is, up to

18. Cf. above, chap. I, p. 37.

the moment of choice, the reverse of the irruption of novelty which brings about freedom's forward movement.

This double aspect of choice is already suggested by the metaphors which can be culled from the etymology of the abstract words pertaining to the idea of choice. To choose is to close off a debate: con-clude, *ent-schliessen;* it is also to cut off, to cut the Gordian knot of hesitation, to de-cide. Just as the word pro-ject refers to a future intentionality, these two images allude to a previous history behind which choice places a concluding period. Future intention thus is not the whole story; it even seems that the more noticeable aspect here is not the thrust but the resolution of hesitation. We can understand this aspect better if we bear in mind that all hesitation, all alternatives stand out of a ground of a willing without alternatives which supports the future-oriented thrust of consciousness, as in the case of the tame decisions proposed by laboratory psychologists to their students: "Here are two numbers, choose for good reason addition *or* multiplication." [19] The alternative is like a hollow core within a broader decision, present in the form of a posture—the subject accepts the experiment, consents to carry out an arithmetic operation and to do it in the form of one of the two alternatives. The voluntary complex is what gives the debate as such a forward thrust and bestows on choice through which it will be expressed a future mark, the sign "to be done by me" which the pure act of attention to ultimate reasons does not include. We assume it equally in the routine decisions of daily life: What shall I do on my vacation? Shall I go to the country or to Paris? But it is certain that I want a change of occupation and a break in the pattern of my work: this alternative is always lodged at the very heart of a broader project which is in some respect univocal.[20] Does it perhaps belong to an absolutely basic alternative, of the form "to be or not to be"? [21]

Thus the moment of resolved attention is the gesture indicating the alternative which will be chosen, of constituting the direction of an action held in suspension by hesitation. By a sort of mental gesture, I show, as by an indication to a fictitious spec-

---

19. Michotte and Prüm, *op. cit.*—Concerning the relation of choice to disjunctive willing, cf. A. Pfänder, *Phänomenologie des Wollens,* pp. 114–18; Shand, "Types of Will," *Mind* (1896); Bradley, "The Definition of Will," Part III, *Mind* (1904).

20. Michotte's subjects accept the univocal task of "working a problem," *op. cit.,* pp. 147–64.

21. Gilson, "Essai sur la vie intérieure," *Rev. Phil.* (1920).

tator who is at the same time myself, the "what" of the action, while at the same time this "what" is cloaked by the spirit of decision with fundamental characteristics of thrust, of "to be done by me in the future." [22] Thus the gesture triggers the thrust of willing which at the same time precedes it and envelops it. By itself it belongs not to the prospective dimension of the thrust towards the future, but to that quasi-reminiscence constituted by attention which considers the "anterior" worth of its values, as if the quest for value were a kind of memory with respect to a thrust of action tending towards the future. But in turn this end of the examination is the beginning of action: the resolution of attention is the launching of the project.

The second image—to choose is to break off—confirms the relation of choice and of resolved attention suggested by the image of cloture. The resolution of a debate which we close off is indeed the resolution of an operation of separating akin to perceptive attention.[23] I break off a part from the web of my perplexities, I "bear it in mind," I "refer" it. By this disjunction I simplify myself and collect myself in a univocal project. This practical separation is the counterpart of the main act of theoretical consciousness, which, however, relates instead of separating. While two ideas are compossible, the two actions which correspond to them are practically incompatible. The law of theoretical thought is the conjunction "both/and"; the law of action is the disjunction "either/or." How do we avoid closing the disjunction of the gesture of ex-traction, of ex-ception in which we have already recognized the essence of attention? If we take away from choice the effort which elaborates it and which we rediscover later, and abstract the future thrust of the project, there remains a resolved vision. It is the same essence of seeing which appears in different contexts, depending on whether we look at an object, a value, or an alternative to take. Undoubtedly no vision makes consciousness tend towards the future and thrust itself towards

22. Michotte's work is interesting because he has isolated choice from all eventual achievement and thus stripped bare the "indications," the mental gesture which fixes the alternative, without interference from a future aim; op. cit., pp. 187–204. In contrast Narziss Ach's work, Ueber den Willensakt und das Temperament (Leipzig, 1910), deals with a future determination. In a concluding note, op. cit., pp. 310–20, Michotte explains very clearly how a simple gesture of "indicating" the chosen alternative, a gesture without a future aim, becomes the condition of realization of an antecedent project, the project of doing what one shall choose; ibid., p. 316.

23. We also find such parallel in Michotte, op. cit., pp. 318–19. Minkowski suggests the same assimilation of indicating and "looking"; looking, he says, "is a phenomenon of a general order of which looking with eyes is no more than one mode." (Vers une cosmologie [Paris, 1936], p. 53.)

an action which depends on it. This is why we have not said that willing means paying attention. Willing, to be sure, is the structure of the project, of self-determination, and of motivation, but the voluntary birth of the project leaves room for the movement and resolution of vision. The same power of preferring, which in the context of investigation of things is properly called looking in a strict sense (looking with my eyes), in the context of investigation of values is called deliberation; finally to cease deliberating is to choose. And yet choice is never only this resolution. Rather, this resolution, in resolving the ambiguity of a divided project, makes it appear as a simple thrust. This is why choice seems to mask the moment of attention, and does not appear to retain anything from the investigation of values, of the inspection of the good. The *resolution* of the attention which becomes fixed on such motives is as if swallowed up in the *projecting* of the project. However, deliberation is completed *in* the choice, as the project is sought *in* hesitation and the preceding debate. In one sense decision does not surge forth from nothing: in hesitation I was already being prepared for a decision; in choice the look which elects an alternative frees from encumbrances the basic, initial thrust of deciding which constitutes me as existence.

Thus it becomes apparent that the movement and the resolution are two sides of one and the same temporal freedom of attention which can consider this or that, or can stop considering and elect.

This paradox of an attention which *resolves* the consideration of its reasons and of a project which *irrupts* rises above the oldest difficulty involved in a psychology of choice: if choice does not issue from examination, what is the point of deliberating? And if choice is not an *original* act, how do we free ourselves from the morass of reflection? Perhaps the continuity and discontinuity, the *ripening* and the *irruption*, are paradoxically imbedded in all voluntary processes, and perhaps it is possible, by starting from this paradox, to include most disparate cases in a single view of the whole, cases in which choice seems to fall like ripe fruit from the very fecundity of internal debate, and cases in which it seems to burst forth like a flash in the night.

This temporal dialectic of process and of the instant borders on pure description and in turn leads to the limits of a genuinely metaphysical problem which we shall reserve for the following chapter, the problem of the *indetermination* appropriate to freedom which does not reduce itself to an absence of "reasons." We are on the verge of understanding that the *sui generis* indetermination of attention is the obverse of self-determination of the act as a leap, as an irruption. We shall here deliberately avoid this final difficulty, and attempt two "readings" of choice, a "reading in terms of continuity" and a "reading in terms of discontinuity," one of which defers to the role of anterior deliberation and the other to the novelty of choice. We shall show at the same time the necessity and the limitations of these two unilateral readings: the failure of a synthesis of these two readings itself constitutes the paradox. This double reading will provide an opportunity to examine the theories of choice whose defect, we shall note, is being unilateral and seeking to escape the paradox. We shall not forget that this temporal and, so to speak, horizontal paradox of continuity and discontinuity in process sums up the vertical paradox of motivation and project, that is, finally, of the involuntary and the voluntary. The event of choice is precisely the practical reconciliation of the paradox in the moment which simultaneously brings the process to a resolution and bursts forth into novelty.

2. A Reading in Terms of Continuity: Choice as the Resolution of Deliberation

THE FIRST READING is that of classical philosophy with an intellectualistic bend. It can be traced back to two propositions. The first is that to resolve on an alternative is to resolve motivation: to choose is nothing other than to cease deliberating. The second is that the resolution of motivation is nothing: the extinction of a movement poses no particular problem.

The first proposition—which is an affirmation—is true and we shall defend it against the negations suggested by the second reading. The second proposition—the negative—is false: it will lead us to the other aspect of the paradox.

The affirmative proposition can easily be understood in light of all we have said above concerning hesitation and deliberation. The project, though it is a novel event, is not a novel structure which appears suddenly at the conclusion of an interior process which makes no allowance for it. Hesitation is a testing of multiple projects. Consequently choice is not created by an irruption of a projecting consciousness but by the simplification of a hesitating one. Now how does the project move forward? By the progress of motivation. I am always a consciousness which attempts a project *because*. . . . To hesitate is to have confused reasons, to deliberate is to disentangle and clarify these reasons, to choose is to bring out a preference among the reasons. We should miss the nature of willing if we imagined that prior to choice I move among reasons without projects and that in the moment of choice I stand amid projects without reasons. The project ripens slowly, together with its reasons. Confused reasons mean an equivocal project, clarified reasons mean a univocal project. Hence we might well say that to choose is to resolve hesitation, to resolve attention on a group of motives. The judgment of preference which is thus found to be the last one *ipso facto* determines choice. It is not just that the judgment of preference weighs externally on the choice after the manner of a physical necessity—we know well that in a decision the motive aspect and the project aspect are distinguished only abstractly: in virtue of the relation of the project to the motive, the determination of the ultimate practical judgment is indissoluble from the expression of the choice. Thus choice is a resolution of deliberation.

This reading prevails in all the cases where deliberation tends to be a complex reasoning and where the choice tends to be a logical conclusion. The eliminated alternative evaporates by itself because it appears incompatible with the rules invoked in the debate. This is the limit indicated by the decisions which Kant related to rules of competence. The more a debate concerns means relative to precise rules and not rules placed in question once more in the moment of decision, the more does the debate tend to be a technical discussion, resolved on the basis of economy. This is also the case, though more rarely, if a debate concerns the ends but introduces only homogeneous ends which are already strongly systematized in a coherent ideal of life. Then deliberation does not lead to those deep-seated conflicts concerning values such as those which we shall analyze presently. Deliberation becomes resolved since one alternative is clearly related to the general maxims of a life habitually and forcibly confined to principles. I recognize my line of conduct in the new decision: I recognize myself, I am in agreement with myself. Choice is the rational recognition of that agreement.

Yet this reading remains basically dependent on a *limit-construction* which is more of an idea in a Kantian sense than an abstraction in an Aristotelian sense: we discover reality as related to a schema of which it is at best a remote approximation. We shall see that the event of choice gives rise precisely to two contradictory limit-constructs. Classical writers usually oriented psychology of will by reference to an integrally clarified idea of the will. In light of this ideal, they understood the complexity of the situations of daily life as a *defect* due to lack of reasons. Thus they held in low esteem what the moderns like to call the grandeur of choice conceived as audacious, as involving risk, even as anxious. Rather they invite us to seek the essence of our freedom not at all in the choice risked amid the shadows, but in the very mastery which we exercise over our judgment when it is clearest. The perfection of freedom is perfection of judgment.

This lasting message of intellectualism is one which contemporary philosophy must not forget, even though it has to complement it with another message. It can be summed up in several formulae. Choice conforms in the end to practical judgment; freedom of indifference, to which risked choice tends by default of adequate reason, is then the lowest degree of freedom. It is defective in comparison with the perfectly clear decision whose freedom is proportionate to the light which makes it clear.[24]

The necessity of returning nonetheless to another reading and to another limit-construct is underlined by the obstacles encountered by all attempts to eliminate from choice all elements which are novel with respect to previous deliberation. Is it true that the resolution of deliberation is nothing in itself?

Here we can reap the fruit of the critique of intellectualism initiated above in light of a consideration of attention: the gesture of resolving examination is itself a positive reality, because it is an operation of that attention in whose free movement consists the freedom of even the most intellectual debate. Thinking is an act, reasoning as an attentive reception of reasons is an act. If, then, a succession of *acts* of thought poses a problem which is not reducible to a problem of the linking of the *contents* of thought, it is understandable that the resolution of attention constitutes an equally irreducible problem. Even if it were true that choice is reached with the last practical judgment, even if this last judgment tended towards the type of rational conclusion, to conclude is to move thought forward by taking a position with reference to premises. I do not have to come to a conclusion: if I do, the conclusion, to be sure, is necessary: but this very necessity is one which I bring out by adding a step to my progression. We can understand the judgment of Thomist psychology in this sense: choice issues from the last practical judgment, but to make a judgment, even the last judgment, is the work of freedom.

24. Cf. texts from St. Thomas, below, pp. 190 and 192; Descartes, *Meditations*, IV; *Treatise on Passions*, art. 20; *Principles*, §§ 32 ff. and especially *Letter to P. Mesland*, May 2, 1644, and February 9, 1645; Malebranche, *De la recherche de la vérité*, Book I, sects. i, ii, Book IV, sect. i.

Thought inspired by Stoicism, by Spinoza, or even by Liebniz tends to omit consideration of acts and to sacrifice it to the consideration of contents of thought and their relation. Thus it misses attention, both its movement and its resolution. Starting with this omission, it wants to lock the philosophy of freedom in a false dilemma of the freedom of indifference which it proscribes and the rational determination which it eulogizes. Ignoring attention, which sustains reasons themselves, it cannot encounter the true indetermination of acts which is rooted in the clearest decision, that is, the decision least indifferent to reasons and most determined by these reasons as to its contents.[25]

The second reading prepares us to understand this indetermination to which we shall devote our final consideration. This reading, however, approaches the problem from a different aspect, taking as its theme choice as a novel event, as an original act.[26]

3. A Reading in Terms of Discontinuity: Choice as the Irruption of the Project

THE SECOND READING is that of voluntaristic and existential philosophies. It makes room for an affirmation which deals with the defects of the preceding negation: to become resolved is something, it is actually the most notable moment of freedom, the moment of the leap, of the jump, of the thrust, of the irruption.[27] But this affirmation in turn leads to a negation. Its proponents like to say that choice is what gives motives their definitive form. Just as the first reading, stressing the guiding role of motivation, tends to make choice into a nothing, so the second reading, starting from choice as a positive act, tends to annul the receptivity of attention and thereby its docility to values. This shift brings us back to the first reading, that of the classics, which measured arbitrary freedom by understood freedom.

This second reading is suggested by all our earlier reflections concerning the project as the projecting of action and projecting of the self ahead of itself. More precisely, the novelty of choice has the appearance of categorical modality within the network of

25. Descartes, *Letter to P. Mesland*, May 2, 1644.

26. Here we can no longer follow Malebranche who reduces "consent" to "cessation of search and examination: to a rest which would be a nothing."

27. William James, *Psychology: Briefer Course* (New York, 1900), pp. 423 f.; Lequier, *Recherche d'une première vérité*, pp. 107–20, 137 f.; "La Feuille de charmille" and Analyse de l'acte libre" (fragments published by Dugas, *Rev. de met. et. mor.* [1922], esp. pp. 296–310); Bergson, *Time and Free Will*, chap. III; K. Jaspers, *Philosophie*, II, 149–209; J.–P. Sartre, *Being and Nothingness*, pp. 73–106, 433–556.

172 / DECISION: CHOICE & ITS MOTIVES

a consciousness which unfolds itself in a conditional mode. Thus discontinuity concerns a change of modality: through choice the three dimensions of decision—the triple relation to project, to self, and to motives—surge forward into a categorical mode. The project, for one, becomes a genuine imperative: I command the event in general. The indicator, "to be done by me," itself becomes categorical. The possible which I open up already bites into things by the power awakened by my body instead of floating at a distance from the actual. At the same time, while the project becomes categorical, I determine myself categorically. I choose *myself* in determining *what* I shall be in my doing. The projected myself gives consistency to my self, to the self which is at present projecting. Before the choice, I was only the unity of a wish to choose and the unity of painful consciousness of my intimate division. I create myself as an actual living unity in my act: in that moment of choice I come to myself, I come out of the internal shadows, I irrupt as myself, I ek-sist. Finally, in the choice the constellation of motives itself is fixed in its definitive order. Motivation itself becomes categorical: I choose because. . . . A preference becomes consecrated beyond return. All the "but's" disappear, contrary reasons are effaced in the background of inattention, henceforth no longer convertible to the foreground, at least as long as the project under consideration is not itself placed in question.

Such is the novelty of choice: suddenly my project is *determinate,* my reasons become *determinate,* I become *determinate.* This triple determination—or resolution—is the irruption of choice.

This reading prevails in all the cases in which some *breakdown* of motivation emphasizes the discontinuity. We have already noted the abrupt deflection of the progression of reasoning in all the instances where we have to find a new solution to an unexpected problem. As psychology of invention stresses, already the progression of knowledge brings out this abruptness. We seek for a long time, test clues, and try out working schemata when suddenly all our data become regrouped in a new presentation: that is the moment of discovery and invention.[28]

If such a rupture is possible in intellectual understanding, it is not surprising that voluntary choice, whose givens are more affective, more disparate, and more indefinite, is always in some

28. Köhler, *Gestalt Psychology* (London, 1930), chap. X ("Insight"); Claparède, "Genèse de l'hypothèse," *Arch. de psych.,* XXIV, 91, 136–38; Duncker, *Zur Psychologie des produktiven Denkens* (Berlin, 1935) studies particularly the structural reorganization in resolution of practical and mathematical problems (reviewed in *J. de Psych.* [1936]).

degree a novelty. We have to dare: freedom is always a risk.[29] While our first reading was suited to the calmer situations in which reflection can show up the *agreement* of the chosen alternative with a cluster of non-contradictory, uncontested values, with the ground of value which gives consciousness its consistence and stability, this new reading fits circumstances in which we confront incommensurable ends, in which even the ground of our values is put in question, in a word, where our choice is ethical rather than technical. To live consistently with oneself was the maxim of choices consistent with our permanent reasons for living; to dare, to risk, is the maxim of those choices which are a response to the incommensurability of values produced in the course of deliberation. Regardless of how we conceive the *a priori* objectivity of values, the order in itself—if this expression means anything—only appears within the confused history of a consciousness in connection with the moral history of humanity. No moral consciousness is free of the conflicts of duty which we have already considered.

These conflicts allow of no solution other than choice. An extended rationalization hardens them into rigid alternatives, personal meditation consecrates them into impasses. There is a point at which there exist no rules for resolving the conflict of rules. Such conflict has at least the virtue of awakening socialized consciousness to itself and saving it from rational automatism. It calls for personal initiative and invention capable of constituting at most a limited jurisprudence, a provisional morality which always remains revocable. Generosity, in Descartes' sense, means not only loving the good, but also deciding amid confusion and conflict what is better, here and now, for me. In this sense indecision is a vice. There are those divided souls whom puzzles and conflicts of action leave disabled: they are the scrupulous. They do not know how to break free from perplexity. On the one hand they are the intellects which endlessly refine their reasons but never succeed at the conversion which leads consciousness from the memory of the good to the anticipation of action, from the multiplicity of reasons to the simplicity of a project. Here belong also the all-embracing minds which cannot resign themselves to the elimination of other possibilities, other aspects of the good, and who wish that the law of action would always be synthesis, never

29. Even Lequier trembles before this awesome power of beginning, of being able to begin (*Recherche d'une première vérité*, pp. 107–20). Note the pages admirably entitled "La Feuille de charmille," in which the power of "doing or not doing," the emotion before the initial characteristics of the act and its unlimited retention assume such an authentic tone.

alternative. This finally is that pure consciousness which has a horror of compromise and compromising and prefers community disaster to an injustice. All are left behind by the events which choose for them and inflict upon them the spectacle of a *fait accompli* which is more painful than doubt itself, at least if they do not finally let themselves be borne along in the wake of collective consciousness. Perhaps scruple errs against human freedom as human, and represents an angelic trait of freedom. Human condition is one of choosing *because* consciousness can never be totally one, completely rational. It is not given to us to convert conspicuous contradictions by faith. Risk is a human rather than a divine form of freedom. It goes without saying that we are not confounding the risk with the altogether organic values of aggressiveness which elaborate the risk and which we encounter in exalted forms in the type of choice we call heroism. There is a simple, calm, extended form of risk which suits the modesty of a consciousness which has never followed out the alpha and the omega of the world and which apprehends values within the network of a confused corporeal condition and from a limited, partial history.

Thus it becomes apparent that the "conflicts of duties" which at first seemed to be only an exception and a sort of limiting instance express the normal condition of the will. Rather, what remains exceptional is coherence of obvious good in a given situation. And even if for the theoretical man who is a stranger to choice, values could belong to an indisputable hierarchy, the sacrifice of an inferior value always appears to the agent as a disputable and even absurd act: organic values are not comparable to other values for the sole reason that for me their essential sacrifice entails the collapse of all other values. There is never a clear debate between life and higher values. I consecrate the hierarchy of values precisely in choosing. Finally, between the least contradicted rule and its application there always remains a hiatus; only the pressure of a concrete decision, which is unique and inimitable, adapts the rule to the standards of a situation which is itself unique.

This second reading does not at first appear as a limit hypothesis. Far from having a normative, ideal character, it seems to come closest to man's actual condition. Because man finds himself in a corporeal, historical situation, because he stands neither at the beginning nor at the end but always in the middle, *in media res,* he must decide in the course of a brief life, on the basis of limited information and in urgent situations which will not wait.[30] Choice surges forward in a context of radical hesitation which is a sign of finitude and infirmity, a sign of the constriction of human existence. I am not divine understanding: my understanding is limited and finite.

But while the moderns are obviously concerned with man's actual condition, they respond to it with another limit construct, corresponding to the previous one: this second reading refers more or less explicitly to a *limit construct* which experience can only approach. To the idea of an essentially transparent will it opposes the idea of a will which decides as a *sovereign* about the meaning of its existence. By the standard of this ideal all automatism, even rational automatism, appears to be an inauthentic form and the lowest degree of freedom. The authentic individual invents an ever new existence from day to day. No model to be copied can take the place of a choice which is new each time for the unique individual. Just as the formulae of intellectualism *universalize* choice in terms of its most clearly understood reasons, so those of voluntarism *individualize* it in terms of its fully sovereign daring. The ideal limit which is clearly posited here is one of an individual who would not be a secondary individuation of a form, a type, or a primary essence, but rather the individual who "individualizes himself" by choosing his existence in every moment. As the contemporary formula puts it, existence precedes essence.

But the impossibility of excluding the other reading—and even the necessity of always holding both readings simultaneously—becomes apparent when we consider how, starting with the affirmation of choice as an irruption, we pass over to the negation of the guiding role of motivation. Consequently, how can we avoid the seemingly natural outcome of the analysis, that choice *determines* the reasons of choice, that I *choose* my motives, that choice is a *creation* of values? Voluntarism carries with it this temptation to annul attention to values as inauthentic, to submerge evaluation in decision, the receptivity of freedom in its activity and, finally, the involuntary in the voluntary.

This temptation finds a descriptive basis in the analysis of the pretext—or "bad reason"—to which voluntarism seeks to reduce motive. It is of course true that the ordering of our reasons is often only a little comedy we put on for others and for our-

---

30. Karl Jaspers, *Philosophie*, I, 1–4. Yet the classics were not unaware of this concrete situation which is not reducible to the evident. Descartes, *Discourse on Method*, Part III; Malebranche, *Recherche de la vérité*, Book I, sect. iii, § 2.

selves. But we know very well, at the same time, that this comedy is secretly denounced by a truer idea of motivation which stands in judgment over it: a pretext is a false reason, a sham motive. A pretext is bad faith in the strict sense, and it is still good faith which qualifies it as bad faith. Yet what is good faith if not the very idea of a choice which appeals truthfully to the conviction of its own motives and bases itself on this conviction? Every pretext gives itself out as an authentic motive.

Here we are not quibbling over words. Since we are trying to understand the concrete condition of freedom, we necessarily measure it by a model. The central theme of this model is an *a priori* idea, the eidetic relation of choice to motive as we have described it at the beginning of this book. I decide because. . . . This *a priori* idea is completed by an ideal implicit in all men which classical authors identified as man himself: the ideal of a perfectly understood choice, with respect to which any other choice is defective. We cannot separate the experience of risk from that of defective consciousness given by the ideal and, so to speak, normative structure of deliberate choice.

But modern analysis appeals to other situations in which choice appears, in a more authentic fashion than in the case of the pretext, as a more or less retrospective elaboration of its own motives. We shall find an attenuated form of this interpretation in William James: here choice appears as an *additional force* which, consequently, falsifies to a degree the spontaneous value of our motives and inclinations. Yet it is still possible to dissociate, in James, his admirable description of the *fiat* from the interpretation which distorts it. The defect of James's analysis seems to us one of language rather than of doctrine.

The *fiat* differs from all other forms of deliberate action (as opposed to non-deliberate or ideo-reflexive action whose elaborations they are).[31] William James seeks no common standard between reasonable decision (Type 1), which is roughly what we described under the title of rational deliberation, and the *fiat* in which the subject is conscious that the decision is a personal and direct achievement of the will which intervenes in order to tip the scales. This type of decision appears "wherever non-instinctive motives to behavior must be reinforced so as to rule the day."[32] Thus what James regards as the privileged situation is very real: it is the experience of victory over the self. The drunkard or the timid man does not ever say that he has conquered sobriety or

31. William James, *op. cit.,* pp. 432 f.
32. *Ibid.,* p. 436.

courage. There is victory where the will follows the line of great-est difficulty; the *fiat* is "the action in the line of the greatest re-sistance." [33] But a most unfortunate imagery immediately seizes upon the experience which James transcribes thus: the *fiat* is the balance of effort towards the ideal, "the additional or super-added force added to the motives which prevail in the end." A quasi-mathematical formulation immediately suggests itself. If we designate the ideal I, the propensity P, and the effort E, we shall write $I < P, I + E > P$. We shall conclude by saying that E is an additional force which is "undeterminate *ante rem*," [34] the problem of free will being one of knowing whether the "quantity of effort" is a determinate quantity or an "independent variable." [35]

This language is obviously the language of mental physics, in which motives are conceived as forces and not as motives of . . . , choice as an addition of forces and not a decision to do this because. . . . Thus there remains only to insert the voluntary element as a supplementary force, free if we specify that it is in no sense to be conceived on the model of physical force.

Yet James himself gives us the means to evade this imagery which he believes to be purely descriptive since he identifies the *fiat* with attention. "The essential achievement of the will, in short, when it is most 'voluntary,' is to attend to a difficult object and hold it fast before the mind. The so-doing *is* the *fiat*. . . . Effort of attention is thus the essential phenomenon of the will." [36] In ef-fect what is difficult is to create silence: passions smother the austere voice of reason, of honor, of duty: "The strong-willed man, however, is the man who hears the still, small voice unflinch-ingly. . . ." [37] It is attention which works against the trend: "If we let it go, [the idea] would slip away, but we will not let it go. Consent to the idea's undivided presence, this is effort's sole achievement." "To sustain a representation, to think, is, in short, the only moral act, for the impulsive and the obstructed, for the sane and lunatics alike." [38]

Thus all effort is concerned with creating silence: the *fiat* which, in a manner of speaking, joins the motives consists of listening to higher motives. In what sense can we say therefore that attention is added to these motives? In the sense that it might not be given, that one could leave them be. Attention is added,

33. *Ibid.*, p. 444.
34. *Ibid.*
35. *Ibid.*, pp. 455–56.
36. *Ibid.*, p. 450.
37. *Ibid.*, p. 452.
38. *Ibid.*, pp. 452–53, 454.

if we can still speak in this way, to its possible omission. This is the true indetermination which is not comparable with a variable magnitude. The additional force is the very control over our attention which can bear *or* not bear on this *or* that.

Thus the *fiat* is not the *opposite* of "reasonable decision": what makes the latter a decision rather than a mental mechanism is the attention which sustains the clarity of reason itself. Let us consider the three other cases: in the absence of an "overwhelming reason," the decision is brought about by an accidental circumstance of an external order (Type 2) or internal order (Type 3), or perhaps by a momentary change of our mood and our vision (Type 4). These types of decision are connected with the *fiat* by the omission or even demission of our attention which already makes us responsible for ourselves and for the course of our thought. In all these cases choice does not overturn motivation as an alien force, but fits it: it is inseparable from the attention which sustained the reasons for the chosen alternative.

William James's analysis still refers to a classical situation. It takes as its theme the difficult choice, the victory of duty over desire. Through an unfortunate choice of words, even freedom could appear as an alien additional force, alien to the life of the self as such. But Bergson directs our attention from the viewpoint of such eruptive choice in which the flux of the deepest existence comes to break up a course of dead thoughts which are the truly alien forces in my life. The idea suggests itself that motive rather than freedom is what is alien. Bergsonian analysis of the period of *Time and Free Will* operates in the privileged climate of convalescence, of juvenile outbursts. What we have to say here is to a great extent prepared by the technical critique which we have carried out above. If, as we believe, Bergsonian freedom cannot be understood apart from attention to the most serious and highest values, the very values which Bergson later teaches us to listen for in the prophetic appeal of wise men and of saints, it becomes apparent that freedom is a genuine revolt against dead values, the values of the mob, only as it appeals to newer, more profound values, the values of heroes. Far from freedom reigning where motivation is in retreat, it is still a naïve, virgin motivation which crops up together with my deepest self. All revolt comes from a more profound obedience than itself which raises it to the pitch of ethical indignation. The error of some romantic views of life is that they do not know how to recognize the spring of values from which freedom drinks when it has thoroughly examined the sand of dried ideas. This equivocation of Bergsonianism makes us attentive to Kant's warning that there is no freedom without law and without respect.

It is precisely the root of all law, namely, value and respect for value, which is undermined by a segment of modern literature: it makes it appear that to appeal to values which the mind recognizes rather than institutes would be the principle of alienation. Freedom then can appear only as a rupture of all nascent fidelity to the point of indignation and revolt, a rejection of the very condition of freedom connected by motivation to a possible order of values. Kierkegaard, who has, in addition, given modern philosophy the anguished significance of individual existence, is in part responsible for this illusion that subjectivity can be posited on the fringes of objectivity in all forms and in particular in its axiological form. Thus his influence joins that of Nietzsche and his transvaluation of values. Their joint influence contributes to the perpetuation of serious confusion concerning the relations of freedom and some order of value in modern thought. The idea of value succumbs to critique together with the idea of dead law, as if freedom were incompatible with any order of values.[39]

In the last instance we have to come back to an eidetics of the will to correct the errors of philosophy of the will. Even if we do not yet know what objectivity is appropriate to values, we can at least read in subjectivity itself the basic relation of decision to motives. This relation can be grasped directly, even in a fictitious example. It is this relation which stands in judgment on all situations and brings their unintelligibility to the light of its primordial intelligibility. In partcular it shows the superficiality of the definition of freedom in terms of the rupture of legitimity and of subjectivity in terms of a break-up of objectivity. It invites us to search patiently for a more fundamental relation of freedom to values, to find it even in the revolt and perhaps even in the arbitrariness of the gratuitous act: when freedom repudiates all value and produces an empty gesture, it invokes itself as the ultimate value which justifies its decision. Freedom becomes its own motive in which a diminished concern for value takes refuge. No matter how ephemeral this justification may be, it institutes a sort of intimate division by which freedom, giving a base to its thrust, divides itself into power and value. In the poverty of its overly sketchy reason the gratuitous act is a caricature of the attention to values of life and their community which give substance to freedom. Freedom acquires substance to the ex-

39. Nabert, *L'Expérience intérieure de la liberté*, pp. 262–323; Dufrenne and Ricoeur, *Karl Jaspers et la philosophie de l'existence*, pp. 211–17, 348–54, 376–78.

tent that it moves further from the self-centered concern with proving its independence to itself and invokes reasons for dedicating itself which radically transcend its subjectivity.

Thus one reading sends us to the other: the irruption of choice is finally in its most authentic form a discontinuity in the very web of motivation, often even a reversal of values, a revolution in valuation. We have to assume this viewpoint of interpretation in order to present the most favorable case for voluntarism, the instance of conflict of duty: objectivity of value is not rejected, it becomes attenuated and *stranded* by irresoluble contradiction. We are thus led back from the unusual instances—pretext, additional effort, eruption of myself from the depth, revolt, freedom without value—to the most genuine instance, that in which choice proceeds not from nullity but from subordination of motivation itself. It becomes evident that the irruption of choice here is nothing else than the product of the last practical judgment. Risk, daring, *are* the resolution of motivation. Thus the debate with oneself is not in vain: the seriousness of choice determines the profundity of the reasons brought to bear. Authentic choice assumes an authentic debate among values which are not invented but encountered. The power of receiving and hearing the good is what raises consciousness to the point of tension from which it is delivered by choice. Hence the leap of option has as its obverse the sudden appearance of a preference in the web of conflicting motives. To choose an alternative is to prefer the reasons for this alternative to the reasons for another. This is why the debate is not in vain: the chosen alternative has no value other than that which motivation brought to light. To risk is something quite other than to wager: we wager without reasons, take a chance when the reasons are not sufficient. The irruption of choice and the resolution of attention on a group of motives which give value to choice are paradoxically identical.

Continuity, discontinuity—conformity to the last practical judgment and the irruption of the event—such is the paradox of the guided process in which each moment of existence invented is based on the preceding one and moves forward as novelty. The act of basing oneself on . . . , which is the essence of motivation, sustains the continuity of consciousness with itself: it is the permanent possibility of being in agreement with oneself. The act of irrupting from . . . introduces the discontinuity of a consciousness moving forward: it is the permanent possibility of taking a risk. The reading in terms of continuity stresses the guiding role of motivation, but cannot show the nullity of the act of choice; the reading in terms of discontinuity brings out the leap of the event but cannot annul the sustaining role of motivation. Thus we must say simultaneously that "choice *follows from* the final practical judgment" *and* "a practical judgment is final when choice *irrupts.*" The act reconciles practically the theoretical discord of the two readings.[40]

This reconciliation in the act rises above the dialogue of the voluntary and the involuntary, at least in its initial dimension. The act of basing oneself, which constitutes the continuity of freedom in process, is the attentive reception of the good which the involuntary describes and transmits. By this reception subjectivity accepts *being transcended* in its body and through it by the other. The act of irrupting and of risking, which constitutes the discontinuity of the moment, is the voluntary existence which *transcends* the motives issuing from its involuntary existence or mediated by it. The paradox of continuity and discontinuity thus sheds light on the paradox of the involuntary and the voluntary; and even practical prereflexive consciousness—which reconciles the irruption of choice and the continuing pondering of motives —reconciles willed existence with received existence.

[4] DETERMINATION AND INDETERMINATION

THE PARADOX of resolution of attention and irruption of the act points to a tangle of difficulties the most serious of which must lead us to the very limits of a philosophy of subjectivity. It seems that philosophy of attention has to introduce a certain *indetermination* into the definition of freedom. But:

1) Does not the introduction of indetermination and hence of a *potestas ad opposita* into freedom lead us back to freedom of indifference, contradicting our rejection of choice without reason?

2) If we locate freedom in a *power*, that is, a potency, can we at the same time locate it in an *act* as our analysis of irruption demands?

3) Is it possible to formulate a theory of *determination* and

40. Just as we have followed Malebranche to abandon him at the point where he reduces the rest of attention to a nothingness of being, we follow J. Lequier up to the point at which he pretends to derive the basic certitude and the "postulation" of first truth from the power of choosing (*op. cit.*, pp. 133–35; "Fragment," *Rev. de met. et mor.* [1902], pp. 74–75). In a general way, if Lequier's theory of choice has in the last instance a desperate rather than a joyous tone, it is because he has tried to erect it beyond the fringe of any motivation and thus of attention, and has tended to derive a doctrine of truth from a doctrine of freedom.

of *indetermination* within a phenomenology of subjectivity without recourse to a theory of *being* and, more precisely, to a system of nature, a *cosmology*, within which theory of freedom would constitute a subordinate chapter?

1. The Indetermination of Willing

WE WOULD SAY that the indetermination which we must introduce into freedom has nothing in common with the other indetermination which characterized freedom of indifference, that is, choice without reason, *willing without motives.*

The terms determination and indetermination of willing have three different meanings. The first, which is basic to the other two, comes directly from eidetics of willing; the two others refer respectively to the two limit hypotheses to which we referred above in order to clarify our description of choice.

1) In the first sense we say that all choice is determined by its motives. In this very broad sense, shared by the two hypotheses outlined above, choice always follows from the final practical judgment, whether it is final because the debate has tapered off or because of an abrupt resolution. To change one's decision means to change one's reasons. It is important not to interpret the words "to depend on . . . ," "to follow from . . . ," or "to be determined. . . ." [41] causally. Determination of willing is nothing other than motivation itself. To say that choice is determined by motives is to say that all choice is motivated. Between the final practical judgment and choice there is no distance, no *exteriority*. That is why this relation could be discerned prior to the reaffirmation of the existing process. Choice does not follow its reasons; it is motivated in the moment. Choice determined by determinate reasons follows not its reasons, but an indeterminate choice which is itself an instantaneous relation to a constellation of confused motives. Consciousness progresses simultaneously towards a judgment of preference and towards the act of election, because the one and the other are only two different dimensions of the same concrete act. The relation between these two dimensions, the *sui generis* relation between the imperative of decision and the indicative of

41. It is rather difficult for us to retain the traditional terminology which relates different moments of decision to different faculties and institutes a causal relation among faculties: "Omnis electio et actualis voluntas in nobis immediate ex apprehensione intellectus causatur." "Motus voluntatis . . . natus est semper sequi judicium rationis" (St. Thomas). Judgment "results from convergence of two causes . . . of my understanding and of my will jointly" (Descartes).

evaluation is so narrow that saying "would it were so" and "this is better for me, here and now," are synonymous.[42]

The indetermination excluded by determination in this first sense is thus the indetermination of a choice without a motive: I cannot decide other than as I prefer; and this involves no constraint, but is a fact of my constitution. I cannot have or be a freedom whose *direction* would be other than that of a motivated willing. A different indetermination, that of the considering attention, is not excluded by this structure of willing: quite the contrary, this indetermination is what makes it a free willing.

2) In a second sense, the determination of choice by clear reasons represents an idea which is not derived from experience by abstraction, as the preceding one which belonged within eidetics of the will, but which is formed by idealization. It represents a limit-form of freedom, a freedom brought about by a perfectly clear and rational motivation. All equilibrium, all indifference of motives would be excluded from this freedom. Hence the determination of willing would mean that the practical evidence which resides in rational evaluation *ipso facto* determines the univocity of the imperative of choice. This new meaning is only a special case of the preceding rule: if there is no choice without motive, clarity of motives constitutes the preference of choice. All that is added is an ideal standard of human willing, according to which perfection of choice is proportionate to the rationality of motivation. No new problem is introduced as concerns the indetermination appropriate to freedom: though, in effect, clarity of reasons necessarily puts an end to hesitation, it still does so in virtue of the axiom which ties the project to its motives and which forbids us to distinguish, except by abstraction, the *meaning* of the decision from the *meaning* of the evaluation. The only necessity which appears here is not a necessity of a succession of acts, but the necessity of a continuity of contents of intellectual meanings, *assuming that we consider them attentively.* The principle of intentionality alone can protect us from all error: in effect it is one thing to derive a necessary consequence and another to derive a conclusion necessarily. The order of ideas is not that of the operations themselves.

In return this limit hypothesis holds considerable interest: it is what permits us to isolate by contrast the genuine indeter-

42. In the language of Descartes, the will can surpass clear understanding, but not understanding in general. (*Fifth Responses* [concerning *Meditations* IV:iii]); *Letter to Hyperastistes*, August, 1641; and especially *Principles*, I, 34.

mination proper to freedom which subsists even though all difference has disappeared from motivation. The trouble with Buridan's famous example is precisely that it confuses two indeterminations, indetermination in the sense of equivocal motivation and the indetermination which we are seeking at the very root of the *operations* which bring motivation to life. The freedom of vision itself has to be sought at the peak of observed necessity.[43]

3) A third meaning of the word indetermination is introduced by the description of choice as irruption and by the second limit construct, that of the individual who chooses himself as sovereign in the insufficiency of his reasons: this is the determination by oneself corresponding to indetermination with respect to reasons, that is, with respect to intentional contents of value judgments which animate motivation. This new determination differs noticeably from the preceding because it no longer concerns the instantaneous eidetic relation of choice to its motives, but the existing event of irruption. This determination by the self *follows* an earlier indetermination and is a sign of positive initiative of freedom which ceaselessly transcends its own confusion by an initiating *sursum*. Yet this existential determination does not render the eidetic rule that the meaning of choice is determined by that of its motives once more questionable because, according to our earlier analysis, I can only determine *myself* by determining my reasons for choosing and because the very decision of a categorical choice remains reciprocal with a momentary categorical evaluation. The determination of the self by the self is thus the existing determination, within existing process, which is homogeneous with the existing indetermination of attention. It is this indetermination which is resolved into *this* determination in the irruption. This temporal determination of the act remains hidden by the first reading of choice. There the mastery over decision was eclipsed by the control which my reasons exercise over me in the limit-hypothesis of fully rational decision. We were even tempted to define freedom by the absence of constraint rather than by the positive power of self-decision. Yet it depends on me to decide.

This indetermination which becomes determined is the indetermination of the vision which can consider *or* not consider this *or* that. It is really a potency for opposites. It is this potency for opposites which St. Thomas, Descartes, and Malebranche find at the root of judgment itself: our acts depend on our judgments, but our judgments depend on our attention. Thus we are masters

43. An attitude close to that of Descartes, with respect to the thesis of P. Petau concerning free choice (*Letter to P. Mesland*, May 2, 1644).

of our acts because we are masters of our attention. This *libertas judicii* is what moves in the examination of motives and becomes resolved in choice.[44]

But the two interpretations of choice can collaborate at this point: it is the second interpretation which shows us with respect to which determination freedom is indetermination and which leads us to this existing indetermination in the process of attention. It is in turn the first interpretation which teaches us that this indetermination of attention has nothing in common with freedom of indifference, that is, with indetermination excluded by the axiom of motivation. It is not an absence of motives, but the freedom of considering either this or that motive within the determination of choice by motives. How can we actually discover this indetermination which is as universal as the determination by motives if we do not seek it in the instances which appear most favorable, in the peak of determination by reasons? The indetermination of attention is this indetermination which universally accompanies the determination by motives and more particularly the determination by evident motives. This is the meaning of Descartes' response to P. Mesland concerning the doctrine of P. Petau: there is no evidence without attention: I believe to the extent to which I look at the reasons for believing; and thus I can suspend my judgment even in the presence of evidence. This is the *potestas ad opposita* with respect to the act which sustains the *determinatio ad unum* with respect to the content of motives and thus also of choice. The indetermination of attention takes the part now of indifference of election, now of invincible preference. It is common to the two hypotheses of determination of the meaning of choice by clear reasons and of the indetermination of reasons preceding the determination of the project by the self. It is the indetermination of reasons preceding the determination of the project by the self. It is the indetermination of an intentional *act* in lived time and not of a content or meaning of intention—of a power of acting in succession.

2. Indetermination of Attention and Determination of the Self by Itself in Irruption

A NEW DOUBT interrupts our difficult reflections at this point. We have affirmed rather lightly that this indetermination fits in with the determination of the self by itself: yet it seems

44. J. Laporte, *op. cit.*, and *La Conscience de la liberté* (Paris, 1947), pp. 183–225.

that we cannot without equivocation locate freedom alternately in an indeterminate power or potency and in an act of self-determination. Doesn't the pure description of our first chapter lead us to seek freedom in the possibility *opened up by* the determinate project rather than in an indecision which *leaves* all possibilities *open*? And does not the indetermination of attention now lead us to select a privileged moment in the growth of the project, to locate freedom in the moment of indecision? If so, then freedom would no longer be the act of choosing but the capacity for choice.

In replying to this objection we have to bring together for the last time the paradox of freedom, the paradox of continuous motivation and discontinuous project, the paradox of attention becoming resolved and of irrupting choice. In effect we have to affirm that the indetermination of attention and the determination by the self are two sides of the same freedom which must be understood as powerful and as act.

Determination of the act and indetermination of the power do not actually represent two different moments: there is no moment of freedom. Indetermination with which we are dealing here does not lie solely in indecision, while the determination of the self does not lie solely in the decision. There is an indetermination of the self, subsisting in decision, which is the continuing ability to consider something else, and there is a determination of the self subsisting in indecision, which is the forward movement of the act itself, moving on to consider something else. In this sense determination and indetermination are strictly contemporaneous and concern the very irruption of acts of valuating and choosing, of choosing in valuation and of valuating in the direction of choice. Determination and indetermination apply equally to the problematic moments of hesitation and to the categorical moment of choice.

What we need to come to understand is that to decide to choose and to be undetermined in my vision are one and the same thing.[45]

For the last time, let us show that this indetermination of

45. This concomitance of the power and of the act is the radical manner of affirming freedom. On the one hand, only the *potestas ad opposita* of St. Thomas, reaffirmed by Descartes, Malebranche, and Pascal (*Pensées, Fragment 99*) saves the *remotio coactionis* of St. Augustine. But in turn the *potestas ad opposita* cannot be dissociated from the event of the act, from the very *forward movement* of existence, as Lequier vainly attempts to do when he wishes to retain the experience of power of choosing on the fringes of the act of choosing ("Discourse du predestiné et du reprouvé," in *Esquisse d'une première vérité,* pp. 233–39).

attention and the determination of choice by the self mutually imply each other.

It would, on the one hand, be a serious illusion to believe that it is possible to conceive of the determination by the self in a choice without referring back to the indetermination of vision. If in effect choice is determined as to its contents by those of the motives, then I determine *myself* in my act inasmuch as the terms opposed to the choice, considered as to their content and as to the content of their motives, have nothing with which to force my vision to turn towards them. To say that I determine myself means that my motives incline without compelling; it always depends on me, in presence of the most evident motive, to look at it *or* not, at it *or* at another. It I look at it, it determines my choice in the first sense of the word to determine, that is, as to its contents. Acts as acts are independent of contents: it is not the determinate object of thought which can win over the capacity of my vision. In this sense determination by the self implies the indetermination of attention as act in relation to motives as contents. Any doctrine which does not distinguish the indetermination of successive acts in relation to their contents from the supposed freedom of indifference which is no more than an impossible indetermination of contents of choice in relation to the contents of motives remains imprisoned in a false dilemma: the dilemma of freedom of indifference and of some determinism, whether rationalistic in Leibnizian fashion, vitalistic in Bergsonian fashion, or sociological after the manner of Charles Blondel. The indetermination of attention is what brings about even the spontaneity of self-determination of choice. Even in the demission of my freedom, I still grasp myself as the act of my non-act, as active demission, because I know that I am determined by nothing as act. Even in the worst bondage I know that I can look at another thing, on a more basic level of myself than the fascination of consciousness. Indetermination is this independence of acts which makes them truly acts. This independence of the act as to its determination as operation does not contradict the intentional meaning of the act of attention which receives values and thus receives even the life of the involuntary into the heart of freedom. Precisely the act has to be independent in order to receive what it does not produce. Thus determination by the self entails the indetermination of attention as *potestas ad opposita*.

But it is no less important to affirm that this power is nothing apart from the act which puts it into execution. It is as difficult to construct a philosophy of freedom on the experience of potency alone as to eliminate this experience from the consideration of acts. As I reflect on my acts, I recognize them as the resolution of a broader power. Remorse particularly is based on the painful certitude that I could have done otherwise. A reproach arises from unused power which could have been devoted to a betrayed value; it besets the act which has wasted freedom and, more than the act, calls the self whose spokesman in the world the act is, to expiation. First comes the irruption, then the reflective return to the used and unused potency.

These remarks carry further our initial analysis concerning the potentiality of consciousness. Thus we shall ask ourselves in what sense consciousness not only opens up possibilities but itself appears as a possibility. We have attempted to approach this difficulty by starting with the effective project which works out possibilities in the world. The possibility I am, we have said then, is one which I open up in myself—that is, in my body and in my future as freedom—in making the leap of the project. The analysis of attention authorizes us to go back, beyond this power of acting which *proceeds* from the very act of the project, to the power for contradictories which lies *at the very roots* of motivation. But we must note that reflection, insofar as it seizes this basic power and suspends the generosity of consciousness which *moves forward* in exercising its potency, becomes imbedded in the sterile anxiety of potency apprehended in the margins of joyful thrust. The consideration of the indetermination of attention allows us to extend and understand this dialectic. Consciousness cannot help choking itself in the endless encroachment on a power which always precedes itself. As soon as I posit this power of willing on the fringes of the powers which *inaugurate* willing, it never stops redoubling itself as a power as being able to . . . , as potential ability. More basically still, it discovers itself as potential being, hidden in the power of willing to act. This power, which strictly is what makes me anxious, is a reserved power, engaged, held in suspension, at the dead point of indetermination.

What does this venture mean? I know well, on the one hand, that it makes me a man. It is not altogether dissimilar from the Cartesian venture of doubt: the *epoché* of judgments of existence concerning the world attests, for Descartes, the immanent certitude of the existence of the self. The same is true of the apperception of my power of looking, beyond my power of choosing, and that of my power of being beyond my power of looking: I suspend, I put in brackets, the possibilities opened up by decision and the world itself as the locus of projects. I accomplish the *epoché* of the projecting of the project and I attest willing itself as possible existence. In such hyper-reflection, in which I myself am, for myself, "the constantly future mold," I indefinitely close a circle with myself in the sterility of an endless return to myself.

Thus it is that I come to suspect that while on the one hand this venture makes me a man, on the other hand and more profoundly, it is a loss of thrust, loss of naïveté and of youth. Yes, a certain youthfulness of willing exults in committing itself and discovers modesty only in the stride of the project of acting in the world and at the heart of the project of a self which envelops the project of action.

The anxiety is irresoluble because uprooted reflection of the project has become a rebellion of potency against act. Introducing the argument of Zeno the Eleatic, it has become the "feathered arrow that hums and flies, yet does not fly." [46] In the whirlwind to which it gives rise the power of willing has become the new Achilles who will never catch up with the tortoise of slow but efficacious decision: only a shadow of the act is left from which it is endlessly separated by an infinitely divisible mental distance, the bad infinity of reflection: "Oh, sun!—Oh what tortoise-shadow to outrun / My soul, Achilles' giant strides left standing." [47] Anxiety is the corrupt blossom of reflection; if freedom is, according to Nietzsche's saying, the disease of being-here, it is not its generous thrust which makes it sick, but its dying reflection which uproots it from the act. O ye dead, "the real flesh-eater, worm unanswerable / is not for you that sleep under the table: / Life is his meat, and I am still his host." [48] Only a leap, such as the leap with which Achilles at one stroke passes the tortoise, an affective leap and neither a contemplated leap nor one unceasingly divided by reflection, can break the motionless march of reflection and its melancholy. But this leap is not the fruit of anxiety, it is wrenched from it as a second immediacy of willing. Yet anxiety itself was not initial, but rather wrenched from the generosity of the thrust. I suspend the parentheses which suspended the act. Bergson teaches that we make no movement with virtual resolution: with the anxiety of indefinite reflection we act not at all. I unmask the potential ability as a castration of an initial willing which discovers its own power in exercising it. That is the second reflection

46. Valéry, "The Graveyard by the Sea," trans. C. Day Lewis, from *Selected Writings of Paul Valéry* (New York, New Directions, 1950¹, 1964), pp. 48–49. Copyright 1950 by New Directions. Excerpts from this poem reprinted with permission of the publisher.

47. *Ibid.*, pp. 48–49.

48. *Ibid.*, pp. 46–47.

which shows that the first reflection was itself secondary with respect to a primordial ingeniousness of willing. Only willing in act reveals the power of willing.

3. Possibility of a Definition of Freedom in the Margins of Cosmology

THE READER may have noticed that we have not attempted to *demonstrate* the indetermination of freedom *a priori* in a Thomist way. Like Descartes,[49] we have sought a living experience of determination by the self and of the indetermination which proceeds from the independence of the Cogito with respect to its objective contents *directly, in the subject himself.* We must justify our avoidance of this well-known doctrine which subordinates indetermination with respect to the finite, to determination with respect to the infinite.[50]

The demonstration of indetermination of willing with respect to finite goods entails a number of moments which, we would say, are all infected with a fundamental flaw as concerns eidetics and existential elucidation of the subject.

1) First of all, such an approach requires that we admit that the will is a species of the genus desire. As all desire, it tends naturally towards its end, that is, towards the form or act which would make it perfect. This initial theme presupposes the general context of a cosmology, of a fundamental doctrine of nature which extends a common system of determinations to subjects and things, mixing the determinations of things as a natural concept with the determinations of the subject conceived as appetite. One vaguely sanctified teleology of human meaning is projected into things and in turn the natural teleology engulfs the fundamental meanings of consciousness. Thus an element of necessity is introduced into the will, considered as a nature; the subject has lost his privilege of being a subject. It has become a part of nature, an outcropping in the hierarchy of appetites which by themselves presuppose no freedom and are moved by their object.

2) Secondly, this approach posits that the degree of desire is a function of the degree of knowledge: thus the will is named rational desire and ranged among rational powers. This second theme dominates the general relation of will and understanding,

49. *Principles,* § 39; *Fifth Responses* (to objections to *Meditations* IV:iii): it is a "first notion"; *Letter to Mersenne,* December, 1640.
50. St. Thomas Aquinas, *De Malo,* Q 6; *De Veritate,* QQ 22, 24; *Summa Theologiae,* I, QQ 82–83; I–II, Q 13; *Contra gentiles,* 48.

conceived as distinct faculties. The will is said to "follow" from and "obey" understanding. In this doctrine we can easily recognize the fundamental relation of the project to motive, but it is transplanted into a cosmological context: on the one hand the will is a form of natural appetite, on the other hand the determinations of understanding are interpreted according to the general spirit of a cosmology of knowledge. Finally, a causal relation is instituted between the two faculties: thus the pure relation between the imperative of decision and the indicative of evaluation, which owes nothing to cosmology, is completely changed by cosmology.

3) Thirdly, the approach characterizes rational appetite as rational insofar as it is *capax omnium*. The will thus tends naturally towards the general good (*universale bonum*): invincible desire, implicit in all particular desire, results in that we do not will anything *nisi sub ratione boni*—unless we conceive of it as good. One object only would then be adequate to the *voluntas ut natura:* this would be the object in which all forms of the good in all respects would be comprised. Only the intuitive vision of God perceived in himself, *per essentiam*, would satisfy us. This thesis, which serves as the point of departure for a demonstration of the indetermination of willing as to particular good, seems to us too infected with the cosmology of the two preceding theses to admit it in this context. We believe that we must have the courage to strike this desire for God from objective cosmology in order to rediscover its true, uncharacterizable, unobjectifiable, metaproblematic dimension. It will constitute the object of the "*Poetics*" of the will. But insofar as we are holding the "*Poetics*" of the will with its ontological mystery in suspension, we lose the means of *demonstrating* the indetermination of the will by starting with the determination of the *voluntas ut natura* by the general good. The "eidetics" of consciousness can depend only on those concepts which can be read in the acts of the subject. Now without invoking the desire for God the indetermination of willing can be read directly in the Cogito as an act. In this respect the Cogito is, for a certain description of subjectivity, a terminus, a last prerequisite, *an absolute from one point of view*. The ultimate consequence of the Cartesian revolution seems to us to lie here, in the discovery that the originality of consciousness with respect to all objectively conceived nature is such that no cosmology can any longer engulf this consciousness. The "*Poetics*" of the will can hereafter rediscover the desire for God only thanks to a second revolution which breaks through the limits of subjectivity, as the latter had broken through the limits of natural objectivity. The second revolution

never takes place in Thomism because the first one has not, either. God, consciousness, things lend themselves to only one universe of discourse, to only one total cosmology which abolishes the leaps between objectivity, Cogito, and transcendence and so avoids the mysteries which underlie these paradoxical transitions.

4) Fourthly, the demonstration strictly speaking of indetermination of the will with respect to finite goods consists in showing that there is no necessary connection between the ultimate end and the particular end. The domain of the contingent is not that of the demonstration. It is this altogether logical Aristotelian thesis which supports the entire edifice. We believe, on the contrary, that there is a hiatus of different significance between Transcendence and terrestrial good, and this good may be freedom itself, taken as the supreme good incarnate in the world: the transition to the *"Poetics"* is already a conversion. The reader will notice that at this point of the argumentation, indetermination of rational appetite with respect to finite goods does not in the least appear as the obverse of determination by the self. It is demonstrated entirely by the default of the finite object proposed to move the power of desiring, that is, *a parte intellectus.* Freedom still is not a positive power for contraries. The originality of Descartes lies in having defined indetermination in terms of the determination by the self, which is natural in a doctrine of the Cogito which starts with the subject's act itself as being the first and last word of subjectivity.

5) The fifth thesis concerns precisely the determination by the self of which Thomism is not unaware, even though it does not dominate its whole system. It is in part subordinated to the preceding, in part linked to another line of reflection. In one aspect the determination of the will by itself in effect corresponds to the *deficit* of determination by the object. When the will turns towards an object, the principle of its determination—*lacking* an adequate object—is itself, since its *virtus activa* as mover exceeds or equals the *virtus passiva* of the object which attracts it. Thus the cosmological matrix of the theory of movers and attracting objects, of passive and active virtues, engulfs the royal intuition of man's power of positive domination of his own acts.[51] Yet on the other hand we should note that indetermination as the power for contraries can be demonstrated directly, as several texts show,[52] by

51. *De Malo*, Q 3 A iii; *De Veritate*, Q 22 A 5, Respondeo and Ad 2'; Q 9 A 3; Q 10 Ad 1'. Texts collected by Laporte, *op. cit.* (1931), p. 70.
52. *De Potentia*, Q 1 A 5 Respondeo; and esp. Q 22 A 6 Ad 1'. Texts collected by Laporte, *op. cit.* (1932), p. 199.

starting with the control which man exercises over his acts, that is, by starting with his own nature as will. To be sure, this domination over his own acts remains the replica of the indetermination which intellect's power of the universal bestows on the will, but it belongs at the same time to another dimension of Thomism, in no way contradictory with the preceding. It is the degree of power itself and not only the type of determination of the appetite by its object which constitutes the increasing dignity of beings on different hierarchical levels of the universe. Yet again the general cosmology of "powers" confounds the rules and distorts the central intuition of the power of willing. Still it is a fact that in many texts which affirm the control of the will over its acts we are struck by the positive nature of this power. St. Thomas here appears to be rather close to a psychology which really takes the "I" rather than nature as the root center of perspective. Thus reflection, understood as power of judging its own judgment, appears tied to the power of moving oneself to judge. Finally, the action on oneself, and of powers on each other, brings out the circle which subjectivity makes with itself. If we then consider the movement of the will as understanding, that is, from the point of view of the "exercise" (*quantum ad agere vel non agere*), we are confronting a true action. Undoubtedly our action is grafted onto the pure Act of the divinity through the natural inclination towards the good in general, but the originality of the movement towards this or towards that is itself indisputable. We are really dealing with a determination of the self to willing. We have recalled above what the points of application of this movement are: the will has to begin to consider, has to consider this or that, and has to choose the final alternative.

In brief we could say that Thomism tends towards the recognition of the power of thinking without recognizing absolute originality in it. Such originality remains submerged in a general theory of second causes which does not fit the Cogito. Nonetheless such a doctrine incorporates the elements of an autonomous eidetics of the subject without recognizing it. This ambiguity of a psychology mixed into a cosmology is particularly visible when we consider how the natural thrust towards the good in general is resolved to form a concrete project involving only particular goods. If we stress the dependence of particular goods on the general good which binds them as *means to their end,* the will appears as if moved by the general good. Thus we can do without the determination of the self by the self. A moved will is not a "self" in the spirit of the cosmology. On the contrary, if we stress the hiatus which separates the infinite good from finite goods, we bring out the indetermination of the thrust towards such finite goods. Then we have to bring out the determination of the self by the self in the first movement of deliberation, in the process itself, and in the resolution of deliberation. St. Thomas goes to the verge of evoking this vertigo which seizes reflection when it takes the fact of deliberation itself for the theme of deliberation. Thus it is quite clear that the desire for the good in general appears as a useless motive from which we could derive anything at all following hypothetical syllogisms. Pure freedom is displaced at the very start of the deliberation: *"quod deliberet vel non deliberet, ... hujus modi etiam est homo dominus."* Thus the first movement of the will which determines *itself* appears alternately wrapped up in the received thrust towards the good in general or again as other than the first movement, so that we should have to insist on including all ends as *means,* within the supreme end or on the impossibility of deriving a finite good from an infinite good: only the last point of view stresses the initiative of the will which *"se habet ad diversa."* This recourse to the determination of the self, if it were truly taken seriously and were truly attached to a radical reflection on the Cogito, could burst open the entire edifice of the cosmology which cannot contain a veritable subject: nevertheless, Thomism appeals to this determination of the self by itself sufficiently to do good psychology, but right away attaches it to the entire order of nature sufficiently to avoid pushing this good psychology to the point of a genuine metaphysics of subjectivity. The subject is always masked by some derivation starting with a received power. This is why we do not believe that the conditions which would enable us to speak of a psychology of attention in St. Thomas are fulfilled. The preoccupation of the system in which the will is inserted limits subjectivity too much in order for it to work its devastating effect and ruin the cosmological *Summa* which we would like to make only one moment. In the *Summa* subjectivity is easily surpassed because it is never fully affirmed. We believe that we must follow the opposite path: to make sure of the subjectivity of the subject itself, to relate all the involuntary to him, broadening subjectivity to the very limits of incarnation. Only thus can we approach the strange bond which joins the subjective power and the creative act and makes them simultaneously one and two, the same and different, according to the extra-systematic relation which Jaspers calls a "cypher."

These are the methodological reasons which keep us from

deriving indetermination with respect to finite goods from a more fundamental determination with respect to the absolute good. Such a demonstration is tied to an unacceptable general cosmology. The indetermination of attention seems to us to be the obverse of determination by the self which is the first and last word of the doctrine of subjectivity. In some respects responsibility must appear without a basis, alone. The discovery of a presence other than the self must remain upsetting for that solitude, as an explosion of the Cogito.

Does this mean that by renouncing a cosmology of freedom which would make it appear as a moment in nature we renounce any "concept" of freedom. By no means. Precisely here Husserlian phenomenology showed itself capable of reappropriating classical cosmologies. We have adopted Husserl's views concerning the plurality of "regions" of being and of regional ontologies. The region "consciousness" and the region "nature" bear with them their appropriate concepts which Descartes would call "primitive." The eidetics of the will which we have elaborated at the beginning of this book presupposes such a regional ontology. Such ontology entails no Platonism, but is the field of meanings understood in terms of some examples or even of a single example, perhaps even an imaginary one. It by no means assumes that these concepts would have an existence analogous with existence in the world and would organize themselves into a *cosmos*. We must notice also that the concepts of nature and the concepts of consciousness, though they belong to different regions, participate in common fields of meaning, such as being, real, possible, object, appropriateness, relation, etc. . . . But these meanings no longer constitute only one region of being, but a formal ontology, that is, the sum of determinations of the idea of object of thought in general.[53] These concepts do not prejudge the difference between being as nature and being as consciousness, they do not prejudge the type of relation among these beings, and in particular they do not demand that these two modes of being should be coordinate and of equal importance, as two absolutes in a fortuitous relation. This is why the completely formal possibility could become divided in our first chapter into several material significations relative one to the objective anticipation, another to the voluntary projects, Even the words, determination and indetermination, belong to this formal sphere and become immediately bifurcated between indetermination as object of nature and indetermination as operation of the act of consciousness. Even indetermination in the

53. Husserl, *Ideas*, §§ 9–17.

physical sense of the word—if there is such—has not the same content as indetermination understood as the independence of the power of thought. This entirely formal community of the sphere of consciousness and of the natural sphere served as the pretext for muddling regional concepts. Aristotelian cosmology is at the same time a mixture of "regions" with each other and with formal ontology. This is how a fantasy-physics is born, loaded with diminished "subjective" concepts which in turn engulf consciousness within a sort of general nature. On the contrary we need to understand that the scientific development calls forth a purification of natural concepts from all foreign concepts, just as the deepening of subjectivity since Descartes, Kant, and Kierkegaard imposes a recognition of primitive concepts relative to consciousness.

Thanks to these formal and material concepts, a certain intelligibility attaches to structures of consciousness. A philosophy of freedom is not purely ineffable and it is not true, as Bergson claims, that all effort to define freedom implicity admits that determinism is right.

But we can readily admit that this intelligibility lets something essential escape: we have forced our way gradually into the mystery of individual existence which is incarnation, process, and irruption. Philosophy of free will appeared to us as oscillation between this lived experience and the higher objectivity brought about by Husserlian method. Undoubtedly, as we affirmed strongly in the introduction, this lived experience is itself obscure and, so to speak, buried; but the bondage of the fault is itself revealed as freedom by the protestations of a deeper certitude, the certitude of having been able to do and be something other. The fault calls attention to a power which makes me responsible even in the very midst of lamenting impotence and calling for deliverance. This is the unarticulated experience which sustains the conceptual interpretation even as it extends it in the direction of living existence of body and freedom. But Husserl has not stressed sufficiently the extent to which meanings in the region of consciousness are fragile and transitory. The experience of freedom is in itself a transitory experience which must ceaselessly be recovered by *action* of the self on the self. I can *hide* my freedom from myself and lie to myself; by this denial which is one aspect of the fault, consciousness imitates the thing and hides behind it. At the same time regional ontology of consciousness dissolves as a vapor trail, "the attitude" which would make the interpretation of regional ontology of consciousness possible having been inhibited by the denial of freedom itself. In contrast, objects are always present; I need not act on myself, respect humanity as an end in itself in my person, in order for them to continue to appear to me as things. The "natural attitude" which conditions their appearance is easy and permanent. This is why the fragile and really veiled experience of my freedom would not support the pure description of this region where freedom rules if it were not completed by the exemplary myths of innocence, by a sort of reminiscence of purity which itself corresponds diametrically to the hope of purity expressed in terms of a Kingdom of God. In the introduction we called attention to the bond between such myths and a properly religious meaning of deliverance, and have shown how they rejoin pure description as illustration or exemplification of the regional ontology of consciousness.

PART II

Voluntary Motion
and Human Capabilities

1 / Pure Description of Acting and Moving

THE WILL IS A POWER of decision only because it is a power of motion. As we said at the beginning of the first part, we can separate these two functions of the will only by abstraction. We must not be misled by classical analysis which distinguished the several phases of voluntary activity, deliberation, decision, and execution, *in time*. Decision does not *follow* deliberation purely and simply, nor does action *follow* decision. Delayed action, separated from decision by an interval, is not normative. There are spontaneous acts, done as soon as we think of them, which we still call voluntary. The extreme cases are the "observed automatisms," as rolling a cigarette while marching. Such acts contain only very implicit intention which we often recognize only after the fact; I say to myself that I might have willed it explicitly. That is enough to let me recognize these actions as mine and not as escaping me completely. The distinction between decision and action is thus one of meaning rather than of time: it is one thing to project, another to do.

The close affinity of action and decision can be shown more precisely still. A projecting willing is an incomplete willing: it is not put to the test and it is not verified. Action is the criterion of its authenticity. A will which does not issue in a bodily movement and through it in a change in the world totters on the verge of becoming lost in sterile wishing and dreams. The man who does not carry through did not truly will. The legitimacy of an intention separated from the efficaciousness of action is already suspect. We need only to remember that all value includes an ought-to-be: in this sense it demands existence. Once consciousness turns into a scornful inwardness, value becomes infected with a sterility which transforms it profoundly. It grows stale and unreal, it hardens and becomes a screen between the inventive genius of the will and the stuff of existence in which values have to prove themselves. Thus the embodiment of values in the world is not an external *addition* to their pure legitimity, but rather an internal part of it. The worth of an action is not secondary; it is not simply a question of subsequently carrying out our plans and programs, but of testing them continuously amid the vicissitudes of reality, that is of things and men, and thereby constituting their authenticity.

The most prophetic visions and the farthest looking utopias demand at least symbolic acts, small-scale testing, a practical dedication by which the body initiates their realization. These are the actual attempts which, by affecting the nascent idea, protect its freshness from moment to moment. Consciousness continues to invent in doing. Thus the artist, according to Alain, does not have the idea of the work of art before having made it. His complete idea is the meaning of the completed work. The project and the work engender each other mutually. An educator or a politician can avoid fixed ideas only through a militant effort which ceaselessly challenges him to recreate his ideas. The obstacles which our ideas encounter in the world should not make us captives of sarcastic reflection on the recalcitrance of the actual, on the decay which action inflicts on the purity of sublime ideas. Such preoccupation with obstacles leaves us no choice other than idealistic evasion or cynical realism. The obvious obstacle ought rather to make us attentive to the more intimate obstacle which consists in the hardening and aging of our ideas when they are removed from the test of the actual. In this way the material obstacle should actually rekindle in us a hope of an ideal vision and actual incarnation of our ideas which would be strictly contemporaneous.[1]

Moving and deciding can thus be distinguished only in abstraction: project anticipates action and action tests the project. This means that the will actually decides about itself only when it changes its body and through it the world. Inasmuch as I have done nothing, I have not yet fully willed.

These considerations lead us to the central idea which we believe to lie at the very core of all consideration of the will. *The genesis of our projects is only one moment in the union of soul and body.*

Action, furthermore, is already present even in the most indefinite project. The feeling of power appeared to us as an essential moment of a project. Deciding, we said, consists of an

1. Nabert, *Éléments pour une éthique* (Paris, 1943), pp. 19–36.

empty intention of a future action which depends on me and which is within my power. I feel charged with the action to be done, I experience myself as its force as well as its intention. What I will, I can. The sign, "to be done," which distinguishes a project from a wish or a commandment already refers to my capacity for the action under consideration. I do not normally notice this capacity as such; it is itself projected in the theme of the action. More exactly, in projecting myself as the subject of an action, I affirm myself capable of that action. To decide, we have said, is to project myself in general as the theme of conduct proposed for the body to obey. My capacity is hidden in the imputation of myself in the context of the project. In this way the possibility opened by the project is not completely empty. It is not a simple non-impossibility; the power gathered in my body orients the project towards action, that is, towards the actual, towards the world. The presence of power in the context of willing means that my projects themselves are in the world. This is what distinguishes will from imagination, at least from that imagination which removes itself and makes itself unreal. In virtue of the power the project is like a pledge of insertion of the possible into the actual. This is the union of soul and body which is already apparent in the project: I feel capable, as an incarnate being situated in the world, of the action which I intend in general. By its connection with capability, willing is grounded in the world, intended in the world, even when it is an empty intention. Capability directs it towards the actual instead of deflecting it towards the imaginary.

Even more basically, a tacit action accompanies even the most indecisive, most hesitant willing: we cannot make a motive count unless we are in control of our body. "Willing to reflect," Hamelin says, "means to keep the body still in some respect." The fact is that voluntary motion does not consist solely of initiating an act, of producing a movement in a muscle which is at rest and in some sense waiting for it. It is just as much a question of ending or subduing action to allow me to deliberate. If the effect of the will is to move an initially immobile body, its first task is to keep the recalcitrant body from carrying us away, from vibrating and starting to escape. Or, alternatively, the will must wake it from the slumber of the customary. The full meaning of these remarks will emerge below, when we shall have understood that effort deals in the first place with a body which is already agitated by emotion and predisposed by habit: thus if to move my body is in the first place to tame it, to domesticate it, to seize it, this function of willing always operates side by side with motivation.

Voluntary motivation is conditioned by willing which is the master of its body. A need or a tendency proposes values only if the flock of nascent movements which accompanies them has already upset the body or made it inaccessible to voluntary impulsion. The body motivates willing only if willing controls the body. Thus the problem of voluntary motion accompanies at every moment the problem of our attitude to values: after the decision, in order to carry it out; before and during the decision, in order to master and guide the body.

But we need to go further still: in some respects motivation is a type of action and even of voluntary motion. It is not only my body which is the terminus of my action, but also all my thoughts which constitute, so to speak, the body of my thought. This is rather difficult to understand correctly: all that I have learned, all that I call my experience and that I bear with me even if I am not actively aware of it at the moment, briefly, all that we can call knowledge in the widest sense of the term, has to be moved like my body. These are the methods, the tools, the organs of thought which I utilize in order to form new thoughts. When I call up my knowledge, not only to think of the same object anew, but also in order to form a new thought with the help of old thoughts of which I am not explicitly aware, I control what I know just as I control my body. This will become clearer when we shall have spoken of habit: my thought, we shall see, constitutes a sort of nature for me. The same ambiguous relation holds between myself and my knowledge as between myself and my body. At first sight this is rather scandalous for a philosophy of the subject, but the body strictly speaking is not the only source of the temptation to objectify the Cogito. Insofar as effort applies to *knowing,* we can find in it the characteristics of recalcitrance applicable to the body. There is here a genuine sense of movement of thought and of effort to think. The essence of voluntary motion is not changed; it is only more intimately involved with motivation, and in some sense grounded in representation itself. Thus by an even more daring abstraction, always to some extent grounded in the direct awareness of acts of the Cogito, we can distinguish within motivation consideration of value and the more or less easy or difficult application of antecedent knowledge. In the preceding chapter we have considered only abstract motivation, detached from the effort which accompanies movement of thought just as much as the movement of body: in the motive we acknowledge only value and not resistance. Yet both body and thought can resist. A complete characterization of will is possible only in context of effort. I cannot *represent* the content of value to myself unless I *master* the movement of the body and the movement of the idea. The first function takes place in the register of practical representation, the second constitutes the original relation of willing to reality which is *acting* strictly speaking.

[1] Intentionality of Acting and Moving

A DESCRIPTION of acting runs into serious obstacles which threaten to reduce it to a discussion of the difficulties of description.

1. The Presence of Acting

THE FIRST DIFFICULTY PERTAINS to the *present and full* character of action. The gesture of picking up a book, of opening it, is distinct from all anticipation, from any project. It is no longer a word, a Logos, it is an act contrived in the fullness of the actual. The action is itself an event. It initiates novelty in the world. It is no longer a possibility moving towards the actual, but an aspect of the actual itself, the flesh of advancing process. The temporal index of action is a constantly renewed present. Thus while future process, indicated by project or anticipation, can be discontinued and reversible—I leap ahead of myself to an event which will happen day after tomorrow, I retrace my steps and envisage an action which I shall do tomorrow, etc.—an action by definition participates in the forward movement of existence itself, of my existence and that of the world: what is happening is present, what I am doing is present. The present thus has at least two aspects, the happening and the doing. It is on the one hand, the present of a full, undeniable presence, of a pre-given world, apart from all expectation, all demands, all ideal construction. But, on the other hand, in this irreducible present I work, I manipulate what is present, I am the author of events: I act.

Just as we can say nothing about pure presence, about the fullness of existence for the sense which receives it—because all discourse remains on the far side of the event, of the pure "this" and stops at possibility or necessity, at the concept in general, at the law—so also with action as an event: I do not state my acts but the intentions which they realize. The only thing which I could say about action is not at all its actualized presence, but its relation to an empty intention which it fulfills at the time or after a delay. "Realization"—that is, the passage from possibility of the project to the reality of action—belongs to the category of "fulfillment" which thus embraces also the accomplishment of a wish or of an order, the satisfaction of a desire or a fear and, in the order of theoretical representation, the effectuation of actualization of a presence of suffering, enjoyment, seeing. Two aspects need to be considered in this relation of fulfillment. In the first place the meaning of the presence or action which "fulfills" the project, the commandment, the desire, the fear, etc., is *the same* as that of the project. I "recognize" the empty intention in the full act. There is a relation of coincidence, a "covering" between the same meaning as full and as empty. Without this, I could not say that "this is or this is not what I wanted." On the other hand this coincidence is one of the empty and the full. This metaphor of the empty and the full is striking. It applies equally to the relation between thinking and seeing and the relation of thinking to acting. In the same way as the countryside I see fulfills what I think only on basis of books on travel and geography, so the excursion I take fulfills the emptiness of my project of a journey. Thus in the narrow sense of the word "to think," which indicates a content of meaning lacking presence, acting surpasses thinking in the same way as suffering, seeing, and all the forms of sensation surpass thinking. In this sense, acting is not parallel to "pure thinking," but rather parallel to enjoying, suffering, seeing: they are all the limit of "pure thinking," of "empty intention": they fulfill it.[2]

2. Practical Intentionality of Acting

THIS IS where we encounter the second difficulty. If it is not discourse about action but the relation of realization which joins it to its project, the appropriate shade of meaning of "realization" is in turn difficult to uncover because of its *practical* character. If acting is the limit of thinking in the narrow sense of empty intention (imagining, projecting, etc.), is it included in thinking in the broad sense, that is, in the Cogito as a whole? In other words, can acting be a part of the Cartesian enumeration along with "I desire," "I will," "I perceive," or "I feel"? This question assumes a precise meaning: can we speak of the intentionality of acting? The question is serious, since we have purported to identify phenomenological psychology with the realm of intentionality itself. We must admit that the problem is not

2. Concerning the "fulfillment" of an "empty intention," see Husserl, *Logische Untersuchungen* (Halle, 1922), vol. II, study V.

clear: at first sight it seems that acting is diametrically opposed to thinking, not as accomplishment of an empty practical representation, but as a vast domain which escapes the realm of intentionality. Marching, taking, speaking would be incomparable to seeing, imagining, desiring. This mutual exclusion of thought in the broad sense and of acting might be justified this way: intentionality as such is adynamic: thinking is a light, acting is a force. The words force, efficaciousness, energy, control, production, effort, etc. would then belong to a different dimension of the subject than the non-productive intention of perception, memory, desire, wish, commandment, and consequently different than the equally non-productive intention of a project.

Such an argument seems inadequate. We need rather to broaden the concept of intentionality and even that of thought. In the first part we have already introduced into intentional psychology the concept of active affect (need and quasi-need) along with sense-affects (pleasure, pain, etc.); already the dynamic concept of tension entailed such extension. Acting seems to us for several reasons an aspect of intentional thought in a broader sense. Thought as a whole, including bodily existence, is not only light, but also force. The power of producing events in the world is a kind of intentional relation to things and to the world. The transitive structure of the verb "to do" (What are you doing? I'm doing this.) and of active verbs in general (I hang a picture, hold a hammer, bend my fingers) cannot be altogether without analogy with the transitive structure of verbs which express acts of representation (I desire a picture, I see a hammer, I look at my hands). Active verbs thus also express a direction from a subject-pole to an object-pole. The verb has a personal subject and object predicate. The analogy goes even further: in common language we call "objects" "tools" which we manipulate It is not simply a question of grammatical meaning of "object" or in a phenomenological sense, of "intentional correlate" (in the sense in which we speak of the "object" of a request, of a concern, of a perception). It is true that this transitive structure of active verbs expresses also relations of objects within nature and in particular causal relations: one billiard ball striking another. This in fact is what obscures the analysis: the terminus of action indicates at the same time what a human subject does with his body and what an object does with respect to another object. This duplicity of the word "action" can be easily explained: human agent, considered as an object among objects, is the cause of change. Empirical causality is the objective indicator of corporeal motion. In virtue of the diagnostic relation which we have recognized between personal body and the object-body, a certain correspondence is established between voluntary action and objective relations of causality. This correspondence, to which we shall return at length, explains the terminological ambivalence. But this ambivalence has become a confusion. Words like action, efficaciousness, force, dynamism are now also loaded with ambiguity. The realm of subjectivity [3] and the realm of objectivity infect each other. In this way physics becomes loaded with anthropomorphisms and forces of nature are conceived as types of human energy. At the same time psychology becomes loaded with physics: corporeal force of willing is conceived as a cause whose effect is movement. Thus the continuous lived relation of idea to movement and the external objective relation of cause to effect fade into each other. If we separate the realm of subjectivity, without forgetting to include the personal body, the transitivity of voluntary action should appear in its purity, without admixture of physical causality. This is an original relation of subjectivity to the world. Acting is a way in which a subject relates himself to objects. In a very broad sense we might well call the relation of acting to the terminus of the action a "practical intentionality." This practical intentionality is no longer one of practical *representation* which decides about the project, nor is it in any sense or to any degree the intentionality of a "representation"—it is the counterpart of the intuition which fulfills a theoretical intention, it is the action which fulfills the project.

This practical intentionality is what permits us to respect the subjective character of the concept of *force*. We have avoided, in the first part, treating willing as a force in order to provide a thorough grounding for phenomenological description and to avoid any confusion with physics, even a mental physics. Now we can broaden the range of phenomenology and thus of intentionality and recognize that *force* is an aspect of the Cogito. But it is singularly more difficult to respect the subjective character of voluntary force than that of decision. In practice we are tempted to believe that only "representation" is not a "fact," observed empirically in nature. Now voluntary force is in no way a representation. It is a production of a change in the world "through" the motion of a personal body, without my representing the movement as an object of perception. We need not be sur-

3. Let us bear in mind that subjectivity has to be understood in its broad sense: myself and yourself; and in its corporeal manifestation: myself-body and yourself-body.

prised that we do not encounter representation in the practical relation of willing to the body which it moves: in principle moving my body does not mean representing my body to myself. And yet we need to understand that acting is an original dimension of the Cogito, a "consciousness of . . ." in a Husserlian sense. It is a non-representative consciousness, no longer even a practical representation, as a project. It is a consciousness which is an action, a consciousness which presents itself as matter, a change in the world through a change in my body. The "naturalization" of this voluntary force seems inevitable because of the objective character of the movement which this force produces and in some sense ex-poses among objects. Further, reflection copies a non-representative Cogito with difficulties; it tends here to desert the active modes of consciousness and turn them over to the process of objectification which, in addition, coincides with the scientific spirit.

3. The "Pragma" or Intentional Correlate of Acting

ALL THIS, we must admit, is not altogether satisfactory: supposing that this intentionality of acting corresponding to that of intuition is not a blind window in the edifice of intentional phenomenology, it is rather difficult to tell what the object of "actualization" is. The temptation is to say that it is a physical movement—what are you doing? a gesture, a movement of the head; I move my body. Such response is doubly faulty. In the first place a movement of the body is a product of analysis. I do not do such or such *movement*—I hang a picture. The action is a form of a totality which has an overall meaning capable of being accomplished by various movements, that is, by starting with different initial postures, and by variable configurations of elementary movements. The action is not a sum of movements; movement is a product of an analysis of a moving form by an outside observer who considers the body as an object. This has been stated forcefully by *Gestalt psychology* [4] and even by certain behaviorists, like Tolman.[5] But this initial reformulation of point

4. [Koffka, *Principles of Gestalt Psychology* (London, 1937), pp. 25–41.] Like Tolman, Koffka distinguishes molar conduct within a "context of behavior" from molecular movements of reflexology.

5. Concerning "molar behaviorism," see Tolman, "A New Formula for Behaviorism," *Ps. Rev.*, XXIX (1922), 44–53. Molar behavior is distinguished from the movement studied by the physiologist by organic unity of action which "persists even when" a physiological rest has been reached. Tolman calls this "persistence even when" "purpose." Cf. *Purposive Behavior in Animals and Men* (Berkeley, Calif., 1932).

of view can still be handled by scientific psychology, which is objective in the sense which we have given to this word in contrast with phenomenology of subjectivity. We need to correct radically the opinion that the "object" of action, the terminus of "realization," is movement. The motive form is not yet the true object of action. Actually, when I act I am not concerned with my body. I say rather that the action "traverses" my body. We shall presently try to recognize the meaning of the body in relation to the terminus of action when we shall have found it. I am concerned less with my body than with the product of the action: the hanged picture, the strike of the hammer on the head of the nail. What is "acted" (coining a term to correspond to "perceived") is a transformation of my environment itself, this is the *factum* corresponding to *facere,* the "done" as passive perfect,[6] the "being done by me," the *pragma.* If the complex movement of my hand which wields the hammer is not exactly *the object* of action, should I say that this object is the wall, the painting, or the nail, or the hammer? Not that, either. These things are themselves implicated in "the acting as such," but in a different way than the body, and do not integrally constitute the pragma.

The complete pragma is "that I hang the painting on the wall." It is expressed by the whole predicate responding to the question, what are you doing? All active verbs, from this point of view, could be analyzed into a "doing plus an action-object." This analysis lets a part of the verb pass over into the object: (I-am-doing)—(I-am-hanging-the-painting-on-the-wall). The pragma is this complete correlate of doing.

This object of action, considered in itself, is the focus of a great number of relations which constitute the complete structure of an action. We find principal elements of this description in widely different psychologies, insofar as the concern with explication has not choked off description. The most remarkable analyses can be found in Lewin and his disciples,[7] Koffka (all belonging to the Gestalt school), and in Tolman.[8]

The pragma becomes detached in the first place as a form from its matter: in the example referred to, the wall is the mat-

6. J.–P. Sartre, *Emotions,* trans. Frechtman (New York, 1948), pp. 51 ff.

7. All these works were published in *Psych. Forsch.,* beginning in 1926, under the title "Untersuchungen Zur Handlungs- und Affekt–Psychologie." See esp. K. Lewin, "Vorbemerkungen über die psychische Kräfte und Energie und über die Struktur der Seele," *ibid.,* pp. 294–329; and "Vorsetz, Wille und Bedürfnis," *ibid.,* pp. 329–85; cf. below, p. 271n70, 324n24, 324n25, and 325n26.

8. Tolman, *op. cit.,* chap. V; cf. Tilquin, *Le behaviorisme* (Paris, 1942), pp. 356–418.

ter of the pragma. Each pragma appears as a solution of a local *difficulty* in the world and thus the perceived and known serve in general as the matter of the pragma. Each difficulty is a tangle to be resolved practically.

The internal articulations of the pragma can be analyzed with the concepts which Tolman uses. These are teleological concepts: the world is a "means-ends field"; the "acted" world appears to me in the first place in perceived forms and qualities. We can call the indices considered in terms of their practical function *discriminenda*, that is, insofar as they serve to differentiate instruments and paths of action. Two other fundamental notions which Tolman employs are *manipulanda* and *utilitanda*. This distinction is interesting. Both of these are "means objects" referring to "goal-objects" (for instance, nourishment which makes hunger cease). But the *manipulandum* is the tractable, practicable function of the object considered independently from its end: the baton can be taken, the course run. The *utilitandum* is the *manipulandum*'s property of *leading to*. . . . It is the relation of means to the end itself: the path which can be run leads to nourishment. Tolman stresses particularly the equivocal, ambiguous character of such teleological relations of discrimination, manipulation, and utility. The world of action is the world of practical probability and consequently the world where "expectations" are often disappointed and one where we have to formulate "hypotheses," risk "attempts." Koffka and Lewin carry out a similar analysis of the easy and the difficult "ways" of this practical world. These authors stress the dynamic rather than the teleological aspect of the field of behavior from a descriptive point of view: when I am peacefully stretched out at the beach, the field is homogeneous, balanced, without tension; a cry of "Help!" is enough to transform the field into a "cone of appeal," drawn out in the direction of the cry. The practical indices of the world refer to this "practicability" of our ways: obstacles, blank walls, openings, scandal (stumbling block), fog, etc.

But there are undoubtedly many other articulations, if we wanted to take into account the multitude of possible technical changes, considered from the point of view of the *object* produced, the *end* to be attained (spatial, social, etc.), of chief *means* used, of *resistance* to be overcome, of *material* to be used, and finally of the type of *bodily motion* (we shall return presently to this last point). Our civilized milieu is particularly complex: it is peopled with the products of human action. Fields, marks, tables, books, etc., are at the same time tasks and utensils involved in new actions. Since the milieu of human behavior has itself been produced by behavior, man reacts to his own works. This eminently technical character of the human milieu and of human action depends, as we know, on the fact that man *works* with tools to produce the "artificial" objects of his civilized needs and even of his vital needs. This is why man's action is typically "artificial": it is *techne,* mother of arts and techniques.

In this way acting stretches between the "I" as willing and the world as a field of action. Action is an aspect of the world itself. A definite interpretation of the world is already included implicitly in every project: I am in a world in which there is something to be done. I have embarked into it in order to act in it. It is the essence of all situations which affect me to pose a question for my activity. A situation calls up an attitude of consciousness and a corporeal task. There is something unresolved within it. Sometimes it is the urgency of the situation which solicits my project and obliges me to act. At other times it is my project which makes me produce the very occasion in which it ingresses by seizing another occasion which leads to a favorable opening. In any case the world is not only a spectacle, but also a problem and a task, a matter to be worked over. It is the world for the project and for action. Even in the most immobile project the feeling of power, of being able, presents the world to me as horizon, as theater, and as matter of my actions.

4. Moving as an Organ of Acting

IF THE TERMINUS of acting is not in my body but in the world, what is the significance of the body in acting? It is not the terminus of action but rather a usually unnoticed stage in my relation to things and to the world. It is in an ebbing of attention that I notice my body and constitute its original meaning: *the body is not the object of action but its organ.* The relation organ-pragma is an absolutely specific relation. We have said above that acting "traverses" the body: it is the original "mediating function" of an organ which is thus indicated.

The hitherto unnoticed organ characteristic and its relation to the terminus of acting creates a new difficulty which descriptive phenomenology encounters: it seems that its chief task should be to distinguish this relation from better known relations and in particular from objective, intra-worldly relations which tend to be substituted for it. Thus for instance it is frequently said that the body is the *instrument* of action. I *use* my hand to write or to take. I take "with" my hand, by means of my hand. Yet even such likening of the organ to a tool is defective.[9] An instrument is what prolongs the organ, it is outside the body; it represents a material rather than an organic mediation between myself and the action produced. This superadded intermediary characterizes properly human action, a technical, artificial action. To act is in great part to work with instruments. Someone who knows how to use his hands is someone who knows how to handle tools, who has the job in hand. This relation, "organ plus tool," gives rise to a new problem which, far from clarifying it, further complicates the "organ-pragma" relation which becomes an "organ-tool-pragma" relation. This extremely ambiguous relation has both an organic and a physical aspect. In effect on the one hand the customary use of a tool in some sense incorporates the tool into the organ: the worker acts at the end of his tool as a blind man extends his sense of touch to the end of his cane. From the point of view of the man who acts, tool in hand, the action passes through the organ extended by the tool as through a single organic mediator. Attention is focused primarily in the pragma, secondarily in the indivisible pair of organ and tool seen as an extension of the organ. But on the other hand the relation tool-work is entirely in the world, and is a physical relation. The tool "acts," "works" as a natural force known according to the laws of physics. Any organic concept is excluded from industrial technique which is a simple application of science by transformation of relations of cause and effect into relations of means to an end. This way the purely objective interpretation of the relation of the tool to the job can regain the level of the relation of organ to tool and finally of the relation of willing to the organ. Muscular force is a physical force comparable with the force of the hammer; the worker's output becomes a part of the output of the tool system. Thus the physical, industrial character of the relation of the tool to the work absorbs the organic character of man to the tool.

In this respect the series will-organ-tool-work is rather ambiguous because it can be read in two directions: starting with the will—and thus from the point of view of phenomenology—or starting with the work—and thus from the point of view of physics. The tool is the point in which these two interpretations meet and so cannot clarify the function of the organ.

In addition, if I treat the organ as a tool, I become involved in an endless regression; for the meaning of the tool is its exten-

9. Marcel, *Metaphysical Journal*, trans. Wall (London, 1952), pp. 242 ff.

sion of the organ. If the organ were the tool of willing, willing would itself become organic, presupposing that the problem has been resolved. We shall see, however, that the dualism of willing-subject and of body-object is largely attested by this more or less explicit tendency to treat the organ as an instrument. The organic nature of the body disappears from sight and the entire body, having become a machine, becomes foreign to willing.

When attention shifts from the pragma, which is the object of acting, to the motive form, which is its organ, the meaning of action is modified. This is the modification of acting which we call "moving." Moving is acting insofar as it applies to the organ and not insofar as it terminates in a pragma, that is, in things and in the world. Besides, this modification of meaning is perfectly natural and the action itself demands it. I pass constantly from one point of view to the other. For instance, I can say that I am hanging a picture, that I am holding a hammer, or that I am bending my fingers. Insofar as I have to learn to use tools and common objects (themselves products of human labor), my attention is ceaselessly led from production of the work or pragma to the utilization of the tool and to the motion of the organ. One part of motor habituation itself takes place "in general," as empty, without tool or task. This is gymnastics in the broadest sense. Here I am concerned exclusively with my body; I make *movements* which are movements for nothing, in order to exercise my body. They correspond to a highly artificial and purely preparatory study in which the results do not count, and in which the moral, professional, and social context of the work disappears. Laboratory attitude, such as I have to assume towards subjects in experimental psychology of labor, is of this order.

But other situations, such as habituation, exercise, psychotechnical inquiry, make us conscious of moving. Action as a whole encounters *obstacles*, resistances which ceaselessly require a re-adjustment of movement. In a general way, it is body's resistance which makes me conscious of its mediating function. This situation, which is propitious to reflection on the body, is what we ordinarily call effort. Effort is the moving itself, made more complex by an awareness of resistance. But while effort is what makes the organ-body available to reflection, it is at the same time effort which can falsify this reflection: it tempts us to reduce the description of moving to one of its forms, namely, to the relation between effort and organic resistance. Here dualism finds further justification: we no longer see anything but the opposition of body and willing, yet the essence of moving is that the body *ceases* to will. Resistance can be understood only as a complication of the very docility of the body which, from another viewpoint, corresponds to willing. We shall return to this point at length in the third chapter.

Finally I reflect on my body apart from action when I inquire concerning its capacities. Here we once again encounter the concept of capacity. A capacity is the moving itself, retained apart from the act, a potential moving. I refer to it when I say that I know how or that I can (swim, dance, climb trees, etc.). I appear to myself as a complex not only of projects, but also of powers (and, as we shall see in the third part, of givens: character, health, etc.). Capacities are at the same time residues of action and promises of action. They become apparent only in reflection and on the margin of action, before or after the act. These powers of doing can also be called skills or know-how, in a practical sense of the term "knowing," exactly coextensive with the word power or being able to (in English and German the expression is "I can swim," "Ich kann schwimmen"; in French this is expressed as "I know how to swim"—"Je sais nager.") In the same way Tolman does not hesitate to say—in a language which he strives to keep within behaviorist bounds—that the rat "knows" the shortest way: all habit, he tells us, can be called "cognitive postulation" of aspects of the environment.[10] We shall frequently use the term skill (knowing how) in the sense of power (being able to). But we might think that the word *knowing* is strictly appropriate only to human powers which have been reflected upon, which have undergone conscious examination. We shall call skill (knowing how) reflected power.

Such then is the reflection concerning body in action: it is a reflection concerning the *organ* of willing favored by habituation, by gratuitous exercise of the body, by the consciousness of resistance to easy execution, or by the hold of consciousness over my powers. Such reflection is always to some extent a modification of acting which normally passes through the body in an *unreflecting* way and bears on its terminus *in things themselves*.

In this modified form of acting or moving the efficacious content is the organ-body, the moved organ, and not a sensed, imagined, represented body, but my body-moved-by-me. In the consciousness of moving the significance of the Cogito is voluntary incarnation and no longer incarnation which happens to me, as in suffering, or implicitly felt as in perception, but rather an active

10. Tolman, "Purpose and Cognition, the Determiners of Animal Learning," *Ps. Rev.*, XXXII (1925), 285–97, as quoted in Tilquin, *op. cit.*, pp. 363–64.

incarnation, control exercised over my body, over I-body. All reasons accumulate to make reflection on the voluntary motion of the body quasi-impossible. Already acting itself is difficult to reach by reflection, and moving, which is but an unperceived stage of acting, is even more so. Reflection naturally duplicates intentions in objects of representation in the broadest sense of the word which includes the intention of the project. It can duplicate the deployment of the "I will" in the pragma only with greatest difficulties, and with even greater difficulty its deployment in the organ. I am so engaged in what I do that I do not think of my moved body. I move it: consciousness of acting and the even more opaque consciousness of moving myself remain a secondary, marginal consciousness with respect to my principal, focal consciousness. When I act, I think of the ends of the action, of the objects of perception and generally of the representation which governs it. Consciousness of acting is in great part a continued decision, persistence, correction, a renovation of the project. The most reflected, most pronominal consciousness of the "I"-moving adheres to this principal intention as a sort of obscure halo. Thus while decision was consciousness eminently *available* to reflection because of its basically pronominal character—"I make up *my* mind," "I decide"—voluntary motion escapes such reflection— consciousness which is expressed in the corresponding statement "I move myself" is "traversed" by the consciousness of action: I do such and such an action—and this in turn, because of its non-representative character, is difficult to reflect upon.

This is why it is difficult to uncover the operation of consciousness *involved in acting organically*.

[2] MOVING AND DUALISM

1. The Dualism of Understanding

WHEN WE HAVE THUS with considerable difficulty recovered the consideration of moving from the intentionality of acting—itself rather difficult to reflect upon—we come upon an unexpected difficulty. The concluding phrase of the preceding paragraph, "operation of consciousness involved in acting organically" is sufficiently striking to convince us that behind the difficulties of reflection lies the paradox and even a certain amount of absurdity of voluntary movement. In fact voluntary motion presents immediate consciousness with a continuous and indivisible operation which understanding can only conceive as a succession of distinct and even heterogeneous moments. Yet immediate awareness is nothing without the understanding which seeks to understand what it experiences in an overall sense. Effort is the application of myself, who am not an object, to my body which is still myself but which is also an object. Now I am not actually conscious of this application which constitutes a sort of physical thickening, an organic spatialization of the "I will." Yet for myself, who move my body and attempt to uncover myself in that very act, willing, being able to, moving, and acting are one. The order addressed to the body, the disposition of the organ responding to that order, the effective response felt in the organ, and the action produced by me together constitute a unitary practical consciousness of which I not only become aware with difficulty, but which I do not comprehend at all without breaking it up. Dualism is rooted in the theory of understanding as such.

In the general introduction we presented an overall critique of epistemological dualism as it emerges from Descartes. We can return to this critique by applying it specifically to the problem of voluntary motion: Cartesian dualism cannot be overcome as long as we assign thought (project, idea, motive image, etc.) to subjectivity and movement to objectivity. This dualism is in all respects an outcome of method. And yet Descartes himself teaches that the continuity of the "I will" and movement also belongs to thought and even to clear thought in its way: "Things which belong to the union of the soul and the body . . . are very clearly recognized by the senses." [11] In some sense we have certain knowledge of the transition from the I will to movement. But Descartes forbids us to introduce into philosophy such practical evidence, supported by the "uses of life" and presented to distinct thought as an enigma.[12] To succeed here we have to reintroduce the body into the Cogito as a whole and to recover the fundamental certitude of being incarnate, of being in a corporeal situation. We always have to reconquer the certitude of being the masters of our body from the disjunctions of understanding. The task of any philosophy of moving is to sharpen this awareness of contrast with divisive understanding. We have to rediscover a single universe of discourse in which thought and movement would be homogeneous.

11. Descartes, *Letter to Princess Elizabeth*, June 28, 1643 (and also May 21, 1643).

12. *Ibid.* "It is by employing solely ordinary life and behavior and refraining from meditation and study of all that makes use of the imagination that we learn to conceive of the union of the soul and the body."

The naturalism frequently professed by scientific psychology imagines that the Cartesian difficulty is brought about in all respects by the metaphysical structure of Cartesianism and that a more empirical treatment of the problem will dissipate it. Actually the duality of substances, far from being constituted on the ontological grounds which naturalism avoids, is introduced and supported by a duality of certitude, the certitude of the Cogito and the certitude of space. All this should be simplified for a psychology which claims to treat the Cogito as a species of empirical fact which it calls "mental fact" or "fact of consciousness" and which it declares verifiable by the methods of observation and induction used in the natural sciences. Yet not only is the difficulty not resolved by the advent of naturalism in psychology, but also the unity of method imposed for the sake of objective consciousness burdens the problem with an additional absurdity inherent in the postulates to which it appeals. There appears a more implacable divorce between two types of physics: a physics of mind and a physics of matter. The intimate and undecipherable certitude that I move my body, transported into this context, becomes an absurd problem: how can an idea, which is a mental fact, produce a movement, which is a physical fact? We are familiar with the embarrassing position of psycho-physiological parallelism: the more it bars itself, in order to satisfy strict methodological demands, from conceiving of any relation between idea and movement, the more it postulates a single phenomenon with two aspects in order to approximate more closely the sense of inner experience which reveals an indivisible operation, oriented alternatively from the body towards thought (as in emotion in which I in fact suffer from my body) and from thought towards the body (as in voluntary movement in which thought manifests its efficacity).[13]

If we want to break the impasse of the problem of effort we have to retrace our steps. We have to give up the attempt to coordinate two orders of facts, psychological and physical, of mental and biological objects, and, starting with the Cartesian Cogito, rediscover the subjective mark of movement, *bodily motion in first person* (and also, as we have said, in second person). This is the place to remind ourselves that the Cogito includes a certain experience of the body. The latter presents itself twice, once from the side of the subject, secondly from the side of the object. In part my body-moved-by-me is included as an organ in the indivisible experience of willing-moving. Both the submission and

13. Blanché, *La notion de fait physique* (Paris, 1934), pp. 49–59, 222–26.

the resistance of my body are part of the experience of my willing as applied force: the "I will" is effectively applied in the lived movement. The Cogito is the very intuition of a soul joined to a body, alternately passive to the fact of the body and controlling it. Undoubtedly we are here going farther than Husserl himself, at least in his second period which is the period of the *Ideas*. His last philosophy and his concept of *Lebenswelt* encourage us to extend intentionality beyond theoretical and even practical representation (representation of the project) and to include in consciousness its own relation to the body. To be sure, this broadening of the descriptive method threatens to explode it—notions which are too close to the body actually lack a clarity of their own. Concepts such as sensing, suffering, or moving serve more as indices, as "signa" of a situation which the mind never perfectly masters and which understanding cannot consider without perverting it. The "essences" here are extremely inexact and "indicate" a mystery which understanding inevitably transposes into an insoluble problem. I experience—rather than know by a direct inspection of meaning of words—what "being able to" and "moving" mean, and that there is no willing without being able. I grasp it in a single example. But this eidetic proposition, which is so clear in itself, refers to a practical certitude which Descartes calls "usage of life" and which repulses understanding. Concepts which gravitate around moving indicate functions which are always, so to speak, "acted," and which unify practically what understanding separates: the thought of movement and movement itself. Phenomenology must go beyond an eidetics which is all too clear, and go on to elaborate the "indices" of the mystery of incarnation.

The most important of these "indices" are precisely those which have to do with the elementary experience of being a voluntary *force*, of being able to move my body and of moving it in fact. "Understanding given to itself" (*intellectus sibi permissus*) falls back into the dualism of the Cogito. It reflects clearly only representations and lacks the indivisible assurance of being a willing which has taken hold of its body. This assurance must always stand in a tension with the reflection which analyzes it and win itself back from it. This is the only way understanding can clarify it, by contrast and paradox, for we can conceive of mysteries only in terms of problems and at the limits of problems.

Here we have to test our conception of *diagnostics*. If corporeal movement (my-body-moved-by-me) is actually inseparable from subject's experience, then the duality of moving in the first person and of movement considered objectively as an event which belongs with external experience raises the question of the precise nature of the dualism of points of view with respect to the body. We have said in general terms that there is no parallelism between personal body and object-body. In effect voluntary motion as it is "acted" presents itself as an application, as a continuous change of plans, as if willing grew from a non-dimensional point to a volume lived as mine, a personal volume, having extension in flesh in first person. Thus it would move without interruption from a non-spatial simplicity to the level of multiplicity and organization. Bodily application of the I will is that by which I *become* actively extended and composed, by which the "I *become*" is a lived interval which is my body (note that the relation into which I enter with the diversity of my ideas and my memories to the extent to which I activate or move them is the same). Now this mystery of the application of effort cannot be strictly compared with knowledge of the object-body. While the personal body presents itself as body-moved-by-a-willing, that is, as the terminus of a movement which *comes down* from the "I" to its mass, the object-body is conceived as simply body, as first of all and only space. It is a link in an even system of objects. The idea which grows from the non-spatial to spatiality has no objective meaning. This impossibility, which clings to the constitution of the world of objects itself, is more basic than the law of conservation of energy of which we can always say that it only applies to the structure of a scientific universe and that it is a postulate limited in its applicability. Consequently the applicaion of effort has no objective correspondent which would be exactly parallel to it. The dependence of the personal body on myself as willing has no opposite on the objective level other than a body which, by definition, is explained by other bodies. This is a more forceful reason than the preceding why the experience of effort should be a scandal to understanding and to the science which remains within the framework of general laws of objectivity, that is, of number and systematic experiment.

This anomaly undoubtedly explains the difficulties encountered by authors who tried to carry over an equivalent of voluntary control to the objective terrain of biology. We can recall the famous example of Maine de Biran: this great philosopher believed that it was possible to treat the myself, as it is included and revealed in the apperception of effort, as a hyperorganic force applied to the organism. The hyperorganic force seemed to him to be to the organic center what the organic center is to organs.[14]

14. Maine de Biran, "Responses à Stapfer," in *Morceaux choisis*, ed. Gouhier (Paris, 1942), pp. 231–53.

Such a proportional relation is totally devoid of homogeneity. Direct examination of the organic series at no point suggests such a hyperorganic force which remains a projection of Cogito's experience on the level of objects. Even the idea of seeking a sign or a physiological symbol of willing contains an intrinsic absurdity.

Undoubtedly the experience of the *imperium* inevitably poses a problem for the biologist. This is what remains interesting in Maine de Biran's attempt. But the enigma which inner experience poses for the scientist is one which the scientist has no means of resolving on his own grounds. There is naturally a temptation to find an objective indication of the power of will, whether a negative indication in some gap in determination, or a positive sign in a force which is superior to organic life and at the same time belongs to its level. But if we explain these attempts clearly, they inevitably become stranded: determinism is always right on its own grounds, the grounds of "empirical facts." This obstacle, which misleads the positivist, calls for a change of attitude, for a passage from the "natural" viewpoint to the "phenomenological" attitude: only here does my body acquire meaning by its submission or resistance to my willing.

The only objective indication of willing is a certain aimed bearing of behavior, a specific *"form"* of action. We shall see in what sense the remarkable studies of the Gestalt school can help us to distinguish this diagnostic function of the object-body with respect to personal body. This function, we have said, is elaborated in a highly empirical manner by a gradual discovery of correspondences between scientific concepts of biology, of behavioral psychology, of Gestalt psychology and the most naïve givens of self-reflection or "communication" (or intropathy) with another. The other's effort in his body, the practiced ease of a dancer, the tension of the athlete straining to the limits of his power, or the struggle against extreme fatigue "present" (or "preserve") to me effort in second person applied in a body in second person. The expression of effort and in a broad sense the expression of the *force of the will* reveal to me the control of the "thou" over his body in a way which is undoubtedly less intuitive than reflection about myself but which is still immediate and indubitable. *Objective* knowledge of man is built up in a relation with this first person *and* second person experience of the *force* of willing on the body.

Thus we must give up the attempt to coordinate a physiological knowledge of movement with the experience of effort: such knowledge and such experience belong to two different universes of discourse. We have even to give up the attempt to establish a one-to-one parallelism between phenomenology of effort in first and second person and objective knowledge of movement. The latter serves only as a diagnostic for reflection about myself and about my body as well as for the intropathy by which I reach your body and you.

2. "Understanding" and "Explanation" of Action

SOME EXPLANATION IS NEEDED of the relationship between the phenomenology of action in which we are engaged and certain forms of behavioristic and Gestalt psychology.

We clearly cannot be content with a behavioristic psychology such as Watson's, already because of its "molecular" character. The most interesting comparison which we should make more precise is with authors whose description is close to ours, such as Tolman, Köhler, Lewin, Koffka, etc., but who ultimately pass from this description to an objective and causal type of explanation on a physiological level.

Tolman has no doubt that his "molar" description of action, which, as we have seen, is teleological in form, cannot be reabsorbed into a physiological explanation which, according to him, is of the "molecular" type. More exactly, he states that the distinguishing signs are in the last instance *effects* of physiological stimuli and means of manipulating *causes* with a view to obtaining the "final object" of intention.[15] But we can ask with Tilquin whether the description does not postpone rather than prepare explanation, and whether the effect of the explanation is not to *reduce* the original and properly "emergent" elements evoked by the description.[16] In reality Tolman's excellent description itself does not come solely from examination of behavior but draws heavily on introspection or more exactly on an implicit phenomenology which we have sought to make explicit. Consequently his causal explanation appears as a destruction and a negation of results obtained by the description.

The Gestalt psychologists have attempted an *explication* which does not regress to the elementary, to the "molecular," but remains on the molar level of description itself. This attempt must occupy us longer because it claims to avoid the perils of Watson's strict

15. Tolman, "Purposive Behavior," *Ps. Rev.*, XLV (1928), p. 538; Tolman and Brunschvicg, "The Organism and the Causal Texture of the Environment," *Ps. Rev.*, LV (1935), pp. 43–77.

16. Tilquin, *op. cit.*, pp. 404–406, 414–39, 457–66.

behaviorism and even those of the modified behaviorism of Tolman.[17] Above we have seen the use which the Gestaltists make of the concept of "context of behavior" as a phenomenal field of action, as opposed to "geographic context" defined in physical terms. This phenomenal field is reciprocal with behavior itself which reveals it as a world of "manipulanda" (to use Tolman's language) as behavior responds to this context.[18] The phenomenal field thus is the context as it appears "behaviorally." Koffka is not unaware of the enormous difficulties raised by the transition to a *realist science* of conduct: he notes himself that the context of behavior of the animal can only be *inferred* by starting with the behavior of the animal in our "context of behavior" and that thus the apparent behavior of the animal is situated with reference to my phenomenal or lived behavior. But in the end science has to include the "apparent behavior" of the other for me as well as my phenomenal or lived behavior and the context of behavior relative to this apparent behavior within an objective system of relations. In the last resort this objective system can only be between the *actual* geographic context and the *actual* organism. Phenomenal behavior and what introspection calls consciousness are thus simply points which reveal *actual* behavior of an organism with respect to geographic context. Thus we are led to say that the context of behavior and phenomenal behavior are *included* in the actual organism and that the "phenomenal ego," far from including the totality of its relations, belongs to phenomenal conduct as a subordinate system. This reversal of perspective leads to the central notion of *psychophysical field*,[19] which is the ultimate and only universe of discourse with respect to description of consciousness or behavior. The transition to this field is facilitated by several factors:

1) First of all the concept of field is already elaborated on a descriptive level: but, from a strictly phenomenological point of view, though the world appears as a total field with forms, forces, a background, and a horizon, it appears as such to me. The total field is the correlate of a total subject (who decides, perceives, acts). The leap, we might even say *coup de force*, here is objectifying the myself with respect to which the total field of perception and action orders itself and in turn placing this myself in the total field which then is no longer *for* anyone but is in some sense in itself. Under the pretext that the conditions of distribution of

17. Koffka, *op. cit.*, pp. 25–41 *et passim*.
18. *Ibid.*, p. 32; definition of conduct.
19. *Ibid.*, pp. 41–68.

the subjective and the objective—for example, in the relative movement of objects with respect to the body—are a part of this very distribution, the myself as it appears and the appearance of all things for him are objectified as parts of the total field. Such argumentation is a pure sophism which allows us to preserve the descriptive and phenomenological intention of the concept of field in an explicative system which, however, ruins it completely by objectifying the very experience *for* which it is a field.

2) Secondly, the description of the field of perception and action as it appears and of the bearing of action within this field require a *dynamistic* terminology: concrete behavior and lived experience which both represent "totalities with temporal extension" (Lewin) can be described in terms of *forces*, tensions, and resolutions of tension. These dynamic concepts called forth by description seem to invite a physiological and even physical transcription. Objectivation of the self is facilitated by the *resemblance* between descriptive and explicative dynamism. Precisely the physiological and physical models to which Lewin and Koffka can appeal are themselves dynamic and not mechanical models. If physiology is not condemned to molecular explanation (mechanical, anatomical), if on the contrary a resemblance of form can be always noted between phenomena of consciousness and of behavior on the one hand and of physiological reality on the other hand, we shall avoid the dangers of classical parallelism and we shall be able to speak of an *isomorphism* between on the one hand the *phenomena* of consciousness and behavior and on the other hand the *inferred* physiological field. This isomorphism does not seem to us capable of masking the real gap between the product of description (carried out and lived) and the physiological level of explication: for neither apparent behavior of the other nor my behavior as it appears to me present themselves as an appearance *of* some objective field of physiological nature. A bad phenomenology of appearance and finally of perception becomes dissimulated in the Gestaltist argumentation. Structural resemblance of physiology and phenomenology of action rests only, as Köhler sees at one point,[20] on the purely *formal* character of dynamic concepts, which are thus superior to the *material* use to which they are put on both sides.

Speaking in Husserlian language, we can say that dynamic concepts are applicable to several regions without belonging to any. In the "region" of things or in the "region" of consciousness there are many other concepts which thus overlap all "regions,"

20. Köhler, *Gestalt Psychology* (London, 1930).

as the terms object, property, relation, plurality, etc.[21] Phenomenology of consciousness requires dynamics, just as it requires other concepts of "formal ontology." It is even possible to construct a purely psychological dynamics, without reference to physics or even psychology. It was to avoid the sliding of psychological dynamics (with its concepts of force, tension, release, etc.) into a physical interpretation that we have held the description of willing as force in suspension until now and that we have considered it as thought, that is, as practical, a-dynamic intention. Now we must not forget that voluntary and involuntary *forces* are also the forces which evoke or actualize a *meaning*.

Finally, the physiological field of the Gestaltists is in great part a construct, not even inferred from behavior but presupposed in its conception and then opposed to it in order to absorb it.

3) The objectification of the Ego in the total field is in addition encouraged by the unconscious character of a great part of the tension and resolution of tension so that we are forced to infer them from certain aspects of action and of consciousness. It would seem that everything invites us to consider the Ego as a system of tensions which is contained within the total field and which becomes "separated" in conformity with general laws of organization of a force field.[22] The problem of action, of the will (for example, in habit, emotion, etc.) then appears as the problem of "communication" between two relatively temporary subsystems of tension and the subsystem of the Self whose tensions are enduring.[23] Thus it becomes possible to have a general concept of action, as Lewin's *motorium* or, better, Koffka's *executive*. Action is a form of suppression of tensions, along with the suppression of tensions without action by sensory organization and by thought: "execution includes all the means by which action can suppress or contribute to suppressing tensions." The works of Lewin's school, a considerable bounty from a descriptive point of view to which we so often refer, are animated by this theory of tensions in affective and volitional psychology. Unfortunately there is reason to fear that Gestaltism and its doctrine of "total physiological field" are only a vast mythology: the existence of unconscious tensions and of "tacit structure" does not in any way

21. Husserl, *Ideas*, §§ 9–17.
• 22. Koffka, *op. cit.*, pp. 319–42. Koffka refers to the beginning of the repossession of consciousness where there is not yet an Ego, and draws an argument from attribution of psychic aspects to other parts of the field (music, countryside, vision of another); he sees here not facts of intentionality but vicissitudes of "separation."
23. *Ibid.*, pp. 342–67.

force us to include the Ego as a part of the field. We shall see in Part III that these facts can be integrated in a doctrine of the subject and that it is on the contrary the tacit structure which is entailed by the personal body.

4) What is interesting about Gestalt psychology with respect to *behaviorism* is that it tries to overcome the classical conflict between introspection and external observation of behavior by integrating both in an ultimate explanation as descriptive moments which reveal and permit us to infer laws of organization of the physiological field. Thus Lewin considers consciousness and behavior as a simple "phenotypical" level in relation to the "psycho-dynamic" level: on this level systems of tensions constitute the "genotype" revealed by consciousness and behavior. Here we reach the unity of discourse which psychology takes great pains to seek.[24] It is also here that our method becomes most radically distinct from the method of the Gestaltists. We seek to understand the voluntary and the involuntary as subjectivity. And, as we have said in the introduction, we do not believe that they are enclosed in introspection. We believe on the contrary that the concepts of subjectivity are alone capable of overcoming the contrast of introspection and behavior. But in order to reconcile these two methods of *description* within one *understanding* of subjectivity, we must radically correct two false ideas which are ordinarily attached to the terms consciousness and behavior. If introspection only reveals states of consciousness of a "myself" which has no effect in the world, which is not incarnate in a body, it reveals only an interior, closed, and in addition fictitious world. If external observation only receives movements deprived of meaning and without roots in the "thou," it only reveals motor display unrelated to a subject. If on the contrary the integral experience of the Cogito includes that of the personal body and through it the experience of acting in the world, if, in addition, the conduct of the other is described as revealing a subject, a "thou," the concepts of action or conduct which we have to formulate really concern *action of a subject in the world "through" his body.* This subject is myself, yourself, it is my fellow man. My own experience of myself and the sympathy (or better, intropathy) for the other are two living experiences which give rise to phenomenological concepts immediately valid for subjectivity in general. To be sure, we could say with apparent justification that personal experience reveals better the meaning of the project and external observation

24. Lewin, "Vorbemerkungen über die psychische Kräfte..." *Psych. Forsch.* (1926).

the meaning of action. This duality of methods unfortunately sustains the false problem of the relation between the (subjective) idea and the (objective) movement. But this distinction is not tenable in the end. The projects, we know, are also capabilities contained in the body and discernible in the body of the other. In turn, we have to say that our actions are incarnate intentions whose meaning is for me. We cannot thus assign the "idea" back to introspection and the "movement" to behaviorism. Thus we reject the false dilemma of introspection and psychology of behavior no less than Lewin, but seek to go beyond it not by objectifying the Ego, but by formulating concepts of subjectivity derived equally from perception of the self and from understanding of the behavior of the other as a second person.

3. The "Dramatic" Duality of the Voluntary and the Involuntary

THE DUALISM of understanding is neither the sole nor the chief division introduced in the texture of subjectivity. The unity of willing and movement which breaks up when it is thought itself includes a certain duality, a lived duality. The bond with the body, even though indivisible, is polemic and dramatic. In actuality as soon as we say with Descartes, "from this alone, that we have the will to walk, it follows that our legs move and that we walk," [25] we also sense the certitude that this submissiveness of the body is entirely a conquest. Initially the body is clumsy, convulsed, and impotent. The idea that to all intentions of willing there correspond appropriate movements simply as a birthright is really untenable: all this has been acquired from an elementary, primitive ineptitude; better, all this has been wrested from a disorder which is the genuine state of the body's childhood. Against Descartes' proposition we have to set down this other proposition: "there are no voluntary acts which we have not accomplished in the first place involuntarily." Every voluntary hold on the body repossesses the body's involuntary usage.

Thus here we introduce a new detour which will be the guiding thread of the next chapter: voluntary motion of the body does not present itself as a native power of an *imperium* over an inert body but as a dialogue with a bodily spontaneity which calls forth the reign of the ἡγεμονικόν. Thus we shall find once more in the register of voluntary motion our principle of reciprocity of the voluntary and the involuntary. Our plan is all laid out.

25. Descartes, *Treatise on Passions*, art. 18.

1) First of all it is important to seek out the functions of movement which effort controls; to show the fundamental aptitude of these functions for being appropriated by the "I will" and thus distinguish the *powers* of the will from causal thought as we have distinguished motives from it. That will be the object of the next chapter.

2) Next it will be necessary to describe the ways in which effort affects the synthesis of different sources of movement. That will be the object of the third chapter of this study of acting.

But if effort is a dialogue with the body, is not our first ambition to discover the actual application of the "I will" in movement, completely misguided? Haven't we introduced a new dualism with the principle of reciprocity of willing and of the involuntary? Undoubtedly; but this dualism or rather this "dramatic" duality, once again hides and masks the genuine connection of thought and movement which must be thought *apart from* effort itself. The living and undecipherable bond of idea and act is effected in the involuntary. This throws a new light on all our earlier analyses. Dualism is not simply demanded by understanding, it is, in its way, a daily reality: "Homo simplex in vitalitate duplex in humanitate," Maine de Biran loved to say. The unity of the human composite is formed at too deep a level to be easily discoverable. What is given in the first place is the debate which we pursue with our body as long as we live. But we must know how to penetrate deeper than the level of this struggle of effort and of the body, to the very organic pact inscribed in the involuntary powers of movement. Here we must seek the ontological unity of thought and of movement, apart from the duality of willing and the involuntary. This means that description of the involuntary will have not only to reveal the first matter of effort, but also this "simplicitas in vitalitate" which is more basic than all duality.

The *involuntary functions* of movement studied here are three —preformed skills, emotions, and habits. The cornerstone of the edifice is not the ideo-motor reflex, that is, the mechanical bond of a movement to the idea of that movement, but the preformed connection of our highly supple motor patterns to regulating perceptions which are absolutely foreign to the idea of movement. Habit would not be comprehensible without an initial pattern of personal body prior to all knowing consciousness of the body and even to all gradual learning of movement.

But such endowment, prior to all knowing and to all acquired experience, would leave man more helpless than any other living being if he did not infinitely multiply his means of action by learning. Here habit will appear as the great mediator between the abstract intentions of a will and the diversity of action.

It is, however, not habit which we place in second place after preformed skills: according to Hegel's beautiful view of *Phenomenology of Mind,* habit can be properly understood only as the educator of different functions which it may be surprising to find in the second rather than first part—emotion. But in emotion we shall not seek the affective motives already considered above but their explosion, the turbulence and disorder of the body which stimulate action. Aristotle said it before Ravaisson: the will only moves by desire. In three different ways the mysterious transition from thought to action is already effected. There is here, in a triple form, a sort of "primitive fact" which is the practical usage which I make of my body; and this primitive fact is situated more deeply than the effort which only adopts it.

4. Pathological Dissociation

PATHOLOGY SHOWS US a new type of dualism, by dissociation, "functional liberation," or "repression." This dualism does not make for a direct comprehension of the normal unity of man and the dramatic duality which it includes: we fail to understand a function if we start from its disorders. Only the normal is intelligible. There is no intrinsic intelligibility of the pathological. But I do understand what a capacity for willing is, since the involuntary powers become fully meaningful only in terms of willing which makes them intelligible in controlling them and bringing them to a human level. It would be a mistake to believe that pathological dissociation brings back a primitive simplicity: the degraded is not simple. The products of illness are for a great part original products.

But at the same time it has to be said that the normal contains the possibility of the pathological—more than its possibility, its threat and its lure. Human reality is a "dramatic" duality constructed on an organic unity. A nascent discord is always inscribed between my will and bodily and mental spontaneity. The unstable relation between the will and the functions which give it a hold over the body contains a permanent possibility of liberation of the tamed functions. This is the principle of all the pathological.

We could object to this priority of the normal and of its definition by the reciprocity of the voluntary and the involuntary that emotional anarchy is prior to voluntary mastery in time and that the equilibrium of the will and of habit is the terminus rather than the starting point of education. That is true, but it does not give any priority to the facts of automatism and emotional agitation from the point of view of *understanding*. What is first in the order of intelligibility may be second in time: reason comes only after childhood, yet it is reason which initially knows itself as reason. The will has a history, but this history is that of man, and we shall never say how man begins. The meaning of man reveals itself step by step but it does not engender itself.[26]

This study is not a *history* of the will; it has to do solely with the *meaning* of man—it is an eidetics. This meaning might not be recognizable except in the adult—it may be even that it remains an unrealizable ideal, the prize of perfected freedom. Yet this history, even though it is unfinished, can only be understood in terms of the unchanging meaning which, step by step, unfolds itself within it.

26. Concerning genesis and meaning, see below, pp. 425.

2 / Bodily Spontaneity

[1] PREFORMED SKILLS

REFLEXES ARE NOT the most elementary components of human conduct: the germ of all the movement which we can learn and which effort seizes upon is a non-reflex type of innate, or better, preformed movement. For reasons which we shall specify later, we shall call these movements preformed skills ("know-how") rather than instinctive movements. Our task is limited: we do not wish to carry out a systematic study of them, but only to distinguish among them from the point of view of a psychological description of the involuntary, that is, to establish in what different ways they are involuntary.

In order to eliminate all ambiguity let us say right away that we understand by reflex a *descriptive type* of reaction and not a theoretical, ideally simple scheme arising from analysis and imposed on explication of complex actions. The criticism to which the *theory of the reflex* has been subjected in the last thirty years is well known: according to the mechanistic interpretation the total functioning of the nervous system would be a sum of partial processes of a mechanical type. A definite stimulus would act on a locally defined receptor and produce a definite response. The form of the response would be governed by anatomical, topographical considerations. To be sure, authors like Sherrington have sought to fill in the distance between actual observation and this conception with a set of laws of composition, irradiation, inhibition, integration, etc.

Weizsacker's [1] and Goldstein's [2] critique of this theory of re-

1. Weizsacker, "Reflexgesetze," *Handbuch der norm. und pathol. Psychologie,* ed. Bethe *et al.* (Berlin, 1922), vol. X.

2. Kurt Goldstein, *Der Aufbau des Organismus* (The Hague, 1934), pp. 44–67, 104–31.

flexes is sufficiently known in France today, particularly through the works of Merleau-Ponty.[3] It is tempting to conclude, at least if these authors' critique is accurate, that the distinction which we shall make between preformed skills (which other authors call instinctive, perceptive, suspensive, etc. conduct) and the reflexes loses all meaning because reflexes do not exist. We must not forget that Weizsacker and Goldstein criticize the idea of a pure, stereotyped reflex, constant for a given stimulus. Such a reflex, they tell us, does not represent a *normal* activity of an organism, but the behavior of a sick organism or laboratory behavior, constrained to respond by dissociated alternatives to artificially simplified stimuli. Even taken in this sense reflexes can be said to exist. But from the descriptive point of view which we assume we shall not compare the first movement capable of being learned to a pure reflex produced by illness or in the laboratory. The *normal* functioning of the organism presents movements which we can characterize as reflexes in terms of certain descriptive criteria.

The criteria we retain apply to the *involuntary type* manifested by diverse types of elementary movements, namely, a certain stereotyping, a relative autonomy with respect to impulsive and affective life and especially a *fundamental incoercibility in relation to the will.* These reflexes can be distinguished even within the structured behavior which Goldstein opposes to the theoretical reflex of classical writers. But our task is not physiology, as Goldstein's, but psychology. The psychology of reflexes begins with the study of functions which they fulfill and more precisely with the *involuntary* character of these functions. What is important in this respect is that reflexes, unlike other primitive movements, are incoercible, inassimilable to a voluntary system. Thus they refer to the circular schema of the voluntary and the involuntary only secondarily, to the extent to which the will can limit their amplitude or delay their development. For consciousness, reflexes of which it becomes aware are produced in spite of itself; they actualize an absolute involuntary rather than an involuntary relative to the will. I am their locus and appear to myself as an epiphenomenal consciousness in an action which escapes me.

The movements which we propose to call *preformed skills* are quite different. Prior to all learning, all knowledge of the body, we possess a primitive pattern of behavior of our body in relation to perceived objects. More exactly, though there are no adult gestures which the adult has not learned, there are also no adult

3. Maurice Merleau-Ponty, *Structure of Behavior,* trans. Fischer (Boston, 1963), pp. 7–60.

gestures which would not come initially from an initial unlearned power of acting, already related to selective signs in the perceived world. Psychology of the very young has revealed the importance of these incontestably preformed units of sensory motors. "Without having learned it, the infant knows how to follow an object by moving his eyes and head, how to stretch out a hand which he does not see in the direction of an object which attracts his attention. At eleven days he knows how to bend his head forward with the upper part of the body. Locomotion, in spite of its tardy appearance due to organic maturing, is yet not learned. The acts of bending, rising again, etc., are learned with a minimum of fumbling and seem directly governed by perception." [4] In such initial functioning of the body, whose prototype is the liaison between hand and sight, coordination of movement and thought is effected prior to all concerted willing. As soon as the world presents itself to me, I know how to do something with my body, without knowing either my body or the world.

Why have we given preference to the term "preformed skills" over the apparently clearer and more traditional term "instinctive action"? We have avoided the word instinct for two reasons: in the first place, it does not clearly enough indicate a *descriptive* type of behavior and is dangerously reminiscent of a principle of explanation which lends itself to inopportune philosophical discussions. But mainly it seemed that the term instinct should be reserved to indicate less a type of conduct than a general *level* of behavior which roughly defines animality. [5] On this level of instinct there does not yet appear an involuntary moment corresponding to a possible will and presented for its control, but a behavior which has an order within it and brings about genuine organic self-regulation. The word skill has the advantage of being purely descriptive and of not prejudging the impulse which moves it, nor, especially, the higher instance which regulates it. We have chosen the qualifier "pre-formed" for all the reasons which make the term "innate" inappropriate. The actions governed by seeing, hearing, etc., on which there will be constructed endlessly new gestures, are fundamentally distinct from movements produced in us without our participation by an action of things on us (taking the words "produced," "action" in their descriptive rather than

4. Paul Guillaume, *L'Imitation chez l'enfant* (Paris, 1925), p. 77.
5. Thus we shall avoid useless discussions about knowing whether man has more or less instinct than the animal: he has more instincts (plural), in the sense of motives and inclinations, but less instinct (singular), in the sense of organic self-regulation.—For a discussion of the animal as a resolved problem, man as task, cf. p. 231.

explanatory or causal sense). We shall go over a few examples before considering their general opposition.

Because our study is psychological and descriptive we shall neglect a vast group of phenomena which the physiologists still call reflexes but which from a psychological point of view do not belong in the class of reflex actions. They have the physiological character of reflex but are incorporated within other functions. Thus the mechanisms of contraction and secretion which physiology reveals at the basis of alimentary needs (trophic reflexes, etc.) [6] do not present themselves as reflexes, but only reach the level of consciousness through the impulse whose obverse they in some sense are. Now it is an impulse of need and not the reflex itself, masked by impulse, which the will encounters. Since our descriptive method demands that we approach functions as they give themselves as involuntary, we shall not speak of it here. More generally, those reflexes which do not refer back to relational life come close to what Koffka rightly calls "tacit structure," that is, the total of the balances and controls which do not as such appear to consciousness but only contribute to the overall awareness of being alive, of being well or ill, of being in such or such a mood, etc. In Part III we shall consider these organic feelings which reveal to us a life which is no longer motive or power *of acting*, but a condition, situation, or basis to which we can only consent.[7]

In contrast with the reflexes discovered by physiology at the basis of need and, more broadly, of structure, the reflexes of protection and defense, of appropriation, accommodation, and exploration present themselves as reflexes *in the body* or as incoercible influences of the *world* on me. They are not entailed by another experience whose objective counterparts they would in some way be. They constitute by themselves an embryo of function with an adaptation of the initial urge. The will thus confronts them in an entirely original manner. These reflexes must be distinguished from corresponding skills: we shall see that though reflexes have an important role in the order of initial defenses, it is the preformed skills which decidedly place them into the order

6. André Mayer, "Excitation physique et secretion," in *Nouveau traité de psychologie*, ed. G. Dumas (Paris, 1930), II, 59–68.

7. In the last instance reflexes of relational life, those which underlie need and which constitute more broadly structural phenomena, all together compose the organic order in us: within this broader framework they take on their definitive meaning. (See p. 425.) They constitute the level of necessity which *supports* the will and serves as its *preliminary*, thanks to their adaptation of the initial urge.

of elementary adaptations. We shall save the purported reflex force of an external model for a special examination which will lead us to examine the famous ideo-motor reflex in which many authors believed they could find the basic material of voluntary movement.

1. Defense and Protection

IT IS EASY ENOUGH to separate reflexes of protection and defense from the corresponding skills: what is remarkable is that the reflexes offer remarkably adapted means of defense. At the head of the list we can place specialized protective reflexes which assure the integrity of functioning of sense organs (blinking of eyelids and flowing of tears following an irritation of the exterior conjunctiva of the cornea and adjacent mucous membrane, sneezing and nasal excretion reacting to an excitation of passages of the tympanum). These are reflexes of the exteroceptive system which are related to the senses only by their protective action. To this group we must add mechanisms of expulsion which serve to protect consummatory organs: cough which expels solids or liquids which irritate the trachea and vomiting which responds to irritations of the uvula by too coarse or especially sharp bodies.[8]

All these reflexes represent such brief and useful actions that the will never has occasion to resist them. They do better what conscious behavior would do very slowly. Nevertheless convenience, will to surmount a danger, or a test could put them into conflict with the will. The will could sometimes bypass and in some way submerge such brief function within the fullness and tenacity of concerted behavior. Thus a man who has decided to pass through a tear-gas barrage cannot, to be sure, stop himself from crying, but it is possible that the occurrence of such reflex will not change the general line of action governed by an overall intention. At other times the will can relatively restrain the unfolding of the reflex (as coughing or sneezing). This is even more so since these mechanisms are not always self-sufficient acts but rather moments of emotional conduct, imitated or suggested by presentation. The soldier on patrol who wants to keep himself from coughing or sneezing finds himself at the border of the irrepressible and the repressible. We can imagine this soldier accused of having wrecked a surprise attack by his clumsiness, and this weighty question discussed by a court-martial: does

8. Pieron, "L'Excitation et le mouvement," Dumas, *op. cit.*, II, 19–26.

coughing or sneezing involve a man's responsibility? In any case the will can only impose itself on the reflex, without truly making it its own. Its control is limited to the muscles situated on a voluntary course and applies to a retardation or a limitation of the fullness of the reflex.

To these specialized reflexes of defense or protection we must add the general defensive reflexes which are strictly speaking pain reflexes. Their non-sensorial character is as evident as that of protection-reflexes. We must remember the great principle of sensation of pain: the perception itself is never painful. Only the organs of general sensibility next to sensorial termini conduct the pain. We have already had occasion to consider instances of conduct stemming from pain. Pain can by its very character be an occasion of reflexes. Need is born of general indigence of being, it is local in a secondary sense, it anticipates and calls for an object, a sensation, or a pleasure. On the contrary, pain presupposes an encounter, it is prior to the defense which is not an action but a reaction. Such a reaction would, of course, be a reflex on which the will could impose itself more or less successfully.[9]

Pain which I undergo acts as exhaustion, shock, or aggression strictly speaking. In effect, if it is prolonged, it wears me out, suppresses and removes the organic basis of will's functioning. This action belongs to the functions conditioning the body which we shall bring up in Part III. As shock, it resembles the feelings of shock. It surprises, overtakes, and upsets the will which requires a delay and a concerted response. There are few limits of willing as brutal as shock, as if an abruptly absorbing presence occupied the capacity of attention, stunned its capacity for turning away and considering something else and brutally lowered the level of effectiveness of willing.[10] What interests us here are the localized and relatively adapted movements which constitute genuine pain reflexes. Without any cortical participation, the reaction presents an astonishing adaptation.[11] The will can do almost nothing. It might well attempt to *repress* or to *limit* the release of the reflexes insofar as the movement finds itself on a voluntary route, the neuro-muscular mechanism permits the or-

9. Pradines, "L'Heterogéneité fonctionelle du plaisir et de la douleur," *Rev. Phil.* (1927).

10. In this sense we could speak of a rain-emotion, adding to these actions the profound changes in vegetative life uncovered by Frank's work. If we added diffuse muscular reactions to this we should have a picture of a reaction of discharge.

11. Cf. Sherrington's "spinal" dog.

gan to respond, and the action of shock and of deprivation still permit it to think and to will.[12]

But the essence of human defense lies not in these reactions to experienced pain but precisely in the forms of conduct which prevent pain and presuppose an anticipation of the noxious agent by senses or imagination. Anticipated pain, as we know, stimulates genuine impulses which can be likened to a negative desire, impulses of fear which lead to fleeing, waiting, hiding, or attacking and which appeal to the will in the same way as needs. Not only reflexes, but also skills, what is currently called "attack and defense instincts," governed by objects perceived at a distance, belong to fear. Thus while pain reflexes do not presuppose advance warning of perception to respond to experienced pain with stereotyped mechanisms which are relatively isolable and largely incoercible, motor impulses of fear proceed from approaching pain and from the threat of duration of present evil. Now the essence of human wisdom concerning pain does not lie in repression of reflexes of pain, but in the courage of acting in spite of pain which must be undergone. Courage here means facing the representations which accompany the threat and devoting all available attention to the passionate or moral idea which demands that we hold out—to the faith whose witness I must remain, to the ambition which I want to satisfy, to the record I want to break, the pole I want to reach, etc. In all this courage ceaselessly precedes present pain and struggles with the vertigo born of imminence. This function of attention has a muscular component: attention to an idea is also an effort of a set of muscles. Now here we do not find reflexes to be mastered but rather partly preformed motive patterns of the skill family. Repression of manifestations reflecting pain has a more spectacular meaning in courage than in morals; ethics of suffering does not really begin until the scornful rejection of attention to danger and repression of possible flight.

What are these preformed skills? In a rudimentary form, the young child presents an outline of the technique of attack and defense mechanism: parrying a blow by raising his hand to his face, avoiding a projectile by a movement of the whole body, extending hands before falling, protecting the abdomen and the pit of the stomach, pushing away, hitting. These are "instinctive" forms of conduct and not "reflexes," as we have said, and are utilized in forms of conduct we learn by chance or even systematically, as for instance in sports of attack and defense: in com-

12. Pieron, *op. cit.*, II, 253.

mon parlance we call them reflexes, but already the fact that we learn to elaborate them, to correct them, and even to reverse them in feints and practiced holds in wrestling, boxing, or fencing should call it to our attention that we are dealing with anything but reflexes. They are highly variable motor units governed by perceptions and constituting an initial pattern of behavior of a body with respect to an object perceived in general and at a distance, an initial adjustment of motor impulsion to the senses. Of themselves they are inert until an impulse, susceptible to being suspended, animates them. I know how to hit, but I only hit in fear or anger. The entire thrust of the act is not in the perceptivo-motor setting, but in the impulse of need, or passion, or of the will.

2. Appropriation, Accommodation and Exploration

EVEN THOUGH in this second class of elementary acts skill decidedly outweighs rigid reflex, it would be erroneous to believe that all reflexes are defense reflexes. Already the appropriative reflexes (sucking reflex of the newborn, salivation, mastication) represent a type of response not related to a noxious stimulus. These reflexes are remarkable enough since Pavlov's investigations of conditioned reflex relate to one of them, namely the salivation reflex. But we must note two points which limit their significance: in the first place, as we shall develop it below with respect to habit, the conditioning by which Pavlov hopes to explain higher forms of behavior does not apply to construction of new forms of conduct but to transferring reflexogenous capacity to associated stimuli. The movement remains one of a rudimentary type of response and not of display.[13] The latter proceeds from elementary movements which are not triggered by contact but are governed by objects perceived at a distance, as for instance in the conduct of an inquiry, of a hunt, etc., which Pierre Janet calls "perceptive conduct."[14] In addition, these appropriative reflexes ingress as partial and easily isolable segments, without becoming truly integrated, in a broader form of behavior —eating, drinking—whose most important and most decisive segments for the course of action—exploring, pursuing, manipulating

13. Guillaume, La Formation des habitudes (Paris, 1936), pp. 54–55; Pradines, Traité de psychologie générale (Paris, 1943), I, 83.

14. Pierre Janet distinguishes suspensive actions from reflexive actions. L'Intelligence avant le langage (Paris, 1937), pp. 42–47. We find an initial definition of these tendencies in the schema of the whole: "Hierarchy of Psychological Tendencies," in De l'angoisse à l'extasse, I, 211–43, esp. 214.

—are not of a reflex type. Undoubtedly with respect to this form of conduct as a whole these reflexes are distinguished from defensive reflexes as "preparatory" rather than "consecutive" reflexes: but they are only one activation of particular organs and not a complete form of conduct governed by perceptions.[15]

In addition there is a group of reflexes whose point of departure is a sensory organ and whose effector is the mobile organ which bears that sense. These are the accommodation and exploration reflexes: blinking my eyes at the sudden approach of an object or under the effect of a strong, sudden light, following an object which remains within my field of vision with my eyes, or focusing my eyes on a near object. Here we have reflexes which in addition are not equally incoercible, many of which are synergetically governed (for instance ciliary contraction, convergence, and accommodation) and which plainly are not defense reflexes but rather orientation reflexes adapting to a situation. They constitute the reflex part of attention. These reflexes do not present themselves as my body's reflexes, but as a seduction of my attention on part of things themselves, as irresistible control of the world over my consciousness. But, as in defense, the reflex outlines an adjustment of the initial urge. The will, which is slower, reigns only when there is a delay, and thus normally does not come into conflict with them (though I might try not to blink my eyes, as a game or as an exercise). Furthermore, as reflexes of appropriation, these accommodation and exploration reflexes become lodged in the broader observation and research forms of conduct whose most important segments are not of a reflex type: thus reflex attention appears to be based on spontaneous or even voluntary attention governed by emotive awareness or effort.

It could be objected that these reflexes are less distinct from skills than the preceding ones, because they react to an object perceived at a distance while pain reflexes proceed from an essentially non-sensory stimulation. Nonetheless they are distinct from preformed forms of conduct of exploration, locomotion, prehension, or manipulation which on a primitive level adjust all relational life to perception. A child a few days old who reaches out with his hand in the direction of a perceived object, the several months old child who attempts the motions of walking, is no longer the seat of an isolable, quasi-inevitable action. His action is subordinated to his needs and can be indefinitely trained. Sensory reflexes are material effects of things upon us rather than

15. Pradines, *op. cit.*, p. 85.

consequences of perception as the subject's act. Thus in perceiving at a distance I pass under the action of the thing. Still the continuity of the reflex and the preformed skill asserts itself here as we describe their differences: accommodation or fixation reflex of our vision, for instance, *prepares* an appropriate form of conduct. To be sure, this still is not an "adaptive response," only an "actuation" of the organs as in the case of assimilatory reflexes, but the conduct which involves the entire organism incorporates the reaction of local organ. From a phenomenological point of view, this last becomes dissimulated in the conduct as the whole of which it is only a part.

3. General Contrast between Reflex and Preformed Skill

WE CAN NOW SPECIFICALLY compare reflex and preformed skill. Above we have affirmed the triple descriptive character of the reflex: it is relatively stereotyped, easily isolable, and always incoercible. Preformed skill can be distinguished from a reflex by three antithetical traits.

1) The stereotypical form of the reflex does not represent the functioning of the basic organism. Goldstein notes that apart from illness and artificial laboratory or medical examination conditions we can best observe these reflexes in "limit-situations" in which the subject, confronted with a sudden threat or an abrupt stimulation such as flash of light reacts suddenly with one of his parts. The suddenness here plays the same role as isolation: if the subject knows the conditions of the experiment in advance, his artificially provoked reflexes are modified. Thus we cannot rightly speak of reflexes apart from the method by which they have been obtained, and it always seems that the conditions of experience bring about some form of isolation. Thus we cannot understand an organism or—what interests us here—a truly organic form of conduct by starting with a reflex. But, reciprocally, by virtue of the methodological principle of which Goldstein reminds us and which we shall always apply in this work, "the progress of knowledge is possible only in the direction of the more 'perfect,' never in the opposite direction." [16]

This is why the initial skills are not chains of invariable movements, but are already supple forms, structures with variable contents, as habits will be later—they have been called "kinetic melodies." They do not respond to simple stimuli (though even reflexes might never respond to a simple and invariable stimulus),

16. Goldstein, *op. cit.*, pp. 1–8, 240–63.

but to discriminated aspects (qualities, forms, etc.) which already represent a complex perceptive organization. Thereby these initial movements can serve as motive themes of indefinitely transposable variations and increasingly more complex compositions.[17]

In addition each form of in some sense local conduct is organically connected with a posture of the whole which serves as its basis and from which it arises as a representative process. Goldstein has even shown that the form-ground configurations expressed in overall postures in which each partial movement is incorporated are not unlimited in number like variations in a situation: action tends in each instant to realize a "privileged form of behavior."[18] Thus to point out an object, to draw a circle, etc., starting from an initial position (standing up, bent forward, etc.) the organism spontaneously assumes a particular posture. Each individual's customary stances which give him a sense of ease, comfort, and mastery, are modifications of this posture. It would seem that this phenomenon must be related to laws of "good form" which we observe in perception. Thus we can say that, given a task, an intention, an initial situation or posture, there is a privileged scheme of action for realizing the "privileged form of behavior."

This *involuntary* distribution of movement between the form and the ground is also important for us as the specific form of various unlearned skills elaborated by habit and taken up by the will in its turn. We can consider this distribution the most general (or, better, overall) and most complete structural aspect of involuntary powers which are available to the will: even if I do what I will, I do it with involuntary skills and following an overall pattern or involuntary privileged form of behavior.

2) The relative independence of reflex with respect to overall behavior has to be related to its partial dependence on needs and other affective stimuli. Thus reflexes are subordinated to a stimulus and, as Pradines says, "organic activity here appears *endowed with a spirit*, but as from the outside and by a type of incantation. The soul remains as if external to its body: it has not yet *taken possession* of it."[19] The skills thus are not at the mercy of external influences because they are themselves relatively inert until a

17. The Gestaltists, as we shall see later with respect to imitation, have even pushed this structural resemblance to the point of complete solidarity of perception and movement.

18. Goldstein, *op. cit.*, pp. 219–40. Goldstein sees in this privileged form of behavior a manifestation of the tendency of living beings to realize their "essential nature," their *So-sein;* see esp. pp. 237–40.

19. Pradines, *op. cit.*, p. 86.

need, an affective impulse, or a voluntary intention comes to animate them, so to speak, from within. I know roughly how to go about hitting without having learned it, but I do not attempt it except in fear or apprehension. The motive element here is not the signal, but *the impulse which the will can make its own*. Here an essential relation to the three termini, need, perceptive sign, skill, comes to light—this schema cannot be reduced to a mechanistic type.[20] Thus the sign does not *produce* the movement in the way in which stimulus produces the reflex, but only regulates it, because the true source of movement is in the tension of need and "quasi-need." But, as the need is experienced as an apprehension of a "desirable characteristic" *in* the object itself, it is in some way the object in the world which draws the initial gestures from me—though it does not wrench them from me as the stimulus of a reflex animating me from the outside. If the object of my desire draws from me the actual gesture of taking and handling it, its desirable characteristic—which is in the world—seduces me as from within me. What is involuntary here is in part the impulse issuing from need, in part the regulation of the movement as to form by external signs. The *incitation* lies within me insofar as it is a lack and a drive and can be coordinated with the incitation of willing. The involuntary bond of skill to sign concerns not the incitation, the launching, but the *form of unfolding* of the movement. We shall return to this distinction with reference to habit.

To complete this second contrast between reflex and preformed skill we need to consider that the regulating object of a skill not only has the distinctive properties of "forms," quality and affective properties, a desirability, but also that it is at a distance. All these traits belong together. I desire available food because it is absent, perceive it because it is at a distance from me. Now the stimulus of a reflex involves contact, permitting only a re-action. A perception, on the contrary, anticipates possible action of the object. The action which it awakens and which it regulates is pre-ventive in nature. It takes place under the sign of a delay. Here lies the source of all improvements and elaborations based on practice. Nothing can be constructed on a reflex because it follows solely the action of things and does not assume anticipation of that action by senses. By its very nature an object at a distance cannot produce a reflex but rather awakens a need which turns first to the absent, then to the distant. Actions gov-

20. Lewin, "Zwei Grundtypen von Lebensprozessen," *Zts. f. Ps.* (1929) 209–38.

erned from a distance by a perceived object and sustained by the awakened need would also fall within anticipated actions whose result is outlined but suspended until contact. Thus the animal leaps and runs before seizing and devouring its prey. Nothing about its actions resembles a series of reflexes. Rather, we are dealing with a combination of tensions arising from need aroused at a distance and the formal properties of an object perceived equally at a distance.[21]

3) Thus we can understand that the involuntary of preformed skills differs from the incoercibility of reflexes. Because of its incoercibility the reflex remains unassimilable to the will. But we must say, as a counterpart, that by its remarkable adaptation the reflex is not an obstacle to the will but its indispensable preface. It does well what the will cannot do. The adaptation which the will must invent in inventing suitable means is here a resolved problem. The reaction is directly tied to the stimulus and the means to the end.[22] This is why the will naturally follows reflex and is in some ways contiguous and continuous with it. This narrow bond, however, does not constitute a reciprocity of the voluntary and the involuntary. It refers back to the specific solidarity between the will and life which we shall study in the third part rather than to control over myself. The reflex is in me apart from me. The skill for its part constitutes a manifestation of the involuntary in the very special sense that the most basic connections between perception and movement have never been willed or learned. All that we can say of walking or of the movement of prehension is that the internal coordination of the movement and its coordination with a system of regulative objects is prior to all willing. This involuntary does not mean that the child cannot (at least in principle) keep from picking up the objects he sees, but that the impulses, themselves susceptible to being appropriated and integrated by the will, are naturally extended in the useful gesture, primitively adapted to the world as he perceives it. Here then, presented as instrumental or, better, structural involuntary, we find the most primitive connection of the perceiving Cogito with the acting Cogito. That I know how to perform certain elementary gestures without having learned them is in addition the condition of all voluntary learning. I cannot learn everything: I cannot learn for the first time to coordinate a movement with

21. Janet, *L'Intelligence avant le langage* (Paris, 1937).
22. Pradines, *op. cit.*, p. 82: ". . . as by the effect of knowledge, innate to the living being, of the conditions of maintaining and reestablishing its vital equilibrium."

my perception. This is the initial given, the initial foundation granted to the will by nature; and already the union of "I can" and "I perceive" is systematically acted out within an inert structure which the impulse of needs, passions, and voluntary intentions can set in motion. We shall find this type of the involuntary at the basis of habits. The problem of acquisition of habits is in great part one of the constitution of increasingly complex motor machinery depending on signals which are more and more removed from primitive signs and themselves increasingly complex.

Skill thus is not produced by a stimulus in the double sense that it is governed by perceived objects and not by physical stimuli and that these objects are only efficacious on the condition of an affective impulsion whose property it is to lend itself to appropriation by willing. Those elementary gestures whose genesis is recounted in the psychology of the young child never constitute complete actions which would have a meaning in themselves. Following an object with one's eyes, walking, talking, etc. acquire their meaning from the intention or need which animate them and use them. Now classical psychology, undoubtedly because it chose its examples by preference among defense reflexes of uniform and rigid character believed that action was entirely derived from a mechanical system of the stimulus-response type. At the same time it condemned itself to seeking elementary forms of action in constructs conceived on a machine pattern. Adoption of these elementary actions by the will became unintelligible. It is to the credit of psychology of form that it substituted a dynamic tension capable of variable resolution for the principle of rigid, preformed series of reflexes. The true instinctive action on which highest habits are built is already characterized by the production of a constant effect by variable means. These are the totalities which we cannot derive by addition of rigid partial movements: description must apply directly to the form of movement in order to relate it on the one hand to tensions of need which open the cycle of action by uneasiness and close it by satisfaction, and on the other hand to structures of perception which govern variable elements of action. Every action is a meaningful gesture and not a mosaic of movements. The pattern of need and the meaning of the perceived world give elementary action its style. Now an action brought about by need is in principle susceptible to voluntary regulation. I can accept a need or reject it, but I cannot accept or reject a reflex. The preformed structure which connects gestures and perceptions is itself inert. Skill is the source of all the bodily aptitudes which alone give substance to the will and allow freedom to inscribe itself into the world.

4. Problems of Ideo-Motor Reflex and of Imitation

WE HAVE NEXT to account for a group of facts which seemingly cast doubt on our analysis of reflex. The so-called "imitative instinct" seems to imply that an action could be triggered by a similar action which serves at the same time as a model and a stimulus for it. Does the similar as such have an efficaciousness comparable to that of reflex stimuli? The psychologists of the last century and still at the beginning of this century never doubted this primitive power. They saw in it only a special case of the ideo-motor reflex in which the presentation of a movement is of itself supposed to be capable of producing a similar movement. In effect, the ideo-motor reflex implies that a representation produces a similar movement. Now the external model seems to be a special case of representation of movement in which the outline of the action is offered by another subject in place of being produced by the subject himself. The motive force of the external model—which is what is currently understood by the imitative instinct—would thus be only a corollary of the general theorem of the motive power of representations of movement. It has to be admitted that if this ideo-motor reflex has the meaning and importance which is still often attributed to it, we would have to do with a type of reflex which would not be reducible to preceding reflexes of which we could say that they remained alien to voluntary movement. Quite the contrary, we should stand here at the very source of *voluntary* movement.

Ribot states without hesitation that the idea of a movement is already a beginning of its execution and that the movement most frequently remains on the level of tendency because it is hindered by the mental context as a whole. Through mutual reinforcement and inhibition the ideo-motor reflex engenders all the suppleness and apparent motor initiative of the will. Thus we should have here one of the major roots of psychological explanation: in effect the ideo-motor reflex would be at the same time the principle of automatisms of distraction, habitual automatisms, pathological automatisms, and of voluntary movement. Automatism would become primary. Briefly, it is on the level of reflex, on the level of an involuntary which does not in principle presuppose a reference to a possible will that we should have to seek the origin of the will itself.[23] All our hypotheses concerning the irreducible character of the "I will" and the reciprocity of the voluntary and the involuntary are here contradicted.

The representation of movement and more particularly its kinesthetic representation would be able to draw on itself and produce a corresponding movement. Furthermore, voluntary movement would be derived from an ideo-motor reflex by inhibition and correction.[24]

Such a reflex is unique in comparison with the two which we have encountered so far: unique in its role in mental life, in its susceptibility to modification which contrasts with the isolable character and ordinary incoercibility of reflexes, and even unique in its structure—all other reflexes are responses to stimuli as such without any reference to the movement produced, the excitant producing the movement without passing through an idea of the movement. Such unexpected character in a reflex is already surprising.

Such a capacity rests on a rather artificial construction which is not borne out by experience. The supposition is that a movement produced by chance or a passive movement is perceived by various external or internal senses and that because of the close connection between the movement and its perception the *marks* of this perception have in turn the immediate power of producing the movement itself. The sensation of movement, in becoming an image of movement, would become a cause of movement. Among these images, the kinesthetic images would have a particular power of causing which would actually have the characteristics of muscular sensations of movement adhering in some way more than any others to movement itself, whether it is passive or impulsive. Thus we arrive at the primacy of the kinesthetic image which could be called motor image in a double sense: image which represents a movement and image which produces a movement. This immediate power presupposes only an accidental production of movement prior to itself, but not learning strictly speaking. In this sense it would be really primitive. This way the strange causal power attributed to resemblance between representation and a movement would be explained.[25]

23. Th. Ribot, *Les Maladies de la volonté* (Paris, 1833), pp. 3–12.
24. William James, *The Principles of Psychology* (New York, 1890), II, 522–28: the ideo-motor action is the type of normal volition, unencumbered by any complication or disguise, without fiat or express decision.
25. Cf. Guillaume, *L'Imitation chez l'enfant*, pp. 1–27; and esp. Johannes Lindworsky, who sums up all experimental work on this question. [*Der Wille*, 3rd ed. (Freiburg, 1923), pp. 125–44.]

Today we can no longer doubt that these "motor images" are pure constructs: here our criticism finds itself unexpectedly allied with the process of image centers which followed the period of "schemata" in the famous quarrel about aphasia. The studies of primitive reactions of the young child and experimental psychology of learning no longer seem to confirm this interpretation of the ideo-motor reflex.[26]

It really seems that the motive power of representations is not primitive but has to be derived from primitive sources of movement which we have already considered, and among them not from excitants, but from external signs which govern our skills and from attraction (or "desirability") emanating from objects of need and corresponding to the tensions of need. This very derivative character of motor efficacy of representations of movement appears less astonishing if we consider their tenuous role in the control of movement. Normally we govern our movements in terms of things, persons, and events which surround us, briefly, in terms of spatio-temporal signs which form the true context of action and whose regulative power is in part preformed. The representations of movement which precede a gesture play a very episodic role in such regulation of movement, frequently having even a parasitic and disturbing effect on correct execution. Most frequently we are incapable of forming an exact representation of movement, in particular of compensatory movements, of overall postures which balance the principal gesture. The normal function of the image of movement is not to initiate movement or govern it, but to appreciate it after the fact (this does not exclude the possibility that this appreciation might be followed step by step by execution according to natural articulations of action). This is the model function of our images. It is what the dancer, the skater, and others do: the model serves to control the movement in its totality in the course of execution. It constitutes a type of imaginary trying out of our acts which in addition can be completely separated from its regulatory function, cutting us off from action and letting us slide into a dream life, no longer controlled. The regulatory signs of the most primitive act thus are not to any degree imaginary anticipations of movement. They subordinate the entire movement to something other than itself.[27] This organic unity of certain perceptions and certain actions is the true source

26. Thorndike, "Ideo-motor action," *Ps. Rev.*, XX (1913), 91–106. The idea of movement according to Thorndike, gains its motive power by association with excitants which are not representations of movement. Contiguity governs resemblance: "not what is similar, but what is associated."
27. Guillaume, *L'Imitation chez l'enfant*, p. 26.

of the actions which a man knows how to do without having learned them: from them, images of movement derive their regulatory power. It is on the level of these preformed skills that action of the body is digested into knowledge of the world.

The critique of the ideo-motor reflex once again raises the question of all interpretation of imitation. If regulation by a model is a special case of ideo-motor reflex, imitation can be justified by the same explanation. Thus P. Guillaume believes that it is necessary to apply the explanation of mental models to an external model and to derive it from the primitive regulative action of these signs which in the case of the young child guide the initial movements of prehension and manipulation.[28] Nonetheless we might ask whether we do not need to dissociate the role of imitation from that of motive image entirely. Though effectively subjective representations of movement regulate human action only belatedly and in an episodic fashion, it is not certain that the external model does not have an immediate regulative power, without passing through motive images and purported traces of kinesthetic sensations. It is quite possible that regulation of an action by a similar action perceived in another could be a very primitive type of skill. This is a view of the type which guides the general spirit of Gestalt psychology. This school stresses structural resemblances between overall perceived forms and motive totalities considered equally as totalities. Classical psychology, too atomistic, neglected such considerations. A form could very well immediately command a similar form by a sort of dynamic continuity from form to form.[29]

Whatever may be the primitive character of action of an external model, the question which concerns us is one of knowing whether this action is of a reflex type, that is, incoercible, or whether it refers back to skills which we have already shown to be always subordinated to impulsions which the will can always assimilate. Whatever explanation is adopted, it has to deny the reflex character of imitation forcefully: imitation never presents the stereotyped, isolable, irrepressible characteristics of a reflex. A similar action has perhaps a primitive motive power, but it is a power of regulation and not of mechanical production. The model, as all regulative objects, functions at a distance. Thus it gives rise to a spontaneous action and not to a reflex reaction.

28. *Ibid.*, pp. 104–36.
29. Cf. Guillaume's corrections already in *La Formation des habitudes* (Paris, 1936), pp. 133–34, and in *La Psychologie de la forme* (Paris, 1937), p. 198.—Thus on a structural level resemblance would imply contiguity.

This action itself is only aroused if the model possesses a desirable characteristic which is the fascination of the "socius." On this condition alone does the form perceived by a subject govern his action. If the desire to imitate is contradicted by misunderstanding or lack of interest, briefly, if no prestige emanates from the model, it does not arouse a similar action. Thus imitation is a part of those actions subordinated to tendencies susceptible to suspension. A model does not appear to have an immediate effect unless it gathers up remarkable formal properties and a fascination which is its specific desirable characteristic. We can see how dangerous it is to push the structural solidarity of perceived forms and motive forms too far. Outside of reflexes strictly speaking, objects only act with the complicity of affective impulses which can be assimilated by the will. The model *regulates* movement but *does not produce* it. Perhaps it regulates it by an immediate power of the like over the like, but this action can in no sense claim the title of a complete and isolable efficaciousness. Thus the action of a model does not belong to the reflex cycle: supposing that it is primitive, it belongs to the cycle of skills.

5. Conclusion

THUS IT IS THE PREFORMED SKILLS which play the ultimate role in human action. It is the schemata of action in agreement with the presence of the world which will serve as the melodic cells of all the body's habits. In turn acquired skills are encountered in a disordered and often disfigured form in emotion which, as a "malfunction" of these preformed skills, still brings about a crude adjustment to the situation. The hold which I can have on the world and which makes freedom efficacious presupposes this initial continuity between the perceiving Cogito and the movement of personal body: knowledge and movement are more fundamentally and more basically bound together than a concerted voluntary movement can bring about. Here the mental and physical Cogito, thought and movement, bring about an undecipherable unity, beyond effort. *Homo simplex in vitalitate,* said Maine de Biran.

At the same time as skill resolves the incomprehensible union of movement and thought in principle and more deeply than all reflection, all knowledge and all will, it presents itself as the matter of possible effort. This is what distinguishes it radically from reflex. And this distinction is one of principle. We might be tempted to deny the radical character of this contrast: the difference between producing a movement and governing it might perhaps appear as a difference of degree and not of kind. We might say, for example, that in isolation perceptive signs would infallibly produce movement the way a reflex does, and that revocable skills are only automatisms impeded by the totality of a mental state. Skill would differ from reflex only by its greater aptitude for being integrated into the actions of the total field (speaking as a Gestaltist). Primary action would be of a unique type, an undifferentiated automatism. Unfortunately this systematic view is only an initial prejudice. In principle the formal, structural elements of perception act only within a constellation of factors which are impulsions accessible to voluntary mastery. A form cannot act in isolation; it only governs action in connection with a characteristic of the object which reflects such impulsion.

The defenders of primitive automatism invoke the conclusion of pathological psychology: fatigue, distraction, psychoasthenesis, major neuroses and certain mental disorders seem to restore a fundamental automatism, as if by simplification of consciousness: the motive power seems to revert to the signs which lost it through mental complication. A disintegrated consciousness or a consciousness on the verge of breakdown seems to show the primitive character of the actions which are initiated in isolation by simple pressure of representation. But we must not forget that the degradations of consciousness do not represent a return to simple and primitive forms from which consciousness and will would have arisen by complication. Degradation of habits and of skills into quasi-reflexes is an original product, resulting in a different consciousness. We cannot hope to explain normal consciousness by a consciousness simplified by disease. We have rather to seek to understand action by starting with definite movements or preformed skills available to the will which in turn can master them.

[2] EMOTION

IT MIGHT SEEM paradoxical to place emotion among the means or organs rather than among the motives of willing. Even the kinship of the words "emotion" and "motive" would seem to suggest the latter. Yet there appear to us various decisive reasons for a different treatment of emotion.

The essence of a motive is to propose ends. Now emotion, as

we shall see, contributes no ends not already present in needs and quasi-needs. Emotion presupposes a more or less implicit motivation which precedes and sustains it. All it can do is give the ends which are already present before consciousness a certain physical prestige whose efficacy is partly of the order of nascent movement. Here emotion appears as the province of involuntary action. On the other hand emotion is so interrelated with habit that these two functions cannot be very well understood except in terms of each other. It is unquestionably habit which provides the will with convenient means it can use. But habit would be incomprehensible if we saw it solely as an extension of the initial unlearned skills: Hegel at one point views it as moderation of an explosive force, a domestication of emotion. Habit itself must be spurred into action by the ill-defined function it appropriates. This is why emotion appears to us as a source of involuntary movement more basic than habit. We propose to show 1) that in emotion there is no hiatus between thought and movement and that, consequently, the passage from thought to movement is mysteriously carried out on the level of the involuntary, this side of effort; and 2) how the involuntary aspect of emotion is comprehensible in relation to a willing which it agitates and which in turn only moves if it is moved. We shall reserve the dialectic of effort and emotion for a later analysis and a similar study of habit.[30] Only then shall we understand the interrelation of all involuntary powers among themselves and in relation to the *hegemonikon:* for meaning comes always from above and not from below, from the one and not from the many.

But what appears undoubtedly most paradoxical is not that we shall speak about emotion here rather than elsewhere, but that we shall speak of it as an involuntary which *sustains* voluntary action, which *serves* it in preceding and limiting it. Contemporary psychology is actually unanimous, if not in explanation, then at least in description of emotion: Larguier des Bancels calls it a miscarried instinct,[31] Pierre Janet,[32] followed by Renée Dejean,[33] calls it a primitive evolutionary stage in functional liberation of rudimentary forms of conduct. Pierre Janet provides a very valuable guiding thread in contrasting the *disordering* character of

30. Cf. below, pp. 280.
31. Larguier des Bancels, *Introduction à la psychologie;* Dumas, *op. cit.,* II, III, chap. VI, 53–57.
32. P. Janet, *De l'angoisse à l'extasse* (Paris, 1928), vol. II; "Les Sentiments fondamentaux," Part III, chap. I; "Les Emotions," pp. 449–96.
33. Renée Dejean, *L'Émotion* (Paris, 1933).

emotion with the regulative character of feeling, understanding by feeling "not actions, but potentially different ways of regulating action." [34] M. Pradines tried to perfect this thesis by seeking affective attitudes and forms of conduct which emotion disorders apart from feelings "which are basic only in asylums." [35] The feelings derouted by emotion are complex affections tied to imaginative anticipations of pleasure and pain. They are not themselves pleasure or pain, but manifest them affectively, developing a thousand affective nuances which are the feelings strictly speaking. In the course of fluid situations they outline an "objective and adaptive circumstantial orientation." [36]

If emotion is a derangement of feeling, how can it lend itself to a *reciprocal understanding* of the involuntary and the voluntary? Would not the only understanding suited to it be one of a *disrupted* order?

Precisely here we shall attempt to uncover a form of emotion *in which the derangement is in a nascent state*. We have reached the conviction that there are here fundamental emotions whose functional role in voluntary life is as decisive as that of habit: they have a power of stimulating action, of moving a being, which consists in the first place not of driving it beside itself but in drawing it out of inertia by a spontaneity which always poses a threat to self-possession. While the will must always recapture itself from this spontaneity, it is nonetheless through it that it moves its body.

We owe the principle of our description to Descartes' *Treatise on Passions*. The "principal passions" (admiration, love and hate, desire, joy and sorrow) shall serve as our guiding thread. While modern psychology derives emotion from a *shock* and describes it as a *crisis*, Descartes derives it from *wonder* and describes it as an *incitation* to action in accordance with the vivid representations which engender wonder. Thus we shall postpone any examination of the emotions of shock and shall eventually show how these extend the disorder nascent in all emotions of wonder and distort its functional significance.

The objection could be made that we are here substituting feeling in P. Janet's sense for emotion, and that emotion remains essentially deranging. We hope to show that already *wonder* allows us to call the affections we are describing "emotions." There is a connection between wonder and shock which assures the

---

34. Janet, *op. cit.*, p. 456. Re Janet's theory of feelings, cf. *ibid.*, pp. 9–43.
35. Pradines, *Traité de psychologie générale* (Paris, 1943), I, 659–733.
36. *Ibid.*, p. 665.

unity of the realm of emotions.[37] Our analysis must focus precisely on showing how the emotion of shock is derived not only from misadaptation of the order of feeling, but also from the *fertile* disordering of the emotion of wonder essential to human life.

Further, the affects which contemporary psychology prefers to describe are not only too disordered, but also rather more complex than is assumed. We would find here a thousand passions which introduce their principle of bondage and of the special vertigo of the will which fits in obscurely with the passions. Yet we believe that this vertigo and this bondage, most often encountered at the roots of fear and anger which are the archetypes of emotion for modern psychology, do not fundamentally belong to emotion.

For all these reasons we shall shift our focus from emotions of shock and passion to the emotions of wonder which are in fact also non-passionate.[38] Thus the meaning of emotion as an involuntary would become apparent here.

1. Wonder as Emotion: Basic Emotional Attitudes

WONDER OR AWE (Cartesian "admiration") is subsequently elaborated by emotive forms of *affective imagination* by which we anticipate some good or evil. It reaches its culmination in the *awakening of desire,* its peak in the emotion of *joy* and *sorrow* connected with the possession of a good or an evil.

a. *Wonder* is the simplest emotive attitude and yet it already contains all the richness of what has been called the *circular phenomenon* of thought and the body. In wonder a living being is awed by a new event to which it yields, *by an other*. This is more primitive, more basic than love and hate, than desire, joy or sorrow. "It has," says Descartes who calls it admiration, "neither good nor evil for an object but only knowledge of the thing I admire." [39] This awe is what colors time; through it objects touch us, through it something happens, through it there are events. What we encounter, what we see as new, might not be real: ab-

37. If we nonetheless wanted to call the emotions of wonder, which we shall describe first, "feelings," their characteristic of nascent derangement would demand at least that we call them *moving* feelings.—Pradines is not convincing when he speaks of them as enduring affective motives: if they are in fact circumstantial, do they not arise from wonder?

38. We are using the word "passion" in a sense different from Descartes', who opposed it to action. We give it a definite meaning in the General Introduction. Thus we shall bracket "passion" in the broad Cartesian sense which includes emotion and passion in our sense.

39. Descartes, *Treatise on Passions*, art. 53, pp. 70–73.

254 / VOLUNTARY MOTION

sence or fiction can meet us, touch us, astonish us in the same way. This remark already warns us against interpreting wonder as a reflex. It is at the same time an impact of knowledge and a disturbance of the body or, better, a shock of knowledge in a disturbance of the body.

Here we must pay close attention to the circular character of the emotion of wonder which we shall encounter again, more diffuse and limited, in emotions of shock. James would make emotion a trait of the human automaton, so that movement would proceed directly from this or that completely physical impression of things on the body, emotion being only the consciousness of a synthesis of reflexes.[40] Wonder is more complicated than a reflex. It is true that a shock emotion follows the pattern of a reflex—the tide of fear or anger, the explosion of joy or the crisis of despair producing further change—but wonder does not permit this confusion.

The new does not affect the body the way pain does: emotive shock is not a contusion, but in the first place a disorder in the course of thought; all we think, feel, and will is generally brought to a halt. The new disarranges a regular adapted course of thought and life. Consequently a lightning valuation of the new, an implicit comparative judgment, accompanies its irruption. Psychologists like to speak of upsetting of tendencies, but what would such an upset be without an implicit judgment with its emotive trait which is precisely wonder, love, hate, or desire? Only the lightning-fast character of judgment of novelty can create the illusion that wonder is an automaton's reflex in response to an external situation.

But in turn a judgment of novelty, no matter how rapid and implicit, is not the emotion of wonder. Emotion is nourished by bodily repercussions; the shock of knowledge affects the flow of disturbance and bodily inertia to thought. How are we to understand this circular process in its two directions? How can a quick judgment about novelty mean for the body of quickened pulse, a diffuse inhibition, a certain stupor which stiffens the face and inclines mobile parts of the senses to receptivity? And, in turn, why is this disposition of the body also a disposition of the mind to consider the object and to linger over it. It is doubtful that more can be done here than to circumscribe the mystery a bit more and, with each moment of emotion, seize it in detail in some respect. The basic fact of astonishment is that attention is overcome by a

40. William James, *Principles of Psychology* (New York, 1890), chap. XXIV, which takes up in greater detail his article, "What Is Emotion?" *Mind* (1884).

body and an object imposes itself on thought. Thus incarnate thought is no longer atomic or reduced to gliding vaguely over things without stopping on any. The body keeps the encounter with the new from remaining only a furtive touch. It leads consciousness to stumble and in a way settle on a representation: we can see in the case of admiration that the function of emotion is, as Descartes has it, to "strengthen and preserve an impression." [41] The body amplifies and magnifies the moment of thought by giving it the time of bodily impression as the substance of duration. Through wonder, thought becomes in a sense physically imposed. There are few passions which do not draw some force from it: respect and scorn, magnanimity, pride, veneration, humility, meanness, disdain. "And its force," says Descartes, "depends on two things: namely, its novelty and the fact that the movement it brings about has its full force from the start. For it is certain that such a movement has a greater effect than those which being faint at first and only growing bit by bit can easily be diverted": [42] willing is surprised, that is, taken unawares. Thus all voluntary attention might have to be recovered from an initial involuntary attention involving even a muscular effort. Since involuntary attention has all the visceral density and a certain muscular inertia as a resounding board, voluntary attention which brings it into action or which opposes it will also have muscular components. Even the most abstract attention is also physical.[43] In this sense Ribot is right: there is no attention which does not in some way involve the body and in particular the mobile organs of sensibility, but this motor aspect of attention is only an articulation of the initial judgment derived from it through the original phenomenon of frustration of control.

But this involuntary aspect of wonder is susceptible to being controlled by an effort of attention: only passions can so fascinate attention that it frequently becomes enslaved to them. There is, however, nothing in emotion which could enslave the power of judging. Involuntary attention is an appeal thrust at the receptivity which is the attention of the judging person itself. In *extreme* cases, as the emotions of shock of which we shall speak

41. Descartes, *Treatise on Passions*, arts. 53 and 70. Of course, though we are following the Cartesian description, the circular understanding we propose departs from Descartes' dualistic explication.

42. *Ibid.*, art. 72.

43. This emotional attention is an extension of reflex attention, described above, which performs only an activating function. Thus there is a hierarchy of attention: automatic, spontaneous, voluntary—all frequently included in the same act.

later, it may be true that the mind can be so distraught that judgment is entirely suspended within it. As we shall see, the mind only thinks within certain limits and by a kind of permission from the universe. The universe can press in on my body to the point of distorting my being as a man and completely turning me over to disorder. But when circumstances have submerged me to such an extent, I am as if released from myself. In a hospitable environment which is not excessively upsetting wonder should be only the first awakening of the power of judgment. This power is in principle its master. According to a suggestive coincidence of words, the one who judges is called upon to consider only when the body is distrained. But the judgment is up to him. This is why Descartes, having described passion as a physician, concludes as a moralist. He does not in the least doubt that it is within our power to "supply its defect by a special reflection and attention to which our will can always oblige our understanding if we judge that the thing is worth the trouble." [44]

b. *Affective anticipation as an emotion.* Astonishment, in the modern sense of the word, is in its purity only an alerting of knowledge. Emotion is rarely cerebral: it generally affects our body, social, intellectual, spiritual, and other interests. Hope, fear, worry, rage, or ambition trouble us only in terms of an anticipated or represented *good* or *evil.* Here lies the second function of emotion, that of echoing and amplifying in the body a rapid, implicit value judgment.

Under the topic of motivation we have already considered affective apprehension of good and evil, but we have left the natural dynamogenesis of this anticipation in suspension. Similarly, we have been able to reduce the will provisionally to a kind of *vision* which sometimes considers, at other times turns away. But emotion introduces into all valuation a visceral, motive element which in turn means that all decision is tinged with some bodily effort. To choose means to hold the assemblage of muscles pressing for an act at an arm's length while I consider motives.

Emotion consists not only in affective, but also in motive anticipation of goods and evils. But love and hate, in Descartes' sense, are still only a more visceral aspect rather than the motor of emotion. Descartes gives their fine, familiar definition: "Love is an emotion of the soul caused by the movement of the spirits which incites it to unite itself willingly with objects which seem desirable to it. And hate is an emotion caused by spirits which incite the soul to desire to be separated from objects which appear

44. Descartes, *Treatise on Passions,* art. 76.

noxious to it." [45] What is remarkable about this definition is the distinction which it introduces between this emotion and desire: it very fortunately isolates a non-militant emotion which is in some sense contemplative. This is the emotive dimension of imagination by which I foresee myself in a situation which the will, impelled by desire, is to bring about or to avoid. "Finally by the word 'will' I do not mean here to speak of desire, which is a distinct passion related to the future, but of consent, by which man considers himself in the present united with that which he loves, so that he imagines a whole of which he believes himself but a part while the beloved object is the other part. Similarly, by contrast, in hate a man considers himself a whole, completely separate from that to which he has an aversion." [46] Thus to understand this emotion correctly we have to grasp it this side of desire, in that unmoving evocation of an absent good and evil. This anticipation goes far beyond anticipated need related solely to nourishment or a sexual object. It covers all possible aspects of human good and evil: love of glory, of money, of reading, etc. are forms of love. It is no longer an illusion in which I take the unreal for the real, but a living representation of that which is not. But, we might say, to imagine a good or an evil with which I would like to be united or from which I consider myself separate is not the same as being moved by love or aversion. Precisely, the emotion is distinguished from simple intellectual anticipation by its host of organic concomitants. I love music or even God with all my body. While it is false that love could proceed directly from an external situation without passing through consciousness, it is still true that the body magnifies the initial judgment of suitability and seems in all respects to precede and prepare the fully developed judgment by heightened pulse, heat in the chest ("soft warmth" in the case of love, "sharp, pointed heat for hate," says Descartes). [47] My body is the fullness and the flesh of anticipation itself.

We have to distinguish the circular process which leaves some sort of initiative to the body from the infinitely more discrete presence of the body absorbed entirely in the matter of an imaginative intention. In what sense can we actually say that an image

45. *Ibid.*, art. 79. Love and hate, as emotions of wonder, are thus simpler than the passionate emotions of the same name: the former is an intermittent stirring of the latter. In addition, Descartes' attempt to discover love and hate beyond desire is significant because all the passionate emotions are highly complex derivatives of desire, the principle of all emotions.

46. *Ibid.*, art. 80.

47. *Ibid.*, arts. 97–98.

includes an affective moment? J.–P. Sartre has shown in *L'Imaginaire* [48] that every image is first of all a form of knowing: I can only imagine what I know, which is another way of saying that I learn nothing new by trying to observe an image. But an image does more than intend the absent object or value generally—it endows it with a quasi-presence. At this point there intervene muscular attitudes and movements which designate and outline what is absent and feelings which grasp its affective nuances. Feelings and movement play the role of an analogon, of a concrete equivalent of the object (what Husserl calls *Darstellung*). The absent manifests itself to me in its affective and kinesthetic presence: the affect and the movement are the matter, the *hyle*, of the image. The relation of knowledge and affect in the image remains one of form and matter.

The circular phenomenon of emotion by which a value judgment incorporates a corporeal disturbance appears to us rather more complex than the relation of knowing to an affective-motor analogon. There the corporeal disturbance acquires an importance and a type of initiative which make it difficult to treat it as flesh, as the fullness (*die Fülle* in Husserl) of the image. This organic amplification, which is more than a *hyle*, is what distinguishes emotion. This suffices to protect the originality of the emotive attitude which we are here describing with respect to the portraying, representative image. There is a continuity from the most intellectual image right up to motive representation and thence to hallucinated anticipation such as we encounter most frequently in shock emotions. The further we move from the image towards emotion strictly speaking, the more does the genuine intentionality of feeling which we have found implicit in the non-emotive image become effaced. Feeling aims at the very expression of things, it is not aberrant. With emotion this authentic feeling for the affective nuance of things retreats before the appearance of a magic world which is no more than a transformation of organic disturbances in the Cogito. The more the corporeal orchestration of emotion makes it outweigh feeling strictly speaking, the more does affective imagination become aberrant. This undoubtedly explains why imagination has occasioned such contradictory judgments. J.–P. Sartre expects much from imagination, perhaps even the secret of freedom. Alain sees in this power of intending the absent only the chief error of classical moralists, the frantic commentary of corporeal disturbance.[49] But Sartre

48. Sartre, *Psychology of Imagination*, pp. 81–96.
49. Alain, *Système des beaux-arts* (Paris, 1920), chap. I, esp. pp. 15–18.

described a peaceful imagination with a faint organic resonance in which the body remains the discrete *hyle* of knowledge, Alain the troubled imagination which lies on the path of a true organic disorder. Both are right; the *spectator* imagination is in fact our freedom which "negates" the real, while the concerned imagination, ties to our goods and our evils, lies on the way of *disorganization* which leads to the quasi-hallucinatory manifestation of good and evil. In this extreme stage, the reflection connected with delay is annulled: the living being finds himself as if in contact with good and evil and prey to agitation.[50] Affective imagination of love and hate lies midway between a spectator-image and a hallucination-image, as wonder stands midway between a circumstantial feeling and shock. It is still a *nascent* disorder which plays a normal role in the dialectic of the voluntary and the involuntary.

How does emotional anticipation affect voluntary and involuntary motion? We have reffered to the frequently painful dialectic of need and image: in acting out satisfaction, image heightens the tension of need. Now in elaborating in some sense corporeally the attractiveness of the image, emotion adds to it a specific corporeal element which specially concerns voluntary motion. In a sense love and hate stimulate a relaxation of effort. The being "united by the will" with an object or other finds the annulled distance in some sense restful. And when we "consider ourselves simply as a whole, entirely separated from the object for which we have an aversion," we shall similarly find the distance we have created restful. For insofar as love and hate are distinguished from desire "which is a distinct passion related to the future," they constitute the rest in which all desire is resolved and dreaming. But love and hate prepare to act in that very repose, in the "charm" of effort which anticipates its own triumph. Thus this relaxation gives rise to the specific tension of desire: as Descartes puts it, while all love invites us to extend our well-wishing to all the objects which are suitable for being loved, its most frequent effect is to give rise to desire.[51]

c. *Joy and sorrow.* It is difficult at first to distinguish joy and sorrow as emotional attitudes from more complex forms of conduct, exultation and despondency, which develop them in space

50. Pradines, who goes directly from regulatory feelings to purely anarchic emotion, describes this movement towards disorder through emotive effects of representation perfectly as the "mental vertigo," the "bewilderment of the imagination," but he passes over the basic stage of motive representation. (*Traité de psychologie générale*, pp. 713–33.)

51. Descartes, *Treatise on Passions*, arts. 119, 120.

and time and which are part of the same cycle as fear and anger. Now if we do not want to miss the true function of emotion, which is to incline the will to action, we have to lay hold of joy and sorrow in the attitudes which initiate actions and not in excessively disordering forms of conduct.

Joy and sorrow are distinguished from other emotional attitudes by containing a note of sanction. Wonder expresses the irruption of the "other" into consciousness, affective anticipation having invoked his absent-presence and his charm. In joy I am with my good, in sorrow I am with the evil: I have become that good and that evil. The good or the evil have become my mode of being. I *am* sad, I *am* happy: these expressions have an absolute meaning which we do not find in expressions like "I am surprised," "I love," or "I hate." To love and to hate means less *being* than being *directed* towards something lovable or detestable which is a possible object of desire, situated in the world and at a distance. Now to be sure joy is also in a sense a way for the world to appear—joyful—but we still say that I *am* my own joy, absolutely. If I discover it outside of myself, that is in part insofar as my joy is projected on the neutral beings around me and recognized in the world in communicating with the joy which is outside of me and which in some sense is also absolutely there. My joy makes my vision sensitive and makes it capable of reading the greatness of being drawn on the physiognomy of things and persons, as if the expression of things betrayed their absolute being and as if joy and sorrow were in the world as they are in me, testifying in some way to the level of being of each thing. We could say even that my sorrow puts me specially in tune and sympathy with whatever there is most degraded, low, wrong, my joy with what there is perfect, pure, and faithful in the universe. This remarkable character of sorrow and joy reveals that these emotions are less affective intentional objects than sanctions of my being.

But the problems posed by sorrow and joy are no different from those posed by other emotions. Do sorrow and joy really include the belief that I have a good and an evil? Does the body here really always play the role of an amplifier of belief which we thought we found elsewhere?

It often seems that sorrow and joy are immediate impressions of consciousness which exclude all judgment and which furthermore seem now to come from the body alone, now to shine in the privacy of consciousness without the body seeming to share in any way. It is really not always easy to distinguish joy and sorrow from pleasure and pain or from the vague mood which a good meal, feeling unwell, or a ray of sun insinuate into the soul. The difference between pain and sorrow is still relatively easy to establish: pain is generally a sensation, it is local; sorrow is neither sensation nor local, it is a way of being. In the same way pleasure, which stresses the moment of encounter and is always associated with the advanced parts of the body, retains something local; but the enjoyment which confirms the completion of the˘ cycle of need, the fusion with the object is in no way localized: in spite of its local indices, it affects the living being in its indivisibility. Is it not the lowest degree of joy? Not at all. Sorrow and joy, while most closely related to pain and enjoyment, are distinguished by several aspects. In a sense enjoyment is still local, no longer in a geographic sense of the word, but in a functional sense: it is always relative to a satisfied function to which I can oppose my self as a whole: I can distinguish myself from my enjoyment, step back from it, judge it, that is, expel it, no longer into some part of the body, but as body and life. I can oppose myself as being to the living and feeling myself, while joy is inherent in the very judgment which I can bring to bear on enjoyment and pain. I can suffer morally from a pleasure for which I reproach myself, find joy in spite of the pain which I suffer in my body. Joy and sorrow affect me as being inasmuch as I am more or less perfect. Similarly the diffuse mood which time exudes like perfume is not at all the emotion of sorrow and joy.[52] There is something flexible and moving and even superficial about mood which distinguishes it from sorrow and from joy. Without being as apparently organic as enjoyment experienced in the mass of the body, mood, more free-floating, still bears the subtle weight of the body. Joy and sorrow affect me more fundamentally: they are the good which I have become, the evil into which I have been transformed. It is here that they re-enter the schema of emotion.

There is always a diffuse view of good and evil which I have reached in sorrow and in joy: it is even the touchstone of the emotion of joy and sorrow with respect to pain or enjoyment, gay or somber mood. The good we possess, the evil with which we are afflicted are its discrete intellectual armor. We always find a shortcut and an infinite capacity for judging in joy and sorrow.

52. Concerning mood, cf. p. 409 below. It refers back to more incoercible and more treacherous involuntary, as the influence of age, sex, personality. Here Maine de Biran recognized the most discouraging form of affectivity. His *Journal* is a touching echo of it.

The judgment, highly implicit itself, seems inexistent by virtue of the very character of its object: in effect a feeling of triumph or obstacle in the soul does not deal with a particular good. It is an over-all appreciation of a relation of suitability between myself and my situation as a whole. In joy, a being feels superior to his situation and tastes his success with respect to his own role, in sorrow he tastes his injury and weakness. But as in all emotion, judgment is only the starting point of a minor disruption of the whole body. What would joy be without that slight acceleration of pulse, that pleasant warmth in the whole body and expansion of the whole being? And sorrow, without the tightness around the heart and a general languor? James is right: take away from joy and sorrow. . . .

At the same time we have to hold that joy and sorrow would be nothing without a hidden appreciation of the level attained by a being and that they would be nothing if the whole body did not act out that unclear thought which it develops in its visceral motive depth. There are not two joys, a bodily joy and a spiritual joy: [53] in reality all joy is intellectual, at least in a confused way, and corporeal, at least as an attempt and as it inscribes into the body the possession of goods and evils normally foreign to any usefulness for the body. In this sense James is right in rejecting a distinction in principle between "finer" emotions and "coarse" emotions. Both have the same bodily texture. Undoubtedly finer emotions have a lived intensity out of proportion with the physical disturbance which orchestrates them, but their intensity and refinement are explained by other reasons—in the first place by the capacity which joy has of opening us to a joy spread out through the universe and drawn in the physiognomy which reveals the degree of being of each thing. Its refinement is the acuteness and power which it brings to our reading of the world. But its character as emotion is complete only in all its bodily resonance.

We still have to find a place for the emotions of joy and sorrow in the realm of the involuntary. If movement born spontaneously in thought is the outstanding trait of emotion, our whole analysis of emotion must focus on desire, the most motive of our emotions. Considered in the register of action, emotion is a disposition of

53. Descartes himself notes that there is no joy born "without the intervention of the soul" (*Treatise on Passions*, art. 93), and, on the other hand, "because the impression of the brain presents it as its own" (art. 93), the good or evil from which the soul suffers or rejoices are not any "purely intellectual joys arising in the soul solely through the action of the soul" (art. 91), as those which come from the good use of our freedom: intellectual joys never fail to evoke those which come from the body and are "like" them (art. 143).

the will to seek or flee things for which it prepares the body. But this is only true to the extent to which emotion culminates in desire. Could we say that joy and sorrow are moving towards desire? Not in the principal sense of these emotions which *sanction* action. In this respect loving, desiring, and enjoying are successive natural moments of emotion and the definition of joy naturally follows the definition of desire. But in a secondary sense, which is more important for our researches into the involuntary, this emotion is also related to desire. In man, the most restless of beings, a cycle of tension is only closed in order to be reopened, or to reopen another one. Consciousness only commemorates its sorrows and its joys in order to anticipate them anew. And thus joy and sorrow, which complete the desire, arouse it over again. In this respect they are like love and hate: to love and to hate is to anticipate the future joy and sorrow of being united with the beloved object or separated from the hated object. And to be sad or joyful is already to begin once again to anticipate a union or a separation which are yet to come. Sanction and anticipation imply each other mutually. Finally it is through the mediation of desire that love and hate, joy and sorrow "rule our ways," that is, incline our will.[54] Man knows no definitive repose. Desire grows in the pauses of sorrow and joy.

d. *Desire as an emotion.* Here at last we have a conquering emotion, the motor emotion par excellence, desire: desire to see, to hear, to possess, to keep, etc. Love anticipates union, desire seeks it and drives towards it; love is triumphant because desire is militant first. Now desire is born from a definite judgment, sometimes most confused, in which we represent to ourselves at the same time the thing's suitability for us and the possibility of obtaining it. Desire means representing to myself the possibility that I can already do something in the direction of the desired object.

But this complex judgment is still not an emotion: the emotion desire is at the same time a profound visceral disturbance and an acute alerting of all our senses and all motor regions. This agitation provokes judgment and makes it that original quality of the Cogito by which I am prepared and carried to a pitch nearer to action than in a simple inspection by the mind of a problem proposed for my initiative. ". . . I notice this peculiar

54. Descartes examines first of all the four passions of love and hate, of joy and sorrow, "in themselves . . . insofar as they bear on no action"—later, starting with article 143, "insofar as they excite in us the desire by means of which they rule our manners." "It is particularly desire which we need to regulate and it is in this that the principal utility of Ethics consists" (arts. 143–44).

quality in desire, that it stirs the heart more violently than any other passion, providing more spirits to the brain which, passing thence into the muscles, make all the senses more acute and all the parts of the body more mobile." [55] Thus I turn towards the object of desire with a body which is "more agile and more disposed to movement." It is an intention of the subject, but reinforced by organic dynamism. Thus to analytic understanding desire is no less disconcerting than astonishment or love.

Two remarks need to be made concerning the nature of desire before we consider its function with respect to the will. It will be undoubtedly surprising to find desire among emotions. We have considered desire in the first part as a *motive*, that is, as revealing an anticipated good. Now we have to consider it as *motor*. We know already that the realm of desire infinitely exceeds the field of organic needs and is not concerned solely with satisfying organic indigence. The realm of desire is as broad as the field of human values which are not only vital, but also social, intellectual, moral, and spiritual. Desire belongs to the body in terms of visceral intensity and muscular alerting which orchestrate, often most covertly, the most subtle movements of the soul. Desire might even be borne out of the world by its intentions, yet the body still accompanies it with its thrust:

> "As a hart longs for flowing streams,
> so longs my soul for thee, O God." (Ps. 42:1)

The soul truly does become longing and movement, which is why such metaphors are comprehensible: the body's power of resounding is so well grounded in the operations of judgment that body moved by desire is a true description of the soul grasped by its values. Ribot did not realize how right he was when he refused to see more than a nascent movement in desire (he forgot, perhaps, only the visceral disturbance in which movement occurs and which gives desire its bodily density and its very quality of emotion). But this definition of desire in terms of nascent movement is only true within the context of the circular phenomenon, that is, insofar as the body improvises under the sign of value. Considered from this motive angle, desire, as Descartes notes, has no counterpart: "It is always the same movement which leads to the quest for the good and thereafter to the flight from evil which is opposite to it." [56] Aversion and desire in the strict sense are distinguished only by the nuances of love, hope, and joy or of hate, fear, and sorrow which color them. Ultimately

55. Descartes, *Treatise on Passions*, art. 101.

they are only distinguished by the horror of evil and the vision of pleasure which motivate the flight or the quest. But desire as such is properly a strong inclination to act which arises from the whole body. It can be oriented towards the object, or in the opposite direction—this does not affect the meaning of desire which is the very disposition of willing to moving in accordance with the represented end.[57] It is desire which redoubles motivation and gives all value the aura of nascent or suspended movement and which, after the decision, keeps fresh the schemes of action which will inscribe it into the world. Undoubtedly, from a strictly biological viewpoint, appetite and defense are not symmetrical, but the imagination which anticipates the object of need and the object of pain makes real opposites of desire and fear.[58] And it is with a similar movement that our whole body incites us to seek the apparent good or flee the apparent evil. Similarly protection of the body presents phases of attack, defense, immobility, or feint which convert desire alternately into quest and flight. The orientation of desire does not belong to its essence: it is simply the acute awakening of all the body to movement.

Here we have reached the highest point of the corporeal involuntary: desire is a type of spirit of adventure which rises from the body to willing, and which is the reason why willing would have little efficacy if it were not sharpened first of all by the prodding of desire, as we can see in the case of bare idea of duty. Plato recognized, under the name of *thymos*, the entire control of desire over the will. The *thymos*, which already he considered related to anger, is "to courage what the dog is to the hunter." The scholastics took up this Platonic conception of *thymos* under the name "irascibility." To be sure, they distinguished precisely between desire and irascibility. Desire strictly speaking—concupiscence—seemed to them to be an original power of the soul in which the soul yields only to the force of affective attraction and repulsion of good and evil. That sums up desire as motive, as we considered in the first part. Irascibility refers more strictly to the tendency which leads us to confront difficulty. Its appropriate object is no longer good or evil as such, but rather the hard or the difficult.[59] That is desire as incitation to action. The scholastics themselves defined the concupiscible and the irascible equally well as types of desire in a broad sense, the concupiscible as desire for union with an object, the irascible as desire for overcoming

56. *Ibid.*, art. 87.
57. *Ibid.*, art. 86.
58. Cf. above, p. 85.
59. Cf. texts in Gilson, *St. Thomas d'Aquin* (Paris, 1925), pp. 113–15.

a difficulty. Descartes laid down two classes of "passions" and introduced characteristics of the irascible into the definition of desire itself. In his case this is based on a refusal to carve up affectivity into two parallel series and especially on an effort to harmonize the two principal moments of emotion into an order. This would seem reasonable: desire is only distinguished from love by its thrust and the type of outburst in confronting an obstacle which brings it to rage, an efficacious rage representing irritation in face of difficulties, as in the exaltation of combat. Desire is the irascible in the concupiscible.[60] This synthesis seems to be confirmed by the very nature of the judgment which we find implicit in desire and which refers at the same time to the end and to the means. We can bring it out more clearly if we consider no longer desire as it is lived, but the desired object in its context of the world: the world of desire is the world where there are things which *demand* to be attained or avoided and difficulties which permit or prohibit passage. The liaison between the characteristics of desirability and the more or less arduous progress takes place precisely in the desired object. Description of the world as it is for desire involves a consideration of the world as practicable or impracticable, easy or difficult, offering openings and obstacles, barriers and detours in time as in space, an opportunity being a kind of breech in time.

It is in virtue of this "irascible" character that desire is of all emotions closest to action: it brings together all the involuntary within the confines of the act. We could even say that it is through the irascible that desire re-enters the register of voluntary motion rather than of motivation, and all emotion with it. Wonder in face of novelty becomes an affective anticipation of promised value and it is here that action offers itself in terms of ready muscles and an eager body. Desire is the body which dares and improvises, body brought to action pitch. Through it, it is the disposition to willing itself. Wonder was already, in spite of its motor aspect and even by its motor aspect, a passivity in the very heart of consciousness and the occasion of the revolt of the body; love gave consciousness over to the charm of value. Desire is the initial thrust, body and soul, towards the object. This is why the full weight of ethics bears in the last instance of desire and on the means of controlling it.[61]

At the same time there appears a reciprocity between the involuntary aspect of desire and voluntary action. On the one hand

60. Mesnard, *Essai sur la morale de Descartes* (Paris, 1936), pp. 109–20.
61. Descartes, *Treatise on Passions*, arts. 134–44.

desire refers to a willing which it inclines to act: this reference belongs to its essence and gives it its intelligibility. It is remarkable that Descartes thought it well to introduce it into the very definition of desire: "The passion of desire is an agitation of the soul caused by the spirits which incline it to wish for the future the things which it represents to itself as agreeable." [62] This relation between emotion and the will can only become apparent on condition that we seize upon emotion in nascent attitudes rather than in elaborated and especially disordered forms of conduct in which the entire consciousness becomes transformed and swallowed up. We can understand rage and fear even better if we seek in them highly complex derivatives of desire, sorrow, and hate. Now in returning to initial emotional attitudes we are led to question whether emotion is a consciousness which understands itself by itself and which confuses the world of action in a magical sense, that is, which is finally aberrant.[63] This world for desire is also a world for the will; this world which tempts me by its enticements and bristles with difficulties, this world full of permissions and prohibitions, is only tempting and arduous for an eventual willing: the world of desire is the world of an agent.[64]

It may be true that in the great forms of emotive conduct, as fear and rage or even joy and sorrow, elaborated and established as durable forms of conduct, the appearance of the world for action is entirely altered. Desire does not go that far: on the contrary it enhances and stresses its articulations. Desire is the exciting aspect of the world. The world is not even easy or difficult except in relation to the poles of attraction or repulsion. A world without desire is a world whose practical structures are effaced because there is nothing attractive or repulsive. It is the outline of "appeal-characteristics" (Lewin) which in turn brings out the arrangement of practicable ways. Or, to put it otherwise, the irascible is always subordinated to the concupiscible. The world only interests me as a means if it affects me as an end.

2. Shock as Emotion

THE VERY BROAD EMOTIONAL COMMOTIONS and highly differentiated forms of emotional conduct like fear, rage, exultation, or dejection (in their active and passive forms) have to be understood by starting from initial emotional attitudes. Only

62. *Ibid.*, art. 86.
63. We shall discuss Sartre's interpretation later.
64. But the world's permissions have its prohibitions as their obverse; this world of necessity and death can only be the object of consent; cf. below, p. 339.

the emotional attitudes we have gone over are intelligible, insofar as the nascent disorder stands in an original relation with the will which it moves. It is this intelligibilty which gives them their priority. From our point of view it matters little whether they come first in time: as in Auguste Comte's sociology, it is the statics which supports the dynamics, order which explains progress, type which gives meaning to genesis.[65]

The emotion of shock constitutes a real trauma of willing: here the function of emotion is entirely obliterated. The disorder assumes a quasi-independence and at the same time becomes entirely unintelligible. Here man becomes unknowable, he becomes a cry, a tremor, a convulsion. We shall say later that willing can be broken that way, that the involuntary with which it stands in a dialogue must remain proportionate to it: willing has its limits. Emotional shock comes within the purview of phenomenology as it follows a line of descent from meaningful to incoherent disorder and as it stretches out, in the margins of the reciprocal relation of the vountary and the involuntary, the movement of functional liberation outlined in initial emotional attitudes.

In the *fit* of rage or *fear,* in the *crisis* of exultation or dejection (among which shocks of sorrow and joy belong as an extension of the wonder of sorrow and joy) the agitation of the body breaks through all the walls of voluntary control, expands, sustains itself for a rather brief duration and of itself retreats in a disengagement. Excess of wonder suppresses the conditions of reciprocity of willing and the involuntary. Just as man is only possible organically within the limits of definite permissions of the universe (temperature, atmospheric pressure, etc.), he is only possible *psychologically* if the unevenness and imbalance of his situation do not surpass certain limits. Man is organically and psychologically fragile. It even appears that this fragility is the price he pays for his evolution. Excess in the imminence of good or evil fortune or excessive impotence in face of dangers throw him into a disorder which, at the time of its discharge, is *quasi-incoercible.* But extreme imminence, extreme privation of means of response only drive man beside himself if his stored-up values are precariously balanced on the narrow platform of his threatened body: one blow and the whole human edifice of goods and evils will collapse. And Pradines reminds us on this occasion that imagination takes possession of our most vital interests from the outside, nourishes them with anticipation, leads them into a kind of hal-

65. Concerning the idea of genesis, cf. below, p. 425.

lucinatory delirium and tends to take the future which it has thus evoked into the field of present threats where all delay is suppressed and where our responses are unpremeditated.[66] Thus the regression in the emotion of shock is a human regression which does not make us fall to an animal level. Animality, we should stress, is lost forever: man can only invent human disorders which are the price of an overly fragile order. The incoercibility of the emotion of shock is a specific incoercibility. It is the incoercibility of a rupture which is only remotely similar to a reflex. It imitates only the incoercibility of the reflex, not its own nature and even less its adaptation of initial need.

Already the mental conditions of "shock" warn us that the general initial level of corporeal disturbance conceals a more subtle and highly compressed course of consciousness.[67] However, a consciousness which simplifies itself becomes rather more complex than a consciousness given over to a simple reflex like a sneeze. Emotion is not a reflex because its occurrence follows thought—often quite elaborate—perception, and a very rapid evaluation of a situation and a value-context, briefly, it follows a motivation which is sometimes quite clearly sketched out. But in the form of shock, emotion, as compared with reflex, brings about a living passage from a nascent thought to a corporeal agitation. Emotion does not refer back to the reflex mechanism which functions between body and body, but to the mystery of the union of the soul and the body. This relates it in an unexpected way to the skills which extend the perceiving Cogito in a gesture. This time, the movement leaves thought and returns to it later under the sign of a certain disorder. It is this *circular* phenomenon which we shall find once more in the emotion of shock, though in the margin of voluntary control. James is irrefutable when he holds that organic disturbance is not the effect of an emotion but the emotion itself. But it is not accurate to say that this disturb-

66. Pradines, *Traité de psychologie générale*, pp. 726–30. The author speaks with justification of a "hallucination of the possible and the contingent."

67. Does this mean that we are going back to Herbart's intellectualistic theory elaborated by Nahlowsky [*Das Gefühlsleben* (Leipzig, 1862)]? No, because (1) the representations of which these authors speak remain *spectator representations* even when it is a question of affective anticipations of goods and evils and of practical representations of the easy and the difficult "manifested" affectively (cf. above, p. 85); and (2) the conflict between representations is not yet emotion inasmuch as it is not taken into organic disturbance. The idea of circular progression avoids the alternatives of a non-affective representation (Herbart, Nahlowsky) or reflexes unprepared by any representation. This false dilemma is based on an erroneous reading on both sides of affective and practical representations which we have studied in the context of motivation. In the same sense, see Pradines, *op. cit.*, pp. 714–19.

ance comes from the situation via the reflex and it is not accurate to say that emotion is the hold of that disturbance on consciousness.

On the other hand there is already a comprehension and affective evaluation even in the most brutal shock.[68] Shock *is* the sudden transformation of the world for feeling and for action. The distraction of imagination which vividly draws the future as present and drives the living being to the level of desperate responses is the intermediate link between shock and bodily rebellion. Starting here, the body goes ahead, and goes alone. The knight is unhorsed: it might seem that emotion is no longer anything more than an epiphenomenon of the body. What is remarkable in this discharge is that in part the motor part of the disturbance escapes control and in part it becomes in a way immersed in the visceral density of the disturbance which escapes all manner of voluntary jurisdiction. If emotion can never be altogether imitated or reabsorbed along the route of muscular control, it is because of its visceral aspect. The will which attacks the motor part of emotion never wins more than a partial and precarious success. The motor aspect of emotion adheres in some way to all the visceral density of the disturbance. On the other hand, it is not quite accurate to say that emotion is the hold of the organic disturbance over consciousness. If we insist specifically on the visceral disturbance we cannot help being struck by the banality and even incoherence of organic disturbance. With respect to the modalities of the Cogito which present themselves in each case as a differentiated and unified attitude—fear, rage, joy, etc.—physiology encounters only a mosaic of secretions, contraction, etc., which reoccur in each emotion with only quantitative variations. Is it enough to stress the structure, the form of conduct which "takes place" in the organic disturbance to bring out even a distorted *meaning* of emotion? This is only a part of the answer, but it deserves examination.

There is always, even in a disorder, a form of conduct which unifies the organic disturbance, an original pattern of behavior which, in order to represent a disordered conduct, cannot be pure chaos. Thus we can seek the *meaning* of such conduct in two directions: first of all from the direction of the *residues* of adapted

68. Cannon, *Bodily Changes in Pain, Hunger, Fear, and Rage* (New York, 1915, 1929) shows that "intentions" and "representations" are necessary in order to bring about emotive adrenalinemy, and that they cannot be provoked in the laboratory without a mental preparation which alerts the subject's habits by representations of good and evil. Cf. Dumas, *op. cit.*, II, 436–37; Pradines, *op. cit.*, pp. 703, 716.

conduct which we still discern in emotion. In effect, emotion releases preformed skills and their habitual extensions. It releases
them in disturbing and disordering them. In each of the "physical
regimes" of emotion, as Alain says, we can rediscover the distorted style of an adapted conduct.[69] But this is undoubtedly a
narrow way of giving meaning to emotion. The Gestaltists,[70] like
Goldstein,[71] have shown that this wreckage of adapted conduct
is taken up in a new pattern which has the value of *substitution*
(*Ersatz*) with respect to adapted conduct. Catastrophic conduct,
substitutive conduct, and emotion have their own structure which
demands that it be described synthetically and not in terms of
analysis and summary.

But it is not enough to oppose to James a synthetic consciousness of a form of conduct as against a consciousness summing
up fragmented reflexes. When I am moved by emotion, I do not
think of my body at all. Whether in the disadapted (negative)
form or in the substitutive (positive) form, emotion is lived as
specific intentionality. Being afraid does not mean feeling my
body shake or my heart beat; it is to experience the world as
something to shun, as an impalpable threat, as a snare, as a terrifying presence.[72]

It is this affective intentionality which incorporates emotion
to thought in its broad sense. Thus the circular progression which
we encounter again in shock emotions becomes specified by a default of the reciprocity of the voluntary and the involuntary. Even
in an extreme form of shock, emotion is an original type of the
involuntary in which a rebellion of the body is governed by a
shock, that is, by a lightning judgment in which all our interests
are alerted and thrown into the balance. The rapid judgment in
which I evaluate a danger which threatens me, a loss which affects me, an injury which wounds me, or an unexpected good
which befalls me explodes in disturbance and disordered gestures.
There is thus no emotion without an evaluation, but there are
no emotions which would be only that evaluation. This is why
it is always true at some time that we have to find representations at the root of emotion and that emotion represents the rule
of the body. But if divisive understanding tends to dissociate the
level of representations and that of automatic behavior, emotion

69. Cf. William MacDougall, *An Introduction to Social Psychology* (Boston,
1908), pp. 46 ff. and Larguier des Bancels, *op. cit.*, "Emotions."
70. Dembo, "Das Aerger als dynamisches Problem," *Psych. Forsch.* (1931),
pp. 1–144; cf. P. Guillaume, *Psychologie de la forme*, pp. 138–42.
71. Goldstein, *Der Aufbau des Organismus*, pp. 23–25, 78–79.
72. Sartre, *Emotions;* see also below.

unites the shock of thought and the bodily revolt in that vital continuity of soul and body which is deeper than all possible effort. The physiologist who analyzes motor disturbances and visceral disturbances and even the Gestaltist who finds an overall form in them give an objective diagnostic in terms of the body-object of an overall experience in which the personal body is involved in a specific way, since on the one hand the intentional object is "taken" into the organic density and on the other hand this density is "transcended" in a new appearance of the world of action. This attempt at a descending linking of shock emotion by starting from functional disorder of emotion of surprise rather than from regulatory feelings in Janet's or Pradines' sense allows us to uncover human invention of disorder in a specific case by starting with the *spontaneity* of the involuntary. It is true that it becomes increasingly difficult to determine where the line between the voluntary and the involuntary lies. The principle of discrimination remains theoretical and difficult to apply in concrete cases. Normal emotion, which is thus also the only intelligible emotion, is one which lends itself to a circular or reciprocal understanding between intellectual and affective evaluation and bodily spontaneity. Finally it is a function of this specific involuntary in relation to the will which in declaring it normal also makes it comprehensible. But it remains the case that a continuity between the normal and the pathological is inscribed in the nature of emotion. Emotion is a nascent disorder which constantly puts us on the way towards the pathological. Habit, we shall see, similarly outlines a different disfiguration: in becoming neutralized, consciousness becomes alienated and provides an opportunity for a mechanistic interpretation. But the nascent disorder of emotion like the nascent objectification of habit are parts of the rhythms of the Cogito. Undeniably there is something troublesome here for a philosophy of the Cogito, but it is in his body that man is astonishing to man: the union of soul and body inevitably scandalizes the natural idealism of analytic understanding. Having a body or being a body means in the first place knowing order only as a task, as a good to be won from nascent disorder. What is initially intelligible is not the disorder left to itself: there is no intrinsic intelligibility of the pathological.

On the other hand, it is in order to give emotion an intelligible meaning and a more positive direction which would distinguish it from a simple disorder that J.–P. Sartre describes moved consciousness as a *magic consciousness,* that is, as a consciousness *structured* according to other relations with the world than rela-

tions of manipulation and practical determination which sub-
jugate our actions to the exigencies of a *difficult* world. Thus
J.–P. Sartre seeks the meaning of the phenomenon of emotion
beyond the formless organic differences, devoid of meaning, with
which physiology stops. He concentrates on facts which give emotion a covert purposiveness and make it a ruse of consciousness.
He takes up again the case of P. Janet's patient who throws
himself into a nervous breakdown in order not to have to go
through an overly difficult form of conduct, a confession. He also
makes use of the descriptions of rage in Dembo's article in which
anger appears also as a least costly solution to a practically insoluble problem. To this he adds a remarkable analysis of active
and passive fear, of joy and sorrow in which each emotion is an
attitude *adopted* by the consciousness *in place of* a superior conduct which is too difficult. In his eyes emotion cannot be at the
same time disorder and meaningful. Rather, consciousness must
move by mutations of its spontaneity from meaning to meaning
and each of these meanings must be a constitution of consciousness in its totality. Least costly solutions, to be sure, but the
entire consciousness becomes involved in them, together with its
body: it is we who degrade ourselves, place ourselves on the
lowest level. It is consciousness which passes from reasonable
form to emotional form. "It alone can, by its synthetic activity,
unceasingly break and reconstitute forms." Thus there would be
only actions of the soul.

It seems to me that the analysis of the circular relation into
fundamental emotions of the type of emotions of wonder does
not allow us to concur with this other extreme of interpretation.
While theories inspired by psychopathology best fit the *deranging*
forms of emotion, Sartre's interpretation best fits the *passionate*
complications of emotion. The magic attitude appears to me tied
to the passionate level of emotion.

If, as we have described it, desire only rearranges the affective
and practical accents of the world and inclines the body to will
in its direction, it is equally distant from a pathological conception of emotion and from an interpretation which would refer
it back to a degradation of consciousness to a magic level. In desire emotion still is not a conduct adopted in order to avoid the
exigencies of a world which is too difficult. It is impatience with
the difficulty: emotion is not essentially a liquidation of an obstacle. That is only an ulterior development and, so to speak,
secondary accident of emotion. Nonetheless one could hold that
desire always includes a nascent magic. That is quite reconcilable

with the primacy of willing. Just as will rules only under the threat of a nascent disorder, we could say that it uses the world in accordance with determining exigencies thanks to a nascent illusion. To leap towards a difficulty—doesn't that mean to experience it as overcome before the act, to deny it with the whole body? Now the magic begins when the interval of time and space is felt as annulled and the levels of means upset. This is true, but then the magic element of desire is not its thrust, the alerting of the body and of the senses, but the love and hate implicit in it: love and hate are precisely this anticipation of union and of separation in which the obstacle is magically suppressed. I am already one with the desired object. Thus through love there is a nascent vertigo in desire. It is militant only because it is triumphant by anticipation. But we can see at the same time that the magic is rather like a germinal state, maintained in suspension in the flux of the energy of desire. Thus if consciousness completely degrades itself in a magic conduct, as might be the case in rage and fear, it is by a decomposition of true emotion and freeing of the magic which runs through all action. But this fits in well with passions and perhaps with an obscure consent.

More fundamentally, this interpretation tends to eliminate the initiative of the body stressed by our circular interpretation in favor of the sole *spontaneity* of consciousness. The body is much more than a simple organ of a consciousness which degrades itself to the level of magic. J.–P. Sartre would like to make consciousness transform its body, change the body in becoming magic.[73] According to him, even when we are dealing with a motive world which invades consciousness, as in case of the horrible or the admirable, it is still consciousness which takes the initiative in changing itself: "Consciousness, plunging into the magic world, drags the body with it insofar as the body is belief. It believes in it." [74] Undoubtedly J.–P. Sartre is not unaware of the fact that emotion is *undergone:* consciousness, he says, is taken into emotion as in dreams and in hysteria, but he has no doubt that it retains a spontaneity. Only a spontaneity binds itself. The unreflective character of this purposiveness of one part and the opacity of personal body which consciousness presents to itself would suffice to account for the passive character of emotion. Consciousness does not think of itself when it is moved, it is completely preoccupied with a magic transformation of the

73. *Ibid.*, pp. 60–66 and esp. pp. 75–77.
74. *Ibid.*, p. 87.

world.[75] It is because the change of intention—from reason to magic—is a change in the appearance of the world that this purposiveness does not become apparent to it. On the other hand, this magic comedy is distinguished from a genuine ruse, from a concerted play, by the weight and seriousness which psychological disturbance gives to it. This is why we are sometimes captivated by belief, enchanted and overcome by it. The man who is acting out an emotion can voluntarily induce in himself only its muscular part, the conduct but not the disturbance. And if, by a kind of contagion, all the visceral accompaniment of an emotional disturbance is reintegrated by the conduct, the actor is no longer acting: he has been captured by his acting; he is really moved. "In order to believe in magic conduct man has to be overcome." [76] Thus J.–P. Sartre admits that consciousness does not create its own physiological disturbance as in feigned emotion. But can we then still say that in the birth of physiological disturbance the body follows the intention of consciousness, that consciousness "quickly realizes and lives this hardening of deterministic relations of the world, and that emotion follows" a spontaneous lived degradation of consciousness in face of the world? The state of the body in emotion is only governed satisfactorily when we make it a kind of matter for consciousness' intention, a "self-presence adhering immediately to its point of view of the world," "the point of view of the universe which inheres immediately in consciousness." [77]

For the idea of spontaneity of consciousness, it seems to me, we have to substitute the idea of a "passion" of the soul from the fact of the body. And there is no "passion" unless it is for a possible action. Emotion brings about a vital inherence of the body in consciousness insofar as the revolt of the body follows thought and outlines in turn an action which agitates and solicits willing.[78]

We could possibly reproach Sartre for the idealism concealed in a theory of personal body which reduces it to being the organ of a spontaneity of consciousness. Human existence is like a dialogue with a multiple protean involuntary—motives, resistances, irremediable situations—to which willing responds by choice, ef-

75. *Ibid.*, pp. 77–78.
76. *Ibid.*, pp. 73–75.
77. *Ibid.*, p. 76.
78. Habit, as we shall see, poses a similarly acute problem: the idea of a corporeal materialization of voluntary intentions leads to a different form of spontaneity which, in its turn, serves as a point of support and of resistance to to any eventual effort.

fort, or consent. I submit to the body which I guide. Still we have to distinguish this *assault* of the involuntary from the captivity of passions. The principle of passion is the bondage which the soul imposes on itself. The principle of emotion, as Descartes well saw, is wonder. But as emotion is most often the bodily paroxysm of passions, it bears the mark of that bondage and brings together the bodily power of emotion and the entirely spiritual power of passion. Magic consciousness is born from this encounter. A will purified of passions would still know emotions because it would still be susceptible to wonder and shock which might break it but cannot enslave it.

Thus our description leads us to *understand* emotion in the context of a general reciprocity of the voluntary and the involuntary and, more precisely, as a circular phenomenon of thought and adjacent bodily agitation. We could not see in it either a deficit pure and simple or a structure, a meaning, which would in its way designate all of consciousness.[79] Even if it is true, on the one hand, that the disorder of the body presents itself in certain patterns which are immediately understood and which are the forms of emotion, these forms do not acquire their complete intelligibility until related to the One of willing. When Descartes said that "the principal effect of all the passions in man is that they incite and incline the soul to willing the things for which they prepare the body," [80] he gave not a trait belonging to comprehension of the "passions" but, in relating passion to action, made man comprehensible by their mutual relation. On the other hand, if it is true that emotion is a nascent disorder, that it belongs to a consciousness which is beginning to *destroy* itself, its meaning only becomes apparent when consciousness reconstitutes itself in drawing a principle of efficacity from it.

Willing only moves on the condition of being moved. The body has to go first and willing must moderate it afterwards, as the fine metaphor of the knight and his mount suggests.

3. Passion as an Emotion

By STARTING from its nascent disorder, we made use of the emotion of wonder as a guide for understanding the disorder involved in emotions of shock. It should serve us equally as a benchmark for understanding the complication of emotion by the phenomenon of passion. The will can be *ravished* in many

79. "It expresses the synthetic totality under one given aspect," Sartre, *Emotions*, pp. 6–15, 92–95.

80. Descartes, *Treatise on Passions*, art. 40.

ways. The majority of emotions, as joy, sadness, fear, or anger, arise from a ground in passion which introduces an involuntary factor other than wonder or shock. Here emotion appears as an ardent moment of passion.[81]

But we believe that there is here an original principle of passion.[82] Passion is consciousness which binds itself, it is the will making itself prisoner of imaginary evils, a captive of Nothing or, better, of Vanity. Since its role is to rule over its body, the will can only be its own slave. Nourished by the wind and victim of the vertigo of fatality, passion is in its essence wholly mental. But it has very close dealings with emotion, which is most frequently its physical stirring. Emotion is normally the epitome and the physical paroxysm of passions. The sliding of passion into emotion and the thrust which it finds there are an application and fundamental verification of the circular schema on a broader scale. But this schema is singularly complicated in it. Already by the sole fact that emotion is born of passion and passion of emotion the bondage to which the soul yields and the bodily agitation which disturbs it are closely intertwined. Hence the ambiguity of most emotions which bring together the truly corporeal involuntary of emotion strictly speaking and the intimate involuntary of passions. We can always find in fear and in rage the emotion of wonder, but also a secret ruse of the will, an obscure complaisance to the vertigo. This is why we could not approach these emotions directly. The hidden purposiveness of fear and rage which consciousness adopts *in order not to* follow a course of conduct of courage and mastery sums up the most tortuous deceptions of passion and far exceeds the context of bodily rebellion. But the disorder of the body which it amplifies gives to passion the alibi it seeks just at the right time. The magic of consciousness is not simple and many passions burn in it. It conceals certain acquiescence of the will of which emotion is never more than an intermittent corporeal flame.

This bond of passion and emotion poses a difficult problem: it might seem at one moment that the field of emotion is dangerously extended in it, and yet this connection of emotion and passion is alone capable of giving an exact measure of the extension of emotion. Certain psychologists reserve the term "emotion"

81. Summing up the thesis of R. Dejean (*op. cit.*, esp. pp. 101–20): emotion does not "rout" what he calls instincts unless an excessive privileged value is attached to the end pursued. This sentimental polarization on an exclusive object drives the being to seek an equilibrium menaced if not condemned by circumstances. Routed by passion, conduct is at the mercy of emotive rout.

82. Cf. above, "General Introduction," chap. II; this will be the subject of Volume II.

for few particularly violent fits, such as fear and rage. There are always emotions which a passion revives from a minor shock. In this sense all passion, which has the entire body to amplify it, takes an emotive form. Thus love which in the ordinary sense of the word can cover long moments in an easy flow of thoughts, dreams, and feelings lacks nothing for being fanned up again by a small upset in which the whole body trembles and shakes. Might love not wither away without this disorder and this agitation of the body which really is emotion? The same is true of hate, ambition, jealousy, envy, or misanthropy: all passions come about through surge of emotion. In this sense emotion is a nascent or renascent passion, because it always is its initial point. Emotion is the youth of our passions, principally in those small tremors of wonder in which Descartes had so well seen the dawn of all passions, in that "admiration" which initiates all thought heavy with flesh.

If the initial emotional attitudes were irreducible to reflexes, there is that much more reason for it in the case of the emotive forms of conduct in which we can recognize embryonic passions. They are never mere imperfect reflexes. The moment of emotion, by releasing the body, confirms all the bondage which the soul imposes on itself through passion, at the same time as it really places the will at the mercy of the body in revolt. Herein lies all the ambiguity of emotion. It is because it is not a reflex but an embryonic passion that it is partly subject to wisdom: though it always takes us by surprise and renders ineffective the very weapons which seek to defeat it on its own ground, that of the body, we can still grasp it from above, in terms of the passions whose ardent moment it is. I do not cure myself of anger without curing myself of excessive self-esteem and of the susceptibility to injury deriving from it: these are the bad imaginations, oppressors of the will which constitute the combustible matter of emotion. If anger did not contain all that, if it were a simple reflex, how could we understand why the moralists have devoted so many maxims and often veritable tomes to it? Even the example of Descartes is striking. Descartes begins as a physician, but as he enumerates the passions he slides progressively from a mechanical explanation to a moral appreciation which makes it apparent that we incite our own passions as much as we yield to them. It is not by chance that fear and rage, which modern psychologists consider prototypes of emotion, only come up long after self-esteem, pride, etc. They are nourished by hate and sorrow while an excessive estimation of the self and of the goods whose lack threatens us dominate the background. This is why according to Descartes the true cure of anger lies in generosity, that is, in the estimate of free choice alone.[83]

Fear calls for the same remarks. Beside the violent fear born of a terrifying encounter—which is a shock emotion—there is a fear which is prior to the encounter in the region of unformed expectation. Such fear is closer to anxiety than to terror: anxiety of the soldier before the attack or of a musician's or an orator's stage fright. "No fear needs to be guarded as carefully as the fear of fear," said Alain.[84] The dread of a terrifying encounter is covertly reinforced by the fear which feeds on fabulous expectations. Now if fear can emanate from the nothingness of the object, from the nothing of waiting, it is thereby also the texture of passions. According to Descartes dread is not an initial passion, but rather always "an excess of cowardice, astonishment, and fear."[85] In this sense it is the inverse of boldness whose object is difficulty. Now if boldness lives on hope, that is, on acute expectation of the end which it proposes to attain in spite of difficulties which would evoke nothing but fear and hopelessness if considered in themselves, fear would outweigh it in case of the man who, being too preoccupied with himself, marks his place in life and its good with an avarice which makes him incapable of great tasks. Anyone who is not preoccupied with his body and scorns its eventual destruction is not far from being delivered from fear as far as it depends on something other than on wonder itself. This is why generosity is still the true remedy for fear: furthermore, since cowardice can be combated by the spirit of adventure, all that accustoms the body to daring is a remedy for fear. This is to say that if in emotion the body deprives me of my control, it is because first some thoughts—and almost always passions—have preceded this revolt.

But while the grand forms of emotion conduct are so closely related to passion that they most frequently take on once more the mark of imaginary evils with which our will has encumbered itself, emotion remains a corporeal form of the involuntary. Thus the tempest of the body provides passion at the same time with its organic paroxysm and with the alibi of a genuine bodily involuntary.

We are here continually abstracting from the ferment of pas-

83. Descartes, *Treatise on Passions*, art. 202.
84. See Alain's beautiful analyses of anger [*Éléments de philosophie* (Paris, 1941), pp. 280–89]. In them Alain does not derive anger from hate but rather from fear of oneself.
85. Descartes, *Treatise on Passions*, art. 176.

sions. We have already explained this method of abstraction in the introduction. We need to *learn* about the world of passions by a method other than existential deepening of eidetics: by daily life, novel, theater, epic. This world constitutes an obscuring of consciousness which does not lend itself to being *understood* as an intelligible dialogue of the voluntary and the involuntary.

[3] HABIT

1. Human Habit

IT IS RATHER DIFFICULT to delimit the domain of habit: we have no impression at the beginning of inquiry, in terms of some well chosen example, of what habit means, as we do when we speak of perception, imagination, feeling, etc., prior to all empirical and experimental exploration. It does not seem to designate any particular function, that is, any original intention in the world, since it is defined as an acquired and relatively stable *way* of sensing, perceiving, acting, and thinking. It affects all the intentions of consciousness without being itself an intention. Habit is precisely like emotion: it represents an alteration of all our intentions. Without being a new class of "cogitata," the habitual is an *aspect* of the perceived, the imagined, the thought, etc., opposed to the new, the surprising.

When I say that I am in the habit of . . . , 1) I designate a characteristic of the history of my acts: I *have learned,* 2) I see myself as affected by this history: I have *acquired* a habit, 3) I indicate the use-value of the learned and acquired act: I *know how,* I *can.*

1) "Learning." It is important to grasp this transformation of the living being by its own activity in all its extension. The French word "apprentissage" ["apprenticeship," used broadly for a period or course of learning] enshrines the unfortunate tendency to narrow down the field of habit to habits of movement. The importance of experimental work devoted to it must not lead us to lose awareness of affective and intellectual habits, of "tastes" and "knowledge." The key idea of habit, the eidetic rule which governs the entire empirical inquiry, is that the living being "learns" in time. To reflect on habit always means to refer to the time of life, to the holds which a living being offers to time and the holds which, thanks to time, he acquires on his body and "through" it

on things. Thus "learning" defines habit not only nominally, but also in terms of origin: habit presents itself as that which is not preformed but "acquired" by mastering an activity.

In the case of man the original involuntary represented by habit is in great part the work of willing. Though this study is limited to voluntarily acquired habits which return back to the will and affect it, this does not in any way imply that, in an exhaustive study, the initial course of habits might not be sought by starting from conditioned reflex or from trial and error.

However, conditioned reflex remains below the level of genuine learning even in the broadest sense which would include both human and animal psychology. A conditioned reflex can only transfer by association the reflex-producing power from primitive (or absolute) stimuli to new stimuli. No new conduct comes from this transfer which does not involve the activity of the living being, making no appeal to a modification of his own self by his own activity.[86]

As for the trial and error method, it undoubtedly represents more of an initiative on the part of the being who encounters the affective sanction and even an "intention" (purpose) in Tolman's sense, but on the human level it remains an expedient to which we resort when a problem can no longer be understood and when no schema, no external or internal model, can guide the analysis and synthesis of movements in direction of a total gesture to be brought about. In addition this method does not account for the inherent characteristic of the majority of human habits—technical habits, habits of civilization and culture, or moral habits— whose affective motivation on the organic level is faint and whose elaboration is largely free from elementary sanctions of pleasure and pain. Their acquisition demands, beside understanding the task, a constantly renewed effort in order to sustain the thrust of practice and in order to maintain the level of pretension or ambition of the subject. These higher habits tend less to develop preexisting tendencies and aptitudes, that is, to *conserve* man's living, than to *form acquired* ways of existing.[87] This is why we

86. Guillaume, *La Formation des habitudes*, pp. 45–55.

87. Pradines, *Traité de psychologie générale*, I, 113. The author distinguishes three tiers of habit: conserving, reforming, and creative. Concerning the last he says, "Only in these is genuine acquisition manifested." (*Ibid.*) These habits constantly confirm the inadequacy of Thorndike's "algedonic law" (*Educational Psychology*, 1913). Thorndike himself admits, in *The Fundamentals of Learning*, that painful sensation can invert its function and *indicate* the right path instead of *sanctioning* the bad choice. P. Guillaume, "Le Problème du learning d'après Thorndike," *J. de. Ps.* (1936).

shall turn immediately to the level of the voluntarily acquired habits.

But while no human habit is acquired entirely apart from the will, the will does not have a direct power of constituting habits: it can only activate or hinder a specific formative function which we might well call involuntary: *practice* is what has this "spontaneous" power—in itself not willed—of disengaging from the activity of perception, movement, imaginative evocation, judgment, etc., *forms* which to the extent to which they are "segregated" become assimilated to my activity as such, precede new operations, and ingress in the living duration which accompanies my present. Among these are the "preperceptions" which aid me in orienting myself among new objects of perception, the "preconceptions" and "prenotions" which, by condensing previous thoughts, become in their turn thinking rather than thought, the forms of motion which become detached from learning a particular movement and facilitate the exercise of related movements, etc. We shall return to these different acquired forms in detail. A. Burloud has devoted a remarkable book ot these "tendencies" and "schemata" which act as intermediaries between effort and organism.[88] Here he rightly stresses that the activity of segregation and integration which disengages and organizes these forms is independent of the will and that the psychic "dynamism" must be sought below effort itself, contrary to Maine de Biran's "monarchic" conception which concentrates all activity in the primitive fact of effort.[89]

2) Habit is *defined* in terms of its *origin*, but also by its manner of affecting the will: habit is either *"acquired"* or *"being acquired."* To say that a habit is acquired does not mean that it has entered the "phase of a state," so called. A nascent habit, a habit being developed is acquired solely in terms of the fact that it affects me afterwards. My ulterior power of decision confronts an unrepairable something which is the work of time. The familiar dicta concerning the first time, the first movement, receive all their significance from the reflexive impact which habit, as it develops, exercises on initiative or simply on prevoluntary activity which engendered it. Habit affects my will as a kind of nature, a second nature. This is what the word "acquiring" means: what had been an initiative and an activity has ceased to be such, functioning thereafter in the manner of the organs created by

88. Burloud, *Principes d'une psychologie des tendences* (Paris, 1938).
89. *Ibid.*, pp. 48–55. Concerning segregation and integration, cf. *ibid.*, pp. 141–224.

living, or better, following that primitive wisdom which governs preformed skills whose realm habit extends at the same time as it adopts its type of the involuntary. The acquired is harmonized with the preformed and participates in the familiarity and at the same time strangeness of life which is so close to us and so disconcerting to the awakened consciousness.

This second aspect of habit must never be sacrificed to the first: an acquisition which does not become inscribed into nature would no longer be a habit. This is the case with certain extreme forms of human conduct, at the extreme of those formative human habits which we shall presently compare with simple adaptive habits of living. The word habit is also used to designate certain *disciplines* of life: getting up when I do not feel like it, taking a cold shower in spite of revulsion, practice of asceticism in all its forms, etc. But the regularity of a discipline is only a habit in terms of external analogy with the regularity of a nature. If this regularity is only sustained by a decision which is made anew in each instance and does not fall obviously back on a nature, we are dealing with bare effort, deprived of the support of habit. What would be the extreme point of human habit from the point of view of acquisition ceases to be a habit from the point of view of acquired involuntary.

Thus we have here a unique form of the involuntary, one of alienation of the voluntary and "subjective assimilation" of products of the activity of acquisition.[90] What I learn becomes "acquired." The will and the activity which dominate "nature" revert to a nature or better invent a "quasi-nature" thanks to the passage of time.

If habit thus extends preformed skill, it has on the contrary an antithetical relation to emotion: habit is *acquired*—emotion *overcomes* me. This contrast prefigures all the interferences of those two great classes of the involuntary: prestige of the old and force of novelty, fruit of process and irruption of the moment—all the dangers and all the recourses are announced in these two powers which wisdom continuously trains in terms of each other.

3) In addition, the essence of habit lies in its use-value: I *know how*, I *can* do.[91] Habit which can be understood is a power, a capacity to resolve a certain type of problem according to an available schema: I can play the piano, I know how to swim.

90. *Ibid.*, pp. 82–83.

91. The equivalence between knowing and being able to in some languages permits Tolman to call the habit acquired in the service of a purpose "cognition, cognitive postulation." "Purpose and Cognition, the Determiners of Learning," *Ps. Rev.* (1925); cf. above, pp. 214–216.

This principle of comprehension first of all puts us on our guard about defining habit in terms of an automatism. It is commonly said that habit makes action mechanical and unconscious, a true habit being completely removed from the will. Not only does habit acquire the rigidity and stereotyped procedure of a machine, but it also starts by itself simply on being triggered by external and internal stimuli.

A similar interpretation is supported by some curiously convergent prejudices. A certain superficial romanticism likes to see in habit a principle of sclerosis and oppose explosions of freedom to the banality of daily activity, as if we could conceive of consciousness entirely in terms of opposition to functions. But empirical psychology, for different reasons, also overestimates the facts of automatism. Here it is the method which does violence to the doctrine. The prestige of natural sciences and the concern to transpose their procedures into psychology have given rise to an enormous effort at experimentation which quite naturally has been applied to the most measurable and most objective aspects of habits which are finally closest to the realm of things. Thus it is that such summary mechanisms as association of ideas or stereotyped handling of laboratory apparatus came to serve as models for all study of habit. Here we can recognize the prejudice in favor of the simple, the elementary, in psychology. In addition, these prejudices of empirical psychology were reinforced by clinical facts which seemed to reveal a primitive automatism by a kind of stripping bare of the skeleton of consciousness. Illness proceeds by simplification of consciousness and in fact manifests an elementary mechanism which normal psychology could only isolate by abstraction, with all the artifices and conventions of experimentation.

Thus everything seems to conspire in making automatism a primitive mental reality and treating so-called higher phenomena as a complication of a simpler reality.

One of the aims of this study is to show that the facts of automatism have no intelligibility of their own and can only be understood as degradation. Rather than automatism, we shall take for our reference the flexible habit which can finally illustrate the original duality of plastic willing and ability. A degraded consciousness does not represent a return to a purported simple primitive consciousness.

This correction of the analysis is similar in all respects to that which we have attempted with reference to the emotion of wonder. But just as the emotion of wonder is always a nascent disorder moving towards an emotional upset, so also habit can hold the seed of a threat of falling into automatism. The drift towards the thing must in some way form a part of habit. Emotional disorder and habitual automatism are both occasions of approaching the central problem of harmony between ourselves and the involuntary spontaneity in the wrong way.

2. The Involuntary in Internal Coordination of Habitual Action

OUR STUDY of the involuntary characteristic of habit deals with two aspects: with the structure of learned conduct or conduct being learned, and with the *triggering* of such conduct, or, if we wish, its leashing and unleashing.[92]

Our study of preformed skills has already led us to make this distinction. But while reflex is strictly subordinated to a stimulus and is incoercible, the so-called "instinctive" acts are *governed* by the objects only as to their form, remaining subordinated to affective impulsions, that is, ultimately to voluntary intentions. Habit is an extension not of reflex but of preformed skill.—The abolition of willing in the voluntarily learned habit also poses quite distinct though sometimes confused problems: the problem of *coordination* of the action both internally and with respect to regulatory signals, and that of the *opportunities* of release it offers.

Internal non-willed coordination of habit poses no radically new problem: already the most primitive skill represented an articulated totality governed by perceptions. It is a characteristic of habit that it brings about the same enigma by leaving behind the intelligence and the will which might have presided at its construction. But it is because acts which were never constructed by knowledge and willing already establish a bond of the motorium and the sensorium that habit can in its turn endow us with powers we find mysterious. It does no more than to extend that primitive relation to our body which precedes all knowledge and all willing relevant to the structure of movement. I neither know nor will the structure of what I am able to do in detail.

Habit thus does not introduce radically new facts. Thanks to the passage of time, to repetition, it indefinitely enlarges body's *irreflective usage*. What once was analyzed, thought, and willed

92. This distinction governs the majority of conclusions of the remarkable work by Van der Veldt, *L'Apprentissage du mouvement et l'automatisme* (Paris, 1928).

drifts bit by bit into the realm of that which I have never known or willed. This is why we can call it a "reversion of freedom to nature," [93] understanding by nature that primitive characteristic of all power over the body of being neither known nor willed.

Thus we need not say that in habit *consciousness* is abolished: only *reflexive* knowing and willing are. The improper expression, "unconsciously," applied to habit, designates *practical, irreflective* usage of an organ "traversed" by an affective and volitional intention which alone is susceptible to being reflected. But such corporeal usage is still a moment of consciousness in the broad sense defined in the first chapter. What could be the object of a voluntary intention falls back to the level of an *organ* of another voluntary intention. I do not think the movement, I make use of it. This is precisely what we mean when we speak of "acquiring" a habit.

Experimental psychology offers frequent testimony to this desertion of habitual structures by reflexive intention: to the extent to which I know better how to make a movement, my intention deals with increasingly broader totalities of movement which alone are intended. In each progress of habit there are internal connections which no longer require special attention based on overall intention subordinated to signs and ends of action which alone are noted.[94]

In Van der Veldt's experimental studies [95] this "short circuit" between initial perception and executed movement is studied systematically: the appearance of artificial syllables or words sets in motion a movement of the subject (or, in the non-"motion" series, called "sensorial" series, representation of movement): namely, touching a bulb (or a series of bulbs in a complex order) whose flashing corresponds to the word; in the experimental session looking at the bulbs was prohibited. In the sensorial series, as in the motion series, the history of learning is confused with that of "awareness of location" of the bulb to be touched. This visual image starts out as a feeling or a knowledge of direction (to the right, below, etc.) and a tendency "in the arms." The subjects themselves said, "I do not know how I know that I know it." Later, it became fused with the word to become its meaning: the word is the place. Thereafter the bond between the word and the movement became even closer. "I truly do not know what

93. Ravaisson, *De l'habitude* (Paris, 1838¹, 1927), p. 62. Intuitions of that great philosopher are the source of many of the reflections in this book.

94. Guillaume, *La Formation des habitudes*, pp. 125–31.

95. Concerning dispositions of experience, cf. the résumé in Guillaume, *ibid.*, pp. 101–4.

happens." "Only after the reaction do I realize what has happened." "The arm is surer than the hand." We would not say that the movement has become associated with the perception: the perception is no longer the same. Its value has changed. In the series of complex movements in an experiment so devised as to require in part analytic, in part synthetic, and in part free-learning periods, the short circuit becomes most noticeable: we can see the guiding scheme which at first helped the subject understand the movement to be carried out volatilize: it becomes a symbol, meaning more than a model to imitate, thereafter it disappears and the word becomes the name of the place and the command to a movement. At the same time, the form of the movement becomes a whole, a stylized harmonious form which adheres to the perceived form without either a guiding image or a special initiating order.

This involuntary of structure or coordination would be almost completely inassimilable to the will, that is, incompatible with voluntary initiation, if its internal and external connections were of a reflex type. Even experiments dealing with stereotyped movements testify to this contrast between habit and reflex sequences. This shows most clearly in daily habits which, unlike rigid gestures brought about by industrial life, are indefinitely variable, "environmental," as the milieu of civilization which gives them rise. They become adjusted to different customary objects produced by human art and almost masking the face of raw nature from us. These objects demand intelligent handling because they are at the same time initial intellectual objects such as those which P. Janet enumerates in his history of intellectual conduct: the road, the door, the basket, the drawer, etc.[96] Unlike automatic mechanisms, they suggest themes for manipulation, walking, etc., which we modify endlessly by unforeseeable innovations. We are not, either entirely or largely, savages with no control over nature. But neither are we living among our works, which are blocks of intelligence left behind, we respond to them with forms of conduct which are also forms of intelligence and of naturalized will.

Here again we have to give credit to form psychology for having stressed the structured and transposable character of true habits. It reacted against the reduction of habit to a simple addition of invariable elementary movements among which repetition introduced or reinforced an associative bond. Habit is a new

96. P. Janet, *Les Débuts de l'intelligence* (Paris, 1934).

structuring in which the meaning of elements changes radically.

More forcefully still, A. Burloud sees in habit a purposive, active "intention"—which he calls "tendency" since it is completely independent from willing—and which is essentially many-valued: it aims not at a gesture, an image, or knowledge, but at a sphere of representations or movements which are essentially variable with circumstances.[97] These are, rather, essentially transposable rules and methods which we could call "schemata" since they are more complex and contain in their turn tendencies which make them specific.

Understandably habit, thus described, could take on a human meaning if its plasticity permitted it to become subordinated to unceasingly new intentions. It is with general habit—and in this sense all habit is general—that there clearly appears the relation of will and habit which Ravaisson outlines. *Description* of habit as a form and its *comprehension* as a power fit together perfectly.

3. Involuntary Release: Facilitation

AN INVOLUNTARY RELEASE of a habitual gesture is something quite different from involuntary structure. The typical habit is not one in which a gesture occurs by itself. Technical habits of high sensor-motor complexity can be extremely "automated" yet entail no tendency to execution. In an extreme case aversion or disgust can even make a skill unavailable though it otherwise has all the internal cohesion of a melody: the movement "takes place" by itself—but only if it is desired and willed.

We have been led to contest categorically the assumption that a habit creates a need.[98] The force of habit does not generally consist of developing needs. That is a secondary effect of habit for which revulsion can be substituted.

And yet there is a specific *spontaneity* of habit which cannot be reduced to desire or to inclination and which can be discovered again even in aversion. When I say that I know how, for instance, to do a trick I not only mean that I shall *certainly do* it if I wish—attesting a future act—but I indicate an obscure presence of a power with which I am in some sense charged. In this conviction I anticipate a certain surprise which the releasing of all the com-

97. Burloud, *op. cit.*, pp. 55–83. In his sense, the Gestaltists have not even studied true form, independent of sensible elements, but rather manifestations which are only opposed to the foundation or ground; for it, the laws of field organization are valid (pp. 143–54).

98. Cf. above, pp. 104. P. Guillaume, "Les Aspects affectives de l'habitude," *J. de Ps.* (1935), nos. 3 and 4.

plex, fragile habits also occasions, the surprise of the *ease* with which, given a sign, a wink, "it" responds to my invitation: the astonishment of seeing figures present themselves spontaneously when I count, or words grouping themselves and acquiring meaning when I speak a foreign language which I have mastered thoroughly, or the astonishment of feeling that "that" body responds to the rhythm of a waltz. To be sure, "it" only works right when I will it, but this willing is so *easy* that it seems no more than a permission granted to a preexisting spontaneity which offers itself to the encounter with my impulsion.

What is hidden behind this enigmatic submissiveness of habit which effaces the traces of its own history? Nothing is more impenetrable than the familiar. Ravaisson compares habit with desire: it is "the invasion of the domain of freedom by natural spontaneity." [99] However, it is not true that habit is not only skill, but also a tendency to act (ordinarily we speak of the "force of habit"). The most neutral terms, "acquired disposition" or "tendency," remove nothing of the equivocity of this habitual spontaneity.

We shall understand something of this spontaneity of habit, which is a spontaneity of life, if we observe the life of our familiar gestures and customs of our thought. Here we discover that spontaneity which sometimes anticipates, sometimes awes, and sometimes perturbs our voluntary actions. [100]

a. A habit only grows through tentative probes in all directions which are not, strictly speaking, willed. We "pick up" manual and mental patterns without actually knowing how. These are the lucky breaks which are always disconcerting to our conscious effort. All the monographs on acquisitions of habits point to this curious relation between the intention which launches out in a specific direction and the response, arising from the body and the mind, which always has the air of an improvisation. This is familiar in the case of skaters, pianists, and even aspiring writers. Habit only grows through this type of germination or inventiveness concealed within it. To acquire a habit does not mean to repeat and consolidate but to invent, to progress. The Gestaltists emphasize the structural changes which affect directing perceptions and motor or mental structures, but even if we add to this an affective reference, lure of better results, the appeal on the "level of pretension" (Lewin), there remains something incomprehensible in

99. Ravaisson, *op. cit.*, p. 62.
100. Ch. Blondel, "L'Automatisme et la synthèse," in *Nouveau traité*, ed. G. Dumas, IV, 341–86.

the growth of a habit: we have to refer to a capacity for probing in all directions which is latent in our acquired powers. Such invention is particularly obvious in the skills which must be acquired at one stroke, without breaking them down, as balancing on a bicycle, jumping rope, or somersaults.[101]

In relation to this inventiveness of habit itself our perceived or represented models play only a secondary or critical role. The guiding scheme creates nothing, only judges the improvisation which approaches what was desired. In this sense it is always true that we do nothing voluntarily unless we have first realized it involuntarily.

b. We can recognize this life of habit even in simple, customary, and apparently most ingrained gestures. The activation of our experience in a novel situation always retains an element of surprise. On the other hand, the call sent out in the direction of this experience is always satisfied beyond what we have actually expected. We only think of general conditions which the gesture or the knowledge should satisfy. "From this point of view," says Charles Blondel, "everything occurs as if we signaled these conditions to our memory as a call to which events and information capable of responding to it offer themselves spontaneously." [102] On the other hand, and this is more interesting, such experiences, in springing forward, immediately assume not their accustomed form, but a useful adapted form. "Everything occurs as if once our appeal is understood [our experience] of its own initiative applied it towards the solution for which our reflection has done no more than prepare and justify its birth." [103] We only will the presence and, in a general way, the bearing of the useful gesture; the form arises as if of itself. There is a wisdom of habit which psychology does not encounter as long as it restricts itself to stereotyped forms of conduct. In their infinite variations, our flexible habits summon up a frequently disconcerting spirit of appropriateness: a reflection on mental or physical dexterity, on conversation or improvised eloquence, on the skill of living or culture, will show that each time that we parry a new situation we discover in ourselves astonishing resources to which it is wisest to trust ourselves.

c. It is true that this spontaneity is often accompanied by a certain exuberance of consciousness and of the body which interferes with intentional action more than it helps it. There are

101. Guillaume, *La Formation des habitudes*, p. 119.
102. Blondel, *op. cit.*, p. 347.
103. *Ibid.*, p. 348.

margins of consciousness rife with inappropriate ideas, impatience, and probing movements. Along with the efficacious spontaneity with its disconcerting improvisations, and pathetic spontaneity with its troublesome anticipations there is, as Ch. Blondel says, an "idle spontaneity." This interfering, clumsy spontaneity is part and parcel of a process of hardening which we shall study later and which is the reason why improvisation quite frequently also repeats and reintegrates the old, or even the mediocre. This is where we encounter mechanical association of ideas. But here we are already dealing with a bent of habit drifting towards waste activity. We shall return to it: in the texture of capability there appears the first hint of unsuitability. Life is invention and repetition: the one is the obverse of the other.

This spontaneity which anticipates, surprises, and sometimes interferes with a voluntary action does not prejudice its affective character, the pleasure we take in it or the revulsion it engenders. Habit does not have the power of creating genuine sources of action, energies similar to those of need. Many "technical" habits are affectively neutral. A professional or personal motive not belonging to the actual doing is needed in order to stimulate their execution. All habit can do is to provide an outlet for the sources of action by providing a form for the power which releases it. Thereafter desire, in the determinate sense which it has in ordinary language, is at the same time a conscious form of need, spurred by the emotion of wonder which drives it to act and encouraged by the ease of familiar means. Thus habit can only reveal needs. Need becomes revulsion when the execution of a task has "saturated" it. But beyond the contrary affective effects, habit always remains a *practical* rather than an affective spontaneity, offering need an easy action along the lines of a privileged form.

Thus if attitude does not create taste, practical spontaneity of habit implies only that the customary gesture has always the lowest threshold of execution and that the will can activate it with minimal impulsion, as from the fringes of consciousness. A habitual act can be carried out inattentively.

We could call facilitation of release [104] the second aspect of the involuntary pertaining to habit in order to distinguish it from tendency strictly speaking. But only with serious reservations

104. This easing could be called clearing of the way if this concept were not a part of a physiological explanation of the phenomena.—The same is true of the idea of a track, even in the sense which the Gestaltists give it. [Cf. Koffka, *op. cit.*, pp. 424–614.]—From a psychological point of view, this facilitation is broader than the "reproductive tendencies" of associationist psychologies. It refers to transposable forms.

could we speak of a "customary desire" characteristic of habit, compared with "wonder desire" characteristic of emotion, in order to stress the specific guidance which comes from capacities concealed in structure insofar as they facilitate the initiative which moves them.

4. The Broader Problem of Habit: Knowledge and the General Problem of Ability

So FAR we have assumed that habit is always a corporeal habit. We have, erroneously, considered the loss of voluntary intentions in the density of the body less surprising than the invasion of intellect itself by habit. But as we have said at the beginning, habit is primarily a way of acquisition, contraction, which provides capabilities for willing. Yet knowledge, no less than motor conduct, comes from habit. In case of a speaking being, motor habit is itself saturated with discourse. An acquired gesture is always joined and subordinated to techniques of thought. Now such techniques of thought are not usually rigid constructions just as corporeal habits are not as a general rule stereotyped movements. The vast mass of work devoted to the act of learning by heart, the systematic use of artificial associations among series of meaningless syllables must not mislead us: all that I know intellectually and that we indicate by the general term "knowledge" is a schema, a flexible method rather than rigid association. Even understanding our native tongue contains more rules, structures, and relations than univocal associations of word-object type.[105]

The resemblance between knowledge and acquired skill is so extensive that we can recognize the structure of the one in the structure of the other. In particular, language, with its verbal, grammatical, and syntactical schemata institutes a continuity and a mutual symbolization between the meaning of my thought, the meaning of my words, and the meaning of my action. Actually the similarity obtains among the structures, the schemata operative on these different levels. Understandably, it favors substitutions so that verbalizing an action and acting out discourse become equivalent. Now we have indeed to admit that such mental tools are living, that they, too, have a *spontaneity* like bodily habits, in other words, that thought constantly improvises without my willing, even though this appears contrary to its status

105. Burloud, *op. cit.*, pp. 306–66.

as pure subject. This improvisation on the part of thought expresses itself particularly in *association of ideas* and more precisely in association by resemblance and contrast (association by contiguity, which is more obviously rooted in automatism and in the object, will be dealt with in the following paragraph). Already Bain has suggested that this association by resemblance and contrast holds the key to all spontaneous thought, as if a need to recognize things and assimilate them and a need to stress them by opposition were endowed with a life of their own and preceded reflexive thought in their syntheses and distinctions. This is what authors like Renouvier [106] and Hamelin [107] have seen perfectly: association, called association by resemblance and contrast, includes in a general way all the diverse relations whose structure forms the very framework of thought; and these relations are living relations, they function spontaneously, before I perceive them. Something reasonable functions even though we are not actually reasoning. Hamelin touches the vital core of the debate raised around association by resemblance: there is nothing to justify denying a true spontaneity to the relation.

After that no timidity need hold us back: all relations are susceptible to spontaneous functioning. Consequently there are as many types of association as there are types of relation. Renouvier stated it already: "First associations are simply first relations." [108] Similarly, resemblance means no more than the role of relation insofar as it relates spontaneously and in a confused way—and there are a thousand ways of relating. Contrast is the same relation insofar as it opposes of itself and in an indistinct way. Let us go further: what is true of these initial relations is also true of the most outstanding intellectual endowments. Original knowledge in each of us is a web of relations which we subsequently treat as a whole. It is not just that these relations are no longer perused for their own sake at the time we use them and apply them to new thoughts, but that in every moment they represent a partial appropriation of all living things with respect to willing. In this sense Delacroix speaks of "the immediate, spontaneous power of comparison which is the dynamic and inventive aspect of association of ideas." [109] Here, at the heart of the Cogito

106. Charles Renouvier, "Traité de logique générale et de logique formelle," *Essai de critique générale* (Paris, 1912), II, 197.

107. Octave Hamelin, *Éléments principaux de la représentation* (Paris, 1907), pp. 360–61.

108. Renouvier, as quoted by Delacroix, "Les Opérations intellectuelles," in Dumas, *op. cit.*, V, 140.

109. Delacroix, *ibid.*, p. 141.

and in the law of habit lies a new manifestation of that *dualitas in humanitate* whose first example we found in emotion.

Then what is the status in thought of rules of language, grammar, style, of the rudiments of science, axioms, and principles especially as concerns tools which serve us in forming other thoughts rather than as capacity for recall and repetition? The status of intellectual habit presents reflection with one of the strangest problems of psychology: what I know intellectually is present to me the same way as the bodily skills I have. What I learn, what is understood in an original act of thought, is constantly being left behind as an act and becomes a sort of body of my thought: thus knowledge becomes integrated with the realm of capabilities which I use without articulating them anew. Each time I form a new thought I call up some old knowledge without being aware of that knowledge as such. We could say that "knowledge" is that which I do not think, but by means of which I think.

The difficulty is to understand, in the first person, this life of the Cogito escaping from itself. As bodily habit, so mental habit is an antecedent, ingenious but also useless spontaneity. Now how can we uncover a spontaneity of relations which precede all active, voluntary apperception? Does not their entire existence consist of being perceived? Understanding does not subsume the law of habit which is a partial alienation of the subject from himself and a capacity for being taken by surprise by my own spontaneity. This is a problem which we shall encounter again, more seriously, with respect to the unconscious.[110] Nothing is more difficult than to sustain this idea of a "knowing how to think," of a second nature in the very texture of thought. Already the idea of an *a priori* structure of understanding common to all thinking beings risks introducing into the Cogito a kind of objectivity which is not transparent to it. Even more, the strange presence within me of my intellectual experience, of means, methods, and organs of thought laid down by the activity of thought itself, briefly, the existence of an intellectual nature which would subsequently make my individuality involuntary, seems to "objectify" thought completely. And yet the paradox which seems ruinous for a philosophy of the subject receives full significance only for it, for what is presented as an enigma is *my self* becoming a nature by virtue of time; an "it thinks" is present in the "I think."

This knowledge brings about no absolutely new difficulty but only makes the general problem of habitual capacity more problematic. I waver between two relatively clear and equally unten-

110. Cf. below, pp. 373.

able positions: on the one hand I am tempted to *objectify*, to *spatialize* completely the characteristic of second nature acquired by an act or by knowledge. Thus I will look for some material "imprints" which the functionings of action and thought leave behind in the brain or in the peripheral organs. On the other hand, being more concerned with satisfying the theoretical demands of a philosophy of subject than with accounting for the facts— which the first position respected more—I might give up locating rules of reasoning, principles of geometry, my familiar gestures, and my bodily aptitudes *somewhere;* I will say that a capacity is not something that exists, that potency is only manifested in the act. These two manners of speaking miss the difficulty of the nascent alienation of the subject. I can neither think myself distinct from my capacities, as if they were outside of me, in the brain-object perceived by the physiologist, nor think myself identical with them, as if they were myself without escaping me in any way.

On the one hand, it is perfectly legitimate to seek the supports of experience in the brain or elsewhere; but such "imprints"— if they are more than a convenient hypothesis—are only external symptoms, an indication in an objective register, of capacities belonging to the register of the Cogito. How, in effect, can we understand such imprints *as* knowledge in the first person, as aptitude in the first person? We need to lay hold of the essential union of my capacities and myself, and the type of alienated existence which nonetheless remains in the first person in the Cogito. Habit is a nature, but a nature at the very core of my self. Now the passage from the imprints, that is, from object-body, to habit, that is, to the nature which I am, is, we know, unthinkable. We have to make a leap to the point of view of personal body from the body which is thought become nature. We should note that the problem of imprints is not different from that of subsistence of ideas. Ideas are types of mental imprints of the act in thought. The reason why so many philosophies find it difficult to resist the temptation to treat thought as a bundle of ideas and ideas as subsisting entities brought to light at a particular time while remaining hidden in the shadows of consciousness in the meantime is that the use I make of my own thought strongly leads me to such a view. Malebranche's doctrine of representative being, Aristotelian doctrine of forms and Epicurean effigies find their perennial source in this quasi-subsistence of knowledge: a certain substantialism of ideas plays the same role as the doctrine of imprints. In the end, it encounters the same difficulties: if ideas are something depicted—in whatever sense—how are these ideas still mine? How can the subject still assimilate them? I am distinct from them, never reunited with them. On the other hand I cannot fully identify with my capacities: there is something in habit which resists me. Everyone feels that there is something artificial in the reasoning which derives the concrete power of habit from the idea of the possible and reabsorbs aptitude in the act. It is not only the materialist instinct of understanding and a naïve use of the principle of continuity which makes me seek a persistence of aptitude beyond the intermittence of my acts, as something which continues to exist unobserved. If I am tempted to give my bodily aptitudes and my knowledge a semi-reality outside of myself, it is because habit has the character of semi-nature which resists my effort to conceive of it in the first person. This type of magic is suggested and imposed by habit itself.

We might assume that the difficulty posed by the involuntary persistence of habit in all its forms would be, if not resolved, then at least correctly posed if we were able to conceive it temporally and not spatially, as an involuntary *continuation* of ourselves and not as a material *conservation* in the space of the brain.[111] Perhaps the "imprint" is only the external symptom of such temporal serialization of moments of time. Such serialization "conditions" at the same time the persistence of individual memories and of aptitudes, methods, etc. It becomes manifest in my duration in the first person, radically inaccessible to my control, following a necessity which I am. Here the constitution of habit returns to a new form of the involuntary, most basic of all, to which we shall turn in the third part: the temporality of my self which is the absolutely involuntary "condition" of all capacity. Habit is one of the intersections at which the polarities of existence—willing and body, existential possibility and natural reality, freedom and necessity—communicate in what Ravaisson calls "ideas of action."

5. Habit as a Fall into Automatism

HOWEVER, the reciprocity of willing and habit is no less fragile and threatened than that of willing and emotion. The practical spontaneity of habit, which insinuates itself even into thought, at the same time constitutes the efficacy of the will and conceals a threat to it; life aids willing, but in a sometimes re-

111. Cf. Burloud, *op. cit.*, pp. 366–86; von Monakov and Morgue interpret the "engrams" in the same sense. [Semon, *Introduction biologique à l'étude de la neurologie et de la psychopathologie* (Paris, 1928), pp. 125, 223, 315.]

bellious spirit. The path of automatization lies open, representing at the same time a temptation to sleep and sloth, as if habit were a weak point offered to what is perhaps the most perfidious of passions, the passion to become a thing. A nascent alienation presents itself. For all these reasons, even our most familiar abilities are up to a certain point distinct from us, as a "having" which does not exactly coincide with our "being." [112]

Here we can see the parallel with emotion. Emotion began with awe and aimed towards sedition just as a habitual ability stimulates an outburst of bodily spontaneity. "This" body, "this" thought are on the verge of becoming an other who is most like me and always ready to swallow me up as he resembles me. "It" is able within me. The *organic unity* of nature and willing to which the naturalization of the will testifies turns constantly to the *ethical duality* of spontaneity and effort. I am one only in a constantly repeated conquest of the renascent scission. In me, personal body and thought as its own body are already nascent objects; desire and power tend to make me impenetrable to myself and even other than myself.

This constantly attempted dissociation is carried out in the process of automatization which is the counterpart of the spirit of appropriateness, of inventiveness, and exuberance of habit. Habit is at the same time a living spontaneity *and* an imitation of the automaton, reversion to the thing. Already here there are two closely interrelated series of facts which support two types of understanding, in terms of life *and* in terms of the machine: in terms of spontaneity *and* in terms of inertia. Through this process, the opposition between the voluntary and the involuntary outweighs continuity. In fact, all the psychologies which have concentrated on automatism have missed this fundamental relation and have sought an intelligibility belonging to an automaton in the spirit of mechanism.[113] But at the same time it becomes apparent that this second type of understanding is no longer an understanding of man, that is, an understanding of the *multiple* involuntary in its relationship to the *unity* of willing. It is no longer really an *understanding* of the multiple by the one, but an *explanation* in terms of the simple, in terms of the simplicity of elements and laws (of recension, frequency, association, etc.). For naturalism, it is inert nature and, in man, inertia and machine which are intelligible, that is, explainable.

112. G. Marcel compares having and being able to in *Being and Having*, trans. Farrer (Westminister, 1949), pp. 150 ff.

113. L. Dumont, "De l'habitude," *Rev. Phil.*, I (1876). This article gathers the facts which justify the assimilation of habit to inertia.

It should be possible to *understand* even automatism, but no longer in terms of itself and of its own laws, but by starting from flexible habit, as an already threatened, disintegrating human order. When an organ becomes isolated and lives an autonomous, reduced life, it no longer means anything because it represents not man but the "disfiguration." In the order of the subject it is not the simple but the one which gives meaning.

This project of understanding automatism fits in with a genuine *genesis* of the simple: the simple, inhuman realm, is the product of simplification. Here illness misleads the psychologist by bringing about the apparent conditions of a naturalistic explanation.

Thus what the process of automatization helps us understand is a "simplification" of man, according to a scheme of understanding which in some sense goes against the grain.

The development of habit from spontaneous to automatic habitual actions—development in a sense of comprehensive, non-explicative genesis whose principles we have just laid down—can follow two directions, depending on whether the automatization concerns the structure of habit or the release of habit.

a. *Automatization of structure* itself involves two stages. It indicates in the first place the very general phenomenon of *fixation* which sooner or later affects our needs, tastes, and tendencies and which makes habit a fundamental *recasting* of their field of vision. Habit gives form and, in giving form, makes the possible crystallize in one exclusive representation. Custom fixates our needs (in the broadest sense) in their rhythm, their quality, and their quantity. In their rhythm first of all: all need runs through a cycle from the phase of lack and tension to repose, passing through quest and satisfaction. The initial occurrence of habit is in fixing these periods. "Habit," as Ravaisson elegantly puts it, "reveals itself as spontaneity in the regularity of periods." [114] By themselves, our needs have a partly evasive character, lending themselves to multiple combinations in time. Hours of rest and sleep vary with culture, professional necessity, and private custom. Our tastes in reading, music, etc., are rhythms whose form habit tends to set. What we call the use of our time is no more than an interweaving of diverse rhythms located at different levels —vegetative, affective, intellectual, and spiritual rhythms—which are satisfied by turns and modify each other mutually in mutual incidences of equilibrium of energy, humor, states of mind, etc. Habit tends to establish a kind of unstable equilibrium among

114. Ravaisson, *De l'habitude*, p. 13.

rhythms by adjusting them with respect to each other. Habit also sets the quantity and quality of the object of need; our individual tastes are an affective crystallization around a privileged object in which our entire history becomes focused. Thus, as Goldstein says, each man tends to develop a personal style which contributes to his "essential nature."

Here we are witnessing the birth of automatism: it is the same process which awakens needs by giving them form and which now fixates them. Our needs are no longer unformed and, correspondingly, the spread of possibilities representing their goals is closed. Their acquired form tends to be exclusive; all determination is negation. Man's life is one long suite of unfolding possibilities and fixations. These two moments can compensate for each other at length. To the extent that one taste becomes fixated other tastes crop up and what each of them loses in breadth is balanced by the broadening scope of the individual. But as adolescence is the age when our scope grows rich, old age (and already maturity) is the time when the hardening of our previously discovered abilities outweighs the awakening of new aptitudes. Aging, from psychological point of view, is the triumph of the phenomenon of fixation over the phenomenon of awakening, of inertia over life. And, when automatization predominates over spontaneity in habit, it is more of a danger than a help: the relation of ability to willing becomes obscure; man is buried under habits.

A second stage of automatization is reached when the form itself ceases to be a general theme with limitless variations. A process of ossification then invades our schemes of action and thought; the form loses the indetermination of its content. Here habit drifts over into stereotype. Laboratory experiments dealing with intentionally stereotyped habits (typing, etc.) do not provide grounds for characterizing this instance of automatization as a phenomenon of aging. Here the automatization of structure is habit itself.[115] That is not the case with variable, circumstantial habits. In them stereotyping is a degeneration of the habit which then becomes a rigid response, invariable in detail, to a strictly determined situation. The least variation of detail changes the situation and presents an entirely new problem which leaves the subject at a loss. The acquired form resists all change and habit becomes what is often described as the process of reintegration of acquired forms by use. Some lives without incidents or occupations without surprises permit the formation of gestures which are rather like a balanced solution between a task, a situation, and an instrument. It is the danger of the "everyday"—whose spiritual significance is considerable—that it will make us resemble vegetables or even minerals. Far from being the model of habit, these facts of stereotyping are rather phenomena of aging. A young habit is only governed by a simple framework of signals to which it responds by a flexible schema. Aging begins when secondary signals, having become invariable, begin to fill up that loose constellation of primitive guideposts. Such aging can also be postponed, as when a teacher, for example, varies the details and even type of problems to be solved as much as possible. Very old habits can thus remain very young habits. Ossification is a threat inscribed in habit, but not its normal destiny.

Here we see the extent of the error of systems which construct habit piece by piece as a chain of reflexes whose articulations become gradually effaced. Apart from the phenomena of aging we encounter no mechanical connections except in circumstances which Goldstein calls "isolation." [116] When a subject submits to laboratory experiments, he in a sense lends one part of himself which consents to let itself work artificially. This is how we can understand the great reputation of the famous association by contiguity, understood in its most intrinsic sense, on which so many chimerical systems have been built. It is not an accident that such views boil down to the already examined alternative of deriving all conduct and all mental life from reflex; a reflexology would find a well prepared terrain in old associationism. There is certainly one form of association which is irreducible to the spontaneity of logical relations discussed in the preceding chapter and of which the old association by resemblance and contrast is itself only one form. Association of ideas straddles spontaneity and inertia, the living and the automatic. But association of mental atoms devoid of intrinsic relations is only a view of mind to which some hothouse flowers are forced to correspond by an artifice of experimentation. Laboratory experiments based on syllables denuded of meaning are far from revealing primordial structures of the mind: instruction engenders suitable, strictly verbal reac-

115. This is the case with Van der Veldt's experiments. The author defines automation as "capacity of bringing about previously learned acts in a state of more or less pronounced distraction." This is why the principal subjective criterion is the disappearance of any guiding representation, any schema. But the author agrees that this criterion is not universal and only fits stereotyped habits; in effect the schema serves to "specify" the movement; if the latter is invariable, it becomes unusable. That is not the case in the plastic movements of prehension, manipulation, walking, etc.

116. Goldstein, op. cit., p. 140.

tion in subjects functioning on a high mental level who will to suspend reflection, pay attention to the indicator, briefly, who consciously apply themselves to the conditions of a highly cognitive experiment in an artificial context, yielding completely to the whims of a laboratory. Here there is a type of association created of all the pieces by the material used and the conventional attitude of the subject. Genuine association by contiguity, which is neither a product of laboratory nor waste product of consciousness, is, as the various psychologies of the whole and the Gestalt psychology in particular have shown, the tendency of a whole to reconstitute itself by starting with an element, oriented towards *privileged*, stable structures.[117] This tendency to restore the old totalities is admittedly irreducible to spontaneous play of relations which is the highest form of association, thought which is living more than thinking. It revives something of the element of inertia built into body and thought, but to the extent to which it is already a structure, it is not as different as is often assumed from the quasi-intelligent spontaneity of other forms of association. It is never entirely disconnected from the general train of thought which offers it definite opportunities and allows it to be a useful organ of a will which is careful with its force. In a repetitious world, it is the least inventive form of spontaneity, yet still a capacity for a willing.

But consciousness brings about a state of isolation naturally as its control is diminished by distraction, fatigue, play or proximity of sleep. The mind, left to itself, functions through partial systems. Thus mechanical association triumphs, and association by contiguity is its prototype. This is why what should have been no more than a curiosity in psychology has become its keystone.

Thus the automatization of structure, even more than that of release, is an extension of a natural propensity of most adaptable habit. This imitation of the thing by the living, of inertia by spontaneity, explains the error of mechanistic theories: if we do not linger over the intermediate link of flexible ability, it would appear as a brutal paradox.[118] The fact remains that inertia cannot be excluded from life and that the temptation to resign my freedom under the inauthentic form of custom, of the "they," of the "only natural," of the already seen and already done lies

117. Koffka *op. cit.*, pp. 556–71, 586–89.
118. That is the case of Pradines who, in a spirit contrary to mechanism, goes directly to the phenomenon of automatism; habit is also defined as the paradoxical building up of mechanisms by non-mechanical beings, as an "organic mechanism." (*Traité de psychologie générale*, I, 89–100, 120–24.)

in the very nature of habit. In this sense we could speak of *passionate habits* as it was possible to speak above of passionate emotions.[119]

b. *Automatization in release* represents a more serious displacement of the will. Automatization which invades the structure of habit does not entail automatic release. A gesture, a professional or mental pattern can constitute a strongly automatized whole, mobilizable by more and more remote signs, without in any way escaping the control of the will. The details of actions come of themselves, take place, as we say, automatically, but the act as a whole proceeds on command. We could even say up to a point that an act is that much more available to willing as it is more automatic in this sense.

We are all familiar with the practiced ease of a good worker, athlete, orator, writer, or technician. The genuine gain for the will is that it can launch an act with minimum effort. Yet it is one thing to act easily, effortlessly, to perform a complex operation with little attention, and another thing to do it without being aware of it, in spite of oneself. Genuine automatisms, whether motor, intellectual, or moral, are the automatisms I observe. They are even a type of perfection of submissive spontaneity. They function only with the tacit authorization and latent control of consciousness which most frequently has already acted to suppress their foibles. This observation should alert us against overestimating the mechanical aspect. We shall return to this liminal, daily will which is the normal counterpart of the spontaneity of habit later; let us only say that the guiding idea underlying our control of such automatisms can be simplified considerably, the mental preparation of the act can be considerably abbreviated, even to the point of being absorbed in the regulatory signals of the act, and the fiat can be reduced to a covert toleration. But this simplification of the voluntary act must not mislead us: such habitual movements, such thoughts which act with practiced ease are not produced *involuntarily*. It is not impossible for us not to produce them. Far from being incoercibles, they are the easiest to keep under observation as from the corner of the eye. And if at times we leave them unattended and trust ourselves to their discretion, as when we let ourselves go on rolling a cigarette while chatting, we find no difficulty in picking them up again.

119. The passion of indolence is perhaps the most perfidious since it is the temptation of a mode of being which will deliver us from the risk of freedom, the temptation of the thing, of non-being of freedom. La Rochefoucauld has said as much already. Similarly Jankélevitch, "Signification spirituelle du principe d'économie," *Rev. Phil.* (1928), pp. 88–126.

We can always reclaim them as ours and do not hesitate to say that we have performed them intentionally.[120] Thus there is a gap between such observed automatisms and reflexes or reflex chains which at no point present themselves as ours.

How can we pass from such observed automatisms to mechanical acts which are activated spontaneously? The facts which can be brought together under the topic of *mechanical* are not as homogeneous as we might believe.

It is curious that it is often the least elaborate habits which give the impression of a machine revolting against the suppleness of life and voluntary intentions. Gestures, words, and ideas most frequently escape our designs in blunders and bungles. It is the least accomplished, least differentiated movement, closest to the spontaneous coordinations of childhood, which responds to our appeal and plunges us into astonishment, sometimes shame or rage. This deserves to be stressed: the mechanical is not necessarily the ultimate stage of automatization; it seems more frequently involved as a constant risk in the very character of all skill: its internal relations escape us whether by nature, as in the initial unlearned gestures, or through the effect of habit. We then yield to totalities which follow a course of their own, do not coincide with our designs, and are even in large part impervious to them. Furthermore, habits do not grow by simple addition of elements but by structural rearrangement, by analysis and synthesis: the resistance of old forms in which the old is preeminent adequately explains why there is not a malleability of mobilized structures corresponding to the malleability of our inventions. The mechanical here corresponds to the inertia of the organ itself, in the broadest sense of the word; the will animates a body and a train of thought which in virtue of their structure have a speed of mutation always less than that of thinking thought— which poets describe as lightning-fast.

But this obviously is not the principal realm of the mechanical: we know well that the majority of gestures which escape us are gestures which in different circumstances would easily obey consciousness and that the mechanical pertains rather more to failure of control than to inertia of organs of execution. Even in the case of a blunder there is always some change of consciousness mixed with such inertia, as in stage fright or bashfulness to which we fall prey, we say, without wishing to do so. A blunder often presents itself as a relapse into habit from a default of

120. Ch. Blondel, "Les Volitions," in *Nouveau traité,* ed. G. Dumas, VI, 380–87.

consciousness: in the groups of facts which we shall now consider, we shall find confirmation of this connivance between inertia and certain failures of consciousness.

A second group includes very strongly entrenched habits whose structure has reached a high level of automatization and which, under certain circumstances, are self-initiating. This occurs normally thanks to a voluntary operation which has something in common with a former automatism. The mechanical presents itself as a "fault," a "defect," as an "error" in the execution of a present task. Thus I will look for the door knob on the right if ordinarily I find it on the right; if I have learned to type on a particular machine, I shall make strike-overs on a different model. Experimental psychology has made a very important contribution to the study of such mistakes of automatic behavior. A large part of Ach's [121] work and of Lewin's [122] early work concerns this problem. Experimental material was that used in laboratories at the beginning of this century: a series of meaningless syllables. The experiment was of a type employing visual stimulus and verbal reaction, introspection was joined with crude notation of mistakes and time measurement. The course of the experiment was the following: it created a conflict between an old habit of an associative type and a contrasting task by introducing among the new inductive words, words which had belonged to the old series and were connected with automatisms constructed in preparatory experiments. Interpretation of these experiments is not without interest for the understanding of the mechanical involuntary: it became apparent that automatism is not as simple a phenomenon as had appeared previously.

At first sight mistakes in execution seemed to come from a very simple conflict between the will and the tendency of the inductor to reproduce the induced which has been strongly associated with it. The mechanical would thus represents a triumph of automatism over the will. Thus Ach thought he had found a measure of the strength of the will in terms of the force of association which it was able to overcome and which he called "associative equivalent." But Ach himself had already observed that

121. Ach, op. cit.; résumé in Lindworski, Der Wille, 3rd ed. (Freiburg, 1923), pp. 86–97.

122. Lewin, "Die psychische Tätigkeit bei der Hemmung von Willensmessung und das Grundgesetz der Assoziation," Zts. f. Ps. (1927), pp. 212–47; "Das Problem der Willensmessung und das Grundgesetz der Assoziation," Psych. Forsch., I (1922), 191–302. Brief résumés in Guillaume, Psychologie de la forme, pp. 156–58; and Van der Veldt, op. cit., pp. 36–39; at greater length in Lindworski, op. cit., pp. 99–106, and Koffka, op. cit., 571–90.

mistakes did not occur as long as the subject thought continuously about the task to be performed: a will attentive to the task is stronger than any association.[123] Mistakes are only possible on one condition (which the instructions of the experiment systematically create): in the "preparatory period" before the appearance of the inductor, the subject must become absorbed in the task; during the "principal period" of the experiment, that is, at the appearance of the stimulus, the subject must let himself go to respond with the induced which appears spontaneously: the execution of the task is thus confined to the in some sense "subterranean," so to speak, subconscious action which Ach calls "determining tendency." Ach conjectures that mistakes occur when the determining tendency is overcome by the reproductive tendency, but he already established that it is not the will which is overcome by associative automatism, but a spontaneous tendency issuing from the task itself. (It is true that the role of attention, combined with such spontaneous action of determinant tendency, is not brought to light by the experimenters of that period.) Lewin had to go further and correct the superficial idea thus formed of the force of association. It is not the associative force as such which overcomes the will (or the determining tendency): in order for the subject to fall back into the rut of an old reaction it is necessary that the identity of the stimulus should make him leave the attitude demanded by the instructions and substitute for it a special attitude which puts him back into the cycle of the earlier experiment, into the "learning complex" (*Lernkomplex*): briefly, the mistake does not result from the will to execute the task being overcome by the force of association, but from the will leaving the "conduct of the task" and no longer carrying out the demanded operation (rhyming, inverting the consonants of a given syllable, etc.) but adopting a repetitive attitude.[124] This in fact is what happens in common life: we are not, strictly speaking, overcome by automatism, we fall back on it. Repetition of daily cycles of action saves the trouble of inventing. For reasons of economy we appeal secretly to old resources and yield to them. Thus it is imprudent to speak of a force of habit as a force identical with itself and one which, at

123. Cf. Ach's discussion with O. Selz in *Zts. f. Ps.*, No. 57, pp. 241–70, and No. 58, pp. 263–76.

124. Van der Veldt arrives at a similar conclusion (*op. cit.*, pp. 251–323). If distraction has the same effect as awaiting a learned movement, this means only that an inhibition exercised by the task on the "reproductive tendency" would be removed; it seems rather that distraction functions by differentiation of task and return to an old attitude thanks to it.

times, overcomes our better intention. This way of reducing the mechanical to the incoercibility of reflex is erroneous: inertia is itself an adopted attitude. It triumphs and comes to the fore when effort is held back. A gesture and even a mechanical association do not initiate themselves thanks to a constellation of familiar stimuli alone. The mechanical which seems to *invade* certain consciousness to the very roots is never completely independent of a definite *desertion* of consciousness. In particular the distracted subject is always a subject with a narrow field of consciousness more or less contracted to an exclusive object. Mechanical "mistakes" thus always correspond to an abandoning of control or, as we shall see, a loss of control of consciousness which is itself involuntary.

A third group of facts brings us close to the pathological: dreaming, errant consciousness, momentary difficulties of attention, fatigue, exhaustion bring about in a progressively incoercible way a loss of control to which we normally more or less consent. Here we can find phenomena of stereotyping, in large part of a verbal type, which are like waste-products of consciousness in the fall of tension. Such constitutional or accidental limitations of consciousness remind us in a way different from that of the disorders of shock emotion which also can bring about such stereotyping that the human synthesis of the voluntary and the involuntary is fragile and that man is only possible within definite limits. Destruction of this synthesis is, in addition, a measure of the human edifice whose skill and knowledge give us such a great idea. It shows, even in their disaster, a human grandeur.

At the extreme of this third group of facts we touch upon facts of automatism which do not come from a *weakness* of consciousness, from a fall of tension, but from dissociations brought about by *repression*. Freud related many aberrations of behavior to the difficulties of affectivity, directing the search for the principle of automatism in a clinical sense of the word to the level of unconscious affectivity. Here we leave the context of normal psychology and at the same time the limts of our method of approach. We shall encounter this group of facts and the difficulties of interpretation they pose again in the chapter devoted to the unconscious.

Thus if we remain within the limits of the *normal*—which are also the limits of our responsibility—the mechanical arises in the margins of all our habits. At its source we find on the one hand a certain *defaulting of consciousness* which tends to draw back from its work and fall back on the power of perseverence and of restoration of the past, on the other hand a certain inertia which is the principle of the automatic and which is exhibited in the most spiritless way in what we have called "observed automatisms." This principle of inertia introduces the threat at the very point of perfection of habit. However, it remains enigmatic: why are the supple organs and docile capacity threatened not only by the spontaneity of life, but also by mechanical inertia? It seems that through our body we participate in an obscure ground of inertia of the universe. In becoming natural, to use Ravaisson's terminology, freedom submits to "the primordial law and most general form of being, the tendency to persist in the act which constitutes being." [125] By making use of the time of life, habit at the same time invents and yields to the fundamental inertia of matter. This resistance of matter at the very heart of organic structure is the ultimate principle of inertia. When abstract thought itself becomes objectified, perhaps it is because there are living means in the life which is translated in them.

Habit is the useful naturalization of consciousness. The possibility that all consciousness can become an object is contained in it. It is enough that it consent to this propensity or that an accident displace it from itself. The question arises whether the terminus of this fall into inertia can still be conceived in the first person: perhaps inertia can only be understood when we awaken from it, as shadows can be understood only through light. Thus the dangers of habits are inverse to those of emotion, as the dangers of order and the dangers of disorder, as the dangers of sleep and the dangers of agitation. These dangers themselves call forth their mutual training under the sign of effort.

125. Ravaisson, *op. cit.*, p. 62.

3 / Moving and Effort

THE ACID TEST of a philosophy of the will is indisputably the problem of *muscular effort*. There is, to be sure, also intellectual effort, as the effort of recalling memories, etc., but in the last instance the terminus of willing is in the muscles. All other effort is finally effort in virtue of its muscular components, of its mastery over a body. A being which is *compos sui* only possesses its thought if it possesses its body.

The entire second part is only a long preparation for confronting this problem.

But it would not be wise, either, to approach the meaning of effort without a detour, as some kind of a sensory register like seeing, hearing, etc. The simple gesture of raising my arm when I want to is a great epitome of enigmas. The disconcerting simplicity of a gesture made without specific purpose, just to assure myself of my power, in which everyone sees a sign of his freedom, *sums up* all of will's conquests. The muscular contraction carried out, for example, in a laboratory and knowingly isolated from the history of the individual, from the emotional and moral context of daily, professional, and private life, conceals all the civilizing of an intelligent adult's body.

To justify this detour, it is important first to recall the conclusions of the first chapter and complete them by those of the second.

1) The feeling of effort is not the simplest consciousness which description encounters. It comes through reflection from a more basic consciousness, the consciousness of acting. We should be going too fast if we simply said that effort is in principle the focusing of a self's consciousness. In the first place action draws me out of myself and holds me in relation to a task. Consciousness

of acting is a consciousness of . . . , consciousness of a passively created endeavor. My activity is visible in the docility of the endeavor which, unlike objects which are simply there and which I encounter, depends on me, derives its being from me. The being-there of the object is joined by the being-done-by-me of an endeavor. Undoubtedly there is here a very definite reference to myself, but as lost in the world. Let us note well that this experience of my action apprehended *in* an endeavor in the process of being carried out must not be confused with some one of the feelings which continue to relate me to the endeavor which has been completed: astonishment, unease in face of the endeavor now detached from me, or reaffirmation of its relation to me. This experience of acting emerges step by step with action and adheres to the endeavor insofar as it is in the process of coming about. It is attuned to retrospection more than to anticipation. We speak of imminent creation, passive pressure of nothingness on the being of the endeavor in process of being carried out.

The feeling of effort appeared under the condition of an attention which *flows back* from the endeavor to the organ "traversed" by consciousness of acting. It is primarily *resistance* of the thing or body or some aspect of myself which brings out such consciousness of effort.

But at the same time as this consciousness of effort passes into the foreground, it becomes obscured. It becomes obscured in two ways. On the one hand, the movement becomes disconnected from its relation to the endeavor: in place of being a "traversed organ" it becomes the "terminus" of the movement. At the same time it loses its essential meaning. Both Biranian introspection and experimental psychology of effort remain preoccupied with such meaningless movements. Torn from the context of an endeavor in the world, production of movement tends to become incomprehensible in its very simplicity and familiarity.

On the other hand, in being reflected in the obstacle, effort is accentuated before consciousness, but in turn the true meaning of voluntary motion is changed. Genuinely voluntary motion is one which passes unnoticed because it expresses *the docility of a yielding body*. Docility is transparent, resistance apaque. It is not an accident that Maine de Biran's philosophy gives precedence at the same time to the perception of the self over self-transcending consciousness, to reflected effort over bodily motion which consciousness of acting simply "traverses," and to bodily resistance over bodily docility.

Yet it is the docility of the body, though most difficult to *de-*

scribe, which enables us to *understand* the body as an organ of willing. What is first and initially intelligible is not the opposition of effort and a resistance, but the actual deployment of the imperium in the docile organ. Resistance is a crisis of the unity of the self with itself. Here we need to add: more basically, what makes man intelligible to himself is his myth of himself, the ancient dream of his fulfillment in innocence and graceful action; the practiced ease of a dance, the supple joy of a Mozart are momentary, fleeting glimpses in the direction of a final stage of freedom where there would be no hiatus between willing and ability, where no effort would ruffle the docile coursing of movement with its misfortunes. What complicates the description is the coursing of passions which have made this happy union of will and all its abilities impossible. It is due to passions that conflict appears as the ultimate verdict on man. The fundamental conflict is the conflict of law and passion. This conflict is what covertly gives resonance to all dramatic description of man. This conflict is what is at stake when we think we are speaking only of muscular resistance to effort. The abstraction of the fault, which defines our method, permits us to bracket this conflict of passion and law which lies at the heart of man's daily reality and to inquire into the intelligible network on which the terrible game of passions is plotted. Here psychological understanding is greatly aided by the myth of innocence. Hence we need to return to a type of understanding in which *resistance* continues to be seen as a moment of *docility.* This is not without its difficulties, since docility shrinks away from attention.

An ordinary *reflection* on external resistance and all organic resistance testifies that it is the unreflecting and not the noted docility which is reflected in effort.

In the first place things resist the effort we deploy to displace them. Impulse among impulses, focus of forces in a field of forces, man inevitably experiences the resistance of things. But we need to note that the force of things is not an absolute interdiction of the exercise of the will, but has only the effect of limiting a partly successful movement: an absolute obstacle which would stop movement from being deployed from the start would be such a constraint that the least contraction would be prevented. This does not mean that things stop my willing: only willing which is already effectively deployed can encounter limitations. External resistance presupposes docility of the body.

Resistance becomes characteristically ours in the form of organic resistance. Effort clashes with different forms of muscular inertia (limitation of intensity of contraction, limits of repition of moderate contraction, limits of speed of execution of contractions). This is accompanied by the inertia of coordinations (resistance to dissociation of primitive muscular synergies). In connection with mechanical activity we have spoken of this failure of the fluidity of structure in relation to the speed of alteration of our projects. Here organic inertia is still a limitation on effective deployment of willing. For the rest these two forms of resistance imply each other mutually: I experience external resistance of things only in the moment when excess effort encounters the inertia of organs. The thing resists me only as a limit of intensity, duration, speed, or differentiation of our movements. Inversely, organic resistance is normally revealed only in contact with an object. Even in an aimless movement it is still in the impossibility of obtaining even a symbolic performance from my body that I experience the body's resistance.

2) On the other hand the hope that a psychology of docile movement can be easily carried out disappears when we add to these conclusions the conclusions of the preceding chapter.

All the power I exercise over my body is at the same time immediate and achieved. The three foregoing studies prepare us for this paradox of effort which brings together organic unity and "polemic duality" of the voluntary and the involuntary. On the one hand preformed skills, emotion, and habit represent in fact or, better, in action the inherence of "movement" in "idea": the bond between skill and perceived sign, the bond between emotional difficulty and the lightning evaluation in surprise, and the alienation of intention in habit confront us with the mystery of the union of soul and body which is *already* "accomplished" quite apart from effort. Through it the body is *available* for voluntary motion. But on the other hand the trinity of practical involuntary is manifest in the triple *spontaneity* which, at every moment, is on the verge of becoming dissociated from the voluntary realm. This is why my *hold* on my body is always in some way a *recapture*. And with the same stroke it becomes apparent that it is not a straightforward problem of understanding how "mind moves the body." I move my body through the *mediation* of desires and schemata presented by habit. The overly condensed difficulty of muscular effort will therefore have to be analyzed; the relation of effort to habit and to emotion is a necessary stage in an analysis of muscular effort.

Now if we coordinate the first group of observations with the second, the task of this preparatory analysis emerges clearly:

the *relation of resistance to docility* is what must be traced on the level of habit and emotion. We must show how the application of effort to functional resistance of habit leads to an understanding of effort in its relation to organic resistance.

[1] EFFORT, EMOTION, AND HABIT

THE KEY to the problem of *docility* and *resistance* lies in the complex relations of habit and emotion whose contrast is all we have noted so far. These two modes of the involuntary function alternately as a basis for and obstacle to the willing which cultivates one in terms of the other. Each represents alternately a *functional* rather than simply external or organic resistance as well as a recourse against the force of the other when it oppresses willing.

The emotion of wonder resists willing insofar as it is a nascent disorder. It becomes insinuated into the core of the field of attention and affects its orientation in such a way that voluntary attention becomes difficult. Free displacement of our vision becomes a struggle against involuntary attention. More clearly still, desire with its obstacles is emotive resistance par excellence. It can assume either of two contradictory forms: at times, in fearful flight, the basic unstable obstacle is the body which is shrinking away so that daring demands an effort. At other times, in the aggression of rage, the obstacle is the explosion: here effort is required to contain myself. Thus effort means either daring or holding back, and resistance accordingly is either inhibition or impulse.

The vertigo of passions is tied to this emotive resistance which has to do with the initiative of the body in emotion. But it comes from the soul itself; the principle of passion is bondage I impose on myself, the principle of emotion is wonder to which I submit. This specific resistance thus has neither the external character of a physical obstacle, nor the intimacy of a passion like envy, jealousy, or ambition. In effect the ambiguity of this resistance is the ambiguity of appearing as this or that, at the very moment when effort becomes distinct from it. Insofar as I am taken up with an emotion, in the world as it appears to an emotionally moved consciousness, emotion does not yet resist me; it is to the extent to which I refer the appearance lent to the object by emotional consciousness—as hostile, injurious, or terrifying—to the body that I resist emotion and constitute it as an obstacle.

In this sense effort is a willing which escapes wonder, love, hate, and even desire. This explains why some authors, like Locke, have attempted—not without risk—to define effort by the absence of desire.[1] This rigoristic definition is obviously only one moment in the entire dialectic; at least there is no effort which would not at least potentially include resistance to emotion.

Yet how does effort break through the *circle* of emotion, the circle which nascent thought forms with its visceral and muscular retention and finally with the belief which reflects bodily disturbance?

The direct struggle which we can carry on against emotion on a strictly muscular level retains a derisory element: motor agitation, which is theoretically capable of being overcome by willing, is taken into the mass of visceral disturbance which is not directly subject to voluntary influence. The will, Descartes tells us, "can easily overcome the lesser passions but not the more violent and stronger ones, until after the emotion of the blood and of the spirits has been appeased."[2] Undoubtedly with respect to the emotion of wonder it is possible "not to consent to its effects and to restrain the numerous movements to which it disposes the body,"[3] in particular thanks to some muscular strategy which consists less in holding back such movement than in keeping the body occupied with other gestures—as getting a glass of water and drinking slowly when one is angry. But this activity of the body, more effective than mere inhibition, leads us to anticipate the sedative action of habit.

But there is a more basic dissolving action than disputing the movement of the emotional wave which tends to carry it along in its flow. Muscular action only acquires its full significance when it is included in a more internal struggle which attacks emotion on its representative level and—if there is a passionate aspect—in the belief in which the bodily disturbance is transcended. I reach the very core of emotion when I turn my attention to values higher than my threatened values or my insulted reputation. This act brings into action all the aspects of motivation of which we spoke above. In particular it engenders a revolution in the imagination which is, as we have said, the common level on which emotion projects its belief and on which thought gives a vitality, flesh, and a quasi-presence to represented objects.

1. Quoted by Maine de Biran, *Mémoire sur la décomposition de la pensée;* Tisserand, *Oeuvres de Maine de Biran* (Paris, 1920–39), III, 190.

2. Descartes, *Treatise on Passions*, art. 46.

3. Descartes adds, "Each of us can discover the strength or weakness of his soul by his success in such struggles." (*Ibid.*, art. 48.)

I can change the course of my thoughts by forcefully imagining the reasons opposed to anger or fear.

Now this action on the level of representation has repercussions right down to the visceral depth to the extent to which the new course of thought tends in its turn to engender a contrary emotion. Descartes showed admirably that the art of living lies in part in playing one "passion" against another; thus the will acts against the emotion it *resists* in its very visceral stronghold by giving itself indirectly to the involuntary spontaneity of an allied docile *emotion*.

But this aid of one emotion against another emotion constituted as an obstacle is itself exceptional. Bare effort would be ineffective without the mediation of the pacificatory function par excellence—habit.

It is habit in all its forms which from infancy calms the muscular storm and diminishes body's susceptibility to wonder and shock. Habit functions through its activities of attrition in all senses, through muscular exercises, through its regulatory action, and finally and especially through its close alliance with effort itself in the form of discipline.

The initial effect of habit is most spontaneous and least willed. It consists of a progressive deadening of the irritating power of emotive impressions. This is the gist of the good expression "passive habit" used by classical authors. It builds up a less affective consciousness which is more representative of our muscular impression and thus works for the subordination of muscular impulse to voluntary initiative (we shall return to this role of such differentiated, identified muscular sensibility localized in the thrust of movement).

After attrition by habit, active exercise of the body: the second effect of habit pertains to this power of muscular exercise over emotivity which, above, we opposed to simple inhibition. Emotion is a convulsion, knotting the muscles; systematic muscular exercise has an anti-emotive effect which is slow but sure. Gymnastics is related to ethics. In unknotting my muscles, in leading to a kind of muscular introspection, gymnastics habituates the body to respond in a docile way to differentiated, impelling ideas. It makes the body better known and more available. There is a great deal of clumsiness in anger.

Perhaps the most important effect of habit pertains to its characteristic of regularity and order. Through the rhythm which it establishes or renews it exercises a flywheel effect on the convulsive soul. As an extension of biological rhythms, social rhythms imposed by the family, school, or job in turn lay the ground for a more concerted use of habit. A sedative habit is one I will constantly. From becoming accustomed to discipline, habit becomes willingness to repeat and to derive a part of the cumulative effect of exercise. In this sense effort is willed habit and habit is the most perfect instrument in civilizing the body. In *Phenomenology of Mind*, which contains a history of infancy of consciousness, Hegel glorifies in habit the first teacher of the "pythic consciousness." In emotion I am on the verge of being forced, possessed. Through habit I take possession of my body, as the words *habere, habitude,* themselves suggest.[4]

Montaigne and Descartes, who among other things have denounced the high esteem of custom and authority, were not unaware of this active possession of the body and of thought through habit which places them at the service of effort: "Virtue," says Montaigne, "is not a momentary outburst of the soul, but resolute and constant habit." [5] There is a great deal of habit in equanimity of the soul.

Similarly Descartes writes: "It seems to me that only two things are required for being disposed to judge well at all times. One is knowledge of the truth, and the other the habit thanks to which we remember and acquiesce to this knowledge whenever the occasion arises." The difficulty of being attentive at all times puts us at the mercy of false appearances "unless by long and frequent meditation we have so imprinted it upon our mind that it becomes a habit." [6] Descartes thus rediscovers the assimilation of virtue to habit, in line with the classical analysis of "habitus." According to this, habit being a "passion of the soul," virtues are one of the moments of the union of soul and body.[7] Thus the continuity of the will and docile habit underlies the *conflict* of effort and emotive resistance.

In turn effort is also what says *no* to habit the on basis of emotion.

Condillac opposed the "reflecting self" to the "habitual self." The danger is great here since the resistance which habit offers to effort does not irritate it at all from the outside, as an obstacle. It is the resistance of an inertia saturating our nature: "mens

4. Cf. Alain, *Idées,* re Hegel, pp. 248–52. "There is a folly in natural consciousness . . . , the initial consciousness is a sick consciousness . . . , habit is a moment of deliverance."

5. Montaigne, *Essays,* II:xxix.

6. Descartes, *Letter to Princess Elizabeth,* September 15, 1645.

7. Thoughts which fortify "disposition of the spirits" are "acts of virtue and of totality of passions of the soul," Descartes, *Treatise on Passions,* art. 161.

nostra imbuta est," says Descartes with reference to prejudices which obscure judgment. An acquired habit is the jarring resistance implying a threat of non-being. It is an awakening of effort which reveals habit as a dream (cf. the dogmatic slumber of which Kant speaks) and constitutes habit as resistance. I become *detached* from my powers and exile myself from all form; in some privileged instances my freedom trembles before its lost and rediscovered fullness. A certain adolescent fear of choice and commitment is frequently a clumsy expression of this horror; to choose means to exclude, man assumes appearance and form in a series of amputations. Escape into the imaginary is a still sterile form of this detachment and already an adumbration of the scope of "possible existence" (to use Jaspers' term). In that moment habit is cast off as the garments of authentic being: custom is costume, says Alain who banishes it to the body as we push back emotion when we recognize it as such, as the tremor and fury of the body. Undoubtedly this easy romantic theme of opposition between an inspired myself and the working, daily myself is itself only a moment in a far broader dialectic; for we cannot break a form except in the name of another form and there is a greater danger than one of being limited—the danger of not being at all: there is no being without choice, no choice without willing, no willing without ability, no ability without a particular being. We have to return to the Cave. At least this negative moment is an essential moment of freedom. In principle, consciousness, not being capable of being engendered by what is in no way itself, has something with which to oppose its own naturalization, and only annuls itself in the passion of sloth which is a fear of self, fear of arriving at the self and of running the risk of inventing its existence. Mingled with this passion of sloth, habit is a way of shrinking away into the "negative labor" in which Hegel recognized an escape from consciousness.[8]

Here we could speak of a curative effect of the emotion of wonder on habit and custom. Descartes said that "all the passions are good insofar as they are governed by consciousness." Wonder, which associates the body with the discovery of the unexpected, the strange, the new, tears us away from the customary. When all is expected, banal, "all too common," "admiration" can still break the tacit pact of disarming familiarity between our life and our environment and lend a new youthfulness to the most familiar

8. Concerning habit as the blunting of the negative, see Hegel, *Morceaux choisis*, trans. Lefebre and Guterman, § 147, p. 217.

gestures as it illuminates with a fresh flash "the fresh, the lively, and the beautiful of this day." We aspire to this transfiguration of the daily which Ines, in Montherlant's *La reine morte*, glorifies: "It is always the same thing and it seems to me that it is always for the first time. And there are acts, too, which are always the same and yet each time I do them it is as if God descended to earth."

Through love and hate the world comes alive with contrary affective accents, the polar landscapes devoid of color and contrast towards which *ennui* drives (cf. Baudelairean "spleen") are broken up by "desirability" and repulsiveness.

But most of all effort is based on desire. Descartes here happily rediscovered the irascible of the scholastics which finally has the same significance as an obstacle. The cutting edge of desire awakens consciousness even as the body improvises. It might seem contradictory to say successively that effort is bare willing, without desire, and that effort is moved by desire. But spontaneity is alternately organ and obstacle to willing. Effort confronts resistance only if, in another sense, it encounters the complicity of this spontaneity. It says *no* only on condition of a *yes*. Virtue, in the classical sense, is alternately a habit and the imprint in the body of the emotional forces of the goods we love. Stoic *ataraxia* is inhuman insofar as it does not recognize the continuity of the soul with the body even in the very struggle against the body. Descartes' inspired idea is on the other hand to have made generosity a synthesis of action and passion. Perhaps even higher than the complicity of effort and of "habitus" he honors the fusion of willing and emotion in "joy." Joy is the emotion which I can no longer oppose, which the "negative labor" cannot broach. It is the flowering of effort: there is a solid harmony between it and effort. This is precisely what distinguishes joy from pleasure: in joy, the habit governed by effort and the emotion immanent in effort are reconciled.[9]

Human being aspires to this quality of habit and emotion which makes the body both retention and, if it were possible, spontaneous expansion of freedom itself. This ultimate synthesis is the unattainable limit, the mythical terminus of the dialectic of the voluntary and the involuntary from which the negative cannot be eliminated.

9. It is remarkable that the joy of "generosity" should be the last word of the *Treatise on Passions*, that even Kant retains an echo of it in the feeling of the sublime, and that it serves as conclusion of such great Bergsonian texts as *Creative Evolution* and "L'Intuition philosophique."

[2] EFFORT AND "MOTOR INTENTION"

How DOES the preceding analysis help us understand voluntary bodily action? In the first place it confirms that the most difficult and most basic problem is the problem of bodily docility, that is, the problem of a *transitive* consciousness—in the sense in which we speak of transitive causality—between unitary effort and multiple movement. The opposition between resistance and effort reflected here represents a crisis of such transitive consciousness. Thus consciousness of moving, of which we have spoken as "traversed" by consciousness of action terminating in the task is itself, so to speak, traversing: it is the passage from idea to movement. But our analysis at the same time orients us towards the solution of this problem and of technical difficulties inherent in it. The schema of interpretation which we shall apply to it is this: effort moves the body through "motor intentions" represented by the intermediate level of desire and habit. In effect effort appropriates the irascible, that is, the impulsive involuntary of desire, and utilizes the structural involuntary elaborated by habit. Without this "mediation" the classical difficulties of the problem of voluntary movement would remain insoluble.[10] (We shall not go back to the radical obstacle confronting knowledge of voluntary movement, namely the dualism of understanding which refers intention to unextended thought and movement to spatial object.)

Our discussion will deal with three critical points:

1) the distinction between "motor intention" and kinesthetic *sensations* or *images;*

2) the continuity between motor intentions and effective action;

3) the *continuity* between voluntary initiative and motor intention.

In other words, the point is to understand the *transitive* action of willing on the body in terms of the *practical* and nonrepresentative character of motor intentions, in terms of the hold which they exercise on the body directly and by their immediate *subordination* to willing.

1) Psychology is on the wrong track when it seeks to interpret experience of effort in terms of representative elements—sensations or images. It does this in two ways, either by inquiring what representations we have *of* effort, or by inquiring what representa-

10. Burloud, *op. cit.,* pp. 95–119, 389–92.

tions *precede* movement so that the movement would warrant the appellation "voluntary."

a. In its first aspect the problem concerns the classical discussions of the feeling of effort, as the familiar discussions between Maine de Biran and Ampère, Bain's "theory of innervation," and especially the famous article in which William James presents his centripetal peripheric theory of effort.[11]

Now once we pose the problem in terms of sensations it is difficult not to agree with James—we have no sensation of effort on the verge of or in the course of being released in the organism. Sensation does not and cannot reveal what a movement does; the register of sensation is the register of *fact*. Furthermore, the register of sensation is the register of the *diverse;* reflection applied to sensation cannot hope to encounter a unique "state," but a multitude of states, a sensual multiplicity strewn about the muscles, tendons, and articulations.[12] Consciousness of effort in principle eludes a description of sensations and states; it represents an entirely different dimension of consciousness, a radically non-representative, radically practical dimension. Deployment of willing in its organs is not itself a sense-consciousness, but, through successive kinesthetic sensation, it is *directed towards* a sense-consciousness, it is the "intention" of a sense-consciousness. To state the same thing in inverse order, sensation *is what* effort produces side by side with the movement. This characteristic of being "produced by" is not external to sensation but qualifies it in itself and completes its meaning. Absence of intention *in* a given sensation and *towards* a nascent sensation is what distinguishes the experience we have of a passive movement (stamped on our members by an external agent) from experience of an active, spontaneous, or voluntary movement: "At one pole a feeling of inertia, consciousness of changing state which is yet included in each particular moment, looking, so to speak, backwards in time—at the other, consciousness of an 'open' state, looking forward." This properly *active* moment in the sensible refers back to the practical dimension of consciousness which we must constantly distinguish from theoretical consciousness (perceptive, representative, intellectual, etc.). But introspection tends to reduce consciousness to representation. In addition, in an easy movement motor intention is concealed in the sensation of the movement performed; it is distinct from it only if the relation of "intention" to the sensation becomes "dis-

11. William James, *Feeling of Effort* (Boston, 1880).
12. Burloud, *op. cit.*, p. 99.

tended," extended in time in the form of a focused waiting, of motor preparation. A simple experiment reveals its presence: when I get ready to raise a weight which turns out to be hollow, my effort is in some way deceived. The sensation I experience surprises me. This surprise arises from the contrast between the effective sensation which resembles that of the passive movement and the sensation which had been expected and prepared. This type of "frustration" shows that motor intention anticipates sensation and that sensation confirms it in some appropriate way. It is recognized to the extent that I simultaneously develop and receive it. If we now recall that consciousness of the body is itself recaptured from the consciousness of acting in the *world* and that it is in some way traversed by it, saying that the organ is traversed by the action is equivalent to saying that kinesthetic sensation is traversed by acting. It is the intentionality of acting, oriented practically to an endeavor, which completes the meaning of moving and of the sensation which it brings to the fore. Thus psychology of introspection misses the sensation of effort when it seeks what it cannot find: a *spectator* representation of effort. Seen from its practical dimension muscular sensation is in some sense *reduced*, reduced to itself, if you wish. Now in itself, precisely, it is nothing more than immediate introspection which will reveal a passive moment and an actively produced moment in similar ways. But on the other hand, we have to agree with Maine de Biran against Ampère when the latter seeks a purely central sensation of effort: the sensation of effort remains that of an action *in* a peripheral sensation.[13] It is finally this action *in* a sensation whose indivisible unity Maine de Biran tried to make his friend Stapfer understand: that is where the "connection of willing and motion" is brought about.[14]

b. In its second aspect, the role of representations in the experience of effort has to do with the debate concerning "motor images." Can motor intention be reduced to an image of a movement to be performed which would have the remarkable ability of engendering the movement it represents?

13. *Correspondance d'Ampère et de Maine de Biran*, ed. Tisserand, VII, 383; and *Revue de met. et de mor.* (1893), pp. 317–19.

14. "Responses à Stapfer," in *Morceaux Choisis de Maine de Biran*, ed. Gouhier, pp. 236–37. The lasting weakness in Maine de Biran's doctrine (beside his exaggeration of resistance which led from contradictory elements into dualism) is that the personal body is never clearly distinguished from the *organism*, from the object-body; the notion of the "organic" retains an ambiguous meaning: it signifies at the same time the object of biology and the lower level of inner experience. This ambiguity is communicated to the correlative notion of hyperorganic force; willing is not beyond organism, it transcends personal body.

Our discussion of the ideo-motor reflex has already provided an occasion to specify the role of the images of movement in the initiation of movement. We still have to relate the conclusions of that analysis [15] to the present problem of motor intentions.

It became apparent to us that movement is not often regulated by kinesthetic image of that movement. There is no room to pre-suppose an unconscious kinesthetic image in the majority of the cases where it is absent. In the preformed skills it is the formal properties of perceived objects, *bearing no resemblance to the movement,* which govern that movement. The regulatory role of the kinesthetic image seems to be derived on analogy with that of external signs. Still, if it is true that the external *model* has a primitive regulatory power over a similar movement, then the motor role of kinesthetic image can take place on analogy with the external model. Kinesthetic image would be a special case of a model: a muscular model. This role of kinesthetic images is manifested in the case of having to complete deficient or absent signs and visual models, as in the case of the person blind from birth. The same is true in case of difficult movements in which all senses have to cooperate in regulation, as in case of the mountain climber, acrobat, etc. One of the effects of exercise, as we have seen above, is precisely to engender an increasingly clearer and less and less affective recognition of our muscular control, briefly, a sort of muscular introspection. When the body is well known and when a specialized muscular sensitivity is separated from the matrix of obscure affects and general impressions, then, Maine de Biran tells us, "the soul preserves a determination of it which is like a kind of memory or imperfect idea." [16] Such imperfect ideas are the kinesthetic images available for their guiding and control-ling function.

Thus there is no question of denying the existence and role of kinesthetic images, but they do not by themselves produce movement. They govern movement in the same way and even less than perceived and imaginary models. They are acquired in exercise, won from affective synesthesis. This means that the kinesthetic image, even reduced to this modest role, is not the motor image we are looking for. Such intention is rather a "di-rected tension," [17] a "method of the body, an actualizing idea

15. Cf. above, p. 245. "Problems of Ideo-motor Reflex and of Imitation."

16. Maine de Biran, *Mémoire,* III, 228, 195; formation of muscular representa-tion is equally won against muscular irritability as against affectivity. (*Ibid.,* p. 212.)

17. Burloud, *op. cit.,* pp. 96–97. "Motor intention is, on the level of the body, the analog of imaginative intention on the level of spirit." (*Ibid.,* p. 97.)

which gets along without any image, even a kinesthetic one, and is activated directly by nerves and muscles in which it finds its point of application." [18] We must understand it as an active mode and not as a representative mode. Representative modes, actual kinesthetic sensations and anticipatory kinesthetic images, perception awaiting external signs and models are as if the "light" of motor intention. They mark out the new difficult, or uncertain movement. These are the representations which are gradually eliminated as an action becomes automatic. Then there remain only some rather fleeting, guiding representations and that covert permission of willing, itself indiscernible from attention in the member which forms the principal part of the action.[19] Thus it is that "motor intention" is step by step reduced to itself. In this way we return to the easy, familar voluntary action which we referred to at the beginning of the discussion, the movement of the head or the arm by which I prove my own freedom of movement to myself. Voluntary movement is thus "motor intention" itself, barely illuminated by kinesthetic images, tendered between given and nascent kinesthetic impressions, and accepted by a permission which itself tends to disappear into an absence of inhibition.

Excessive attention to *representation* in the initiation of movement has as a consequence a gradual loss of the *transitive* character of voluntary motion: image produces nothing, it only illuminates the motor intention which passes through it, sometimes outlives it, and which alone produces action. It is remarkable that psychologists who sought the specific difference of voluntary movement in the type of representations which precede it have been led, often against their initial intention, into dualism. William James's declarations are characteristic in this respect—after having stated that sensations and thoughts are only abstractions with respect to action, "cross sections as it were of currents whose essential consequence is motion," he comes to write of them, "volition is a psychic and moral act pure and simple, and is absolutely completed when the stable state of the idea is there. The supervention of motion is supernumerary phenomenon and depending on executive ganglia whose function lies outside the mind." [20] But this scission must be attributed to his definition of voluntary movement: "A movement is voluntary only if a repre-

18. *Ibid.*, p. 210.
19. Cf. above, the short circuit, perception-action, in automated operations.
20. William James, *Psychology: Briefer Course* (New York, 1900), pp. 426, 432, 449. Similarly, "moral effort is not transitive between internal and external world"; *Feeling of Effort* (Boston, 1880). [French translation, "Le Sentiment d'effort," *Crit. Phil.*, II (1880), 123.]

sentation of it precedes its execution." [21] Thus on the one hand effort is reabsorbed into attention to ideas whose characteristic is being inefficacious, that is, unproductive in their own right, while on the other hand movement remains *foreign* to representation: it is an absolutely automatic *reflex*—the purported ideo-motor reflex—which follows an attention which has absolutely no hold on the body. Thus, once separated from representation, voluntary movement becomes indistinguishable from automatic movement. It differs from it only by an *antecedent* which is external to it.

But at the same time as movement is separated from representations and prepared for being turned over to the physiologist, there is an overly narrow psychological criterion imposed on voluntary action and easy, voluntary movements which are automated in their execution and released by a simple permission without antecedent representation of either articulations or even general design—movements which we have called, with Charles Blondel, "observed automatisms" [22]—are excluded from it.

This obstacle justifies Ch. Blondel in seeking the criterion of voluntary movement not in its psychological antecedents, but in its opportuneness, that is, in its *social convenience,* which seems to him the only common denominator between the difficult movements of the mountain climber and the automatic movements of the smoker rolling a cigarette while chatting.

Referring motor intention to faint permissive willing dispenses with this abdication of psychology. Motor intention is transitive action—whether or not governed by a representation of movement to be executed—through which a specific effort or a covert permission moves the body.

2) But how does motor intention *move* the body? A part of the answer comes to us from the *hierarchic* character of desires as well as of schemata and adjustments which mediate between willing and the body. This trait has been forcefully described by Tolman under the name of "determining adjustments," and later "behavioral adjustments." [23] Our skills are telescoped practical schemata the highest of which (for example, professional adjustment) are contiguous and continuous with an intention or *purpose* (for example, the intention of earning a living). It con-

21. James, *Psychology: Briefer Course,* p. 443.
22. Blondel, "Les Volitions," in *Nouveau traité,* ed. G. Dumas, VI, 387–95.
23. Tolman, "Instinct and Purpose," *Ps. Rev.* XXVII (1920), 217–33; *Purposive Behavior in Animals and Men,* chaps. XIII–XIV. Cf. also the concept of "levels of consciousness" which traverses effort in Bergson, "Intellectual Effort," *Mind-energy,* trans. Carr (London, 1920), chap. VI.

tains more precise adjustments (curiosity, anger, walking, then movement of legs, etc.). *Purpose* is the persistence of the superior adjustment *"until"* an appropriate act puts an end (release) to the one and the other. Thus the "determining adjustment" accounts for variability of subordinate movements capable of achieving a purpose.

This variable fulfillment conforms in part to the schematic character of skills acquired through practice such as we have described in the context of habit, and on the other hand to the structuring of our "tastes" and our "desires" in degrees of increasing and decreasing generality. Psychology of affectivity and psychology of action converge towards the same description.

From a purely motor point of view our skills are methods ranging from very vague "aptitudes" through general "schemata" to specific skills and completely specialized automatisms.

From an affective point of view our urges are ranged similarly from highly indeterminate "aspirations" and "tastes" through general "tensions" up to precise desires which keep us alert with respect to an increasingly more concrete "problem." The works of Lewin and his pupils offer a remarkable illustration of such resolution of tension by action. These works are in a great part directed against associationist theories of action which explain its unfolding by rigid association between a *specific* stimulus *and* a specific reaction.

In his principal work Lewin [24] shows how the same intention (the project of a conversation) finds variable ways of satisfaction. Even if the project were precise (to inform a friend by a letter), a new circumstance (encountering a telephone on the way) can lead to resolution of the tension of the project in a different way. Most remarkable are the cases of research in initiation, premature action (start of a race though the signal is delayed), or resumption of interrupted action. [25] What we speak of as "satisfying" a project and what we have examined from the point of view of general and specific significations presents itself

24. Kurt Lewin, "Vorsatz, Wille, und Bedürfnis," *Psych. Forsch.* (1926), pp. 329–85.

25. Maria Osvianskina, "Die Wiederaufnahme unterbrochener Handlungen," *Psych. Forsch.* (1929), pp. 302–79. In these researches interruption is provoked by an interesting action, an interdiction, a vexatious accident, introspection, etc. The author studies resistance to interruption, attempts at resumption, the equivalents of resumption, weakened or substitutive resumption, etc. Cf. also Zeigarnik, "Ueber das Verhalten von erledigten und unerledigten Handlungen," *Psych. Forsch.* (1927), pp. 1–86: the author studies particularly the pressure exercised on memory by actions which have not been "satisfied."

to the dynamic point of view as a satisfaction of a quasi-need. Release by a process of substitution testifies that the forces to be released accommodate themselves to relatively indifferent means. Thus while an action may function as vicarious satisfaction (initials which have the value of a signature), it also happens that the initial project (finishing and signing a work) can be "forgotten." The vicarious satisfaction can be appropriate (giving a letter to someone in place of posting it), partial (making a note of a promise in place of keeping it), fictitious (deprived of command, the imprisoned general writes history of battles), etc. Study of psychic fatigue or "saturation" confirms this analysis.[26] Such fatigue (which is distinct from muscular fatigue since a change of task using the same organs of execution can suffice to dispel it) also shows a hierarchy: I can be tired of drawing hatch-marks in a ratio of 3:5, or of drawing hatch-marks in general, or of doing manual labor, etc.

All such works are of considerable interest which, due to the choice of tasks and actions to be studied, far surpasses the interest of earlier works about "reproductive tendencies" based on mechanical and artificial tasks (lists of meaningless syllables). Unfortunately the physical interpretation of the concept of "tension" and the correlative reduction of myself to a special system of tensions makes utilization of these excellent studies difficult apart from the central hypothesis of Gestaltist dynamism. In order to correct its interpretation it is important not to separate the "causal-dynamics" of tension from the properly phenomenological concept of "intention" whose objective symptom it remains.[27] In this respect A. Burloud is right in seeking the model of "motor intention" in those intentions which we can seize live when we try to complete a memory in time or space.[28] These intentions operating on the level of imagination are the key to the problem of voluntary motion: "Here action appears as if directed and the direction as if active"; intention here appears as "active determination of the subject, a form of thought at work, thinking before being thought and in relation more than relation itself." [29] Production of movement is a similar realization of intention, in terms of movements rather than of images.

26. K. Lewin and A. Karsten, "Psychische Sättigung," *Psych. Forsch.* (1927), pp. 142–255. Concerning the distinction of the two "fatigues," along same lines, see Blondel, *op. cit.*, pp. 327–28.

27. Concerning this methodological discussion, see below, p. 355.

28. Burloud, *op. cit.*, p. 55.

29. *Ibid.*, p. 57.

Nonetheless the hierarchical character of this satisfaction and the comparison with the functioning of imaginative intention offer us only a fragment of an answer, as we said at the beginning. In effect the ultimate satisfaction of a motor intention is known objectively as a neuromuscular mechanism. The subject remains absolutely unaware of this mechanism. Our study of pre-formed skills and reflexes confronts us with the initial perceptivo-motor coordinations whose structure eludes consciousness absolutely. Thus the realization of intention depends in the last analysis on the *structure* of the living being which subordinates motor "montages" to intentions. Yet this structure is revealed to consciousness only by a general feeling of being alive, of being affected by my bodily situation.[30] Entire physiology records the objective symptoms of our being-alive. Here the diagnostic is more important than the tangled affective revelation of our incarnate existence; and yet it is that revelation of our living presence by the fundamental affectivity of the synesthesis which, on the level of the Cogito, bears the whole meaning of our body. Thus the motor intention of desire and of skill is "immersed" in the absolute involuntary of structure. We can alternately read the relation of the relative involuntary (motive, ability) to the absolute involuntary (situation as personality, the unconscious, and life) as a relation of "immersion," when, for example, motor intention *descends* into structure, or as a relation of "emergence," when, for example, a need "rises" from the tacit structure of trophic reflexes and vital intraorganic compensations and is born, arises as lack and as a lived thrust in the direction of the world. Feeling of effort reveals precisely this delicate articulation. In it I experience this feeling at the same time as product of intention and as received from the body which locates me. Effort lies at the confluence of the activity which *descends* from the self into its corporeal density and of "simple affection," as Maine de Biran said, which always reveals to me that even in the highest mastery over my body I do not *give* myself my body. This is why kinesthetic sensation, of which we have said that it was in no way an experience of effort, remains in turn the indispensable medium of passivity in which active intention of movement becomes incarnate.[31] But this hierarchic continuity of practical intentions, increasingly specific and immersed in the absolute involuntary

30. Cf. below, p. 355 concerning life as *resolved problem* and as *task*.
31. "Effort contains two elements, action and passion. . . . Effort is carried out in contact." Ravaisson, *De l'habitude*, p. 23.

of structure, is complicated in effort by a feeling of resistance, by mutual exaltation of bodily activity and passivity. This *contrast* is on the verge of obliterating the *transitive* consciousness of voluntary motion.

[3] BEING ABLE AND WILLING

IF WE now consider motor intention from the viewpoint of willing, the continuity between motor initiative of willing and tendency has to be stressed just as much. Motor intention is the power of willing. There can be no willing without ability, and in the same way there is no ability without possible willing. In this respect there is no difference in kind but only in degree between motor initiative of observed automatisms which reduces itself to a covert permission and the intense effort applied to resistance. Here willing remains an initiation of motion through abilities or powers.

This reabsorption of specific initiative in an implicit permission is considered an "effect of habit." Human habit is for a great part, as we have seen, a fall of willing into nature: but in turn it is a nature subordinated to willing as its organ. This understanding of willing and ability in terms of each other, which is the conclusion toward which the second part is moving, was expressed by Aristotle in his famous formula, *"the will moves by desire."* Even Descartes echoes this when he understands desire and generally all passions as a *disposition* of the soul to willing. "For it is good to note that the principal effect of all passions in men is that they incite and dispose their soul to willing those things for which they prepare their body." [32]

But it is Ravaisson, in that extraordinary small book entitled *De l'habitude* who expresses the continuity of willing and ability perhaps most forcefully. Here it becomes apparent that the naturalization of the will is the condition of its functioning in the world; the will can rule only through the abolished will:

It is the natural spontaneity of desire which is the very substance and at the same time the source and initial origin of action. The will constitutes the form of action, the unreflected freedom of love constitutes all its substance. . . . Here is the ground, the basis, and the necessary beginning, the state of nature whose primordial spontaneity all will includes and presupposes. Understanding and will are only related at the limit, at ends, at

32. Descartes, *Treatise on Passions*, art. 40.

extremes. Movement measures the intervals. Understanding and will determine nothing except the covert and the abstract. Nature constitutes concrete continuity, fullness of reality. The will deals with ends, nature suggests and provides the means.... In all things natural necessity is the cord around which freedom is spun.[33]

It is this subordination which appeared to us as the first of two aspects of habit (the second being the involuntary of facilitation). As we have said in the first chapter, the *structure* of acting is not *what* I want, but that *through which* I want. The terminus of acting is the change in the world, it is the notes which come from my fingers and which in some way "passively demand" to be played. I do not explicitly will the articulation in the movement of my hands, but the execution of a piece of music through it. What does this "through" mean? This question concerns specifically the *structural* involuntary of an acquired gesture: an involuntary structure is an ability traversed by acting. This is what senses as organs are. Strictly speaking, I do not know *how* I do what I know how to do.

This situation is normal and even essential for the practical relation which I have with my body. In order to understand it we have to go back to the initial unlearned skills: in the first gesture of every young child who stretches out his hand in the direction of a desired object, the internal connection of movement and its regulation by perception are already a resolved problem. When reflection awakes the problem is always already resolved. The initial clumsy gesture was already the organ, albeit neither willed nor known in its articulation, of a purpose or a desire. Thus the enigma of habit is preceded by and contained in that of the preformed gesture which is already an articulated totality governed by perception. This primitive fact of a practical relation to my body, irreducible to a knowing and a willing, can in some sense be rediscovered through a reduction *ad absurdum:* if in effect I ought to know each time the means for attaining an end, I should have to have a complete awareness of the structure of my body, exhausting even the last means. But a complete knowledge of anything and especially of the body remains the governing principle of a permanently incomplete effort of thought. We might just as well say that there has never been a voluntary movement in the world. Voluntary movement is a kind of movement which is never exhausted by thought or traced by voluntary intention and yet one which in a single stroke sums up the body's func-

33. Ravaisson, *op. cit., passim,* pp. 50, 59, 60–61.

tioning. In this sense all willing presupposes an ability which presents itself as non-knowing and non-willing.

This relationship of ability to willing extends considerably beyond voluntary movement. An entire segment of my thought goes to sustain a practical relation which is rather like that of a pianist and his fingers when he is completely preoccupied with drawing from nothingness, "through" his fingers, the notes which the piano contains only as possibles: in the same way, when I hear a questioner or when I speak, I pass through grammar and style and without thinking of them as such directly to the meaning. To think is always to bring to life knowledge forged by former thought which I utilize as an intellectual nature. Here in the texture of the most abstract Cogito is the condition of progress. I formulate new thought only on condition of having thoughts which I no longer need to formulate. There is no present Cogito without a former Cogito which I have left behind as act: there is a type of thought as movement which cannot be run through anew but which is summed up practically each time I think actively.

Thus the efficacy of the will is proportionate to the intricacy of the hierarchies of abilities of which we spoke above, from general methods to specialized automatisms. To the extent to which the will in the first place activates former, abolished willing, to the extent, consequently, that it is naturalized, it can turn to more and more abstract ends, that is, ends increasingly removed from the movement variety. The place of these intentional hierarchies is thus fully indicated in case of a being capable of seeing into the distance: they *mediate* the abstract project and the variety of movement. Already in the organic structure we can see a prefiguration and an antecedent condition[34] of this development of human action. To the extent that we go up the scale of living beings the circuit of action from objects to individual response takes longer, and, as Ravaisson notes, this delay is correlative with organic development. Its consequence and homologue in history of individual psychology is the prolongation of intermediaries between projects which are ever more abstract and actions which are ever more complex.

In this sense the simple movement by which I prove my freedom to myself can contain the epitome of the entire history through which the will as abstract loses itself in its own organs. This is why we can say equally well either that our most general abilities are a type of will constituted through relation to the

34. Concerning this concept of condition, cf. p. 341.

constitutive will or that our will becomes the form of our body.[35]

In becoming subordinated to willing as an ability, the structural involuntary appears also as the involuntary of facilitation. Here the identical nature of effort and permission becomes apparent. The more docile an ability is the more capable it is of being carried out by a faint and in some way subliminal willing. Voluntary possession of the body becomes an insignificant control, yet it may be here that willing is most noticeable.[36] One of the inconveniences of experimental introspection has been that it placed great stress on the forms pregnant with effort and neglected the covert form of voluntary motion which is a simple, vigilant "posture" of consciousness, corresponding to the availability of its body. This common will of observation and permission, this subdued effort, represent an unattainable harmony of willing and ability and graceful improvisation of a nature not divided between its humanity and its vitality.

This relation between effort and permission can be included within the relation of actuality and potentiality as it is revealed in the field of attention. Husserl insisted strongly on the universal character of that relation: the flux of lived experience, he said, cannot be constituted of pure actualities.[37] The distribution of emphasis, familiar in the order of perception, must be extended to all operations of the Cogito. There are memories, judgments, and marginal desires, a non-actual willing. All the while that I am perceiving, judging, or willing, there is something which is co-perceived (mitgeschaut), co-judged, co-willed, and with which I am not specifically concerned. The observed automatisms are authentic voluntary actions "at the horizon" of willing. To call them unconscious or absolutely involuntary is erroneous. It is the nature of marginal (or non-actual, if we wish to speak that way of an act) acts to be capable of becoming focal acts in virtue of the temporal implication between the potential field and the

35. Pushing the idea that habit belongs to embodied will to the limit, Ravaisson sees in it the principle of reconciliation between thought and reality, "substantial idea," "thought in the members." "It is from these organs that such inclinations, such ideas become increasingly the form, the mode of being, even the very being: spontaneity of desire and intention are in some way disseminated in being developed in the multiplicity of a structure." (Op. cit., p. 37.)

36. Baruk, "Le Problème de la volonté: nouvelles données psychologiques," J. de Ps. (1939), pp. 397–423: catalepsy and catatony reach electively the initial incitation of voluntary movement, physiological method makes it possible to confirm our distinction between release and structure and to show the universality of such initiative of movement even in the most familiar gestures; cf. in particular pp. 400–2 and 410: "It does not seem that the initiation of movement could be related to a determinate zone of the brain."

37. Husserl, Ideas, §§ 35 and 169.

actual vision. The smoker who automatically rolls a cigarette knows very well that he does it "expressly" because he is capable of recognizing his act as his and to take it up again as a focal act. He does not need to have recourse to a sociological interpretation to understand the voluntary character of this observed automatism. The possibility of converting faint willing into forceful willing constitutes the unity of permission and effort. In one sense, it is forceful willing which helps us understand faint willing, but in turn effort is a reflexive reiteration of faint willing which masks the meaning of voluntary motion: thus it is most frequently with faint, potential willing that the continuity between willing and being able to and the transitive action of willing in the world "through" ability becomes most apparent.

[4] LIMITS OF A PHILOSOPHY OF EFFORT: EFFORT AND KNOWLEDGE

THERE IS A TEMPTATION against which few philosophies of effort have guarded: the temptation to derive a theory of knowledge from consideration of action, to derive seeing from doing. For is not knowledge bound up with an action, and itself an action? Is not the world a system of resistance to contact in which the self is reflected in such a way that it posits the nonself in contrasting itself with it? There immediately comes to mind Maine de Biran, who believed that he could derive an entire theory of perception from the "primitive fact" of effort.

It is useful to remind ourselves that a philosophy of effort does not suffice to constitute a theory of knowledge. Thus it is rather a limit of our problem which we shall now take into account: the limit at which a theory of action can no longer present us with the actual *presence* of the world.

Knowledge includes a definite action, and *attention* is, in this respect, a type of effort. The organs of sense are organs which I move: I see *by* looking, I hear *by* listening, I smell *by* inhaling, I feel *by* touching, *by* fingering, *by* grasping, and *by* embracing. I am aware by a diffuse effort; while it is by a localized effort that I take in only the painted form, music, or the perfume of a rose. In all this we do not distinguish the new effect from the perennial effort to hold the mass of muscles in check against lateral effect of emotion and habit. As all sustained effort, attention is not an act terminating in the organ. It is not aware of itself: the intent passes through it to the object: attention is attention to. . . . I am not at all concerned with myself but rather with the object. Nor is this extraordinary. On the contrary, the novel element is that the broader intentionality in which this effort is lost is not one of acting but *one of knowing*. The light effort of looking becomes lost in the very presence of the object seen. This type of effort in which knowing completely absorbs the subject's action is attention strictly speaking. Its modifications have as their correlate a modification of the actual aspect of the object ("clarity" of attention, "relief," etc.).

I am obscurely aware that something depends on me in the world's appearance. But it is not whether an object shall be such or such: my entire ability consists of questioning it, by turning to or from it, by singling out this or that characteristic from it or by letting it be. My sole initiative is one of exploring my universe, or orienting the process in which objects are progressively sketched. This initiative in exploration distinguishes voluntary attention from a passive attention in which I am absorbed by the object, occupied, captivated, or perhaps even fascinated by it. But this initiative does not produce the essential part of perception which is properly seeing, hearing, and which is related to the actual presence of the object. Here lies the limit of a psychology of effort. There comes a moment when action yields to knowledge and becomes its servant, when effort becomes receptive to the world as a questioning openness. Doing reinforces seeing, but in order to make it more docile, more available. Attention is the homage which effort pays to the reign of knowledge, and this reign has demands of its own which cannot be derived from the properties of action. The order of presence has its own laws which cannot be reduced to those of actions and passions.

In the light of these principles Maine de Biran's proposal to derive the essential elements of a theory of knowledge from a consideration of effort becomes once more questionable. It is not possible to reduce the presence of the world to a system of limits, of resistances which our effort encounters.

We are familiar with Maine de Biran's thesis: without effort I should know nothing, I would only become this or that impression, but I should not know it. By this we shall understand that 1) this impression would bear no stamp of an external object, 2) it would not be related to any localized organ in the body, and 3) it would not be elucidated by self-conscious consciousness.[38] Only an effort applied to a more or less resisting organic terminus gives birth at the same time to a subject who perceives himself,

38. Maine de Biran, *Mémoire,* IV, sect. II; cf. esp. general summary, pp. 245–56.

to a feeling of localization of the sense impression, and to the belief in the exteriority of the resisting object. Thus Maine de Biran treats the properly cognitive element of perception as an affection which by itself is not the presence of an object, is devoid of intentionality, yet constitutes a mode of the subject which the latter does not perceive as such but to which he yields or, better, which he "becomes."

Only through effort does "everything become related to a person who wills, acts, evaluates the results of his acts, distinguishes, through contrast, enforced modes of passive sensibility from those it produces by willing and from which it can thus acquire, either directly by touch or through some sort of induction (using all other senses) an idea of some foreign existence or force conceived on its own model." [39]

This attributes considerable dignity to effort which is seen as engendering self-consciousness and, by contrast with it, knowledge of the world which is not myself.

We can discern a kind of hierarchy in this induction of the non-self: what is other than myself is revealed progressively, as a vague limit, as contrast, and especially as resistance to effort. Thus in case of the sense of smell it is only through the voluntary effort of smelling that the perfume of a rose first becomes a perception. Since even the impression of an odor does not always respond to the effort I exert to recall it, the effort is distinct from the impression. "A distinction arises between the acts which my self perceives in producing them and the modifications it experiences without producing them." Hence "the resistance of desire must lead not to knowledge but to a belief in something which exists outside the sensing being, not a perception, but rather a persuasion of a non-self." [40]

This vague existence suggested by the sense of smell is more purely intuited in the functioning of hearing whose motor part is properly voice: the sounds which I have not produced are referred to a non-self by a simple contrast with the entirely negative index of "absence of effort." [41]

Biranian interpretation of external knowledge triumphs with active touch: without any properly representative element in touch, through the simple experience of resistance, active touching constitutes a direct relation, force against force, with a resisting outside:

39. *Ibid.*, pp. 7–8.
40. *Ibid.*, p. 44.
41. *Ibid.*, p. 59.

Active touch alone establishes a direct communication between the moving being and other existences, between the subject and the external term of effort, because it is the first organ with which moving force, being constituted in the first place in the direct and simple relation of action, can still be constituted in the same relation with strange existences.[42]

Thus the world is only a resistance to our control. The strictly speaking tactile sensations (the rough and the smooth, the cold and the warm, the dry and the moist, etc.) only dress up this level of resistance and become reduced to the role of signs of possible action.

To exist is to act. This applies to me in terms of effort, to objects in terms of the resistance they offer me.

The initial judgment of existence comes from apperception of effort which in the same intuition constitutes the subject of effort and the alien terminus which *exists* solely as the force of resistance; through it . . . the *myself* becomes capable of knowing its own limits and of circumscribing them.[43]

In this way a philosophy of perception is included in a philosophy of effort, positing the world is entailed in the "judgment or simple, primitive relation of personal existence" [44] and the existence of the world is entailed in the perception of effort.

We might ask whether Maine de Biran does not miss the essentials of knowledge and ask too much from a consideration of effort and resistance. The essentials of perception do not become manifest in the extension of effort but along an absolutely original and, we could say, adynamic line. The pair, action-passion, effort-resistance, does not govern my relation to the world either exclusively or even essentially. The presence of the world in perception has a mystery of its own, a mystery of sense intuition which does not permit itself to be absorbed in that of effort. The existence of the thing is not purely the counterpart of my existence as force. To exist, for a thing, is to *be there* for me. We can say the same thing in other words: being perceived is not a form of passivity or inertia, of resistance to my action. An object does not act, it is perceived. An object is not *non-self* but a presence of an *other*.

This, precisely, is the reason why the intentional relation of knowledge does not essentially reduce to the pair action-passion, because to know is neither to act nor to be acted upon so that

42. *Ibid.*, p. 102.
43. *Ibid.*, p. 115.
44. *Ibid.*, p. 125.

perception could be lived now in a passive, now in an active mode. Passive attention (and its extreme, fascination) is at the same time receptivity in what it knows and passivity insofar as it does not direct the being of the object but remains its captive. On the contrary in the effort of attention, perception is receptivity in its adherence to the object and activity in its inherence in effort, that is, in the initiative of the subject who orients himself and moves his body to turn the object. (The scholastics rightly distinguished the point of view of practice, which is that of effort or passivity and the point of view of specification which expresses determination of knowledge by its object. Unfortunately they have their own way of yielding to the temptation of naïve realism and finally treat the intentional relation as a type of action and passion.)

This failure to understand the properly representative significance of perception leads Maine de Biran to underestimate attention: since the presence of the world is not an orginal dimension of the Cogito but a moment derived from effort by the experience of resistance, attention which presents itself as a complete poverty before the object can only be a type of reflection or self-perception, though inverted and alienated. We should then say that effort is no longer perceived in its deployment but is lost in sense impulse, the "force is not perceived itself except in the transformed result." [45] Action is concealed in the passivity of the senses. Attention is like an observation, but this observation is in reality a disguised action, it is a ruse of effort and of self-consciousness putting on the garments of alien existence. Attention triumphs with sight, as effort becomes revealed without alteration in active touch and even in hearing and smell.

Yet Maine de Biran came close to recognizing the limitations of his theory of effort and of the originality of a pure receptivity: in effect sight has the remarkable quality that passive impressions in it are only minimally affective. Effort in it is almost nil, and "as if unperceived in its minimally intense deployment." [46] Thus the simple or objective perception reaches its maximum purity when affection tends towards zero and when effort is almost nil. The philosopher of action does not fail to be astonished at this point:

The individual neither senses nor acts, and yet the phenomenon of representation takes place; there is an external or internal object, passively

45. *Ibid.*, p. 30.
46. *Ibid.*, p. 14.

perceived. At this point the idea of sensation seems to exist of itself and to come ready made from the outside.[47]

The philosopher has to concede that the visual object is represented rather than sensed. He endeavors to consider this representative function a property of the sense of sight, making allowances for touch in which it also appears to a small extent. "Now if the affect is faint, the effort is also faint, for the eye is the least inert organ; effort surely is not reflected but uniquely perceived in the represented world itself. Attention belongs to this mode as one of its elements." [48] In reality Maine de Biran here presents a pure receptivity which is not derived either from voluntary action or from passive affection and which constitutes perceiving itself. A consideration of the various sensory registers will show in each of them the irreducible presence of such receptivity. Far from exhausting the problem of sense knowledge, an exploration of active and passive modalities of perception does not even allow us to pose the problem correctly. It is only in the function of pure representation that the effort of attention acquires its full significance as *an action in the context of a presence.* Its characteristic as something observed and received is in no sense a degradation of effort.

Now we are in a position to appreciate the significance of a philosophy of effort within its proper limits.

1) Our stated refusal to derive a theory of knowledge from a theory of effort has an incalculable significance: *the key to the problem of truth does not lie in a consideration of the will.* A philosophy of the will has no right to become a voluntarism and to exercise a kind of imperialism over all the sectors of philosophical reflection. To discover the "I will" in the "I think" does not mean sacrificing the "I see" to it. There is also "theory," that is, a seeing and a knowing which the will does not produce. We must not ask more from a line of reflection than it can give.

2) In turn an elucidation of active and voluntary modes of perception remains of considerable interest from a double point of view:

a. We need to become aware of whatever there is of the voluntary in knowledge worthy of that name in order to put an end to the pretensions of superficial sensualism which would make the self into a simple bundle of impressions, a "polypary of images." If all the acts of the Cogito constitute regions of the same self, it is because they participate in a unity of effort, of a covert tension

47. *Ibid.*
48. *Ibid.,* p. 87; also pp. 85, 94.

which keeps up awake, alert, and in harmony with the world. Vision reveals seeing as an act. Here Maine de Biran is invincible.

b. The same reflection which frees us from sensualism also frees us from an intellectualism which pays attention only to impersonal structures of knowledge (categories of understanding and ideas of reason): the philosopher who takes as the theme of his considerations universal conditions which make knowledge in general possible always runs the risk of missing the personal level of the "I think." The effort of attention which none can make in my place gives to knowledge the personal mark of "I" and reveals in it at the same time a solitary action and a universal function. All the modes of the Cogito can be justified by effort: it is their common inheritance in the "I will" which relates them to the unique and irreplaceable destiny of a person.

We need not sacrifice either of the two aspects of attention: on the one hand, effort here bows before a presence; on the other, effort binds knowledge as well as acting to the same vigilant Cogito.

PART III

Consenting: Consent and Necessity

1 / The Problems of Consent

[1] THE THIRD CYCLE OF THE INVOLUNTARY

THE FORMS OF THE WILL, as of all the acts of a subject, are distinguished primarily by their object and the way they
intend it. But previous knowledge of the involuntary with which
they are reciprocal is enough to direct our vision to the most concealed forms. Our attention is drawn to the third form of the will
—the act of consenting—by a consideration of the third cycle of
the involuntary. Deciding is the act of the will which is based on
motives; moving is the act of the will which activates abilities or
powers; consenting is the act of the will which acquiesces to a
necessity—remembering that it is the same will which is considered successively from different points of view: the point of
view of legitimity, of efficacy, and of patience.

This new aspect of the involuntary first appears as a residuum
of preceding analyses. More than once we have come up against
a set of facts which seemed to block the three guiding ideas of this
book, the *reciprocity* of the voluntary and the involuntary, the
necessity of going beyond psychological dualism and seeking the
common standard of the involuntary and the voluntary in *subjectivity*, and finally the primacy of *conciliation* over paradox. Let
us recall these facts summarily. They deserve, par excellence, the
name of *facts*; they share the common element of escaping all
appreciation as well as all alteration by the will; they can be
neither compared as motives, nor taken hold of by effort as docile
organs.

All motivation is in the first place irremediably particular:
every consciousness has its own style which distinguishes it from
all others. This particularity, which is each man's character, far

from being able to figure in a scale of values, is rather the angle from which values will appear to a particular consciousness. Character, we shall say, is neither a value nor a value system, but my perspective which is not reducible to values. A second limitation of motivation was its irremediable incompleteness. I must always decide amid an impenetrable obscurity. Decision brings to a halt, more or less arbitrarily and violently, a course of thought which is incapable of definitive clarity. A decision is never more than an islet of clarity in an obscure, moving sea of unknown potentialities. A total motivation seems impossible. The unconscious functions as a horizon of any system of motives. It is not a motive, but a source of motives. Motivation encounters a third limitation in its dependence with respect to biological life. The initial evaluation of values is effectively constituted by needs, and though other values are not reducible to them, they must in the last instance be measured against these basic values whose force is an initial given with respect to willing. Now this initial contribution of value has the remarkable quality that it is at the same time the condition of the being of any values: I might well measure my life by other values and, according to Plato's saying, "exchange" it for them, but it is still necessary to be alive in order to sustain the project and the realization of the sacrifice: by suppressing life, sacrifice suspends all other values. This dependence of the will on life appears yet more simply: a definite condition of my life is always in the background of all voluntary thought. It is a commonplace that sickness, fatigue, or sleep change the quality of a man's decision and effort. Life is the given which makes it possible that there can be values for me.

In a different way the study of effort confronted us with the same difficulties. All efficacy has its conditions and its limits in character, the unconscious, and life. I might well increase and change my abilities, but in accordance with a formula which is my way of being effective rather than the terminus to which such effectiveness applies. The same character, which a moment ago we considered as the particularity of motivation is also the incoercible mode of being of my abilities and of my effort itself. The unconscious potentialities in which all the motives are immersed are also the obscure and hidden spontaneity which animates emotion and habit and explains their peculiarities, stiffness, and certain automatic aspects. Finally the life from which all value arises is also the source of all force: all power is immersed in life and seems superimposed on a "tacit" structure which assures the essential tasks of life before all reflection and all effort.

The reflex from which we have distinguished the initial hold of consciousness on movement and of which we could make no use in the theory of habit and emotion, testifies, insofar as it is conscious, to a prevoluntary wisdom without which I could not even begin to will. We understand, without knowing what the metaphor conceals, that all will is borne up by a system of regulations and equilibria whose disorder or absence scatters or destroys it. It is enough to place a hand on our side to feel the heart whose beating makes willing possible until the day it fails us. The heart which beats and which stops beating summarizes that involuntary world which is so close to us and which life gathers for us and in us. It is life which permits us to choose and to make an effort. Without it, we should not be men capable of willing. We shall refer to these diverse forms of the involuntary which are neither motives nor organs of willing by the general term *bodily necessity*.

Character, the unconscious, and life are the three principal directions of this new realm of the involuntary, at least of the bodily involuntary: for the factual position of other wills, of history, and of the course of nature constitutes the immense context of this invincible involuntary. Here we shall abstract from this context; nonetheless this abstraction is imperfect for, in part, character, the unconscious, and even life retain the imprints of other wills, of history, of men, and the structure of life sums up the order of nature for us and in us. On the other hand, the awareness of these relations of the will to this form of the bodily involuntary gives us access to the meaning of nature taken as a whole, in relation to freedom. It is to the extent to which the entire world is a vast extension of our body as pure fact that it is itself the terminus of our consent.

[2] CONSENT: PURE DESCRIPTION

1. Structure of Consenting

WHAT THEN is this act of consenting which completes willing? An act can be only understood by its intention, that is by its object. Now pure description of consent is singularly difficult. At first sight it does not seem that there is room for a new practical act in addition to the decision whose essence it is to be directed practically but in general to a project, and to the effort whose essence it is to fulfill a project practically through an action. What is disconcerting is that consent seems to have the practical character of the will, since it is a type of action, and the theoretical character of intellectual consciousness, since this action stumbles against a fact it cannot change, a necessity. Thus we shall take a chance on surrounding the essence of consent by a sequence of approximations, comparing it with theoretical representation of necessity and the practical attitude implied by voluntary motion. In the beginning a more direct language is not possible.

Consent indisputably resembles theoretical representation of necessity. "That," it states, "is the way it is"—"muss es sein? Es muss sein." In fact wise men have always construed the recognition of necessity as a moment of freedom. The grandeur of Stoicism lies in having mediated these two, and this is also what gives the mechanistic doctrine an ethical significance. I judge the necessity and thus am delivered from it: that is, I deliver the judging "I" from it.[1]

But consent cannot be said to be a judgment of necessity since it does not consider the fact in the least theoretically. It does not place it at a distance as sight, it is not a spectator's view of inevitability, but a contemplation devoid of distance, or better, it is an active adoption of necessity. In what sense does consent still constitute an action? As judgment of necessity expels that necessity from the subject who considers it, so consent links it with the freedom which adopts it. To consent is to take upon oneself, to assume, to make one's own. Undoubtedly we have to discover the individual judgment surpassed and preserved in consent. Consent seeks to fill the gap which judgment opens up, to make necessity an expression and so to speak an "aura" of freedom. What follows will show sufficiently that such perfection is the unattainable limit of consent.

Such active adoption of necessity recasts consent in terms of the practical modes of the Cogito. Actually it is not without an analogy with decision. Like decision, it can be expressed by an imperative: let it be; a strange imperative, to be sure, since its terminus is the inevitable. At least in willing the pure fact, I change it for myself since I cannot change it in itself. In this respect consent is always more than a knowledge about necessity: I do not say, as from without: "It is necessary . . . ," but passing in some sense over the necessity, I say, "yes, let it be." "Fiat." I will thus.

But is an imperative which does not terminate in a project,

1. Alain, *Idées*, pp. 199–200.

that is, in a new possibility engendered by the being who wills that it should be, an imperative which does not anticipate a change in the order of the world in conformity with its project, still an imperative? Consent anticipates nothing; we can say that it has no future. It commands in the present, and as if after the fact; for what it commands is already given, determined. Thus the same will which leaps into the future and decides it, that is, resolves it—acquiesces to a situation which bears the marks of being prior and which leads us to consider causes which push it from behind and not the ends which call it forward. I cannot will the new without finding the old and finding myself already given. Necessity is a situation which is all complete and in which I find myself involved.[2] If, as the study of the most fundamental condition of willing—life—will show, it is sensation in the broadest sense of the word which shows me my situation, we can say that consent is an imperative resolved to cooperate with sensation.[3] We shall have to say later how choice as a decision turned towards the future and consent granted to the facticity of a situation fit together.

This conspiracy of will with the order of the body, and, beyond the body, with the order of the world, is what ultimately reconciles consent and effort. I change nothing in the texture of things in accepting the implacable context of necessity. It is the very texture of reality which either lends itself or does not lend itself to voluntary motion, which presents lacunae favorable to action and confronts it with unbreachable limits. Moving and consenting means confronting reality with the entire body to seek its expression and realization in it. To consent is still to do, as expressions like taking on or assuming indicate. It is an engagement in being. But this resemblance is clearly at the same time an opposition. Consent is even the reverse of effort; it is specifically willing without being able, a powerless effort, but one which converts its powerlessness into a new grandeur. When I transform all necessity into my freedom, then that which limits and perhaps breaks me becomes the principle

2. Cf. the analysis of *Befindlichkeit, da, schon,* in Heidegger, *Being and Time,* pp. H.137–67, H.339–46. The concept of "situation" is common to all the "existentialisms." We shall try here (1) to give it a precise content by applying it to the third cycle of the involuntary, that is, giving it specific form with respect to a theory of character, the unconscious, and life, and (2) to delineate precisely the dialectic between choice and consent to a situation, using the descriptions of the three cycles of the voluntary and the involuntary.

3. The apparent proximity of the words "sensing" and "con-sen(t)ing" has no etymological value since the connotations of the Latin *sentire* are far more intellectual than those of "sensing" or of the French *sentir*.

of an entirely new effectiveness, an entirely stripped, disarmed effectiveness. Thus consent, which is so close to the effort whose extension it is, is at the same time its counterpart.

A very different relationship, that between man and things, can give us a proximate image of this and give rise to a final distinction of its essence. The expression "making a necessity my own" suggests a comparison of consent with a kind of possession. What is "mine" bears the stamp of myself; it is like a person's radiation upon things. Possession, like consent, does not transform the order of the world but the relation of certain of the world's objects to me. This "to me" stands midway between "outside myself" and "within me." In the same way necessity tends to become an expression and almost a possession of my freedom. But consent lacks the inflexibility and rigidity of possession. In effect what I possess has always some relation to an eventual enjoyment prior to which it can become corrupt or changed and implies a reference to other subjects who are excluded from my use and who can in turn exclude me from it. This is why possession is the seat of passions—the passions of having—and does not account for the essence of consent. Necessity is not aimed at a consummation, and so is incorruptible, and can be neither divided nor envied or taken away. Necessity is always with me, and each of us has life and death in totality. I make them mine in an inimitable way which is consenting, strictly speaking. It is patience rather than possession. Patience actively supports what it undergoes. It acts inwardly according to the necessity to which it yields. Consent is patience, as effort is effectiveness, and choice legitimity.

In this way we have progressed towards increasingly positive determinations: to consent is less to state a necessity than to adopt it; it is to say "yes" to what is already determined. It represents converting, within myself, the hostility of nature into the freedom of necessity. Consent is the asymptotic progress of freedom towards necessity.

Now we can fathom what is at stake in consent: it is the ultimate reconciliation of freedom and nature which both theoretically and practically appear to us torn apart. It is this reconciliation which we have pursued patiently through the forms of the will. Decision pertains still only to the value of action. Between a project of action and the action which inserts it into the actual there is still all the difference between an action which is merely contemplated and an effective action. A decision projects an act in some sense as blank, general, without confronting the hardness of the real. Thus effort appears as a specific mediation between thought and action; by practical fulfillment of decision, effort terminates among actual things. When I move my body, I bear witness before myself that freedom has a hold on nature, that nature is relatively unresisting to it, in brief, I practically realize the continuity of freedom and nature. But in addition to the fact that effort remains a struggle with involuntary forces which will yield only to discipline, the docility of bodily nature appears to be limited on all sides by an incoercible necessity which limits and at the same time supports the flexibility of natural order for human rule. We have encountered three forms of it which we designated by the traditional names of character, the unconscious, and life. Thus it is that consent here comes to take the place which the incomplete attempt has in the order of voluntary motion, to embrace the real and to extend the realm of freedom even into the region of necesity where nature no longer confronts our will with the docility of bodily powers. Consent is the movement of freedom towards nature in order to become reunited with its necessity and convert it into itself.

2. A Psychological Difficulty: The Spell of Objectivity

PURE DESCRIPTION gives rise to more problems than it resolves or than it presents as resolved. Conversion of necessity into freedom presupposes in the first place that there be, for thought, some kind of proportion between the two terms united in consent, secondly, that behind the difficulty of understanding there does not lie an irreconcilable practical hostility between necessity experienced within ourselves and our freedom's wish, and finally that there is no incompatibility between the new form of the will and the preceding ones whose meaning it inverts as soon as it reaches them. The third difficulty is new: it has to do with the ultimate agreement among the forms of freedom. By contrast, we are familiar with the first two: they only become more acute to the extent to which we raise motives and abilities to necessity. The first—more psychological because it is related to the treatment of the three forms of the involuntary contained in necessity by scientific psychology— poses in new terms the problem of psycho-physical dualism. The second—more philosophical because it refers to the treatment of the concepts of freedom and necessity by classical philosophy—is an extension of the well known problem of the union of soul and body and has to do with the very possibility of actually consenting to necessity.

The opposition between the voluntary and the involuntary is in the first place an opposition for the understanding: the involuntary seems in principle to demand an objective treatment and there seems to be no common standard between *object* and *subject*. Yet the reconciliation between motives and decision, between abilities and effort demanded in the first place that the involuntary which presents itself naturally as an objective reality among the objects of the world should be discovered once more at the very core of the Cogito's integral experience. To what extent can we discover necessity again in the subject? This would in many respects seem contrary to the demands of the problem. 1) Man's condition, insofar as it is irrevocable, is principally knowable from without; intimate experience of what I call character, the unconscious, and biological life is crude, fleeting, or even null. Some of the realities which these three words bring up are even known only by an external observer and by means of appropriate scientific techniques. The aura of subjective experience which still clings to these concepts is quickly overshadowed by the infinitely finer, more differentiated, and more coherent objective knowledge we have of it. 2) Necessity seems to demand that the mind should place it outside of itself in order to consider it and reduce it through explanation since it is unable to subdue it through action. More intimate experience seems to repel it while only the distance of objectivity seems suitable to it. It is not an accident that wisdom engendered by meditation on necessity is hard to guard against the temptation to assume with respect to all things the distance of observation and critique. 3) Submission of the body to necessity suggests more pressingly still a recourse to objective explanation. A healthy body to be cared for is like a tool which must be maintained; in terms of nutrition it belongs to the cycles of carbon, nitrogen, etc. A sick body is like a machine needing to be fixed. Fatigue, sleep, or suffering give the body over to things, and death marks its return to dust, that is, to the most formless of things. Here the appeal of objectivity is no longer the appeal of method or of wisdom, but of urgency. 4) Ultimately objectivity works a spell, and as a spell it is a passion. Total objectification of man is an invitation to betray the responsibility I have for my body itself. Consideration of the inevitable from a spectator viewpoint is my refuge when I am tired of willing and when the daring and danger of being free weigh upon me. As we shall see, the hypostatization of character type, of the unconscious, and of life as fundamental, exclusive natures are an alibi for fear and sloth, a pretext for non-being.

Thus it becomes apparent that the progression of this spell of objectivity determines the order of appearance of the forms of necessity in accordance with a kind of dialectic of alienation. Character, the unconscious, and life are not on the same level and mark a regression towards a more fundamental nature where I am more radically abolished. The unconscious is in some way farther than character, as the residuum of ethological explanation; life lies beyond the unconscious as the principle of all mental energy. On each of these levels the claim of the will is hidden behind a blinder objectivity. Am I not a projection of my character? This character is still a law made to my measure. Yet is this not itself an expression of unconscious forces which deceive me? And here already the unconscious begins to fascinate and frighten me by its way of approaching and engulfing consciousness. Finally it is life which is the terminus of psychological explanation. Still, it too presents to the gaze of psychology and from the point of view of the involuntary a new progression of the dialectic of alienation. Life is in the first place structure: in this respect it is perhaps the most crushing marvel for the will: that we consider it only one of those surprising hormone balances which regulate the tenor of calcium and water in blood. It seems that consciousness would be no more than a fragment emerging from a vast, unselfconscious wisdom. But this structure itself has an individual history. My will is tied to the very general fact of growth, what I am I have become, and I have been "a child before I became a man." Now childhood is the first dawn of consciousness; I proceed from this childhood. Finally all genesis leads back to an origin, growth to birth. The I who says "I" had been born one day; the I who claims to initiate acts does not initiate its own being. I have come forth from unknowns from which I derive and on which I depend, and am posed on the inexorable current of the laws of the species. Thus my being appears completely dissipated, volatilized in the crisscrossing of lines from which I come more radically than from my childhood, and which once more bring up the multiple origins of the first epoch of my life. I am no longer a being but an encounter among a considerable number of possible genetic combinations. And thus necessity has undergone its last mutation and won its last claim: it has become blind and absurd chance.

In proposing an order among character, the unconscious, and life the spell of objectivity imposes also the initial task, more properly psychological, of our examination of consent: to find the subjective indices of necessity within us, necessity such as it affects us and such as we experience it as a mode of our existence. It is useless to try to escape the devouring need of objective necessity by coupling objective necessity and inner freedom. This new form of psycho-physiological dualism is as untenable as the one we traced in the order of decision and voluntary motion. The progression of dualism finds here its supreme stage.

There is, in effect, a temptation to take up the relation of causality which we tried to apply to the passage from thought to movement, and to orient it in the opposite direction: posing the question of how necessary conditions could be imposed on the will. At first it could be thought that it would be enough to restrict the meaning of causality by giving it the negative form of a condition *sine qua non*—no life, no will. This is the relation expressed positively in expressions like infrastructure, lower levels, support, ground, or permission. Necessity would then be a fundamental causality, its hierarchy of causes thus forming a series of partial causes in which each would complete the preceding and would be completed by the following. Such concept of partial cause would provide us with the appropriate response to the spell of necessity. Character, the unconscious, structure, growth, descent would be only successive degrees, in that order, of such partial causality. The broadening of explanation in crossing waves which seem to disperse our unity in the actual cosmic totality and in the shadows of a geological past of life should no longer surprise any but the romantic minds, for the progression of explanation marks regression towards causes so much more incomplete that they appear more basic. This descending movement would call forth its opposite, an inverse movement of ascending composition of partial causes of which the last, at least on the human scale, would be that of the will which completes the subordinated causes with its choice and effort and which, failing an effective change of direction, completes them in consent.

This harmonious scheme is completely illusory: necessity conceived objectively is determinism. To conceive of an object is to conceive of it under a law. A partial or permissive determinism makes no sense. To conceive of determinism means to conceive of a total determinism. We shall show, at each level of necessity, that once character, the unconscious, and life are conceived as objects of science, it is no longer possible to limit their demands and explicative force and to reintroduce a subject consciousness. Such consciousness must necessarily be an element or a product of the personality type, a result of unconscious forces, an effect of structure, of genesis, and finally of genetic composition of the original embryo. Determinism is either total, or it is not at all. There can be no knowledge of man unless it first of all takes into account this *a priori*. The hiatus between objective knowledge of the world and internal experience of freedom cannot be bridged by understanding. All the attempts to coordinate heterogeneous causalities with each other can only conceal the paradox. There is no objective cosmology in which my will, reduced to consent or even to simple judgment of necessity, could figure as a reality of a higher degree and being articulated from realities of a lower degree according to a coherent relation. The condition *sine qua non* between objective necessity and freedom is a deceptive and untenable form of causality applicable only between object and object. This reductive power of causality and the blocking of all compromise is what we have to test on the various levels of explanation. Thus the obstacle itself leads us to preserve the internal experience of necessity in all its forms, especially where our body does not appear to us as source of values or abilities. We have to say what it means to undergo, to experience the incoercible, the inevitable. Existence is imposed on us in different ways: only necessity experienced within ourselves can be matched with the freedom of consent, for only an internal experience can be partial with respect to freedom and call forth an act of the will which it completes. Let us state right away that our effort to find necessity once more in the Cogito will be guided by the consideration that bodily necessity is always in some way intertwined with our motives and abilities whose subjective significance we have already discovered. This clinging of necessity to the docility of the body should constantly remind us and guarantee to us that necessity can be the locus of our responsibility.

Does that mean that in reverting from the objective to the subjective we lose the benefit of scientific knowledge of character, of the unconscious, and of life? Not in the least; we experience nothing subjectively unless we try, at the risk of failure, to conceive of it along causal lines. The detour through objective knowledge is necessary; at its limit we begin to sense necessity for us and in us. It is always a definite objective knowledge which lends its inadequate language to Cogito's experience. We shall thus be led to retain the language of causality as an index of that investment of freedom by necessity subjectively experienced; in this sense we are, we shall say, determined by our character, our unconscious, and our life. This is expressed in the fine term, "human *condition*," which articulates well the necessity to which I yield by the very fact that I have not chosen to exist. But we must not lose sight of the improper and indirect character of such language: it is transposed from the level of explanation, where causal necessity is not limited and made complete by any freedom, to the level of the lived where necessity is the condition of a freedom. Such language is useful to indicate and announce a fleeting experienced necessity which freedom in principle confronts, refuses, or adopts. The relation of the inevitable to consent comes first, but understanding breaks it up and reconstructs an order of the inevitable according to the objective schema of causal necessity from which freedom is excluded. Thus the psychologist makes use of concepts in which necessity is without reciprocity to express the reciprocal necessity of consent. This inadequate use of language of causality then allows us to rediscover the notion of condition *sine qua non* and to make use of it without being deceived. Applied naïvely, it implies the fusion and confusion of internal necessity, which is partial and reciprocal with freedom, and objective or causal necessity which is without limit and without reciprocity.

Condition sine qua non *is one of the indices of necessity which mark freedom*. But it is only one of these indices. The possibility of having recourse to other equally inadequate concepts testifies to its imperfect character: thus the language of topography provides the concept of *situation*. We shall say that freedom is immersed in necessity, that necessity is the locus of freedom. These spatial representations are obviously improper; their inadequacy even has an advantage over causal concepts because it is obvious and so to speak unequivocally equivocal.

But the concept of causality, once restored to its inadequate meaning and its indirect use, not only loses all exclusive character, but even in this new use does not fit all the forms of necessity which the will undergoes. Necessity which pertains to the limited perspective of character is one thing, the necessity indicated by the unconscious potentialities of mind is another, and the necessity which characterizes the dependence of consciousness with respect to life is something else still. We shall be led by close analysis to renounce the language of causality, even in its inadequate sense, in order to express the two initial forms of necessity. With respect to the infinite of choice and effort the finite perspective of character stands in a relation which is difficult to express by the idea of condition *sine qua non;* and the same is true of the indefinite virtualities of the unconscious with respect to the form which will imposes on all acts worthy of a conscious subject. It is in order to resolve these difficulties that we shall try to return to the classical concept of *finite manner* (or *mode*) for character and of *indefiinite matter* for the unconscious. Thus it will appear that the index of symptom function of causality does not cover all the fields of relation of necessity and freedom.

Thus our first task will be to criticize, step by step, the dualism of the involuntary and the voluntary on the level of character, of the unconscious, and of life. This will be the object of Chapter 2, "Experienced Necessity." This relation of nature to freedom is undoubtedly here more than elsewhere a paradoxic relation. At least the paradox will fulfill its function if, in wearing itself out, it will succeed in showing the basic adherence of necessity and freedom.

3. A Philosophical Difficulty

ASSURANCE OF RESOLUTION is always the covert reason for paradox: in a certain way we are always confident of the unity of what we break up as we conceive of it. The conviction that there is a final agreement between nature and freedom in which from the beginning we have seen the moving spirit of all philosophy of the voluntary and the involuntary has a specific meaning: it tends to restore, on a higher level of consciousness and freedom, the initial harmony of spontaneous consciousness with its body independent of reflection and will. It is this initial continuity of consciousness and body which makes a higher conciliation possible, one which will then appear as a reconciliation: I am alive, I am my life. But the birth of reflection is the rupture of this initial intimate coordination of consciousness and the body; hereafter it is the very act of freedom assuming its reasons, its abilities, and its conditions in a new practical conciliation. Now it will become apparent that the antecedent unity of the will with its ethological, unconscious, and vital roots (a unity which the three monographs concerning the unconscious, character, and life will suggest) seems definitely broken. The incommensurability of necessity and freedom for understanding has as its background a practical conflict that we can present in two different yet parallel ways.

If understanding tends inevitably to expel necessity out of itself it is because necessity always to some degree injures freedom. Necessity is essentially ambiguous: condition is at the same time limit, what grounds me also destroys me. Necessity involves a *practical negation* of freedom whose possible spread it breaks. Our task in Chapter 3, "The Way of Consent," will be to bring out this experience of negation in all the forms of necessity. After the three monographs, this exploration of the negative will provide the germ of a synthetic view of necessity. This obscure presence of negation in necessity has at least an extreme overt form (whose relation to other forms we must state): this life which supports me abandons me; I am mortal, my condition includes something negative. Here is the touchstone of consent and the ultimate test of wisdom.

This discovery has a particularly more serious significance than that of the *resistance* of our abilites: my powers resist me, necessity breaks me. To be sure, the constantly threatening disharmony between my abilities and myself includes the permanent possibility of the pathological which we have called the psychological *terrible*. But folly does not have the same urgency in life as evil which arises daily from the mortal condition. Here the *terrible* is normal. Its result is that the "yes" of consent can only be pronounced in the extremes of misfortune and that it is the essence of consent to be always on the way and of conciliation to be incomplete.

This conclusion, which we shall try to base on a rigorous analysis of different forms of negation entailed in necessity, can be reached by a different way: while man's condition includes a certain hostility with respect to freedom, this in turn bears with it an absolute demand diversified according to the three limits to which it yields. This demand, which calls for a careful analysis, tends to recast the will in terms of refusal. Freedom first says NO in wresting itself from misfortune and absurdity; it attempts to reject the pact which binds it to the earth. Thus the last turn in the drama of freedom and nature is the most violent: freedom and values seemed congeneric, freedom and ability proportionate, freedom and necessity negate each other mutually. *Thus the yes of consent is always won from the no.*

Yet why say yes? Does not consent mean giving up, capitulating? Here we are in the last cycle; psychology here is infinitely surpassed by properly philosophical options.

2 / Experienced Necessity

1. Ambiguities of Common Sense

CHARACTER IS the necessity closest to my will. Not even the most elementary and least elaborate consideration can fail to encounter difficulties which philosophy in its turn inevitably clarifies and brings to their most virulent pitch unless it is prepared to give up the resources of analytic understanding. Unable to reconcile freedom of choice and the inexorable limitations of nature, common sense successively affirms a false unlimited and unsituated freedom, and a false determination of man by nature which reduces him to an object. On the one hand common sense produces a fictitious conception of an indefinitely plastic human nature in which there would be no fate and in which even character would be chosen and could be changed through effort; on the other hand it claims that each man's lot and the use he makes of it is inscribed in it. What common sense does not succeed in formulating is a conception of freedom which *is* in some respect a nature, the conception of character which is an *individual mode* —neither chosen nor modifiable by freedom—of freedom itself.

This uncertainty and these contradictions of common sense concerning the relations of character and freedom are based on uncertainties and contradictions which we can call primary:

1) For common sense character is at the same time each man's external manifestation, what permits us to recognize him, to identify him in space and time—and his own nature as he experiences it. On the one hand this individual stamp is established externally, as an anthropometric reference. However, com-

mon sense, which functions this side of the separation of subject and object, does not in the least doubt that my character does not adhere to me so closely that I could not oppose it. My character is myself—it is my nature, what is most stable about me, beyond changing mood and bodily and mental rhythms. Thus it is at the same time my manifestation for others and my secret existence: in one case it has the consistency of a terminated, fixed portrait, in the other it is a fleeting reality which can only be discovered at the heart of my actions.

2) A second hesitation of popular thought before the enigma of character deserves notice. Popular thought holds in suspension diverse methodological possibilities which no science can develop simultaneously, but which the man in the street tries out in a confused way without distinguishing them. On the one hand popular thought tries to understand character by addition of distinct traits. Such "character traits" are the product of a rather advanced abstraction elaborated by conventional wisdom: shifty, gossipy, demonstrative, etc. Now such concepts are formed in conversation, epic, tragedy, elegy, or the novel and express human possibilities which, prior to being suited to a particular individual, are conceived with reference to man in general in all his scope. I come to the individual armed with signs and attempt to capture him in the increasingly tighter mesh of my abstractions. An individual character thus is a composition of abstract, universal character traits. But common sense adds to this rather clear procedure a more subtle effort to reach the nature of the individual at a single stroke. Thus it uses metaphors whose suggestive power is finally more penetrating than the analytic spirit of a combination of character traits. In this way the image of speed or thrust evokes promptness or ease with which feelings and acts flare up, burn, and go out. An excitable, irritable, lively type differs by its basic *tempo* from a calm, unsusceptible, slow character type.[1] The image of a surface makes it possible to distinguish depressed, worn natures; the image of depth contrasts superficial, light beings with deep, serious ones. Some men are extroverted, others live withdrawn into themselves. Dynamic images of equilibrium, of harmony, of disruption, conflict, instability, of birth and decadence, of rigidity and flexibility, suggest a swarm of semi-abstractions of an analogical order grafted onto the world of solids, liquids, plants, flowers, and butterflies, as to geometry and dy-

1. Ludwig Klages, *Science of Character*, trans. Johnson (London, 1929), retains these concepts of speed and development in which he sees the best of the old classification of temperaments. Compare the expression, "having a temper."

namics. The suggestive power of these metaphors compensates for the analytical spirit which governs the elaboration of character traits.

3) This indecision between the subjective and the objective, between undivided intuition and abstract sympathy, is extended in a hesitation between the individual and the genus. Through my character I am unique, inimitable, and yet in terms of it I belong at the same time to a collective type, to one of those composite portraits which Theophrastus or La Brueyère have elaborated. Common sense, we can say in Spinozistic terms, brings together an implicit philosophy of unique essences and general ideas.

4) These primary uncertainties cumulate in the fundamental hesitation of popular thought over the relations of freedom and character as we have stated it at the beginning: is character an infinitely flexible nature which makes a freedom without fate possible or is it a determinate reality such that it includes in itself even the use which a will, claiming to react to its own conditions of functioning, can make of it? Common sense does not know how to bind together the inexorable and the free.

2. Science of Character: Methodological Critique

SCIENCE of character resolves the ambiguities of common sense by choosing in each instance those of the spontaneous interpretations which have closest affinity with the method of natural science and which are most suitable for conceiving of character on the model of a stable object, external to the observer. We shall use as our reference the classification and explanation of character by the school of Groningue, Heymans, and Wiersma.[2] We do not intend to present a summary of the works of the Dutch scientists, but to show, by a careful examination of their method, that an objective science of character poses the problem of man in such terms that it is impossible to relate character scientifically constructed in this way directly to the freedom of a subject. Such objective character must rather serve as an index for discovering and diagnosing a certain nature in

2. Biographical research: "Ueber einige Korrelationen," *Ztschr. f. ang. Ps. u. psych. Sammelforschung,* I (1908), 313–81. Statistical research: "Beiträge zur speziellen Psychologie auf Grund einer Massenuntersuchung," *Ztschr. f. Ps. u. Physiol. d. Sinnesorgane* (1909). In French, Gerardus Heymans, *La Psychologie des femmes,* trans. R. Le Senne (Paris, 1925). [Original, *Die Psychologie der Frauen* (Heidelberg, 1910.)] Page numbers refer to French edition. R. Le Senne introduced Heymans' typology of personality in France in his *Le Mensonge et le caractère* (Paris, 1930), and *Traité de caractérologie* (Paris, 1945).

the first person, whose subjective status is finally more obscure but which alone can be related in some way to will in the first person.

1) According to ethology, a character type is in principle a portrait containing the distinctive features of the individual for an *external* observer—an observed portrait, distinct from the actual movement of inner life which would overtake it as the background of its initiatives, as included in its own actions. Science demands this; that is the meaning of the biographic method and especially of the extensive statistical research [3] initiated by Heymans. The attempt to build up complete psychographs, including habits, aptitudes, passions, virtues, vices, bodily dispositions, etc., presupposes a total objectification of the individual and suspension of precisely that communication through which alone we would have some hope of reaching the other as an existence, indivisibly free and necessary. Science demands it, but at the cost of an ultimate problem: for there is no discoverable relation between the "I will" and a psychograph which is only the portrait of the other.

2) In order to arrive at a rational and clear view, ethology has to sacrifice all the fleeting metaphors by which common sense attempts to uncover the undivided spirit of the individual. It tries to reunite the individual by combinations and mutations of simple components. Already the way the questionnaire for biographic and statistical research is made up presupposes an initial elaboration of abstractions which remain close to common observation. But the most stable correlations [4] among character traits which make a classification possible can only be systematized by means of a small number of general properties—*emotivity, activity, secondarity*—which, in different combinations, provide the principal ethological types.[5] At this point, ethology moves beyond the descriptive stage towards a genuine explanation of character types

3. Concerning the conditions of the two approaches and the comparative heuristic and demonstrative value of the methods, cf. Heymans, "General Introduction," *op. cit.*, esp. pp. 1–13, and "Methods of Research," *ibid.*, pp. 26–42; and Le Senne, *Le Mensonge et la caractère*, pp. i–xi, and *Traité de caractérologie*, pp. 26–42. The questionnaire of the statistical method can be found in the Annex of *La Psychologie des femmes*, pp. 285–89, and in *Traité de caractérologie*, pp. 637–49.

4. The notion of correlation designates a relation of necessary coexistence between forms, qualities, and functions of a being. It belongs to the area of classification.

5. We shall recall only the eight combinations of emotivity (or non-emotivity), activity (or non-activity), and secondarity (or primarity): EnAP, nervous; EnAS, sentimental; EAP, choleric; EAS, passionate; nEAP, sanguine; nEAS, phlegmatic; nEnAP, amorphous; nEnAS, apathetic.

represented by formulas it elaborates. At least systematic classification and quasi-spontaneous distribution of individuals into classes mutually support each other. In addition, abstract factors whose permutations compose the ethological formulas are either suggested directly by certain traits appearing in the inquiry or produced by a more informed elaboration on the level of theories of general psychology.[6]

It is not hard to see the systematization which these three factors bring to explanation,[7] but in turn they make ethology a tributary of postulates of mental physics to which, as we shall see, free willing succumbs. In the first place mental life is construed on the model of an interplay of tendencies, that is, of mental realities considered as facts in the same sense as material movement. We know that psychology as a science is born in the act of raising these beings of reason to an undecided status, half subjective, half objective, sufficiently subjective to distinguish psychology from physiology, sufficiently objective to authorize scientific treatment of consciousness and especially a causal deterministic explanation. These are the tendencies which the ethologist marks with the coefficient of emotivity and whose motor power and unconscious action he considers. The second postulate is the primacy of automatism over reflected, voluntary action: [8]

6. Concerning the definition of the three gradual factors which affect tendencies, cf. Heymans, *La Psychologie des femmes*, pp. 41–99; Le Senne, *Traité de caractérologie*, pp. 61–103. See the critique in Burloud, *Le Caractère* (Paris, 1942), pp. 125–40.

7. These three factors do not eliminate the possibility of dichotomy. (1) We need to add the normal extent of the field of consciousness (Heymans, *op. cit.*, pp. 44–53; Le Senne, *Traité de caractérologie*, pp. 104–14); (2) In addition, what is the significance of the differences of intelligence which play a major role in *La Psychologie des femmes* (pp. 99–100) with respect to a more affective classification? (3) Even more serious is the fact that these three factors deal only with the "general availability of motives," independently of their preferred orientation. *La Psychologie des femmes* rests in great part on a particular type of motives to which the feminine character is sensitive in its natural scale of values (*ibid.*, p. 210), that is, "the ends which this activity preferentially poses for itself" (*ibid.*, p. 228): concrete altruism, sense of duty, truthfulness, patience in suffering, all the virtues which the dominant emotivity of the woman ought to contradict testify to a disposition of tendencies themselves not reducible to other ethological givens (pp. 230–63 and esp. p. 281). Heymans does not take this into account in his classification of character types, and when he approaches the question of the system of tendencies he reproduces the classification proposed by Paulhan (organic, egotistic, social, and abstract tendencies). The relationship of formal characteristics affecting tendencies in general (emotivity, activity, secondarity, etc.) and material characteristics which have to do with the privileged order of tendencies themselves calls for further specification.

8. Heymans, *La Psychologie des femmes*, pp. 191–93; Le Senne, *Le Mensonge et le caractère*, pp. 25–30.

activity is the motor power of a representation whose impulse can only be hindered by the inhibitive action of other tendencies. Secondarity is called a remote subconscious effect of representations; secondary functions and breadth of the field of consciousness function as shock-absorbers of primitive automatism. We are quite aware to what extent this physical imagery fails to do justice to the more sutble nature of the involuntary. But the postulate fits with the initial one: it is the material principle of mental physics as the objectification of the Cogito under the name of tendencies is its formal principle. The third postulate is the one which defines consciousness as a fragment of a wider unconscious field.[9] It is invoked in order to define secondarity and extent of the field of consciousness. We shall rediscover the meaning of the unconscious later, but at no point will it ever be possible to define consciousness as a part of a broader whole.

These three postulates of scientific psychology in turn make it impossible to relate character type, thus reconstituted, *directly* to a free subject. Character type and freedom are reached from two incommensurate points of view: on the one hand the self apprehends its own subjective realm and senses its limits and conditions, but is unable to treat them as an object of observation or a portrait; on the other the psychologist offers us a table of tendencies built up from without and elaborated according to the postulates of mental physics.

3) Thus the task of ethology is to reach the individual in terms of his ethological *class*, free from considering him ultimately as ineffable at the limit of an endless approximation. As against the unique essence it chooses the general idea. Consider, for instance, Heymans' eight classes: these classes are in the first place empirical types based on the functioning of correlations and suggested by the inquiry itself: the first meaning of character is *class* to which an individual *belongs*. A second, more precise meaning of character is average type, a bundle of traits to which statistics allow us to attribute coefficients of probability and a statistical value on basis of statistical inquiry: in this second sense character is a *probable* type which an individual more or less *approximates*. In a third, still more precise sense, character type is a formula systematically elaborated by composition of three variables, EAS [emotive-affective-secondary]. This triple way of understanding, as class, as probable type, and as synthetic formula, lies at the root of the complexity of that being of reason we call the amorphous type, the nervous type, the apathetic type,

9. Heymans, *ibid.*, pp. 3–27, 41, 44–53.

etc., and permits a triple qualitative, statistical, and systematic speculation.[10]

Let us pause over these three forms of speculation: they provide us with the best access to our central problem of character and the will. In the first sense, then, to *have* a given character means to *belong to* a definite class which *has* certain properties and which is a collective portrait, a composite image. Yet how do we obtain this composite image? By superposition of completed portraits, that is, of psychographs representing the totality of an individual's reactions. This is important for understanding the harmony with the will. It is often said that character is the totality of stable *dispositions* offered to a will. Do we ever arrive, by the psychographic method, at something like a disposition to . . . ? The research does not have to do with dispositions, but with actual reactions manifesting forms of conduct which can be classed by comparisons. Psychographs, on the basis laid down by the investigators, affirm or deny the presence of a given pattern of conduct in the case of an observed subject. It is impossible that the composite image based on such psychographs could show us character as a simple disposition related to a sovereign willing, as an instrument of freedom. How in effect could an average of *actual* individual *conduct* lead to a *disposition*, a *potentiality*? Character up to now does not indicate a disposition of the subject to such conduct, but his belonging to the class which most frequently exhibits it.

It is precisely the transition to the second meaning which can bring about a change: the ethologist resorts, thanks to statistics, to a concept of average type which at first sight seems to provide a scientific equivalent of the popular notion of disposition. Does not having truthfulness of 32% mean having a strong propensity to lying without yet being hopelessly addicted to this defect? But let us see how this judgment of probability is built up: in each individual psychograph, the subject has replied yes or no to questions posed. Thus (quantitative) judgments of probability are made possible by (qualitative) rough attributive judgments. When we say that the phlegmatic has a rate of truthfulness of 87% it means only that 87 of 100 individuals whose various correlations permit them to be classed as phlegmatics have been judged truthful in terms of an undifferentiated "yes." Thus it is a frequency of attributive judgments within the class which is transformed into a judgment of inherence of the individual level (one who *is*

10. Extension, comprehension, "concept" were terms used by L. Brunschvicg in accord with the thesis of *La Modalité du jugement*.

phlegmatic *has* a truthfulness of 87%). Thus statistical method provides equivalent to the subjective concept of a disposition to . . . ; it never gives more than frequencies within a class which in its turn is derived from a superposition of overall portraits. Frequency of a conduct *exhibited* by individuals within a class cannot be equated with a *disposition* of one *individual* in that class with respect to this form of conduct.[11]

The transition to the fully developed formula (EAS [emotive-affective-secondary]; nEnAP [non-emotive-non-affective-primary]; etc.) puts an end to ambiguity. Necessity is introduced in the correlations, the empirical class being only a composite image devoid of necessity, the probable type a statistical concept. The fully developed formula tends to make character into a system in which a certain factor governs definite traits; the individual who could be simply *"located in"* the class and more or less *"approach"* the average is the ideal terminus of an infinitely complex formula. In principle there is no limit to an explanation of all the aspects of an individual in terms of the major regions of emotivity, activity, and secondarity and by such other regions as a less limited science would add to them. Once it is handed over to objective methods, character appears as a concrete whole susceptible to unlimited synthesis. It is absurd to try to introduce freedom into it; determinism of the object is limitless and unopposed. The incompleteness of ethology indicates only that explanation is inexhaustible, but not that something eludes this type of explanation. We shall verify these methodological considerations concretely by considering the difficulties of ethology in confronting the problem of the will.

4) It can be easily shown directly by examination of ethological investigations and systematizations that methodological necessity forces ethology to conclude with a limitless, unopposed determinism and that the ethological formula must include will itself. The will itself is taken up into the network of correlations characteristic of a type: thus we learn that the nervous type is most impulsive, least circumspective, has lowest correlation between his thoughts and acts, weakest sense of long-range goals of action, that his action is turned successively in contradictory

11. Concerning this discussion, see Heymans' article about his statistical research. [*Ztschr. f. Ps. u. Physiol. d. Sinnesorgane*, XII (1909), 1–72 §§ 7, 8]; "Des Méthodes dans la psychologie spéciale," *Ann. psych.*, XVII (1911); *La Psychologie des femmes*, p. 10. Le Senne also recognizes that personality traits are "beings of reason" derived from statistics. (Preface to *La Psychologie des femmes*, pp. 23–27; *Le Mensonge et le caractère*, p. 33.) But in the last instance all use ethological factors as conditioning aptitudes inscribed in the individual.

directions, that he is most inclined to procrastinate, to become discouraged, etc. Statistics even allow us to class the different types with respect to decisiveness, perseverance, aptitude to carry through long-range tasks, tendency to put off obligations, etc.[12] Finally the three fundamental factors in Groningue's ethology have to explain will just like fear, lying, etc.; will is only an elaboration of the ideo-motor phenomenon.[13] There is, in this respect, no difference in principle between Heymans and Ribot: for the one as for the other, the problem of the will is a problem of forces in conflict, in equilibrium, and in disruption of equilibrium. What is new in ethology is the quest for a principle of permanent individual differences among certain ethological constants. In this respect a comparative study should permit evaluation of the effect of each factor.[14] Such different constants are composed rather subtly, anyway: often it is the figures produced by grouping them two at a time which should be considered, often also the three term formula is itself original. In any case will is inhibition, composition, and integration.[15]

Thus explanation of the whole individual, voluntary and involuntary, is in principle exhaustive, even if in fact it can never be completed because of the complexity of the object. Whatever may be the ethologist's convictions as a man, for the scientist everything occurs *as if* the individual could be reduced to his own portrait and his portrait to his ethological formula, infinitely elaborated.

Le Senne, to be sure, suggests in *Le Mensonge et le caractère* and in *Traité de caractérologie* a synthesis of a metaphysics of freedom and a science of character. But it seems precisely that this synthesis, with which we are also concerned, is reached too

12. To Question 8, concerning decisiveness, statistics yield the following results: nEAP, 76.6%; EnAS, 65.8%; EAP, 61.1%; EnAP, 36.2%; nEnAS, 27.6%; nEAS, 26.5%. To Question 6, concerning tendency to discouragement: EnAP, 52.9%; EnAS, 52.2%; nEnAS, 31.5%; EAP, 31.5%; EAS, 28.3%; nEnAP, 24.5% nEAP, 15.8%; nEAS, 9.1%.

13. Heymans, *La Psychologie des femmes*, p. 191.

14. Constriction of the field of consciousness explains certain stiffness, clumsiness, obstinence. Secondarity augments the availability of more numerous and older motives; primarity favors fanaticism, imitation favors crude habits. Emotivity increases impulsiveness. It is activity which is the most important factor for psychology of the will, as we can imagine after the distribution in Questions 8 and 6.

15. Thus EnA favors fear, discouragement, premature resignation in face of an obstacle; EA altruism, ES attachment to the past, force of habits, affective force of abstract motives, etc. (Le Senne, *Le Mensonge* ... pp. 191–226.) As to the three-term formulae, synthesis of three positive forces in case of the passionate personality type gives the richest formula, as the primacy of the impassioned in history testifies.

easily and covers over serious differences. His entire ethological study of lying, for instance, is carried out in deterministic language: he inquires "what influences are added to the conditions of affirmation of the truth in order to determine its change, as the physicist seeks what factors are added to conditions of free fall to vary its application." [16] But at the same time Le Senne develops the conviction that character can be an instrument of freedom: thus the lying of the nervous, favored by emotivity, inactivity, and initiativity, represents a poor use of a system of dispositions whose good use is, for instance, a work of art. [17] In the same way the legality and punctuality of the phlegmatic are a snare from which good or evil can come, depending on whether freedom abandons or grasps itself. [18] But have we really introduced a coherent relation between a *method* which attempts to explain lying causally and a *doctrine* according to which it is freedom which abstains, permits, consents, or yields? The ambiguity arises repeatedly [19] and betrays the difficulty of harmonizing a science of character *directly* with a metaphysics of freedom. Between *the* character, which is a being of reason elaborated by the ethologist, and *my* concrete freedom there exists only an indirect relationship: ethology has to serve as a mediator for discovery of a subjective moment of the Cogito, for a definite though rather fleeting experience of my personality intertwined with my freedom.

Is assigning ethology to the object and freedom to the subject enough to resolve the difficulty? Not at all, for in the subject himself there is something which lends itself to a theory of character: it is my self as a character, and my character is not an invention of science, but an aspect of myself which cannot be reabsorbed into the voluntary which we have just examined. It is something irremediable which I do not know how to take into account without altering the fleeting experience I have of it. Let us move to the context of subjectivity: it is there that we can discover the nexus of freedom and destiny and, by the way, the good use of ethology.

3. Deliverance of Freedom

ANYONE who has no more than a superficial acquaintance with the theory of character cannot help playing a game of portraits with himself and others: am I a nervous type? and

16. *Ibid.*
17. *Ibid.*, p. 186.
18. *Ibid.*, pp. 300–4.
19. *Ibid.*, pp. 16, 22, 91, 174, 258, 285–86, 299.

is a man like that a phlegmatic? It is impossible to keep such objective knowledge from turning on me and from being grasped by an internal dialectic which wants nothing more than a scientific alibi to elaborate its destructive claims. This dialectic never fails to test itself any time we linger around the irremediable. Its effect follows close upon it: if I have an immutable and invincible character, who am *I*? Isn't my willing inscribed in my character and prescribed by it? Worse still, isn't the illusion of freedom one of the most insidious inventions of my character? But I do not want to be deceived any longer, and thanks to ethology, I now know it. I know that each of us plays the role which nature imposes on him. Or better still, I shall no longer be deceived by ethology that my nature develops thanks to some fortunate combination of emotivity and secondarity combined with faint activity. Here the suspicious and at the same time petrified consciousness becomes silent.

But this dialogue, carried to its highest degree of clarity, at least engenders its own deliverance. To allege a determinism is to include myself in it, but only as long as I do not think it forcefully; to think of my character consistently as an object is already to deliver myself from it as subject: it is I who thinks it, it is I who wills to be an object comprehensible within laws.

I understand very well that this inverse dialectic of deliverance is only a token: it sets free only a formal, transcendental will, that point of the will which makes the abstract "I think" in every man a free act of attention. I still have to set myself free as concrete freedom, as control over my body, as daily ability to decide. At least the spell is broken; I have rediscovered something of the subject. Starting from this precarious and in a way dimensionless freedom I can widen the breach and break the other, less reasonable claims which prepared the way for the fascination exercised by personality. Objective necessity is the reasonable mask of a fatality which is no longer simply one of understanding but of society and passion. It is principally vanity and fear which imprison me. They make me assume responsibility for the idea which the other forms of me—when it is flattering. In seeking to live up to the other's opinion, I become a slave of the image which he gives me of myself. But it is especially fear which really condemns me to being nothing but this character: Alain says:

We must not be hasty in judging character as though decreeing that one man is a sot and the other lazy forever. If you mark a galley slave, you are giving him a kind of right of the savage. At the basis of all vices there lies undoubtedly some condemnation which the man believed; and in human relations this leads rather far: in being appealed a judgment is experienced, and the experience reinforces it. I try never to judge from high up, nor even from below, for relations and attitudes always say too much; and I expect good after evil, often through the same cause. In this I am not far wrong; men are always fertile.[20]

Thus through the diverse converging passions I forge my *fatum;* it is they which give weight to the temptation of objectivity which, however, seems far removed from the bondage of passions. But reflection itself is already a passion when it takes the place of action: in being overly concerned with myself, I keep myself from living, that is, from doing and from making myself. I constitute myself a victim of what I have been and of a nature which devours me. It seems that the irremediable must never be looked at by itself but rather as a counterpart of that which it is up to me to change, as the background of an involuntary relative to the voluntary, as the fringe of motivation and ability. Thus it is this power of deciding and moving which I must rescue from fascination, and not only the pure will of thought. All remains to be done, since we still do not know how an absolute involuntary could be included in a relative involuntary, nor what legitimate use can be made of ethology. At least we know that freedom cannot be lodged in the interstices of ethological determinism, and that we must start from this freedom of deciding and moving to discover within it a finite nature strangely coupled with its infinite initiative. Thus it is that, making our way between determinism which governs the object and excludes freedom and fascinating subjective fatality, we reach a destiny which is never other than the obverse of freedom.

4. The Significance of My Character

EVERYDAY THOUGHT senses the way my character presents itself to me. We need only to return to the theses which we have set aside in deriving character types on empirical scientific grounds:

1) My character is not only my outward aspect, but also my nature which clings to me so closely that I cannot contrast my-

20. Alain, *Propos sur l'éducation* (Paris, 1932) pp. 47–48. What follows is important: "With this I believe strongly that each individual is born, lives, and dies according to his own nature, as the crocodile is a crocodile, and that he changes not at all." (*Ibid.*) We shall later rediscover and adopt the same train of thought.

self with it as, for instance, with an inferior part of myself. The very decision I make, the way I exert effort, the way I perceive and desire, all bear its mark. It affects me as a whole. Bearing, gestures, inflection of my voice, my handwriting, etc., all point to the omnipresence of character down to the way my mind works. This intimacy of character makes of it, for the mind, an unseizable, intangible reality.

2) My character is as indivisible as my self, but its indivisibility is one of brute existence rather than of initiative. This is why the truth of images, analogies, and metaphors which attempt to grasp its style or overall aura is more suitable than ethology's mosaic of abstractions. But as they overlap and mutually annul each other, they represent a knowledge which is as fleeting as the reality they try to capture is itself intangible. What is interesting in an attempt like Klages', it seems to me, is that it tries to stress the plurality of viewpoints concerning character. Knowledge of character types demands more than well planned and well answered questionnaires: a consideration of myself, of the opposites to which I respond, and sensitivity, an imaginative experimentation by which I try out other feelings and motives, a consideration of language, of its intent, etymology, metaphors. An idiomatic expression can often lead further than a laborious psychological inquiry.[21] Hence analysis of character demands more than one approach: Klages distinguishes the matter (*Stoff, Materie*), that is, forms of unfolding, the *tempo* of feelings and of action (having or not having a temper), vivacity, depth, richness, ease, etc. —the order (*Aufbau*), that is, compatibility or incompatibility of dispositions: unity, balance, contradiction, maturity, etc. It is not a bad idea, after reading Heymans and his very simple schemes, to let Klages remind us of the complexity of points of view of character.[22]

3) My character is not a class, a collective type, but my unique self, inimitable; I am not a general idea, but a singular essence.

21. "Reflecting on himself systematically, man discovers an entire universe of traits belonging to different character types which are his own." (Klages, *Les Principes de la caractérologie*, p. 45.) "We consider a critical elaboration of characteristic names of quality an indispensable element of reflection about oneself." (*Ibid.*, p. 49.) For instance, indignation is termed *Entrüstung*: that an indignant man should be defenseless is suggestive. We should note that Le Senne also admits, in addition to objective induction, an ethological induction which consists of seeing sympathetically the type we have reached inductively and of sketching its consequences. (*Traité de caractérologie*, pp. 34–41.)

22. In contrast the very study of impulses ("nature" of character) leads directly beyond the cycle of questions dealt with here and introduces a metaphysics of life for which will is a non-creative, critical, regulative power, hostile to life; cf. the *table of impulses* at the end of the work.

Yet we are all familiar with the obstacles which thought encounters in pursuing what is individual.

Thus my character clings to me (it is not an anthropometric chit which could circulate from hand to hand); it is a concrete totality (and not a combination of isolated, abstract traits); it is this individual who I am.

4) Here we stand on the verge of a problem which common sense does not know how to resolve, though its very contradictions hint at the concreteness of what it senses. Character is in a sense fate. We cannot meditate too much on Democritus' old principle—'Ηθos ἀνθρώπῳ δαίμων: man's character is his fate. That is how Kant and Schopenhauer have understood it. And yet, in Schopenhauer's presentation, my freedom is complete (at least apart from the bondage of passions). Present in all I will and can, indivisible, inimitable, this fate is invincible. To change my character would actually mean becoming someone else, becoming alienated; I cannot become detached from myself. My character situates me, casts me into an individuality. *I yield to myself as a given individual.* And yet I am only as I make myself and I do not know where the limits of my sovereignty lie unless I exercise it. I sense that freedom and fate are not two juxtaposed realms, one starting here and the other there, but that my freedom is present throughout and imprints its stamp even on my constitution. I sense without being able to articulate it correctly that my character in its changeless aspects is only *my freedom's mode of being.* It seems to me that I am capable of all virtues and all vices if I take them in their full scope, beyond the partial representation presented by this or that character, that I am barred from nothing human, but that it is my fate to be generous or avaricious with the same gesture, to lie or to tell the truth in the same tone of voice, to do good or evil with the same bearing, that is, in an inimitable *manner* which is my self given to my self, prior to or independent of all choice. I have a way of choosing and of choosing myself which I do not choose. The possibility that fate might be the clinging, indivisible, individual, and unwilled manner of my freedom is what transcends the subtlety of common sense—and of the philosopher.[23]

23. Alain, *Propos sur l'éducation:* "In any human body all passions are possible, all errors are possible . . . , always, to be sure, according to the inimitable *pattern of life* which is each man's lot. There are as many ways of being bad and unhappy as there are men on the earth. But for each man there is also salvation appropriate to him, of the same color, of the same texture as he" (pp. 218–20). "But this nature belongs to the order of life; it is well below the level of our judgments. It is the ground of moods, and, so to speak, the ordering of life which

This is why my character is never perceived itself but always as interwoven with some movement of the will in relation to its motives or its powers. I have first of all to believe in my total responsibility and my unlimited initiative, and then recognize that I can only use my freedom in accord with a finite, immutable mode. Thus I can arrive at my character as an invincible *aspect* of my controllable motives, as an incoercible *aspect* of my coercible powers, as a non-willed *aspect* of my decision and of my effort. Like my freedom, it is always present.

Let us sketch the bond between my character and the involuntary of my capabilities and motives. My desires and my habits, which are my principal powers, have an order of life, a way of arising, erupting, functioning, surviving, and becoming extinguished which changes not at all as long as I live: but this style, this permanent way, says nothing about which desires, which habits concern me at any time. Ideally (that is, apart from passions which are truly contractions of the soul) and within the limits of the normal, there are no desires or habits which could not give way to discipline; but this very plasticity of desires and habits and this discipline can only be produced in agreement with the formula of development. The finite and the infinite do not limit each other but are present to each other and in each other.

This will become more apparent if we consider the life of motives: I should think that there are no reasons inaccessible to me, no virtues or vices prohibited to me or imposed on me except by my passions. Motivation is unlimited, but my character forces me to encounter value only in my own way.[24] If at times it seems that a particular character type is more at home in a particular moral region, this is not false; it shows that we have not considered value in its full human scope, but already according to the partiality of a character type. It is perhaps true that abstract, cold

---

by itself entails neither good nor evil, neither virtue nor vice, but rather an inimitable unique way of being frank or devious, cruel or charitable, avaricious or generous." (*Ibid.*, pp. 87–88.) Along the same line, Le Senne, in *Traité de caractérologie*, speaks of "invariable systems of necessity which we find, so to speak, within the limits of the organic and of the mental" (pp. 1, 9–18, 26–28, 580–86). On the other hand, Burloud, *Le Caractère*, misses this immutable manner because he identifies character with dispositions of personality as such pp. 14, 51, 70, 162). It is said that character is a "kind of realization of my deep self" (p. 162). If we distinguish character from personality and even from dispositions as its invincible mode, then character can in no way be our doing.—These pages had been written before I became acquainted with E. Mounier's *Traité du caractère*. That great book, which is a genuine anthropology, makes room for the invincible necessity in the dramatic existence of man.

24. Alain, *Propos sur l'éducation, op. cit.*, pp. 221–25.

duty is more accessible to phlegmatic than sentimental types, but duty without the urge of the good expresses only the unilaterality of a character. We have to believe that all values are accessible in some respect to all character types. We have to believe that there are no minds excluded from all morality; nor are there character types which possess morality as a natural right. This only becomes apparent if we respect the power of appeal of the totality of values. Each value is a universal which each individual stamps with his individual mark. If character does not itself appear in the course of motivation, it is because in deliberation I do not think of this special mark but of the purpose of the value, which is another way of saying that I never think of the individuality of my reasons. Character is always my own way of thinking, not what I think.

My character affects my effort and my decision in no other way. As we have said, my character is not in some respect inferior to myself; it is not a part at all: nothing escapes individuality. This is why the way of terminating a discussion, the ease or brusqueness of resolution, the vigor or tenacity of offort are ethological characteristics. Otherwise we could not understand how a morphology of the will would be possible. Capacities, motives, willing, and all within me bears the mark of a character type. Freedom itself, as "possible existence," has a structure which makes it a given nature. This is why I should be greatly mistaken if I proposed to change my character: I cannot know it in order to modify it, but in order to consent to it.

Thus in order to understand the presence of my character I would have to succeed in the hardly conceivable synthesis of the universal and the individual, which means that all value is accessible to me only in a manifestation—and the synthesis of freedom and nature, which means that all decision is at the same time an unlimited possibility and a constituted particularity. The idea of an infinite finite, of a situated initiative, situated not only by the lateral character of its motives but by the individuality of its special way of ingression, remains ineffable and inconsistent to the mind. My fate clings to my freedom without destroying it. All is possible, though in a limited, narrow way. Only passions can destroy this infinity.

But it soon becomes obvious on the other hand that the nature I am, considered as an objective nature, loses its meaning. As I observe it, it devours me. This is how the dialectic of fascination with character type is born. Only in the shelter of a doctrine of freedom can a meditation concerning nature reach its fullness and be restrained from turning into psychological determinism. That to which consciousness yields can only become *its own* when it is appropriated *through* what it does. This is why, as we shall explain presently, consent to the inexorable is not an autonomous act, but the obverse of an initiative actively assumed by consciousness. I only have the right to recognize the conditions and limits of sovereignty when I actually exercise it.

5. The Function of Ethology: Character Types and My Character

AT THE CONCLUSION of this difficult analysis which is not, on the whole, overly satisfying to the mind, we have to point out that ethology, which for a while appeared questionable, can and must be rediscovered. Our inner experience of character is in fact fleeting and lacks, for the mind, the stability and coherence of the experience of need or desire which consciousness can place before itself, compare, or repudiate. Actually all the involuntary of motives and capacities had an intentional structure which fitted into a doctrine of subjectivity. Objective knowledge, too—knowledge of psycho-physiology or of objective psychology constructed on the model of natural science—was of no use except as a diagnostic which pointed to the constitutive intentional structures of the Cogito from without. The experience of character has no definite status in intentional psychology. We can all the more find a place for it in what Husserl called hyletics. It would be a *hyle* of the Ego itself as there is a *hyle* of perception, desire, and feelings. This is why I can only maintain the notion of *my* character by forming a conception *of* character types in sketching an ethology which would play not only a diagnostic but a mediating role. What is true of character will be so of all the aspects of the "condition" of the will which we shall study subsequently: the subterranean activity of the unconscious, the order of life which supports consciousness, childhood, birth, heredity, all this is uncovered, sensed, and awaits the help of distinct knowledge from the distance of an object. I always approach these confused, clinging experiences with clues from the study of character, psychoanalysis, and biology. Who could conceive of his character without using a more or less spontaneous or learned classification of character types, without referring to an average type with a more or less quantitative scale of properties?

Thus in order to give the validity of thought to the theses of common consciousness concerning character which objective knowledge rejects we have finally to clarify them by other theses which function as a criterion of such objective knowledge itself. Common sense does not know whether character is an external portrait of my own nature, an unanalyzable order of life or an analyzable formula, a genus or an individual. In the last instance it does not know how to reconcile fate and freedom. We are obliged to conclude that in order to understand this clinging nature we have to conceive of it as an anthropometric token. In order to grasp the omnipresence of character in each gesture we have to analyze it and reconstitute it. In order to understand the inimitable character types we have to conceive of them as genera and surround them with differences. In the last instance the immutable way in which I sense, think, and wish has determinism itself as its objective medium. But determinism must break down as an objective concept in order to become the sign of fate, the manifestation outside myself of the fate within me. Since determinism considered as an objective concept has neither a counterpart nor a limit, in serving to mediate character in first person, the necessity at the heart of the Cogito, it gives rise to the fleeting concept of destiny which is only the *particularity* of freedom. Thus appropriated and converted into myself, ethology which started out by condemning me by placing me on a chart of ethological formulas leads me rather to respect, to love, and finally, as Alain said, to set free the immutable nature in each man and first of all within me.[25]

This living adoption of the teachings of ethology is not without its problems. It is not without a danger to adopt the laws of nature as an indication of subjectivity. Inevitably the spell of objectivity is constantly reborn. Passions, which make me prisoner of a role, are always capable of making the objectification, which ought only to mediate my destiny, destructive. This is why a science of character is doomed to remain *ambiguous,* always equally available to a work of degradation or a work of deliverance whose double power an educator wields. Science never absolves the educator from the need for sensitivity. R. Le Senne forcefully stressed the part which sensitivity plays in good use of ethology: knowledge of character must serve not only for psychotechnics, but for a genuine education based on sympathy and on the appeal to freedom. Genuine ethology would be "a method of spiritual life

25. *Ibid.,* pp. 88–92. "Willing that there be natures is charity itself. Not virtue of the neighbor which he need only do, but his virtue in himself, which shares the color of his hair and has the same texture. His own virtue which resembles his own vice as a brother ..."

in which knowledge would be based on sympathy, in order to permit the individual not to find a job but to develop and extend himself." [26] Through this and other similar formulations, R. Le Senne returns to Alain's insight: "All that is given is good. . . . Differences are invincible, they have to be loved."

Such then is the invincible mode of being—of desiring, willing, moving—to which I must consent: but as contemplated necessity is always on the point of devouring me, consent is always itself on the verge of becoming spellbound. When consciousness lingers to meditate upon its conditions and limits, it is not far from being overwhelmed. It is still an act, the act of "yes," which preserves the force of refusal and of challenge overcome, it is an act which saves it from becoming spellbound by what it observes. It is never free of either the spell or the "yes"; apart from this adhesion, this consent to my own rigidity, there is, for pure understanding, no *harmonious* resolution, no *system* of nature and freedom, but always a paradoxical, precarious synthesis of intentional structures which support free will and the idea of nature understood as this infinite freedom's way of being finite. A freedom situated by the fate of a character to which it consents becomes a destiny, a vocation.

[2] THE UNCONSCIOUS

1. A False Dilemma

BECOMING AWARE of character is not the most serious crisis of freedom. In its immutability, character retains something direct, unconcealed. It seems that a bit of attention to myself and others, and a certain familiarity with ethological inquiry can strip it of all its claims and make it completely transparent. This is not so. Analysis of character leaves a residuum: factors envisioned for example by Heymans only concern the way tendencies function, not their matter, that is, their preferred directions. (We have alluded to the various reappearances of this ethological uncertainty.) We still have to decide whether these preferred directions are not in the main *hidden* and do not require a completely different method of unveiling than that of these inquiries, and if the appearance of my nature is not the mask which conceals my being. This doubt brings up a new detour: the already ambiguous relation between the *immutable* and the free is still

26. Le Senne, *Le Mensonge*, p. 325.

only the outer shell of a far more enigmatic relation between the "hidden" and the free. When the inexorable seems to be redoubled by a capacity for concealment, when appearance becomes suspect and is no longer the way a being becomes exposed but rather refuses itself, there arises a radical disturbance in my consciousness of freedom, the suspicion of having been not so much hedged in as deceived.

In the first place the realm of the "hidden" is far broader than the unconscious of the psychoanalysts. These are two principle foci which can only be separated in abstraction: the lie of passions which moralists like La Rochefoucauld denounce, and the unconscious strictly speaking. Nietzsche, who masters these two themes above the point of their bifurcation, had the vivid feeling that consciousness is a surcharged text, that consciousness of myself is an infinite which in its ferocity never ceases to strike down masks, to wipe off make-up. But in this deciphering it is important to distinguish exorcism of the fundamental lie derived from the fault and the exploration of a hidden nature.

In this work we shall not follow out the first direction but shall present only a very superficial conception of it. A complete analysis would presuppose a general theory of the passions and finally a consideration of the close link which the fault institutes between bondage and lie. Consciousness bound to vanity is duped by nothing, fascinated by nothingness. This deception of consciousness is not easily understood. It leads back to a conscious, concerted lie made possible by language. It is language, that is, voluntary expression, which grafts an appearance onto a being by convention and artifice. Thought can withdraw into a discourse in which the body is covered over, just as the body gives the other a lying word. Thought is naturally hidden from *the other:* every secret can be guarded, every confidence can be kept. To be sure, it is a long way from this clear lie to a deceived consciousness. But at least by starting from it we can come back to and illuminate this strange power which freedom has of being mistaken, of hiding from itself, by losing the key to its own devices.

The other pole of the "hidden" will no longer be my freedom insofar as it deceives itself, but my nature insofar as it is concealed from consciousness. Here the "hidden" applies to the very condition of being conscious and is not related to a defect of consciousness. Its discovery does not demand an *ascesis* of self-consciousness, but rather a method of exploration and investigation akin to that of the natural sciences. Is it possible that prior to any lie—that is, prior to any intention of deceiving the other —what I think and will has a meaning hidden from my consciousness, a meaning different from that which I think I give it? Is it possible, as the examples of posthypnotic suggestion would suggest, that my decisions are false decisions, my reasons sham motives which *stand for* unconscious motives which I cannot compare because of some mysterious hindrance?

Here already we can see, at least tentatively, the fundamental opposition of the two poles of the hidden even though they can only be dissociated by abstraction. We always construe all the deception in consciousness and in the world on the model of intentional lie, transparent to itself. As the dangerous psychoanalytic metaphors like censorship, guardian consciousness, disguise, etc. show, any relation between appearance and being of human thought which is not immediately transparent is presented as a kind of lie. When the being resists a discovery, it is likened to a secret which refuses to yield, while appearance is likened to a faked confession. In turn, while the analysis of the unconscious tends to be expressed in the language of disguise and lie, the true lie tends to hide behind the involuntary deception which the unconscious produces in consciousness: it is rather tempting to shift all responsibility to the ruses of that unconscious demon which I claim to bear within me. In this way the two extremes of the hidden meet and mix. Thus it is only at the cost of a forcible abstraction that we can confront the unconscious of the psychoanalysts as distinct from all the lies which can be reduced by self-searching.

The genuine relation which can be instituted between a definite unconscious and freedom of decision and motion can only be uncovered at the end of a long detour and at the cost of encountering a double obstacle: the obstacle of a dogmatism of the unconscious which commits the error and the fault of attributing *thought* to the unconscious, and the obstacle of dogmatism of consciousness which commits the error and perhaps also the fault of pride, of assigning to consciousness a transparence which it does not have. We must first of all reject this apparent dilemma of a definite realism of the unconscious and a definite idealism of consciousness in order to pose correctly the new paradox of an *indefinite matter* of signification and an *infinite capacity* of thought.

I should say at the start that reading works on psychoanalysis has convinced me of the existence of facts and processes which remain incomprehensible as long as I remain prisoner of a narrow conception of consciousness. But, in turn, I am not convinced by the *doctrine* of Freudianism, in particular by the realism of the unconscious which the Viennese psychologist developed in connection with his methodology and his therapeutics.[27] The facts which Freud brought to light cannot be suppressed by a stroke of the pen. Only a long use of his method of analysis might correct their inventory. In other words, only psychoanalysis can rectify the psychological and therapeutic conceptions issuing from psychoanalysis.[28] Here the philosopher learns from the physician and in the first instance listens and learns. But in turn, while he is led to enlarge his objective knowledge of man to the limit, his task is to take the new facts which he could not have discovered alone into the purview and healing context and atmosphere of a philosophy of man which cannot deny the guiding principles which I learn not in the consulting room or in a clinic but by a constant return to myself.

2. The Obstacle of the Doctrine of Transparence of Consciousness

WE HAVE NO opportunity to integrate authentic results of psychoanalysis unless we first *reject* the prejudice, parallel to the realism of the unconscious, which holds that consciousness is transparent to itself. If there is no thought which would have a meaning apart from consciousness, it follows that there are only actual, formed thoughts, *forms,* within it. The ambition of idealism is to identify responsibility with a *self-positing* of consciousness and to reach an exact equation of reflection with intentional thought in all its obscure density. This wish comes undoubtedly from the Cartesian Cogito. If it is true, as we have to maintain against Freud's doctrine, that it is always *myself,* conscious of myself—which thinks—and never some unconscious within me and independent of me, is it not legitimate to suppose that the act of thought is perfectly transparent to itself, that it is only a consciousness of being? "By the word thought," Descartes says, "I understand that which is formed in us in such a way that we perceive it immediately by ourselves." I might well doubt that an

27. R. Dalbiez, *La Méthode psychanalytique et la doctrine freudienne* (Paris, 1936). The author teaches a dissociation of Freudianism as a doctrine from psychoanalysis as a method. But as the discussion below will show, we shall attempt to integrate the facts brought to light by psychoanalytic method and therapeutics with the philosophy of will by starting from a different general philosophy.

28. J. Boutonier, *L'Angoisse* (Paris, 1945), pp. 123–30.

object exists as I believe it to exist: I can believe that I am walking and actually not walk.

While if I mean to speak only of the act of my thought or feeling, that is, of knowledge which is within me, which is the reason why it seems to me that I see or walk, this conclusion is itself so absolutely true that I cannot doubt it because it is related to the soul which alone has the faculty of feeling or thinking, in whatever way this may be.[29]

Is not the suspicion that I may be perpetually deceived by a hidden principle excluded by consciousness once I no longer compare the phenomenon of thought and its being? Is not transparence of consciousness entailed by freedom? Does it not in effect demand that the motives which confront it be whatever they appear to be, that is, a distinct idea of a Cartesian sense, "which comprehends in itself that which appears manifestly to anyone who duly considers it"?

It would seem that all that is left to do is to assign the unconscious and its purported effects back to bodily mechanism and to refuse it all psychological status, not only that which realism of mental physics attributes it, but any possible psychological status. Thus Descartes explains the unreflected dispositions of love and hate in terms of mechanical movements, by action of impressions in the brain.[30] Alain echoes this in this clear declaration:

We resolve these phantoms by saying simply that all that is not thought is mechanism, or better still, that all that is not thought is body, that is, something subject to my will: a thing for which I am responsible. This is the principle of rigor. . . . The unconscious thus is a way of dignifying my own body, of treating it as like me, as an inherited slave with whom I must come to terms. The unconscious is an erroneous approach to myself, it is an idolatry of the body.[31]

In its extreme form, the doctrine of the transparence of thought to consciousness leads to according spontaneity only to consciousness: if consciousness is self-constituting, then its only being is its appearance. Therefore there are no passions of the soul, in the sense that some passivity could insinuate itself into the experienced flux of consciousness. In changing, consciousness changes its body.[32] Here we have the most radical consequence which can be drawn from the idea that consciousness posits itself.

29. Descartes, *Principles*, I.9.
30. Descartes, *Letter to Chanut*, June 6, 1647.
31. Alain, *Éléments de philosophie, op. cit.*, "Note sur l'inconscient."
32. Sartre, *Emotions*, p. 76.

We believe that the philosophers who have for good reason refused to attribute any thought to the unconscious were subsequently wrong when they refused to attribute to thought this obscure ground and this spontaneity hidden within it which blocks its efforts to become transparent to itself. We believe on the contrary that consciousness reflects only the form of its actual thoughts. It never perfectly penetrates a certain *principally affective matter which presents it with an indefinite possibility for self-questioning and for giving meaning and form to itself*. The unconscious certainly does not think, but it is the indefinite *matter*, revolting against the light which all thought bears with it. The unconscious allows us to name, after the finite manner of personality, another aspect of this absolute passivity inherent in all activity of consciousness, another aspect of that absolute involuntary which cannot be held at a distance, evaluated as a motive, or moved as a docile ability.

In the first place we shall show the obstacle of the doctrine of transparence of consciousness concretely by confronting it with opposite readings of psychology of need, emotion, and habit. These facts, related to psychology of consciousness, still remain distinct from problems posed by the Freudian unconscious. Nevertheless they ought to lead us to the limits of those enigmatic facts brought up by psychoanalysis and clear the way for their difficult exegesis in terms of subjectivity.

Many aspects of our earlier description of an involuntary which remains relative to a possible will led us close to the absolute involuntary. Relative obscurity points to a limit-obscurity which would be the hidden, while resisting spontaneity points to a dissociated spontaneity which is the permanent principle of the *terrible* at the core of consciousness and which ceaselessly engenders a pathological mode of existence.

Starting with *need*, we hardly need to be reminded that it is the principle of all obscurity in us. Affectivity is obscurity itself. This obscurity is something we would gladly dissolve into mechanism and attribute to the body. But, if we are not to lose the psychical, that is, intentional dimension of need, its lack and its desire which are prior to the light of intellectual image representation of its object, we have to discern in it a tangled density of anticipation which no image and no knowledge can eliminate. There is in the experience of need an indefinite possibility of asking "what is it I want?" or "would that do?" "what is the point?" I can endlessly forge representations of the lack and the desire of need. Thus need is not at all transparent insofar as consciousness reflects clearly only the representation which cloaks it. It is a consciousness of . . . and with it the body participates in consciousness, but it does not belong to clear consciousness. Hence, passing to the extreme, isn't it possible that the unformed existence of all need continues in the absence of all representative forms, hidden, perhaps, within some other representation? Such is the possibility of the hidden posed at the limit of the obscure. Yet such possibility is not abstract, general. It is prompted by other events of voluntary life which suggest such hidden existence as a lower limit: the adoption of a group of motives by the will has as its counterpart and so to speak residuum the exclusion of other motives. The rejected tendency disappears as motive, that is, as value. It no longer figures among that of which I take account, but assumes an obscure existence—whose status is difficult to establish precisely—which gives it a power whose frightening images we encounter already in deep regret, rancor, or resentment. The lower limit of the reciprocal spontaneity of willing is a dissociated spontaneity which prepares us to admit, beneath subconscious existence, an unconscious existence inaccessible to the most obscure consciousness of myself, which, though it is not a formed thought, is nonetheless a form of unreflected subjectivity.

Emotion is no less obscure than need, and yet it has an undeniable psychical character: in it consciousness encounters the amiable, the detestable, the joyful, the sad, etc. In this sense it really is a disorder of the body penetrating into the mind. At the same time a consideration of the affective qualities correlative with emotional consciousness is limitless: they can always have new meaning as I examine them. Could not this obscurity become purely unreflective and live on in a *hidden* way under the incognito of new affective qualities which would show only their form to consciousness? There is, to be sure, a hiatus between the obscure and the hidden. Considering emotion as disorder and as rebellion, that is, as nascent dissociation, prepares the way for extrapolation and leap. Great affective crises, emotive shocks of childhood undoubtedly leave "impressions" which in one way or another pass through consciousness and blend in with its actual life. Here, too, everything prepares us to come up once more against the facts presented by psychoanalysis as a lower limit.

Undoubtedly it is habit which brings us closest to our problem. *Habit* actually is the power of forgetting. As it is "acquired," its origin is effaced; and yet the past, even though abolished as representation, subsists in an obscure way as awareness of a capacity. This awareness rebels against the clarity of reflection. In the first place practical intention, aimed at an endeavor which has to be brought about by it in the context of objects, passes through the skills I use, as through a means. But chiefly I have lost the key to what had once been orderly and patiently built up —it has become body, acting, unreflecting body: in this sense no gesture is in vain, no thought is lost; rather, it is received into the living actuality. Undoubtedly habit itself is not unconscious, it is only a form of unreflecting, inattentive, practical Cogito; but consideration of habit, of that enigmatic familiar ability, is like an invitation to endless memory which becomes lost in shadows.[33] Aren't we thus led almost by hand from the forgotten to the forbidden? Once again, this possibility is suggested by the strange vitality of habits: their initial, pointless spontaneity always surprises and often disturbs voluntary action. Their exuberance reveals more stereotypes and repeated associations than inventions. If not controlled, they lead to automatism and become dissociated from living consciousness. The mechanical due to distraction thus carries us to the threshold of the pathological or quasi-pathological mechanical which the vigilance of consciousness can no longer master: acts of which we are not aware, tics, forgotten acts, etc. Thus I sense that I am barred from an area of my self, and that its reconquest calls for a purification which is no longer of a moral order but requires the help of a technique of a medical order. There must be some rejected spontaneity at the origin of such unsurmountably automatic behavior.

Thus psychology of need, emotion, and habit shows in different forms the inadequacy of the principle of transparence and the complete mastery of consciousness over itself. At the same time, it provides a path of approach, by extrapolation and exaggeration, to the existence of a matter of thought which is no longer accessible to consciousness of myself.

Let us recall in a few words the facts brought to light by psychoanalysis. By facts we mean in a broad sense the totality of enigmatic phenomena submitted to investigation (dreams, neuroses, etc.) and the theoretical and practical results of analysis: psychological techniques and therapeutic results.

Almost everyone is familiar at least with Freud's *Psychopathology of Everyday Life*. This old work, devoted to unnoticed acts,

33. Leibniz, *New Essays*, I, II, chap I, § ii: "Each soul retains all preceding impressions. . . . The future in each substance is perfectly tied to the past. This is what constitutes the identity of an individual. However, memory is neither necessary nor even always possible because of the multiplicity of impressions present. . . . We can forget much, but we can also remember far if properly led."

lapses, forgetting, tics, and stereotypes situated at the fringe of the normal, already focused interest on phenomena devoid of apparent meaning and involuntarily carried out. We shall constantly encounter these two characteristics in what follows: they already are signs revealing a disorder.

A new type of intelligibility suggests itself if instead of taking the viewpoint of the subject's intentions we now deal with these phenomena as objects and approach them from a causal viewpoint. In this way it is possible to see in them signs or *effects* which reveal certain hidden affective tendencies. The psychoanalytic method thus consists of gathering indications whose convergence leads us to the hidden *cause*. Once we adopt this perspective it is possible to consider the psyche as a locus of conflict, that is, of mutually opposing and inhibiting forces. Repression is the most remarkable case of this fundamental phenomenon of intersection of psychic forces. It becomes equally possible to assume that certain among these forces are unconscious, that is, that they function without being known. Indisputably the *psychoanalytic method* is impracticable unless we adopt this "naturalistic" point of view which is the working hypothesis of analysis. This is a point we cannot overstress. It does not constitute a part of the doctrine but of the analytic method itself, in the same way that biology is only possible if we treat the body as an object. Thus we confront facts which become apparent only if we adopt a particular viewpoint and method. Even though in the end it becomes necessary to integrate them into a psychology of the subject, this psychology of the subject has no means of discovering them. All the heuristic capacity belongs to naturalism. My task is to try to understand myself subsequently as a subject capable of such phenomena and accessible to such objective and causal treatment.

The case of dreaming deserves more extensive consideration. We shall limit our discussion to this example which is by itself sufficient to undermine any narrow psychology of consciousness and sums up the entire problem of the unconscious. Freud in fact builds his theory of neuroses on the model of dream analysis. Finally dream is the normal expression of the nocturnal existence which alternates in every normal man with a daytime existence whose responsible master he wishes to become. For consciousness it is an enclave of disorder par excellence, it has no logical meaning and does not lie within my power. But if I wish to *understand* myself, I cannot be content with these two negative traits; I must not neglect to add to what I *sense* what I can *know* by assuming a different perspective on myself. What can in no way be understood in terms of its intentional aim can perhaps be *explained* in terms of its causes.

These causes cannot be sought too far down on the organic level: external or internal stimuli of a somatic order cannot explain the *imaginary mode* which consciousness uses in dreams. Most of all, they do not explain why these rather than other images should present themselves to the sleeper. An explanation must be at the same time psychical and share the positive marks of a dream itself: a deficit, an impoverishment, a deflection of control functions alone cannot account for an activity, even if such deficit lies at the origin of a "functional liberation" which permits the release of such activity.

The working hypothesis of psychoanalysis is that dream has *a meaning, that is, can be explained by causes*. It has to be capable of being considered a psychic symptom of relatively stable affective themes related to the history of the individual. The individuality of dream images is explained by the individuality of a psychic history.

In addition the possibility of analyzing a dream by the method of free or spontaneous association presupposes that associative relations have a relative stability so that the thematism which emerges progressively in analysis approximates the assumed thematism of the dream. It is evident that here we can speak only of a working hypothesis. Only psychoanalytic practice can decide whether the hypothesis is a good one. As we have said, the considerations which follow presuppose conviction communicated from the psychoanalyst to the reader.

The causal order which now becomes apparent where before there appeared only disorder of intentions of consciousness is a *scientific* achievement, as those of physics or biology. All is yet to be done to transform it into a subjective comprehension of myself.

In effect all explanation is developed in the universe of discourse of mental physics and can in principle *be stabilized only on that level*. Since Freud studies what he calls the "dream work" (*Traumarbeit*) whose elaboration is entirely unconscious, he analyzes only the mechanism in which relations of contiguity or resemblance function not only without being known (which is not surprising, since we have already observed such spontaneity of relations on the level of habit and, we might say, even of all relations and not of continuity and resemblance only), but also function as forces rather than meanings. From this point of view alone can we give meaning to these mechanisms by which we explain the distance between latent and manifest content of the dream. Ethical and social *values* which inhibit incompatible tendencies function as a psychic *force,* construed by the analyst on the model of physical forces. Censorship is a psychic barrier which results in a compromise, demands the alteration and disguising of repressed desires. (We shall leave aside the question of knowing whether there are repressed desires.) This way we explain "condensation" or abbreviation of latent contents, "sublimation" in terms of which affective charge of a representation is transferred to a less important affective object at the same time as the latter replaces the former, and the "dramatization" which transposes all the relations enacted by the dream into images. This process is particularly remarkable since the relation of resemblance functions automatically, without being perceived and since the relations which are only implied in waking life are, in the dream, represented, "visualized" as much as possible without being understood.

There would be little need for speaking of neuroses in order to bring about a personal consideration of the unconscious if the nature of psychoanalytic cure did not introduce an absolutely decisive element into the discussion. As far as the etiology of neuroses is concerned, we have said, the principle of explanation is already given in the dream. (In turn we must not lose sight of the fact that Freud is interested in dreams *in order to* understand neuroses.) Freud does not deny the importance of somatic causes, of heredity, or of simple psychic deficits (psychoasthenesis, etc.) but concentrates on the search for psychic factors connected with the history of the individual. The highly symbolic and associative method which served the analysis of dreams led him to the constantly confirmed conviction that affective impressions left by psychic incidents are made unconscious by repression, that is, by a defensive reflex which itself can belong to the non-conscious level of the psyche.[34] Neurosis comes from the inner conflict within the psyche and from disruption of the balance of opposed tendencies. The origin of neuroses would thus be "historical" modification of great instincts and primarily of the "libido." The same mechanism of condensation, displacement, and dramatization would fill the interval between unconscious themes and the aberrant symptoms of consciousness.

34. In the *New Introductory Lectures on Psychoanalysis,* trans. Sprott (New York, 1933), the theory of the "superego" in part shifted interest from the repressed to the repressing unconscious.

What has to make us pause here is the remarkable character of psychoanalytic cure. As we know, it involves in effect at least three important elements: on the one hand the subject must collaborate in the therapy by voluntarily relinquishing autosuggestion and critique: he yields to the disordered flux of his memories, associations, and emotions, oscillating among several levels of consciousness from walking to a state akin to hypnosis. On the other hand the analyst's principal and irreplaceable task is *interpretation:* that is analysis in the strict sense, applied to the thematism of dreams, of post-dreaming associations and neurotic symptoms. But the decisive factor of cure is the reintegration of traumatic memory in the field of consciousness. Here is the heart of psychoanalysis. Thus, far from being a negation of consciousness psychoanalysis is on the contrary *a means of extending the field of consciousness* of a possible will by dissolution of affective contractions. It heals by means of a victory of memory over the unconscious. We cannot overstress the importance of this twist of Freudian therapy: in particular we can never stress enough that the grasp of consciousness is not reducible to a simple theoretical understanding, a simple *knowledge* in etiology of neurosis such as a doctor can work up for himself or even communicate to his patient's convictions. Interpretation is not repression: it is the intuitive reintegration of memory which "purifies" consciousness. But in turn interpretation by the other is a necessary detour between a sick and a healthy consciousness. It is psychoanalysis which must dissolve repressed automatisms, repressing resistance, and manifestations of "transference" which are only consequences of these two kinds of difficulty to be overcome. Someone *other* (this other can be myself, in some special circumstances, difficult to bring about) has to interpret and know in order for me to be able to become reconciled with myself. Someone other has to treat me as an *object,* as a field of causal explanation, and to consider my consciousness itself as a symptom, as the sign-effect of unconscious forces, in order for myself to become the master of *myself* once more.

3. Critique of Freudian "Realism" of the Unconscious:
   The Mode of Existence of the Unconscious
   in Consciousness

THIS GROUP of facts, of psychological interpretations, and of therapeutic results, even as it dispels any idealistic interpretation of consciousness, seems inseparable from a theory and even from a system in which the unconscious appears as the explanatory principle *of* consciousness itself. We are led, as R. Dalbiez for one attempted to do, to dissociate the psychoanalytic method and its working hypotheses on the one hand, and the Freudian system and its implicit philosophy of being on the other hand.[35]

Three traits in particular attract our attention. Let us stress in the first place the *realism* according to which the unconscious desires, imagines, and *thinks*. The concept of the "meaning" of unconscious thought itself is at stake here.

Secondly we shall examine the "causalism" implied equally by the method of association and by the "mechanisms" of dream or neurotic work.

Finally, we shall consider the "genetic and evolutionary" principle by which Freud tends to *reduce* the superstructures of the psyche to its instinctive infrastructure.

It is rather easy and in some respects inevitable to slide into a *realism* of the unconscious. Even the fleeting experience of *my* immutable personality was immediately seized upon by an objective schema and its intimate connection with freedom was lost in ethology. It seems that in principle the unconscious escapes all subjective experience and can only be reconstituted by another, thanks to a method of converging indications. It seems that the unconscious belongs from the start with those objective constructs of mental physics about which we have sought to show throughout this work that they are at the same time metaphysically precarious and methodologically necessary.

Realism of the unconscious represents a real Copernican revolution: the center of human being is displaced from *consciousness and freedom* as they give themselves to the unconscious and the absolute involuntary of which we are ignorant and which are known by a new natural science.

This displacement seems to be demanded by psychoanalytic explanation. The enigmas of consciousness are explained, it seems, if we abandon the point of view of consciousness and posit the existence in oneself of a psychological unconscious which perceives, remembers, desires, imagines, perhaps wills the death of another and its own, but is not aware of itself. The principle of homogeneity of the conscious and the unconscious, which is demanded by causal explanation of the conscious by the unconscious, is interpreted in a simplicistic way and becomes translated

35. Dalbiez, *op. cit.*, I, 1–8; II, 1–4, 439–44. Also Charles Baudoin, *Essais de psychanalyse* (Paris, 1922[1], 1936), pp. 4–5.

386 / CONSENT AND NECESSITY

into rather coarse images: consciousness is understood as a part of the unconscious, as a small circle included within a larger circle. Freud represents the unconscious as thought homogeneous with conscious thought and lacking only the quality of consciousness. In this sense the unconscious is really the essence of the psyche, the psyche itself, and its essential reality.[36]

To the explicative power of the concept of the unconscious construed like the physical hypotheses as ion or electron has to be added the practical success of this hypothesis: psychoanalysis in fact is not only a diagnostic art, but also a healing one, and the success of a cure is equal to a verification of the theory by the totality of its practical consequences.

We must start out by attacking this chimerical interpretation in its principle; after that, it will be possible to dispel it in each particular case for no interpretation of dreams or neurosis, even in the sense of Freudian psychoanalysis, implies such a mythical unconscious.

The refusal to conceive of the unconscious as thinking is a foregone conclusion of freedom itself, of that Cartesian generosity which is at the same time knowledge, action, and feeling. A knowledge beyond suspicion: namely that in every man "there is nothing which belongs to him truly other than this free disposition of his will, nor for which he could be praised or blamed except for the good or bad use he makes of it." A promise: "a firm and constant resolution to use them well, that is, never to lack willingness to undertake and execute all the things which he judges to be best; this is what following virtue perfectly means." A feeling: respect for myself as free "so that we do not lose, through cowardice, the rights it gives us." [37] When I conceive of my unconscious as thinking, I yield to this "cowardice," to this "misconception of myself" which in Descartes' eyes is the opposite of generosity.

The root of the illusion lies in the very conception of consciousness as explicit self-knowledge added to a prior operation, unconscious in principle, of consciousness oriented towards other than self. R. Dalbiez, who attempted to bind the fortunes of psychoanalytic method to a realistic metaphysics, even believes that an integral realism entails such an unconsciousness-in-principle of cognitive operation on level below that of judgment.[38]

36. Cf. the two texts by Freud quoted by Dalbiez, *op. cit.*, II, 68.
37. Descartes, *Treatise on Passions*, arts. 152–53.
38. Dalbiez, *op. cit.*, II, 4–83, esp. pp. 12, 21, 42, where he affirms the intrinsically unconscious character of exteroceptive sensations.

Yet a careful phenomenology of perception reveals no such thing; on the contrary, it warns us against the simplicistic dilemma: either perception or awareness of oneself is identified and all I ever know is myself, or perception deals with the other than self and is unconscious, consciousness being posterior and super-added. This dilemma rests on a quasi-spatial representation of successive directions which mental observation is supposed to adopt. When I am turned towards the outside, it seems to say, I cannot be turned inwards.[39] Phenomenology must stop with *a priori* impossibilities; perception appears more like a "non-reflexive" consciousness. What perception does not in any sense include is an explicit judgment of reflection, such as "It is I who perceives, I am perceiving." But apart from such explicit reflection, perception by its nature includes a diffuse presence to the self which is not yet a conscious grasp. In terms of this it *lends itself to* a more complete reflection which is not an added operation, grafted onto perception from without, but the explanation of an intrinsic moment of perception. It is this conception of unreflected consciousness which justifies the use of the word consciousness to designate perception itself. As Husserl says, consciousness is consciousness of. . . . Intentionality and consciousness belong together.

What shall we conclude from this—that there is no unconscious? Not at all: but the unconscious does not think, does not perceive, does not remember, does not judge. And yet, "something" is unconscious, something which is akin to perception, akin to memory, akin to judgment, and which is revealed in the analysis of dreams and neuroses. We can cite numerous examples of dream images or hallucinations which represent "perceived" objects unknown to the subject in his waking state. These facts do not force us to the hypothesis of an instantaneous consciousness followed by forgetting, in the sense of an unreflecting perceptive consciousness.[40] These impressions fall within the function of the real, within the most unreflected perception. There is in that "something" *that which* sustains an act of perception, but that is not yet an act of perception but an impressional matter not yet brought to life by an intentional aim which would at the same time be a light for the self. Briefly, it is not yet a consciousness of. . . . Psychoanalysis forces us to admit that the

39. *Ibid.*, II, 33–34: "In knowing a tree, we do not at all know our seeing, we only seize that after the fact, in a second act."

40. Our study of project in Part I and of acting in Part II has familiarized us with this concept of unreflective consciousness.

infra-perceptive "impressions" can be dissociated from their corresponding intentionality and undergo alterations such that they
are cloaked by an apparent meaning which seems absurd.

The Freudian will say that he asks no more, and that this
amounts to the same thing except for philosophical hairsplitting.
But the difference for a philosophy of subject is considerable:
our responsibility, we shall see, is entirely on the level of acts,
of authentic awareness. Thus a separation between the object of
consciousness and the matter of impressions is essential. To be
sure, the status of the unconscious is most difficult to establish;
perhaps it is the greatest difficulty which psychology faces. But
the "working realism" of a psychoanalyst is not philosophically
tenable. This is not the first time that the implicit philosophy of
the scientist had to be corrected by a phenomenological *critique*
leading back "to things as they present themselves." Husserl has
shown, for example, that the "physical entity" (ion, electron)
refers to an original perception, correlative with intentional perceiving, contrary to the naturalist illusion which dissipates the
perceived in the "physical entity" as the scientist determines it.[41]
In the same way the psychoanalytic unconscious is a "psychological" object which refers to certain impressional aspects implied
in some way by the unreflecting consciousness.

The objection could be made that the search for an infra-
perspective, infra-memory, infra-affective factor leads to forging
precarious entities to fit the needs of the cause. In fact a reflection
which does not want to reduce consciousness to an impotent
epiphenomenal unconscious is forced, at one point or another, to
elaborations of this kind. Those who admit unconscious perceptions will object to admitting unconscious pains or judgments and
will interpose a special stage between disposition and act. Thus
R. Dalbiez who rejects the idea of unconscious proprioceptive
sensations has to resort to sensations which he calls organoceptive
and which reveal our body as organic but not as ours.[42] Freud
himself, in *The Ego and the Id*, even though he denies the possibilities of unconscious affective states, comes up against dreams in
which pain, which only becomes conscious upon waking, gives rise
to dream images in which the pain is attributed to a person other
than the dreamer. In order to account for the phenomenon he
admits that before pain strictly speaking there is "something" we
could call a "pre-pain." [43] The case of judgment is no less inter-

41. Husserl, *Ideas*, §§ 40 and 52.
42. Dalbiez, *op. cit.*, II, 47, 81–83.
43. *Ibid.*, p. 82.

esting: R. Dalbiez rightly calls it naturally conscious and always accompanied by a beginning of reflection, while for Freud the "most complex activities of thought can be produced without consciousness taking part." [44] If then the unconscious seems to invent new thoughts of a rational order its role would become reduced to a "work of elaboration which never reaches the point of judgment strictly speaking." [45] Thus other authors, and sometimes even Freud himself, have been led to seek a "something," a pre-pain, pre-judgment which would account for the enigmas of the unconscious. We believe that this precarious notion has to be generalized to all the alleged desires, images, and thoughts of the unconscious.

If the unconscious does not think and if in spite of this we can, through psychoanalysis, *give* a "meaning" to dreams and neuroses, what is this "meaning"? Let us note first of all that the dream becomes a complete thought only upon awakening, as I recount it. It is a complete image, that is, representation of the unreal, only on the basis of the real and in the form of a recounting. The dream was not that recounting minus the quality of consciousness. What was it? That is hard to say, since I can only speak of it in waking, in a memory directed towards my nocturnal being from my waking being. In any case it was less than image, but lent itself to being received into a waking image. While the dreamed dream, seen in waking thought, now receives meaning from the psychoanalyst, this latent meaning, itself enunciated in a retelling, though in a coherent retelling, was not present in that form "in the sleeper's unconscious." Desires expressed in waking language—hate of father, love of mother, return to the womb, etc.—are only desires as conceived by the psychoanalyst or by the subject himself as he adopts them. It is convenient for the psychoanalyst to imagine that this meaning was already given "in the unconscious," that the "dream work" (*Traumarbeit*) has changed it in a way to produce the apparent content of the dream, and that analysis undoes what the dream had done. The "latent meaning" would then be a rediscovered meaning, such that it would be the basis of the moral of the dream. This is not altogether wrong. The "latent meaning" is that "some-

44. Freud, *Interpretation of Dreams*, trans. Brill (London, 1913), quoted by R. Dalbiez, *op. cit.*, II, 78.
45. Dalbiez, *op. cit.*, II, 51. The author here cites a text from Delacroix concerning the elaboration of "obscure syntheses which are in principle judgments." "Its data only become judgments through the work which accompanies consciousness." ("Les Operations intellectuelles," in *Nouveau traité* . . . , ed. G. Dumas, V, 151.)

thing" which, if it were thought completely by a waking consciousness, would be what the psychoanalysts call "meaning." It must be that, since associations posterior to the dream are not simply random and since their thematism manifests an order, a structure which would fit the dream itself. Hence everything takes place *as if* this latent meaning, conceived by the waking consciousness, were already hidden behind the manifest contents. This is only an abbreviated way of saying that the nocturnal consciousness, itself known by waking consciousness, has the wherewithal to engender the waking retelling, the wherewithal to engender the post-dreaming thematism, the wherewithal to engender the analyst's coherent exegesis: but it is the analyst who thinks, who is intelligent, and his patient after him.

Here we could undoubtedly invoke, in favor of the preexistence of a hidden *meaning* in the unconscious, the role played in psychoanalytic cure by the reintegration of forgotten memories, the personal adoption by the sick person of the meaning gleaned by the analyst. Isn't there here a genuine recognition of representations, desires, and forgotten memories?—It is not necessary to locate thoughts in the unconscious in order to understand this phase of psychoanalytic cure. We do need to say that for the sick person the difficulties and dreams which inhabit him receive meaning for the first time from him. By adopting the analyst's convictions in an intimate way the patient forms the thought which frees it. We could say, if we wish, that he recognizes something in himself which has been banned but *it* is not yet a fully formed thought which would lack only consciousness. It was no thought at all: it is in becoming a thought that *it* ceases to be a weight on his conscience. Only now do the difficulties and dreams have the dignity of thought, and that thought marks the reconciliation of man with himself. This promotion to thought is what in the last instance has curative value.[46]

We do not know enough to insist on the significance of bringing to consciousness: reintegration of the unconscious in the field of consciousness is the only guarantee that the uncon-

46. It is true that an exercise of imagination on anxiety-producing themes, for instance, by suggestions of movement of rise and descent—as in Desoille's method of waking dream—can have direct cathartic effects without the reintegration of pathogenic events in consciousness and even without conscious interpretation of the imagery called up. But, as J. Boutonier notes in *L'Angoisse* (pp. 197–201), it is the patient who reaches the elaboration of a new psychic *synthesis;* psychotherapy, in the last resort, appeals to the constructive force of my self. "There is no analysis without synthesis. . . . We ought not to claim to be *doing* a psychosynthesis, but placing the subject in favorable conditions which make it possible for him to carry it out." (*Ibid.,* pp. 200–1.)

scious, interpreted by analysis, reached by inference, is not a mythical construct. At the same time bringing to consciousness connects the unconscious with the conscious and confirms its psychic nature in the moment when it subordinates it to consciousness. Yet we can assume that the interpretation of the relations of the unconscious and the conscious proposed here not only is compatible with the reversal which takes place in analytic cure, but also accounts for it better than realism of the unconscious. If analytic therapy acts "by transforming the unconscious into the conscious," [47] this means that consciousness is much more than an added quality which does not change the essence of the psychic. It is not true that the cure shifts the pathogenic "memory" from the unconscious to the conscious; rather, it guides the conscious in *forming* a "memory" where there had only been a "something" which oppressed consciousness, "something" issuing from the past but remaining infra-memory, oppressing consciousness undoubtedly because consciousness could not form a memory out of this mnemonic and affective psychic matter. That "something" is closer akin to habit than to memory.[48] When we say that cathartic cure enlarges the field controlled by consciousness the word consciousness no longer means only that meager knowledge of myself attached to intrinsically unconscious memories; it designates the very emergence of memory which unites me with my past and thus *collaborates* in the synthesis of myself which would not exist without at least the unreflected consciousness thanks to which it becomes apparent in a confused way. The "conscious" consists in forming liberating representation of past events whose "psychic trace" troubled my consciousness without being able to rise to the dignity of a memory. Thus nothing in psychoanalysis forces us to attribute thought to the unconscious, but the fact remains that consciousness has an obverse, a nether side, inconceivable outside of it or without it, which is not thought in any sense but which still is not body. Is it possible to throw

47. Freud, *A General Introduction to Psychoanalysis*, trans. Hall (New York, 1920).

48. Dalbiez moves in the same direction when he writes, "Analytic cure consists essentially in dissolving morbid habits by reducing them to memories of the events which gave them birth. Habit becomes dissolved into memory. Automatism yields to consciousness." (*Op. cit.*, I, 328, 333.) But he also speaks like the Freudians of "pathogenetic memories," "kept unconscious," and states that the problem is to "rediscover them." (*Ibid.*, pp. 330–31.) These two ways of speaking are not identical: according to the second, memory is complete in the unconscious, lacking only consciousness; according to the first the "conscious" itself is the memory both as a vision of the past and as presence to myself. Thus the *formation* of memory represents genuine progress of consciousness.

more positive light on the status of this "hidden" in consciousness?

It is more difficult, we said above, to formulate a philosophy of the hidden than it is to formulate a mythology of the unconscious. In many respects it is a wager on finding even the motives of the elaboration of the "objective" and technical concept of the unconscious in consciousness. There is no subjective, experienced equivalent which corresponds in my conscious experience to the psychoanalyst's unconscious. There is no *my* unconscious as there is *my* personality.

We can give a status in consciousness to the hidden only by an *abstract* decomposition of the act of consciousness, by distinguishing a conscious form or intention and affective memorial matter in all thought. All thought is thought of this or that, to some degree attentive or inattentive, reflected or unreflected, and as we shall say later, responsible for itself in terms of an intention. It is in terms of this matter that all thought is given the task of perpetuating the whole of my past experience, having a density, an endless potentiality which lends itself to a limitless exegesis. This matter can be called unconscious when it is *dissociated* from the "form" which gives it life and its true meaning. But there is no subsistence of the matter as such because the matter is always "hidden" in some "form" or other—dream, neurotic symptom, etc.—which has an apparent meaning. Nothing can be posited at the core of this concept, the way Freudians believe they can posit the concept of the unconscious. The consequence of the past is never more than a potentiality of thought and meaning in the actual form of *my* thought. It can only be spoken of in terms of a relation to a form which brings it to life. We might well say that it is a non-conscious moment of consciousness. This is why, if this matter becomes *dissociated,* if the affective and memorial *flux* becomes cut off from consciousness (we shall return to this dissociation presently), such aberrant matter represents anything only in terms of the *meaning* which a consciousness elaborates with respect to it. The unconscious which assumes the form of a dream was, apart from my vigilance, only a material flux—the memorial, affective matter—capable of receiving the meaning elaborated by analysis.

Hence this notion of *matter* of thought is reached in three steps, starting from consciousness. In the first place, it is reached by *extrapolation.* All that we have said in preceding pages concerning the obscure constitutes a kind of propaedeutic for the hidden. This extrapolation is then extended by an *abstract* analysis of the precarious concept of *dissociated* affective and memorial matter. Finally this distinction is confirmed by a quasi-recognition of the unconscious as mine at the end of psycho-analytic cure. This quasi-recognition, which is a kind of conscious-ness after the fact, of retrospection on the hidden, tends to give a subjective meaning to this "object-unconscious," a first person mark which is *almost* equivalent to the fleeting yet indubitable experience of my own character. The realistic Freudian concep-tion of the unconscious thus appears as an objectification of that unconscious in the first person which we can only sense and suggest. It attributes an intelligibility and stability of its own to a concept which neither does nor can have it. This achievement of psychology is indispensable for integrating the facts, the methods, and the results, but it is unacceptable as such to the philosopher who must try to say that it represents a mode of existence in the subject itself, a mode of existence of which the Freudian unconscious is only an objective equivalent.

The extreme precariousness of this analysis is related to the very condition of consciousness which remains consciousness even in the very shadows in which it elucidates itself and in which it operates. It is at the same time prior and situated as to its manner (personality) and its matter (the unconscious). The problem of habit led us to a similarly unstable concept in this respect. It was not a reasonable answer to a question like "where is our knowledge when we are not using it?" All explanation in terms of material imprints is too far removed and touches only the corporeal condition of memory and habit, but not the very status of unperceived capabilities. Thus we come up against two stumbling blocks: either we "substantify" such capabilities and treat them as birds in a cage which we need but seize, or we reduce abilities to acts. The continuity of abilities which assure the identity of the self with itself can be conceived only abstractly —since it is not experienced—as an unemployed aptitude in-herent in the act of consciousness. Thus we come back to the difficulties which the problem of the unconscious presents if we want to resolve it in the manner of a philosophy of the subject: the problem is to distinguish in the act of thought itself some potentiality which, assuring the continuity of consciousness with itself and its total presence to itself, is the contiguous foundation "on" which responsible thought imposes form and meaning to its contents.

It is remarkable that Descartes and Husserl themselves come

up against the same difficulty in different circumstances. Descartes encountered the problem of potency in thought with respect to innate ideas:

When I say that some idea is born with us or that it is naturally imprinted in our soul, I do not mean that it is always present to our thought, for nothing is that, but I mean only that we have within ourselves the faculty of producing it.[49]

Husserl, in order to account for some aspects of perception, elaborated more explicitly and more systematically a distinction between intention and the *hyle* whose fertility in all sectors of phenomenology he sensed. It is this distinction to which we have referred in our disquisition on integration in psychoanalysis. In particular our attempt is an extension of an observation in the *Ideas* concerning the possibility of dissociating *hyle* from the corresponding *Auffassung*.[50]

4. Critique of Freudian "Physics" of the Unconscious: The Mode of Necessity Appropriate to the Unconscious

THE REALISM of the unconscious seeks to save itself by causalism. In the "causalist" language, the "meaning" of the dream and of neurotic symptoms is their value as effects indicating an unconscious psychic cause.

It has to be admitted that at this point Freud's own language remains ambiguous. He himself comes to institute a relation of "translation" between the apparent and the latent meaning, as between two different languages. The thoughts of the dream would be "translated" in the coded language of the conscious. He also says that the dream is a "puzzle" in relation to the thoughts of the dream.[51] (We shall not repeat what we have said about the expression "thought of the dream.") If one speaks of a puzzle or a translation, the *relation* between the unconscious and the conscious remains one between two "meanings," a relation of

49. Descartes, "Sixth Objection," *Reply to the Third Objections*. Also, *Letter to Clerselier*, April 17, 1647. The case of the innate ideas of God is discussed in *Reply to the First Objections*, § 4. In the *Reply to the Fourth Objections*, §§ 119–21, the problem is taken up again. Descartes also explains his views of what he calls the "species of thought" which are "imprinted in memory." (*Letter to Meysonnier*, January 29, 1640; *Letter to Mersenne*, April 1, 1640.)

50. Husserl, *Ideas*, § 85, p. 227. "Whether such sensile experiences in the stream of experience are of necessity everywhere the subjects of some kind of 'animating synthesis' . . . , or, as we also say, whether they ever take part in *intentional function*, does not here call for decision." [Quotation from the English translation by R. Boyce Gibson.]

51. Freud, *Interpretation of Dreams*, quoted by Dalbiez, *op. cit.*, I, 78–79.

meanings implied and in some sense immanent in each other. This is a relation between two thoughts, between a puzzle and its meaning. Yet the fertility of analysis demands a change of perspective: the "meaning" of the dream is the "cause" which produces this sign-effect of the apparent symptom. Here the relation is an altogether external causal relation.[52] Psychoanalysis constantly plays on this double use of the word "meaning." As all mental physics, it preserves a psychological accent by the first use and assumes a scientific posture by the second. We encounter this double use again in the interpretation of the "mechanisms" which change and disguise repressed desires and inclinations. These "mechanisms" must at the same time characterize existence as "psyche" and must be presented in the language of physical laws. Thus repression is at the same time an incompatibility of values and a physical exclusion, and the corresponding disguise of the libido is simultaneously a quasi-lie and a filtering of energy.

However, if the facts revealed by psychoanalysis are correct, this equivocation seems to be rooted in the nature of things. As we have said since the beginning, psychoanalytic method is inseparable from a mental physics in which aberrant images and representations are treated not as intentions whose absurdity itself constitutes an intentional content, but as "facts," as "things" to be explained causally. We would even add that all heuristic power belongs to this naturalism: no one can make discoveries in psychoanalysis or conduct a psychoanalytic treatment successfully unless he adopts this "naturalistic," "causalistic" view of man.[53]

Throughout this work we have fought against such "naturalization" on the level of "formed" thought, that is, on the level of the conscious voluntary and involuntary. Is this position still tenable on the unconscious level?

R. Dalbiez has made the most interesting attempt at combining psychological determinism and a metaphysical conception of freedom in a system which he tries to make homogeneous.[54] He does not hesitate, as a first step, to systematize the "causalistic" methodology which analytic interpretations and therapeutics presuppose. The right to treat dreams and neurotic symptoms causally is connected with their lack of object, their "dereistic" character (to use Bleuer's expression). A dream is not a thought, but the *effect* of a thought. It is a psychic product, not knowledge.

52. Sartre exposed this equivocation clearly. (*Emotions*, pp. 44–46.)
53. "The principle of causality was Freud's guiding star. Every effect is a sign of its cause. This old Aristotelian axiom condenses in short all the psychological researches of the Viennese master." (Dalbiez, *op. cit.*, I, 331.)
54. *Ibid.*, I, 76–80, 153–60, 196–201; II, 143–244 (esp. 152–70), 406–37.

It is derived not from objects but from thoughts. We shall say that a dream or a neurotic symptom are "psychic expressions," that is, psychic sign-effects of unconscious psychic states. In other words, dream is a natural, individual psychic language. The method of association is therefore the technique suited to thoughts which cannot be understood in terms of their object but which can be explained in terms of their causes. There is no reason to hesitate to treat "psychic states" as things among which real, unconscious causal relations obtain. Associative mechanisms are normally unconscious, even though the elements they bind together are not. "The relational unconscious is a fundamental law of mind's functioning." Thus for R. Dalbiez causalism is a natural complement of realism of the unconscious.

The ground for this reconciliation of determinism and freedom is laid by the observation that a thought can be subject to a double regulation, by principally affective causes from the side of the subject, by knowledge from the side of the object. We are finally brought back to the distinction between "acting" and "determination" of psychic acts:

Psychic truth and expressiveness go together perfectly. A mathematical thesis is a system of true propositions, but it is also an effect of intellectual curiosity or ambition of its author. Presumably, also, a psychoanalysis of it would be of little profit.[55]

The result of this is that psychotherapy is placed midway between healing of the body and training of the will: "Just as ethics and religion use freedom, so psychotherapy makes use of determinism." [56] In this respect we should not denounce too vigorously the incompetence of educators who confuse neurosis with insufficient will and aggravate mental difficulties by insisting on applying morality to what belongs to medicine.

I, too, believe that such reconciliation of freedom and determinism really is a task of a doctrine of man. Yet I doubt that it can be so that *directly*. R. Dalbiez believes that he can succeed in it within the context of a cosmology conceived on an Aristotelian model in which different types of causality are combined. We have already criticized in principle schemes in which "physical causalities" (about which we can never be sure, in addition, whether they have been purged of all anthropomorphism) are

55. *Ibid.*, II, 159.
56. *Ibid.*, II, 407, 409, 413: "What in effect differentiates analytic psychology from training the will is that the latter endeavors to promote good use of psychic possibilities found already at their normal level by freedom, while analysis seeks to lead dynamically disturbed possibilities to that normal level."

combined with "mental causalities" tainted with a "thingism." [57]
We cannot repeat here the critique which we have carried out
on several occasions and in several different forms. Perhaps we
can at least add to that general critique several aspects bearing on
the problem at hand.

It is doubtful whether the distinction between "specification"
and "operation" can be turned into a distinction between a metaphysics of truth and freedom and deterministic psychology. If
the point of view of acting is applied to "acts," it leads to the idea
of motivation and not to the idea of causality. Motivation and
intentionality belong to the same universe of discourse, the
phenomenological universe, while causality and intentionality do
not. Causality and intentionality could themselves be harmonized,
as "acting" and "determination," though the difficulty arises
again since within the point of view of "determination" we shall
have to reconcile free production of acts with their deterministic
production. Only the two modes of motivation, voluntary and
involuntary, can be harmonized, causality of objects and voluntary motivation cannot.

Nor is the right to introduce causality and determinism in
psychology guaranteed by the fact that dreams have no object.
Dreams have no "logical" object but do have an intentional correlate
since the absurdity of their apparent meaning is a characteristic
of that correlate. The discussion is ultimately based on the possibility of extending the idea of causality to the acts of a subject
and I believe that this extension is the fruit of an objectification
of unfree motivation which suspends its "subjectivity." R. Dalbiez,
on the other hand, starts with a cosmological idea of causality
which presupposes, "material" homogeneity between the realm
of subjects and the realm of objects.

Yet precisely such "objectification" is not only a possible
detour, but also an inevitable one, indispensable for the advance
of understanding of the absurd and radically involuntary motivation of dreams and neurosis. *Causality is the objective equivalent
of an absolutely unfree motivation.* It is this unfree motivation
which belongs to the same sphere as freedom—not the determinism in which it is "objectified." To put it in other words:
the unconscious and unconscious mechanisms are not immediately "objects," "things," but affective automatisms make them as
much as possible like physical entities whose determinism they
simulate. Thus while the determinism of "things" is incompatible
with consciousness and its freedom, this *quasi-determinism* is the

57. Cf. above, pp. 66, 216, 343.

obverse of consciousness and freedom. The unconscious indicates within me that not only my "body," but also my psychic functioning lend themselves to objective treatment: there is an object-psyche as there is an object-body. Here mental physics is ineradicable. *The unconscious is the object par excellence of psychology as a science.* Yet a distance, no matter how small, always separates an automatic motivation from the determinism of things.

This difficult and fragile interpretation can be clarified at several points:

1) What Freud had called the "dream work" (*Traumarbeit*) entails, besides, unconsciousness of affective themes which nourish dreams, unconsciousness of mechanisms of elaboration: the multiple "relations" of associative type in which the diverse mechanisms are summed up function without being known. But we have already encountered this phenomenon on the level of habit. It is entirely independent from the myth of unconscious thought and can be interpreted as a type of motivation rather than causality. Here automatism has to do with a dissociated affective and memorial matter. Our psyche is constituted by such stable thematisms assuring the stability of unconscious "relations" which in turn is the condition of analytic technique. Analysis is an instrument of investigation suited to this foundation of affective automatisms which lend themselves to "objectification."

2) Such unconscious "mechanisms" are essentially related once again with the "dynamism" of repression. We cannot see how we could speak of endopsychic conflicts without a quasi-physical language. In its unconscious aspect, subjectivity is *like* a physical nature. It imitates the object. It lends itself to the schemata of conflicts, compromises, products of forces, or, as the psychoanalysts put it, of "drives." But "force" in the language of subjectivity is, as we know, the thrust of a need or sovereignty of effort. When it becomes automatic, the force of need is *like* a force of nature—direct analysis of habits also leads to this. What psychoanalysis forces us to add to our study of habit is that a part of ourselves is dissociated and proscribed in virtue of an incompatibility of values. Hence the instrument of investigation forged by psychoanalysis is irreplaceable. For a great part of consciousness has no access to its own foundations. It is unable to do an exegesis of its own enigmas. It remains given over to an absurd, incoercible impulsiveness. More than that, the psychoanalyst who cannot force us to call this dissociated unconscious thought does force us to recognize, on the level of this invincible

impulsiveness, the mark of a purposiveness which is itself absolutely involuntary and unconscious. Repression indicates this function of control, repression, "censorship" about which it is difficult to speak without lapsing into mythology. It is actually quite tempting and undoubtedly inevitable in medical *practice* to resort alternatively to the language of consciousness and to that of physics, or even to mix the two, to imagine an intelligent guardian who is more cunning than a malicious demon, or to construct a play of forces which repulse each other and balance each other, are derived mutually, break through the barrier at some points or lend themselves to a filtering operation. What status should we give to this dynamism in a philosophy of subject if not one akin to that of natural objects?

On the level of affective and memorial matter of consciousness, repression appears to be an aspect of these functions of structure and regulation which govern life itself below the level of consciousness. But this structure has not only a strictly "biological" level, but also a "psychic" level which becomes apparent at this point. The next chapter will confront us with this new aspect of the absolute involuntary, that I am alive and that the wisdom of life precedes all the wisdom gathered by willing. Living affects consciousness; it is the living myself given to my self. Censorship is a psychic level of the structure at whose mercy I am placed by this life which I have not chosen. Hierarchic, selective, and repressive, the structure introduces a new aspect into the absolute involuntary: the purposiveness of life itself. Here there is a residuum of a consideration of the obscure and the hidden: it refers us back to a different level of explanation and a new round of problems.

3) The possibility of psychosomatic illness is inscribed in the nature of these unconscious conflicts at the same time. A disorder is possible when we confront a plurality of forces. The "hidden" and the dynamism which cloaks it entail the existence of a psychological *terrible* and call for a mental *cure* which is not reducible to ethics or disciplining of the will.

There is a psychological *terrible* because the will has no hold over the function of vigilance on which it depends and whose failures unleash ravages in consciousness to which major neuroses testify and to which the small anomalies of daily life point. A mental pathology is possible because even consciousness is a tributary of a spontaneity which is the seat of intestinal crises, and can be divided against itself. Existence of an affective *hyle* is one of the sources of the pathological by its possibilities of dissociations, of internal conflict, and of incomprehensible and invincible eruptions in the course of consciousness. The philosopher will not attribute thought to the unconscious, but he will admit the dependence of thought, which is consciousness itself, on a hidden psychic dynamism whose dramas often erupt at the very heart of consciousness and remove an entire region of intentions and actions from its control. All power is surrounded by impotence.

Hence if consciousness is not capable of its own exegesis and cannot restore its own control, it is legitimate to think that someone *other* can explain it to itself and help it win itself back. That is the principle of psychoanalytic cure. At the point at which effort only intensifiies a morbid impulsion a patient uncovering of the morbid themes by the analyst is needed to release it from its sterile effort. Sickness is in no sense the same as the fault, cure is not morality. The profound meaning of a cure is not an explanation of consciousness in terms of the unconscious, but a triumph of consciousness over its own proscriptions by the detour through a deciphering consciousness other than itself. The analyst is the midwife of freedom, aiding the patient in *forming* the thought which fits his disease. He unravels his consciousness and restores its fluidity. Psychoanalysis is a healing by the mind. The true analyst is not the despot of the diseased consciousness but a servant in the restoration of freedom. In this the cure, though not an ethic, is no less the condition of ethics rediscovered where the will had succumbed to the *terrible*. An ethic in effect is always only a reconciliation of my self with its own body and with all the involuntary powers. While the eruption of proscribed forces marks the triumphs of the absolute involuntary, psychoanalysis places the patient back in normal conditions in which he can attempt such a reconciliation anew with his free will.

The critique of the Freudian "physics" is as difficult and precarious as the critique of Freudian "realism" of the unconscious. We have been led to say that the unconscious is made up of infra-perceptions, infra-images, and infra-desires. Now we can say that its mechanisms and dynamism function *like* a physical nature.

Here it might still seem that only a linguistic subtlety separates us from Freudian realism and causalism. But this is not so. If the unconscious were purely and simply a "thing," a "reality" homogeneous with the nature of objects subject to the law of determinism, it would no longer have room for a voluntary and free superstructure. Man in his entirety would be given over to determinism. This is in fact how the Freudians interpret human psychic life. Freud's entire work breathes his mistrust of the place of the will and of freedom. This, let us note well, is not only a sign of the psychotherapist's professional deformation, but it is also the strong conviction that determinism cannot remain isolated, and that we can never leave it.[58] Determinism devours all because it is not reciprocal with a freedom. This is why methodological determinism which lies at the basis of psychoanalysis can be interpreted as the inevitable and legitimate objectification of a *necessity* which is the obverse of free subjectivity.

5. Critique of Freudian "Geneticism": The Concept of Affective "Matter"

A THIRD TRAIT, decisive for our inquiries concerning the will, completes the Freudian system. We have said nothing of the mechanism of sublimation which, in the psychoanalytic schools, serves to link *genetically* the ends which higher human psychic life assigns to itself with lower instincts and fundamentally with the libido.[59] Freudianism is in effect an evolutionistic explanation which reduces higher energies, considered derivative, to lower energies which it considers elementary. And as the unconscious is vital, sexual, infantile, perhaps even ancestral, consciousness is led to suspect that it itself might perhaps be only a disguise of its own unconscious. Sublimation in this respect is the privileged process which assures the transition from vital to non-vital ends. Unlike dreams and neuroses or therapeutic return to the forgotten which in one way or another brings out the repressed in consciousness, sublimation applies tendencies (primarily sexual) on a less instinctive level, with respect to the objects of aesthetic, moral, and religious spheres. This interpretation gives a new guise to evolutionism by seeking in the unconscious not only the primitive sources of energy, but also the mechanisms of their superelevation. Thus the beautiful has its origin in the libido by derivation from the same energy in a new direction. Does that mean that higher values are *only* ends substituted for sexual ends? Freud himself seems to hold a prudent position, stressing only the contribution of energy

58. "By breaking down universal determinism even in a single respect we would disrupt the entire scientific conception of the world." Freud, *A General Introduction to Psychoanalysis*, quoted by Dalbiez, *op. cit.*, II, 464.

59. Baudoin, *Études de psychanalyse*, pp. 62–71.

which sexuality, in virtue of its aptitude for sublimation, provides for other activities. But his whole interest concerns the affective complexes which it would be the function of higher activities and principally of art to discharge.[60] Still more forcefully, moral and religious values are referred to taboo-prohibitions and these are identified with obsessional neuroses. In particular, we are familiar with the importance which the psychoanalysts, as well as Freud himself in *Totem and Taboo,* attach to the Oedipus complex (killing of the father and sexual attachment to the mother) in order to explain the beginnings of religion, morality, and society. The conception of the "superego," which, starting in 1920, corrects the older conception of "censorship," articulates the way these prohibitions can be transmitted: parental conduct of repressive nature is adopted by the unconscious in a process of identification (or introjection). In this way a repressive unconscious is elaborated which is superimposed on the repressed unconscious.[61] Sublimation of the Oedipal concept, introjection of parental training, self-punishment, etc., hold an increasingly large place in the psychoanalysts' recent speculations which already overflow the therapeutic context of psychic derangements.

Thus Freudianism has entered into our mores as the prototype of descending explanation, of the reduction of the higher to the lower: nothing hinders us any longer from going to the very end of a total explanation of man in terms of this repressed and repressing unconscious, sexual and autopunitive, infantile and ancestral. Freudianism serves as a vehicle of a general mentality according to which all non-vital values are considered a disguised manifestation of the unconscious. The Cogito means something else than what it thinks it means: consciousness is a coded appearance of the unconscious. The generosity of the consciousness which *gives* a meaning to its thought and *receives* values is suddenly distorted. This in fact is the threat sensed and perhaps obscurely wished for by all who seek in Freudianism not a help for understanding and healing the shipwrecked consciousness,

60. Cf. texts quoted by Dalbiez, *op. cit.,* I, pp. 597–98, 607–8.

61. In the *New Introductory Lectures* (Lecture III) the unconscious is very neatly divided between the repressed id and the repressing superego (*Es* and *Ueberich*) which in addition also overlaps into the subconscious. Freud is thus lead to correct his conception of anxiety (Lecture IV): the libido is no longer the sole psychic danger, but also the superego whose threats make consciousness anxious. The idea of the superego is central for therapeutics. Its resistance is what has to be conquered in order to reach the repressed and to dissolve it by analysis. Thus the field of control of consciousness can be won back from the repressing and the repressed.

but an explanation which rescues it from the charge of being free. We must admit that this doctrine has an appeal which ethology lacks completely because it is not content with locating the individual in a class but claims to explain him in his individuality, leading him to first sources of his thought and acts. In exploring the hidden and proscribed regions of his self, it gives rise to that mixture of curiosity and fear of doctrines of salvation, specifically of mystery religions. Freudianism has something fascinating for the feeble consciousness which accounts for its popularity. This popularity is not alien to its essence, but expresses its inevitable incidence in modern consciousness. Modern consciousness senses in it its ruin, and perhaps all passion, which is a certain vertigo of freedom, finds in it with a diabolical perspicacity its best alibi. Consciousness seeks an irresponsibility in principle in its own regression to the level of vitality, to the infantile and the ancestral. The taste for Freudian explanations, insofar as they represent a *total* doctrine of man in every man is the taste for descent into hell in order to invoke the fatalities from below.

But this taste for abasing oneself and explaining oneself by the beast, which is one of the forms of self-denial, can lead to an awakening of freedom when this temptation is understood as a threat. By this threat we can engender a dialectic of deliverance similiar to those which we have wrested from the appeal of a false metaphysics of personality.

It is I who think, give meaning, weigh my motives, wish, and move my body. This assurance, infected with the suspicion that I am acting out a comedy on the stage of a mythical opera and am a dupe of a conjuration of hidden forces in some mysterious wings of existence—this assurance, that "I" which I was tempted to sacrifice into the hands of the decipherers of enigmas, must be won back constantly in the *sursum* of freedom. I confront the unconscious as Descartes confronted the great deceiver: I save myself by the affirmation of the Cogito and the refusal to make my thought conform to something which is not *also* consciousness—free then to integrate into this refusal whatever can be legitimately retained of psychoanalysis. But this integration can be carried out from within consciousness and from the assurance of the "I will." This refusal, which still represents only a negative moment in a more discriminating and more equitable position with respect to Freudianism, is at the same time a critique and an ethic, that is, an examination of the concept of the thinking and willing subject, and an appeal to this very freedom.

"The unconscious," says Alain, "is an effect of contrast in consciousness." [62] A consciousness can denounce itself as dupe only before an undeceived consciousness: for the deceived consciousness the apparent meaning and the hidden meaning inevitably coincide. In fact the critical consciousness must take itself for granted. If he who deciphers meaning is deceived by his unconscious in the moment when he denounces the devices of the other's unconscious, the suspicion becomes endless: ἀνάγκη στῆναι in some sense consciousness and thought form a circle in an indivisible unity. This argument is rather abstract: it exists only for the Freudian. For me it means that I do not think at all except when I believe that I think and that what I think has no other meaning than what I believe it to have. This is no longer an argument but a pledge to myself: I shall not attribute thought to the beast in me and instead of me, and I shall not flee into irresponsibility. Having said this, must I reject the entire doctrine of sexual and infantile origin of my higher sentiments. Not at all. In this respect we have sufficiently affirmed the originality of the acts by which consciousness makes itself sensitive to ethical, æsthetic and religious values that it is not difficult to clarify another aspect of this perspective on value. It is one thing to recognize the original *form* of various values, such as the vital, the noble, the elegant, the beautiful, the sacred, and another thing to discover by analysis the *special* affective matter through which such values are intended. It can be the same affective potential which nourishes infantile sexuality and adult morality. The *origin* of affective "matter" and the *meaning* of the intentional "form" pose two radically different, irreducible problems. There is nothing scandalous in the fact that the psychoanalysts discover, at the root of a discontinuous series of values which consciousness runs through, from the vital to the sacred, a unity of identical affective matter. If the psychoanalyst had been led to *formulate*, in this affective matter, the idea of a regret of infancy or the idea of desire of return to maternal womb, he will find it convenient to say that the origin of the higher sentiment is the desire to return to the womb. It will be enough if we are not deceived by this language. Evolutionism of instinct is only an abbreviated form of saying that it had been possible to stake out, in terms of a special affec-

62. Alain, "Note sur l'Inconscient," *Éléments de philosophie.* We need to notice that in the case of a dead artist, a psychoanalytic interpretation remains unverifiable since resolution is the sole criterion of good analysis. It is furthermore contrary to the therapeutic spirit of analysis to undertake it without the collaboration of the interested party.

tive energy, the ascending and discontinuous series of consciousness, intentions of the vital, the noble, the beautiful, the sacred,
etc.: this very energy is the memorial and affective matter which
remains relatively stable throughout existence but which is animated by different levels and perspectives of nature. This does
not mean that the sacred is reduced to the vital, but that I intend
the sacred with the same lack and the same thrust which are
awakened on the level of vital values. In Husserlian language,
psychoanalysis is only a hyletics of consciousness. It must remain
subordinate to the phenomenology of its intentions, that is, its
"forms." This, I believe, is the most favorable interpretation we
can give to Freudian sexualism and to the process of sublimation.

The fact remains that psychoanalysis must be used with greatest caution when it has to do not with *disordered* products but
with higher creations of consciousness. In the case of dreams or
neuroses the "latent meaning" formulated by the psychoanalyst
in the course of interpretation and by the patient in his recovery
has a value as deliverance—which was the very reason for analytic therapeutics. From this point of view we could say that the
"latent meaning" is a *better* meaning than the "apparent meaning" because of its curative value. But with respect to, for instance,
a poem, the meaning which the psychoanalyst formulates is a
lesser meaning with respect to that which the poet had *given* and
which refers to the æsthetic aims of a work of art.

An example will help us understand this better:

No poet could choose and govern his language better than
Mallarmé. A poem, he said, is "chance conquered word by word."
To understand a poem means for the reader to overcome in turn
the fortuitous appearance and to rediscover, not necessarily by
understanding but by poetic sensitivity, the "spirit of the song
beneath the text which leads divination from here to there," the
network of relations and correspondences which constitute the
"glitter beneath the surface" in the poem. This hidden meaning
can be sought in two ways, one philosophico-literary, the other
psychoanalytic. According to the first, we shall ask what quality
of the soul, what shading of innocence can suggest the insistent
evocation of palms, of wings of angels, of white plumage, of old
tools, of old locked chests, and those glances of yesteryear and
the grace of faded things. Thus we shall attempt an odyssey of
consciousness in the direction of a certain lost purity which once
was easy, naïve, and faultless. The play of symbols thus goes from
the sensible to the intimate, from emotions to feelings. Its

meaning, which we formulate in ourselves, is Mallarmé's message. Then comes the psychoanalyst:[63] obscurity of the poem for him will be only a coding effect of the subconscious or the unconscious. In place of following the ascendant movement of the symbol to poetic and religious sentiment, he will adopt a movement which descends from the symbol to the sublimated instinct. The entire cycle of "obsessing metaphors" which revolve around paradise lost will be explained by the nostalgia for infancy and for the womb. These two trajectories of explanation cannot be compared with each other: the first goes from the minimal meaning of first reading to the poetic surplus which is the treasury of spiritual signification: that is the true meaning which joins and extends what Mallarmé intended. The second goes from the same minimal conscious meaning to an unconscious meaning which had been neither thought or willed and which is only suggested to an external observer by the affective matter *out of* which Mallarmé independently of any chance, in full clarity, composed the most voluntary poetic text that had ever been written. The observing stranger who denies to himself that ascendant movement going from the symbol to poetic meaning attempts a different exegesis according to a new system of postulates, but one which is equally motivated by the affective matter of the poem. A limitless possibility of new meaning which one had neither thought nor willed clings to all meaning. Consciousness clarifies only the form, not the matter which more or less resists light.

Yet though these two attitudes in face of an apparent meaning are not *comparable,* it is not indifferent whether consciousness adopts the one or the other since it itself wants to understand or communicate with another consciousness. In effect, with respect to each other they stand on *different levels.* One attempts to bring out the values which are often intended in a concealed way and to expose them explicitly before consciousness. It represents an awakening of consciousness to itself and to its loftiest goods. The other, by evoking the energy mobilized by lower values, attempts a regression of consciousness to its lower values. Systematic recourse to different complexes and incidents which gather around sexuality always runs the risk of conditioning consciousness to placing itself on a level which was not in reality the one on which it had chosen to place itself. This is why we

63. Charles Mauron, *Mallarmé l'obscur* (Paris, 1941): "I believe that for each of Mallarmé's poems there exists an objectively true meaning, that which the poet had in mind in writing it and which determined his corrections" (p. 26). This phrase contains all the ambiguities which we shall try to remove.

posit a principle of hygiene which is already an article of ethics: consciousness should not consider an explanation of desires of higher values in terms of sublimated need of lower values a good exegesis of its own meanings *whenever this explanation does not have a curative value.*[64] It is a good use and the limit of psychoanalysis to be defined by its therapeutic function: it is good that consciousness actively adopts and formulates for itself the thoughts of return to the womb, of Oedipus complex, etc. when these thoughts *free* it from the weight which burdens its flight. Apart from this function, the influence of Freudianism can be inauspicious, even degrading. It can support precisely the meanness and misunderstanding of myself which are the opposites of Cartesian "generosity" and from which we should have broken free in rejecting the realism of the unconscious.

6. Responsibility for Form and Consent to the Hidden

OUR STUDY of character led us to a paradoxical proposition: all freedom is an infinite possibility tied to a constitutive particularity. *It is an infinite finite.* It is inseparably a capacity for being and a way of being given. The study of the hidden has led us to a similar thought: I am responsible only for the form of my thoughts ("we need account only for our thoughts," says Descartes) and at the same time thought is nourished by an entire obscure and hidden presence which makes each initial act a consquence of what I have been.

Now this paradoxical synthesis of *definite form and indefinite matter* can only be read and understood in one irreversible direction. Just as my immutable nature which is my character can be recognized only under the protection of the affirmation which makes me will and consciousness, I am, I will—in the same way the existence, appeal, and even power of the hidden can only be proffered in the context of the thought which affirms itself as consciousness and will. Any reading in the opposite direction, from character to will, from the unconscious to consciousness, represents a suicide of freedom which gives itself over to an object. Prior to investigating psychoanalysis I posit that thought is my act. It is the first option by which I am born and awake to existence as voluntary subject. As we have adumbrated it with

64. In the same sense, see Dalbiez, *op. cit.*, II, 401–38, 491–511. Hence the limited force of his conclusion: "Freud's work is the most profound analysis which history has known of that in man which is no longer human,, (*ibid.*, II, 513).

respect to character, only he who exercises an ability can recognize its limits. To the very end, I believe in my total responsibility within the limits of the apparent good, that is, in proportion to the intentional form of my motives. Within these limits, my responsibility has no degrees and is, for me, only the question whether I have used as much as possible the free choice which had been the pledge of generosity.

An example, grafted onto the old theme of the double, will clarify our thought. In *Amphitryon 38* Giradoux had shown the fidelity of Alcmène in grips with Jupiter's ruses when Jupiter assumed the form of her husband Amphitryon. It is possible to see in Jupiter the unacknowledged, errant desires which seek to restrain clear, voluntary love and which had been said to issue from the unconscious. Now it does not matter for the faithfulness of Alcmène that Jupiter had taken the *form* of Amphitryon and that unwittingly she had taken Jupiter *for* Amphitryon. Jupiter is nothing yet, insofar as Alcmène has no idea of it, just as the so-called unconscious desires which drift into our motives. There is really a problem only when the temptation is recognized, when Jupiter and Alcmène are face to face, "I knowing your virtue, you knowing my desire." After that there is no more fatality, except in the vertigo of freedom which gives a consistence to the semi-acknowledged desires and which seeks an alibi in the unconscious. In themselves, they are *nothing*, in the fall of freedom they are *everything*.[65] Insofar as Alcmène does not know that the appearance of Amphitryon can represent another being, it is only for the *other* that Alcmène had been deceived; for herself, for Amphitryon and for any being capable of communicating intimately with her, Alcmène has remained a faithful wife.

Giradoux's great lesson is no different from that of Descartes on repentance. The pride of the "generous" who advances into the demi-shadows of the apparent good, is to "become accustomed to forming certain, determinate judgments concerning all things which present themselves and to believe that one has always done one's duty as long as one does what he judges to be best, even though it is possible that he misjudges."[66]

65. "Speak to me no more of fatality," says Alcmène, "it only exists through the flabbiness of men. Ruses, men, desires have no power against the will of a faithful woman. Think you not so, Echo, you who have given me the best advice? What have I to fear of God and men, I who am loyal and sure? Nothing, is it not so? Nothing, nothing." Echo: "Everything, everything." Alcmène: "What did you say ... ?" Echo: "Nothing, nothing."

66. Descartes, *Treatise on Passions*, arts. 152–70, *Letters to Princess Elizebeth*, October 6, 1645; January, 1646.

But while in the moment of decision I should allow no access within me to thoughts capable of destroying my resolution, such as the suspicion of being deceived by forces hidden behind the apparent reasons I invoke, it is good that, in the leisure which is not concerned with action I should consider the irremediable *condition* of my freedom which condemns me to playing my role in an undecipherable context. After the epic, the elegy of freedom. I must *consent* to produce all meaning on the basis of the meaningless, to exercise all power in the context of threatening inefficaciousness and perhaps, in some extreme cases, to seek a midwife of my freedom in a master of deciphering. Thus, after the most extreme demands with regard to myself before the decision, perhaps I should use extreme patience and indulgence when I consider the very *condition* of a responsible agent. To be sure, in dealing with these invincible shadows, I shall refrain from making them speak the language of men, but I shall consent to shelter, at the foot of the tower of free choice, an animal periphery sensed without complaisance and intuited without terror, which only becomes fascinating when the spell of passions gives it form and fatality. At the end of *Amphitryon 38*, Jupiter is not banished but retained as friend. This consent is not contrary to generosity: evoking the obscure inclinations which carry us towards a being and which are not based on his merits but come from some unperceived kinship with the other, once desired and loved being, Descartes counsels us to trust ourselves to these impulsive impressions if at the same time reason perceives a good in them.[67]

Thus if the errant, unformed and unformable, unwished and unwishable desires cannot be called myself, thought, or even desires, they cannot be denied simply in the name of transparence of consciousness: we have to consent to the obscure, to the hidden which can always become the terrible—but with a consent which remains the counterpart of resolute spirit.

[3] LIFE: STRUCTURE

1. Being Alive

WHILE CHARACTER is necessity closest to my will, we can call life basic necessity. It sustains the potentialities of

67. "...the chief good of life being friendship, we are right to prefer those to whom our inclinations draw us, provided we also notice merit in them." Descartes, *Letter to Chanut*, June 6, 1647.

the unconscious and their conflicts, it gives privileged directions to character. In the last instance, everything is resolved in it. In the last instance? Isn't the animal in us in some respects vegetable and finally mineral? To be sure, but it is with the animal alone that I deal; it is only from the viewpoint of objective consciousness that life involves the physico-chemical order. In myself and for myself, the union of soul and body is the union of freedom and life. I am "alive"—as the French expression *"en* vie," "in life," suggests, it is enough to be "in life" in order to enter "into the world"—in order to "exist." [68]

Haven't we already said everything concerning life that phenomenological knowledge of man permits us to say in speaking of that spotaneity of need which comes to sustain our motives, or the spontaneity of our body's initial capabilities expressed in emotive explosion or in the construction and tenacity of habits? No, life is more than the spontaneity of motives and powers—it is a certain necessity of existing which I can no longer hold at an arm's length to examine and control. I cannot go to the limit of that act of self-expulsion which is consciousness, of that appreciation and sovereignty which are motivation and effort. Life in all respects escapes from the judgment and commandment in which it is covertly present. Life is not only a lower part of my self over which I rule. I am alive as a whole, alive in my very freedom. I have to be alive in order to be responsible for my life. What I control is what makes me exist.

Let us attempt to suggest concretely this movement of inclusion, of the investiture of consciousness by life. This life which I judge has a remarkable characteristic: it is not a value like others, but at the same time it is the condition of all other values. When I destroy my life, all other values are scattered: "The entire universe totters and trembles on my stem."

In this trait we can already sense the peculiar necessity which belongs to life: it is an extrasystematic motive on which all other motives depend even when we prefer them to it. This potentiality of life, this grace of life whose flow and ebb constitute the force or weakness of my courage, are manifested in yet other traits, akin to the preceding one: all motives, all capabilities have a more or less precise outline which stands out as a form out of the ground, out of the confused and unformed background of *mood* (taking this word in its most natural sense as in the expressions

68. The Kierkegaardian sense of the word "existing" is not satisfactory. As all human condition, existence is bipolar: willed and undergone; as such it is the living mystery whose expression is inevitably paradoxical.

of being in a "good" or "bad" mood). A need has an intentional object which I can circumscribe and name; a desire, a habit have a determinate structure; a mood is rather a general tone which functions as an underlying web for all the definite modes of the Cogito. In this it reveals that necessity which I can no longer hold at arm's length: it is unformed and constantly insinuating, it acts more like a perfume which drifts in the air and bathes the forms. Like a scent, it is an influx, a diffuse influence.[69] We shall say that all motivation is basically influence. Influence is already a relation without distance in which we sense the invincible and irrefutable positing of an existence which escapes me. Maine de Biran was well aware of this: his theory of passivity or "simple affection" is constructed almost entirely on this desperate experience of the movements of the serpent mood which he reports a thousand times in his *Journal*. It is this experience which will reveal to us the essential character of life, of my life at the core of my consciousness.

1) Life is enjoyed (*erlebt, sentie*) rather than known: a certain diffuse affectivity reveals my life to me before my reason can explain it to me. In his study of *Befindlichkeit* Heidegger strongly emphasizes the capacity of affectivity for preceding all distinct ideas.[70] I sense myself alive before I know myself as animal. Yet the status of that affectivity is rather difficult to establish, since it can be said to be devoid of intentionality. In it, I intend nothing. It is an essential characteristic of a perceived object that it is present itself in a multiplicity of sketches, of perspectival profiles; whether I turn it or whether it turns before me, it offers a plurality of "aspects"; it itself is only the unity of such retained and anticipated aspects. Yet my life is in no sense an object which presents itself under different expressions; I apprehend it always from the same side or, better it has no sides for me and is grasped without perspective. In experiencing my life, I possess the very center of perspective in terms of which there are different perspectives on objects. I can observe things but I do not observe my life. *Ein Erlebnis schattet sich nicht ab*, says Husserl: a lived experience does not present itself in perspectives.[71] At every moment, I grasp as much of it as I can ever grasp of it. We can say the same thing differently: the object seen from

69. Valéry, "Ébauche d'une serpent," *Poésies*, *loc. cit.*, "I was present as a scent, as the aroma of an idea whose insidious depth cannot be made clear." (Trans. Kohák.) Concerning influence, cf. Minkowski, *Vers une cosmologie*, pp. 111–21.

70. Heidegger, *Being and Time*, pp. H. 130–40.

71. Husserl, *Ideas*, § 42, p. 77.

an angle is also an object seen from outside, in terms of its outside: I do not penetrate the object, I move around it, I envelop it and pass through it, I divide it and still remain outside the fragments. The phenomenon of transparence is only for sight and not for touch, it does not represent a co-presence of the look with the objects through which it passes. My look passes through the glaze and rests *on* opaque objects. My consciousness penetrates my life better than transparent glass: when I feel my breath raise my chest, my blood pulsate in my temples, I am, so to speak, in my breath, at the center of my pulse, co-present and coextensive in the volume felt and the movement experienced. This is the meaning which we can assign to Descartes' expression that "the soul is united with all the parts of the body conjointly," [72] which can in no way express the relation of two heterogeneous substances but rather the nonperceptive consciousness of my body or, if we wish, the experienced rather than perceived presence of my body to my consciousness. It means that consciousness of life is not consciousness of an object but of my self. This affectivity is the elementary form of the apperception of myself. As all consciousness of myself, it accompanies in an original way all consciousness of something, sometimes muted, sometimes as an exalting or painful orchestration of the presence of the world.

2) This affective consciousness of the myself-body reveals life to me as indivisible: I am a living totality. Life is the unity which circulates among the functions. I might well say that I have members, feelings, ideas, but life is never plural. The Cogito lends itself to an enumeration of parts, of functions, and of acts; only freedom and life, that is, willed existence and existence undergone, transcend enumeration. I exist as one. We can see this in all the forms of organic or "proprioceptive" affectivity: the best localized synaesthetic sensations arise out of a global, non-localizable affective ground. Pain, while wounding me here or there, affects me as a vital totality (experienced totality whose objective symptom is the radiation, the diffuse reflexes and the generalized reactions which disperse the localization). This is why I can say "I have a pain in my foot" and not "my foot has a pain." There is a special pain consciousness which is not strictly somewhere *in* the body—as the individuality of experienced space—and which brings together local feelings of pain. This strange mixture of the local and the non-local can be encountered again in hunger, thirst, and in all needs. The obstacles encountered by any attempt to localize pleasure are well known—perhaps it approaches an overall

72. Descartes, *Treatise on Passions*, art. 30.

consciousness without a counterpart of localized sensations. Thus I should say that I am divisible as space and as a machine, and indivisible as life. Life is susceptible to levels and tonalities but not to parts; or, if we wish, it is the indivisibility of extension and of movement in the first person. And when I fear being wounded, that is, divided, I fear for my life, for its division is its end, that is, its reduction to the level of dead things, and as such divisible and divided. My death itself presents itself to me as a return to the divided object par excellence: dust.

3) The necessity involved in life is a consequence of these two initial characteristics: what is felt as indivisible is the non-willed positing of myself, the brute fact of existing: I *find* that I exist.

We shall attempt to encircle this necessity gradually by inquiring into some *metaphors* which are its indirect language. These metaphors are that much more suggestive since they are devoid of subjective claims. There is, in the first place, the spatial metaphor: I am alive, or, in French, I am "en vie"—"in life," I find myself there. This image is one of insertion or immersion in a "medium" at the heart of the mass of my vitality. This imagery is unmistakable: an aura surrounds the geometric language and testifies to a transgeometric intention of topography. The spatial metaphors are, so to speak, a residuum of that intention.[73] The I is at the basis of life, all representations which I form have, as their horizon, the ἄπειρον, the indefiniteness of a gratuitously given life. This inability of consciousness to bestow being on itself and to persevere in it is sometimes suffered as an original wound, at other times experienced as a joyous complicity with a thrust which comes from without: "Harmonious Self," says the youngest of the Fates. This spatial metaphor thus suggests a delimitation of all power of being by a non-power of existing. This feeling of being delimited by my life is augmented by the assurance that my life is in the world, that it comes from beyond me and passes through me only in giving me existence. At the extreme, it appears to me as a conditional loan, as a revocable gift. We can already sense the religious repercussions of this idea which, however, we shall neglect. Whatever it means, I have the obscure feeling of belonging to a unique life in the universe.

If we pursue one image by another, as Bergson recommends, another metaphor, that of support, suggests itself. I am brought and *placed* into the world by my birth, *carried away* by death. Because I do not posit my life, I am posed on it, I stand on it as

73. Minkowski, *op. cit.*, pp. 69–88.

on a foundation. I rest on my breathing as on the waves of a sea, and I "fall back on it" even more when I cease willing and abandon myself to the wisdom of life which guards me in my sleep. It is not hard to slip from this metaphor to the more consistent conception of a ground. But we shall not yield to this yet: it would take us too rapidly to a discussion of cosmology and its superimposed causalities. Let us stay a while with the imagery of foundations and superstructures. What does it add to what preceded? This: I not only *basically am* life, I also *rest on it as on my foundation.* The life I basically *am* is unstable, while as a foundation it represents almost an effort of supporting. A building stands on its foundation, but in turn it adds novelty without, however, being able to subsist without it. This is what an architectural and hierarchic conception of degrees of being and of causality attempts to stabilize in a rational cosmology.

If we remain faithful to living experience, barely elaborated by metaphors, we shall have to say that existence is a paradox for analytic understanding and a mystery for a more covert unifying consciousness, for it is both willed and undergone. It is a focus of *acts* joined to the *state* of living. The expression, state of consciousness, which is otherwise so erroneous, finds its justification here. The state of living is the state of consciousness par excellence.[74] The act and the state of existing are conceived as two and lived as one: my act and my state are one for us in the "I am." In this sense alone the Cogito as act includes the fact of existing: "Cogito, ergo sum." But "ergo" is not a logical connection: it is a paradox encroached upon by a feeling of mystery. Existence in the Kierkegaardian sense includes existence in a Kantian sense, but this implication is a supra-logical bond which holds by connivance and *pact,* and which breaks up as soon as it is thought into act and state, into freedom and necessity of existing.

Thus we reach the third and ultimate expression which the paradox of freedom and necessity assumes. Freedom is bound not only to a finite manner and an indefinite matter, but also to the pure fact of existing "in life."

For the third time we shall seek, in the objectification of life, first of all the remnants of this paradox replaced by a radical

74. By an extension I can speak of a "state of the world" because I am in the state of living: I find myself there, alive, in the world which I find there and of whose reality I had neither willed nor produced a single grain. In this sense the consent which acquiesces to necessary existence within and without me is akin to perception which finds and receives a "state of things" which is does not produce.

determinism, then the fleeting rational indication of a relation which is lived more than thought: the relation of the act of the Cogito to its own factual existence. Reason's mediation is more necessary than ever, even though it becomes stranded. The affective nature of life is obvious: without object and blind, feeling calls for commentary by understanding. Its richness constitutes its confusion and its depth is sanctioned by its absence of language.

The first effect of objectification is to divide life, if not into parts, then at least according to different points of view.

1) We could, first, consider an instantaneous segment in a given moment: that is, a transverse segment in the process of living: life appears then as the indivisible unity of a structure which astonishes me, takes me by surprise, as a wisdom which is unaware of itself.

2) Then we can reintroduce consideration of time and of the evolution of the living: life presents itself then as the unity of a *growth* which bears me without interruption from infancy to old age. The unity of life is simultaneously one of order in space and order in time.

3) Finally we have to make room for the decisive fact that the time of the living has a beginning and an end. I am born, and I shall certainly die. Provisionally we shall set aside any consideration of death which is better placed at the conclusion of an inquiry into the diverse forms of negation entailed by the necessity of existing.

Thus an examination of life involves three moments: structure, growth, and birth. A consideration of the condition of the living thus involves the triple temptation of placing necessity outside the subject and, subsequently, of burying freedom itself there: the will can appear as an effect of structure, as a product of evolution of the living, or even as a result of its heredity.[75]

2. The Objective Concept of "Structure"

OBJECTIVE KNOWLEDGE of life reaches a scientific level which neither the study of personality nor psychoanalysis

75. We must eliminate from the experience of being alive all the harmonies which already point to the "poetics" of the will. In our language, life has an ambiguous meaning: it designates at the same time the order of limits and the order of sources or creation. In this new sense life brings up a new method, namely, a "poetics" of the will which we are here abstracting. One of the crucial, difficult problems posed by such "poetics" of the will will be to know why the spontaneity of life below serves in turn as a metaphor for higher life, and what secret affinity unites those two meanings of the word "life."

have yet attained. Thus the exegesis by science of the obtuse feeling of being alive confronts us insistently.

Here we are interested only in biological concepts which precisely distinguish biology from the class of physico-chemical sciences. We cannot know whether these concepts—first of all the concept of structure—are themselves explanatory or whether they still have only a descriptive value, that is, whether the phenomena of balance, regulation, or adaptation of all types call in the last resort for a physico-chemical explanation, both necessary and sufficient. For us it is enough that biological concepts have a genuine intellectual consistency and give a *meaning,* an intelligibility to life as an original phenomenon, that they make vital order *comprehensible* to our understanding.[76]

If we wish to distinguish the living from the object, it is the *biological functions* which give it its original meaning. These are what unify the different physico-chemical materials and the diverse anatomical tissues. Function is the indication of an organ, and physiology gives anatomy its significance. Life as indivisible presents itself finally as a higher harmony of diverse functions in the unity of the individual's structure: more exactly, the task of life is to maintain the unity of internal relations of the organism in relation with its external milieu: internal equilibrium and adaptation to environment are the two solidary aspects of that *factual purposiveness* which gives life its intelligibility. Once more, it is enough for us that this *factual purposiveness* in its double aspect has at least a descriptive value so that we can pose the problem of knowing whether it can include all the elements of human conduct.

Now once we have adopted this level of understanding, nothing in fact prohibits a limitless generalization of the use of the fundamental concepts which characterize this level. Everything, including the allegedly free will, can be seen as a structural problem resolved by life. Undoubtedly, the prototype of organic structure is found in the system of balance and regulation which in no way involves the will and in which, we can say at least approximately, the structuring power of life is completely self-sufficient. I need do nothing voluntarily to assure normal balance of calcium: this autonomy of life consists here in the maintaining of internal bonds of the organism, certain exchanges with the

76. Concerning the teleology of fact, cf. Lucien Cuenot, *Invention et finalité en biologie* (Paris, 1941), chap. 1; E. Goblot, "La Finalité en biologie," *Rev. phil.* (Oct., 1903); A. Burloud, *Principes d'une psychologie des tendences,* pp. 224–64; H. Vernet, *Le Problème de la vie,* pp. 47–125; L. Bournoure, *L'Autonomie de l'être vivant* (Paris, 1949), *passim* and esp. pp. 201–2.

environment being presupposed. But we can consider the whole of the relations of the organism with its environment as a structural problem whose balance will be constantly redefined and in process. And since psychic life enters the picture on the occasion of so-called relational activity, it is always possible to include psychology of conduct within a vast structural problematic, to bring the balance between the organism and its geographic environment into a total structural system.

This extension of biological interpretation is even more legitimate since the external adaptation of reaction to stimulation (and even of stimulation to reaction, to the extent to which the organism reacts to its own conditions to suit them to its own action) is finally organically governed. This precisely is the principal significance of the nervous system and, to a certain extent, of the hormone system: to harmonize the terminus of *all* centripetal stimulations and the starting point of *all* the centrifugal actions and reactions within the living being. In one sense, everything takes place within the living being, both intraorganic balance and adaptation to environment.[77]

3. My Life as Task and as a Resolved Problem

THERE IS LITTLE point in recalling the general reasons which must lead us back to a doctrine of pure subjectivity and assure us of being that which says "I." On the other hand it is important to lay out before consciousness the particular reasons which can put us on guard against the ultimate power of fascination issuing from the idea of system.

Why does the order of life, assiduously observed, invite us so strongly to alienation in the object? Let us go back to that factual purposiveness which characterizes functional explanations: it is not without reason that mechanistic biologists have been critical of its psychological overtones. Yet this analogy of organic purposiveness and man's intentional activity which attracts biology to anthropomorphism also draws consciousness into the vertigo of objectivity. This curious effect of contamination in two directions deserves consideration, for on the one hand it makes purposiveness suspect for the biologist; on the other hand—and that is what interests us here—it lies at the origin of the reversal of viewpoint at the end of which the will is reduced to a forward

77. This harmony between internal equilibria (completely alien to the will) and motor adaptation (in part subject to the will) would come up physiologically in the neuro-humoral connections which are as if the intersections of vegetative and relational life. R. Collin, *Les Hormones* (Paris, 1944), pp. 299–331.

movement of the system. If, in fact, we compare invention and purposiveness in biology with human invention and purposiveness, it will necessarily seem astonishing: compared with the difficult progress of human construction, organic growth is stupifying. While man makes tools from without by addition of parts, life builds up its organisms from within through a guided growth. Everything takes place as if an unself-conscious though infinitely more clear-sighted and infinitely more powerful intelligence governed matter. This "as if" has to be bracketed by the biologist who forces himself, albeit with difficulty, to elaborate a scientific description of structure. It remains as a faint glow around scientific concepts.[78] And man, more than the scientist, gets away from this thought with difficulty: if life does what it does voluntarily, there ought to be a will quite unlike ours, in a word, "demiurgic." This is the beginning of our astonishment, our fascination, and of the temptation to annex the works of which the will has charge gradually to the structuring power of life. In effect, it is extraordinary that life functions in me without me, that the multiple hormone balances which science reveals constantly reestablish themselves within me without my help. This is extraordinary because at a certain level of my existence I no longer appear to myself as a *task*, as a project. I am a *problem resolved* as though by a greater wisdom than myself. This wisdom is a nourishing one: when I have eaten, it is not up to me to make the food into myself and grow on it. It is a wisdom of movement: the circulation of my blood and the beating of my heart do not depend on me. To be sure, life in me is not always such a benevolent, protective power. In sickness I fear it as a sly power which saps my strength and draws out my existence, but even then it presents itself as a power of reparation, of compensation and healing. The marvelous spectacle of healing, sleep, and convalescence confound my will with its feeble means and its meager patience. Life builds life—the will only constructs things. The spectacle of life always humbles the will. And so I take to dreaming of an existence—which would perhaps be an animal existence—"where there would be no more problems," no more tasks, no more responsibility, no more freedom. I picture the animal as a problem resolved by life. This is what we usually call instinct, but I am no longer an instinctive being. I might well dream of an animal

78. It is not an accident that Cuenot draws his most striking examples of biological invention and teleology from consideration of *organs* which resemble *tools* (saw, pliers, pushbutton, etc.). But organs which do not resemble tools pose the problem of adaptation perhaps more radically still, as the eye with respect to vision.

paradise which would free me from the weight of my humanity, but I can no longer revert to being an animal: I remain a task for myself.[79]

We have spoken of life in this scientifically suspect language intentionally. It had to be shown that the very source of the vertigo is in life as lived, in life in the first person. It is a strange thing, the more anthropomorphic life is, the more it invites me to deny myself as man. I have to awaken as freedom at the very heart of the subjective experience of "being-alive-myself."

Thus it is in a decision that I put the human dialectic "on its feet." In place of thinking of the subject in terms of the object and, in our particular case, of the will in terms of biological structure, I take as the center of perspective my existence as a *task* and as a project and I seek to place the partial and subordinate experience of my life as pure fact, as a *resolved problem*, in relation to this central experience.

On the path of this rediscovery of the meaning of my life, I reassure myself that the absolute involuntary is only the background of the involuntary which is relative to my needs and capacities. It is in the dialogue with my needs and capabilities that I perceive my life as that which is no longer either motive or organ for willing but the body which I move in its aspect as *the other*.

Let us press closer to the difficulty: life does not belong wholly to the necessary, to the absolute involuntary, it also belongs to the relative involuntary, docile to willing. In other words, the paradox is not only one of will and life in general, but also is already present at the core of my experience of my life. My life is ambiguous: it is at the same time a resolved problem, insofar as it is structure—*and* a problem to be solved, insofar as it is spontaneity of need, of habit, and emotion. It is the marvel of structure and a pressing appeal to the sovereignty of decision. I have nothing to do with the beating of my heart, and everything with nourishing, caring for, and guiding this body. Thus I constantly experience within myself the mixture of two involuntaries: the

79. A "poetics" of the will always finds the *myth* of the animal as the myth of innocence and freedom from care: "We're not at one," says Rilke in the Fourth Elegy, "we've no instinctive knowledge, like migratory birds." [Rainer Maria Rilke, *Duino Elegies*, trans. J. B. Leishman and Stephen Spender (London, 1948), pp. 48–49. © 1960, The Hogarth Press. Reprinted by permission of the publisher, New Directions Publishing Corporation.] The myth of the animal which "sees the open," of the birds who neither sow nor reap, the myth of the lilies of the field, the myth of the child to which we cannot literally return—all these myths are parables, similes, in which the presence of freedom points in symbols to a certain beyond-the-Self.

absolute involuntary of the life which gives me existence as consciousness—and thus is the *preface* to my humanity—*and* the involuntary relative to a life which seeks my decision and effort —and thus waits upon my humanity. There is the resolved *and* the unresolved. My life at the same time constitutes a part of those things which do not depend on me and of those which do depend on me. This is what the Stoics could never understand since they assigned the entire body to the realm of objects and expelled pleasure and pain, need and emotion, into the sphere of "things which depend on me." [80]

Thus my life is *ambiguous*. Only the apperception of the Cogito reveals this interweaving of the two experiences of my life as a task and as a resolved problem, the solidarity of the two involuntaries in which the necessity of being alive remains always the *other* with respect to the spontaneity which I control. When I suspend the relation of my structure to my responsibility, when I forget myself as task and contemplate in myself a simple epiphenomenon of the fact of vital structure, I abolish my own subjectivity in an objectively encountered and known biological order.

4. Structure as an Index of the Absolute Involuntary: the Condition *Sine Qua Non*

THIS RELATION between the two meanings of my life is still only a vague feeling as ambiguous as the life it reveals. How can my life be that which grows by itself, sustains and repairs itself, and *at the same time* a question posed for my will? Before this confusion and this ambiguity I retrace my steps and ask, is what I know about structure purely and simply ejected from experience? Is clarity of knowledge excluded from the depth of feeling? Not at all: objective knowledge has to attempt to mediate the most obscure anticipations of affective experience until it encounters an obstacle.

To be sure, I must give up harmonizing the subjective experience of willing and the objective knowledge of structure in a coherent knowledge. I have to give up harmonizing in a single universe of discourse the concepts of Cogito and those of biology,

80. In the direction of effort we have discovered one of the delicate junctions between an order which depends on me (movement) and an order which does not (structure). We have spoken in this respect of the "emergence" of practical consciousness of acting in relation to organic structure, and of the "immergence" of effort in structure. In a similar vein, see Pradines, *Traité de psychologie générale*, I, 76.

which belong to two incommensurate universes of discourse. Only within the Cogito are willing, the relative involuntary, and the absolutely involuntary mysteriously harmonized, but this mysterious pact cannot be expressed directly.

Yet it remains possible to give to objective, constraining knowledge the secondary function of an index or *signum* expressing the subordinate place of life in the building of consciousness. Just as we have formulated concepts of finite manner (character) and indefinite matter (the unconscious), so we shall now elaborate the concept of *conditio sine qua non. We shall say that life is the condition* sine qua non *of will and of consciousness in general.*

The most remarkable illustration we could give of this "conditioning" of the will by structure can be derived from the facts of *integration* and *subordination* which characterize cerebral activity and more generally nervous activity. Nervous structures, we know, present a functional hierarchy such that lower level systems are incorporated into higher level systems. This subordination presents at the same time some aspects of inhibition, as Hughlings Jackson showed some time ago in his studies of the phenomena of "functional liberation." This subordination emphasizes the accession of the telencephalic to the summit of the nervous hierarchy. Should we say that this *telencephalization* by which cerebral centers are subordinated to the most rudimentary nervous activity explains the will? We could in effect say so, if throughout we understand by the will an objective aspect of behavior which is characterized by integration of reflective and instinctive conduct in a *purposive behavior* representing "ideation" and "invention." [81]

But if the explanation which links behavior to a nervous structure is relatively homogeneous, it is at the cost of a reduction of the will to its objective concepts of behavior, grafted, in addition, underhandedly to a phenomenology of the subject (I and thou). Perhaps we will have to add that this relation among nervous structures and those of behavior is less a causal one in the sense of constant succession than an *isomorphic* one.[82]

But if we keep to the descriptive givens of practical consciousness in their authenticity, we have to attribute to this isomorphism the significance of that diagnostic relation which we have constantly encountered between objective concepts of psychology and the living experience of a subject. More exactly, physiological

81. Tolman, *Purposive Behavior* ... , chaps. XIII and XIV.
82. Cf. above, p. 216.

structure performs a diagnostic function for the absolute involuntary of life (which itself stands in a relation of immergence and emergence with conscious action). In capsule form, we can say that such structures are the condition *sine qua non* of will and consciousness. But this abbreviated expression condenses a double relation: a diagnostic relation between objective knowledge of life and subjective experience of being alive, and an intra-subjective relation of immergence of willing in living. We can speak of a conditioning of the will by nervous structure, by telencephalization of this structure, only with these reservations.[83]

Thus we must not have any illusions about the pure objective significance of the concept of condition *sine qua non*. Literally it expresses a form of partial causality, or, if we wish, of limited causality. It seems to indicate that a different causality, a psychic causality, is combined with organic causality. Now by right there is no reason in principle, within the plan of structure, for not including a total explanation of man in it. For while purposiveness is only one aspect of causality itself and cannot be understood as the directed posture of causal series or rather of a multitude of causal series, the generalization of organic purposiveness to the human totality is in the last resort only a generalization of causality itself. Yet as we have said on several occasions, causality and the determinism which is the rule of its intelligibility cannot be partial; they can only claim to embrace the totality of phenomena.

Thus the totalitarian claim of explanation by structure can be limited by a sort of reverse impact of phenomenology on biology. The concept of condition *sine qua non* expresses only this *limitation*. We shall say that the laws of structure do not explain the *whole* man because I discover *my* life as a part of myself by a method different than biology or Gestalt psychology which generalizes the laws of structure. The laws of structure are an index of that experience of my life as the absolute involuntary: yet this experience always remains a subordinated, entailed experience. It is the *total* experience of the Cogito which declares the experience of necessity partial.

We can see that this concept of condition *sine qua non* introduces some *intelligibility* into the experience of necessity. It makes science of structure an external diagnostic, objectively revealing one isolated moment which in the Cogito has no autonomy. Since this relation is separated, since the knowledge of life loses its function as an index, and at the same time nothing

83. For an example of such ambiguous language, justifiable only as an abbreviation, see J. Boutonier, *Les Défaillances de la volonté* (Paris, 1945), pp. 27–29.

warns us any more that man is more than his life, the pretentions of biology to total explanation have no counterweight. Thus the concept of condition *sine qua non* is not purely objective. It is what we call an index. It can be only the indirect language of an extrasystematic relation which is no longer a category of objectivity, namely the *pact* of freedom with factual existence.

5. A Note about Cosmology

Is IT POSSIBLE to go further than this fragile relationship of a *signum* between the objectivity of biology and the subjectivity of absolute involuntary? Is it possible to stabilize the relationship between life and will in an ontology of degrees of being? This has been attempted periodically in the grand classical cosmologies whose secret Ravaisson tried to rediscover in his turn.

The principle of cosmologies is to articulate the world in a hierarchy of levels or degrees of being in which the human order is linked to the vital order depending on it, in a double relation of dependence and emergence. They attempt at the same time to give meaning to the differences among levels of reality and to their continuity. Life and consciousness are ordered in a ladder of causalities which are one and diverse as a preparation and a completion. What we have said metaphorically above here takes on a rational meaning: the image of foundation becomes the concept of the ground in a hierarchic view of the universe in which life is the ground of consciousness while consciousness is the perfection of life.

The question we pose for such cosmologies is this: does there exist a universe of discourse which would be "neutral" with respect to objectivity and subjectivity? This would mean a universe of discourse which would be something other than a purely formal concept of being in the sense of object in general (understanding here by the object in general whatever can be thought with all its formal significations: quantity, whole and part, property, state of things, etc.).[84] Does there exist a material ontology common to the region of nature—known by external perception and objective natural sciences—and to the region of consciousness known by reflection and by phenomeology of the subject?

To this ultimate question we believe we have to answer *negatively, at least provisionally.* We do not believe that there exist actually thought concepts which would unite nature and Cogito in one homogeneous hierarchy. We believe, on the contrary, that

84. Husserl, *Ideas,* § 13.

the "models" in which some thinkers claim to articulate, for example, biology and phenomenology (that is, objectively considered structure and subjectively experienced freedom) can only *alter* the purity of the one and the other, and *mask* the fundamental hiatus which separates the Cogito from objective nature. It is always a demi-subjective biology which is thus integrated with cosmology; an animistic or vitalistic mythology is always the price paid for this type of harmonization. The example Maine de Biran and the "hyperorganic force" is an eloquent warning in this respect. Biology progresses only by not letting such cosmological implications drift into its autonomous structural concepts. Inversely, it is always a demi-objectivized psychology which is thus superimposed on such biology. There are, of course, concepts of subjectivity, and subjectivity is always thinkable up to a point, but such concepts must always be "integral" concepts (intentionality, perception, imagination, willing, need, etc.), proportionate concepts, that is, proportionate to the apperception of the subject by himself and the apperception of the other subject. Once we "place the subject into nature," his quality of subjectivity is obliterated. Subjects and objects do not fit together: nature as a totality of objects and subjects is a contradictory idea.

This does not mean that knowledge of nature and of the subject are completely unrelated. The subject, insofar as incarnate, is precisely nature in the first person: personality, unconscious, and life. I can say that it is the *same* life which is experienced as the absolute involuntary in the *total* Cogito and which is known objectively as structure. This identity of the same life known in two ways as object among objects and as part of a subject makes it possible to institute the only relation which, provisionally, seems to us compatible with the discontinuity of the universes of discourse: the relation of the *signum* or diagnostic.

Thus I might well speak the language of cosmology, but on the condition of not being deceived by its false homogeneity. Projecting knowledge of nature into the knowledge which I have of myself, I might well say that I am the living hierarchy of being: mineral, vegetable, animal, and human. I sum up the degrees of nature. But I cannot show the degrees of nature and conceive of these realities as constructed one on the other unless I can descend within myself along the degrees of existence from my freedom which extends from the absolute involuntary to the confines of an existence which would be the *analogon* of animal existence. It is this descent into the kingdom of shadows which is the implicit justification of a cosmology. That is the grand intuition of

Ravaisson's chief work, *De l'habitude* and his famous *Rapport*. It reminds us that a cosmology is always ambiguous, at the meeting of two systems of concepts.

Does this mean that cosmology has no other significance? We do not mean to deny it. A different unity might exist between the subjectivity of willing and life and the objectivity of natural knowledge. The unity of *creation* might bring together all the forms of being beyond all fragmenting knowledge. A unity of creation might be discovered by an entirely different dimension of consciousness than that which proceeds to "regional eidetics" of the Cogito and of nature. I, too, am a reader of ciphers, as Jaspers puts it. It is not accidental that a unity of inspiration animates the great medieval cosmologies: it is a unique desire which starts with God and returns to God through all the degrees of being. This unity, lost as knowledge, must be rediscovered in some other way in the "poetics" of the will. But, in the eyes of sober eidetics, the pretension of cosmology is something quite different.

[4] LIFE: GROWTH AND GENESIS

TO BRING OUT the structured character of life it is enough to carve out an instantaneous segment in the development of the living: in each instant life *tends* towards equilibrium and adaptation. Consideration of process introduces a new dimension which is itself a dimension of life. My life is temporality: birth, growth, aging; adolescence and senescence, to put it more strongly.

Yet this growth is not my work. I experience it as sheer fact, as a dimension of brute existence. This sheer fact of growth poses difficult problems for a philosophy of the will.

1. Essence and Genesis

IN EFFECT there seems to be a contradiction between a *description* of the will which regards it as an *essence,* that is, as in some sense underivable or even non-temporal meaning of man, and an *explanation* of the will which shows its *genesis* as a function in the growth of the body.

Let us push this seemingly disastrous contradiction to the end, in order to derive from it the living paradox which must lead us to the limits of a new experience of that necessity which clings to our freedom.

Eidetics would seem to exclude the possibility that the will could have, or better, could be a history. It describes an essence. The "I will" is an essence—an integrating essence, we can say. Emotion, habits, etc. are subordinate essences. The will does not become, it is; it does not begin since the meaning of a function, the meaning which makes man comprehensible, man's intelligibility, is not at the mercy of time. The order of understanding is not a temporal order. Not only are reason and will not derived from something other, not only are they primary and make subordinate powers comprehensible by giving them the seal of unity and totality, but they neither wax nor wane. Eidetics excludes history. We might actually be tempted to draw these conclusions from our effort at elaborating the *meaning* of the will.

On the other hand a genetic psychology seems to exclude the possibility of doing a phenomenology of the will. The will is not —it becomes. In effect we could show concretely that in the first place the involuntary does have a history: new tastes develop in succession just as others disappear. William James has given what has become the classical description of this birth and death of instincts. And our capabilities change with our tastes: psychology of habit gave us some idea of that history of our capabilities with which, for one part, the "image of our body" is identified. But most of all we cannot assume that such a history would only be a history of our body, a history of the involuntary, as if each age posed a new question to an internal arbiter who himself would have the privilege of escaping from process. The will grows, matures, becomes senile. Just as I as a whole am living, so I as a whole am history. Thus it is not possible to speak in general of what "man" is: we can speak only of the ages of man, elaborating a psychology of childhood, of adolescence, of maturity, and of old age. The partiality of each age can similarly be compared with the partiality of each character type. Each age is defined by a privileged cluster of motives and capacities and by a manner of willing: there is a childish will, an adolescent will, etc.

Thus it is tempting to accuse an eidetics of emphasizing and preferring one moment of this evolution, specifically maturity, orienting the psychology of each age by a reference to this form which it has made normative. Eidetics would represent only the psychology of the adult, that is, description of a kind of psychological peak placed roughly between the two phases of integration and regression, *being* adult placed between *becoming* an adult (or adolescence) and *becoming* old (or senescence). However, for a psychology which would take each age seriously, just as personality types, this particular movement has no greater value than the others, and all ages, such as they *are,* deserve equally to be studied and recognized according to their own proper structure.

As we enlarge the perspectives of genetic psychology to the dimension of an evolutionism, we shall bring out the fact that eidetics tends not only to make the adult normative, but also to isolate him in the history of life as a discontinuous essence, that is, as a signification separated by a hiatus from the animal signification focused on instinct. The force of genetic explanation on the other hand lies in the fact that it resolves discontinuities into continuous development. The child becomes an adult and, perhaps, animal becomes man. It is the continuity of stages of development which gives intelligibility to the passage from the bounds of animality to humanity, and from the bounds of childhood to adult humanity.

The function of history is in effect to fill in the intervals which seem unbridgeable to eidetics. What cannot be engendered intemporally can be engendered in time. Thus the implicit philosophy of all *genetistic* interpretations of man seems to be to reject any allegedly *ingenerable* entity and to derive, thanks to time, the higher from the lower. This rejection of irreducibles, of discontinuities, in its extreme form implies a rejection of essences. There is no essence of reason or freedom because an essence would be timeless. Yet everything becomes; there is nothing which is not derived from something simpler. Thus genesis is the temporal line from the simple to the complex. This at least is how Spencer understood it, but Spencer undoubtedly only gave a systematic form to a conception of becoming which comes naturally to understanding. All genesis is a form of reduction of the higher to the lower. Understanding develops in time what it first reduces and flattens out in a single stroke of mind. A genetistic explanation is an effort to dispense with the "leap" in the doctrine of man. Thus in contrast with eidetics which claims to *understand* the lower in terms of the higher, genetic psychology *explains historically,* the highest in terms of the lowest. Reason and will, which are primary for a description of *meanings,* are secondary for a *history.* The alleged human *being* is only a moment in human *becoming* from birth to death. A meaning is built up and lost. Only what becomes, is. Here we can see a new devouring objectivity being constituted, an objectivity of genesis or evolution. I lose myself in my own growth which makes and unmakes me. I have no basic meaning, I am only a history, or, better, *there is* a history which I call "I," and which immediately has a structure which engulfs the "I" as one of its subordinate sectors.

This uneasiness must be dispelled if we wish to catch a glimpse of the possible significance of the absolute involuntary of organic time, of that *necessity of growth* which clings to the being which I am as freedom. In order not to become lost in an altogether abstract dialectic we shall base our analysis on some examples drawn from a comparison of adolescence with adulthood.

2. Psychology of Ages

CAN PSYCHOLOGY OF AGES basically avoid orienting itself by referring to some definite *meaning* of man? It would not seem so. There is an unacknowledged phenomenology behind the evaluation of different ages. Thus psychology of adolescence spontaneously assigns a place to this age—which it considers in relation to maturity—to the extent to which maturity represents an approximation, approaches a fulfillment of a definite *meaning of man* which frequently remains implicit in the interpretation. (We shall presently see precisely that maturity does not exhaust the meaning of man who in turn judges it and depreciates it in contrast with some traits which constitute the pride of other ages.)

Adolescence strives towards the *equilibrium* of maturity. It is with respect to this equilibrium that, for instance, the exaltation of the self on part of some adolescents is described as a "crisis," as the "crisis of juvenile originality." [85] When Maurice Debesse studies the "structure of the crisis," which he first describes at length and relates to the formation of personality,[86] he emphasizes factors of "organic discord" [87] and "social misadaptation" [88] at the source of the exalted affirmation of the I which characterizes the crisis. He distinguishes this crisis from pathological constitutions in terms of its capacity for preparing, among other traits, a new adjustment to reality and to social environment. A certain idea of man is presupposed, namely, that consciousness of the self is the factor which integrates all tendencies, that objectivity applies it to the ferment of subjectivity and that adaptation to environment and social tasks follows mistakes, revolt, etc. This is the idea of

85. M. Debesse, *La Crise d'originalité juvenile* (Paris, 1941).
86. *Ibid.*, pp. 210–85.
87. *Ibid.*, p. 210.
88. *Ibid.*, p. 217. Speaking of the overestimation of themselves on the part of the adolescents he had studied, Debesse notes, "There is as yet only an imperfectly ordered structure of an 'I' badly adhering to reality" (p. 131).

man which we encounter again in the ideal of adaptation in which the behaviorists see the criterion of the complete man, or in Janet's conception of "reality function."

It is not surprising that this idea of man should be based on a normative conception of human evolution derived from Comte's law of three stages. Man is positive man. Such views are really abbreviated in many respects, to the extent that the criteria of output and socialization reduce man to a functional normality of a biological or social order. Nonetheless they contain an element of phenomenological truth. Even the behaviorist criterion of adaptation or Janet's reality function are genuine aspects of what appeared to us to be the central criterion of man, namely, the control of the voluntary over the involuntary, conceived as a harmony and reconciliation of willing and the body. This meaning of man thus includes both the subjective *feeling* of an internal unity as well as the *functional* criterion of adaptation. It is always a question of integration and mastery, external or internal. Without such presuppositions, it would be hard to see what right a psychologist would have to say that in becoming an adult the adolescent becomes a *man*,[89] unless it is because he in his turn falls prey to the prejudices of the adult associated with the concept of man. To the extent—and only to the extent—to which maturity is normative, it is maturity which has itself to serve as a point of orientation for a concept of man which conceives of the will as the one integrating the many.

But it is precisely phenomenology which does not purely and simply make the preferences of the adult age normative. There is still the implicit phenomenology which allows us in some respects to give precedence to other ages over maturity: thus the ancients honored, in old age, prudence and counsel in which they saw a good which man can attain only in his declining years. Similarly a balanced psychology of adolescence is led to recognize in it a stage which "has its own perfection"[90] that cannot be recaptured in a later age. This precious ambiguity in the evaluation of adolescence can only be protected by the acute awareness that while in principle the adult age offers the greatest biological opportunity of reaching a human equilibrium, in terms of other traits it is itself defective: something of a man is lost with adolescence. Undoubtedly a certain aggressive non-conformism, an arrogance and a skittish susceptibility, a certain overestimation of the self made up of complaisance and anxiety, might later

89. *Ibid.*, p. 156.
90. *Ibid.*, p. 259.

appear ridiculous to a young man past adolescence. But is that sense of uniqueness, of solitude, of a desire for purity and the absolute, the capacity for wonder and awe, the very energy and avidity which we normally attribute to youth not a human good which the experienced, practical, slightly blasé adult lets wither away? [91] Yes, maturity is in some respects atrophy. Joubert writes, in the fine passage quoted by M. Debesse, "In our youth there is often in us something better than we ourselves—our desires, our pleasures, our consents, our approbations." [92] This quotation brings us back to the fear, expressed above, lest we reduce man to the criteria of productivity and functioning which already represent the adult atrophy of man.

Each age is in its way a peak: happy adolescence which has not accommodated itself to reality, and for which the world still holds the power of amazing, for which it is not yet true that "the desire for adaptation leads to being a self"! [93]

Thus on the one hand psychology of ages is guided by an anticipation of man's broader possibilities, and this anticipation helps it evaluate ages in terms of the *opportunities* which each offers for realizing a certain aspect of humanity. On the other hand, psychology of ages reveals those multiple aspects and makes it possible to respect the fullness of humanity which none of the ages exhausts.

These observations, drawn from a comparison of adolescence and adulthood, bring us close to our point: there is no opposition, we believe, between a genetic psychology pertaining to a *history* of structure and a *descriptive* phenomenology pertaining to the *meaning* of human structures. For if the object of psychology were completely fluid, psychology could not even speak of *man*. Only stable significations can serve as references for history. Thus we shall refrain from making genetic explanation into a dogma which would exclude other forms of understanding. Already Leibniz, with respect to another problem, that of innate ideas, attempted to hold together what is called innatism of faculties (and even of ideas) and a certain empiricism according to which all experience is acquired. We are proposing to maintain a similar paradox: the paradox of a *genesis* which derives all the culminating forms of man from something lower than they, and

91. Debesse often attributes certain genuine philosophical values to adolescent mentality. (*Ibid.*, pp. 122, 139, 140, 144, 232–36.) There is in it that "extraordinary will" which Delacroix contrasted with "daily will" and which permits possibility of self-creation to subsist alongside habit.

92. Joseph Joubert, *Pensées*, II, 87, cited by Debesse, *ibid.*, p. 140.

93. Debesse, *ibid.*, p. 160.

an eidetics which describes the *meaning* which is made actual in this history.

It is, I believe, this paradox which we anticipate each time we say that humanity is nothing other than itself but that it awakens, that it *develops*. For man can only become what he is. But in turn he can *be* only within the conditions of time which reveal him bit by bit. In respecting this paradox we keep genetic psychology from reducing the higher to the lower. Far from deriving the highest from the lowest, it reaches, in the development from the infant to the man, the progressive revelation of man who in himself is ingenerable. There is an infant freedom, as there is an infant fate, in the words of Giradoux' mischievous Eumenides. The meaning of man is "historialized" in growth.[94] It does not rest solely in maturity, but is always in some respect a possibility for every age. Man grows, but it is his being which becomes manifest in the appearance of his becoming: man *advenit:* man comes about.

Thus the idea of development appears as a fundamental concept of genetics which does not reduce the higher to the lower but which shows the progressive realization of a meaning. This meaning is nothing extratemporal, it is, rather, something that *comes about* in the great *events* of growth.

3. Age as Fate

THUS MAN IS SITUATED by his age. Age is one of the modes of that constitutive construction which we have summed up in the general term necessity. This means two things:

On the one hand my age at a given moment is fully comparable to the lasting particularity of my character: only it is a particularity in the course of evolution, a particularity which makes me kin to individuals of my generation rather than those of my character type. We can say about it what we have said about the finite manner of character: nothing human is foreign to me, but the fate of my age is to encounter all the motives of my decisions and all the capabilities of my action in terms of the profile which my age chooses, in a choice which is in a way given and foreign to my choice. I will what I will in an adolescent, adult, or old age style, and this style is the invincible limitation of my power of freedom. Age is a fate like character; as the latter, it is not only a proscription which excludes me from this or that

94. Relating "historialization" of the subject to the "historialization" of his values in good and finally in motives, see p. 55.

form of life, but also an opportunity: every age orients itself in a given direction and opens the scope of values and capacities from one definite angle. The field of an unlimited freedom opens only within these finite bounds.

But my age at this moment is a privileged instant in the sweep of life. It represents the initial derivation from my growth in life. The specific experience which we have to isolate here is the same as what we indicate with the words growth and aging. To be sure, I do not see this process as a block: any panoramic view of it is a spatial projection and thus a substitute. But I have the experience of being borne by life in an invincible way which is properly the experience of organic time. I see multiple traits in that vague experience of growing and aging. I notice in the first place the ascending or descending direction of this "impetus" of life: I shall frequently refer to it as the second consequence of my age in terms of which I mount towards or descend from a peak. This experience is, however, rather complex: while in overall terms the movement towards maturity is the grand ascent of my existence, every age, as we have said, is a relative "peak" in some respects. Every age is an ascent towards a horizon of values and power which finds its perfection in it. But in relation to these relative peaks, the summit of maturity is the absolute peak and life is the inexorable ascending movement towards maturity and descent towards old age. I notice also another trait of that "impetus" from childhood to old age: its rhythm, or better, its "tempo." There is nothing absurd in saying that life does not move at the same speed in all ages [95]—unless in the words or in relation to physical concepts of speed and acceleration. This rhythm makes me particularly attentive to the inexorable character of time which I undergo simply because I live.

In this sense I shall say concerning organic time what consideration of structure led me to say concerning life in general: time is both a resolved problem and a task. On the one hand, it is a "passion of the soul": consciousness no more engenders its temporal "impetus," its ascent, its descent, or its "tempo" than it engenders the order and equilibrium which support it in space. It lasts as long as consciousness lives, in spite of it. And yet, on the other hand, this process advances through a decision: it is a dimension of my projects which put memories behind. This is really true: in certain respects the thrust of freedom consti-

95. Lecomte du Nouy, *Le Temps et la vie* (Paris, 1936), diagnoses this confused experience of subjective speed of organic time in terms of objective speed of formation of scar tissues.

tutes process, but the thrust of the organic involuntary at the same time presents me with process as the fundamental situation of my freedom.[96]

That is the absolute involuntary of growth: being alive entails the relentless abduction of organic time. But this vague experience requires mediation, and it is here that a genetic psychology lends us its basic concepts, first of all the concept of *development*. The laws of development are the objective index of that experience of growth and aging which I bear at the heart of my freedom.

[5] LIFE: BIRTH

PHILOSOPHERS DO NOT commonly concern themselves with birth. Death is more pathetic; the worst threats seem to come from before us, and our birth, because it is accomplished, does not threaten us. But it is precisely because it is accomplished that it holds the germ of the full growth of the necessity which casts a shadow on my freedom. Unfortunately the reflection for which it calls is almost impossible: the word birth evokes a collection of confused ideas none of which correspond to a subjective experience and which seem susceptible only to a scientific elucidation.

1) My birth is the beginning of my life: in it I was placed, once and for all, into the world, and posed in being before I was able to posit any act voluntarily. Yet this central event to which I refer in dating all the events of my life leaves no memory. I am always *after* my birth—in a sense analogous to that of being always *before* my death. I find myself alive—I am already born. Furthermore, nothing shows me that there had been a beginning of myself: my birth is precisely what remains hidden from my consciousness. I might well say that I am already alive, but not that I am after my birth, unless in terms of a knowledge of general laws of life external to me or in terms of the memories which those around me have of my entrance on the scene of existence. Thus I am initially called to leave behind the level of experience as I live it and place myself as a spectator over an objective event: the birth of a man.

2) My birth does not mean only the beginning of my life, but also expresses its dependence with respect to two other lives: I do not posit myself, I have been posited by others. Others have

96. Cf. p. 41.

willed this brute existence which I have not willed. What is worse, they did not exactly will it, since I know very well that a responsibility was undertaken which is never measured because it functions in the region of possibilities impossible to calculate—a monstrous collusion of chance, instinct, and another's freedom cast me up on this shore. Yet how do I experience my sonship? It was abolished materially on the day of my birth, and I abolish it more surely still in each act of consciousness. Is it not therefore more certain to look for a point of view external to the individuals from which I could grasp their connection? The same consciousness which abolishes the more or less umbilical relation of beings to each other at the same time creates the perspective on life which makes possible a scientific linking, a truly rational relation in terms of causality.

3) A third consideration will steer us still more definitely towards an objective consideration of causes. I have not received only a beginning, but a nature, that is, the law of a growth, the structuring principle, an unconscious structure, and finally the form of a personality type. To be born means to receive from another the *capital of heredity*. An ancestor is like a donor; and I do not even know whether this legacy is not a mortgage. Here all the forms of necessity become entangled. Yet who knows about heredity if not the biologist?

A beginning of myself, a relation hidden from my consciousness, and an individual existence burdened by my ancestors all invite me to search for the obscure beginnings of the individual on biological grounds, by a study of the ovum and ontogenetic factors, then in terms of sexual cells and their encounter, finally and especially through an adoption of a higher level than that of the individual, the level of lineage or of the species in which all description of consciousness is extinguished: for, it seems, consciousness is an individual and not a species.

1. Objectification of My Birth

CAN I HAVE an objective equivalent of my birth? Not at all:

1) First of all I have to give up attributing an objective meaning to the idea of a beginning. Through a strange paradox, it is only for subjectivity that birth can be a beginning and not only connection: in effect it is only my subjectivity which makes me unique, and only a unique entity can be said to begin rather than merely continuing some other entity. Yet it is precisely sub-

jectivity which a beginning misses. For biology, on the other hand, birth is only an incident between the intra-uterine and external life of the same individual, while conception is only a union of two cells which themselves continue the life of germination. There is in no sense here a beginning in the radical sense in which "I" begin to be. The idea of a beginning which passing to the objective point of view was supposed to save disappears here already.

2) The idea of filiation, to which the idea of beginning becomes reduced, is in turn profoundly altered. What is it I wish to clarify? The feeling which, starting with myself understood as the center of an absolute perspective, extends my ancestry upward from me just as my descendants spread out downstream from me. Yet biology only clarifies this feeling by reversing the perspective: the center of perspective is the ancestor; I explain my filiation not as *my* ancestry, but as my ancestor's posterity. This observation, innocent at first glance, is of decisive importance. It implies that the explanation of my being will be *alienation.* I leave myself in order to place myself in a being outside my control, my ancestor, and follow out a chain of effects down to myself. Yet this chain of effects has the remarkable quality that it is exactly what Cournot means by chance, that is, not the chance of indeterminism, but chance defined as encounter of independent causal series. Thus I appear to myself as an effect of chance. Even if I know nothing about genetics, I will already be bothered by the idea that the one I am derives from two beings who, it would seem at first, could have been other and could have made me other. A knowledge of elementary determinations which preside at the formation of the embryo gives this doubt a positive basis and a certain monstrous massiveness: I am fascinated by the immense combination in which determinism takes the form of statistical determinism, alien to me since it places me in a causal sequence. Every statistical anticipation presupposes as sheer fact such antecedent introduction: two given parents, given reproductive cells with a particular chromatic structure, a given ovum chosen in the combinations in the course of the initial ovulation, particular sperm issuing from chromosomic reduction, and finally this sperm reaching the ovum in question. At the end of these considerations I myself shall appear as a possible combination out of a considerable number of combinations which did not come about. The spell of objectivity has become the spell of combinations. *Why is this possible combination me?* and why are these individuals bearing these genes my parents? Absurdity follows me into the very con-

fines of genetic rigor. On the descending trajectory of causality I am derived from the other, and discover that I could myself have been an other, an other as the other possible combinations are other. This is the alienation which I inflict on myself in genetics.[97]

3) This tie with my ancestor which alienates me at the same time places me on a level suited to a science of heredity. Once I speak in terms of genes it is the history of these genes, so precociously differentiated in ontogenesis, which alone interests me. The individual no longer comes into consideration except as the bearer of the seed, itself coming from a parental seed. Thus a new posture develops a consistency, the posture of the species. Through it the individual is basically servant of the species. The facile lyricism which follows from this is familiar enough: the flow of the species rolls on beneath me and I am only its fleeting manifestation on the surface. Yet such false pathos expresses well enough the type of spell which this change of level brings about. On this new level of necessity a self-sufficient reading of man becomes possible. It is possible to stay on this level once we have chosen it and to follow out a limitless explanation, just as it was possible on the level of the science of personality, of psychoanalysis, and of psycho-physiology. On this last level the same encroachment of objective necessity on the certitudes of subjectivity, that is, on the self-affirmation of freedom, can be consummated: I am an effect produced by my heredity. The ethological formula, explained first by unconscious complexes, then by the structure of the individual and finally by his history dissolves into a genetic formula whose microscopic chart it might some day be possible to construct and so explain its structure in a physico-chemical way. It is not even absurd to think that one day it will be as easy to know an individual's genetic formula as his character type, since it has a material, geometric and physico-chemical meaning. Hence the same unease which character typing engendered arises on another level: are consciousness, reason, and will contained in this formula? On the terrain chosen by the geneticist, we have undeniably to reply in the affirmative, since any harmony between subjective freedom and objective necessity is unthinkable: determinism is either total— or it is not at all.

97. Jean Rostand has expressed this theme of chance with a rare force and made it the basis of his sober, clear pessimism. [*Pensées d'un biologiste* (Paris, 1954), pp. 16, 27, 72, 82.]

2. Philosophical Consideration of My Birth

BIOLOGY, without the compensation of a apperception of the Cogito, alienates me. And yet the study of genetics must become a guide in my consideration of myself: in effect the experience of existing, included confusedly in the "I," seems to contain no subjective assurance of birth whose objective equivalent a science of heredity would be. At least we have given up hope of finding it directly. Hence it is possible that this objective consideration of my birth will clarify aspects which so far have been too obscure for the Cogito. I must at the same time break through the nascent dogmatism which follows from genetics and convert genetics philosophically into an index of my birth.

But, we shall object at the start, there is no experience of my birth. To be sure. But if the idea of heredity is to have a subjective meaning, the ultimate level of necessity must be characterized for the consciousness which is subject to it as a limit level, as a point of necessity which we always approach and never reach. Thus here is the theme which we shall attempt to elucidate at least faintly: my birth in the first person is not an experience but the necessary presupposition of all experience. This necessity of being born in order to exist remains a horizon of consciousness but it is demanded as a horizon by consciousness itself. The Cogito implies the anteriority of its beginning apart from its own perception. How shall we engender this sense of beginning as limit in the womb of consciousness, failing a memory of my birth? There is no other means than to follow the objective scientific knowledge which constitutes our knowledge of birth, and to attempt to apply it to ourselves, to interiorize it in some way. This effort at the limits of possibility of objective knowledge is in a sense an obstacle to knowledge, but as that knowledge vanishes, something will be suggested as necessity in the first person of *my* beginning.

One initial observation will indicate the order of our endeavor: scientifically the chief idea is not one of beginning but of heredity: it is explanation of myself in terms of another. Philosophically the central idea is most obscure, it is that of beginning, since heredity is finally only one aspect of *my* beginning. Thus our reflection must follow a reverse direction from that of objectification and move up from the secondary to the principal idea. And not only the order must be reversed, but also each of the three moments examined represents itself a reversal of perspective, since I have to understand in myself what I had explained in terms of the other.

1) What does my heredity mean for me? The geneticist in me says that existence is capital received from the other and that this capital is a collection of genetic properties inscribed in a chromosomic structure; thus this capital is a diversity which, while possessing some functional unity, remains fundamentally multiple. The philosopher in me translates this: this multiple capital is the indivisible unity of my life, of my sheer existence; this capital received from the other is not the burden of an external nature, it is my self given to myself. This moment of deliverance is a decree which is not unknown to us. It is this that breaks the spell of character and of the unconscious. I have first of all to conceive of heredity as in me, and I have to conceive of it as the idea of my character and my unconscious more than anything else. My heredity is my character and my unconscious received from another, that is, *my* character and *my* unconscious plus a representation of my ancestor. I can say therefore that philosophy is always a return to the level of intuition and the regression from combinations to the unity and identity of the self. I am not another among others, I am myself, receiving and doing myself. I must constantly repeat that my heredity is only my character externalized, that is, the finite mode of my freedom alienated in the ancestor. I must furthermore say that my heredity is my unconscious externalized; the shadow of my ancestor only persecutes me as the shadow of myself which psychoanalytic doctrine leads me to make think in my place. A mythology similar to that of the unconscious can be derived from a poor use of genetics. Against such conjuring, I must decide that I form no thought except by the power of thinking—of willing thought—which is the Cogito itself. The ancestor whose gesture or thought I repeat no longer exists as ancestor: he is founded on the most unformed level where the voluntary consciousness feeds. It is I who think. Heredity is at the same time the finite mode and indefinite matter of freedom—plus the idea of an ancestor.

2) I still must conquer in myself the specific force of the idea of heredity: the idea of the ancestor. It is here that the philosopher, turning inward, must try to conceive of the filiation of individual consciousness which gives the beginning, birth, its special meaning: to be born means to be engendered. Self-consciousness seemed to us to abolish this dependence, while objective knowledge of heredity conceals it by explaining it:

biology makes my ancestor the foundation of my existence. Filiation conceived according to a descending causality makes me an effect, a tributary to a causal chain. Even as geometry is born through the abstraction of the center of perspective from the body, so genetics adopts a point of departure and follows the series of growth by starting from that arbitrary starting point. But I alone am my own center of existence from which I illuminate what is behind me as well as what is ahead of me. Now the Cogito demands that I should understand this necessity in myself. It is I who have come from . . . , and not the ancestor who is the cause of. . . . It is because I am myself that I can speak of my parents; would have to leave this absolute presence of my body to myself in order to illuminate its presence in all my ancestry. The ancestor is in a sense my *subjective* anterior and my self is his subjective descendant. But the expression, "born of . . . ," expresses an original bond, beyond causality, an adherence which I can clarify and bring to life with any precision only as I think of it as objective descent, as posteriority in a descending order. Thus I discover that this foggy consciousness of being suspended from other beings and of owing my being to them, this consciousness of my attachments is not entirely overcome by the act which institutes the autonomy of consciousness. There sleeps within me an umbilical consciousness which biology can reveal at the cost of its own effacement and of the inversion of its rule of thought. It is in my child-soul that I retain the mark of this dependence and quasi-corporeal adherence. For clear consciousness this childhood is nothing but an obscure infra-structure out of which consciousness arises and from which it becomes distinct. Descartes in the theoretical part of his philosophy taught us to reject our childhood as the source of all false fascinations—those of the senses, of custom, and of passions. This is a strong position. However, the philosopher should not suspect childhood. Childhood is not only puerile. This does not mean being unfaithful to the Descartes of the *Treatise on Passions* but rather to seek in it glimpses of the mystery of unity of soul and body because the bond which binds me to my parents is only one aspect of the pact which I have made with my life and of which Descartes was not unaware. Being born of definite parents and being united to this definite body is one and the same mystery: these beings are my parents as my body is my body. Considered as a problem, this central mystery disappears into absurdity: it becomes the accident of my body. My infant-consciousness bears a scar which indicates at the same time the lesion of birth and the suture which binds me to my parents by a non-arbitrary bond. The family is the refuge, perpetuation, and consecration of that crepuscular consciousness of childhood. Perhaps the obscure imprint and tender nostalgia of this vital continuity are never erased from our affection for our mother. Freud is rather interesting in this respect when he shows, in our dreams and in our attitudes as waking men, something like a desire to return to the womb. This does not mean that the sleeping man or the unconscious have a better memory or remain children longer, but the unconscious, which bears the mark of oldest impressions, gives matter to our thought so that the waking man can free himself from its heavy, unformed nostalgia only by formulating, with the help of a decipherer of dreams, the idea of a return to the womb. That is a waking man's thought, but it is based on the byways of the unconscious. The un-knowledge of our unconscious which is an extension of our childhood represents a valuable testimony for the philosopher seeking roots and ways of approach. Perhaps we should add to this double testimony of childhood and the unconscious—and the unconscious is infantile—the very vivid impressions of paternity itself. It illuminates the feeling of filiation by a curious recurrence of feelings. In acting out the protective role of a father in relation to a child I renew in myself the assurance of having myself received being from my parents: filiality and paternity in effect form a unique bipolar relation which I anticipate in its totality when I approach it at one or the other extreme: thus sexuality, turned towards the part of my life yet to come, is also a retrospective evocation of my life so far. This affective recurrence takes place through that indetermination or surplus of desire which never exactly fits the determinate form in which it is posited. In one of the admirable *Duino Elegies* Rilke sang of "that hidden guilty river-god of the blood," the "Neptune within our blood" who, beyond the reassuring love of a mother opens in me a "surging abyss," I sense the "savage chaos" in me, "the primal forest," the "innumerable fermentation." [98] Thus it is that every history sums up a prehistory. But this prehistory is the very seat of the Cogito, concealed from its apperception. Thus heredity adds to the sense of *my*-life-*in*-me, the unease of *the*-life-*behind*-me-clinging-to-me. A special fear accompanies every descent into the abyss of consciousness. When Pelleas, pushed by a bothersome curiosity, forces his way into the nether regions of the castle, an acrid odor chokes him.

Fear of the self can always be born out of necessity. This

98. Rilke, The Third Elegy, *op. cit.*, pp. 40–41.

fear is the beginning of the fascination emanating from objectivity, for objectivity is only necessity detached from us and turned against us. It is this fear which we have already noticed coming from consideration of character and which became more insidious in the case of the unconscious, and which now acquires the limitless fullness of my prehistory. It is fear before my impotence, before the power of necessity which in some sense deprives me of all the initiative of consciousness. Consent can calm that fear by reconciling me to my roots.

3) The capital of heredity and the bond which binds me to myself are finally only two aspects of *my* beginning. In beginning as an "I," I participate in a lineage. My ancestry is another name for the beginning of my existence. It is really there that our study of necessity comes to an end. This beginning which escapes memory, which is not rationally conceivable, which biology hides in the succession of generations, this beginning must finally be suggested at the heart of consciousness as the fleeting limit beyond my oldest memories. At first sight it seems that I have to give up hope of finding in consciousness the least testimony to its birth. Even the most obscure consciousness finds me already alive. And yet this flight from my birth which escapes the hold of my memory is precisely the most characteristic trait of my experience—if we can call this lack of experience experience. This flight illuminates the nature of a living being such as I. I experience life as having begun *before* I began anything whatever. Anything I can decide comes after the beginning, and before the end. All beginning by freedom is paradoxically tied to a non-consciousness of the beginning of my existence itself. The word beginning, like the word existence, has a double meaning. There are beginnings which are always imminent, which is the beginning of freedom: it is my beginning as act. And there is a beginning which always precedes, the beginning of life: it is my beginning as a state. I am always in the process of beginning to be free, I have always begun to live when I say "I am." [99] As birth, all necessity is prior to any actual act of the "I" which reflects on itself. The "I" is at the same time older and

99. Necessity pertains to the past: it is birth which bestows this mark on all the other degrees of necessity. All determination is predetermination. The world itself is "perfect" until I think and wish, for it was there before I became aware of myself as perceiving. Innateness of knowledge, according to Plato, is attested in the myth of prior life, of reminiscence. The non-temporal nature of intelligible character according to Kant expresses itself as a choice of myself prior to my life; finally, Divine Omnipotence, which is like a transcendent beginning, is the primordial past of predestination. This will be one of the themes of the *Poetics of the Will.*

younger than itself. This is the paradox of birth and freedom.

Thus the experience of my receding birth is rich in its poverty. However, we have yet to show that what it does is a beginning, a fixed limit. What, in effect, testifies that what escapes me is precisely my birth? I might well say that I am *already* alive, but can I say that I am *subsequent* to my beginning? Isn't the experience of being already born also one of never having been born? How can we posit a beginning when objective knowledge only takes into account transformations of life and when consciousness misses this beginning? Thus we have to establish the *limit* character of this ultimate necessity.

Two converging ways aim at this limit. It is indicated on the one hand as the terminus of a half-successful effort to apply to myself the objective event of my birth: it is the particular instance of a biological law and object of my neighbor's remembrances. In applying to myself the objective law and the memories of others—neither of which are a testimony to the beginning of an "I" but simply a change in the state of my parents' life—my attention is turned towards a point which is not an event for me, but which is designated by a certain essential characteristic of my memory. I notice in effect that the regression to the womb of my own memories is not endless. My past, while not exactly delimited and not showing a precise beginning, forces its way into a crepuscular consciousness or into the dark memory and becomes extinguished: certainly my oldest memory is still my childhood, but I have at least a feeling of losing my own tracks. The silence of my memory at the end of more and more enigmatic and intermittent memories is, undoubtedly, not the equivalent of an experience of my birth. An absence of memory is not the memory of a beginning; but this silence nonetheless has something specific about it. This silence beneath the shadows of earliest childhood attests negatively that the flight of my origin is not endless. My birth is the terminus which I sense as limit by the spacing of the last points of memory in its direction. It is intended by that bubbling, trifling beginning consciousness of earliest childhood—which itself is a complete man's memory. It remains the case that my birth is never reached by my consciousness as an experienced event. However, this obstacle is not purely negative: it reveals the lower limit of the Cogito.

Because I never reach it as a memory, my birth cannot be repeated by memory as a choice which I could have made. A limit can only be integrated into consciousness in consent. Yet, to consent to being born is to consent to life itself, with its opportunities and its obstacles. In assuming a limit which escapes me, I take upon myself the individual nature which presses on me so intimately: I accept my character.

But can I consent to my life, to my consciousness, to my character?

3 / The Way of Consent

1. The Reciprocal Negation

WHY IS THE DUALISM of soul and body the doctrine of understanding? Why is this dualism, in the virulent form of dualism of freedom and necessity, seemingly invincible? Why does the paradoxical unit of freedom and necessity remain a scandal to the intellect, incapable of engendering through obstacles it presents even an ultimate assurance that the human being is mysteriously one? Why? if not because the rent lies not only in the weakness of the intellect in grasping the mystery of the union of soul and body, but also up to a certain point is a lesion in being itself. We do not break man's living unity only by thinking it: a secret wound is inscribed in the human act of existing. Or, if you wish, it is really in thinking that we break the living unity of man, but to think, in the broadest sense, is the fundamental act of human existence and this act is the rupture of a blind harmony, the end of a dream. This is why the common proportion which we have sought between freedom and necessity in the fabric of subjectivity itself is still not a reconciliation. We have resolved only the problem of reflection, not the problem of existence. In the background of epistemological dualism there is the *practical* incompatibility of necessity and freedom. Freedom and necessity negate each other mutually. The *negative* moment is what must be clarified. This turn of events is not without importance because the moment of the *no* will always be retained in some way in the *yes* of consent. Thus an understanding of negation is essential for a consideration of freedom. In turn a full consideration taking into account the doctrine of character, of the unconscious, and of life can undoubtedly make a concrete contribution to a general philosophy of negation with which we are not concerned at present. The sources of negation are in fact so complex that it is dangerous to try to embrace them too rapidly within a systematic construct. In particular it seems inexact to consider freedom the sole source of negation, as if freedom were brought about by nothingness by the very act in which it breaks away from the blind innocence of life. It seems to us rather that negation finds a double entry or, if we prefer, a reciprocal entry just as existence, as beginning, etc., following the reciprocity of the voluntary and the involuntary which we have taken as the theme of this philosophy of the will. On the one hand necessity is essentially injurious and appears always in some degree as an active negation of freedom: we shall see this at length in taking up carefully all the signs which testify to the minor key of necessity on the three levels of personality, the unconscious, and life. Everything that constitutes my particularity limits me. The obscure richness of my consciousness is also its default. Life which supports me is heavy with threats and will fail me one day. I am borne up by what at the same time ties me down. Thus negation rises up from the body, invests and penetrates consciousness. Just this possibility of non-being at the base of consciousness has weighed on us since the opening pages of this work. The conflict lay in the heart of motivation as a challenge hurled at the unity of the act. The resistance of the body blocked the thrust of my effort like an obstacle. But it is here that negation comes to the surface. Just as conflict of motives was the goad of choice and as resistance of the body to motion was an invitation to greater effort, so it seems that character, the unconscious, and life signal a constitutive misfortune of man's existence.

On the other hand, negation is the response of freedom and freedom's own declaration to necessity: *no!* The *no* is prefigured in every recoil from oneself. Freedom is the possibility of not accepting myself. Freedom's *no* had itself been suggested in the preceding chapters: there is no choice which would not be an exclusion, nor effort which would not say *no* to the disorder of emotion and inertia of habit. Will is the capacity for saying *no,* since it is itself born in withdrawing. That is the message of Descartes and Kierkegaard, that is, the two aspects of philosophy which we seek to reconcile. The initial act of freedom for the classical thinker is suspicion: it is a doubt, and that doubt is an act of withdrawal: the "I think" withdraws from the snare of the body and the world. It is exalted in defying the malevolent demon. In the same way freedom, according to the existential thinker, trembles since it is the crisis of being, it is anguished by the wide spaces it creates through possibility, it is anguished by the negation which it introduces into the fullness of antecedent being. Starting with its own infinity, it is the permanent possibility of disproportion, it experiences itself as its own temptation, the temptation to exalt itself infinitely, just as it experiences the world and its body as temptation, the temptation to sink into and lose oneself in the object. Thus freedom dissolves the pact and in dissolving it, dissolves the paradox of freedom and necessity. Need we repeat nonetheless that the philosophical faith which animates us is the will to restore, on a higher level of clarity and happiness, that unity of being which negation killed more radically than reflection? Philosophy for us is a meditation of the *yes*, and not a surly intensification of the *no*. Freedom does not will to be a leper, but the completion of nature insofar as it is possible in this age through which we pass as pilgrims. This is why we consider negation only with the ardent hope of overcoming it.

One last point will delay us before bringing out the negation in various moments of necessity. We have admitted that negation can be bipolar, negation underwent and negation as willed, non-being suffered by freedom and refusal posited by freedom. We have to admit that this reciprocity of negation is not, so to speak, symmetrical and in a way even the thesis according to which negation is unilateral is not altogether false: we shall notice with reason that the limits of all sorts which necessity imposes on freedom are not yet negations insofar as consciousness has not yet clarified them and that, anyway, it is consciousness itself which universally reveals negation. We shall even add that consciousness only clarifies these insidious threats as it denies them with the full force of its proud freedom: we could even say that this negation instituted by freedom is what constitutes character, the unconscious, and life as negation. This kind of argumentation is not false: it prohibits us to consider the two poles of freedom as equivalents, and gives to the *no* of freedom a preferred place in the genesis of all negation. But this useful corrective further reinforces our thesis: negation is bipolar. For the refusal reveals precisely an *other* pole of negation. Once freedom is born to itself it appears negating and already negated. What remains true is that the other pole of negation is related to the active pole of negation. Non-being which bears all necessity with it is not such except as it *affects* a freedom. This characteristic of non-being should not surprise us, since we have ourselves held in preceding pages that authentic necessity is one which we experience as a mode of the Cogito. But what we held is that the Cogito is not wholly action, but rather action and passion. This is why freedom only discovers or aggravates its wound in becoming rigid in its active negation, as one irritates a wound by scratching it. But the evil which affects it is no less painfully undergone as the most elementary passivity from which it can suffer: the passivity of bodily existence.

Let us take up successively the three moments of necessity in order to emphasize the double negation, suffered and willed.

2. The Sorrow of Finitude

AT FIRST GLANCE it seems strange to look for any negation in the fact of being or having a character, a particular nature. Have we not spoken of character as my finite being? As language suggests, what is finite is altogether positive; only the infinite *lacks* an outline. Since I have a character I am something determinate and not nothing, or rather I am someone who, in evaluating values and in the application of his effort, constitutes a primal originality which distinguishes him from all others and which gives him the initial consistency of an incomparable being. And yet it is this very particularity which gives rise to a painful negation: character is also the occasion of the simplest commentary we could give, closest to the human condition, the classical adage "Omnis determinatio negatio." I suffer from being one finite and partial perspective of the world and of values. I am condemned to be the "exception": this and nothing else, this not that. Character makes me a "someone," a "Jemeinigkeit"; personality denies man and the singular denies the universal. I suffer from being condemned to a choice which consecrates and intensifies my particularity and destroys all the possibles through which I am in contact with the totality of human experience. This dialectic, visible in great destinies—of a Goethe, a Rilke, a Gide—can be discerned even in the humblest ones. Adolescence is each man's inspired moment, in some way Goethean or Gidean. Ah! If only I could grasp and embrace everything!—and how cruel it is to choose and exclude. That is how life moves: from amputation to amputation; and on the road from the possible to the actual lie only ruined hopes and atrophied powers. How much latent humanity I must reject in order to be someone! And when suddenly the young man discovers that back of his inventions—even back of his revolts—hides the inexorable pattern of a character, a fear grips him: here before him is all he will not do, all he cannot have, all he will not be. He experiences the "Ohnmacht der Natur"; for character is not only a broken growth, but also an impossible metamorphosis. Who has not faced the question "Why am I?" Even consent will be no answer, but rather a reaffirmation, "So be it, let me be that!" Insofar as I seem an answer, the original fact—the "Urfaktum"—of being thus confronts me with the sorrow of the absurd which is forever without a theoretical remedy. The "why" is born of the negation in which my finite nature is submerged. For, as Heidegger observes in *Von Wesen des Grundes*, the full question presents itself in the form of "Why is there something *rather than nothing?*" Most often this question is not formally posed: it remains implicit in the whole gamut of passions which are born of the comparison with the other, from jealousy to resentment. It is implied in the uneasiness felt by a few vulnerable natures—like Vigny or Rilke—who experience themselves as a charge they cannot sustain: something seems lost from the beginning because something had been decided for me before me, or worse, because something is *found to be* decided without *having been* decided by anyone. Though in his secrecy the freely choosing man is alone, in a proud and modest freedom, the invincible nature to which he is united isolates him in a heavier solitude because here freedom submits before it can do. It is sometimes unbearable to be unique, inimitable, and condemned to resemble only oneself.

3. "Bad Infinite" or the Sorrow of Formlessness

IT IS ASSUREDLY EASIER to bring out the feeling of the negative if we start with a reflection on the unconscious. If the unconscious is not another actual "I" which gives me (or takes away) my thoughts, but the indefinite matter which confers an impenetrable obscurity and a suspect spontaneity on all thoughts I form, we shall be able to name this second moment of negation, this second mode of the "Ohnmacht der Natur" which clings to freedom the sorrow of formlessness (or the "bad infinite," as Hegel calls it). I am ἄπειρον, the living indefinite which afflicts the "good infinity" of my freedom. This new dialectic of the indefinite and the infinite must also be approached very concretely and simply. The unconscious is in part the obscure and in part the spontaneous; in one way or another, it presents itself as negation. The obscure is non-being: this is so evident that it is difficult to escape the lure of an imagery as simple as that of light and shadows. The oldest myths play endlessly on this powerful opposition which even the great rhythms of nature thrust at us. Freedom is light and clarity, it is the "lumen naturale," while in terms of the unconscious we are shadows. We shall understand the significance of this elementary image if we supplement it with another symbol, that of the horizon, whose endless flight illustrates before our eyes that more basic flight of the terminus of all reflection and all motivation. We shall lose ourselves in ourselves as in the depth of a forest—Descartes knew that it is always in the forest that the generous decide—or as on a vast, starless sea—Kierkegaard and Nietzsche evoke a hundred times this long wandering upon the "sea of reflection" which resides at the birth of the courage to be. We are not only sustained by our nature, but also, in another sense, limited by it; it is this non-being which gives rise to the fear of the unconscious in which the formless receives form. This is why consent, which is the right love of the self and of being in the self, is already present in all self-consciousness which has conquered the fear of the monstrous potentialities crouching in consciousness and can look at them without shame and without disgust.

The unconscious in me is also the spontaneous power of unrecognized tendencies. This power is my impotence, this spontaneity is my passivity, that is, my non-activity. I am always the knight on the point of being unhorsed or the sorcerer's apprentice faced with a revolt which he had not always called up first. The strange part of responsibility is that it presupposes the sovereignty of a Cogito and yet applies only to an indomitable life of motions and movements. The ἡγεμονικόν is sovereign only in that ambiguous interval whose existence the Stoics had not suspected: the obscure life for which I am responsible lies between the judgment which depends on me and the external good which does not. I am responsible only because I am two and because the second is concealed (as in Gabriel Marcel's fine analysis of fidelity: I promise something only about things which I do not control absolutely; I am my own sagacious elder and my own turbulent youngest son). Thus all self-possession is fringed with non-possession, the terrible is only a step away and with it all discord and all folly. There is an extreme point where the dialectic of freedom and the unconscious ceases by submersion of reason and effort in folly. This possibility is inscribed in the human condition: I can be so dispossessed that I become what older language called "possessed" —the extreme witness that all freedom bears its own negation at its side.

4. The Sorrow of Contingence

IT IS TEMPTING to speak of the negations to which life gives rise as an orator. It is more difficult to speak of them as a philosopher: an emotionally moving philosophy contains many perils. Life wills it so: it is feeling which awakens me. Only poetry—elegy—can, with the magic of words, purify the lament of the body and guide reflection to the *contingency* of a living being. Here the sorrow of the negative reaches its culmination. Life sums up all that I have not chosen and all that I cannot change. It is the sheer positing of fact at the root and at the heart of freedom. All that we have tried to think of as a moment of the Cogito must now express its non-being.

The *structure*, product of cellular differentiation, reminds me that I am a plurality and thus divisible and threatened. To be sure, life is the indivisibility of a living being itself, but its obverse is the very *space* which unifies it. If we use Bergson's comparison of life with the indivisible gesture which my hand imprints in metal filings, we have to say that the more life produces a functional unity and hierarchy, the more does the tissue which it animates become differentiated: I am the simple gesture and the complex filings. I am diverse, I am legion: and here my future as dust announces itself. Undoubtedly only a composed being is capable of lesions. This negativity is revealed to me by *suffering*. The relation of suffering as active revealing to space as the rational schema of my divisibility deserves to be emphasized. In effect suffering presents itself as negative. Already Plato, at the beginning of the *Phaedo*, points to pleasure and pain as a true introduction to the problem of contraries. Descartes and Spinoza see here a diminution of being, a lesser being.

Suffering is non-being sensed before it is thought; I am given over to it, abandoned, and so more perfidiously negated since suffering is one of the most vivid forms of self-consciousness. The cruel man who causes suffering in order to make the consciousness of his misfortune more acute knows this well. In suffering, consciousness becomes separated, focused, and sees itself negated. I am subject to pain as extended. Pain reveals the lack of being and the threat included in extension. This is its contribution to a consideration of the union of soul and body. To suffer and to undergo are synonyms. Descartes was not unaware of this:

Thus we must conclude also that a certain body is more closely united with our soul than all the others which there are in the world, because we perceive clearly that pain and various other feelings happen to us without having been foreseen, and that our soul, by a knowledge natural to it, judges that these feelings are not derived from itself insofar as it is a thinking substance, but insofar as it is united with an extended object which is moved by the disposition of its organs, which we properly call a man's body.[1]

But Descartes, striving to indicate this connection of suffering to extension, refers the latter to physical knowledge of things. By reintroducing the body into the Cogito, we also include the extended as a mode of subjective existence and not only as form of sensibility, as structure of objective things. While effort deploys from the focus of volition in a docile volume, suffering is concentrated, starting with the injured volume, in a narrow focus of pained consciousness. This is only a metaphor, for the focus of volition and the focus of pain are not points; but this metaphor brings up the mystery of the union of suffering and extension. This mystery governs that of existence of the world: if the world exists, it means that all extended bodies function as a horizon of that extended body which I am. It is this body which gradually communicates to them its mark of existence, that dense presence which distinguishes existence from essence; and in communicating to them its undeniable existence apart from any deduction confers on them its own negativity as extension: it is non-self, non-thought, non-willed.

Thus it is that space constitutes my misfortune: it is the exteriority which threatens intimacy, exposing and prostituting the secrecy of consciousness, excluding the here from the elsewhere, intercepting the "winged word," separating and dividing consciousness from itself and from other consciousness. Thus I am for myself "partes extra partes"; in placing myself on a certain level of my self, I have to apply to myself what Leibniz had said of space: "The whole is only a collection or amassing of parts to infinity, and consequently it is impossible to discover a principle of genuine unity in it."

Growth includes the same dialectic: a different plurality—that of time—gives rise to it. Here time, too, presents itself as negativity and as threat, and it is again affectivity which reveals

1. Descartes, *Principles*, II:2.

it. The vague experience of aging reveals time as the "impotence of nature." Aging is the obverse of growth. It does not follow growth, it is the shadow which accompanies it. To grow is to age, but because growth is the major key of organic process, we associate it with the happy image of childhood and adolescence and reserve "aging" and "age" for old age. From birth to death, aging is the minor key, the sorrow of process. Thus a reflection on aging can be a new contribution to a concrete study of necessity as undergone and of the negation which is its sting.

Bergson sang of creative process: it is, he said, a continual creation of unforeseen novelty. But we also have to speak of destructive process: to ignore it or to pass over it in silence would be to miss one of the great contrasts of freedom and necessity, and finally the very transcendence of willing with respect to life: freedom and process mutually say *no* to each other.

This negativity can be approached along two different paths, depending on whether we consider, in aging, only the drift of every event from before to after, or whether we notice the endless replacement of events in the continual flux of the present which is always accompanied by a double horizon of future and of past. In either aspect, process is indicated by negative feelings, as space was indicated by suffering. The sorrow of process is thus in the first place the sorrow of its irreversibility, which is the obverse of its thrust and its joyful burgeoning: the future, for example, which is the dimension of the project, the future domesticated by our rational and volitional anticipations, is also what I can neither speed up nor slow down: the temporal interval crumbles away irresistibly; the event approaches at its own speed in accord with the irresistible tempo of dates. Time is always to some degree a time of impatience, when I burn to imprint my act into history and await only the sign of the times—"not yet!" —or time of fear, when the event will be disastrous for me— "too fast!" To having, says Gabriel Marcel, the future is a threat, the chasm at the bottom of which is my loss. The past, in another way, negates me in my wish to retain the moment: "Linger a while, you are too beautiful," I say to myself. But the response is always the "Nevermore," as in Edgar Allan Poe's *Raven*. The past also negates me in my wish to erase it: for the past is what is no longer to be done: it is done. It is the true limit of my thrust. It is the same thing not to be able to retain a moment and not to be able to destroy it: he who says "never again" is also saying, "for ever." What I can no longer change is at the same time abolished and consecrated: what I have done can never be either redone or undone. Life at the same time effaces and receives. Thus the irrevocable is born of objects and of ourselves.

But we cannot speak only of aging as if a single event were susceptible to coming up at us out of the ground of the future and, once accomplished, to falling upon us with the necessity of indestructible objects. In this same experience we live in a continuous present. Time is not only the event which happens to us, but also the process which we are. Now this very flux of the present which is always present is invincible and carries its own negative index with it. It is here that in spite of the distinction which Bergson rigorously introduced between process and extension there appears another analogy between time and space. Time is experienced as a principle of alienation and dispersion. We create fidelity in defiance of time and its tendencies. The vow to remain true to myself, which is the principle of constancy, is opposed to the destructive action of the flow of feelings. Change constantly makes me other than myself. This dialectic between the same I want to be and the other which I become takes place daily in each of us: anyone who commits himself confronts his own change and discovers the ruinous process. My own metamorphoses are enigmatic and discouraging. Now this change is equally dispersion. My life is naturally discontinuous: without the unity of a task, of a vocation which would be sufficiently great to draw it together, each note would really have to retain the preceding ones and engender the following ones. Yet life is more often a cacophony than a melody, without a unique intention which would give it form from end to end as a theme for improvisation. Bergson evoked to too great an extent the process of heroes, a creation under the sign of an idea, of an endeavor, of a love, rather than the daily process which threatens to become degraded into an analogy of space. Undoubtedly the divergence of process is always other than that of space, a succession and not a juxtaposition, but it is an analogous experience. Even though the awareness of transitions, of passages must lead to that of potential halts, as the Bergsonian method of intuition of process suggests, the most remarkable "passages" of our process are often the crises, the hiatuses, in brief, the forms of "distention" from which we must win back the "intentions" capable of unifying them.

In this sense Descartes is not wrong in presenting process as an imperfection and as the very sign that we are not given being: the process of our life, he says, "being such that its parts do not depend one on the other and never exist together, it does not ncessarily follow from the fact that we at present are what we shall be a moment later, unless some cause, namely, the same cause which had produced us, continues to produce us, that is, conserve us." [2] Descartes, with the same self-assurance, discerns in suffering the index of our union with extended nature; there is a profound insight hidden in these lines which have been so often criticized. These lines are what the most Bergsonian of the French novelists echoes when, referring to Vinteuil's sonata, he evokes "the melancholy of all that becomes in time." "For not being able to love except through successive moments all that this sonnet brought me, I have never possessed it as a whole, it resembled life itself. But less deceptive than life, these masterpieces do not begin by giving us the best they have." [3] Hamelin, thanks to his feel for the dialectic, was not unaware of the destructive moment of process: it is "something which is found at the same time and inevitably in connection and in dispersion, a collection of discrete and yet not separate terms, . . . time is always a plurality of parts on the way to becoming distinct and, correlatively, to becoming united." This synthesis of number, which is distinction, and of relation, which is connection, accounts for the vivid and often painful experience of process better than all Bergsonian efforts to volatilize the distinction of parts of duration and raise the past to the dignity of eternal present (as we can see in *Perception du changement*). Behind Hamelin's abstraction I can hear the eternal elegy of a Ruteboef, Villon, Baudelaire, Verlaine, J. Laforgue, or P. Valéry. This non-being of process to which my aging makes me sensitive also constitutes the drama of Amiel: his thirst for an "interior a-chrony" which would liberate him from the division and inner dispersion is profoundly motivated by the human condition. His dream of non-temporality is pain, insofar as it is in process that we have to create and be faithful; his evil at least reduces neither to an anomaly of character nor to a philosophical error about the meaning of time; for through this anomaly and error, Amiel has brought the sorrow of process to its most lucid.

My structure speaks to me of suffering, my growth of aging—of what form of nothingness does my *birth* speak? Of the nothing-

2. *Ibid.*, I:21. Cf. also the *Third Meditation:* "For all the time my life can be divided into an infinity of parts, each of which does not in any way depend on the others." Cf. also *Entretien avec Burman,* where thought is said to be "extended and divisible with respect to duration because its duration can be divided into parts."

3. Proust, A *l'ombre des jeunes filles en fleur* (Paris, 1919). [English translation by Moncrieff, *Within a Budding Grove* (New York, 1924).]

ness of death—it is tempting to respond with a facile play of opposites. However, this relationship, which we tend to take for granted, runs into great difficulties. If birth should reveal some negation, would it not be the nothingness of origin from which existence proceeded, the *ex nihilo* of existence? In effect birth does not seem to have to indicate any other defect to consciousness than that of having once arrived in the world and thus of having passed from nothing to something. We might object—and not without reason—to this nothing of origin that it is meaningless since, as has been said above, our birth is outside the reach of memory and is not given by any experience. That is true, but though the event of birth is completed and inaccessible, the necessity of being already born is a present and permanent trait of consciousness which conceals a present and permanent negation which I can call my *contingence*. My past birth implies a present structure which includes non-being of contingence: "man born of a woman" (Job) lacks aseity.

My contingence can be presented in two languages: my existence is pure fact, and my existence is not aseitous, even though of myself I necessarily possess sovereign control of choice and of motion. (Compare Jaspers: I am "aus mir," not "durch mich.") I do not posit myself in existence: I have nothing out of which to produce my presence in the world, my *Dasein;* consciousness is not creative, to will is not the same as to create. Thus my enigmatic, ungenerable presence, this brute existence which I find in me and outside of me, secretes the most radical negation—the absence of aseity.

Thus nothingness-past, nothingness before birth, which is not a consistent thought, can become the presented and, we could say, coded expression of my contingence. You are not your own, says contingence; you come from nothing, comments my birth. Between the two negations, one in abstract language, the other in mythical language, we find the unifying trait of contingence: for what is not of itself might not be. The contingent has nothing with which it could necessarily exclude its opposite. We are here at the root of the troubling thoughts which we have formulated with respect to character: I might have been an other, had other parents, other body. These thoughts are illusory in themselves, since I always speak from a given condition, a factual situation; but this situation presents itself with the character of contingence, that is, the character of that which might not have been. A contingent being endowed with reflexion inevitably arrives at these thoughts in which he loses his footing. I cannot imagine another body, but the nascent thought of another body, though it is pushed back by the undeniable presence of this body, serves to draw me on to become aware of contingence of this unique body, its own insufficiency. My factual existence inevitably plunges me into this abyss of reflection, seduces me in the first place by the thought that the pure fact is indisputable, and, as we say, "given," "datum," then drives me to the other thought that the pure fact might not have been. When I have been in turn attracted and repelled by this double thought of the undeniability of fact and its precariousness, I have entered anxiety: I am here, and that is not necessary.

Such, in our view, is the negation implied by the necessity of being born: it is the non-necessity of being, synonymous with contingence. Thus it is not in principle necessary to refer to the feeling of death to account for it.

5. Experience of Contingence and the Idea of Death

WHAT PLACE then shall we assign to the idea of *death*? Is it a supernumerary negation which no symmetry allows us to construct so that no reflection on necessity gives rise to it? Yet it would be strange if we could carry out a reflection on necessity and the negation contained in necessity without referring to death. Nor do we believe that, but we wanted to show in the first place that this consideration can be carried a long way without recourse to that ultimate source of fear, and that the idea of death need not preoccupy us as soon as we turn to negation. We need to remember this when we attempt to understand consent which is not only a freedom towards death, or before death, or in light of death. We also wanted to suggest that the idea of death differs from everything we have considered up to now. I have an experience of character and its limits, I even have an experience of the unconscious—if, that is, we can still speak of that sense of obscure potentialities which covertly animate consciousness as "experience." I have a massive experience of life, of its structure and of the passive experience which this structure implies. I have a vague experience of growth and aging; and finally I have a confused sense of being already born, of coming from other beings and not giving being to myself. On the other hand, I have no experience of death and no means of anticipating the actual event of dying itself. Death is not a limit like birth which is already accomplished. Because consciousness is already born, its birth, even though it is inaccessible to consciousness of the self, is entailed in the Cogito. Death is not entailed in it, not even obscurely: it is not symmetrical with birth. The idea of death remains an idea, learned altogether externally, and without any subjective equivalent inscribed in the Cogito. But perhaps it is still not unrelated to the anxiety of contingence which we have approached in our analysis.

That the idea of death is radically foreign to self-perception can be confirmed easily by inquiring into the various subjective experiences which at first sight seem possibly to contain a vague experience of "having to die." These experiences must be selected among those which reveal a diminution of our being: suffering, aging, loss of consciousness (extreme fatigue, fainting, sleep, etc.). We might think that such diminution of being is a tentative non-being, and that by a type of imaginative extrapolation we can anticipate our future nothingness in all the forms of decline of consciousness. But in reality there is no "little death." Far from suffering pointing out my end to me, it presents me at once with a sense of diminution and with the blinding experience of being still here to suffer. It might even be that my presence in the world and especially in myself is never as vivid as in suffering. Thus death is the interruption and deliverance rather than the consummation of suffering; it is death which extinguishes the burning consciousness lit by suffering. For its part aging is not an anticipation of death: death remains an accident with respect to the design of life. Death is never altogether natural; it always requires a small external impulse to push us. That is the "deception" of death. Assuredly more bothersome are the experiences in which consciousness, caught in a spell, becomes blinded and extinguished: extreme fatigue empties me and "nihilates" me; fainting is an "absence," and sleep an extinction of waking consciousness. And yet these experiences mask our death more than they reveal it: we speak of sleep, which Marcel Proust patiently describes, only after the fact, upon awakening—but we do not return from death: it is always ahead of us. More than that, for the waking consciousness sleep is not nothingness but a more or less refreshing interval inhabited by dreams: it is an other, unreal consciousness which relieves the waking consciousness. Fainting, which Montaigne [4] or Rousseau [5] depicts so vividly, escapes us when we seek in it an experience of the "nearness" or "passage" of death.

4. Montaigne, *Essays*, II:6.
5. J.–J. Rousseau, "The Reveries of the Solitary Walker," in *Confessions of J.–J. Rousseau* (London, 1783).

It is not an accident that the most pathetic moment of the story is the "return" to oneself and not the "departure." It is always a consciousness returning to itself which speaks of it in a past tense; and all that can be said retrospectively about this crepuscular consciousness testifies precisely that I am still there, this side of death. Death is always the superadded accident in which I shall take that incommensurable step from something to nothing. There is some truth in the saying of Epicurus: when I am here, death is not yet, when death is, I am no more. Nothing in the inner experience of Cogito shows me my death; even my limitations are still a qualification and perhaps even an exultation of my presence. Death is the end, the interruption of limitations as well as of capacities. Thus it is an extra-systematic negation which interrupts the Cogito from without.

Then whence comes this negation? We do have to admit that it presents itself as an irrecusable necessity: "You must die." And yet this necessity cannot be deduced from any characteristic of existence. Contingence tells me only that I am not a necessary being whose contradiction would imply a self-contradiction; it allows me to conclude at most that I can not-be one day, that I can die—for what *must* begin *can* end—but not that I *must die*. How can we account for this certitude which cannot be assimilated to an anticipated experience of dying itself?

I shall note in the first place that this certitude is a *knowledge* rather than an *experience*, the most certain knowledge concerning my future but still only knowledge. Passionately accepted, this knowledge can become fear or anxiety, but unlike life, revealed first by feeling, death is first discovered in knowledge. The anxiety which clings to contingence and which it originally reveals is secondarily associated with this abstract, bare knowledge. The idea of death actually penetrates into me from the outside; I learn it through the elementary biology which intercourse with other living beings and the observed event of their death teach me. In them I discover an empirical law without exception: all organic living beings are mortal. I need no enumeration, which would be by definition incomplete, to arrive at the law of mortality. I grasp it, like any empirical law, from several well chosen examples, by the simple examination of the processes of wear and reparation of life. It is especially clear that illness, objectively defined, implies death (as subjective experience of suffering does not). The concentric circles of disease which a living being must necessarily enter lead him towards the last circles, those of the incurable and fatal illness: at the center of these circles probability equals 1.00. I can approach the circles of death from day to day, or leap in one leap from today to the center of the whirlpool: *mors certa, hora incerta*. In the thought of death there is nothing more than a biological necessity which is strictly empirical in character, not based on the anticipations of existence, and motivated entirely by external experience. If I never thought as a biologist, I should never think of death. It is an empirical, not an essential law. There is no intrinsic absurdity in the dream of indefinite longevity whose echo we find even in the work of Descartes. We are not essentially mortal—that is why we have no subjective equivalent of this necessity.

Having said this, we must recognize that, once introduced in us, this idea develops without limit and with such pathetic persistence that it tends to appear as an original experience. In virtue of its examplary character death becomes the necessity that I die: I am immediately intended by that law as a particular case among others. Starting with the vague feeling of being involved, I strive to take this necessity seriously. This learning of *my* future death is never complete. We must note in the first place that biology does not tell me of the death of something unique, irreplaceable; the substitution of one living being for another gives death its significance as the end of the individual. In it one living being is like another while life continues. Sexuality attends to that, giving the species a virtual immortality which the individual lacks. In part it is social life which teaches me at the same time the value of the individual and the meaning of individual death, but this lesson remains impure, for the historical continuity of social tasks and the anonymity of transferred roles hides from me what there is irreparable in individual death. Society continues as a system of vacant places, of hollow roles with provisional, interchangeable occupants. We cannot even say that the observed social experience of death is enough to bring home to us that necessity of death which presents itself to us as an abstraction and remains without a hold on the warm certitude of our presence in the world. Funeral rites hide death as death under the tinctures of aesthetics and actions. A funeral distracts us as mortals: furthermore, such rites are addressed less to the dead who is no more than to the dead as being other than the living. He is an overly real being, suspect, even dangerous, who must be appeased and excluded. I do not even think that the sight of a corpse would incline me particularly to apply the common rule to myself: its presence is so stupefying that it suppresses all reflection. A corpse is too ambiguous: analogous to a living being and to a thing, neither living nor a thing, it is there and it is not there. I can only conceive of death and of my death as I turn my eyes away from it. Would the final agony have greater persuasive power than funerals or the sight of a corpse? I doubt it: in description or because of its extreme pathos which shakes me to the core, agony destroys all thought. A gross initial impact obfuscates all consideration: agony is not the end but the struggle toward the end, for the end. We share in this struggle in aiding the dying man in his struggle. (As Heidegger puts it, we are not present at death, we await death.) At least, struck into a torpor, we are not included in the horrible wait in which the silence and peace of death will finally interrupt the tumult of agony: the final act and the resolution are two different things. Thus the death of the other, in the triple experience of the funeral, of the corpse, and of dying, illustrating the far too abstract law of mortality, leads me only imperfectly towards a personal conviction of my own mortality.

And yet death is not only solitary and incommunicable as the act of dying: it is also exemplary as the illustration of the law of mortality which includes the entire species. This man who dies alone is other than I, but he is also another myself, a man like me with whom I share the same human condition: I see man dying in Callias. This is why the more the other is a man like me through love, the more the law of mortality will touch and wound me. The decisive encounter with death is the death of a being I love. Here death is really sensed as my end—irreparable. Death in second person is the true illustration of death as the law of the species. And this end has repercussions in me as the end of communication: the dead is one who no longer responds—he is absent, vanished. For this radical experience we need neither an elaborate colorful image of agony nor the equivocal spectacle of a corpse, nor funeral rites. It spreads out in the sheer absence which is only in the heart; and it is this silence which lends gravity to the final agony which it makes a separation, which lends the corpse its desolation, lamenting its false absence, and grief to funeral rites which it makes a solemn farewell. And because of it also pain is independent of the image, flows back towards itself and confronts the sheer absence. And yet the fact remains that this poignant illustration of the law of the species is not a communication of dying itself. The experience of death as a final end does not pass from the "thou" to the "I." Love suffers precisely because one is gone and the other remains: each man dies alone and each man is left alone on the shore.

Thus the experience of dying is like a word which I have at the tip of my tongue: I am on the verge of discovering it, and yet it always escapes me. For me it lies beyond the experience of suffering, aging, sleep, fainting, even beyond all the echo of the death of the other within me, though the other be the most precious half of my soul: it is always my life, my wounded life, which offends my sight. The death of the other speaks to me of my death, not giving me an anticipated experience of it, but reminding me of its empirical necessity. *Memento mori.* And this necessity remains one of a law of the species which I never completely apply to myself, assimilate, and make mine. It is a thought, not an experience; it is a thought to be transformed into a belief, into personal conviction, but one which always intends my nothingess in general; because the other is man like me, death has the value of a reminder, of a recall, of a mirror.

But then this occurs: this conception of my necessary death, always general, becomes mingled with the most subjective experiences of my impotence and my negativity to which I submit passively—and this thought, which becomes a personal conviction, contaminates these experiences and gives them the odor of death. Through this contamination they seem all to anticipate, by a quasi-experience, the event of dying. It is this certitude of having to die which gives illness, age, and loss of consciousness the value of anticipation. Because I must die, my days are "numbered" and aging is like a subtraction from a diminishing capital, even though so far no human knowledge has been able to determine the exact number of my days. Finally sleep and fainting would not have that power of simulating an always future death if this certitude of death, derived from elsewhere, did not lend them this symbolic significance. Thus nothingness and death cast their shadow over the sleeper who already suggests a corpse. Thus there is a mixture of various subjective experiences and of the objective certitude of my mortality: the latter lends its altogether abstract necessity, the former makes the conviction of my future death a kind of concrete presentiment. The certitude of my death thus seems to be secreted by my consciousness itself and by the most moving experiences of my daily life just as it is the conviction of my death which sheds light on them, always from without, as *knowledge* and not as experience.

By a similar confusion the certainty of my death is based on the unclear experience of my contingency. It turns my attention towards the most basic negative traits involved in my condition of living and loving, breathes and coagulates all the actual negation involved in being devoid of aseity. The anxiety of sensing myself unnecessary, a fortuitous and revocable fact, is aroused by the news of my future death. The nothingness which always accompanies me and which expresses my very contingence mingles with that other nothingness beyond my reach, my nothingess to come which is only grasped by most abstract knowledge. Thus there arises a confusion between the *knowledge* of my necessary mortality and the *feeling* of my contingence. Knowledge of mortality lends to the feeling of contingence its metallic clarity of knowing "You must die," a clearer sound than "You are not of yourself." In turn, anxiety of contingence, illuminated by the knowledge of death, lends its sting and grief to the thought of death. Thus it becomes true that death is my death and that my death is anxiety. This is the latent anxiety of contingence which completes the assimilation of the thought of death to an intimate experience and lends truth to Rilke's strange intuition that each of us bears and feeds his future death within him, a unique death fit for him, a death in his image. And yet a discrete rent always separates the thought of death from the awareness of contingence. This thought remains always a rather cold conception which is never totally adopted and assumed because *death is not in me like life—and like suffering, aging, and contingence—it always remains a stranger*. This to me is the profound reason why the philosopher's predications find it hard to reach the hearts of men when they try to make them find their own death in themselves. They might well say that men "hide" their fate from themselves by diversion or flight into anonymity. For my part, I do not recognize in myself a primitive anxiety of death. In me it is only a cold thought, devoid of force, and in some sense without roots in existence. By contrast I do experience something like a trembling in face of my lack of a foundation which would be my own. No matter how close this thought and this feeling may be, no matter how apt they might even be to join their forces, something within me separates them. What separates them is more basic than the opposition of feeling and thought, of necessity perceived in the Cogito and necessity learned from empirical observation of objects; it is the different metaphysical significance of these two necessities. I sense from the first that anxiety of contingence can belong to a religious view of brute existence: for a being who is a creature lacks his own foundation to the precise extent to which he has a transcendent foundation in his Creator. This is how Descartes understood the poverty of the Cogito, the divisibility of its duration and its deficiency of being; for him this lack was the sign and, if we can put it that way, the negative aspect of the Omnipotence on which the Cogito depends.[6] On the contrary, if the anxiety of death were an original experience, it would reveal a nothingness which would be in some sense without analogy and without counterpart, and would belong already to the death of God. We are in no position to elucidate these difficult subterranean connections. For what we could call the fair play of analysis it is enough that we have now brought to light the most remote points to which we can push in these lower metaphysical levels of our experience. Whatever might be in such remote extensions, the analysis seems to have justified our first impression: a meditation upon necessity and the negation it implies can go to its limit—that is, the feeling of contingence—without involving the idea of death. But in turn this idea has become, by the force which objective knowledge of the laws of life confer upon it, the particular revelatory instance of this anxiety of contingence. This is why the idea of death has become in some way the objective equivalent, the lure and the stimulus of that eminently subjective anxiety of *my* contingence.

6. Freedom's Response: Refusal

FREEDOM RESPONDS to the *no* of condition with the *no* of refusal. Our consideration of character, the unconscious, and life have helped us make the meaning of refusal specific and to detach it from generalities. In effect *what* we refuse, is always, in the last analysis, the limitation of character, the shadows of the unconscious, and the contingence of life. I cannot tolerate being only that partial consciousness limited by all its obscurity and discovering its brute existence. Thus we know the initial content of the refusal: the most remarkable trait of this triple refusal is that it does not present itself at first as a refusal but conceals itself in an affirmation of sovereignty whose implicit negativity it is important to bring to light. The disguised form of refusal is the haughty affirmation of consciousness as absolute, that is, as creative or as self-producing. It is the very sorrow of negation of all experienced parts which stimulates the passion of freedom to engender itself as sovereign, to posit itself as being of itself. Briefly, exaggeration is the privileged form of refusal.

The initial moment of refusal is the wish for totality in which I repudiate the constrictions of character: I want to have the

6. Cf. esp. *Principles*, I:20–21; the eloquent title of I:21, "That the duration of our life is sufficient to demonstrate that God is."

full stature of man. This was the dream of *Sturm und Drang:* the titan was to gather the full human fate on his broad shoulders.

Thus it is that the fear of being an individual and the frequently painful awareness of limitations of character are transformed into excess. In penetrating into this dangerous region, freedom denied becomes a denying freedom and converts its horror into scorn. Freedom thinks itself Promethean, and thus becomes it. This is the possibility from which consent must be wrested.

The second wish of absolute freedom is that of total transparence. This is troublesome: must we admit that the "know thyself" can become a form of titanism when it is not tempered by a tenacious patience with respect to its own dark places? Must we go even farther and admit that all idealism is Promethean and conceals a secret rejection of the human condition? In all the instances when idealism posits an equation of the self-consciousness of the Cogito and absolute transparence of consciousness, it rejects this ring of shadows which surrounds the focus of consciousness. We have criticized such idealism on psychological grounds, that it makes the adherence of the unconscious to the Cogito incomprehensible. In light of the refusal, this critique becomes singularly clear: it is a wish that there would be no "passions of the soul," that the soul would be pure action and that no passivity would corrupt its pure activity. The philosophical Prometheus wants to be free of shadow. This philosophical titanism is not aware of itself as refusal: this is either its lie or its illusion. In positing a fictitous and in a sense dimensionless subject, without shadows and without body, idealism gives consciousness a triumphant appearance. Today the criticism of such idealism is classic: it was not unprofitable to test it in relation to a concrete study of personality, the unconscious and life. We must stress especially that this philosophical titanism is tied up with the first movement of freedom. Similarly we should encounter no problem in understanding that the basic act of refusal is indiscernible from the self-positing of consciousness: it is by this decree—which we could call the third wish of absolute freedom—that freedom responds to that fundamental passivity which is the factual existence or the contingence of the Cogito. Consciousness refutes its own anxiety of possible non-being by a gesture of power. We need to reread Fichte in the light of this idea: it is intolerable to find oneself existing and not-necessary; we need to *posit* ourselves as existing. This initial demand which considers itself a cry of victory governs all the *ideal derivations* which claim to attest the fecundity of consciousness. If I posit myself, I posit also my limits and my contingence at the same time as the basic determinations of life. But since feeling is rather the mode of consciousness which testifies to what we do not do but rather find complete in ourselves, consciousness will instinctively turn away from those vague feelings which indicate our factual existence. It will pass over these feelings in silence and substitute their rational schema for them. We have said in effect that space is the rational schema of structure, just as mood and suffering are its affective revelation; in the same way, time is the rational schema of growth, as the feeling of the burgeoning of life and the feeling of aging are its affective revelation. Finally the completely pure idea of facticity, of pure fact, is the concept which gives form to the primary joy of existing and to the anxiety of being contingent. The hallmark of idealism is precisely this effort, taken up a thousand times over, to engender space, time, and contingence. This effort would not arise over again if it did not correspond to freedom's most basic wish, which is to respond to its own condition by positing itself as sovereign.

But what this feeling has taught us concerning the underivability of the human condition at the same time indicates the derisory and secretly painful aspect of this wish for power about which we do not know whether it is the philosopher's vocation or temptation and which makes the philosopher definitely kin to Prometheus bound. Any *ideal* derivation of consciousness is a refusal of its *concrete* condition. It is this refusal which lends dramatic grandeur and "existentielle" significance to the least "exististial" of all systems. This refusal to be in a situation can remain indefinitely unaware of itself as a refusal: it is understood implicitly that we are not speaking of the essential, that we are deriving not the body but the *idea* of space, not concrete duration but the *idea* of time, not spontaneity of vital functioning which is always prior to consciousness but the *idea* of contingence as long as we remain unaware of the transcendence of the body with respect to its own idea, of duration with respect to the temporal schema, and of existence itself with respect to every idea.

This close connection between the refusal with which freedom arms itself and the self-positing of consciousness undoubtedly adequately explains why a philosophy of triumphant consciousness contains the seeds of a philosophy of despair. All that is needed is to recognize the refusal spread throughout the wish of self-positing as a refusal and the vanity and the breakdown of that wish suddenly transform the claims of this titanic freedom into despair. Such grasping of the awareness of refusal is facilitated by a direct and concrete meditation on the true condition of man and his misery. The first function of non-being is to sharpen the refusal and to make it erupt into consciousness. When the wish for an excess of freedom is concretely wounded, the ignored condition is finally transformed into a *refused* condition. "Black existentialism" is perhaps only a disappointed idealism and the suffering of a consciousness which thought itself divine and which becomes aware of itself as fallen. Thus the irritated and in some way maddened refusal assumes the posture of defiance and scorn. In the eyes of defiance, human condition becomes absurd; in the eyes of scorn it becomes vile and base. Freedom then tries to seek its highest values precisely in refusal and in scorn. Suicide presents itself to it as one of the highest possibilities: it is in effect the only total action of which we are capable with respect to our own life. I can suppress what I cannot posit. Suicide can appear the highest consecration of that act of rupture introduced by consciousness. It can appear as the act of a master who has shaken all tutelage, of a master who no longer has a master: "Stirb zur rechten Zeit! Die at the right time!" proclaimed Nietzsche. Thus the *no* would no longer be a word but an act. But suicide is not the only expression of refusal. There might be a courage to exist in the absurd and to face up to it, in comparison with which suicide itself would be only an evasion like those of myths and hopes. This courage of disillusion refuses suicide in the sole intent of affirming—and persevering in the act of affirming—the *no* of freedom in face of the non-being of necessity.

Refusal marks the most extreme tension between the voluntary and the involuntary, between freedom and necessity. Consent must be wrested from it: it does not refute it, but transcends it.

[2] FROM REFUSAL TO CONSENT

WHY SAY YES? Does not consenting mean giving up, laying down arms? Is it not surrender, in every sense of the word —whether surrender to an opinion, to an order, or finally to necessity?

Here psychology is infinitely transcended by a metaphysical choice which does not fall within its competence.

It is a choice concerning the fault: the fault is posited either as a withering of the wish for absolute scope contradicted by the human condition, or as withering of the consent which breaks that wish.

And it is a choice concerning Transcendence: it is not possible to reach a doctrine of conciliation without involving the final decision confronting Transcendence. It seemed possible to push the study of decision and effort a long way without involving major philosophical decisions—though not at least a theory of values and a more or less explicit conception of the union of soul and body. How can we justify the *yes* of consent without passing a value judgment on the totality of the universe, that is, without evaluating its ultimate suitability for freedom? To consent does not in the least mean to give up if, in spite of appearances, the world is a possible stage for freedom. When I say, this is my place, I adopt it, I do not yield, I acquiesce. That is really so; for "all things work for the good for those who love God, those who are called according to his plan."

Thus consent would have its "poetic" root in hope, as decision in love and effort in the gift of power.

But if these are the roots of the *yes,* how can we insert such a radical and broad affirmation into a simple psychology of the will? We have here at least a methodological difficulty: to what extent is it *permissible* to introduce hope into the scope of even a largely philosophical psychology? and in turn to what extent can we leave it out?

In any case it is clear that the unity of man with himself and his world cannot be understood integrally within the limits of a description of the Cogito, that phenomenology is transcended in a metaphysics. Husserl believed that he could separate the problems of rigorous science from the problems of wisdom,[7] but once we reintroduce the existence of the body into the Cogito, the problems of science lead to those of knowing. Descartes was sufficiently aware of this to see the promise of all wisdom in a *Treatise on Passions,* that is, in an understanding of the union of soul and body. A psychology of conciliation, itself implied in a *critique of dualism,* already includes a theory of the fault and a "poetics" of the will.

But we admit readily that this transcending of description in wisdom and in poetics, whose intermediate link is the rediscovery of personal body, is not an uncovering, as if the description *con-*

7. Husserl, "Philosophy as a Rigorous Science" in *Phenomenology and the Crisis of Philosophy,* ed. Quentin Lauer (New York, 1965), pp. 71--147.

tained the solution of metaphysical problems. It is really a question of a movement of deepening in which new insights appear. This deepening of the Self is really an aspect of that second reflection of which Gabriel Marcel says that it is a *reflection* more than a critique. Nor do we hesitate to admit that this reflection implies a leap—the leap, in Jaspers' terms, from existence to transcendence.

But though this leap seems arbitrary and superadded to one who does not make it, for the one who makes it it appears immediately inseparable from the very meaning which subjectivity assumes in *response*. A philosophy of the subject and a philosophy of Transcendence—which is what a philosophy of man's limitations is in the last resort—are both determined in one and the same movement. Thus to Descartes the progression appears articulated in two steps which are two decisions: from doubt, which is a defiance thrown at the existence of material objects and of the body, he *advances* to the affirmation of the Self, then from the Self he *advances* by a new act to the affirmation of God which will ultimately permit him to reaffirm the world and his body. This vast circular movement from refusal to reaffirmation finally implies only one decision, a double decision, if you wish: the Cogito affirms itself but is not its own creator, reflection attests itself as subject but not as self-positing. The central intuition of Cartesianism is the bond between the "Cogito" and the ontological argument.

It nonetheless remains true that though from the point of view of a "poetics" of the will the leap from the self to existence and the leap to the being of Transcendence are but one and the same philosophical act, from the point of view of a doctrine of subjectivity like the one which we are developing in this work the movement of deepening and reflection remains another leap, the leap towards the wholly other. We clearly reject the pretensions of an overly zealous apologetics which would pretend to derive God from nature or from subjectivity by a simple rational implication.

Thus we shall show rather the reverse impact of a philosophy of Transcendence (whose development we shall reserve for another work) on a philosophy of subjectivity. Our plan is limited to showing how, by starting with such a philosophy of Transcendence, philosophy of subjectivity is completed as a doctrine of *conciliation*. But by *showing*—rather than demonstrating—this completion, we are reading this philosophy of Transcendence, which erupts from above downward, in reverse. In reading it thus from the lower to the higher we shall discover the *response* of subjectivity to an appeal or a grasp which surpasses it.

1. Stoicism or Imperfect Consent

Two HISTORICAL landmarks will help us surround, by default and by excess, the conciliation of freedom and necessity under the aegis on an invocation of Transcendence. On the one hand Stoicism will represent the pole of detachment and scorn, on the other hand Orphism the loss of the self in necessity. But the one and the other nonetheless indicate in their way the continuity of consent and of a philosophy of Transcendence. From the one and from the other we learn that the road of the self as freedom to itself as necessity lies in a consideration of the *totality* of the world, not, to be sure, as knowledge but as a cipher of Transcendence. I become reunited with my body through love of the Earth. It is this detour which we shall try to understand as the road of consent, and, in understanding it, we shall attempt neither to misunderstand that body which is but a part of the whole, nor to lose our subjectivity which is not a part of the whole.

Initially, Stoic consent seems to destroy itself because it is not reconciliation but rather detachment. The axiom which dominates all this wisdom is the opening of Epictetus' *Manual:* "Of things, some are in our power, others are not." [8] On the one hand judgment, on the other, things. Stoicism does not suspect that my body has precisely the unexpected significance of being neither judgment nor thing, but life in me without me; ignored as the flesh of Cogito, it is pushed back among indifferent things. The whole Stoic strategy is tied to these two corollaries: reduction of the body to "already a corpse" [9] and of affection to opinion; [10] there are no "passions of the soul" in the fact of the body, there are only actions of the soul: the body is inert, the soul impenetrable. [11]

This, through contagion, leads to a depreciation of effort

8. Epictetus, "Manual," in *Moral Discourses,* trans. Elizabeth Carter (New York, 1910¹, 1950), I:1, 255. Reprinted with permission of Chatto and Windus Ltd. and E. P. Dutton & Co. Inc., publishers of Everyman's Library.

9. "You are but a little soul, carrying a cadaver, as Epictetus said," Marcus Aurelius, *Thoughts,* IV:4. Thus the Stoics attempted to dislodge themselves in their own body. (*Ibid.,* X:33.)

10. "Suppress opinion and you will suppress your saying, 'They have done me harm.' Suppress the word and you will suppress evil." *Ibid.,* IV:39; IX:31; Epictetus, *Manual,* V:37. Concerning this illusionism, cf. Max Scheler, *The Nature of Sympathy,* trans. Heath (London, 1954).

11. Marcus Aurelius, *Thoughts,* V:19, 26; VI:42; VII:55; VIII:28, 47; IX:15; 16, 31; XI:16; etc.

which is conceived exclusively as a struggle against resistance and never as a hold on a partially docile nature. Step by step all nature is depreciated.[12] Wisdom is the circularity of the soul reposing on itself, the "wisdom of the stranger, of the pilgrim in the hostel." [13] How in effect can the union of soul and body be "repeated"? Any pact between two incommensurate principles is impossible.

Yet what saves Stoicism on every page is that on the other hand it gives necessity the splendor which it initially depreciates. Just reread Cleanthe's verses with which Epictetus concludes the *Manual:*

> Upon all occasions we ought to have these maxims ready at hand:
>> Conduct me, Jove, and thou, O Destiny,
>> Wherever your decrees have fixed my station.
>> I follow cheerfully; and, did I not,
>> Wicked and wretched, I must follow still.[14]

This note, which remains discrete in Epictetus, sets the tone of Marcus Aurelius' entire work. Necessity taken as a whole can be loved, it is reason, it is God. The force of Stoicism is that it transfers to the whole the prestige it takes from the part. The change which rends each object and my insignificant body is surmounted and preserved in the substance of the whole. The good itself, which had been so deliberately referred back into opinion, suddenly resumes its absolute and in some way transcendent meaning.[15]

The idea of insignificance of transient objects is itself purificatory; joined to that of the total order, it becomes pacificatory. At the same time, the accent of Stoicism—at least that of Marcus Aurelius—passes from a heroic tonality to lyric nuances; its severity smiles in admiration and invocation.[16]

Thus Stoic consent would appear as a kind of detachment and scorn through which the soul retires into its own circularity,

12. "It is the combination and then the dissolution of always the same elements." (*Ibid.,* IV:36, 42; V:4, 13.) "Vanity of all achieved form." (*Ibid.,* IV:13; IX: 36; X:18; VIII: 37.)

13. *Ibid.,* VIII:41; XI:12; XII:13. Epictetus, *Manual,* X ; III:2; III:8; the theme of theater, play, banquet. These basic errors of Stoicism might be explained in terms of a reaction to a theory of passions on the doctrine of man. The danger of a philosophy lured by a reflection on passions is to remain a *critique of vanity* and to miss the initial *innocence* of nature and of the involuntary.

14. Epictetus, *op. cit.,* p. 247.

15. Marcus Aurelius, *op. cit.,* II:3; V:24; VI:1; *et passim.*

16. In particular that magnificent maxim (*ibid.,* IV:23) "... and you, say not, Dear city of Zeus!"

ceaselessly compensated by a reverent admiration for the totality which engulfs necessary things and for the divinity which dwells in this totality.

But if it is admiration for the whole which saves consent from scorn, what is the significance of this detour? If I consent to my personality, to my unconscious, and to my life only by adopting the whole world in which I am, then 1) what is the relation between the whole and my subjectivity? and 2) what makes this totality valuable and admirable?

These are considerable difficulties: their solution can be only sketched here in anticipation of a "poetics" of being and of the will in being. A critical examination of Stoicism will allow us at least to foresee the answer to the first question. We shall bring up the second when we are speaking of Orphism.

What relationship is there between the whole and subjectivity? At first sight it does not appear that consideration of totality could be of any help. I am not a part of the whole. Subjectivity gives me a privileged position which forbids me to dissolve into the sum of objects. Only the "corpse" of the Stoics, that is, my body, completely objectified as I exile myself from the world as a point of judgment devoid of carnal density, can be treated as part of a whole.

Hence even the idea of the whole itself disappears as the sum obtained by addition of parts. I cannot give an accounting of being in which I am included. The world is where I entered in being born. It is not an enumeration of objects—about which, in addition, I do not know whether it is finite or infinite—but the indeterminate encompassing my subjectivity. I do not *know* the whole, I am *in* the whole. The Earth—to speak like Nietzsche—is only the surrounding of my absolute involuntary. Thus if the whole seems to be only the horizon of my body, which is myself, the surrounding of that corporeal existence which I am, how then can I consent to the world before consenting to myself? Do I not, on the contrary, have first to accept myself, with my greatness and my faults, to be able afterwards to extend to the very horizons of my existence the love of my own seasons?

And yet the Whole has a different meaning which is the hidden meaning of Stoic philosophy and the reason for the *detour* of consent. The beginning of philosophy is a Copernican revolution which centers the world of object on the Cogito: the object is for the subject, the involuntary is for the voluntary, motives are for choice, capacities for effort, necessity for consent. The whole is the horizon of my subjectivity in the sense of this first Copernican revolution. This entire work is carried out under the sign of that first Copernican revolution.

But the deepening of subjectivity calls for a second Copernican revolution which displaces the center of reference from subjectivity to Transcendence. I am not this center and I can only invoke it and admire it in the ciphers which are its scattered symbols. This decentering, which demands a radically new method, enters into a philosophy of subjectivity in ways which can only be paradoxical. It is this decentering which presents itself in the Stoic notion of the Whole. The Stoic escapes the shriveling of his scorning effort because he knows himself to be a part of the Whole. The relation of part to the whole is here a cipher of a more subtle relation which is the "ontological mystery" itself, and whose expression in our universe of discourse can only be paradoxical. The Stoics who did not rise to the level of a logic—or an a-logic— of paradox have given it only a naturalistic expression which is precisely the relation of the part to the whole. But this language, although it breaks down, conjures up what is essential: I am not the center of being. I myself am only one being *among* beings. The whole which includes me is the parabola of being which I am not. I come from all to myself as from Transcendence to existence.

This is how the cipher of the Whole mediates the consent which I can give to my limits. To discover the Whole as cipher of Transcendence is no longer to choose, no longer to act; it is not even to consent. It is to admire and contemplate. Contemplation, admiration are the *detour* of consent. Is this a diversion, a simple relapse into the excessive attention to myself which makes my limitations obsessive? A diversion is not always without substance. The least forgetting of myself and my limits, if it has not lost all fervor, can be the obverse of attention to the immense, engender a love of the unlimited. I love my misery engulfed in the grandeur of the world which Marcus Aurelius called the "health of the universe."

To be sure, I must not stabilize this mysterious relation of participation in the Whole in the form of a *knowledge* which would make it banal. An excessively clear idea of the whole and the part tend to turn against the initial primacy of the subjectivity which is transcended rather than annulled. My limits are never compensated for or corrected at the end of a final reckoning. But my sorrows, which always remain inexplicable and scandalous, are surmounted in the invocation whose form in this world is adoration.[17]

The Stoics could only accord such adoration parsimoniously. While their philosophy of the Whole saves their philosophy of effort, in turn the latter infects the former with a surly gall. Why deprecate nature the moment it penetrates the soul? It is not possible to practice at the same time scorn for little things and admiration for the whole. The ultimate limit of Stoicism is remaining on the threshold of the poetry of adoration.

2. Orphism or Hyperbolic Consent

THE POETRY of adoration is the soul of Orphism, if not of historic Orphism, then at least of the Orphism of modern lyric tradition to which belong the final philosophy of Goethe, the final philosophy of Nietzsche, and especially R. M. Rilke's *Sonnets to Orpheus* and *Duino Elegies*.

Let us yield for a moment to the Orphic intoxication: we have enough confidence in our *fiat* not to lose it in an excessive fervor. There will always be time to grasp it again if, through a subtle by-way, consent returns to the spell of objectivity.

> Tell it to no other wise man
> For the crowd is quick to rail:
> I sing praises to the living
> Who aspires to death in flame.
>
> If you have not understood
> The command, "Die and become!"
> You are but an obscure transient
> On a shadow of an earth.[18]

Highly coded language: the incantation suggests what we dare not translate: the *no* and the *yes* are bound in all things according to a dialectic law which is not at all one of arithmetical compensation but one of metamorphosis and transcendence. The universe travails under the hard law of "Die and become." This majestic task in which ruin, loss, and death are always surpassed in some

17. This banalization by knowledge can take the form of a naturalism: the cycle of nature, death which passes into flowers, etc.—but it can also take one of a religious apologetic: evil is only in the part, it is only a defect, there is no light without shadows, etc.

18. Goethe, *West-ostlicher Divan: Gedenkausgabe der werke, Briefe und gesbräche*, ed. Ernst Beutler (Zürich, 1948–54), Vol. III (Trans. Kohák.)

organic forms which do not know consent; not by will but by other being is offered to my contemplation in the mineral and nature. I who will am bound to a universe in which the integration of the *no* in the *yes* is accomplished without consent. Not only the life in me, but also the whole is a resolved problem.

"Hier sein ist herrlich . . ." exclaims Rilke towards the end of that itinerary which throughout the *Duino Elegies* leads him from the distress of man separated from perfection to the extreme joy of man when he is buried in the depth of the Mountain of Primal Pain.

> Praise this world to the Angel . . .
>   . . . show him
> some simple thing, refashioned by age after age
> till it lives in our hand and eyes as a part of ourselves.
> Tell him *things* . . .
> Show him how happy a thing can be, how guileless and
> Ours . . .[19]

Already Nietzsche spoke of the "innocence of becoming." "The heart of the earth is of gold," he said in calling those around him to be "faithful to the Earth."

But Rilke, better still than Nietzsche, knew that this transfiguration of necessity is not at all for the judgment which weighs and already misunderstands, but for the song which conjures up and celebrates. Orpheus is the God of the Song:

> Song, as you teach it, is not desire,
> not suing for something yet in the end attained;
> Song is existence! [20]
> Praising, that's it! One appointed to praising . . .[21]

And what sing we of things when, yielding to Orpheus, we celebrate them? That by death everything is metamorphosed, that all negation is surpassed:

> Set up no stone to his memory.
> Just let the rose bloom each year for his sake
> For it is Orpheus. His metamorphosis
> In this one and in this. . . .
> Oh how he has to vanish, for you to grasp it! [22]

19. Rilke, *op. cit.*, p. 87.
20. Rilke, "Gesang ist Dasein," *Sonnets to Orpheus*, I:3, trans. M. D. Herter Norton (New York, 1942), p. 21. Norton translation used throughout in text. Reprinted by permission of the publisher, W. W. Norton & Co., Inc.
21. *Ibid.*, I:7, p. 29.
22. *Ibid.*, I:5, p. 25.

Orpheus joins the "double kingdom" of negation and affirmation, of death and of life.

> Does he belong here? No, out of both
> realms his wide nature grew.[23]

For the negation which lacerates being cannot be what it is not, and its simple being is its splendor:

> But you, divine one, you, till the end still sounding
> When beset by the swarm of disdained maenads,
> You outsounded their cries with order, beautiful one
> From among the destroyers arose your upbuilding music.[24]

> The earth—ah, who knows her losses?
> Only one who with nonetheless praising sound
> Would sing the heart, born into the whole.[25]

Here Rilke rejoins Goethe, even the Goethe of *Faust I*. In the "Prologue to Heaven" the angels sing, "Und deine hohen Werke sind herrlich wie am ersten Tag."

In this prosaic, skeptical age we need not fear the great Orphic poetry. For it, existence is still enchanted and sacred. Still we need to understand how admiration of the whole, which seeks to mediate between consent and necessity, goes beyond Stoic teleology and providentialism so often rejuvenated by apologetics and how it avoids the defects of metaphysical optimism. When Goethe exclaims, "Wie es auch sei das Leben, es ist gut" and when Rilke proclaims "Hiersein ist herrlich," they do not claim to be evaluating the whole on a scale of objective values on which it would be compared with other possible worlds: the world is not evaluable because it is incomparable. Exterior necessity of the world as sheer fact is too intertwined with the subjective necessity of my body to let me consider the world as one universe among others. Another world would make another body and another myself: I should no longer know what I am speaking of. Thus I do not say that "this is the best of all possible worlds" but that this unique world, uniquely for me, this incomparable world is good with a goodness which itself knows no degrees, with a goodness which is the *yes* of being. Its goodness is what it is. *Ens et bonum convertuntur*. It is because it becomes, it becomes because all destruction is surpassed. The goodness of the world is the "Die and become," it is metamorphosis. Nature is majestic in its sheer

23. *Ibid.*, I:6, p. 27.
24. *Ibid.*, I:26, p. 67.
25. *Ibid.*, II:2, p. 73.

existence. Focused in my body, all non-willed existence is neither a catastrophe nor a prison, but an initial generosity and an initial victory.[26]

Shall we now say that admiration *is* consent? Can the *yes* of admiration as a vision release us from the obligation of the *yes* of consent as willing? At this point Orphic poetry leaves us unsatisfied. It conceals a great temptation, the temptation to lose ourselves as subjectivity and to sink in the great metamorphosis. Borne by the chant of Orpheus, consent to necessity annuls itself as an act and becomes joined to its primitive opposite, the spell of objectivity from which the power of refusal wrested it. It is no accident that Orphism tends to a nature worship in which the unique status of the Cogito evaporates in the cycle of the mineral and the animal. Thus if there remains a tension between the self and the whole even in contemplative participation, I do not find myself resolved in this resolved total problem. Orphism for me remains a limit which I neither can nor dare reach. It is the hyperbolic consent which *loses* me in necessity just as Stoicism was the imperfect consent which exiled me from the whole which it nonetheless strove to admire.

Thus if admiration is not to become alienation, I have to reconsider the meaning of that second Copernican revolution in which I remove myself from the center in favor of being whose nature is cipher. I need to understand that there remains a paradoxical tension between the subjective existence of the Cogito, taken as central according to the first Copernican revolution, and Transcendence with its cipher, the whole of nature. As Jaspers well understood, a philosophy of subjective existence and of Transcendence mutually include each other in a ceaseless reversal.

We shall develop this dialectic elsewhere in its double aspect of mystery and paradox, and from the point of view of a doctrine of the will. Here we shall limit ourselves to suggesting its incidence in the relations of admiration to consent. Admiration (or contemplation) removes me from the center and places me back among the ciphers. Consent gives me to myself and reminds me that no one can absolve me from the act of *yes*. This is why ad-

26. Inversely the world as absurd and freedom as refusal are of a piece: "The divorce between man and his organism, the actor and his costume, this properly is the feeling of absurdity." [Camus, *The Myth of Sisyphus* (New York, 1961), p. 6.] This modern Manicheanism confronts the meaninglessness of the world and human consciousness, "seals them to each other as only hate can rivet beings." (*Ibid.*) The great Orphic poetry sings of the pact of freedom and necessity, of myself as fervor and of nature as a miracle.

miration and consent are circular. In a sense admiration remains incomplete if consent is not attained: if I do not accept myself as nature with my capacities and my limitations, I do not accept the whole. This is finally why the world is not evaluable, for a still more basic reason than its uniqueness: such evaluation would not be an autonomous operation. The evaluation is impossible without a giving of myself which is already implicitly a consent to my limitations.

But, we could say, if admiration already in some way presupposes consent, does not this constitute an admission that nothing can help me surmount the *no* of refusal and scorn? Admiration becomes a help because it is beyond willing; it is the incantation of poetry which delivers me from myself and purifies me. In the circle of consent through the will and of admiration through the hymn, the initiative remains with the hymn. "Gesang ist Dasein. . . . Für den Gott ein Leichtes. . . ."

> Youth, this is not it, your loving, even
> If then your voice thrusts your mouth open,—learn
> To forget your sudden song. That will run out.
> Real singing is a different breath.
> A breath for nothing. A wafting in the god. A wind.[27]

Consent by itself remains on an ethical and prosaic level; admiration is the cutting edge of the soul, lyric and poetic.

This then is how incantation aids the will. It delivers it in the first place from its own refusal by humbling it. At the core of refusal is defiance and defiance is the fault. To refuse necessity from below is to defy Transcendence. I have to discover the Wholly Other which at first repels me. Here lies the most fundamental choice of philosophy: either God or I. Either philosophy begins with the fundamental contrast between the Cogito and being in itself, or it begins with the self-positing of consciousness whose corollary is scorn of empirical being.

But poetry does not think in concepts: it does not posit God as a limiting concept but veils him in *myths*. The Goethean myth of the *Erdgeist* which crushes the titanism of Faust: led on by the dream of total insight, the giant feels himself measured from on high:

> Schreckliches Gesicht . . .

The superman must be humbled:

> Du gleichst dem Geist, den du begreifst,
>   Nicht mir . . .

27. Rilke, *op. cit.*, I:3, p. 21.

How can we help comparing the Goethean *Erdgeist* and the Rilkean angel? "Jeder Engel ist schrecklich. . . ." The poetic figure of the angel here reveals our limitations.[28]

But poetry never humbles except to heal: its hymn provokes a conversion as consciousness, renouncing the attempt at self-positing, receives being with wonder and seeks in the world and in the involuntary a manifestation of Transcendence which is given to me as the mighty companion of my freedom!

In effect, Orphic poetry never separates humbling and exultation. And this exultation aids my freedom as it offers to it myths of its own consent. To consent is to say *yes* to necessity. The law of metamorphosis is painted before my eyes as death surmounted. Thus all metamorphosis in the world is the model or the parabola of my possible consent, it is *like* a consent which is unaware of itself. In myth a philosophy of man and a philosophy of the Whole encounter each other in symbolization. All nature is an immense "as if."

The Stoics were not completely unaware of it: Descartes comments for Princess Elizabeth on Seneca's maxim: to "live in accord with my nature" I must "conform to the law and to the example of nature of things" (*Ad illius legem examplumque formari sapientia est*).[29]

The myth of the animal—the animal complete on the level of organic life with which we have constantly contrasted man— man, incomplete and thrown back on his will as a task to be resolved. The very reason which continually forced us to reject animal psychology as a guide to human psychology and to construct a human psychology to fit the Cogito now leads us back to the animal as the metaphor of consent. Because the animal is complete, it does not rebel against the law of metamorphosis, and death is not a wall for it: as Rilke says, the animal lives "in the open" ("Eighth Elegy"). This has no strictly biological or even animal psychological significance, it is the truth of the animal as myth. The myth of the child—to which Rilke strangely enough related Marionette after the manner of Kleist. "Unless ye become as little children. . . ."

But the inhuman—from the star to the animal—remains a myth which invites and calls me to something other than to sidereal or animal life, to a consent which is always other than the

28. Concerning the "figures" in Rilke, cf. Romano Guardini, cited by G. Marcel in *Homo viator*, pp. 247. In Dostoevski the fool, the epileptic, the "Idiot" are such figures which surpass and transcend.

29. Descartes, *Letter to Princess Elizabeth*, August 18, 1645.

metamorphosis which it nevertheless symbolizes. For any being which is not a subject metamorphosis remains a transformation *into something other* than itself: mortality is transcended in sexuality, the corpse in the flowers of the field. The transformation is really an alienation. For me, to assume my character, my unconscious, and my purposiveness with their being and non-being is to transform them *into myself.* The transformation is not an alienation but an interiorization. No longer "Become all things!" but rather "Become what you are." My task is to raise the "Die and become" to the level of spiritual transcendence where my limitations are transformed in receptivity and patience. This is no longer perceiving, but willing, contemplation paves the way to consent by making the tense power of refusal gentle and tender, but it does not take its place. Contemplation can only paint the negation surmounted in affirmation outside me, in cipher script. To say *yes* remains my act.

Yes to my character, whose constriction I can change into depth, consenting to compensate its invincible particularity by friendship. *Yes* to the unconscious, which remains the indefinite possibility of motivating my freedom. *Yes* to my life, which I have not chosen but which is the condition which makes all choice possible.

Thus I can remain the only one to say *no* while all nature in its way says *yes,* and exile myself for infinity in refusal. But my clarity must be limitless. He who refuses his limitations refuses his foundation, he who refuses his foundation refuses the absolute involuntary which is also a shadow of the relative involuntary of motives and capacities. He who refuses his motives and capacities annuls himself as act. The *no,* like the *yes,* can only be total.

3. Consent and Hope

YET WHO COULD LIVE in this authentic tension between a consent focused on oneself and an admiration careless of the self?

Who can escape the spell of scornful exile or the spell of the joyous consummation in a metamorphosis free of consciousness?

If there is but a narrow path between exile and confusion it is because consent to limitations is an act which is never complete. Who can say *yes* to the end, without reservations? Suffering and evil, respected in their own shocking mystery, protected against degradation into a problem, lie in our way as the impossibility of saying an unreserved *yes* to character, the unconscious, and life and of transforming the sorrow of the finite, the indefinite, and of contingence perfectly into joy. Perhaps no one can follow consent to the end. Evil is the scandal which always separates consent from inhuman necessity. Perhaps we need to understand that the way of consent does not lead only through admiration of marvelous nature focused in the absolute involuntary, but through hope which awaits *something else.* Here the Transcendence implied in the act of consent assumes an altogether new form: admiration is possible because the world is an analogy of Transcendence; hope is necessary because the world is quite other than Transcendence. Admiration sings of the day, reaches the visible miracle, hope transcends in the night. Admiration says, the world is good, it is the *possible* home of freedom; I can consent. Hope says: the world is not the *final* home of freedom; I consent as much as possible, but hope to be delivered of the terrible and at the end of time to enjoy a new body and a new nature granted to freedom.

4. From Orphism to Eschatology

BUT THOUGH HOPE is the soul of consent, it is consent which gives it body. Hope is not an illusion. A lofty evasion would finally be no different from refusal and scorn. Hope which awaits deliverance *is* consent put to the test. Immanent patience —which *lives in* the running—is a manifestation of transcending hope. Thus hope is not the triumph of dualism but sustenance on the way of conciliation. It does not detach itself, but becomes involved. It is the mysterious soul of the vital pact which I can close with my body and my universe. It is the pledge of reaffirmation. Herein a philosophy of hope can always remain in rhyme with the nocturnal themes of Orphism. The Tenth *Duino Elegy,* depicting its restless fervor for suffering and death, protects hope against the temptation of a consolation outside the walls. It seems that for Orphism it would be on the basis of death accepted and that brute existence wins all its splendor by a sort of retrospection which starts from nothingness. Orpheus is speaking of return to Hell when he cries, "Hier sein ist herrlich." This is why

> Only in the realm of praising may Lament
> Go, nymph of the weeping spring.[30]

30. Rilke, *op. cit.,* I:8, p. 31.

And though a fleeting distance always separates freedom from necessity, at least hope wills to convert all hostility into a *fraternal tension* within a unity of creation.

A Franciscan knowledge of necessity: I am "with" necessity, "among" creatures.

CONCLUSION:
AN ONLY HUMAN FREEDOM

AT THE END OF THIS REFLECTION about the voluntary and the involuntary it might seem that the dualism which we have successively expelled from all its positions has found a refuge in the subtler but also more radical duality at the very core of the subject, the duality of aspects or moments of willing.

It might seem that freedom of choice is something quite other than freedom of movement, that freedom of consent is something quite other than the freedom which governs an event in a project and in effect imposes it on things through an effort passing through the body.

As our reflection on consent developed, this difference of rhythm seemed accentuated. We have constantly moved away from that freedom which gives rise to being and moves from the possible to being, finally reaching a freedom which passes over into necessity, becoming subordinate to the initiative of things. This freedom, it seems, no longer dares: it consents, it yields.

It will be well to pause over these disparate aspects before transcending them in the direction of the radical paradox of human freedom.

It does not seem possible to emphasize the moment of choice and effort and the moment of consent at the expense of each other. In this age, wisdom itself is finally paradoxical. An appeal to daring and risk, an ethics of responsibility and involvement end in a reconciled meditation of the incoercible exigences of our bodily and terrestrial condition. But in turn a meditation on irreducible necessity ends in the exultation of freedom in the assumption of responsibility in which I cry, it is I who move this body which bears and betrays me! I transform this world which situates me and engenders me after the flesh! I give rise to being within and without myself by my choice.

Descartes summed up this diversity of wisdom for Princess Elizabeth in the three maxims in which he transposed for her the three precepts of *Discourse on Method* and in which we can distinguish the successive stages of a virtue of decision, a virtue of effort, and a virtue of consent:

The first [rule] is to use our mind as best as possible in order to know what to do and what not to do in all the events of life. The second, a firm and constant resolution to execute all that reason counsels, undistracted by passions or appetites. . . . The third, to consider that while conducting oneself as much as possible according to reason, all the goods which one does not possess are equally outside one's power, thus becoming accustomed not to desire them, for there is nothing except desire, regret, or repentance which could prevent us from being content.[1]

But we must not stop with this contrast which risks hardening an abstract distinction and breaking up the will into several acts. In reality each moment of freedom—deciding, moving, consenting—unites action and passion, initiative and receptivity, according to a different intentional mode.

The analysis of consent simply throws a more vivid light on the same meaning of *choice* which became apparent at the conclusion of the first part. The reader will remember that we were not able either to resolve or to reduce the *irruption* of choice to the impulsion of inclinations or even to the rationality of motives, nor sacrifice the *attention* we bestow on an apparent good to the *fiat* of choice.

Choice appeared to us as a paradox, a paradox of initiative and receptivity, of irruption and attention. In some respects it is an *absolute*, absolute irruption, in other respects it is *relative*: relative to motives in general and through them to values in general, relative to bodily motives in particular and through them to values of organic life. The grandeur and misery of human freedom were already joined in a kind of dependent independence. This independence of willing is no smaller in effort and consent than in choice. In turn, the dependence of willing changes only in direction when it constitutes itself successively as a *value* offered in the course of motivation, as an *organ* offered by corporeal spontaneity, and as a *necessity* imposed by character, the unconscious, and life.

The paradox thus is not between moments of willing which

1. Descartes, *Letter to Princess Elizabeth,* August 4, 1645.

are only distinct in terms of different intentional object but between the triple form of initiative and triple form of receptivity.

This is why we can finally mix the expressions suitable to
different moments and say that willing which acquiesces to its
motives *consents* to the reasons for its choice; and, inversely,
that consent which reaffirms an existence which is not chosen,
with its constriction, its shadows, its contingence, is like a *choice*
of myself, a necessary choice, as the *amor fati* celebrated by
Nietzsche. Daring and patience never cease to alternate in the
very heart of willing. Freedom is not a pure act, it is, in each
of its moments, activity and receptivity. It constitutes itself in
receiving what it does not produce: values, capacities, and sheer
nature.

In this our freedom is *only* human and reaches a complete
understanding of itself only with respect to some limit concepts
which we also understand in general as Kantian ideas, regulatory
and not constitutive, that is, as ideal essences which determine
the limit degree of essences of consciousness (which, as we have
seen, are already of a limit purity with respect to the fault).

1. The idea of God as a Kantian idea is a limit degree of a
freedom which is not creative. Freedom is, so to speak, on the
side of God by its independence from objects, by its simultaneous
character of indetermination and self-determination. But we have
in mind a freedom which would be no longer receptive with
respect to motives in general (of capacities and of a nature), a
freedom which would not constitute itself by beholding and disturbing a spontaneity, by bowing before a necessity, but a freedom which would be itself by definition. Shall we say that such
freedom creates the good, or that it is the good? This distinction,
central in many respects, has little significance for us: such a
freedom would no longer be a *motivated freedom,* in the human
sense of a freedom receptive to values and finally dependent on
a body, it would no longer be an *incarnate* freedom, it would no
longer be a *contingent* freedom. Thus this motivated, incarnate,
contingent freedom is an image of the absolute in its indetermination, identical with its power of self-determination, but *other*
than the absolute in its receptivity.

This first limit concept governs a flow of subordinate limiting
concepts whose implications would themselves constitute a difficult problem.

2. In effect I can also understand in general a motivated
freedom like that of man, but motivated in an exhaustive, transparent, absolutely rational way. We have several times alluded

to this ideal of perfectly enlightened freedom. I am other than such perfectly enlightened freedom; my type of temporality, which belongs to my incarnate situation, separates me from this limit. In the three analyses of indecision, of process, and of choice we have insisted on this connection of human temporality with confusion of motives issuing from the body: first of all I am a freedom emerging ceaselessly out of indecision because values appear to me always *in* an apparent good which affectivity shows me. Affectivity has a problematic character which gives rise to an endless clarification. It is comparable in the practical order with the disparity of a perception through contacts, sketches, perspectives. Only time, we have often said, can clarify it. Thus our freedom is secondly a kind of process. To be sure, inasmuch as we carry on the process, this mastery is not an imperfection but actually a perfection or an image of perfection. But, as the clarification of motives is ever incomplete, as decision is forced by urgency, as information always remains limited, this freedom of attention is of a piece with the limits of corporeal existence themselves. It perceives only apparent goods; it is only capable of an inadequate reading of values. Hence, thirdly, the peculiar character of human choice: it comes from a risk and not from a decree. A risk is a perfection only if we consider it as independent termination of an attention coming to a resolution; but for a motivated and not creative freedom, risk is only a caricature of a free divine decree and remains defective with respect to it. Arbitrary termination of attention finally resembles less God's free decree than a less audacious choice, sustained more by reason, in which persuasiveness of the good joins the spontaneity of vision. Such perfectly motivated freedom would be the highest approximation of divine freedom compatible with motivated freedom.

3. I further understand the limit concept of an incarnate freedom as man's freedom, but one whose body would be absolutely docile: a *gracious* freedom whose bodily spontaneity would be allied with the initiative which moves it without resistance. The athlete and the dancer perhaps sometimes give me a vision of it and a longing for it.

4. Finally I understand in general a freedom which would be the full human scope, which would not have the particularity of a character, whose motives would be absolutely transparent and which would reduce its contingence fully to its initiative. But this final "utopia" of freedom reveals that the entire circle of limiting concepts is focused around the idea of creative freedom.

These limit concepts have no other function here than to help us understand, by contrast, the condition of a will which is reciprocal with an involuntary. They do not yet constitute a surpassing of subjectivity; they still belong to the description of subjectivity. A genuine Transcendence is more than a limit concept: it is a *presence* which brings about a true revolution in the theory of subjectivity. It introduces into it a radically new dimension, the *poetic* dimension.

At least such limit concepts complete the determination of a freedom which is human and *not* divine, of a freedom which does not posit itself absolutely because it *is not* Transcendence.

To will is not to create.

Le Chambon-sur-Lignon
Easter, 1948

Bibliography

Ach, Narziss. *Ueber den Willensakt und das Temperament*. Leipzig, 1910.

Adler, Alfred. *The Neurotic Constitution*. Translated by Glueck and Lind. New York, 1917.

Alain [Émile Chartier].

Aron, Raymond. *Introduction à la philosophie de l'histoire*. Paris, 1937. Translated by George J. Irwin. *Introduction to the Philosophy of History*. Boston, 1961.

Aurelius, Marcus. *Meditations*. Translated by George Long. Garden City, 1961.

Bachelard, Gaston. *Dialectique de la durée*. Paris, 1936.

Baruk, "Le Problème de la volonté, nouvelles données physiologiques." *Journal de psychologie* (1939).

Bergson, Henri. *L'Energie spirituelle*. Paris, 1919. *Mind-energy*. Translated by Carr. London, 1920.

———. *Essai sur les données immediates de la conscience*. Paris, 1889. *Time and Free Will*. Translated by R. L. Pogson. New York, 1910.

———. *L'Évolution creatrice*. Paris, 1907. *Creative Evolution*. Translated by Arthur Mitchell. New York, 1911.

———. *L'Intuition philosophique*. Reprint from *Rev. Met. Morale*, XIX (1911).

———. *La Pensée et le mouvant*. Paris, 1934.

———. *Perception du changement*. Oxford, 1911.

———. *Les Deux Sources de la morale et de la religion*. Paris, 1932. *The Two Sources of Morality and Religion*. Translated by R. Ashley Audra and Cloudesley Brereton. New York, 1935.

Blanché, Robert. *La Notion de fait psychique*. Paris, 1934.

Blondel, Charles. "L'Automatisme et la synthèse." *Nouveau traité de psychologie*. Edited by G. Dumas. Vol. IV.

———. "Les Volitions." *Nouveau traité de psychologie*. Edited by G. Dumas. Vol. VI.

Bournoure, Louis. *L'Autonomie de l'être vivant*. Paris, 1949.

Boutonoier, Juliette. *L'Angoisse*. Paris, 1945.

———. *Les Defaillances de la volonté*. Paris, 1945.

Bradley, Francis. "On Active Attention." *Mind* (1902).

———. "The Definition of Will." *Mind*, I (1902); II (1903); III (1904).

———. "On Mental Conflict and Imputation." *Mind* (1902).

Brunot, Ferdinand. *La Pensée et la langue*. Paris, 1922.

Burloud, Albert. *Le Caractère*. Paris, 1942.

———. *Principes d'une psychologie des tendences*. Paris, 1938.

Camus, Albert. *Le Mythe de Sisyphe*. Paris, 1942. *The Myth of Sisyphus*. Translated by Justin O'Brien. New York, 1955.

Cannon, Walter. *Bodily Changes in Pain, Hunger, Fear, and Rage*. New York, 1915[1], 1929.

Cellerier, Les Éléments de la vie affective." *Rev. phil.* (1926).

Chartier, Émile ["Alain"] *Éléments de philosophie*. Paris, 1941.

———. *Idées*. Paris, 1932.

———. *Propos sur l'éducation*. Paris, 1932.

———. *Système des beaux-arts*. Paris, 1920.

Claparède, Jean. "Does the Will Express the Entire Personality?" *Studies in Honour of Morton Prince* (1925).

———. "Genèse de l'invention." *Arch. de psych.* (Genève) XXIV (1933).

———. "L'Invention dirigée." *L'Invention*. Neuvième semaine international de synthèse. Paris, 1938.

Collin, Rémy. *Les Hormones*. Paris, 1944.

Cuenot, Lucien. *Invention et finalité en biologie*. Paris, 1941.

Dalbiez, Roland. *La Méthode psychanalytique et la doctrine freudienne*. Paris, 1936. *Psychoanalytic Method and the Doctrine of Freud*. Translated by Lindsay. New York, 1941.

Debesse, Maurice. *La Crise d'originalité juvenile*. Paris, 1941.

Dejean, Renée. *L'Émotion*. Paris, 1933.

Delacroix, Henri. "Les Operations intellectuelles." *Nouveau traité de psychologie*. Edited by G. Dumas. Vol. V.

Dembo. "Der Aerger als dynamisches Problem." *Psych. Forsch.* (1931).

Descartes, Renée. *Oeuvres de Descartes*. Edited by Charles Adam and Paul Tannery. Paris, 1910. *Philosophical Works of Des-*

cartes. Translated by Elizabeth S. Haldane and G. R. T. Ross. Cambridge, 1931–34.

Dufrenne, Mikel, and Ricoeur, Paul. *K. Jaspers et la philosophie de l'existence*. Paris, 1947.

Dumas, Georges, ed. *Nouveau traité de psychologie*. Paris, 1930–46.

———. "L'Excitation et le mouvement." *Nouveau traité de psychologie*. Vol. II.

Duncker, Karl. *Zur Psychologie des produktiven Denkens*. Berlin, 1935.

Epictetus. *Enchiridion*. "The Manual of Epictetus." *Epictetus, Moral Discourses*. Translated by Elizabeth Carter. London, 1910[1], 1950.

Freud, Sigmund. *The Ego and the Id*. Translated by Wolf. London, 1927.

———. *A General Introduction to Psychoanalysis*. Translated by G. Stanley Hall. New York, 1920.

———. *Interpretation of Dreams*. Translated by A. A. Brill. London, 1913.

———. *New Introductory Lectures on Psychoanalysis*. Translated by W. J. H. Sprott. New York, 1933.

———. *Psychopathology of Everyday Life*. Translated by A. A. Brill. New York, 1917.

Gilson, Étienne. "Essai sur la vie intérieure." *Rev. phil.* (1920).

———. *Saint Thomas d'Aquin*. Paris, 1925.

Goblot, E. "La Finalité en biologie." *Rev. phil.* (Oct., 1903).

Goethe, Wolfgang. *West-östlicher Divan: Gedenkausgabe der Werke, Briefe und Gespräche*. Edited by Ernst Beutler. Zürich, 1948–54. Vol. III.

Goldstein, Kurt. *Der Aufbau des Organismus*. The Hague, 1934.

Guillaume, Paul. "Les Aspects affectifs de l'habitude." *Journal de psych.* (1935).

———. *La Formation des habitudes*. Paris, 1936.

———. *L'Imitation chez l'enfant*. Paris, 1925.

———. *La Psychologie de la forme*. Paris, 1937.

Hamelin, Octave. *Essai sur les éléments principaux de la représentation*. Paris, 1907.

Hegel, Georg. *Morceaux choisis*. Translated by Lefebvre and Guterman. Paris, 1939.

Heidegger, Martin. *Sein und Zeit*. Halle, 1928. *Being and Time*. Translated by John Macquarrie and Edward Robinson. New York, 1962.

Heymans, Gerardus. "Beiträge zur speziellen Psychologie auf Grund einer Massenuntersuchung." *Ztschr. f. Ps. und Physiol. der Sinnesorgane* (1909).

———. "Ueber einige Correlationen." *Ztschr. f. ang. Ps. und psych. Sammelforschung*, I (1908).

———. "Des Méthodes dans la psychologie specialle." *Ann. psych.* XXVII (1911).

———. *Die Psychologie der Frauen.* Heidelberg, 1910. *La Psychologie des femmes.* Translated by R. Le Senne. Paris, 1925.

Hildebrand, "Die Idee der sittlichen Handlung." *Jahrbuch f. Phil. und phänom. Forsch.* Vol. III.

Husserl, Edmund. *Ideen zu einer reinen Phänomenologie und phänomenologischen Philosophie.* 3rd ed. Halle, 1928. *Ideas.* Translated by R. W. Boyce Gibson. New York, 1931[1], 1962.

———. *Logische Untersuchungen.* Halle, 1900–1901[1]; 3rd ed., 1922.

———. "Philosophie als strenge Wissenschaft." *Logos*, I (1910–11). "Philosophy as a Rigorous Science." *Phenomenology and the Crisis of Philosophy.* Translated and edited by Quentin Lauer. New York, 1965.

———. *Vorlesungen zur Phänomenologie des inneren Zeitbewusstseins.* Halle, 1929. *Phenomenology of Internal Time-consciousness.* Translated by James S. Churchill. Bloomington, Ind., 1964.

James, William. *The Emotions.* Baltimore, 1922.

———. *Feeling of Effort.* Boston, 1880.

———. *The Principles of Psychology.* New York, 1890.

———. *Psychology: Briefer Course.* New York, 1900.

Janet, Pierre. *De l'angoisse à l'extasse.* Paris, 1926.

———. *Les Debuts de l'intelligence.* Paris, 1938.

———. *L'Intelligence avant le langage.* Paris, 1937.

Jaspers, Karl. *Philosophie.* Berlin, 1932.

———. *Reason and Existenz.* Translated by William Earle. New York, 1955.

Joubert, Joseph. *Pensées.* Paris, 1842. *Thoughts.* Translated by Calvert. Boston, 1867.

Kant, Immanuel. *Critique of Judgment.* Translated by J. H. Bernard. New York, 1951.

———. *Critique of Practical Reason.* Translated by Thomas K. Abbot. London, 1898.

———. *Fundamental Principles of Metaphysics of Morals.* Translated by Thomas K. Abbot.

Klages, Ludwig. *Vorschule der Charakterkunde.* Leipzig, 1937. *The Science of Character.* Translated by Johnson. London, 1927.

Koffka, Kurt. *Principles of Gestalt Psychology.* London, 1935.

Laporte, Jean. *La Conscience de la liberté.* Paris, 1947.

————. "La Liberté selon Descartes." *Rev. met. morale* (1937).

————. "La Liberté selon Malebranche." *Rev. met. morale* (1938).

————. "Le Libre-arbitre et l'attention chez St Thomas." *Rev. met. morale* (1931, 1932, 1934).

Larguier des Bancels. *Introduction à la psychologie.* Paris, 1834.

Le Senne, Rennée. *Le Mensonge et le caractère.* Paris, 1930.

————. *Traité de caractérologie.* Paris, 1945.

————. *Traité de morale générale.* Paris, 1942.

Lecomte du Nouy. *Le Temps et la vie.* Paris, 1936.

Leibnitz, Gottfried. *New Essays Concerning Human Understanding.* Translated by A. G. Langley. New York, 1896.

Lequier, Jules. "Fragments." Edited by Dugas. *Rev. met. morale* (1922).

————. *Recherche d'une première vérité.* Paris, 1924.

Lewin, Kurt. "Das Problem der Willensmessung und das Grundgesetz der Assoziation." *Psych. Forsch.* I (1922).

————. "Vorbemerkungen über die psychische Kräfte und Energien und über die Struktur der Seele." *Psych. Forsch.* (1926).

————. "Vorsatz, Wille, und Bedürfnis." *Psych. Forsch.* (1926).

————. "Zwei Grundtypen von Lebensprozessen." *Zts. f. Ps.* (1929).

————, and A. Karsten. "Psychische Sättigung." *Psych. Forsch.* (1927).

Lindworsky, Johannes. *Der Wille.* 3rd ed. Freiburg, 1923. *Training the Will.* Translated by Steiner. Milwaukee, 1929.

McDougall, William. *Introduction to Social Psychology.* Boston, 1908.

Maine de Biran. *Oeuvres de Maine de Biran.* Edited by Tisserand. Paris, 1920–39.

————. *Journal intime.* Paris, 1927–31.

————. *Morceaux choisis.* Edited by Gouhier. Paris, 1942.

Malebranche, Nicholas. *Oeuvres completes.* Edited by A. Robinet. Paris, 1958.

————. *De la recherche de la vérité.* Paris, 1952.

Malinowski, Bronislaw. *Sex and Repression in Savage Society.* New York, 1927.

Marcel, Gabriel. *Être et avoir.* Paris, 1935. *Being and Having.* Translated by Katherine Farrer. Westminster, 1949.

————. *Homo Viator*. Paris, 1944. *Homo Viator*. Translated by Emme Crauford. Chicago, 1951.

————. *Journal de metaphysique*. Paris, 1927. *Metaphysical Journal*. Translated by Bernard Wall. London, 1952.

————. *Du refus à l'invocation*. Paris, 1940. *Creative Fidelity*. Translated by Robert Rostal. New York, 1964.

Mauron, Charles. *Malarmé l'obscur*. Paris, 1941.

Mayer, A. "Excitation psychique et secretion." *Nouveau traité de psychologie*. Edited by G. Dumas, Vol. II.

Merleau-Ponty, Maurice. *La Structure du comportement*. Paris, 1942. *Structure of Behaviour*. Translated by Alden L. Fisher. Boston, 1963.

————. *Phénoménologie de la perception*. Paris, 1944. *Phenomenology of Perception*. Translated by Collin Smith. London, 1962.

Mesnard, P. *Essai sur la morale de Descartes*. Paris, 1936.

Michotte and Prüm. "Le Choix volontaire et ses antecendents immediats." *Arch. de psych.* X (Dec. 1910).

Minkowski, Eugene. *Vers une cosmologie*. Paris, 1936.

von Monakov and Mourgue. *Introduction biologique à l'étude de la neurologie et de la psychopathologie*. Paris, 1928.

Montaigne, Michel. "Essays." *Works*. Edited by Hazlitt. London, 1842.

Mounier, Em. *Traité du caractère*. Paris, 1946.

Nabert, Jean. *Éléments pour une éthique*. Paris, 1943.

————. *L'Expérience intérieure de la liberté*. Paris, 1924.

Nahlowsky, Joseph. *Das Gefühlsleben*. Leipzig, 1862.

Osvianskina, Maria. "Die Wiederaufnahme unterbrochener Handlungen," *Psych. Forsch.* (1929).

Pfänder, Alexander. *Phänomenologie des Wollens* (1899), and *Motive und Motivation* (1911) In one volume. Leipzig, 1930.

————. "Zur Psychologie der Gesinnungen." *Jahrb. f. Phil. u. phän. Forsch.* Vol. III.

Pradines, Maurice. "L'Hétérogeneité fonctionelle du plaisir et de la douleur." *Rev. phil.* (1927).

————. *Philosophie de la sensation*. Vol. II. *La Sensibilité élémentaire. Les Sens du besoin*. Paris, 1928–34.

————. *Traité de psychologie générale*. Vol. I. Paris, 1943.

Rauh, Frederic. *L'Éxperience morale*. Paris, 1903.

Ravaisson-Mollien, Felix. *De l'habitude*. Paris, 1838[1], 1927.

Reiner, Hans. *Freiheit, Wollen und Aktivität*. Halle, 1927.

Renouvier, Charles. "Traité de logique générale et de logique formelle." *Essai de critique générale*. Paris, 1912.

Ribot, Theodule. *Les Maladies de la volonté*. Paris, 1883.

Ricoeur, Paul. *G. Marcel et Karl Jaspers*. Paris, 1948.

Rilke, Rainer Maria. *Duino Elegies*. Translated by J. B. Leishman and Stephen Spender. London, 1948.

————. *Sonnets to Orpheus*. Translated by M. D. Herter Norton. New York, 1942.

Rostand, Jean. *Pensées d'un biologiste*. Paris, 1954. *The Substance of Man*. Translated by Brandeis. Garden City, 1962.

Rousseau, Jean-Jacques. "The Reveries of the Solitary Walker." *Confessions of J.–J. Rousseau*. London, 1783.

Saint-Exupéry, Antoine de. *Terre des hommes*. Paris, 1939.

St. Thomas Aquinas. *Summa Theologiae; De malo; De veritate; De potentia*.

Sartre, Jean-Paul. *L'Être et le néant*. Paris, 1943. *Being and Nothingness*. Translated by Hazel Barnes. New York, 1948.

————. *Esquisse d'une theorie des émotions*. Paris, 1939. *Emotions*. Translated by Bernard Frechtman. New York, 1948.

————. *L'Imaginaire: psychologie phénoménologique de l'imagination*. Paris, 1940. *Psychology of the Imagination*. New York, 1951.

————. *L'Imagination*. Paris, 1936. *Psychology and Imagination*. New York, 1948.

Scheler, Max. *Formalismus in der Ethik und die materiale Wertethik*. Halle, 1927.

————. *The Nature of Sympathy*. Translated by Peter Heath. London, 1954.

Schopenhauer, Arthur. *On the Four-fold Root of the Principle of Sufficient Reason*. Translated by Hillebrand. London, 1891.

Shand. "Analysis of Attention." *Mind* (1894).

————. "Attention and Will, a Study in Involuntary Action." *Mind* (1895).

————. "Types of Will." *Mind* (1896).

Stout. "Voluntary Action." *Mind* (1896).

Thorndike, Edward. "Ideo-motor Action." *Psych. Rev.* XX (1913).

————. *The Fundamentals of Learning*. New York, 1932.

Tilquin, André. *Le Behaviorisme*. Paris, 1942.

Tolman, Edward. "Instinct and Purpose." *Ps. Rev.* XXVII (1920).

————. "A New Formula for Behaviorism." *Ps. Rev.* XXIX (1922).

————. "Purpose and Cognition, the Determiners of Learning." *Ps. Rev.* XXXII (1925).

————. *Purposive Behavior in Animals and Men*. Berkeley, 1932.

————, and Brunschvicg. "The Organism and the Causal Texture of the Environment." *Ps. Rev.* XLII (1935).

Valéry, Paul. *Poesies*. Paris, 1936.

———. *Selected Writings of Paul Valéry*. Translated by Denis Devlin *et al.* New York, 1964.

Van der Veldt. *L'Apprentisage du mouvement et l'automatisme*. Paris, 1928.

Vernet, H. *Le Problème de la vie*. Paris, 1947.

Weizsacker. "Reflexgesetze." *Handbuch der norm. und pathol. Psysiologie*. Vol. X. Edited by Bethe *et al.* Berlin, 1927.

Wundt, Wilhelm. *Principles of Physiological Psychology*. Translated by E. B. Titchener. London, 1904.

Zeigarnik. "Ueber das Verhalten von erledigten und unerledigten Handlungen." *Psych. Forsch.* (1927).

Index

Abstraction, 3, 29, 32, 33, 37, 44, 75. *See also Epoché;* Bracketing

Ach, Narziss, xxxiv, 166n, 304, 304n, 305, 305n

Adler, Alfred, 116

Affectivity, 86, 88, 105, 110

"Alain" (Émile Chartier), 202, 258–59, 271, 279n, 315–16, 344, 365–69, 372–73, 377, 404n

Alienation, 65, 179, 349

Ampère, 319, 320

Appetite, 88, 117

Aquinas, Thomas, 149n, 170, 182, 184, 186, 190, 192–94

Aristotle, 81, 99, 169, 192, 196, 229, 295, 327, 396

Aron, Raymond, 125n

Attention, 76, 149, 151–63, 187, 212, 237, 239, 255, 263, 365, 483

Augustine, Saint, 186n

Aurelius, Marcus, 469, 470, 472

Bachelard, Gaston, 49n

Baudelaire, 317, 454

Bergson, Henri, xxxv, 30–31, 54, 67, 69–70, 74, 122, 127, 129, 151, 160–63, 172, 178, 187, 189, 196, 317, 323n, 413, 450, 452, 454

Blanché, Robert, 218n

Blondel, Charles, 123n, 187, 289–91, 303, 323

Blondel, Maurice, 31

Body, personal, 10, 14, 46, 87–88, 92, 112, 125, 208, 214, 220, 228, 272, 295, 297, 320, 468

Bournoure, Louis, 416n

Boutonier, Juliette, 212, 376, 390, 422

Bracketing, xiii, xxv, 3. *See also* Abstraction; Epoché

Bradley, Francis, 38, 40, 60, 154, 165n

Brunot, Ferdinand, 46

Brunschvicg, L., 222n, 316

Burloud, A., 282n, 288, 292n, 296n, 318–19, 318n, 319n, 321n, 325n, 359n, 369n, 416n

Camus, Albert, 476

Cannon, Walter, 270

Causal explanation, 68, 350, 382

Character, 355–64, 366–73

Chartier, Emile. *See* "Alain"

Choice, 163–68

Christianity, 25, 103

Claparède, Jean, 69n, 172n

Cogitatio, as intentional, 91, 120, 153, 280

Collin, Rémy, 417n

Comte, Auguste, 61, 123, 268, 429

Conciliation, 467–68

Concupiscence, xiii, 138

Condillac, 10, 315

Consciousness, xix, 6, 27, 48–54, 61, 65, 68–69, 72, 98, 105, 117, 125, 138, 141, 143, 155, 216, 316, 365, 406, 412, 437, 442

Constitution, 53

Copernican revolution, xxvii, xxviii, 5, 31–32, 398, 471, 476

Cosmology, 68, 190–97, 414, 423–25
Cuenot, Lucien, 416, 418n

Dalbiez, Roland, xxv, 121, 376, 385–
    86, 388–89, 391, 395–97,
    402, 407
Darwin, Charles, 117
Death, 456–63
Debesse, Maurice, 427, 430
Dejean, Renée, 251, 277
Delacroix, Henri, 293–94, 389, 430
Democritus, 368
Descartes, Renée, xii, 9, 14–15, 20,
    24, 41–42, 56, 62, 65, 149, 153,
    155–56, 170–73, 175, 182–86,
    188, 190–92, 195–96, 206, 217–
    19, 227, 252–53, 255–59, 262–
    66, 276–79, 313–17, 327, 376–
    77, 386, 393–94, 403, 407–9,
    412, 439, 445, 449–54, 459, 462,
    467–68, 478, 483
Description, phenomenological, 3–5,
    14, 27–28, 32–37, 52, 85, 135–
    36, 163, 167, 186, 197, 244
Determination, 62, 78, 143–49,
    168–71, 182–90, 441n
Diagnostics, xv–xvii, xxxii, 13, 15,
    87–88, 117, 207, 219, 221–22,
    272, 326, 351–52, 371–86, 421–
    24, 437
Dialectic, 60, 164, 403
Don Quixote, 119
Dostoevski, Fedor, 31, 478
Dualism, xxvii, 12–13, 17, 341, 444
Dufrenne, Mikel, 19, 27n, 179n
Dumas, Georges, 90n, 270n
Dumont, L., 297n
Duncker, Karl, 172n
Durkheim, Émile, 124

Ego, 32, 52
Eidetics, xi, xiv, xx, xxix, 4, 25, 32,
    37–41, 44, 71, 124, 135, 142,
    179, 182, 190, 219, 230, 380,
    425
Empathy, 10
Empiricism, 10, 70
Empirics, xi, xvi, 34
Epictetus, 469, 470
Epicureanism, 103, 295, 458
Epoché, 188, 201. See also Bracket-
    ing; Abstraction

Essence, 16, 218, 368, 371, 484
Ethics, 22, 74, 130–34
Explanation, xxxv, 348, 352

Fault, xvi, xvii, 3, 21–25, 158, 196,
    310, 374, 426, 444, 467, 476
Faust, 477
Fichte, 465
Freedom, 171–82, 189, 364–66, 441,
    463–66, 482–85
Freud, Sigmund, xxv, 116, 306,
    375–78, 380–407, 440

Gestalt psychology, xx, 69, 145n,
    209, 210, 222–26, 241, 248, 250,
    271–72, 288–91, 300, 325, 423
Gide, André, 447
Gilson, Étienne, 165n
Giradoux, Jean, 408, 431
Goblot, E., 416n
Goethe, Wolfgang, 447, 473, 477–78
Goldstein, Kurt, 6, 231, 232, 240,
    241, 271n, 299, 300n
Guillaume, Paul, 114n, 233n, 246,
    246n, 248, 271, 281, 286,
    288, 290, 304n

Hamelin, Octave, 203, 293, 454
Harmony, 22
Hedonism, 103
Hegel, Georg, 229, 251, 315–16, 448
Heidegger, Martin, xxiii, 25, 62,
    345, 411, 448, 460
Herbart, Johann, 269n
Hermeneutics, xii, xv, xxx, 404
Hesitation, 84, 165, 137–43
Heymans, Gerardus, 357–60, 362–
    63, 367, 373
Hildebrand, Friedrich, 38, 59
Horizon, 16, 27, 73, 144–45, 151,
    156, 223, 230, 342, 413,
    449, 451, 472
Hume, David, 10
Husserl, Edmund, xiii–xv, xxxii–
    xxxvi, 4, 6–7, 13–16, 19, 28, 43–
    44, 51, 57, 59, 97, 149, 151, 154,
    156, 195–96, 206, 209, 219, 224,
    225, 258, 330, 367, 371, 387,
    388, 393, 394, 405, 411, 423
Hyle, xv, xxvi, 64, 258, 259, 371,
    394, 399

Imagination, 90, 97, 98, 102, 105
Incarnation, xii, xxii, xxiii, 15, 136, 143, 149, 215, 219, 227
Intellectualism, 70
Intelligibility, 3, 6, 229, 268, 272, 280, 310
Intentionality, xiii–xx, 6, 42, 44–45, 49, 53, 55–56, 58–59, 69, 89, 91, 99–102, 145, 150, 165, 168, 176, 177, 183, 185, 203, 205, 219, 260, 271, 280, 286, 288, 290, 308, 319, 320, 326, 332, 335, 341, 373, 381–82, 387–88, 394–95, 397, 404, 411, 424, 483

James, William, 69, 171, 176–78, 246, 254, 262, 269, 271, 319, 319n, 322, 323, 426
Janet, Pierre, 69, 93, 238, 243, 251, 252, 272–73, 287, 429
Jaspers, Karl, xxv, 17, 25, 62, 71, 172, 175, 194, 316, 425, 455, 476, 568
Joubert, Joseph, 430

Kant, Immanuel, 19, 76–77, 80, 126, 127, 130–33, 151, 155, 169, 179, 196, 316–17, 368, 414, 441, 484
Kersten, A., 325n
Kierkegaard, Søren, 27, 145, 179, 196, 410n, 445, 449
Klages, Ludwig, xxxiv, 356n, 367, 367n
Koffka, Kurt, 210–11, 222–25, 234, 291n, 301n, 304n
Köhler, Wolfgang, 172n, 222, 224, 224n

La Rochefoucauld, 302n, 374
Laporte, J., 185
Larguier des Bancels, 251, 271
Le Senne, Renée, 72, 357–59, 362–64, 367, 369, 372–73
Lebenswelt, 219
Leibniz, Gottfried, 171, 187, 380n, 430, 451
Lequier, Jules, 171, 173, 181
Lewin, Kurt, 38n, 210, 211, 222, 224–27, 242, 267, 289, 304–5, 324–25
Lindworsky, Johannes, 246n, 304n
Locke, John, 313

MacDougall, William, 271n
Maine de Biran, 145, 220–21, 228, 249, 261n, 282, 309, 313n, 319–20, 321n, 326, 331–36, 411, 424
Malebranche, Nicholas, 149, 155–56, 159, 170–71, 175, 181, 184, 186n, 295
Malinowski, Bronislaw, 121
Mallarmé, Stéphane, 156, 405, 406, 476
Marcel, Gabriel, xii, 15, 17n, 20, 31, 57, 75, 79, 133n, 213, 297, 449, 452, 468, 478
Mauron, Charles, 406n
Mayer, André, 234n
Meaning, xiv, 4, 43, 195, 201, 270, 292, 405, 406
Merleau-Ponty, Maurice, 232, 232n
Mesnard, P., 266n
Michotte, and Prüm, 55n, 67n, 165n, 166n
Minkowski, Eugene, 166n, 411n, 413n
Montaigne, Michel, 98, 118, 315, 457n
Motives, 66–69, 78, 86, 93–100
Mounier, Em., xiii, xxxiv, 369n
Mystery, 15, 17, 94, 219
Myth, xvii, xxx, xxxi, 119, 138

Nahlowsky, Joseph, 269n
Need, 87, 89–100
Nietzsche, Friedrich, 21, 105, 116–19, 143, 179, 189, 374, 449, 466, 471, 473–74, 484
Nogue, Jean, 86n
Nothing, 23

Ontogenesis, 5n, 6n
Ontology, 19, 22, 30, 196, 224–55, 423
Orphism, xxviii, 469, 471
Osvianskina, Maria, 324n

Parallelism, 91, 218, 347, 350
Pascal, Blaise, 31, 51, 98, 186
Passion, 3, 276–80
Paul, Saint, 22
Pavlov, Ivan P., 238
Pfänder, Alexander, 38, 40, 48, 67n, 68, 78, 165n
Phenomenon, xiv, 16, 67

Phenomenology, xi, xii, xiv, xv, xvi, xxv, xxxii, 13, 17, 30, 52, 182, 207, 208, 212, 224–25, 387–88, 410, 421, 427, 429, 430, 438, 467
Phylogenesis, 5
Physics, mental, 218, 136, 208, 359, 360, 382, 395, 398
Plato, xvii, 74, 85, 195, 265, 342, 441n, 450
Pleasure, and pain, 99–104, 106–11, 118–19
Poe, Edgar Allan, 452
Poetics, xi, xvi, 26n, 30, 34, 129, 191, 415, 425, 441, 467, 468, 471
Possibility, xi, 3, 21, 24, 26, 28
Pradines, M., 5n, 6n, 86n, 88, 90n, 92, 100n, 105, 106n, 112n, 118, 236, 238n, 239, 241, 243n, 252, 253n, 259, 268, 269n, 270n, 272, 281n, 301n, 420n
Presence, 16, 96
Prometheus, xvii, 464, 465
Protention, 51
Proust, Marcel, 454n, 457
Psychoanalysis, xxvi, 116, 124, 208, 374–78, 383, 406
Psychology, 118, 124

Rauh, Frederic, 80, 132
Ravaisson-Mollien, Felix, 286n, 288, 289, 296, 298n, 307, 326n, 327, 328, 328n, 329, 330n, 423, 425
Reiner, Hans, 38n, 40n, 78n
Renouvier, Charles, 293n
Ribot, Theodule, 245, 246n, 255, 264, 363
Rilke, Rainer Maria, xxxvii, 419, 440, 447, 462, 473–75, 477n, 478, 480
Rostand, Jean, 436n
Rousseau, J.-J., 436
Royce, Josiah, 75

Saint-Exupéry, Antoine de, 82
Sartre, Jean-Paul, xii, xix, 62, 72, 90, 97, 97n, 172n, 210n, 255, 258, 267, 271–73, 377, 395
Schopenhauer, Arthur, 68, 368
Selz, O., 305n
Seneca, 478
Sherrington, Charles, 231, 236n
Sin, 25
Spencer, Herbert, 123, 427
Spinoza, 171, 357, 450
Stoics, xxviii, 5, 14, 87, 103, 144, 171, 317, 344, 420, 449, 475, 476, 478
Subjectivity, 226, 472

Theophrastus, 357
Thorndike, Edward, 247n, 281n
Tilquin, André, 210n, 215n, 222, 222n
Tolman, Edward, 209–11, 215, 222–23, 281, 283n, 323, 421n
Transcendence, xvi–xviii, xxix, 3–4, 16, 29, 30, 78, 192, 467, 468, 469, 472, 476–77, 480, 486
Transcendentalism, 32

Understanding, xxxv, 3, 76, 222–27
Universalization, 133

Valéry, Paul, 62, 96, 144, 189, 411, 454
Value, 74, 79, 85, 102, 130–34
Van der Veldt, 285n, 286, 299, 305
Vernet, H., 416n

Watson, John B., 222
Weizsacker, 231, 232
Wesenschau, xiv
Wundt, Wilhelm, 153n

Zeigarnik, 324n
Zeno the Eleatic, 189